Law for Accountancy Students

Law for Accountancy Students

by **RICHARD CARD**, LLM,
Reader in Common Law at the University of Reading

and **JENNIFER JAMES**, LLB, BCL,
Lecturer in Law at the University of Reading

London
Butterworths
1978

England London	Butterworth & Co (Publishers) Ltd 88 Kingsway WC2B 6AB
Australia Sydney	Butterworths Pty Ltd 586 Pacific Highway, Chatswood, NSW 2067 Also at Melbourne, Brisbane, Adelaide and Perth
Canada Toronto	Butterworth & Co (Canada) Ltd 2265 Midland Avenue, Scarborough M1P 4S1
New Zealand Wellington	Butterworths of New Zealand Ltd 77—85 Customhouse Quay
South Africa Durban	Butterworth & Co (South Africa) (Pty) Ltd 152/154 Gale Street
USA Boston	Butterworth (Publishers) Inc 19 Cummings Park, Woburn, Mass 01801

ISBN Casebound 0 406 70881 9
Limp 0 406 70880 0

Typeset by Butterworths Litho Preparation Department
Printed in England by Billing & Sons Ltd, Guildford and Worcester

Preface

We have been prompted to write this book by the belief that there is a need for a comprehensive textbook for accountancy students studying foundation or similar courses in law, particularly one which treats the subject-matter in some depth. Clearly, a knowledge of the relevant branches of the law is an important ingredient in the training of an accountant, and we consider that there is no virtue, practical or academic, in the mere recitation of a list of legal rules. Consequently, we have endeavoured to explain the law and to show how it is derived from the decided cases and from statutes. We hope that this has resulted in a book which is not only educationally useful but also brings the law to life.

We have had in mind the syllabuses for the foundation examinations of the Association of Certified Accountants, the Institute of Chartered Accountants in England and Wales and the Institute of Cost and Management Accountants, as well as those of comparable examinations for degree courses in accountancy. Despite its title, this book should also prove useful for those following similar courses in law for other types of qualification.

This book is divided into four parts. Part II, which deals with the Law of Contract, is the most substantial since this branch of the law appears, universally, to be the most significant part of the syllabuses mentioned above. Part I outlines the English Legal System. Part III is concerned with the Elements of the Law of Tort and Part IV with Commercial Law. We estimate that the material in this book covers all matters dealt with in the various accountancy syllabuses. However, while the material in Parts I, II and III covers a core common to all of them, the particular chapters in Part IV which a student will have to study in detail will depend on the particular syllabus which he is following.

We thank all who have helped us. We owe special debts to our colleague, Mr. Peter Schofield, who contributed Chapter 28 (the Law of Employment), Mrs. Rachel Card, who assisted in many ways with the preparation of this book, and finally the publishers, not only for compiling the table of statutes and cases and the index, but also for placing their faith in this new venture. For the imperfections which remain in spite of all this help we are responsible.

We have tried to summarise and explain the law as it was on 1st January 1978, although by footnotes inserted in proof we have been able to indicate important changes made by cases reported in the period up to 31st March 1978.

Richard Card
Jennifer James
May 1978

Contents

Preface   v
Table of Statutes   xi
List of Cases   xxi

Part I Outline of the English Legal System   1

Chapter 1 Classification of the Law   3
Chapter 2 Administration of the Law   10
    The Courts   10
    Specialist Courts and Tribunals   29
    Arbitration   30
    The Legal Profession   34
    The Jury   35
    Legal Aid and Advice   36
Chapter 3 Sources of English Law   39
    Legislation   39
    Judicial Precedent   56
    Custom   65
Chapter 4 Persons and Property   67
    Persons   67
    Property   87

Part II The Law of Contract   91

Chapter 5 Agreement   93
Chapter 6 Consideration and Privity   108
    Consideration   110
    Privity of Contract   120
    Consideration: Discharge and Variation   128

Chapter 7 Form 134
  Contracts which must be under seal or in writing 134
  Contracts which must be evidenced in writing 136
Chapter 8 Contractual Terms 147
  Express Terms 147
  Implied Terms 153
Chapter 9 Discharge by Performance 159
  Performance 159
  Tender of Performance 164
  Performance by a Third Party 168
Chapter 10 Breach 171
  Rescission for Breach 172
  Exemption Clauses 184
Chapter 11 Discharge by Frustration 205
Chapter 12 Remedies for Breach of Contract 217
  Damages 217
  Quantum Meruit 228
  Specific Performance 229
  Limitation of Actions 234
Chapter 13 Mistake 239
  Shared Mistake 240
  Mistakes Not Shared by the Parties 245
  Mistake and Documents 249
Chapter 14 Misrepresentation, Duress and Undue Influence 253
  Misrepresentation 253
  Active Misrepresentation 253
  Misrepresentation through Non-disclosure 269
  Duress and Undue Influence 271
Chapter 15 Void and Illegal Contracts 277
  Wagering and Gaming Contracts 277
  Other Contracts Void on Grounds of Public Policy 283
  Illegal Contracts 305
Chapter 16 Capacity to Contract 318
  Minors 318
  Mentally Disordered and Intoxicated Persons 329
  Corporations and Unincorporated Associations 330
Chapter 17 Quasi-Contract 331
Chapter 18 Agency 337
  Principal and Agent 338
  Principal and Third Parties 353
  The Authority of Agents 353
  Agents and Third Parties 359
  Types of Agent 361
Chapter 19 Assignment 363
  Voluntary Transfer 363
  Involuntary Assignment 373

Part III Elements of the Law of Tort 377

Chapter 20 Negligence 379
  Negligence: Related Topics 394
Chapter 21 Other Torts and Procedural Matters 401
  Breach of Statutory Duty 401
  Some Other Torts 403
  Vicarious Liability 406
  Death 412
  Joint Tortfeasors 413
  Defences 414
  Remedies 418

Part IV Commercial Law 421

Chapter 22 The Sale of Goods 423
  Contract of Sale of Goods 423
  Transfer of Property 428
  Perishing of the Goods 434
  Transfer of Title 436
  Terms of the Contract 444
  Delivery and Acceptance of the Goods 456
  Remedies for Breach of Contract of Sale 461
  Particular Types of Contract of Sale 472
Chapter 23 Consumer Credit 475
  Definitions and Special Characteristics 476
  Controls over Consumer Credit or Consumer Hire Business 483
  Entry into Regulated Agreements 487
  Matters Arising During the Currency of an Agreement 492
  Enforcement and Termination 495
  Judicial Control 503
  Specific Rules Outside the Act 508
Chapter 24 Negotiable Instruments 513
  Rules Common to Bills of Exchange and Cheques 514
  An Outline of Rules Relating to Bills of Exchange but not
    Cheques 536
  Banker and Customer 540
  Cheques and Other Bills 550
Chapter 25 Elements of Insurance Law 551
  General 551
  Indemnity Policies 552
  Life Assurance 558
Chapter 26 Bailments and Securities 562
  Bailment 562
  Securities Generally 566

Contents

Pledges 566
Liens 571
Guarantees 573
Chapter 27 Contracts of Carriage 577
Carriage on Land 577
Carriage of Goods by Sea 582
Carriage by Air 598
Chapter 28 The Law of Employment 602
The Employment Relationship 602
Terms of Employment 605
Continuity of Employment 609
Wages 611
Employment Protection 615
Discrimination in Employment 615
Dismissal 619
Redundancy 627
Liability for Safety at Work 634
Social Security 642

Index 647

Table of Statutes

References in this Table to *"Statutes"* are to Halsbury's Statutes of England (Third Edition) showing the volume and page at which the annotated text of the Act will be found.

Para.

Act of Parliament (Commencement) Act 1793 (32 *Statutes* 412) 3.8
Acts of Parliament Numbering and Citation Act 1962 (32 *Statutes* 778) 3.7
Administration of Estates Act, 1925 (13 *Statutes* 38) . . 19.22
Administration of Justice Act 1969 . . . . . 2.29
Administration of Justice Act 1970 (40 *Statutes* 373, 1098)—
  s.4 . . . . . 2.42
  Sch. 1 . . . . 2.19
Administration of Justice Act 1973 (43 *Statutes* 250, 255)—
  s.7 . . . . . 2.48
  12 . . . . . 2.14
Administration of Justice Act 1977 (47 *Statutes* 113)—
  s.17 . . . . . 2.12
Administration of Justice Miscellaneous Provisions) Act 1933 (25 *Statutes* 749)—
  s.6 . . . . . 2.53
Adoption Act 1976 (46 *Statutes* 718)—
  s.40 . . . . . 4.19
Appellate Jurisdiction Act 1876 (7 *Statutes* 529) . . . 2.28
  s.6 . . . . . 2.28

Para.

Arbitration Act 1950 (2 *Statutes* 433) 2.41, 2.45
  s.4 . . . . . 2.41
  6, 8, 10 . . . . 2.42
  15 . . . . 2.45, 2.48
  16 . . . . . 2.45
  18 . . . . . 2.45
  21 . . . . . 2.44
  22, 23 . . . . . 2.45

Bankers Books Evidence Act 1879 . . . . . 24.78
Banking and Financial Dealings Act 1971 (41 *Statutes* 1554)—
  s.3 . . . . . 24.9
Bankruptcy Act 1914 (3 *Statutes* 33) 19.26
  s.38 . . . . . 19.24
  48 . . . 19.16, 19.24
  54 . . . . . 19.27
  56 . . . . . 19.26
Betting and Loans (Infants) Act 1892 (17 *Statutes* 422)—
  s.5 . . . . . 16.14
Betting, Gaming and Lotteries Act 1963 (14 *Statutes* 539) . 15.4
  s.52, 55 . . . . 15.4
Betting, Gaming and Lotteries (Amendment) Act 1971 (41 *Statutes* 608) . . . 15.3

	Para.			*Para.*
Bills of Exchange Act 1882		Bills of Exchange Act 1882		
(3 *Statutes* 188)	6.4, 12.15, 19.3, 24.2	(3 *Statutes* 188) (*cont.*)		
s.2 . . 24.5, 24.17, 24.26, 24.65		s.42, 43 . . . . .24.55		
3 . . . . . 7.5, 24.4		44 . . . . .24.54		
(1) . . 24.4, 24.8, 24.21		45 . . . . .24.42		
(2) 24.8		(3) 24.43		
(3) 24.5		(4), (5) 24.42		
(4) 24.11		46 . 24.42, 24.43, 24.44		
4 . . . . . .24.46		47 . . . . .24.44		
6 . . . . . 24.6		48 . . . . .24.45		
7 . . . . . .24.10		49 (12), (15) . . .24.45		
(3) 24.10		50 . . . . .24.45		
8 (1) 24.19		(2) 24.45		
(3), (4) 24.10		51 . . . . .24.46		
9 . . . . . 24.8		(9) 24.46		
(2), (3) . . . 24.8		52 . . . . .22.42		
11 . . . 24.5, 24.9		53 . . . . .24.47		
12 . . 24.11, 24.37		54 . . . . .24.54		
13 . . . . .24.11		(2) 24.37		
14 . . . . . 24.9		55 (2) . . 24.37, 24.48		
15 . . . . .24.46		56 . . . . .24.51		
16 . . . . .24.49		57 (1), (2) . . .24.53		
17 . . . 7.5, 24.54		58 . . . . .24.52		
19 . . . . .24.54		59 . . 24.23, 24.71		
21 . . . . .24.17		60 . . . . .24.73		
(2) 24.37		61 . . . . .24.22		
22 . . . . .24.14		62 . . 6.36, 24.22		
(2) 24.14		63 . . . . .24.24		
23 . . . . .24.15		64 . . 24.25, 24.37		
(2) 24.15		65 . . 24.46, 24.48		
24 . . . . .24.16		66, 67 . . . .24.48		
25 . . . . .24.15		73 . . . 7.5, 24.4		
26 . . 18.47, 24.15, 24.49		74 . . . . .24.44		
(1) 24.15		75 (1) 24.69		
27 . 24.2, 24.13, 24.26, 24.31		76 . . 24.58, 24.62		
(1) 24.12		77 . . . . .24.59		
(2) 24.12		78 . . . . .24.60		
29 . 6.20, 24.13, 24.26, 24.38		79 (2) . . 24.60, 24.61		
(1) 15.10		80 . . . . .24.61		
(2) . . 15.10, 24.32		83 . . . 7.5, 24.88		
(3) 23.34		90 . . . . .24.30		
30 . . . . .24.12		Bills of Lading Act 1855 (31		
(2) . . 15.10, 24.32		*Statutes* 44) 19.3		
31 . . 24.20, 24.85		s.1 . . . 27.9, 27.36		
32 . . . . .24.20		3 . . . . .27.28		
(1), (2) 24.20		Bills of Sale Act 1878 (Amend-		
(5) 24.21		ment) Act 1882 (3 *Statutes*		
33 . . . . .24.21		261) 26.22		
34 (4) 24.21		s.7 . . . . .26.22		
35 . . . . .24.21		9 . . . . . 7.5		
38 . . 24.27, 24.28, 24.38		Schedule 26.22		
(2) 15.10		British Nationality Act 1948		
39 . . . . .24.55		(1 *Statutes* 861) . . . 4.19		
40, 41 . . . . .24.55		s.1, 2 . . . . 4.18		

	Para.
British Nationality Act 1948 (1 *Statutes* 861) (*cont.*)	
s. 4, 5	4.19
5A (1), (2)	4.19
10	4.19
19, 20	4.20
32	4.18
Sch. 19	4.19
Carriage by Air Act 1932	27.41
Carriage by Air Act 1961 (2 *Statutes* 604)—	
Sch. 1	27.41
Carriage by Air (Supplementary Provisions) Act 1962 (2 *Statutes* 639)	27.45
Carriage of Goods by Road Act 1965	27.7
Schedule	27.7
Carriage of Goods by Sea Act 1971 (41 *Statutes* 1312)	27.33
s. 1	27.33
Schedule	27.32
Carriage of Passengers by Road Act 1974 (44 *Statutes* 1326)	27.7
Carriers Act 1830 (3 *Statutes* 540)	27.5, 27.6
s. 1, 4, 6, 8	27.5
Cheques Act 1957 (3 *Statutes* 238)—	
s. 1	27.74
2	24.85
3	9.6, 24.86
4	24.80, 24.82, 24.83, 24.84
(3)	24.83
Children and Young Persons Act 1933 (17 *Statutes* 435)	2.7
Coinage Act 1971 (41 *Statutes* 225)	9.13
Commonwealth Immigrants Act 1962 (4 *Statutes* 24)—	
s. 12	4.19
Companies Act 1948 (5 *Statutes* 110)	4.3, 13.18, 19.7, 26.24
s. 1, 2, 4	4.9
5	4.12
31	4.6
38	14.27
108	24.15
161	4.15
119—121	4.15
150—153	4.6

	Para.
Companies Act 1948 (5 *Statutes* 110) (*cont.*)	
s. 222	4.7
245	19.16
322	4.6
434	4.15, 4.16
Companies Act 1976 (46 *Statutes* 187)	4.3
Consumer Credit Act 1974 (44 *Statutes* 746)	3.11, 3.14, 9.9, 14.38, 22.55, 23.1, 23.3, 23.70, 23.73, 23.77, 24.65. 26.16
s. 1	23.2
8	23.5
9	23.6
10	23.7
11	23.8
12, 13	23.9
14	23.10
(1)	23.10
15	23.12
16 (1)—(5)	23.11
(6)	23.12
17	23.13
18	23.8
19	23.15
21—42	23.17
43—51	23.20, 23.21
52—54	23.20
55	23.24, 23.25
56	23.24, 23.28
57	23.24, 23.31
58, 59	23.24
60	23.24, 23.26
61	23.24, 23.26
(2)	23.28
62—64	23.24, 23.27
65	23.24, 23.25, 23.26, 23.27
66	23.24
67	23.24, 23.28
68	23.24, 23.29
69	23.24, 23.29, 23.30
70—73	23.24, 23.30
74	23.24
75	23.32
76	23.43
77	22.33
78	22.33
(4)	23.34
79	22.33
82	23.37
86	23.38
87	23.39
88 (1), (2), (4), (5)	23.40

	Para.
Consumer Credit Act 1974	
(44 *Statutes* 746) (*cont.*)	
s. 89	. 23.40
90 (1), (2), (5)—(7) .	. 23.41
91	. 23.41
92 (1), (2) . . .	. 23.42
(3)	. 23.42
94	. 23.45
96, 97	. 23.46
98	. 23.43
99, 100 . . .	. 23.47
101	. 23.49
103	. 23.50
105 . . .	23.52, 23.53
106	. 23.52
107—109 . .	23.52, 23.54
110	. 23.52
111 . . .	23.52, 23.55
112	. 23.52
113	. 23.52
(1), (2) . . .	. 23.56
(7) . . .	. 23.56
114 . .	23.52, 26.16
115—122 . .	23.52, 26.16
123 . . 23.52, 23.57, 24.65
124, 125 . . .	. 23.52
126 . . .	23.52, 23.58
127 . . .	23.52, 23.60
(4) . . .	. 23.27
128	. 23.38
129	. 23.61
130	. 23.61
131 . . .	23.62, 23.63
132	. 23.64
133	. 23.65
135, 136 . . .	. 23.66
137 (1) . .	23.59, 23.67
(2) . . .	. 23.67
138 (2)—(4) . .	. 23.68
139 (1) . . .	. 23.67
(2), (4) . .	. 23.69
141 (1) . . .	. 23.59
145—149 . . .	. 23.19
153, 154 . . .	. 23.23
171 (1) . . .	. 23.7
(7) . . .	. 23.68
173 (1) . . .	. 23.45
(3) . . 23.41, 23.42
189 . . 23.3, 23.71, 23.78
(1) . . .	. 23.52
Sch. 2	. 23.3
Example 6, 7 . .	. 23.7
8 . . .	. 23.8
10 . . 23.6, 23.8

	Para.
Consumer Credit Act 1974	
(44 *Statutes* 746) (*cont.*)	
Sch. 2 (*cont.*)	
Example (*cont.*)	
12—14, 16—18 .	23.8
20 . .	. 23.12
21 . .	. 23.8
Sch. 4 22.33, 22.34, 23.75, 23.78
Contracts of Employment Act	
1972 (42 *Statutes* 310)—	
s. 1 . . . . 28.38, 28.39
2	. 28.16
4—6, 8 . . .	. 28.16
Copyright Act 1956 (7 *Statutes*	
128)	. 19.7
County Courts Act 1959 .	. 2.9
s. 47	. 2.11
92	. 2.12
93	. 2.48
108	. 2.25
Courts Act 1971 (41 *Statutes*	
285)—	
s. 2	. 2.15
5	. 2.21
10	. 2.18
16, 17	. 2.8
21	. 2.21
Criminal Appeal Act 1968	
(8 *Statutes* 687)—	
s. 1, 2	. 2.26
9, 10	. 2.26
11	. 2.26
(3)	. 2.26
33	. 2.30
Criminal Justice Act 1972	
(42 *Statutes* 99)—	
s. 36	. 2.26
Crown Proceedings Act 1947	
(8 *Statutes* 844) . .	. 4.17
Currency and Bank Notes Act	
1954 (2 *Statutes* 770) .	. 9.13
Defective Premises Act 1972	
(42 *Statutes* 1395) . .	. 20.6
Diplomatic Privileges Act 1964	
(6 *Statutes* 1013) . .	. 4.2
Domicile and Matrimonial	
Proceedings Act 1973	
(43 *Statutes* 231)—	
s. 1, 3, 4	. 4.23
Employers' Liability Act 1880 .	16.6

Para.

Employers' Liability (Compulsory Insurance) Act 1969
(40 *Statutes* 553) . . . 28.70
s.1. . . . . . 25.17
Employer's Liability (Defective Equipment) Act 1969 (40
Statutes 551) . . 20.30, 28.69
Employment Protection Act
1975 (45 *Statutes* 316, 2371)
2.38, 28.19, 28.26
s.34, 35 . . . . . 28.47
61 . . . . . 28.63
70 . . . . . 28.37
71 (1)—(7) 28.49
72 . . . . . 28.50
(5) 28.51
73—76 . . . . . 28.51
81, 82, 84 . . . . 28.19
90, 91, 93 . . . . 28.23
99 . . . . . 28.60
100 . . . . . 28.62
102, 103 . . . . 28.61
104, 105 . . . . 28.62
Sch. 8 . . . . . 28.23
Sch. 11 . . . . . 28.25
Equal Pay Act 1970 (40 *Statutes*
561) 28.29, 28.32
s.1 . . . . . 28.32
(3) 28.34
2 . . . . . 28.34
European Communities Act
1972 (42 *Statutes* 24, 59, 78) . 3.11
s.2 (1), (2) 3.28
(4) . . . 3.28, 3.32
3 (1) 3.39
9 4.11, 4.12, 4.14, 18.5, 18.10,
18.37, 18.48, 24.14
Sch. 2 . . . . . 3.32

Factories Act 1961 (13 *Statutes*
400) . . . 21.27, 28.71
s.12, 13 . . . 28.78, 28.79
14 . 28.78, 28.79, 28.80
15 . . . . 28.78
16 . . 28.78, 28.80
175 . . . . 28.77
Factors Act 1889 (1 *Statutes* 94) 22.31
s.1 . . . . . 18.52
(4) 22.30
2 . . . . . 18.36
(1) 22.30
8 . . . . . 22.31
9 . . . . . 22.32

Para.

Fair Trading Act 1973 (43
Statutes 1618) . . 10.60, 14,38
Family Law Reform Act 1969
(17 *Statutes* 792)—
s.1 . . . . . 16.1
19 (1) 25.23
Fatal Accidents Act 1976 (46
Statutes 1115) . . 21.31, 21.33
Finance Act 1960—
s.44 . . . . . 3.19
Fires Prevention (Metropolis)
Act 1774 (17 *Statutes* 829)—
s.83 . . . . . 25.12
Foreign Judgments (Reciprocal
Enforcement) Act 1933 (6
Statutes 365)—
s.8 . . . . . 3.26

Gaming Act 1710 (14 *Statutes*
519) 15.10
s.1 . . . . . 15.10
Gaming Act 1835 (14 *Statutes*
522) 15.10
s.1 . . . . . 15.10
Gaming Act 1892 (14 *Statutes*
533)—
s.1 . . . 15.7, 15.11
Gaming Act 1845 (14 *Statutes*
523)—
s.18 . . 15.5, 15.6, 15.8
Gaming Act 1968 (14 *Statutes*
696) . . . 15.4, 15.11
s.16 . . . . 15.4
(4) 15.10

Health and Safety at Work etc. Act
1974 (44 *Statutes* 1083) 3.2, 28.77
s.2 . . . . . 28.72
3, 5 . . . . 28.73
6 . . . . . 28.74
7 . . . . . 28.75
21, 22, 24, 25 . . 28.82
33, 47 . . . . 28.72
Hire-Purchase Act 1938 . 8.18
Hire-Purchase Act 1964 (30
Statutes 55) . . . 22.34
s.27 (1)—(3) . . . 22.34
29 (2) 22.34

Immigration Act 1971 (41
Statutes 12) . . . 4.18
s.1—3 . . . . 4.18
Sch. 1 . . . . 4.19

	Para.
Income and Corporation Taxes	
Act 1970 (33 *Statutes* 17)	3.3
s. 49—51	4.26
108	4.25
Income Tax Act 1952—	
s. 25 (3)	3.19
Infants Relief Act 1874 (17	
Statutes 412)	16.1, 16.2
s. 1 16.1, 16.12, 16.13, 16.14, 16.15	
2	16.14, 16.15
Innkeepers Act 1878—	
s. 1	22.37
Insolvency Act 1976	19.24
Interpretation Act 1889 (32	
Statutes 434)—	
s. 1 (1)	3.17
11 (1)	3.9
19	3.17
38 (2)	3.9
Ireland Act 1949—	
s. 2	4.18
Judicial Pensions Act 1959	
(7 *Statutes* 711)—	
s. 2	2.14
Juries Act 1974 (44 *Statutes*	
566)—	
s. 1, 3	2.54
17	2.55
(5)	2.55
Sch. 1	2.54
Labourers Articifers (1349)	3.7
Land Charges Act 1972 (42	
Statutes 1590)—	
s. 4	4.29
Law Commission Act 1965 (32	
Statutes 803)	3.2
Law of Property Act 1925	
(27 *Statutes* 341)—	
s. 2	4.29
40 1.12, 7.16, 7.18, 18.32	
(1)	7.10
(2)	7.18
41	9.17
52	7.2
53 (1)	19.12
54	7.2
56	6.24
78, 79	6.20
101, 103	26.21
136 19.4, 19.6, 25.8, 25.24	
(1) 19.3, 19.4, 19.6, 19.7	

	Para.
Law of Property Act 1925	
(27 *Statutes* 341)— (*cont.*)	
137 (3)	9.13
141, 142	6.20
Law Reform (Contributory	
Negligence) Act 1945 (23	
Statutes 789)—	
s. 1 (1)	21.39
Law Reform (Frustrated Con-	
tracts) Act 1943 (7 *Statutes* 9)	
11.8, 17.7, 22.26, 22.27, 27.19	
s. 1 (2) 11.15, 11.17	
(3) 11.17, 11.18	
(4)	11.15
2 (2)—(4)	11.18
(5) 11.18, 22.26	
Law Reform (Married Women	
and Tortfeasors) Act 1935	
(35 *Statutes* 543)—	
s. 6	21.34
Law Reform (Miscellaneous	
Provisions) Act 1934 (13	
Statutes 115; 25 *Statutes* 752) 21.31	
s. 1 19.22, 21.32	
3	12.15
Laying of Documents before	
Parliament (Interpretation) Act	
1948 (32 *Statutes* 677)	3.12
Legal Aid Act 1974 (44 *Statutes*	
126, 1035)	2.56
s. 1—5	2.57
6—10	2.58
28—40	2.59
Life Assurance Act 1774 (17	
Statutes 827)—	
s. 1 25.2, 25.21	
3	25.21
4	25.2
Limitation Act 1939 (19	
Statutes 60) 9.10, 12.25, 21.46	
s. 2 (1), (3)	12.26
(7)	12.32
22	12.27
23 (4)	12.29
24	7.5
(1), (2)	12.30
25 (5)	12.30
(6) 12.31, 12.32	
(8) 12.30, 12.32	
31 (2)	12.27
Limitation Act 1975 (45 *Statutes*	
847)	12.26, 21.46
s. 1	12.26
2	12.27

	Para.
Limited Partnership Act 1907	
(24 *Statutes* 525) . . . 4.15	
s. 4, 6 . . . . . 4.15	
Litigants in Person (Costs and	
Expenses) Act 1975 (45	
Statutes 1639) 2.56	
Lotteries and Amusements Act	
1976 (46 *Statutes* 643)—	
s. 1—6 . . . . . 15.3	
Magistrates' Courts Act 1952	
(21 *Statutes* 181) . . . 2.2	
s. 56—58 . . . . 2.5	
87 (6) 2.18	
Marine Insurance Act 1906	
(17 *Statutes* 836) . . . 8.18	
s. 4 . . . . . 15.3	
6 . . . . . 25.2	
18 (1), (2) 14.24	
22—24 . . . . 7.5	
Married Women's Property Act	
1882 (17 *Statutes* 116)—	
s. 11 . . 6.20, 25.21, 25.23	
Matrimonial Causes Act 1973	
(43 *Statutes* 539)—	
s. 34 . . . . . 15.16	
Mental Health Act 1959 (25	
Statutes 42) 2.37	
s. 103 . . . . . 16.19	
Mercantile Law Amendment Act	
1856 (7 *Statutes* 8)—	
s. 3 . . . . . 7.12	
5 . . . . . 26.36	
Merchant Shipping Act 1894	
(31 *Statutes* 57) . 27.23, 27.34	
s. 24 . . . . . 7.5	
502, 503 . . 27.24, 27.26	
Merchant Shipping (Liability of	
Shipowners and Others) Act	
1958 (31 *Statutes* 646)—	
s. 3 . . . . . 27.23	
Misrepresentation Act 1967	
(22 *Statutes* 675) . . 3.7, 14.13	
s. 1 . . . . . 14.19	
2 (1)—(3) . . . 14.14	
3 . . . . . 14.21	
4 (2) 22.40	
Occupiers' Liability Act 1957	
(23 *Statutes* 792) . . 21.41	
s. 1 . . . . . 21.35	
(1) . . . 10.41, 20.39	
(2) 20.37	
2 . . 20.35, 2.40, 21.35	
(4) 20.41	

	Para.
Occupiers' Liability Act 1957	
(23 *Statutes* 792) (*cont.*)	
s. 2 (*cont.*)	
(6) 20.37	
3 (1) 20.41	
4 . . . . . 20.42	
Offices, Shops and Railway	
Premises Act 1963 (13 *Statutes*	
584) 28.71	
Partnership Act 1890 (24	
Statutes 500) . . . 3.2, 4.15	
s. 1 . . . . . 4.15	
5 . . . . 4.15, 18.39	
9 . . . . . 4.15	
20, 24 . . . . 4.15	
33 . . . . . 4.15	
Pawnbrokers Act 1872 (24	
Statutes 703) . . . 26.16	
Pawnbrokers Act 1960 (24	
Statutes 731) . . . 26.16	
Payment of Wages Act 1960	
(12 *Statutes* 190) . . 28.20	
Policies of Assurance Act 1867	
(17 *Statutes* 831) . . 25.24	
s. 1, 3, 5, 6 . . . 25.24	
Schedule . . . 25.24	
Powers of Attorney Act 1971	
(41 *Statutes* 2)—	
s. 1 . . . . . 18.6	
4 . . . . . 18.25	
7 . . . . . 18.6	
Powers of Criminal Courts Act	
1973 (43 *Statutes* 288) . . 1.3	
Race Relations Act 1976 (46	
Statutes 389) . . . 28.35	
s. 3 . . . . . 28.35	
Redundancy Payments Act 1965	
(12 *Statutes* 236)—	
s. 1 . . . . . 28.54	
2 (2) 28.53	
(3), (5), (6) . . 28.55	
3 . . . . . 28.53	
(3), (8) . . . 28.55	
4 . . . . . 28.53	
5, 6 . . . . 28.57	
9 . . . . . 28.54	
22 . . . . . 28.53	
30, 32 . . . . 28.59	
Refreshment Houses Act 1860	
(17 *Statutes* 947)—	
s. 6 . . . . . 3.24	
Rehabilitation of Offenders Act	
1974 (44 *Statutes* 148) . . 21.8	

	Para.
Resale Prices Act 1964 (37	
Statutes 158) 15.42	
Resale Prices Act 1976 (46	
Statutes 2033) . . 12.14, 15.42	
s. 1 . . . . 15.34, 15.48	
9 . . . . 6.30, 15.43	
11–13 . . . .15.43	
14 . . . . .15.45	
16 . . . . .15.44	
25 . . . . .15.43	
26 . . . . . 6.30	
Restriction of Offensive Weapons	
Act 1959 (8 *Statutes* 472) . 5.4	
Restriction of Offensive Weapons	
Act 1961 (8 *Statutes* 499) . 5.4	
Restrictive Trade Practices Act	
1956 (37 *Statutes* 77) . .15.33	
Restrictive Trade Practices Act	
1976 (46 *Statutes* 1955) 2.36, 15.33	
15.40, 15.48	
s. 1 . . . . 15.36, 15.37	
2 . . . . .15.37	
5 . . . . .15.40	
6 . . . . .15.33	
7 . . . . .15.34	
8 . . . . .15.38	
10 . . . . .15.37	
11 . . . . .15.33	
12 . . . . .15.34	
16 . . . . .15.38	
19 . . . . .15.37	
21 . . . . .15.40	
24 . . . . .15.36	
28–31 . . . .15.35	
35 . . . 15.36, 15.37	
Sch. 1 . . . . .15.34	
Sch. 3 . . . . .15.35	
Restrictive Trade Practices Act	
1977 (47 *Statutes* 1467) . .15.33	
Road Traffic Act 1960 (28	
Statutes 219)—	
s. 151 . . . . . 27.7	
Road Traffic Act 1972 (42	
Statutes 1633)—	
s. 143–147 . . . .25.18	
148 . . . . .25.18	
(3) 21.35	
149 . . . . .25.18	
Sale of Goods Act 1893 (30	
Statutes 6). 3.2, 3.3, 3.7, 8.18, 10.20	
12.7, 12.18, 13.5, 22.1, 22.39,	
22.48, 23.79	
s. 1 . . . . . 22.2	
(3), (4) 22.3	

	Para.
Sale of Goods Act 1893 (30	
Statutes 6) (*cont.*)	
2 . . . . 16.5, 16.20	
6 . . . . 2.24, 22.25	
7 . . 11.18, 22.26, 22.27	
8 (1) 22.7	
(2) 5.25, 22.7	
9 (1), (2) 22.7	
10 . . . . . 9.17	
(1) 22.41	
11 (1) 10.19, 22.40, 22.44, 22.69,	
22.70, 22.77, 23.75, 23.78	
12 10.47, 22.42, 22.49, 22.99,	
23.75, 23.78	
(1) 8.18, 17.7, 22.43, 22.44,	
22.45, 22.46	
(2) 22.46	
13 10.31, 10.47, 22.42, 22.47,	
22.49, 22.99, 23.75, 23.78	
(1) . . . 9.2, 22.47	
(2) 22.47	
14 10.47, 22.42, 22.99, 23.75,	
23.78	
(1) 22.51	
(2) 8.18, 22.49, 22.51, 22.59	
(3) 8.18, 22.49, 22.50, 22.55,	
22.56, 22.59	
(4), (5) 22.51	
15 10.47, 22.42, 22.49, 22.99,	
23.75, 23.78	
(1), (2) 22.60	
16 . . . . .22.19	
17 . . . . .22.14	
18 . . . . .22.14	
r. 1 . 22.15, 22.17, 22.22	
2 . . . . .22.16	
3 . . . . .22.17	
4 . . . . .22.18	
(a), (b) . . .22.18	
5 . 22.19, 22.21, 22.22	
(1) . . 22.19, 22.21	
(2) 22.21	
19 (1), (2) 22.22	
(3) 22.33	
20 . . . . .22.12	
21 (1) . . . 22.28, 22.29	
(2) 22.37	
22 (1) 22.35	
23 . . . . .22.36	
24 (1) 22.35	
25 (1) 22.31	
(2) . 22.32, 22.33, 22.34	
26 (1) 22.38	
27 . . 22.63, 22.65, 22.69	

Para.

Sale of Goods Act 1893 (30
Statutes 6) (*cont.*)
29 . 9.11, 9.14, 9.15, 22.65
30 . . 10.14, 10.15, 22.70
(1)—(3) 22.70
31 (1) 22.69
(2) 27.71
32 . . . . .22.66
33 . . . . .22.67
34 . . . 9.11, 22.40
35 . . . . .22.40
36 . . . . .22.70
37 . . 9.14, 22.82, 22.87
38 (2) 22.88
39 (2) 22.89
41 (1) 22.89
42 . . . . .22.89
43 . . . . .22.90
44 . . . . .22.91
45 . . . . .22.92
(1), (5), (7) . . .22.92
46 . . . . .22.91
47 . . . 22.90, 22.93
48 . . . . .22.94
(1)—(3) 22.94
49 . . . 22.87, 22.94
50 . . . 22.87, 22.94
(1) 22.83
(2), (3) . . 22.83, 22.84
51 . . . . .22.73
(1)—(3) 22.73
52 . . . . .22.74
53 (1) . . . 10.19, 22.80
(2), (3) 22.80
54 . . . 22.75, 22.78
61 (2) . . . 22.1, 22.40
62 . . . . .22.64
(1) . 10.19, 22.4, 22.10, 22.31,
22.39, 22.51
(1A) 22.52
(3) 22.89
Settled Land Act 1925 (30
Statutes 344)—
s.18, 72, 75 . . . . 4.29
Sex Discrimination Act 1975 (45
Statutes 221) . 28.29, 28.32, 28.35
s.1, 2 . . . . .28.27
3, 4 . . . . .28.29
5 . . . . . .28.27
6 . . . 28.27, 28.33
7 . . . . .28.28
8 . . . . .28.33
Short Titles Act 1896 (32
Statutes 472) 3.7

Para.

Social Security Act 1975 (45
Statutes 1071)—
s.14, 17. 18 . . . .28.83
19 . . . . .28.84
20 . . . . .28.85
41 . . . . .28.83
44 . . . . .28.83
50 . . . 28.86, 28.87
52—55 . . . .28.88
56 . . . . .28.86
57—63, 67 . . . .28.86
76 . . . . .28.89
93—109 . . . .28.90
Sch. 6 . . . . .28.83
Statute of Frauds (1677) (7
Statutes 6)—
s.4 7.7, 7.8, 7.9, 7.10, 7.16, 26.31
Statute of Gloucester (1278) . 3.7
Statute of Labourers (1349)
See Labourers Artificers (1349)
Statutory Instruments Act 1946
(32 *Statutes* 668)—
s.3 . . . . . 3.11
4, 5 . . . . . 3.12
Statutory Orders (Special Procedure) Act 1945 (32 *Statutes*
658) 3.12
Statutory Orders (Special Procedure) Act 1965 (32 *Statutes*
806) 3.12
Suicide Act 1961 (8 *Statutes* 519) 25.22
Supply of Goods (Implied Terms)
Act 1973 (43 *Statutes* 1337)
8.18, 10.47, 22.42, 22.55
s.5 (2) 22.99
7 . . . 22.51, 22.52
8—11 . . . 10.47, 23.75
14 (1), (2) 23.78
16 . . . . .22.61
Supreme Court of Judicature Act
1873
1.10, 2.14, 9.17, 12.32, 19.4, 19.9
s.25 . . . . . 1.13
Supreme Court of Judicature Act
1875 . . .1.10, 2.14, 9.17
Supreme Court of Judicature
(Consolidation) Act 1925
(7 *Statutes* 573; 25 *Statutes*
708)—
s.7, 9 . . . . . 2.24
12 . . . . . 2.14
31 (1) 2.25
44 . . . . . 1.13
56 . . . . . 2.16

Para.

Taxes Management Act 1970
(34 *Statutes* 1245)—
   s.20 .   .   .   . .24.78
Theft Act 1968 (8 *Statutes* 782)—
   s.31 (2) 22.35
   Sch. 3 .   .   . .22.35
Third Parties (Rights against
Insurers) Act 1930 (3 *Statutes*
175)—
   s.1 (1), (3) .   .   .25.16
Torts (Interference with Goods)
Act 1977 (47 *Statutes* 67) . 21.9
   s.12, 13. .   . 22.37, 26.10
Trade Descriptions Act 1968
(37 *Statutes* 948) .   .22.48
Trade Union and Labour
Relations Act 1974 (44
Statutes 1766).   .   .   3.2
   s.2.   .   .   .   4.14
     (5) 15.17
   3 (5) 15.17
   13   .   .   .   4.14
   16   .   . 12.18, 12.22
   18   .   .   . 6.2, 28.7
   Sch. 1 .   . 28.17, 28.18
   para. 4 .   .   .28.41
     5   .   .   .28.42
     6 28.43, 28.44, 28.45, 28.46
     7   .   .   .28.48
     10, 11 .   .28.41
     15 .   .   .28.44
Trading Stamps Act 1964 (37
Statutes 170)—
   s.4.   .   .   . .22.61
Transport Act 1962 (26 *Statutes*
925).   .   .   .   27.8
   s.43 (6).   .   . 27.6, 27.8
Transport Act 1968 (26 *Statutes*
1126)—
   s.2 (2) .   .   . 27.6
Transport (London) Act 1969
(20 *Statutes* 821)—
   s.6 (2) .   .   . 27.6
Truck Act 1831 (12 *Statutes* 11) 28.30
   s.1—4, 9 .   . .28.20
   23   .   .   .28.21
Truck Act 1896 (12 *Statutes* 42) 28.21
   s.1.   .   .   .28.22

Para.

Unfair Contract Terms Act 1977
(47 *Statutes* 84)
     10.53, 21.35, 22.5, 22.42
   s.1 (1) 10.41
    (3) .   .   .10.40
   2   10.44, 10.50, 10.52, 20.13,
     20.41, 20.45
   (1), (2) . 10.41, 10.44
   3.   . 10.42, 10.44, 10.47
   (1) .   .   .10.42
   4.   .   .   .10.44
   (1), (2) .   .10.43
   5.   .   20.34, 22.62
   6. 10.46, 10.47, 10.49, 10.52
   (1)—(3) .   .10.47
   7. 10.46, 10.48, 10.49, 10.52
   (2)—(4) .   .10.48
   8.   .   .   .14.21
   9.   .   .   .10.58
   (1), (2) .   .10.58
   10   .   .   .10.51
   11 (1).   . 10.45, 14.21
   (2).   .   .   .10.49
   (4), (5) .   .10.45
   12 (1).   . 10.42, 10.47
   (2).   .   .   .10.47
   13 (1).   .   .   .10.52
   14, 20.   .   .   .10.40
   26 (1)—(4) .   .   .10.50
   Sch. 1 .   . 10.41, 10.44
   Sch. 2 .   .   .   .10.49
   Sch. 3 .   .   .   .22.51
   Sch. 4 .   .   .   .22.99
Uniform Laws of International
Sales Act 1967 (30 *Statutes*
128). 22.99
Unsolicited Goods and Services
Act 1971 (41 *Statutes* 1277) . 26.6
   s.1.   .   .   .   . 26.6

Wages Councils Act 1959 (12
Statutes 148)—
   s.12   .   .   .   .28.23
   Sch. 2 .   .   .   .28.23
Wills Act 1861—
   s.3.   .   .   .   . 3.23

List of Cases

A

Para.

Acme Wood Flooring Co Ltd v
  Marten (1904) 25.13
Adams v Lindsell (1818) . . 5.15
Addie & Sons (Collieries) Ltd v
  Dumbreck (1929) . 3.40, 20.38
Addis v Gramophone Co (1909) 12.2
Acrial Advertising Co v
  Batchelors Peas (Manchester)
  Ltd (1938) 10.22
Aiken v Short (1856) . . 17.4
Alan (W.J.) & Co Ltd v El Nasr
  Export and Import Co (1972) 6.32
Albemarle Supply Co Ltd v
  Hind & Co (1928) . . . 9.10
Alderslade v Hendon Laundry
  Ltd (1945) 10.33
Aldridge v Johnson (1857) . 22.7
Alexander v Rayson (1936)
  . . . 15.58, 15.61, 15.63
Allan (J.M.) (Merchandising)
  Ltd v Cloke (1963) . . . 15.61
Allcard v Skinner (1887) 14.32, 14.38
Allen v Rescous (1676) . . 15.58
Alliance Bank v Broom (1864) . 6.7
Amber Size and Chemical Co
  Ltd v Menzal (1913) . . 28.11
American Surety Co of New
  York v Wrighton (1910) . 25.6
Amoco Australia Pty Ltd v
  Rocca Bros Motor Engineering
  Co Pty Ltd (1975) . . . 15.23
Amos v Max-Arc Ltd (1973) . 28.54
Anderson (W.B.) & Sons Ltd v
  Rhodes (Liverpool) Ltd
  (1967) 20.14
Anderson Ltd v Daniel (1924)
  . . . . 15.53, 15.54

Para.

Andrews v Hopkinson (1957) . 6.21
Andrews Bros (Bournemouth)
  Ltd v Singer & Co Ltd (1934) . 10.31
Angelia, The (1973) . . . 10.59
Anglesey, Re (1901) . . 12.15
Annefield, The (1971) . 27.10
Annesley, Re (1926) . . 4.22
Anns v London Borough of
  Merton (1972) 20.8, 20.11, 20.32
Appleby v Myers (1867) . 11.17
Applegarth v Colley (1842) . 15.4
Applegate v Moss (1971) . 12.28
Apthorp v Neville & Co (1907) . 15.58
Arab Bank Ltd v Ross (1952) . 24.28
Archbolds (Freightage) Ltd v
  S. Spanglett Ltd (1961)
  . . . 15.49, 15.55, 15.61
Archdale (J.) Ltd v Comservices
  Ltd (1954) 10.33
Archer v Hudson (1844) . 14.36
Arcos Ltd v E.A. Ronaasen &
  Son (1933) 9.2
Ardennes, The (1951). . 27.9
Arenson v Casson, Beckman,
  Ruttey & Co (1975). . 20.7
Armstrong v Jackson (1917)
  . . . . 14.11, 14.26
Ashbury Railway Carriage and
  Iron Co v Riche (1875) . 4.9, 18.11
Ashby v Tolhurst (1937) . 26.4
Asfan & Co v Blundell (1896) . 22.23
Ashford Shire Council v
  Dependable Motors Pty Ltd
  (1961) 18.7
Ashington Piggeries Ltd v
  Christopher Hill Ltd (1972) . 22.58
Ashley v Ashley (1829) . . 25.25

	Para.
Ashmore, Benson, Pease and Co Ltd v A.V. Dawson Ltd (1973)	15.55
Assam Railways and Trading Co Ltd v IRC (1935) . . .	3.26
Atkinson v Cotesworth (1825)	18.25, 18.26
Atkinson v Denby (1862) .	.15.63
A-G of South Australia v Adelaide Steamship Co Ltd (1913)	.15.27
Attwood v Lamont (1920) .	.15.30
Attwood v Small (1838) .	. 14.6

B

	Para.
Bailey v Thurston & Co Ltd (1903)	.19.25
Baily v De Crespigny (1869)	.11.12
Bainbridge v Firmstone (1838) .	6.9
Bainbrigge v Browne (1881)	14.32, 14.38
Baker v Willoughby (1970) .	.20.25
Baldry v Marshall (1925) .	. 17.7
Baldwin v London, Chatham and Dover Rly Co (1882).	. 27.2
Balfour v Balfour (1919) .	. 6.2
Ballett v Mingay (1943)	16.16, 26.3
Bamfield v Goole and Sheffield Transport Co Ltd (1910) .	. 27.4
Bank Line Ltd v Arthur Capel & Co (1919) . . .	. 11.4
Bank of England v Vagliano Bros (1891) . . .	.24.10
Bannerman v White (1861) .	. 8.11
Barber v Meyerstein (1870)	.27.31
Barclay v Messenger (1874)	. 9.17
Barclays Bank Ltd v Astley Industrial Trust (1970) .	.24.31
Barker v Bell (1971) . .	.22.34
Barrett v Chelsea and Kensington Management Committee (1969)	20.24
Barrow & Bros v Dyster, Nalder & Co (1884) . . .	.18.46
Barrow, Lane and Balland Ltd v Philip Phillips & Co Ltd (1929)	22.24
Bartlett v Sidney Marcus Ltd (1965)	.22.52
Barton v Armstrong (1975)	14.29, 14.30
Basma v Weekes (1950) .	.18.39

	Para.
Baumwoll Manufacturer Von Carl Scheibler v Furness (1893)	27.28
Bavins Junr and Sims v London and South Western Bank (1900)	24.80
Bayliffe v Butterworth (1847)	.18.32
Beach v Reed Corrugated Cases Ltd (1956) . . .	. 12.8
Beal v South Devon Rly Co (1864)	.18.18
Beattie v Lord Ebury (1872)	14.4, 18.50
Beaumont, Re (1893) . .	. 4.23
Bechervaise v Lewis (1872) .	.26.36
Becke v Smith (1836) . .	. 3.20
Beckett v Nurse (1948) .	. 7.12
Begbie v Phosphate Sewage Co (1875)	. 14.6
Behn v Burness (1862)	10.20, 27.22
Behnke v Bede Shipping Co Ltd (1927)	.22.74
Belfast Ropework Co Ltd v Bushell (1918) . . .	. 27.2
Bell v Kennedy (1868) .	. 4.23
Bell v Lever Bros Ltd (1932)	. 13.5
Bell v Travco Hotels Ltd (1953) .	20.1
Bell Houses Ltd v City Wall Properties Ltd (1966) .	. 4.10
Belvoir Finance Co Ltd v Stapleton (1971) . .	.15.63
Belsize Motor Supply Co v Cox (1914)	.22.32
Beningfield v Baxter (1886)	.14.32
Bennett v Bennett (1952)	15.29, 15.61
Bentley (Dick) (Productions) Ltd v Harold Smith (Motors) Ltd (1965)	. 8.14
Bents Brewery Co Ltd v Hogan (1945)	.28.11
Bentsen v Taylor Sons & Co (1893)	. 10.8
Beresford v Royal Insurance Co Ltd (1938) . . .	.25.22
Berry v Berry (1929) . .	. 6.35
Berry v Peek (1889) . .	.14.14
Beswick v Beswick (1968) 3.25, 6.24, 6.25, 6.26, 6.27, 12.18	
Bevans v Rees (1839) . .	. 9.13
Beveridge v Burgis (1812) .	.24.45
Biddell Bros v Horst Co (1911)	.22.97
Bigos v Bousted (1951) .	.15.63
Birch v Paramount Estates Ltd (1956)	. 8.7
Bird v Brown (1850) . .	. 18.9
Bird v Holbrook (1828) .	.20.45

Para.

Birkmyr v Darnell (1704) . . 7.8
Bishop and Baxter Ltd v Anglo-
Eastern Trading and Industrial
Co Ltd (1944) 5.24
Bishopsgate Motor Finance
Corpn Ltd v Transport Brakes
Ltd (1949) 00.00
Bissett v Wilkinson (1927) . . 14.4
Bize v Dickason (1786) . . 12.25
Blackburn Bobbin Co v T.W.
Allen & Son (1918) . . . 11.4
Black-Clawson International Ltd
v Papierwerke Waldof-
Aschaffenburg A.G. (1975) . 3.26
Blades v Free (1829) . . . 18.27
Blake v Concannon (1870) . . 16.11
Blaustein v Maltz, Mitchell &
Co (1937) 18.20
Blower v Great Western Rly Co
(1872) 27.2
Blumberg v Life Interests and
Reversionary Securities Corpn
(1897) 9.13
Boardman v Phipps (1967) . . 18.19
Boardman v Sanderson (1964) . 20.9
Boden v French (1851) . . 18.17
Bolton v Mahadeva (1972) . . 10.16
Bolton v Stone (1951) . . 20.19
Bolton Partners v Lambert (1889)
. . . . 18.8, 18.9
Bonita, The (1861) . . . 18.12
Bonsor v Musicians Union (1956) 4.14
Borrows v Ellison (1871) . . 12.27
Bosch v De Gens: 13/61 (1961) . 15.40
Boston Deep Sea Fishing and
Ice Co v Ansell (1888) 18.19, 28.12
Bosten Deep Sea Fishing and
Ice Co Ltd v Farnham
(Inspector of Taxes) (1957) . 18.10
Boston Fruit Co v British and
Foreign Marine Insurance Co
(1906) 18.10
Bottomley v Bannister (1932) . 20.6
Bourhill v Young (1943) . . 20.9
Bourne v Gatliffe (1844) . . 27.3
Bowater v Rowley Regis Corpn
(1944) 21.36
Bowes v Shand (1877) . . 22.41
Bowmakers Ltd v Barnet
Instruments Ltd (1945) . . 15.63
Brace v Calder (1895) . . . 12.9
Bradbury v Morgan (1862) . . 5.21
Bradford v Robinson Rentals
Ltd (1967) . . 20.27, 28.68

Para.

Brandao v Barnett (1846) . . 26.28
Brandt (H.O.) & Co v H.N. Morris
& Co Ltd (1917) . . . 8.23
Brandt's Sons & Co v Dunlop
Rubber Co Ltd (1905) 19.9, 19.12
Branford v Saunders (1877) . 25.21
Brass v Maitland (1856) . . 27.21
Breach v Epsylon Industries Ltd
(1976) 28.15
Brewer Street Investments Ltd v
Barclays Woollen Co Ltd (1954) 17.3
Briddon v Great Northern Rly
Co (1858) 27.3
Bridger v Savage (1885)
. . . . 15.5, 15.6, 15.7
Briggs v Calverly (1800) . . 9.13
British and Beningtons Ltd v
North Western Cachar Tea Co
Ltd (1923) 6.35
British and Mercantile Insurance
Co v London, Liverpool and
Globe Insurance Co (1877) . 25.6
British Broadcasting Corpn v
Joannou (1975) . . . 28.41
British Railways Board v
Herrington (1972) . 3.40, 20.45
British Railways Board v Liptrot
(1969) 28.80
British Reinforced Concrete
Engineering Co Ltd v Schelff
(1921) 15.22
British Road Services v Arthur V
Crutchley & Co Ltd (1968) . 26.7
British School of Motoring v
Simms (1971) . . . 8.23
British Syphon Co Ltd v
Homewood (1956) . . 28.12
British Transport Commission v
Gourley (1956) . 12.8, 21.47
British Waggon Co v Lea & Co
(1880) 9.20
Brogden v Marriott (1836) . . 15.3
Brogden v Metropolitan Rly Co
(1877) 5.9
Brook v Hook (1871) . 18.11, 24.75
Brook's Wharf and Bull Wharf
Ltd v Goodman Bros (1937) . 17.2
Brough v Nettleton (1921) . . 7.17
Brougham v Dwyer (1913) . . 4.12
Brown v Harper (1893) . . 16.15
Brown v Raphael (1958) . . 14.4
Brown v Staton (1816) . . 18.40
Brown (B.S.) & Son Ltd v
Craiks Ltd (1970) . . . 22.52

Para.

Brown Jenkinson & Co Ltd v
  Percy Dalton (London) Ltd
  (1957) 27.29
Browning v Morris (1778) . . 15.63
Brownsea Haven Properties Ltd
  v Poole Corpn (1889) . . 3.24
Bruce v Warwick (1815) . . 16.15
Bryant v Richardson (1866) . 16.3
Buchanan (James) & Co Ltd v
  Babco Forwarding and
  Shipping (UK) Ltd (1977) . 3.27
Budgett v Binnington (1891) . 27.13
Bull v Pitney-Bowes Ltd (1966) . 15.19
Bullock v G. John Power
  (Agencies) Ltd (1956) . . 28.80
Bulmer (H.P.) Ltd v J. Bolinger
  SA (1974) . . 2.33, 2.34, 3.34
Bunker v Charles Brand & Son
  Ltd (1969) 20.36
Burges v Wickham (1863) . . 8.4
Burgess v Cox (1951) . . . 7.12
Burn v Boulton (1846) . . 9.8
Burnand v Rodocanachi (1882) . 25.6
Burnard v Haggis (1863) . . 16.16
Burnett v Westminster Bank Ltd
  (1966) . . . 10.28, 24.69
Burns, Philp & Co Ltd v Gillespie
  Bros Pty Ltd (1947) . . 18.13
Burrell v Jones (1819) . . 18.39
Burrows v Barnes (1900) . . 22.37
Byrne v Schiller (1871) . . 27.37
Byrne v Van Tienhoven (1880) . 5.18

C

C.H.T. v Ward (1965) . . 15.11
Cahn v Pockett's Bristol Channel
  Steam Packet Co Ltd (1899)
  . . . . . 22.33, 22.93
Campbell v Edwards (1976) . 5.26
Cannon v Hartley (1949) . . 12.18
Capital and Counties Bank Ltd v
  Gordon (1903). . . . 24.5
Capper Pass Ltd v Lawton (1977) 28.34
Car and Universal Finance Co Ltd
  . . . . 14.10, 14.11
Cargo ex Argos (1873) . . 27.37
Carlill v Carbolic Smoke Ball
  Co (1893) . 5.3, 5.5, 5.12, 15.2
Carlton Hall Club v Laurence
  (1929) 15.11
Carpenters Co v British Mutual
  Banking Co (1938) . . 24.73

Para.

Carpenters Estates v Davies
  (1940) 12.18
Carr v Mercantile Produce Co
  Ltd (1949) 28.80
Carter v Boehm (1766) . . 14.24
Cartwright v Cartwright (1853) . 15.14
Case of Proclamations (1611) . 3.16
Casey's Patents, Re, Stewart v
  Casey (1892) 6.4
Cassell & Co Ltd v Broome
  (1972) 3.41
Cassidy v Ministry of Health
  (1951) . . 3.38, 21.16, 28.4
Castellain v Preston (1883). . 25.4
Caswell v Powell Dyffyn Quarries
  Ltd (1940) 21.40
Caton v Caton (1865). . . 17.18
Cattle v Stockton Waterworks
  Co (1875) . . . 20.8
Cavalier v Pope (1906) . . 20.6
Cavanagh v Ulster Weaving Co
  Ltd (1960) 28.66
Cellulose Acetate Silk Co Ltd v
  Widnes Foundry (1925) Ltd
  (1933) . . 12.11, 12.14
Central London Property Trust
  Ltd v High Trees House Ltd
  (1947) . 3.37, 6.14, 6.15, 6.33
Central Newbury Car Auctions
  Ltd v Unity Finance Ltd (1957) 22.29
Cesarini v Ronzani (1858) . . 9.6
Ceylon Government v Société
  Franco-Tunisienne
  D'Armement-Tunis (1962) . 27.13
Chamberlain v Young and Tower
  (1893) 24.10
Chandler v Webster (1904) 11.13, 11.14
Chandler Bros Ltd v Boswell
  (1936) 11.10
Chapelton v Barry U.D.C. (1940) 10.28
Chaplin v Hicks (1911) . . 12.7
Chaplin v Leslie Frewin
  (Publishers) Ltd (1966) . . 16.7
Chappel & Co Ltd v Nestlé Co
  Ltd (1960) 6.6
Chapple v Cooper (1844) . . 16.4
Chaproniere v Lambert (1917) . 7.18
Chaproniere v Mason (1905) . 22.56
Charles v Blackwell (1877) . . 24.73
Charlotte, The (1861). . . 18.12
Charter v Sullivan (1957) . . 22.84
Cheshire & Co v Vaughan Bros
  & Co (1920) 15.7

Para.

Chess (Oscar) Ltd v Williams
  (1957) .   8.9, 8.11, 8.14, 10.14
Chesworth v Farrar (1967) . . 26.2
Chichester v Cobb (1866) . . 6.17
Christy v Row (1808) . 10.15, 27.35
Ciampa v British India Steam
  Navigation Co Ltd (1915) . 27.18
City and Westminster Properties
  (1934) Ltd v Mudd (1959) . 8.7
Clark v Lindsay (1903) . 13.2, 13.3
Clark v Newsam (1847) . . 21.34
Clarke v Cobley (1789) . . 16.17
Clarke v Dickson (1858) . . 14.11
Clarkson, Booker Ltd v Andjel
  (1964) 18.43
Clayton v Ashdown (1714). . 16.9
Clayton (Herbert) and Jack
  Waller Ltd v Oliver (1930) . 28.15
Clements v London and North
  Western Railway (1894) . . 16.6
Clifford Davis Management Ltd
  v W.E.A. Records Ltd (1975)
  . . . . . 14.37, 15.25
Clifford (Frank W.) Ltd v Garth
  (1956) 15.54
Clink v Radford (1891) . . 27.16
Clore v Theatrical Properties
  Ltd (1936) 6.31
Close v Steel Co of Wales (1962) 28.80
Clough v London and North
  Western Rly Co (1871) . . 14.11
Cogent v Gibson (1864) . . 12.18
Coggs v Bernard (1704) . . 26.7
Cohen v Kittell (1889) . 15.7, 18.16
Cohen v Roche (1927) 7.14, 22.74
Coldman v Hill (1919) . . 26.7
Collen v Gardner (1856) . . 18.32
Collen v Wright (1857) . . 18.50
Collier v Sunday Referee
  Publishing Co Ltd (1940). . 28.15
Collins v Associated Greyhound
  Racecourses Ltd (1930) . . 18.42
Collins v Godefroy (1831) . . 6.11
Combe v Combe (1951) . 6.15, 6.33
Commercial Banking Co of
  Sydney Ltd v Jalsard Pty Ltd
  (1973) 6.20
Compania Colombian de Seguros
  v Pacific Steam Navigation Co
  (1965) 19.16
Compagnie de Commerce et
  Commission SARL v Parkinson
  Stove Co Ltd (1953) . . 5.14

Para.

Condon, Re, ex parte James
  (1874) 17.5
Cooke v Eshelby (1887) . . 18.42
Cooper v Micklefield Coal and
  Lime Co Ltd (1912). . . 19.16
Cooper v Phibbs (1867) . 13.3, 17.5
Cope v Rowlands (1836) . . 15.49
Cornwal v Wilson (1750) 18.9, 18.12
Cornwall v Henson (1900) . . 22.71
Corpe v Overton (1933) . . 16.11
Cory (William) & Son Ltd v
  London Corpn (1951) . . 8.23
Cosgrove v Horsfall (1945) . . 10.36
Cotman v Brougham (1918) . 4.10
Coughlin v Gillison (1899) . . 26.11
Coulls v Bagot's Executor and
  Trustee Co Ltd (1967) . . 6.23
Coulson v City of London
  Polytechnic (1976) . . . 28.18
Coulthart v Clementson (1879)
  . . . . . 5.21, 26.37
Coutts & Co v Browne-Lecky
  (1947) . . . 16.14, 26.31
Couturier v Hastie (1852)
  . . . . . 7.9, 13.2, 13.4
Cowan v Milbourn (1867) . . 15.61
Coward v Motor Insurers' Bureau
  (1963) 6.2
Cowell v Simpson (1809) . . 26.28
Cowern v Nield (1912) . . 16.8
Cox v Philips Industries Ltd
  (1976) 12.2
Crane v London Dock Co (1864) . 22.35
Craven v Ryder (1816) . . 27.28
Craven-Ellis v Canons Ltd (1936)
  . . . . . 4.12, 17.8
Craxfords (Ramsgate) Ltd v
  Williams and Steer Manufac-
  turing Co Ltd (1954) . . 3.24
Cricklewood Property and
  Investment Trust Ltd v
  Leighton's Investment Trust
  Ltd (1945) . . 11.7, 11.12
Croft v Lumley (1858) . . 9.8
Crompton v Truly Fair
  (International) Ltd (1975) . 28.56
Cross v Lewis Hillman Ltd
  (1970) 14.5
Croydon Gas Co v Dickinson
  (1876) 26.37
Cumming v Ince (1847) . . 14.30
Cundy v Lindsay (1878)
  . . . 5.3, 13.11, 13.16, 14.9

Para.

Cunliffe-Owen v Teather and
Greenwood (1967) . . . 8.17
Currie v Misa (1875) . . . 6.3
Curtice v London City and
Midland Bank Ltd (1908) . 24.70
Curtis v Chemical Cleaning and
Dyeing Co Ltd (1951) . .10.34
Cyril Leonard & Co v Simco
Securities Trust Ltd (1971) . 28.40
Czarnikow v Roth, Schmidt &
Co (1922) . . 2.41, 15.15

D

D. and C. Builders v Rees (1966)
. . . . 6.13, 6.15, 6.33
Daborn v Bath Tramways
Motor Co Ltd (1946) . .20.21
Da Costa en Schaake NV v
Nederlanske
Belastingadministratie (1963) . 3.39
Daimler Co Ltd v Continental
Tyre & Rubber Co (Gt
Britain) Ltd (1916) . . . 4.6
Dakin v Oxley (1864). . .27.35
Dakin (H.) & Co Ltd v Lee
(1916) . . 10.14, 10.16
Dalby v India and London Life
Assurance Co (1854) . .25.21
Daley v Radnor (1973) . .28.21
Daniels and Daniels v White &
Sons Ltd (1938) . . .20.33
Davidson v Handley Page Ltd
(1945) 28.68
Davies v Beynon-Harris (1931) . 16.9
Davies v Collins (1945) . .10.54
Davies v Powell Dyffryn
Collieries Ltd (1942) . .21.33
Davies v Rees (1886) . . .26.22
Davies & Co (Wines) Ltd v
Aja-Minerva (E.M.I.) Ltd
(1974) 14.14
Davis v Johnson (1978) . 3.26, 3.41
Davis (Clifford) Management
Ltd v W.E.A. Records Ltd
(1975) . . . 14.36, 15.25
Davis Contractors Ltd v
Fareham UDC (1956) . . 11.2
Dawson v Great Northern and
City Rly Co (1905) . . .19.16
Dearle v Hall (1828) . . .19.13
Debenham v Mellon (1880) . 18.7
De Bussche v Alt (1878) . .18.20
De Francesco v Barnum (1889) . 16.6

Para.

Defries v Milne (1913) . .19.16
De Geus v Bosch (1962) . .15.40
Delaney v T.P. Smith Ltd (1946) 7.16
De Mattos v Gibson (1858). . 6.29
Denman v Brise (1949) . .11.12
Denmark Productions Ltd v
Boscobel Productions Ltd
(1969) 10.9
Denney Gasquet and Metcalfe
v Conklin (1913) . . .19.17
Denny Mott and Dickson Ltd v
James B. Fraser & Co Ltd
(1944) 11.13
Derry v Peek (1889) . . .14.14
Deuchar v Gaslight & Coke Co
(1925) 4.9
Devaynes v Noble, Clayton's Case
(1816) 9.10
Deverges v Sandeman, Clark &
Co (1902) 26.21
Devonald v Rosser & Sons (1906) 28.15
Deyong v Shenburn (1946) 8.23, 20.5
Diamond v Campbell-Jones
(1961) 12.8
Dickinson v Dodds (1876) . . 5.18
Diggle v Higgs (1877) . 15.7, 15.8
Dimmock v Hallett (1866) . . 14.4
Director of Public Prosecutions v
Schildkamp (1971) . . . 3.23
Ditcham v Worrall (1880) . .16.15
Dixon v British Broadcasting
Corpn (1977) 28.42
Dolphin v Robins (1859) . . 4.23
Donaldson v Donaldson (1854) .19.10
Donoghue v Stevenson (1932)
. 3.47, 20.4, 20.6, 20.9, 20.31, 26.11
Dooley v Cammell Laird & Co
Ltd (1951) 20.9
Doughty v Turner Manufacturing
Co Ltd (1964) . . 3.47, 20.27
Doyle v Olby (Ironmongers)
Ltd (1969) 14.14
Doyle v White City Stadium Ltd
(1935) 16.7
Drew v Nunn (1879) . . .18.28
Drive Yourself Hire Co (London)
Ltd v Strutt (1954) . . . 6.24
Driver v William Willett
(Contractors) Ltd (1969). .20.32
Dugdale v Kraft Foods Ltd (1977) 28.34
Du Jardin v Beadman Bros Ltd
(1952) 22.32
Dulieu v White & Sons (1901) . 20.9
Dungage v Dungate (1965) . .12.29

Para.

Duncan (W.W.) & Co, Re (1905) 9.6
Dunlop Pneumatic Tyre Co Ltd
  v New Garage and Motor Co
  Ltd (1915) 12.14
Dunlop Pneumatic Tyre Co Ltd
  v Selfridge & Co Ltd (1915) 6.3, 6.18
Dunmore (Countess) v
  Alexander (1830) . . . 5.16
Durham Bros v Robertson (1898)
  . . . . 19.6, 19.11
Dutton v Bognor Regis UDC
  (1972) 20.32

E

Eaglehill Ltd v J. Needham
  Builders Ltd (1973) . . .24.45
Easson v London and North
  Eastern Rly Co (1944) . .20.22
Eastern Distributors Ltd v
  Goldking (1957) . . .22.29
Eastham v Newcastle United
  Football Club Ltd (1964)
  . . . . 15.20, 15.21
Eastman Photographic Co v
  Comptroller of Patents (1898) 3.21
Eastwood v Kenyon (1840) . 7.9
Ebrahami v Westbourne Galleries
  Ltd (1972) 4.7
Ecay v Godfrey (1947) . . 8.12
Eddis v Chichester Constable
  (1969) 12.28
Edgington v Fitzmaurice (1885)
  . . . . . 14.4, 14.7
Edler v Auerbach (1950) . .15.63
Edwards v Carter (1893) 16.9, 16.10
Edwards v Newland & Co (1950) 9.20
Edwards v Railway Executive
  (1952) 20.38
Edwards v Sheratt (1801) . 27.2
Edwards Ltd v Vaughan (1910) .22.33
Egg Stores (Stamford Hill) Ltd v
  Leiborici (1976) . . . 11.6
Elbinger AG v Armstrong (1874) 22.80
Elcock v Thomson (1949) . . 25.4
Elder, Dempster & Co Ltd v
  Paterson, Zochonis & Co Ltd
  (1924) 27.18
Ellerman Lines Ltd v Murray
  (1931) 3.23
Ellesmere v Wallace (1929) 15.3, 15.4
Ellesmere Brewery Co v Cooper
  (1896) 26.34
Elliott v Box-Ironside (1925) .18.47

Para.

Elliott v Turquand (1881) . .18.29
Elton Cop Dyeing Co Ltd v
  Robert Broadbent & Son Ltd
  (1919) 6.36
Entores v Miles Far East Corpn
  (1955) 5.11
Erlanger v New Sombrero
  Phosphate Co (1878) . .14.11
Errington v Errington (1952) . 5.19
Ertel Bieber & Co v Rio Tinto
  Co Ltd (1918) 11.9
Eshelby v Federated European
  Bank Ltd (1932) . . .10.16
Esso Petroleum Ltd v Customs
  and Excise Comrs (1976) 6.2, 22.7
Esso Petroleum Co Ltd v
  Harper's Garage (Stourport)
  Ltd (1968)
  . 15.17, 15.23, 15.24, 15.26, 15.27
Esso Petroleum Co Ltd v Mardon
  (1976) . . 8.13, 14.14, 20.14
Eugenia, The (1964) . . .11.10
Evans v Llewellin (1787) . .14.37
Evans (J.) & Son (Portsmouth)
  Ltd v Andrea Merzario Ltd
  (1976) 8.6, 8.10, 8.11, 10.35, 10.54
Evenden v Guildford City
  Association Football Club
  Ltd (1975) 28.17
Eyles v Ellis (1827) . . . 9.6

F

Fairlie v Fenton (1870) . .18.48
Fardon v Harcourt-Rivington
  (1932) 20.19
Farquharson v Pearl Insurance
  Co Ltd (1937) 9.13
Farrell v Federated Employers'
  Insurance Association (1970) .25.17
Farrow v Wilson (1869) 18.27, 19.25
Fawcett v Smethurst (1914) . 16.5
Felthouse v Bindley (1862) . 5.13
Fenton v J. Thorley & Co Ltd
  (1903) 28.87
Ferguson v John Dawson &
  Partners (Contractors) Ltd
  (1976) . . . 28.2, 28.5
Ferrier, Re, ex parte Trustee v
  Donald (1944) 22.18
Fibrosa Spolka Akcyjna v
  Fairbairn Lawson Combe
  Barbour Ltd (1943) . 11.14, 22.26
Fielding, Platt Ltd v Najar (1969) 15.61

	Para.
Finch v Brook (1834) . . .	9.13
Finch v Miller (1848) . . .	9.13
Fisher v Bell (1961) . . .	5.4
Fisher v Bridges (1853) .	15.64
Fisher v Ruislip-Northwood UDC and Middlesex County Council (1945). . . .	3.41
Fisher & Co v Appollinaris & Co (1875)	15.60
Fitch v Dewes (1921) . .	15.19
Fitzgerald v Dressler (1859) .	7.9
Fitzmaurice v Bayley (1856) .	18.12
Fitzfleet Estates Ltd v Cherry (1977)	3.40
Flavell, Re, Murray v Flavell (1883)	6.25
Flight v Bolland (1828) 12.18, 16.15
Flynn, Re (1968) . . .	4.23
Foakes v Beer (1884) . . 6.13, 6.32
Foley v Classique Coaches Ltd (1934)	5.26
Footman Bower & Co Ltd, Re (1961)	9.10
Foreman & Co Pty Ltd v The Liddesdale (1900) . .	18.12
Forman v Wright (1851) .	24.35
Forster & Sons Ltd v Suggett (1918)	15.19
Foster v Driscoll (1929) .	15.60
Fothergill v Monarch Airlines Ltd (1977) . . .	27.43
Frank W. Clifford Ltd v Garth (1956)	15.54
Franz Grad v Finanzant Traustein (1971) . .	3.31
Freeman and Lockyer v Buckhurst Park Properties (Mangal) Ltd (1964) 18.34, 18.35
French & Co Ltd v Leeston Shipping Co Ltd (1922) .	18.26
Froom v Butcher (1976) .	21.39
Frost v Aylesbury Dairy Co Ltd (1905)	22.62
Frost v Knight (1872). .	10.13
Fry v Lane (1888) . .	14.38
Fuld, Re, Hartley v Fuld (1968) 4.23
Furby v Hooey (1947) .	22.20
Furnivall v Andson (1893) .	18.1
G	
G(A) v G(T) (1970) . .	18.5
Galbraith and Grant Ltd v Block (1922)	22.68
Galloway v Galloway (1914)	13.3

	Para.
Gardiner v Heading (1928) .	18.48
Gasque v IRC (1940) . .	4.23
Gasson v Cole (1910) . .	18.23
Gaussen v Morton (1830) .	18.25
Geddling v Marsh (1920) .	22.53
General Billposting Co Ltd v Atkinson (1909) . .	10.4
General Publicity Services Ltd v Best's Brewery Co Ltd (1951) .	8.23
George v Surrey (1830) .	24.7
Giacomo Costa Fu Andrea v British Italian Trading Co Ltd (1963)	2.45
Giblin v McMullen (1868) .	24.79
Giertsen v Turnbull & Co (1908)	27.18
Gilbert-Ash (Northern) Ltd v Modern Engineering (Bristol) Ltd (1974) . . .	10.14
Gilchester Properties Ltd v Gomm (1948) . . .	8.14
Gillespie Bros & Co v Cheney, Eggar & Co (1896) . . 8.4, 8.7
Gillett v Peppercorne (1840) .	18.19
Ginty v Belmont Building Supplies Ltd (1959). .	21.4
Glasbrook Bros Ltd v Glamorgan County Council (1925) .	6.11
Glasgow Corpn v Taylor (1922)	20.38
Gledhow Autoparts Ltd v Delaney (1965) . .	15.18
Glyn, Mills & Co v East and West India Dock Co (1882) .	27.31
Godsall v Boldero (1807) .	25.21
Goldman v Cox (1924) .	24.25
Goldsoll v Goldman (1915) .	15.30
Gompertz v Bartlett (1853) .	24.52
Gonin, Re (1977) . .	7.18
Goode v Harrison (1821) .	16.9
Goodinson v Goodinson (1954)	15.29
Goodman v Chase (1818) .	7.8
Goodman v Harvey (1836) .	24.30
Gordon v Gordon (1821) .	14.25
Gore v Van der Lann (1967) 6.8, 6.26
Gorringe v Irwell India Rubber Works (1886) . . .	19.13
Gorris v Scott . . 3.21, 21.2
Gorse v Durham County Council (1971). . .	10.10
Gosling v Anderson (1972).	14.14
Goss v Lord Nugent (1833) .	6.35
Gould v South Eastern and Chatham Rly Co (1920) .	27.2
Graham v Johnson (1869) .	19.16
Grainger v Gough (1896) .	5.4

Para.

Grant v Australian Knitting Mills
  Ltd (1936) . . 22.52, 22.56
Grant v Norway (1851) . . 27.28
Grant & Co v Coverdale, Food &
  Co (1884) 27.13
Gratitudine, The (1801) . . 18.13
Gray v Barr (1971) . . . 25.15
Great Northern Rly Co v
  Witham (1873). . . . 5.10
Great Western Rly Co v London
  and County Banking Co Ltd
  (1901) . . . 24.62, 24.83
Greaves & Co (Contractors) Ltd
  v Baynham, Meikle & Partners
  (1975) 20.17
Green v Portsmouth Stadium
  Ltd (1953) 15.63
Green v Russell (1959) . . 6.25
Greenwood v Martins Bank Ltd
  (1933) 24.75
Greenwood v Sutcliffe (1892) . 9.13
Gregory v Ford (1951) 8.21, 28.14
Grenfell v Dean and Canons of
  Windsor (1840) . . . 19.16
Griffiths v Brymer (1903) . . 13.3
Griffiths v Peter Conway Ltd
  (1939) 22.56
Griffiths v Fleming (1909) . . 25.21
Griffiths v Ystradyfodwg School
  Board (1890) 9.12
Grist v Bailey (1967) . . 13.6, 13.9
Groom (C.) Ltd v Barber (1915) 22.97
Groos, Re (1904) . . . 3.23
Groves v Lord Wimbourne (1898) 21.1
Guild & Co v Conrad (1894) . 7.8

H

H. v H. (1857) 15.14
H. v W. (1857) 15.14
Hadley v Baxendale (1854)
  . . . . 12.3, 12.6, 22.73
Haley v London Electricity Board
  (1965) 20.16
Halford v Kymer (1830) . . 25.21
Halley v O'Brien (1920) . . 7.13
Hamilton, Re (1921) . . . 19.14
Hamilton Finance Co Ltd v
  Coverley Westray Walbaum
  and Fosetti Ltd (1969) . . 24.45
Hampden v Walsh (1876) . . 15.2
Hang Fung Shipping and Trading
  Co Ltd v Mullion & Co Ltd
  (1966) 27.18

Para.

Hansa Nord, The (1976)
  . . 10.20, 10.21, 22.40, 22.52
Hansen v Harrold Bros (1894) . 27.16
Harburg India Rubber Comb Co
  v Martin (1902) . . . 7.9
Harbutt's 'Plasticine' Ltd v Wayne
  Tank and Pump Co Ltd (1970)
  . . . . . 10.57, 10.58
Harding v Harding (1886) . . 19.15
Harding v London Joint Stock
  Bank Ltd (1914) . . . 24.83
Hardy & Co v Hillerns and
  Fowler (1923) 22.40
Hargreave v Spink (1892) . . 22.35
Harley & Co v Nagata (1917) . 8.17
Harman v Clarke (1815) . . 27.13
Harmer v Armstrong (1934) . 18.45
Harold Wood Brick Co Ltd v
  Ferris (1935) 9.17
Harris v Birkenhead Corpn
  (1976) 20.39
Harris v Nickerson (1873) . . 5.5
Harris v Poland (1942) . . 25.10
Harris and Russell Ltd v Slingsby
  (1973) 28.38
Harrison v Harrison (1910). . 15.14
Harrison v Harrison (1953). . 4.23
Harrison v Holland (1921) . . 17.7
Harrison v Wells (1967) . . 3.41
Harrison and Jones Ltd v Bunten
  and Lancaster Ltd (1953) . 13.6
Harse v Pearl Life Assurance Co
  (1904) . . 15.63, 25.2, 25.21
Hart v A.R. Marshall & Son
  Bulwell Ltd (1977) . . . 11.6
Hartas v Ribbons (1889) . . 18.9
Hartley v Hymans (1920) 6.34, 22.41
Hartley v Mayo & Co Ltd (1954) 21.2
Hartley v Ponsonby (1857). . 6.12
Hartog v Colin and Shields
  (1939) . . . 13.15, 13.16
Harvey v Facey (1893) . . 5.3
Harvey v Farnie (1882) . . 4.23
Haseldine v C.A. Daw Ltd (1941)
  . . . . . 10.38, 20.36
Hastings (No 3), Re (1959). . 2.14
Hathesing v Laing (1873) . . 27.28
Hatton v Car Maintenance Co
  (1914) 26.27
Hawkins v Price (1947) . . 7.12
Haynes v Harwood (1935): 20.29, 21.37
Head v Tattersall (1871) . . 5.28
Healy v Howlett & Sons (1917) . 22.21

Para.

Heatons Transport (St Helens)
Ltd v Transport and General
Workers' Union (1973) . . 21.30
Hebdon v West (1863) . . . 25.21
Hedley Byrne & Co Ltd v Heller
& Partners Ltd (1964)
3.37, 14.14, 18.51, 20.4, 20.13, 20.14,
20.15, 24.79
Heil v Hedges (1951) . . . 22.57
Heilbut, Symons & Co v
Buckleton (1913) . 8.7, 8.11, 8.17
Helby v Matthews (1895) . . 22.33
Hely-Hutchinson v Brayhead
Ltd (1968) 18.32
Henderson v Henderson (1967) . 4.23
Henderson v Henry E. Jenkins &
Sons (1970) 20.22
Henry Kendall & Sons v William
Lillico & Sons Ltd (1969) . 22.56
Herbert Clayton and Jack Waller
Ltd v Oliver (1930) . . . 28.15
Herbert Morris & Co Ltd v
Saxelby (1916) . 15.18, 15.19
Hermann v Charlesworth (1905)
. . . . . 15.14, 15.31
Herne Bay Steamboat Co v
Hutton (1903) 11.8
Heron II, The (1969) 12.3, 12.5, 12.6
Hewison v Ricketts (1894) . . 26.37
Hewlett v Allan (1894) . . 28.20
Heydon's Case (1584) . . . 3.21
Heyman v Darwins Ltd (1942)
. . . . . 10.7, 11.13
Heyworth v Hutchinson (1867) . 10.13
Hick v Raymond and Reid (1893) 27.13
Hill v C.A. Parsons & Co Ltd
(1972) 12.23
Hill v William Hill (Park Lane)
Ltd (1949) 15.6
Hillas & Co Ltd v Arcos Ltd
(1932) 5.24
Hillas-Drake, Re, National
Provincial Bank v Liddell
(1944) 3.44
Hilton v Thomas Burton (Rhodes)
Ltd (1961) 21.19
Hinton v Dibbin (1842) . . 27.5
Hinz v Berry (1970) . . . 20.9
Hirachand Punamchand v Temple
(1911) 6.16, 9.19
Hirji Mulfi v Cheong Yue SS Co
Ltd (1926) 11.13
Hivac Ltd v Park Royal Scientific
Instruments Ltd (1946) 8.20, 28.11

Para.

Hobbs v London and South West
Rly Co (1875) 12.2
Hochster v De La Tour (1853) . 10.12
Hoenig v Isaacs (1952) . . 10.16
Hoffberger v Ascot International
Bloodstock Bureau Ltd (1976) 12.9
Hollier v Rambler Motors
(A.M.C.) Ltd (1972) . . 10.33
Holme v Brunskill (1877) . . 26.37
Holroyd v Marshall (1862) . . 19.15
Holt v Heatherfield Trust Ltd
(1942) . . . 19.7, 19.15
Holt v Markham (1923) . . 17.5
Holwell Securities Ltd v Hughes
(1974) 5.15
Home Office v Dorset Yacht Co
(1970) . . . 20.4, 20.5, 20.6
Honeywill and Stein Ltd v Larkin
Bros Ltd (1934) . . . 21.26
Hong-Kong and Shanghai
Banking Corpn v Lo Lee Shi
(1928) 24.25
Hong Kong Fir Shipping Co Ltd
v Kawasaki Kisen Kaisha Ltd
(1962) 10.20, 10.21, 27.18, 27.22
Hooper v Treffry (1847) . . 18.23
Hooper v Keay (1871) . . 9.10
Hop and Malt Exchange and
Warehouse Co, Re, ex parte
Briggs 14.11
Hopkins v Tanqueray (1854) . 8.12
Horn v Anglo-Australian etc
Assurance Co (1861) . . 25.22
Horn v Minister of Food (1948) . 22.23
Horton v Horton (1961) . . 6.7
Houghland v R.R. Low (Luxury
Coaches) Ltd (1962) . . 26.7
Houghton v Trafalgar Insurance
Co (1911) 10.32
House Property and Investment
Co (1954) 3.47
Howard v Harris (1884) . . 26.6
Howard v Patent Ivory
Manufacturing Co (1888) . 18.10
Howes v Bishop (1909) . . 14.32
Hubert v Treherne (1842) . . 7.13
Huddersfield Police Authority v
Watson (1947) . . . 3.43
Hudson v Ridge Manufacturing
Co Ltd (1957) . . . 28.67
Hughes v Hughes (1971) . . 18.12
Hughes v Liverpool Victoria
Friendly Society (1916) . . 15.63
Hughes v Lord Advocate (1963) . 20.27

Para.

Hughes v Metropolitan Rly Co
  (1877) 6.33
Hulton v Hulton (1917) . .14.11
Humble v Hunter (1848) . .18.42
Hunt v Silk (1804) . . . 17.7
Hutton v Warren (1836) . . 8.17
Hyde v Wrench (1840) . . 5.8
Hyman v Hyman (1929) . .15.16

I

Imperial Chemical Industries Ltd
  v Shatwell (1965) . . .21.35
Imperial Loan Co v Stone (1892) 16.19
Inche Noriah v Shaik Allic Bin
  Omar (1929) 14.36
Industrial Development Consul-
  tants Ltd v Cooley (1972) .18.19
Industrial Properties (Barton
  Hill) Ltd v Associated Electircal
  Industries Ltd (1977) . . 3.41
Industries and General Mortgage
  Co Ltd v Lewis (1949) . .18.19
Ingham v Emes (1955) . . 22.5
Ingham v Primrose (1859) . .24.24
Ingram v Little (1961) 13.13, 13.16
IRC v Hinchy (1960) . . . 3.19
IRC v Lysaght (1929) . . . 4.26
Introduction Ltd, Re (1970) . 4.10
Ironmonger & Co v Byrne (1928) 15.3

J

J. and F. Stone Lighting and
  Radio Ltd v Haygarth (1968) .28.20
Jackson v Horizon Holidays Ltd
  (1975) 6.27
Jackson v Rotax Motor and
  Cycle Co (1910) . 10.17, 22.52
Jackson v Union Marine
  Insurance Co Ltd (1874) . . 11.4
Jacobs v Batavia and General
  Planations Trust Ltd (1924) . 8.4
Jacobs v LCC (1950) . . .20.38
James Buchanan & Co Ltd v
  Babco Forwarding and Shipping
  (U.K.) Ltd (1977) . . . 3.27
Jarvis v Swan Tours Ltd (1973)
  . . . . . 12.2, 14.14
Jennings v Rundall (1799) . .16.16
Joel v Law, Union and Crown
  Insurance Co (1908) . .14.24
John Summers & Sons Ltd v
  Frost (1955) . . 21.3, 28.80

Para.

Johnson v Nottinghamshire
  Combined Police Authority
  (1974) 28.54
Johnson v R. (1904) . . .12.15
Johnson v Sargant & Sons (1918) 3.11
Jon Beauforte (London) Ltd, Re
  (1953) 4.10
Jones v Gardiner (1902) . . 9.17
Jones v Humphreys (1902) . . 19.6
Jones v Lipman (1962) . . 4.6
Jones v Livox Quarries Ltd
  (1952) 21.39
Jones (R.E.) Ltd v Waring and
  Gillow Ltd (1926) . 17.4, 24.34
Joscelyne v Nissen (1970) . .13.18
Joseph Travers & Sons Ltd v
  Cooper (1915) . . 10.33, 26.7
Joseph Watson & Sons Ltd v
  Firemen's Fund Insurance Co
  of San Francisco (1922) . .27.38

K

Kafi Sunkersette Obu v Strauss
  & Co Ltd (1951) . . .18.21
Karsales (Harrow) Ltd v Wallis
  (1956) 10.53
Kay v ITW Ltd (1968) . .21.19
Kearley v Thomson (1890) . .15.63
Kearney v Eric Waller Ltd (1967) 20.36
Kearsley v Cole (1847) . .26.37
Keeping v Broom (1895) . . 9.9
Keighley, Maxsted & Co v Durant
  (1901) 18.10
Keir v Leeman (1846) . 15.60, 15.61
Kekewich v Manning (1851) .19.15
Kelly v Solari (1841) . . . 17.4
Kelver v Baxter (1866) . .18.10
Kemble v Farren (1829) . .12.14
Kendall v Hamilton (1879) . .18.43
Kendall (Henry) & Sons v
  William Lillico & Sons Ltd
  (1969) 22.56
Kenyon, Son & Craven Ltd v
  Baxter Hoare Ltd (1971)
  . . . . . 10.54, 10.57
Kerr v Lister & Co Ltd (1977) .28.34
Kimber v William Willett Ltd
  (1947) 8.23
Kings Norton Metal Co Ltd v
  Edridge Merritt & Co Ltd
  (1897) 13.11
Kingswood, The (1942) . .11.11

Para.

Kingswood Estate Co Ltd v
  Anderson (1963) . . . 7.18
Kiriri Cotton Co Ltd v Dewani . 15.63
Kirkham v Attenborough (1897) 22.18
Kirkham v Marter (1819) . . 7.8
Knight v Burgess (1864) . . 19.26
Knight v Crockford (1794) . . 7.13
Knox v Gye (1872) . . . 12.32
Kores Manufacturing Co Ltd v
  Kolok Manufacturing Co Ltd
  (1959) 15.20
Kray, Re (1965) 2.14
Krell v Henry (1903) . 11.8, 11.16
Kuenigl v Donnersmark (1955) . 15.61

L

L, Re (1968) 2.14
Lacave & Co v Credit Lloynnais
  (1897) 24.65
Ladbroke & Co v Todd (1914) . 24.83
Lakeman v Mountstephen (1874) 7.8
Lampleigh v Braithwait (1615) . 6.4
Lampleigh Iron Ore Co Ltd, Re
  (1927) 26.36
Lancashire Loans Ltd v Black
  (1934) 14.38
Langbrook Properties Ltd v
  Surrey County Council (1969) 20.6
Langston v Amalgamated Union
  of Engineering Workers (1974) 28.15
Larner v Fawcett (1950) . . 26.29
Larner v LCC (1949) . . . 17.4
Latimer v AEC Ltd (1953)
  . . . . 20.19, 28.65
Laurie and Morewood v Dudin
  & Sons (1928) 22.19
Law v Redditch Local Board
  (1892) 12.12
Laws v London Chronicle
  Indicator Newspapers) Ltd
  (1959) 28.39
Laythoarp v Bryant (1836) . . 7.12
Lazard Bros & Co Ltd v Fairfield
  Properties Co (Mayfair) Ltd
  (1977) . . . 12.19, 12.32
Lazenby Garages Ltd v Wright
  (1976) 22.84
Leach v R (1912) . . . 3.25
Leaf v International Galleries
  (1950) 14.11
Leduc & Co v Ward (1888) . . 27.10

Para.

Lee v Bayes (1856) . . . 22.35
Lee v Lee's Air Farming Ltd
  (1961) 4.4
Lee v Showmen's Guild of Great
  Britain (1952) . . 2.41, 15.15
Leeman v Stocks (1951) . . 7.13
Leeson v Leeson (1936) . . 9.8
Lennard's Carrying Co Ltd v
  Asiatic Petroleum Co Ltd
  (1915) 27.26
Leonard (Cyril) & Co v Simo
  Securities Trust Ltd (1971) . 28.40
Les Affréteur Réunis SA v
  Leopold Walford (London)
  Ltd (1919) . . . 6.25, 8.17
Leslie (R.) Ltd v Sheill (1914)
  . . . . 16.16, 16.17
L'Estrange v Graucob (1934) . 10.25
Levene v Broughan (1909) . . 16.17
Levene v IRC (1928) . . . 4.26
Levey & Co v Goldberg (1922) . 6.33
Levison v Patent Steam Carpet
  Cleaning Co Ltd (1978) . . 10.54
Lewis v Averay (1972) . . 13.12
Lilley v Barnsley (1844) . . 26.27
Lilley v Doubleday (1881) 18.17, 26.8
Lilley v Rankin (1886) . . 15.10
Limpus v London General
  Omnibus Co (1862) . . . 21.19
Lister v Romford Ice and Cold
  Storage Co Ltd (1957)
  . . . . 8.20, 8.21, 28.13
Liverpool City Council v Irwin
  (1977) . 8.19, 8.20, 8.21, 8.22
Liverpool Victoria Legal
  Friendly Society (1916) . . 25.2
Lloyd v Fleming (1872) . . 25.10
Lloyd v Grace, Smith & Co
  (1912) . . 18.1, 18.37, 21.30
Lloyd v Sulley (1884) . . . 4.27
Lloyds and Scottish Finance Ltd
  v Modern Cars and Caravans
  (Kingston) Ltd (1966) 22.38, 22.45
Lloyds Bank v Bundy (1975)
  . . 14.32, 14.34, 14.37, 24.65
Lloyds Bank Ltd v E.B. Savory
  & Co (1933) 24.83
Lloyd's v Harper (1880) 6.25, 26.37
London and Globe Finance
  Corpn (1902) 26.29
London and North Western Rly
  Co v Bartlett (1861) . . . 27.3
London Assurance v Mansel
  (1879) 14.24

Para.

LCC v Agricultural Food
Products Ltd (1955) . . 18.1
London Graving Dock Co Ltd v
Horton (1951) 20.36
London Joint Stock Bank Ltd v
Macmillan and Arthur (1918) . 24.66
London Tramways Co Ltd v
LCC (1898) 3.40
Long v Lloyd (1958) . . .14.11
Looker v Law Union and Rock
Insurance Co Ltd (1928) . . 25.4
Lord Strathcona SS Co v
Dominion Coal Co (1926) . 6.29
Lovelock v Franklyn (1846)
. . . . . 10.11, 10.12
Lowery v Walker (1911) . . 20.38
Lowndes v Specialist Heavy
Engineering Ltd (1976) . . 28.44
Lucan (Earl) Re (1890) . .19.15
Lucas v Beale (1851) . . .18.39
Ludgater v Love (1881) . .18.42
Lumley v Wagner (1852) . .12.22
Luxor (Eastbourne) Ltd v
Cooper (1941) 18.22
Lynch v Thorne (1956) . . 8.20
Lyell v Kennedy (1889) . .18.12
Lyons (J.L.) & Co Ltd v May
and Baker Ltd (1923) . . 22.78
Lynch v Nurdin (1841) . . 20.38

M

M. and S. Drapers v Reynolds
(1956) 15.19
Mac Andrew v Chapple (1866) . 27.19
McArdle, Re (1951) . . 6.4, 19.15
Macaura v Northern Assurance
Co Ltd (1925) . . . 4.5, 25.11
McCall v Australian Meat Co Ltd
(1870) 18.29
McConnel v Wright (1903) . .14.14
McCutcheon v David Macbrayne
Ltd (1964) 10.27
MacDonald v Green (1951) . .15.11
McEllistrim v Ballymacelligott
Co-operative Agriculture and
Dairy Society Ltd (1919) . .15.27
McFarlane v Royal London
Friendly Society (1886) . .25.21
McGregor v McGregor (1888) .15.60
Mackay v Dick (1881) . . 5.27
Mackenzie v Royal Bank of
Canada (1934) 14.11

Para.

McKew v Holland and Hannen
and Cubitts (Scotland) Ltd
(1969) 20.29
M'Kinnell v Robinson (1838) .15.11
McManus v Cooke (1887) . .17.18
McPherson v Watt (1877) . .18.19
McRae v Commonwealth
Disposals Commission (1950) . 13.2
McWilliams v Sir William Anal &
Co Ltd (1962) 20.24, 21.4, 28.66
Maddison v Alderson (1883)
. . . . . .7.16, 7.18
Magee v Pennine Insurance Co
Ltd (1969) . . .13.6, 13.9
Mahmoud and Ispahani, Re
(1921) . . . 15.48, 15.49
Major and St Mellons RDC v
Newport Corpn (1952) . . 3.21
Manchester Diocesan Council
for Education v Commercial
and General Investments Ltd
(1969) 5.14
Manchester Ship Canal Co v
Manchester Racecourse Co
(1901) 12.21
Maple Flock Co Ltd v Universal
Furniture Products (Wembley)
Ltd (1934) . . 10.21, 22.71
Marcel (Furriers) Ltd v Tapper
(1953) 22.5
Mare v Charles (1856) . . .18.47
Marfani & Co Ltd v Midland
Bank Ltd (1968) . . .24.83
Maritime National Fish Ltd v
Ocean Trawlers Ltd (1935) .11.11
Market Investigation Ltd v
Ministry of Social Security
(1969) 28.5
Marles v Philip Frant and Sons
Ltd (1954) 15.55
Marryatts v White (1817) . . 9.8
Marshall, Re (1920) . . .16.19
Marshall v Green (1875) . . 7.10
Marshall v Harland and Wolff
Ltd (1972) 11.6
Marten v Whale (1917) . . 5.27
Martin v Pycroft (1852) . . 7.12
Martin-Baker Aircraft Co Ltd v
Murison (1955) . . .18.25
Marzetti v Williams (1830) . .24.68
Maskell v Horner (1915) 17.4, 17.6
Mason v Provident Clothing and
Supply Co Ltd (1913) 15.19, 15.30

Para.

Massey v Crown Life Insurance
Co (1978) 28.2
Mather, ex parte (1797) . .18.23
Matthews v Baxter (1873) . .16.19
May v Lane (1894) . . .19.16
May and Butcher Ltd v R (1934) 5.26
Mayson v Clouet (1924) . . 17.7
Meadow Schama & Co v C.
Mitchell & Co Ltd (1973) .18.19
Mecca, The (1897) . . 9.9, 9.10
Mendelssohn v Normand Ltd
(1970) 10.35
Mercantile Union Guarantee
Corpn v Ball (1937) . . . 16.8
Mercer v Denne (1905) . . 3.52
Merchant v Morton Down & Co
(1901) 19.13
Merchant Shipping Co v Armitage
(1873) 27.37
Mersey Docks and Harbour
Board v Coggins and Griffith
(Liverpool) Ltd (1947) . .21.17
Mersey Docks and Harbour
Board v Hay (1923) . . .27.25
Mersey Steel and Iran Co Ltd v
Naylor, Benzona & Co (1884)
. . . . . 10.10, 22.71
Metropolitan Asylums Board of
Managers v Kingham & Sons
(1890) 18.12
Metropolitan Asylum District
Managers v Hill (1881) . .21.45
Metropolitan Electric Supply Co
v Ginder (1901) . . .12.21
Metropolitan Water Board v
Dick, Kerr & Co Ltd (1918)
. . . . . 11.4, 11.9
Microbeads A-G v Vinhurst Road
Markings Ltd (1975) . .22.45
Midland and Low Moor Iron and
Steel Co Ltd v Cross (1965) .28.80
Midland Bank v Reckitt (1933) . 18.8
Midland Motor Showrooms Ltd
v Newman (1929) . . .26.37
Mihalis Angelos, The (1971)
. . . . . 10.20, 12.16
Miesegaes v IRC (1957) . . 4.26
Miles v New Zealand Alford
Estate Co (1886) . . . 6.7
Miliangos v George Frank
(Textiles) Ltd (1976) . . 3.40
Millan, Son & Co v Radford
(1903) 18.22
Millard v Serck Tubes Ltd (1969) 28.80

Para.

Miller v Jackson (1977) 20.19, 21.48
Miller v Karlinski (1945) 15.58, 15.61
Miller v Race (1758) . . . 24.2
Miller's Case (1876) . . .19.19
Mills v Fowkes (1839) . .12.25
Milward v Earl of Thanet (1801) 12.32
Mirams, Re (1891) . . .15.60
Mitchell v Homfray (1881)
. . . . . 14.32, 14.38
Mitchell, Cotts & Co v Steel
Bros & Co Ltd (1916) . .27.21
Mitchell-Henry v Norwich Union
Life Insurance Society (1918) . 9.5
Monk v Warbey (1935) . . 21.1
Monnickendam v Leanse (1923) . 7.16
Montgomerie v United Kingdom
Mutual SS Association (1891) .18.39
Moorcock, The *1889) . 8.22, 8.23
Moore v Hart (1682) . . . 7.14
Moore & Co v Landauer & Co, Re
(1921) 22.47
Morgan v Ashcroft (1938) . . 17.4
Morgan v Manser (1948) . . 11.5
Morgan v Russell & Sons (1909) . 22.5
Morgans v Launchbury (1973) .21.30
Morison v London County and
Westminster Bank Ltd (1914) .24.84
Morley v Loughman (1893) .14.34
Morren v Swinton and
Pendlebury BC (1965) . . 28.3
Morris v Baron & Co (1918) . 6.35
Morris v C.H. Bailey Ltd (1969) . 28.7
Morris v C.W. Martin & Sons
Ltd (1966) . . 10.39, 21.20
Morris (Herbert) & Co Ltd v
Saxelby (1916) . 15.18, 15.19
Morritt, Re (1886) . 26.15, 22.37
Morton Sundour Fabrics Ltd v
Shaw (1966) 28.38
Moschi v Lep Air Services Ltd
(1973) 10.5
Motor Traders Guarantee Corpn
Ltd v Midland Bank Ltd (1937) 24.83
Motion v Michaud (1892) . .18.25
Mount (D.F.) Ltd v Jays and Jay
(provisions) Co Ltd (1960) .22.90
Mountford v Scott (1975) . . 6.6
Mourton v Poulter (1930) . .20.45
Muir v Keay (1875) . . . 3.24
Murray v Legal and General
Assurance Society (1970) .25.17
Mutton v Peat (1899) . . 9.10
Mutual Life and Citizens'
Assurance Co Ltd v Evatt (1971) 20.14

Para.

Myers (G.H.) & Co v Brent Cross
  Service Co (1934) . 8.21, 22.5
Myers v London and South
  Western Rly Co (1869) . . 27.3

N

N. and J. Vlassopulos Ltd v Ney
  Shipping Ltd (1977) . .18.39
Nanka-Bruce v Commonwealth
  Trust Ltd (1926) . . .22.17
Nash v Dix (1898) . . .18.42
Nash v Hodgson (1855) . . 9.10
Nash v Inman (1908) . . 16.3, 16.5
National Bank v Silke (1891) .24.63
National Coal Board v Sherwin
  and Spruce (1978) . . .28.34
National Pari-Mutual Association
  Ltd v R (1930). . . . 17.5
National Permanent Benefit
  Building Society (1869) . .16.13
National Westminster Bank Ltd
  v Barclays Bank International
  Ltd (1975) 24.77
Navy Army and Air Force
  Institutes v Varley (1977) .28.34
Nettleship v Weston (1971)
  . . . . . 20.17, 21,36
New Windsor Corpn v Mellor
  (1975) 3.52
New Zealand Shipping Co Ltd v
  A.M. Satterthwaite & Co Ltd,
  The Eurymedon (1975) 6.17, 10.37
Newbigging v Adam (1886) .14.15
Newfoundland Government v
  Newfoundland Rly (1888) .19.16
Newsholme Bros v Road
  Transport and General
  Insurance Co Ltd (1929) . . 18.7
Niblett v Confectioner's Materials
  Co Ltd (1921) 22.44
Nicholls v F. Austin (Leyton)
  Ltd (1946) 28.80
Nicholson and Venn v
  Smith-Marriott (1947) 13.5, 22.47
Nickoll and Knight v Ashton,
  Edridge & Co (1901) . . 11.3
Nicolene Ltd v Simmonds
  (1953) 5.25
Nocton v Lord Ashburton (1914) 20.13
Nokes v Doncaster Amalgamated
  Collieries Ltd (1940). . .19.16

Para.

Nordenfeldt v Maxim Nordenfeldt
  Guns and Ammunition Co Ltd
  (1894) . . 15.18, 15.22, 15.30
Norman, The (1960) . . .27.26
North v Loomes (1919) . . 7.12
North and South Wales Bank v
  Macbeth (1908) . . .24.10
North Riding Garages Ltd v
  Butterwick (1967) . . .28.54
North Western Rly Co v
  M'Michael (1850) 16.9, 16.10, 16.11
Northumberland and Durham
  District Banking Co, Re, ex
  parte Bigge (1859) . . . 14.6
Norton v Ellam (1837) . . 9.12
Norton Tool Co Ltd v Tewson
  (1972) 28.51
Nugent v Smith (1876) . . 27.2

O

Oakes v Turquand (1867) .14.11
Offord v Davies (1862) . . 5.19
Oldendorff E.L. & Co GmbH v
  Tradax Export SA (1974) .27.13
Olley v Marlborough Court Ltd
  (1949) 10.27
Omnium D'Enterprises v
  Sutherland (1919) . .10.11
Orbit Mining and Trading Co
  Ltd v Westminster Bank Ltd
  (1963) 24.83
Ord v Ord (1923) . . . 17.5
Ormrod v Gosville Motor
  Services Ltd (1953) . . .21.30
Oropesa, The (1943) . . .20.29
Oscar Chess Ltd v Williams
  (1957) . 8.9, 8.11, 8.14, 10.14
O'Shea, Re (1911) . . .15.11
Ottoman Bank v Chakarian
  (1930) 28.14
Overend and Gurney Co v Gibb
  (1872) 18.17
Owens v Liverpool Corpn (1939) 20.9

P

Pacific Motor Auctions Pty Ltd
  Motor Credits (Hire Finance)
  Ltd (1965) 22.31
Page One Records Ltd v Britton
  (1967) 12.23
Paine v Colne Valley Electricity
  Supply Co Ltd (1938) . .20.32

Para.

Palmer v Temple (1839) . . 17.7
Panorama Developments Ltd v
 Fidelis Furnishing Fabrics Ltd
 (1971) 18.32
Paris v London Borough of
 Stepney (1951) . . .28.65
Paris v Stepney Borough Council
 (1951) 20.20
Parker v Gordon (1806) . .24.42
Parker v Ibbetson (1858) . .18.25
Parker v South Eastern Rly Co
 (1877) 10.29
Parkinson v College of Ambulance
 Ltd (1925) 15.62
Parsons v B.N.M. Laboratories
 Ltd (1964) 12.8
Parsons (H.) (Livestock) Ltd v
 Uttley Ingram & Co Ltd (1978) 12.4
Parvin v Morton Machine Co Ltd
 (1952) 28.80
Paterson v Candasequi (1812) .18.43
Payzu Ltd v Saunders (1919) . 12.9
Pearce v Brain (1929) 16.13, 16.14
Pearce v Brooks (1866) 15.59, 15.61
Pearce v Stanley Bridges Ltd
 (1965) 28.80
Peek v Gurney (1873). . . 14.5
Penman v Fife Coal Co Ltd (1936) 28.21
Pennington v Crossley (1897) . 9.5
Penny v Northampton Borough
 Council (1974). . . .20.45
Performance Cans Ltd v Abraham
 (1962) 20.25
Performing Right Society Ltd v
 London Theatre of Varieties
 Ltd (1924) 19.10
Peters v Anderson (1814) . . 9.8
Peters v Fleming (1840) . . 16.3
Peters v General Accident and
 Life Assurance Corpn Ltd
 (1937) 19.16
Pharmaceutical Society of Great
 Britain v Boots Cash Chemist
 (Southern) Ltd (1952) . . 5.4
Pharmaceutical Society of Great
 Britain v Dickinson (1970) 4.8
Philips v Lamdin (1949) . .12.18
Philips v William Whileley Ltd
 (1938) 20.17
Phillips v Brooks Ltd (1919) .13.12
Phipps v Rochester Corpn (1955) 20.40
Pignataro v Gilroy (1919) . .22.20
Pilkington v Wood (1953) . . 12.9
Pilmore v Hood (1838) . . 14.5

Para.

Pinnel's Case (1602) 6.13, 6.14, 6.32
Pirie & Co v Middle Dock Co
 (1881) 27.38
Planché v Colburn (1831) . .12.16
Plant v Bourne (1897) . . 7.12
Plowman (G.W.) & Son Ltd v
 Ash (1964) 15.19
Poland v John Parr & Sons (1927) 21.19
Pontypridd Union v Drew (1927) 16.5
Poole v Smith's Car Sales
 (Balham) Ltd (1962) . .22.18
Port Line Ltd v Ben Line
 Steamers Ltd (1958) . . 6.29
Porteus v Watney (1878) 27.10, 27.13
Portuguese Consolidated Copper
 Mines Ltd (1890) . . .18.12
Postlethwaite v Freeland (1880). 9.14
Poteliakhoff v Teakle (1938) . 6.7
Potinger v Wightman (1817) . 4.23
Poussard v Spiers and Pond
 (1876) 9.2, 10.4
Powell v Kempton Park
 Racecourse Co Ltd (1899) 3.23, 3.24
Price v Easton (1833). . . 6.18
Printers and Finishers Ltd v
 Holloway (1965) . . .15.19
Proclamations (Case of) (1611) . 3.16
Prosperity Ltd v Lloyds Bank
 (1923) 24.65
Prosser v Edmonds (1835) . .19.16
Punton v Ministry of Pensions
 and National Insurance (No 2)
 (1963) 28.84
Putsman v Taylor (1927) 15.18, 15.30
Pym Campbell (1856). . 5.27, 8.4

Q

Qualcast (Wolverhampton) Ltd v
 Haynes (1959) 28.66
Qureshi v Qureshi (1972) . . 4.23

R

R v Chapman (1931) . . . 3.25
R v Clarke (1927) . . . 5.8
R v Hassall (1861) . . . 26.5
R v Industrial Injuries Comr, ex
 parte Amalgamated Engineering
 Union (No 2) (1966) . .28.87
R v Kelt (1978) 3.23
R v Leeds Crown Court, ex parte
 Bradford Chief Constable
 (1975) 2.18

Para.

R v Midland Rly Co (1885) . 3.24
R v National Insurance Comr,
  ex parte Michael (1977) . . 28.87
R v Newsome and Brown (1970) 3.42
R v Northumberland Compen-
  sation Tribunal, ex parte
  Shaw (1952) 3.43
R v Orpen (1975) . . . 2.21
R v Randall (1811) . . . 24.10
R v Taylor (1950) . . . 3.42
R v Wilson (1879) . . . 16.14
Raffles v Wichelhaus (1864)
  . . . . . 13.14, 13.16
Ramsay v Liverpool Royal
  Infirmary (1930) . . 4.22, 4.23
Ramsgate Victoria Hotel Co v
  Montefiore (1866) . . . 5.20
Rann v Hughes (1778) . . 7.3
Rawlinson v Ames (1925) . . 7.18
Reader v Kingham (1862) . . 7.9
Ready Mixed Concrete (South
  East) Ltd v Ministry of
  Pensions and National
  Insurance (1968) . . . 28.5
Redgrave v Hurd (1881) . . 14.6
Redland Roof Tiles Ltd v
  Harper (1977) 28.34
Reed v Dean (1949) . 8.21, 26.11
Reed v Royal Exchange
  Assurance Co (1795) . . 25.21
Reeve v Reeve (1858) . . . 18.21
Regal (Hastings) Ltd v Gulliver
  (1967) 18.19
Reid v Police Comr of the
  Metropolis (1973) . . . 22.35
Reigate v Union Manufacturing
  Co (Ramsbottom) Ltd (1918) . 8.22
Rely-a-Bell Burglar and Fire
  Alarm Co v Eisler (1926) . . 12.22
Reuss v Picksley (1866) . . 7.14
Reuter, Hyeland & Co v Sala &
  Co (1879) 9.17
Reynolds v Atherton (1921) . 5.21
Rhodes v Forwood (1876): 18.22, 18.26
Richard West & Partners
  Inverness Ltd v Dick (1969) . 4.2
Richardson v Koefod (1969) . 28.38
Richardson v Moncrieffe (1926)
  . . . . . 15.9, 15.10
Richardson v Williamson and
  Lawson (1871). . . . 18.50
Ripon (Highfield) Housing Order
  1938 (1939) 3.26
Ritchie v Atkinson (1808) . . 27.35

Para.

Riverlate Properties Ltd v Paul
  (1975) 13.18
Roberts v Gray (1913) . . 16.5
Roberts v Havelock (1832) . . 10.14
Roberts (A.) & Co v Leicester-
  shire CC (1961) . . . 13.18
Robinson v Beaconsfield RDC
  (1911) 21.28
Robinson v Davison (1871) . 11.5
Robinson v Graves (1935) . . 22.5
Robinson v Post Office (1974) . 20.28
Roe v Minister of Health (1954) 20.17
Roles v Nathan (1963) . . 20.40
Rom Securities Ltd v Rogers
  (Holdings) Ltd (1967) . . 11.12
Rondel v Worsley (1969) . . 20.7
Romer v Haslam (1893) . . 9.4
Rondel v Worsley (1969) . . 3.37
Rookes v Barnard (1964) 3.41, 14.30
Rose v Ford (1937) . 21.32, 21.47
Rose v Plenty (1976) . . . 21.19
Rose and Frank Co v J.R.
  Crompton & Bros Ltd (1925) . 6.2
Rosenbaum v Belson (1900) . 18.32
Rosenthal (J.) & Sons Ltd v
  Esmail (1965) 22.40
Ross T. Smyth & Co Ltd v
  Bailey & Son & Co (1940) . 10.10
Rossiter v Miller (1878) . . 7.12
Roth & Co v Taysen Townsend
  & Co (1895) 12.10
Rothermere v Times Newspapers
  Ltd (1973) 2.53
Routledge v Grant (1828) . . 5.18
Rowland v Divall (1923) 17.7, 22.44
Rosburghe v Cox (1881) . . 19.16
Rubel Bronze and Metal Co Ltd,
  Re (1918) 28.15
Ruben (E. and S.) Ltd v Faire
  Bros & Co Ltd (1949) . . 22.60
Rushforth v Hadfield (1805) . 27.4
Ryan v Mutual Tontine
  Westminster Chambers
  Association (1893) . . . 12.18
Ryder v Wombwell (1868) . . 16.3
Rylands v Fletcher (1866)
  . . . 21.12, 21.25, 21.26

S

Sachs v Miklos (1948). . . 26.9
SCM (United Kingdom) Ltd v
  Whittall & Son Ltd (1971) . 20.8

	Para.
Sadler v Smith (1869). . .	17.9
Sadler's Co v Badcock (1743) .	25.10
Sagar v H. Ridehalgh & Son Ltd	
(1931)	28.8
St Enoch Shipping Co Ltd v	
Phosphate Mining Co (1916) .	27.35
St John Shipping Corpn v	
Joseph Rank Ltd (1957)	
. . . 15.49, 15.52, 15.53	
St John Shipping Corpn v	
Joseph Rank Ltd (1961) . .	15.49
Salford Corpn v Lever (1891) .	18.19
Salomon v Salomon & Co (1897)	4.4
Sanders v Ernest A Neale Ltd	
(1974)	28.40
Sard v Rhodes (1836). . .	9.4
Satanita, The (1897) . . .	5.22
Saunders v Anglia Building	
Society (1971). . 13.19, 13.21	
Sayer v Wagstaff (1844) . .	9.4
Saxon v Blake (1861). . .	18.41
Scammel v Ouston (1941) 5.24, 5.25	
Scaramanga v Stamp (1880) .	27.20
Scarfe v Morgan (1838) .	26.27
Schack v Anthony (1813) .	18.45
Schawel v Reade (1913) . .	8.12
Schebsman, Re (1944) . .	6.25
Schmaltz v Avery (1851) .	18.48
Schroeder Music Publishing Co	
Ltd v Macaulay (1974) 14.37, 15.25	
Schuler A.G. v Wickman Machine	
Tool Sales Ltd (1974) . .	10.20
Scothorn v South Staffordshire	
Rly Co (1853)	27.3
Scotson v Pegg (1861) . .	6.17
Scott v Avery (1855) . 2.41, 15.15	
Scott v Bradley (1971) . .	7.12
Scott v London and St Katherine	
Docks Co (1865) . .	20.22
Scott v Shepherd (1773) .	20.28
Scottish Petroleum, Re (1883) .	14.11
Scrimshire v Alderton (1743) .	18.41
Scriven & Co v Hindley (1913)	
. . . . 13.14, 13.16	
Scruttons Ltd v Midland	
Silicones Ltd (1962) . .	10.36
Secretary of State for Employ-	
ment v Associated Society of	
Locomotive Engineers and	
Firemen (No 2) . .	28.11
Seymour v Pickett (1905) . .	9.9
Sharmia v Joory (1958) .	17.9
Shanklin Pier Ltd v Detel	
Products Ltd (1951) . .	6.21

	Para.
Sharp v Avery (1938) . . .	20.12
Sharpe v Crispin (1869) . .	4.23
Sheikh Bros v Ochsner (1957) .	13.3
Shell UK Ltd v Lostock Garages	
Ltd (1977) . 8.20, 8.22, 8.23	
Shepherd v Kottgen (1877) .	27.38
Sherry, Re (1884) . . .	9.10
Shipton, Anderson & Co v Weil	
Bros & Co (1912) . . 9.2, 22.70	
Shirlaw v Southern Foundries	
(1926) Ltd (1939) . . .	8.22
Siboen, The, and The Sibotre	
(1976) . . . 14.30, 14.31	
Sigsworth, Re (1935) . . .	3.20
Silverman v Imperial London	
Hotels Ltd (1927) . .	8.23
Simpkins v Pays (1955) . .	6.2
Simpson v Eggington (1855) .	9.19
Simpson v Kodak Ltd (1948) .	28.24
Sims & Co v Midland Rly Co	
(1913)	27.3
Simson v Ingham (1823) . .	9.9
Sinclair v Brougham (1914) .	4.12
Sinclair v Neighbour (1967) .	28.39
Sinclair's Life Policy, Re (1938)	25.23
Singh v Ali (1960) . . .	15.63
Siqueira v Noronha (1934) .	16.13
Skaife v Jackson (1824) . .	9.6
Sky Petroleum Ltd v VIP	
Petroleum Ltd (1974) 12.18, 22.74	
Smallman v Smallman (1972) .	5.27
Smally v Smally (1700) . .	18.5
Smeaton, Hanscomb & Co v	
Sasson I. Setty & Co (1953) .	10.54
Smith v Butler (1900). . .	5.27
Smith v Charles Baker & Sons	
(1891) . . . 21.36, 28.66	
Smith v Calogan (1788) . .	18.9
Smith v Cox (1940) . . .	9.19
Smith v Hughes (1871) 13.15, 13.16	
Smith v Kay (1859) . . .	14.35
Smith v King (1892) . . .	16.15
Smith v Land and House	
Property Corpn (1884) . .	14.4
Smith v Mawhood (1845) . .	15.49
Smith v Monteith (1844) . .	14.30
Smith v Scott (1973) . . .	20.5
Smith v Sheppard (1776) . .	24.23
Smith v Surman (1829) . .	7.10
Smith v Union Bank of London	
(1875) . . 24.60, 24.73	
Smith v Wood (1929) . . .	26.37
Smith & Co v Bedovin Steam	
Navigation Co (1896) . .	27.28

Para.

Smyth (Ross T.) & Co Ltd v
Bailey & Son & Co (1940) . 10.10
Snelling v John G. Snelling Ltd
(1973) 6.26
Snook v London and West Riding
Investments Ltd (1967) . . 26.23
Snowdon, ex parte (1881) . . 26.34
Solle v Butcher (1950) 13.1, 13.6, 13.9
Sowler v Potter (1940) 13.13, 13.16
Spartan Steel and Alloys Ltd v
Martin & Co (Contractors)
Ltd (1973) 20.8
Spears v Hartley (1800) . . 26.29
Spector v Ageda (1974) . . 15.64
Spence v Crawford (1939) . . 14.11
Spencer v Harding (1870) . . 5.6
Springer v Great Western Rly Co
(1921) 18.13
Spruce v National Coal Board
(1977) 28.34
Spurling (J.) Ltd v Bradshaw
(1956) 10.27
Stansbie v Troman (1948) . . 20.5
Stanton v Austin (1872) . . 27.13
Stapley v Gypsum Mines Ltd
(1953) 21.42
Staton v National Coal Board
(1957) 21.19
Startup v Macdonald (1843) 9.11, 9.14
Steadman v Steadman (1976) . 7.18
Steel v Post Office (1977) . . 28.27
Steel v State Line SS Co (1877) . 27.18
Steel Wing Co Ltd, Re (1921)
. . . . . 19.10, 19.11
Steiglitz v Egginton (1815) 18.1, 18.6
Steinberg v Scala (1923) . . 16.11
Sterling, ex parte (1809) . . 26.28
Stevenson v MacLean (1880) . 5.8
Stevenson, Jordan and Harrison
Ltd v MacDonald and Evans
(1952) 28.4
Stewart v Reavell's Garage (1952) 9.21
Stickney v Keeble (1915) . . 9.17
Stilk v Myrick (1809) . . . 6.12
Stocks v Dobson (1853) . . 19.13
Stocks v Wilson (1913) 16.14, 16.17
Stoddart v Union Trust Ltd
(1912) 19.16
Stone (J. and F.) Lighting and
Radio Ltd v Haygarth (1968) . 28.20
Strange (S.W.) Ltd v Mann (1965) . 15.19
Strang Steel & Co v A. Scott &
Co (1889) 27.39

Para.

Strathcona (Lord) SS Co v
Dominion Coal Co (1926) . 6.29
Strongman (1945) Ltd v Sincock
(1955) 15.57
Strutt v Whitnell (1975) . . 12.10
Stuart v London and North
Western Rly Co (1852) . . 12.19
Stuart v Stephen (1940) . . 15.10
Stubbs v Holywell Rly Co Ltd
(1867) 11.5, 19.23
Studds v Watson (1884) . . 7.15
Suisse Atlantique Société
D'Armement Maritime SA v
NV Rotterdamsche Kolen
Centrale (1967)
. . 10.52, 10.54, 10.57, 10.58
Summers (John) & Sons Ltd v
Frost (1955) . . 21.3, 28.80
Sumpter v Hedges (1898) 10.14, 10.15
Sutcliffe v Great Western Rly
Co (1910) 27.2
Sutcliffe v Hawker Siddeley
Aviation Ltd (1973). . 28.54
Sutcliffe v Thackrah (1974) . 20.7
Sutton & Co v Grey (1894) . 7.9
Sutton's Hospital Case (1912) . 4.8
Swiss Air Transport Co Ltd v
Palmer (1976) . . . 18.35

T

Tamlin v Hannaford (1950) . 3.25
Tamplin v James (1880) . . 13.17
Tancred v Delagoal Bay Rly Co
(1889) 19.26
Tarry v Ashton (1876) . . 21.23
Taten W.J. Ltd v Gamboa (1939) 11.10
Tatlock v Harris (1789) . . 19.17
Taylor v Allon (1966). . . 5.9
Taylor v Bowers (1876) . . 15.63
Taylor v Caldwell (1863) . . 11.3
Taylor v Chester (1869) . . 15.63
Taylor v Laird (1856) . . . 10.17
Taylor v National Union of
Seamen (1967). . . . 28.40
Taylor v Walker (1958) . . 18.19
Tetley v Shand (1871) . . 9.14
Texaco Ltd v Mulberry Filling
Station Ltd (1972) . 15.24, 15.25
Tesco Supermarkets Ltd v
Nattrass (1972) . . . 4.7
Thacker v Hardy (1878) . . 18.5

Para.

Thairlwall v Great Northern Rly
  Co (1910) . . . 9.5, 24.17
Thin v Richards & Co (1892) . 27.18
Thirkell v Cambi (1919) . . 7.14
Thomas v Brown (1876) . . 7.16
Thomas v Evans (1808) . . 9.13
Thomas v Harris (1947) . . 19.12
Thompson v London Midland
  and Scottish Rly Co (1930) . 10.29
Thompson (W.L.) Ltd v Robinson
  (Gunmakers) Ltd (1955) 22.83, 22.84
Thomson v Davenport (1829)
  . . . . 18.41, 18.43
Thorley (J.) Ltd v Orchis SS Co
  Ltd (1907) 10.54
Thorn v Comrs of Public Works
  (1863) 12.18
Tidman v Aveling Marshall Ltd
  (1977) 28.51
Tiedemann and Ledermann
  Frères, Re (1899) . . 18.11
Timmins v Moreland Street
  Property Co Ltd (1958) . . 7.15
Tinn v Hoffmann & Co (1873) . 5.8
Tiverton Estates Ltd v Wearwell
  Ltd (1975) 7.14
Tolhurst v Associated Portland
  Cement Manufacturers (1900)
  . . . . 19.16, 19.19
Tool Metal Manufacturing Co
  Ltd v Tungsten Electric Co Ltd
  (1955) . . . 6.15, 6.33
Torkington v Magee (1902) 19.2, 19.4
Total Oil (Great Britain) Ltd v
  Thompson Garages (Biggin Hill)
  Ltd (1972) 10.9
Tote Investors Ltd v Smoker
  (1968) 15.3
Touche v Metropolitan Railway
  Warehousing Co (1871) . . 18.10
Tournier v National Provincial
  and Union Bank of England
  (1924) 24.78
Trans Trust SPRL v Danubian
  Trading Co Ltd (1952) . . 6.20
Travers (Joseph) & Sons Ltd v
  Cooper (1915) . . 10.33, 26.7
Trickett v Tomlinson (1863) . 18.36
Tsakiroglou & Co Ltd v Noblee
  Thorl GmbH (1962) . . 11.3, 11.4
Tufton v Sperni (1952) . . 14.34
Tulk v Moxhay (1848) . . 6.20
Turner v Goldsmith (1891) . . 18.26
Turpin v Bilton (1843) . . 18.16

Para.

Turner v Green (1895) . . 14.22
Turriff Construction Ltd v
  Bryant (1969) . . . 28.16
Tweddle v Atkinson (1861) . 6.23

U

Uddin v Associated Portland
  Cement Manufacturers Ltd
  (1965) . . 21.41, 28.80
Udny v Udny (1869) . . 4.22, 4.23
Underwood (A.L.) Ltd v Barclays
  Bank (1924) 24.80
Underwood Ltd v Burgh Castle
  Brick and Cement Syndicate
  (1922) . . 22.15, 22.16
Unit Construction Co Ltd v
  Bullock (1960) . . . 4.27
United Dominions Corpn
  (Jamaica) Ltd v Shoucair (1969) 6.35
United Dominions Trust v
  Kirkwood (1966) . . 6.20
United Dominions Trust Ltd v
  Western (1976) . . . 13.20
United Kingdom Mutual SS
  Assurance Association Ltd v
  Nevill (1887) . . . 18.42
United Overseas Bank v Jiwani
  (1977) 24.66
United Railways of Havana and
  Regla Warehouses (1961) . . 3.40
Universal Cargo Carriers Corpn
  v Citati (1957) . . . 10.11
Universal Stock Exchange Ltd v
  Strachen (1896) . . . 15.3
Urquhart v Butterfield (1887) . 4.23
Urquhart Lindsay & Co Ltd v
  Eastern Bank Ltd (1922) . . 6.20

V

Valentini v Canali (1889) . . 16.14
Vanbergen v St Edmund's
  Properties Ltd (1933) . . 6.32
Vancouver Malt and Sake
  Brewing Co Ltd v Vancouver
  Breweries Ltd (1934) . . 15.22
Van Duyn v Home Office (1975)
  . . . . 3.31, 3.34
Varley v Whipp (1900) . . 22.47
Vaughan v Menlove (1837) . . 20.17
Vaux and Associated Breweries
  Ltd v Ward (1969) . . 28.54

Para.

Victoria, The (1888) . . . 27.25
Victoria Laundry (Windsor) Ltd
  v Newman (1949)   12.3, 12.4, 12.6

W

Wade's Case (1601) . . . 9.13
Wagon Mound, The (1961) . . 20.26
Waggon Mound, The (No 2)
  (1967) 20.19
Wah Tat Bank Ltd v Chan (1975) 21.34
Wait, Re (1927) . .22.10, 22.19
Wakeham v Mackenzie (1968) . 7.18
Walker, Re (1905) . . . 16.19
Walker v Bletchley Flettons Ltd
  (1937) 28.80
Walker v Perkins (1764) . . 15.59
Wall v Rederaktiebolaget Luggude
  (1915) 12.13
Wallis, Son and Wells v Pratt
  and Haynes (1911) . 10.31, 22.47
Walsh v Lonsdale (1882) 7.2, 12.19
Walters v Neary (1904) . . 24.20
Walthew v Mavrojani (1870) . 27.38
Walton v Mascall (1844) . . 9.2
Walton Harvey Ltd v Walker and
  Homfrays Ltd (1931) . . 11.10
Ward v Byham (1956) . . . 6.11
Ward v Tesco Stores Ltd (1976) . 20.22
Ward (R.V.) Ltd v Bignall (1967)
  . . . . 10.5, 10.8, 22.94
Warehousing and Forwarding Co
  of East Africa Ltd v Jafferali &
  Sons Ltd (1964) . . . 18.9
Warman v Southern Counties
  Car Finance Corpn Ltd (1949) 17.7
Warmstrey v Tanfield (1628) . 19.15
Warner Bros Pictures Incor-
  porated v Nelson (1937) . . 12.22
Warrington v Early (1853) . . 24.25
Waters v Monarch Fire and Life
  Assurance Co (1856) . . 25.11
Wathes (Western) Ltd v Austins
  (Menwear) Ltd (1976) 10.53, 10.56
Watkins v Evans (1887) . . 26.22
Watkins v Rymill (1883) . . 10.29
Watson v Swann (1862) . . 18.10
Watson (Joseph) & Sons Ltd v
  Firemen's Fund Insurance Co
  of San Francisco (1922) . . 27.38
Watt v Hertfordshire County
  Council (1954). . . 20.21
Watts v Spence (1975) . . 14.14
Waugh v Morris (1873) . . 15.61

Para.

Wauton v Coppard (1899) . . 14.4
Way v Latilla (1937) . . . 18.21
Webster v Cecil (1861) . . 13.17
Weigall & Co v Runciman & Co
  (1916) 18.17
Weiner v Gill (1906) . . . 22.18
Weir & Co v Girvin & Co (1900) . 27.37
Welby v Drake (1825) . . . 6.16
Weld-Blundell v Stephens (1920) 12.3
Wertheim v Chicoutine Pulp Co
  (1911) . . . 12.2, 22.80
Wessex Dairies Ltd v Smith
  (1935) . . 8.20, 15.19, 28.11
West (H.) & Son Ltd v Shephard
  (1964) 21.47
West (Richard) & Partners
  Inverness Ltd v Dick (1969) . 4.2
West London Commercial Bank
  v Kitson (1884) . . . 14.4
Western Excavating (EEC) Ltd v
  Sharp (1978) 28.42
Westerton, Re (1919) . . . 19.4
Westminster Bank Ltd v Zang
  (1966) 24.85
Westminster Fire Office v
  Glasgow Provident Investment
  Society (1888). . 25.11, 25.13
Wharton v Walker (1825) . . 19.18
Wheat v Lacon & Co Ltd (1966) 20.39
Whincup v Hughes (1871) . . 17.7
Whistler v Forster (1863) . . 24.40
White v Garden (1851) 14.9, 14.11
White v Spettigue (1845) . . 26.29
White v John Warwick & Co Ltd
  (1953) 10.33
White and Carter Ltd v Carbis
  Bay Garage Ltd (1941) . . 11.7
White and Carter (Councils) Ltd
  v McGregor (1962) 10.9, 10.13, 12.10
Whittaker v Ministry of Pensions
  and National Insurance (1967). 28.4
Whittington v Murdy (1889) . 16.9
Whittington v Seale-Hayme
  (1900) 14.15
Whitwood Chemical Co Ltd v
  Hardman (1891) . . . 12.21
Wilbeam v Ashton (1807) . . 12.13
Wilkie v London Passenger
  Transport Board [1947] 1 All ER
  258, CA 5.4
Wilkinson v Downton (1897) . 20.10
Wilkinson v Lloyd (1845) . . 17.7
Williams v Atlantic Assurance
  Co Ltd (1933) . . . 19.6

	Para.
Williams v Bayley (1866)	. 14.31
Williams v Carwardine (1883)	. 5.8
Williams v Jordan (1877)	. 7.12
Williams v Reynolds (1865)	. 22.73
Williams v Rider (1963)	. 24.9
Williams Bros v Ed T. Argius Ltd (1914)	. 22.73
Willis v Barrett (1816)	. 24.10
Wilson v Jones (1867)	. 15.3
Wilson v Keating (1859)	. 9.6
Wilson v Maynard Shipbuilding Consultants AB (1976)	. 28.41
Wilson v Rickett, Cockerell & Co Ltd (1954)	. 22.53
Wilson v Tunman (1843)	18.8, 18.10
Wilson v Tyneside Window Cleaning Co (1958)	. 28.65
Wilson v United Counties Bank Ltd (1920)	. 19.25
Wilsons and Clyde Coal Co v English (1938)	20.30, 28.65
Winn v Bull (1877)	. 5.27
Wishart v National Coal Board (1974)	. 28.18
With v O'Flanagan (1936)	. 14.4
Wolstanton Ltd and A-G of Duchy of Lancaster v Newcastle-under-Lyme Corpn	. 3.52
Wolverhampton Corpn v Emmons (1901)	. 12.18
Wood v Scarth (1855)	13.16, 13.17
Woodhouse v Peter Brotherhood (1972)	. 28.56
Woodworth v Conway (1976)	. 26.27
Woolf v Collis Removal Services (1948)	. 10.54

	Para.
Woolf v Hamilton (1898)	. 15.10
Woollatt v Stanley (1923)	. 24.25
Worcester Works Finance Ltd v Cooden Engineering Co Ltd (1972)	3.47, 22.31
Wrexham, Mold and Connah's Quay Rly Co (1899)	. 4.12
Wright v Carter (1903)	. 14.32
Wright v Laing (1824)	. 9.9
Wroth v Tyler (1974)	. 12.4
Wyatt v Kreglinger and Fernau (1933)	15.19, 15.29

X

Xenos v Danube and Black Sea Rly Co (1863)	. 10.13

Y

Yangtsze Insurance Association Ltd v Lukmanjee (1918)	. 22.98
Yeoman Credit Ltd v Apps (1962)	. 26.11
Yeoman Credit v Latter (1961)	16.13, 16.14
Young v Bristol Aeroplane Co Ltd (1944)	3.41, 3.42, 3.43
Young v Grote (1827)	. 24.66
Young v Kitchin (1878)	. 19.16
Young & Co Ltd v White (1911)	. 18.43
Young and Marten Ltd v McManus Childs Ltd (1969)	. 22.5
Yonge v Toynbee (1910)	18.5, 18.28, 18.50

Part I

Outline of the
English Legal System

Chapter 1
Classification of the Law

1.1 It must be stressed at the beginning that this book is concerned with aspects of *English* law. The laws and legal system of Scotland and, to a lesser extent, Northern Ireland are distinct from those of England and Wales, and while Scots and Northern Irish law may coincide with English law in certain fields it cannot be assumed that this will be the case.

It is usual to divide English law into categories. These categories, which may flourish or decline as circumstances change, are used because they are convenient divisions of the law. Categories may overlap and there may be differences of opinion as to the category into which some area of the law falls. For example, the rules relating to vicarious liability, whereby the law regards one person as liable for the torts of another, may be regarded as a distinct category of law, or as falling within the larger categories of labour law or the law of tort.

One set of facts may involve more than one category of law. If A, a taxi driver, hits a lamp post while driving you to the station, and injures you, the law of contract, the law of tort and criminal law may all be applicable. A has certainly broken his contract to drive you to the station, and if his driving was careless this may occasion criminal liability and also tortious liability for any injury occasioned by it. This example illustrates classification of law by reference to the subject-matter of the dispute. Common examples of 'subject-matter classification' are: contract, tort, criminal law, commercial law, and the law of property. Law may also be classified by reference to the source of a particular rule.

Classification by reference to the subject-matter of a dispute

1.2 When using this method of classification, a major distinction can be drawn between civil and criminal law. It is criminal law which occupies most of the attention of non-lawyers, but lawyers are frequently more. concerned with non-criminal, or civil, law. Civil law can be subdivided into categories, for example, contract and tort, and these categories of civil law are no less important than criminal law.

1.3 It is surprisingly difficult in theory, though not in practice, to distinguish between civil and criminal law. As we show in Chapter 2, to some extent, most courts have both a civil and criminal jurisdiction. Criminal cases, which are called prosecutions, are normally initiated by the State, but they may be brought by a private citizen, although this is rare. If a prosecution is successful the accused, or defendant, is liable to punishment. This affords no direct benefit to the victim of the crime since he does not receive fines payable or the fruits of a criminal's labours in prison. The victims of some crimes, for example, an attempted theft or blackmail, may have suffered no loss from the commission of the crime anyway. Some crimes can be committed without there being a victim to suffer loss, for example, treason and some offences involving obscene publications. Although punishment does not compensate victims, it is now possible for the criminal courts to order the criminal to make reparation directly to his victim under the Powers of Criminal Courts Act 1973[1]. The victim of a criminal offence cannot prevent a prosecution nor order its discontinuance, unless it is a private prosecution, however much he may wish to avoid a criminal trial.

In contrast, civil actions are brought by an individual (the plaintiff) who is seeking compensation for the loss he has suffered or to establish his legal rights. If damages are awarded as the result of a successful civil action, they are payable to the plaintiff and are assessed on the basis that they should compensate and not punish. In certain restricted circumstances the courts may award punitive damages which are designed to compensate the plaintiff and punish the defendant but all the damages are payable to the plaintiff and not merely the compensatory element. A plaintiff is not required to commence a civil action and he can discontinue it at any time before judgment.

Facts which disclose a criminal offence may also constitute a potential civil action but the victim cannot have both claims adjudicated by the same court. It is necessary to bring a separate civil action as well as any prosecution which the State may initiate.

We now discuss some categories of civil law.

---

1 Victims of crimes may also receive compensation from the Criminal Injuries Compensation Scheme.

Contract

1.4 A contract is an agreement which the parties have entered into voluntarily, which they intend shall be legally binding and which is enforceable in law if certain requirements are complied with. We make a contract when we buy goods, purchase a railway ticket, employ a plumber or order a ship to be built. All contracts, whatever their subject-matter and however large or small are the sums of money involved, are subject to the same basic rules. Once the existence of a valid contract has been established, an inexcusable failure to perform the contractual obligations, or defective performance of those obligations, constitutes a breach of contract for which an action can be brought. The usual, but not only, remedy for breach of contract is an action for damages. Oral agreements which comply with the legal requirements for the formation of a legally binding contract are no less binding, except in certain recognised cases, than a contract made in writing or by deed. The principle disadvantages of oral contracts are the difficulty of proving that they have been made and what their terms are.

The facts of a particular case may disclose both contractual and other obligations imposed by law. For instance, if you request a dentist to effect proper dental treatment and his treatment is carried out negligently, he will be in breach of contract and liable in tort.

Tort

1.5 There is no universally accepted definition of a tort, perhaps because English law does not have a law of tort but a law of torts. These different torts share many characteristics but can also vary dramatically from each other. Perhaps we can best explain what is meant by tort if we say that the law imposes certain duties on all of us, for example, not to injure other people, physically, financially or by lowering their reputation. If X injures Y, X will be liable in tort provided that he owed Y a legal duty not to injure him, the injury suffered by Y was a type which the law recognises and the injury was caused by X's failure to comply with his duty. The usual remedy for the victim of a tort is to seek damages but other remedies are available.

The most frequently encountered tort is negligence and its most common manifestations are in road accidents and accidents at work. Other torts seek to prevent us from being a nuisance to our neighbours or a hazard to those who visit our homes.

Property

1.6 The rules relating to property are an amalgam of two varieties of rule:

a. special rules relating purely to property; and

b. special applications of general legal rules. For example, there are rules of contract which apply specifically to property and which form a gloss on general contractual principles.

Property can mean movable property (i.e. chattels, such as cars and books) or immovable property (land and buildings). Immovable property can also be described as real property or realty and movable property as personal property or personalty. Personal and real property do not correspond exactly with movable and immovable property in that for historical reasons land held on a lease is called real personalty or sometimes just personalty.

Property can also mean a legal interest in goods or land, i.e. a proprietary right. Property in the sense of realty and personalty can be subject to proprietary rights. For example, if A is buying a car by means of a loan from B, and A hires the car to C, A, B and C all have legal interests in the car.

The rules relating specifically to land were much modified by statute in 1925 but are generally outside the scope of this book. The specialised rules for the sale of goods are discussed later[1].

---

1 Chap. 22.

Some Other Divisions of Civil Law

1.7 There are many other generally accepted divisions of civil law. Particular topics may fall into more than one category, for example, agency, which is a branch of contract and commercial law. Some other divisions of civil law are:

a. *Commercial law* This is concerned with special contractual situations — agency, sale of goods, consumer credit and other matters relating to business transactions.

b. *Labour law* This again involves special and general rules of contract but also embraces statutory rights and obligations between employer and employee. It includes such topics as health and safety at work (which is also covered by the laws of tort) and unfair dismissal.

c. *Company law* Companies are legal persons[1] and are subject to special rules both common law and statutory, partly because they are artificial legal persons and partly because of the need to regulate their dealings with shareholders, employees and creditors.

d. *Constitutional law* This is a slightly different category of law in that it is that body of rules regulating the affairs of Parliament and the Government and their impact on the individual citizen, rather than rules for regulating the lives of citizen and citizens.

These categories are merely illustrations of the diversity of civil law; other categories are evidence, revenue law, trusts and family law. New categories arise when an area of life develops a sufficiently large and distinct body of legal rules; a recent arrival has been welfare or poverty law.

---

1 Para. 4.3.

Classification by reference to the source of the legal rule

1.8 It is also possible to classify law by reference to its source. Common law, equity and legislation are sources of law. All classification is merely a matter of practice and convenience and the two systems described in this chapter overlap.

The principal distinction is between common law (which has more than one meaning) and legislation.

Common Law and Legislation
1.9 Common law means judge-made law. It is contained in the decisions or judgments made by the judiciary over many centuries. Legislation comprises Acts of Parliament and subordinate legislation, for example, bye-laws and statutory instruments deriving their authority from Acts of Parliament. Legislation can change the common law, but judges cannot change or ignore legislation, although their interpretation of it may occasionally stultify or modify the wishes of Parliament. Some categories of law, contract and tort for example, are almost entirely based on judicial decisions, such legislation as amends the common law is narrow in its scope. Much of labour law and commercial law are statutory in origin. Sometimes statutes seek merely to clarify and codify existing common law rules and legislation, but statutes may create a body of rights and duties where none existed before[1].

---

1 Many of the provisions of labour law are of this type.

Common Law and Equity
1.10 The common law can be further subdivided into common law and equity. If both are branches of the common law and therefore both judge-made law, wherein lies the difference between them? The difference between them is that of their origins. Prior to the Judicature Acts of 1873–1875 there were two systems of courts in England, the common law courts and Court of Chancery.

1.11 The common law courts had developed from the centralised system for the administration of justice developed by a powerful monarchy between the eleventh and thirteenth centuries, which had gradually ousted the jurisdiction of the local courts. Therefore, common law is that body of law developed by the common law courts, for example the Court of Exchequer (whose judges were called Barons), the Court of Common Pleas and the Court of King's Bench, prior to the fusion of the administration of justice in 1875, and subsequent modifications and extensions effected since 1875. The common law is not static but subject to constant affirmation, revision and development by modern judges.

It is generally accepted that it was only the administration of the law and not the law itself which was fused in 1875 and thus it is still possible to speak of common law and equity as distinct bodies of law. Since 1875 a case involving both common law and equitable principles can be heard in one court which can, where necessary, apply both sets of rules. Prior to 1875 the unfortunate litigant might have to bring two actions — one to establish his common law rights and another before the Court of Chancery to establish his equitable rights. An even more unfortunate party might succeed at common law, but have the efficacy of such judgment nullified on equitable judgment.

1.12 Equity is that body of law developed in the Court of Chancery prior to 1875 and its subsequent amendments and developments. The Court of Chancery developed later than the common law courts because of defects in those courts and the law they administered. Common law developed an extremely rigid procedure which made it difficult to initiate actions, and the remedies available for the successful litigant were inadequate. Thus, the habit arose in the fourteenth and fifteenth centuries of petitioning the King to remedy injustice and this function gradually came to be exercised by the Lord Chancellor. Until 1529, the Lord Chancellor was an ecclesiastic whose decisions were supposedly guided by conscience. This jurisdiction of the Chancellor crystallised into the Court of Chancery, presided over by the Lord Chancellor who was by then a lawyer. The procedure in the Court of Chancery was originally less rigid than that of the common law courts; and the basis of decisions was supposed to be the merits of each action and what was just between the parties, with little reference to previous cases. Subsequently, both procedure and substantive law became more rigid and the notion of creating a remedy to fit the particular case before the court disappeared and the Court of Chancery became as much influenced by previous cases as the common law courts. By the nineteenth century the Court of Chancery had a well deserved reputation for tardiness. This was due to the fact that until 1813 all cases were heard by the Lord Chancellor, quite apart from the innate conservatism and caution of some Lord Chancellors[1].

The rules of equity developed by the Court of Chancery, were either entirely new rights totally unknown to the common law or remedies designed to counter the inefficacy or injustice of the common law, for example, rectification and specific performance. Equity did not amend the common law but enabled a litigant who had failed to establish a claim at common law, or been disappointed by the remedies available there, to seek an equitable remedy which made good the defects of the common law in a particular case. For example, sales of real property, if they are to be effective at common law, must comply with s.40 of the Law of Property Act 1925[2], but a sale of property ineffective at common law for failure to comply may be enforced in equity because of its doctrine of part performance[3]. The common law rule is not abrogated by the equitable doctrine: it is merely circumvented by equity in appropriate cases.

---

1   For an illustration of the delays of the Court of Chancery see *Bleak House* by Charles Dickens.
2   Para. 7.10.
3   Paras. 7.17 and 7.18.

1.13   Even modern courts, which administer both common law and equity, will tend to consider the common law first and then see if it is affected by equity. This process is reversed where a case is concerned with a body of rules developed almost entirely by equity, for example the law of trusts. If there is a conflict between the rules of the common law and those of equity, the rules of equity prevail[1]. It cannot be emphasised too much that the remedies developed by equity cannot be demanded as of right (unlike common law remedies) but, reflecting the origins of equity in conscience, are discretionary and may or may not be awarded by the court. A litigant who has acted unfairly or inequitably may find the court will decline to award an equitable remedy and must be content with common law remedies. If, for example, you delay completing the purchase of a house, so that the vendor refuses to proceed with the sale, you have a right to damages for breach of contract of sale but no right to have the completion enforced by an order for specific performance of the contract.

---

1   Judicature Act 1873, s.25, re-enacted in the Judicature Act 1925, s.44.

Chapter 2
Administration of the Law

THE COURTS

2.1 The first thing to be noted in any discussion of the court system is that not every type of court exercises both a civil and a criminal jurisdiction. Moreover, within the sphere of either of these jurisdictions, the particular type of court which will try the case (or hear an appeal) will depend on a number of disparate factors. Opposite is a chart which shows the outline of the court structure and the following paragraphs explain this, beginning at the bottom.

Magistrates' courts[1]

2.2 A magistrates' court is constituted by justices of the peace. The terms 'justice of the peace' and 'magistrate' are synonymous[2] and henceforth to avoid confusion we shall use the word 'magistrate'. Normally a magistrates' court must be composed of at least two magistrates. The most important exception is that one magistrate can conduct committal proceedings[3] in his capacity of examining magistrate.

Magistrates, of whom there are about 19,000, are appointed by the Lord Chancellor or by the Chancellor of the Duchy of Lancaster in the name of the Queen as magistrates for a particular area (normally, a county). Each county is divided into a number of petty sessional divisions (i.e. magistrates' courts districts). Lay magistrates are unpaid, but get an allowance for loss of earnings and for expenses. They are not required to possess any legal qualifications: for legal advice they rely on their clerk, who is usually a solicitor or a barrister, but even though the clerk to the magistrates is legally qualified an individual court may be served by an unadmitted assistant. In the inner London area, and in some other places, jurisdiction is exercised both by stipendiary

THE COURT STRUCTURE

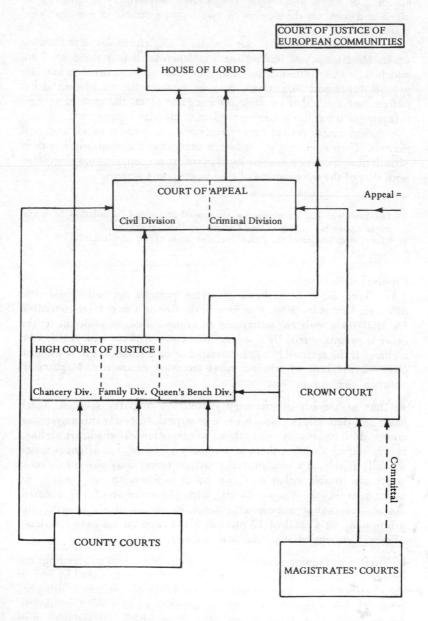

COURT OF JUSTICE OF
EUROPEAN COMMUNITIES

HOUSE OF LORDS

COURT OF APPEAL

Civil Division | Criminal Division

Appeal =

HIGH COURT OF JUSTICE

Chancery Div. | Family Div. | Queen's Bench Div.

CROWN COURT

COUNTY COURTS

MAGISTRATES' COURTS

Committal

11

(i.e. salaried) magistrates, who are barristers or solicitors of seven years' standing or more, and by lay magistrates. Stipendiary magistrates sit alone and have all the powers of two lay magistrates in a magistrates' court.

The Lord Chancellor can dismiss a magistrate without showing cause. Magistrates are put on the supplemental list at the age of 70, which is *de facto* retirement in that they cease to be entitled to exercise judicial functions. Magistrates may be put on the supplemental list before that age either at their own request or on the ground of 'age, infirmity or other like cause' or neglect of judicial duties.

Magistrates' courts have jurisdiction in both criminal and civil matters. Their summary procedure is inexpensive and speedy but their jurisdiction only extends to matters of minor importance compared with that of the other courts of trial in the court system.

1　The principal statute governing the constitution and jurisdiction of magistrates' courts is the Magistrates' Courts Act 1952, as amended.
2　Except that 'justice of the peace' includes those of the supplemental list.
3　Para. 2.3, b.

Criminal jurisdiction
2.3　There are two methods of trying persons accused of criminal offences. One is by judge and jury in the Crown Court after committal for trial on a written accusation of crime called an indictment; the other is summary trial by a magistrates' court without a jury, either on a charge if the accused has been arrested or on a summons if he has not. Over 96 per cent of criminal cases are tried summarily. Magistrates' courts have two functions:

a. That of a court of summary jurisdiction or petty sessions, which hears and determines cases, subject to appeal. Not only do magistrates' courts deal summarily with those minor offences which are defined in the statute creating them as summary offences (i.e. offences which are only triable in a magistrates' court) but they may also try offences which are 'triable either way' (i.e. either in a magistrates' court or on indictment in the Crown Court) with the consent of the accused. Magistrates cannot impose a sentence in excess of six months' imprisonment, or a total of 12 months if the accused has been convicted of more than one offence triable either way.

b. That of examining magistrates by whom committal proceedings are held as a necessary preliminary, in almost all cases, to a trial by jury in the Crown Court. The function of examining magistrates is different from that when they sit to hear and determine a case. All they have to decide is whether there is evidence upon which a reasonable jury properly directed could convict. It matters not that the magistrates themselves would not have convicted on the evidence before them. The system acts as a filter so that persons against whom there is no evidence upon which a reasonable jury could convict are spared the anxiety and expense of a trial. If the magistrates decide that there is no *prima facie* case against the accused they decline to commit him for trial and discharge him.

2.4 A person convicted by a magistrates' court may appeal to the Crown Court against conviction, or against sentence, or against both on a question of fact or law, except that if he pleaded guilty or admitted the truth of the information against him he may appeal to the Crown Court against sentence only. An alternative avenue of appeal is to appeal to the Divisional Court of the Queen's Bench Division. This is open to the prosecution or the defence, or any other party to a proceeding before a magistrates' court, if aggrieved with the determination of the magistrates as being wrong in law or in excess of jurisdiction. This type of appeal is solely concerned with questions of law or jurisdiction, but is usually the preferable course to adopt when the appeal is founded on such questions alone.

Civil jurisdiction
2.5 This is very varied. It extends over the recovery of certain civil debts such as income tax, electricity and gas charges, and rates; the grant and renewal of licences; and 'domestic proceedings'.

'Domestic proceedings' are probably the most important aspect of the civil jurisdiction of magistrates' courts. Magistrates' courts have powers in matrimonial proceedings to make maintenance orders for the complainant spouse on proof that the defendant spouse has failed to provide reasonable maintenance, or has behaved in such a way that the complainant cannot reasonably be expected to live with the defendant, or is in desertion. In such proceedings the magistrates may also make orders concerning the separation of the spouses and, whether or not one of the above grounds is proved, concerning the custody and maintenance of any child of the family. Apart from these matrimonial proceedings, magistrates' courts also have powers under a number of statutes to make orders concerning adoption and the custody and maintenance of children. When hearing domestic proceedings, a magistrates' court must be composed of not more than three magistrates, including, so far as practicable, both a man and a woman. Unless the court otherwise directs, only the officers of the court; the parties to the case and their legal representatives; witnesses, and news reporters may attend. There are strict limitations on the particulars which may be published in a news report of domestic proceedings[1].

---

1 Magistrates' Courts Act 1952, ss. 56, 57 and 58.

2.6 Appeals in civil proceedings in magistrates' courts generally lie to the Crown Court with a further (or alternative) appeal on a point of law to the Divisional Court of the Queen's Bench Division by case stated, except that in domestic proceedings appeal is to the Divisional Court of the Family Division and there is no alternative of appeal to the Crown Court.

Juvenile courts[1]
2.7 Generally, someone aged under 17 who is charged with a criminal offence, whether indictable or summary, must be tried in a juvenile court.

A juvenile court also hears civil 'care proceedings', in which a variety of orders can be made concerning those under 17 on the ground that they are in need of care and control.

Essentially, a juvenile court is composed in the same way as a magistrates' court hearing domestic proceedings and similar restrictions apply concerning attendance and news reporting. Appeal from a juvenile court lies to the Crown Court with a further (or alternative) appeal on a point of law to the Divisional Court of the Queen's Bench Division by case stated.

---

1 Juvenile courts are governed by the Children and Young Persons Act 1933, as amended.

County courts

2.8 The jurisdiction of county courts is exclusively civil. England and Wales are divided into 336 county court districts, each with their own court house, office and staff, which are grouped into 63 circuits.

Each county court circuit has assigned to it one or more Circuit judges. Circuit judges are appointed by the Queen on the recommendation of the Lord Chancellor to serve in the Crown Court[1] and in the county courts, and to carry out such other judicial functions as may be conferred on them. Generally, only Circuit judges specifically assigned to a county court circuit sit in the county court. Those qualified to be a Circuit judge are barristers of at least 10 years' standing or Recorders[2] who have held office for three years. They retire at the end of the completed year of service in which they reach 72, although the Lord Chancellor may retain the services of a Circuit judge until he is 75. A Circuit judge can be dismissed by the Lord Chancellor on grounds of incapacity or misbehaviour[3].

There are county court registrars, solicitors of seven years' standing appointed and removable by the Lord Chancellor, in each circuit. They supervise the administrative business of the court and also have jurisdiction to try claims not exceeding £200, unless the parties object, and any other action with the consent of the parties. With leave of the judge of the court a registrar has the full jurisdiction of the judge where the defendant admits the claim or does not appear at the hearing. He also deals with interlocutory applications which are necessary before an action can be tried and with other ancillary matters. An appeal lies from the registrar to the judge.

1 Paras. 2.21–2.23.
2 Para. 2.21.
3 Courts Act 1971, ss. 16 and 17, as amended. To reduce delay in the administration of justice, the Lord Chancellor can appoint deputy circuit judges on a temporary basis. Deputy circuit judges and Recorders can deputise for a circuit judge in a county court.

Jurisdiction
2.9   Under the provisions of the County Courts Act 1959, as amended, county courts have a wide jurisdiction which includes:

a. Jurisdiction over actions in contract or tort, except defamation, or for money recoverable by statute, where the debt or damages claimed do not exceed £2,000. A county court has jurisdiction over defamation or a claim in excess of £2,000 if either the parties agree to accept the jurisdiction of the county court or the case is remitted to it by the High Court.

b. Over actions for the recovery of land where the net annual value of the land for rating does not exceed £1,000.

c. An equity jurisdiction up to £15,000, e.g. in cases of administration, foreclosure and specific performance, where the amount of the estate mortgage or purchase price, as the case may be, does not exceed £15,000.

d. Contentious probate jurisdiction where there is a contested application for the grant or revocation of probate (will) or letters of administration (intestacy), or where there are actions as to the validity of a will, and the net value of the estate is less than £15,000. In practice, this jurisdiction is rarely exercised; trial nearly always being in the Chancery Division of the High Court.

e. Some county courts have a limited jurisdiction in admiralty matters. e.g. damage to a ship or its cargo, or pilotage disputes.

2.10   Types of jurisdiction under other statutes include:

a. (in designated courts) undefended divorce and annulment of marriage cases and proceedings ancillary to them;

b. guardianship and adoption;

c. bankruptcy;

d. winding-up of companies; and

e. matters under the Consumer Credit, Housing, Rent, and Landlord and Tenant Acts.

2.11 The procedure in the county courts is simpler, speedier and less costly, than in the High Court. To discourage the conduct of minor litigation in the High Court which could have been brought in a county court, a party, who succeeds in the High Court on a matter falling within county court limits, may in certain circumstances be awarded no costs or only awarded costs on the county court, as opposed to High Court, scale[1].

---

1 County Courts Act 1959, s.47, as amended. This rule only applies to actions in tort and contract.

Small claims[1]

2.12 A county court registrar can refer an action to arbitration if one or other of the parties to the proceedings so requests, provided the action is for a sum of money not in excess of £200. If referral to arbitration occurs the hearing takes place before an arbitrator, generally in private, without the formalities associated with a trial. The arbitrator will usually be the registrar, but the parties can agree on the appointment of any other suitable person. If the amount in dispute exceeds £200 the matter can still be referred to arbitration if the parties agree to this or one of the parties does not object to the registrar deciding the application for arbitration. If a party does object then the Circuit judge can decide whether the case should be dealt with by arbitration. The award of the arbitrator is entered as a judgment in the court proceedings, and is binding as such. The Circuit judge has power, on application, to set the award aside.

   The advantage of the arbitration procedure is that it is eminently suitable for the litigant in person in small claims cases, which are mainly 'consumer disputes', since it is even more informal and inexpensive than trial in the county court. The arbitration may take place round a table, the oath may not be administered and each party normally bears his own costs. Formality is kept to the minimum necessary to protect the interests of each party.

---

1 Administration of Justice Act 1977, s.17, amending s.92 of the County Courts Act 1959; County Court (Amendment No.3) Rules 1973.

2.13   About two million actions are commenced in county courts each year, 65 per cent of which are debt collecting claims concerning goods and services. The great majority of actions commenced concern undisputed claims which are settled before or without trial. The percentage of judgments entered after trial before a judge or registrar or after arbitration was only 2 per cent, 2 per cent and 0.9 per cent respectively in 1976.

Appeal from a county court judge lies to the Court of Appeal (subject to certain conditions), except in bankruptcy where the Divisional Court of the Chancery Division is the appellate court.

The High Court of Justice

2.14   The High Court is part of the Supreme Court of Judicature, the Crown Court and Court of Appeal being the other two constituent parts. The High Court was established by the Judicature Acts 1873—1875, replacing the separate Courts of Chancery, Queen's Bench, Common Pleas, and Exchequer, and also the Courts of Admiralty, Probate, and Matrimonial Causes.

The High Court consists of three divisions, each of which, by virtue of the rules of procedure and practice, has a separate jurisdiction. High Court judges are assigned to a particular division but, since they are judges of the High Court, they can exercise any jurisdiction appertaining to a High Court judge, irrespective of the division to which they have been assigned[1].

High Court judges are appointed by the Queen on the recommendation of the Lord Chancellor. Those qualified for appointment are barristers of at least 10 years' standing. A High Court judge has greater security of tenure than a Circuit judge since he is only removable on an address presented by both Houses of Parliament to the Queen[2], except that the Lord Chancellor may, with the concurrence of senior judges, declare vacant the office of a 'superior' judge who is subject to permanent medical incapacity and is unable to tender his resignation[3]. High Court judges must retire on attaining the age of 75[4].

---

1 See *Re Hastings (No 3)* [1959] Ch 368, [1959] 1 All ER 698, *Re Kray* [1965] Ch 736, [1965] 1 All ER 710, *Re L*, [1968] P 144, [1968] 1 All ER 20, CA.
2 Supreme Court of Judicature (Consolidation) Act 1925, s.12. To reduce delay, the Lord Chancellor can appoint deputy High Court judges on a temporary basis.
3 Administration of Justice Act 1973, s.12.
4 Judicial Pensions Act 1959, s.2.

Chancery Division

2.15 The Chancery Division consists of the Lord Chancellor, as its nominal head, although he never sits at first instance, a Vice-Chancellor and, at present, 11 judges (the permitted minimum is four). Theoretically, the Chancery Division could hold sittings anywhere in England and Wales[1] but, apart from exceptional cases, it sits in the Royal Courts of Justice in London. However, the Vice-Chancellor of the County Palatine of Lancaster (who is a Circuit judge) sits as a High Court Judge in certain northern towns to hear business assigned to the Chancery Division.

There are seven Masters of the Chancery Division, who are solicitors appointed by the Lord Chancellor. Applications are made to the Masters in Chambers in the preliminary stages of litigation, and they make orders thereon in the name of the judge to whom they are assigned. Complicated accounts and inquiries are also referred to them. If a party is not satisfied with the Master's ruling, he may adjourn the matter to the judge.

---

1 Courts Act 1971, s.2.

2.16 The jurisdiction of the Chancery Division is entirely civil and can be split into original and appellate jurisdictions.

a. *Original jurisdiction* By virtue of s.56 of the Supreme Court of Judicature (Consolidation) Act 1925 jurisdiction over the following matters is assigned to the Chancery Division:

   i.   the administration of estates of deceased persons;
   ii.   the execution of trusts;
   iii.   the redemption and foreclosure of mortgages;
   iv.   the rectification and cancellation of deeds;
   v.   specific performance of contracts for the sale or lease of interests in land; and
   vi.   partnership actions.

Other heads of jurisdiction have been added by statutes and rules of procedure, e.g.

   vii. winding-up of companies;
   viii. bankruptcy;
   ix. revenue matters; and
   x.   contentious probate.

As can be seen, apart from the absence of financial limits, there is some concurrence between the Chancery Division's original jurisdiction and some of the heads of jurisdiction possessed by the county courts.

b. *Appellate jurisdiction* This is much more limited. Certain statutes empower a single judge to hear appeals of various kinds, e.g. income tax appeals from the Commissioners of Inland Revenue. A Divisional Court of the Chancery Division hears appeals from county courts in bankruptcy matters and has a few other functions which are rarely exercised.

Queen's Bench Division

2.17   This division is the largest of the three divisions and has the most varied jurisdiction. Its head is the Lord Chief Justice and 45 judges are assigned to it at present. The original civil jurisdiction of this division is exercised in first-tier Crown Court centres[1] as well as in London.

There are eight Masters of the Queen's Bench Division, who must be barristers. These Masters supervise the Central Office of the Supreme Court in which official documents are issued and registered. Applications are made to a Master in Chambers in preliminary stages of litigation in the Queen's Bench Division, appeal lying from his order to a judge.

---

1 Para. 2.21.

2.18   The jurisdiction of the Queen's Bench Division can be divided into four heads, the first of which is the busiest:

a. *Original civil jurisdiction* The principal aspect of this are actions in contract and tort. Commercial matters are dealt with by specialist judges in the Commercial Court which sits in London, Liverpool and Manchester and whose procedure is more flexible and speedier than the normal High Court procedure. Similarly, admiralty matters, such as salvage claims, are heard in this division by specialist judges (who often sit with lay assessors). Financial limits apart, there is concurrence between the Division's original civil jurisdiction and some heads of jurisdiction possessed by county courts.

b. *Appellate civil jurisdiction* A single judge has jurisdiction to hear appeals from certain tribunals. The Divisional Court of the Queen's Bench Division hears appeals by way of case stated on a miscellaneous collection of civil matters from the magistrates' court (excluding domestic proceedings), the Crown Court and certain other bodies. The Divisional Court consists of two or more judges, normally three and usually presided over by the Lord Chief Justice. The appeal must be on the ground that the determination or decision is wrong in law. The case is not re-heard, the Divisional Court merely hearing legal argument.

c. *Appellate criminal jurisdiction* The Divisional Court hears appeals in criminal matters by case stated from magistrates' courts and the Crown

Court (in that court's appellate capacity). The appeal must be on the same ground, and is conducted in the same way, as in b. above.

d. *Supervisory jurisdiction* This jurisdiction is also exercised by the Divisional Court. The most important aspect of this is the jurisdiction to issue the writ of *habeas corpus* and to make 'prerogative orders' against inferior courts (magistrates' and county courts and the Crown Court, except in respect of trials on indictment[1]), tribunals and other decision-making bodies. The prerogative orders are *mandamus,* prohibition and *certiorari.* An order of *mandamus* is used to compel any body to carry out a definite duty imposed on it by law. The order cannot be used to compel the body to exercise its discretion in a particular way, but it may be used to compel it to hear and determine a case, or to state a case for the opinion of the High Court[2]. An order of prohibition or *certiorari* will issue only in relation to an order or decision of a body which is under a duty to 'act judicially' or 'act fairly' in making that decision, as opposed to purely administratively. This does not mean that they issue only to courts or tribunals, for many other bodies, such as local authorities, may sometimes be required to act in such a way. The order of prohibition is used to *prevent* such a body from acting in excess of jurisdiction or otherwise acting improperly. The order of *certiorari* covers much the same ground but *after* such a body has done something and it is desired to review it and, if necessary, quash it on the ground of excess of jurisdiction, denial of natural justice, clear evidence of fraud or apparent defect. Natural justice will be denied if a party is not given a chance to state his case, or if the case is heard by a person who is a judge in his own cause, or if a party is not informed of the reasons for the decision in the case.

---

1 Courts Act 1971, s.10; *R v Leeds Crown Court, ex parte Bradford Chief Constable* [1975] QB 314, [1975] 1 All ER 133, DC; para. 2.22.
2 Magistrates' Courts Act 1952, s.87(6).

Family Division
2.19 The Family Division, which came into being on 1 January 1972, replaced the Probate, Divorce and Admiralty Division and took on most of the jurisdiction of that Division. It consists of the President of the Division and, at present, 17 judges (the permitted minimum is three). The jurisdiction of this division is entirely civil, and is exercised in London and at first-tier Crown Court centres. It is set out in the First Schedule to the Administration of Justice Act 1970, and can be divided into original and appellate jurisdictions:

a. *Original jurisdiction* The Division deals with all aspects of family law; the following are the most important examples:

i. proceedings for divorce, annulment of marriage and judicial separation and ancillary (e.g. financial provision and custody proceedings) connected therewith. Undefended divorce etc. proceedings are heard in divorce county courts[1] unless referred to the Family Division;

ii. proceedings for a declaration of legitimacy, or the validity of a marriage, or of a person's right to be deemed a British subject;

iii. proceedings for the determination of title to property in dispute between spouses;

iv. proceedings concerning the occupation of the matrimonial home;

v. wardship of court, guardianship and adoption proceedings;

vi. variation of maintenance agreements.

b. *Appellate jurisdiction* This is principally concerned with appeals by case stated to the Divisional Court of the Family Division (which normally consists of two judges) from the decisions of magistrates' courts in domestic proceedings[2].

---

1 Para. 2.10, a.
2 Para. 2.5.

2.20 Appeals from the original jurisdiction of any division of the High Court lie to the Court of Appeal (Civil Division), as do appeals from the appellate jurisdiction of any Division[1], save that appeals from the criminal appellate jurisdiction of the Divisional Court of the Queen's Bench Division go straight to the House of Lords.

In 1976 the number of proceedings *commenced* and appeals entered in the High Court was, respectively:

Chancery Division	15,677	86
Queen's Bench Division	211,464	618
Family Division (including proceedings started in Divorce County Courts)	261,767	283

---

1 But note the 'leap-frogging' exception mentioned at para. 2.29, b.

The Crown Court

2.21 The Crown Court in England and Wales is divided into six circuits. In each circuit it sits in a large number of towns, which are divided into first-tier, second-tier and third-tier centres. The first- and second-tier centres are served by High Court and Circuit judges and by Recorders: the distinction between the two centres being that in the former High Court civil cases[1] are heard as well as Crown Court cases. Like the second-tier centres, third-tier centres are limited to Crown Court work but they are only served by Circuit judges and Recorders with the result that a few very serious offences, such as murder, cannot be tried at them.

The jurisdiction and powers of the Crown Court are exercised by:
a. any judge of the High Court;
b. any Circuit judge;
c. any Recorder; and
d. in some circumstances any judge of the High Court, Circuit judge or Recorder sitting with lay magistrates.

Recorders are part-time judges of the Crown Court appointed by the Queen on the recommendation of the Lord Chancellor. They must be either barristers or solicitors of at least 10 years' standing. A Recorder cannot continue in office after the end of the completed year of service in which he reaches 72. His appointment can be terminated by the Lord Chancellor on the grounds of incapacity, misbehaviour or failure to comply with the terms of his appointment[2].

Lay magistrates cannot act as judges of the Crown Court by themselves but only with a High Court or Circuit judge or with a Recorder. They must form part of the Crown Court when it hears appeals from magistrates' courts and also when it is sentencing persons who have been committed for sentence by magistrates' courts but the Lord Chancellor has power to dispense with this requirement. The number of magistrates so sitting must be not less than two nor more than four[3]. Rulings on questions of law are for the judge but decisions on other questions, e.g. sentence, are the product of all members of the court[4].

---

1 Para. 2.18, a.
2 Courts Act 1971, s.21.
3 *Ibid.*, s.5.
4 *R v Orpen* [1975] QB 283, [1974] 2 All ER 1121, CA.

Criminal jurisdiction
2.22 The Crown Court has exclusive jurisdiction over all offences tried by jury on indictment, an appeal by a convicted person lying to the Court of Appeal. About 68,000 people a year are tried in the Crown Court.

The Crown Court also has jurisdiction:

a. to deal with persons committed for sentence by magistrates' courts because their sentencing powers are inadequate; and

b. to hear appeals from magistrates' courts, including juvenile courts, against conviction or sentence. The appeal takes the form of a re-hearing of the case, i.e. the case is tried all over again, witnesses being called etc. Where the Crown Court has given its decision on such an appeal, either the prosecution or the defence, if dissatisfied with the determination of the Crown Court as being wrong in law or in excess of jurisdiction, may appeal to the Divisional Court of the Queen's Bench Division by way of case stated.

Juries are not used in these cases.

Civil jurisdiction

2.23 The civil jurisdiction of the Crown Court is far less important. It is principally concerned with betting, gaming and liquor licensing appeals, but other appeals within its jurisdiction are appeals from various administrative decisions and from affiliation proceedings in the magistrates' courts.

The Court of Appeal

2.24 The Court of Appeal is composed of the Master of the Rolls and, at present, 16 Lords Justices of Appeal (the permitted minimum is eight and the maximum 16). Lords Justices are appointed by the Queen on the advice of the Prime Minister. They must have been judges of the High Court or barristers of 15 years' standing[1]. The tenure of their office is the same as for High Court judges[2]. In addition, certain holders of high judicial office are *ex officio* members of the Court of Appeal, for example the Lord Chief Justice, and any High Court judge may be required to sit in the Court of Appeal if this is necessary[3]. The Court of Appeal is divided into a civil and a criminal division.

---

1 Supreme Court of Judicature (Consolidation) Act 1925, s.9.
2 Para. 2.14.
3 Supreme Court of Judicature (Consolidation) Act 1925, s.7.

Court of Appeal (Civil Division)
2.25 This hears appeals from:

a. The decisions in civil matters of all three divisions of the High Court. An appeal from the determination of an appeal by a divisional court requires leave to be given either by the divisional court or by the Court of Appeal[1].

b. The decisions of a county court judge, except bankruptcy. In most cases where the claim does not exceed £20 the county court judge's leave is required[2].

c. The decisions of the Employment Appeal Tribunal, Restrictive Practices Court, Lands Tribunal and certain other tribunals[3].

Except in the case of certain appeals from tribunals and appeals from the Restrictive Practices Court (which are by case stated), the method of appeal is by way of re-hearing. This means that the court reviews the whole case from the shorthand notes of the trial and the judge's notes: it does not mean that the witnesses heard in the trial court are re-called, nor that fresh evidence will normally be admitted.

Appeals are normally heard by three members of the Court of Appeal, in most cases this is the minimum permitted number, and the Division may be sitting simultaneously in as many as five courts. While most appeals are on points of law, an appeal may be against a finding of fact or the exercise of a discretion by the trial judge or against the damages which have been awarded, except in the case of appeals by case stated.

In 1975 1,302 appeals were set down for hearing in the Civil Division.

---

1 Supreme Court of Judicature (Consolidation) Act 1925, s.31(1)(f).
2 County Courts Act 1959, s.108.
3 Paras. 2.36, 2.38 and 2.39.

Court of Appeal (Criminal Division)
2.26   This Division normally sits in two courts: one composed of the Lord Chief Justice, a Lord Justice and a judge of the Queen's Bench Division and the other a Lord Justice and two Queen's Bench judges. In 1976 6,499 appeals to this Division were registered.

The Criminal Division hears appeals from persons convicted by the Crown Court after trial on indictment. The prosecution has no right of appeal against an acquittal on indictment[1]. The convicted person may appeal on any of the following grounds:

a. without any leave, against conviction on a question of law alone;

b. with the leave of the Court of Appeal (Criminal Division) or of the trial judge.
    i. on a question of fact alone, or
    ii. on a question of mixed law and fact;

c. with leave of the Court of Appeal (Criminal Division) on any other ground which appears to the court to be sufficient; and

d. with leave of the Court of Appeal (Criminal Division) against sentence, unless the sentence is one fixed by law[2].

In the case of an appeal against conviction the court will allow the appeal if it thinks *a*. that the jury's verdict was under all the circumstances 'unsafe or unsatisfactory', or *b*. that there was a wrong decision on any point of law, or *c*. that there was a 'material irregularity' in the course of the trial[3]: but an appeal may be dismissed if the court is of the opinion that 'no miscarriage of justice has occurred' even though the ground of appeal is good[4]. On appeal against sentence, the Court may reduce it or vary it, provided that in the result the appellant is not dealt with more severely than he was in the court below[5]. In other words, unlike the Crown Court in its appellate capacity, the Court of Appeal cannot increase a sentence on appeal. A detailed discussion of these and other powers of the Court of Appeal (Criminal Division) is outside the scope of this book.

---

1   However, by the Criminal Justice Act 1972, s.36, the Attorney-General may refer to the Court of Appeal, and ultimately to the House of Lords, a point of law arising at a trial on indictment where the accused was acquitted. The opinion of the court does not affect the acquittal but provides authoritative guidance on the point of law for the future.
2   Criminal Appeal Act 1968, ss. 1, 9–11.
3   *Ibid.*, s.2.
4   *Ibid.*, Proviso to s.2.
5   *Ibid.*, s.11(3).

2.27   Subject to certain conditions there is a further right of appeal from either division of the Court of Appeal to the House of Lords.

The House of Lords

2.28   While the House of Lords has original jurisdiction over disputed claims to peerages and breaches of privilege, such as contempt of the House or wrongs committed within its precincts, this is of minor importance compared with its appellate jurisdiction. The House of Lords' appellate jurisdiction is discharged by its Appellate Committee. The Appellate Jurisdiction Act 1876 provides that at the hearing of an appeal there must be present at least three of the following – the Lord Chancellor, the Lords of Appeal in Ordinary and such peers who hold or have held high judicial office (e.g. ex-Lord Chancellors). Normally, five Lords of Appeal in Ordinary hear an appeal and by convention peers other than the above do not attend meetings of the Appellate Committee. Lords of Appeal in Ordinary (commonly called 'Law Lords', and not to be confused with Lords Justices of Appeal)[1] must have held high judicial office for two years or be practising barristers of not less than 15 years' standing[2]. They are appointed by the Queen on the advice of the Prime Minister and have the same security of tenure and retirement age as High Court judges[3]. At present there are nine Lords of Appeal in Ordinary (the permitted minimum and maximum being seven and 11). Normally one or two of the Lords of Appeal are appointed from Scotland. The House of Lords has both a civil and a criminal appellate jurisdiction. In 1976, 50 appeals to the House of Lords were entered.

---

1 Para. 2.24.
2 Appellate Jurisdiction Act 1876, s.6.
3 Para. 2.14.

Civil appellate jurisdiction
2.29 The House hears:

a. Appeals from the Court of Appeal (Civil Division), provided that leave has been granted by that Court of by the House.

b. 'Leap-frog' appeals from the High Court. To save cost and delay the Administration of Justice Act 1969 provides that in most civil cases appeal may be made direct from the High Court to the House of Lords. This procedure may only be used:
   i. where the parties agree to it; and
   ii. the trial judge grants a certificate to sanction it (which he may only do if he is satisfied that a point of law is involved which is of general public importance and which either relates to a matter of construction of an Act or of a statutory instrument or else is one in respect of which he considers that he is 'bound' by a decision of the Court of Appeal or of the House of Lords); and
   iii. the House of Lords gives leave to appeal.

Criminal appellate jurisdiction
2.30 The House can hear an appeal by either the prosecution or the accused from the determination of an appeal by the Court of Appeal (Criminal Division) or by the Divisional Court of the Queen's Bench Division provided:

a. the court below (i.e. the Court of Appeal or Divisional Court) has certified that a point of law of general public importance is involved and that court or the House of Lords is satisfied that the point of law is one which ought to be considered by the House; and

b. either the court or the House of Lords has granted leave to appeal[1]. As can be seen, an appeal on a question of fact is not possible to the House of Lords in a criminal case.

---

1 Criminal Appeal Act 1968, s.33.

2.31   The House of Lords also hears appeals from the appellate courts of Scotland (civil matters only) and Northern Ireland.

The Court of Justice of the European Communities (European Court)

2.32   The European Court operates under the Treaties of the European Communities, viz. the Treaty of the European Community, the Treaty of the European Coal and Steel Community and the Treaty of the European Atomic Energy Community[1]. The Court consists of nine judges and is assisted by four Advocates-General, a type of official unknown to English law. The duty of an Advocate-General is, with complete impartiality and independence, to make reasoned submissions in open court on cases brought before the Court in order to assist it in the performance of its functions. The Court must generally sit in plenary session to hear cases.

Judges and Advocates-General are appointed for six year periods by the governments of member states acting in agreement and are eligible for re-appointment. They are chosen from those who fulfil the conditions required for the holding of the highest judicial office in their respective countries or who are jurisconsults (i.e. persons learned in the law) of recognised competence.

---

1   The relevant provisions are arts. 164–188 of the EEC Treaty, arts. 136–160 and arts. 31–45 of the ECSC Treaty. The provisions of the first two treaties are very similar.

2.33   Before 1973 the House of Lords was the final court of appeal in all cases in this country but the accession of the United Kingdom to membership of the European Communities meant that the European Court became the ultimate court *in matters within its jurisdiction, which does not extend to purely internal disputes between subjects,* so that in the great majority of cases arising within the United Kingdom the House of Lords remains the ultimate court. The fundamental point that the treaties under which the European Court operates are concerned only with those matters which have a European element, that is to say matters affecting people or property in the member countries of the Communities and not matters which solely concern people and property in this country, must be firmly grasped in order to understand the relationship of the Court to the rest of our legal system[1].

---

1   See *H. P. Bulmer Ltd v J. Bollinger SA* [1974] Ch 401, [1974] 2 All ER 1226, CA.

Jurisdiction

2.34   The jurisdiction of the European Court can be divided into two categories:

a. Matters concerning the conduct of member states or of the institutions of the Communities, such as –

   i. the hearing of complaints brought by member states or by the Commission of the European Communities that a member state has failed to fulfil its obligations under the Treaties;

  ii. the review of the legality of the regulations, directions and decisions of the Council of Ministers of the European Communities and of the Commission;

 iii. the hearing of disputes between member states which relate to the subject-matter of the Treaties, provided the states in question agree.

b. Matters of direct concern to litigants or prospective litigants in this country. Three matters are enumerated –

   i. preliminary rulings on the interpretation of the EEC and Euratom Treaties;

  ii. preliminary rulings on the validity and interpretation of the regulations, directives, decisions and other acts of the institutions of the Communities;

 iii. preliminary rulings on the interpretation of certain statutes of bodies established by an act of the Council.

Where any such question is raised in a case pending before a court or tribunal of a member state, against whose decisions there is no judicial remedy under national law (which means the House of Lords in this country), that court or tribunal *must* refer the matter to the European Court for a ruling, but where the matter is raised before any other court or tribunal it has a discretion as to whether or not to refer. In terms of the relationship between the European Court and English courts it is important to distinguish between the task of interpreting the Treaties – to see what they mean – and the task of *applying* them to the case in hand. The English judges have the final say in applying the Treaties: only they are empowered to find the facts and give judgment for one side or the other. However, before they can apply the Treaties they have to see what they mean, and in this task of interpretation English judges are not the final authority: the European Court is[1].

Under the second category of jurisdiction mention can also be made of the fact that the European Court has jurisdiction over claims for compensation for damage caused by institutions of the Communities or their servants and over disputes between the Communities and their servants. Here, of course the Court applies law as well as interpreting it.

---

1   See *H. P. Bulmer Ltd v J. Bollinger SA* [1974] Ch 401, [1974] 2 All ER 1226, CA.

SPECIALIST COURTS AND TRIBUNALS

The Judicial Committee of the Privy Council

2.35   The Judicial Committee of the Privy Council is the final court of appeal from the courts of some Commonwealth countries. It also entertains appeals from the disciplinary committees of the medical, dental and related professions, and certain other appeals. The Committee is normally composed of five Lords of Appeal, but other holders or past holders of high judicial office in this country or a Commonwealth country may, and do occasionally, sit.

The Restrictive Practices Court

2.36   This court deals with applications under the Restrictive Trade Practices Act 1976 for the validation of cartel agreements and other restrictive or unfair trade practices[1]. The courts consists of three High Court judges (of whom one is president of the court); one judge of the Court of Session in Scotland, one judge of the Supreme Court of Northern Ireland, and not more than 10 lay members appointed by the Lord Chancellor.

---

1   Paras. 15.33–15.38 and 15.42–15.45.

The Court of Protection

2.37   This court can assume jurisdiction over the management and administration of the property and affairs of a person whom it is satisfied is incapable of managing his property or affairs by reason of mental disorder. Its jurisdiction is conferred by Part VIII of the Mental Health Act 1959. Certain orders (e.g. those authorising proceedings for divorce or the making of a will on the patient's behalf) can only be made by the Lord Chancellor or one of the Chancery judges whom he has nominated to the Court. Otherwise, the jurisdiction including the assumption of responsibility, is, in practice, exercised by the Master, Deputy Master and other officers of the Court, subject to appeal to a judge.

The Employment Appeal Tribunal

2.38   This tribunal was established by the Employment Protection Act 1975. It consists of judges from the High Court and Court of

Appeal (one of whom is president) nominated by the Lord Chancellor, at least one judge nominated from the Court of Session and lay members with specialised knowledge of industrial relations. The lay members may be removed by the Lord Chancellor, after consultation with the Secretary of State for Employment, on specified grounds, e.g. incapacity or misbehaviour. The tribunal can sit anywhere in Great Britain in any number of divisions and is duly constituted when sitting with a judge and two or four lay members (or a judge and one member if the parties consent).

The tribunal's jurisdiction is entirely appellate. It can hear appeals on points of law from industrial tribunals under legislation relating to the following matters: redundancy payments; equal pay; sex discrimination; contracts of employment; trade unions and employment protection. In addition, the tribunal can hear appeals on questions of law or fact concerning the certification of a trade union as independent. The tribunal's procedure is designed to be as speedy, informal and simple as possible.

Tribunals

2.39 A large number of different tribunals have been created to deal with matters arising under modern legislation, particularly social welfare legislation. These are usually composed of legally qualified chairmen and lay members. Their hallmarks are speed, informality and cheapness.

In addition, a number of 'domestic tribunals' have been established by private or professional associations to resolve disputes between their own members or to exercise disciplinary powers over them. The jurisdiction of these tribunals is sometimes derived from statute but in other cases rests solely on contract in that, by joining the association, a member contracts to accept the jurisdiction of its domestic tribunal.

ARBITRATION

2.40 Whether it is used as an alternative to proceedings in court or as part of such proceedings, arbitration is a method for the settlement of civil disputes, other than those affecting status, such as divorce and bankruptcy. Arbitration is generally more informal and private, and cheaper and quicker than a trial in a court, although, where the main issues are questions of commercial law, trial in the Commercial Court may be cheapest and quickest, and certainly the most appropriate.

A dispute may be referred to arbitration in three ways: by agreement out of court; by statute or by order of the court.

Reference by agreement out of court

2.41 Particularly in commercial matters, the parties to a dispute may prefer to go straight to arbitration rather than become involved in court proceedings. Hence, they may voluntarily agree before or after the dispute to refer it to arbitration, and many commercial contracts provide for such a reference. If an arbitration agreement (or 'submission', as it is technically called) is in writing, as is usually the case, it is governed by the Arbitration Act 1950 and we now proceed to consider the position under that Act.

An arbitration agreement will not necessarily bar proceedings in a court but if a party institutes such proceedings without referring the dispute to arbitration, the other party may, after entering an appearance but before taking any further step in the proceedings, apply to the court for an order staying the proceedings[1]. The order is discretionary but, in the absence of some good reason, the court will stay the proceedings.

An arbitration agreement which gives the arbitrator the final power to decide a question of law is void on grounds of public policy[2], but there is no objection to a '*Scott v Avery*[3] clause', which is an agreement to refer a dispute to arbitration as a condition precedent to an action in the courts, and since no right of action in the courts accrues until the arbitration has taken place non-observance of the clause will afford a defence to a court action[4]. In addition, an agreement which simply makes the arbitrator's decision on questions of fact final is valid[5].

---

1 Arbitration Act 1950, s.4.
2 *Czarnikow v Roth, Schmidt and Co* [1922] 2 KB 478, CA; para. 16.15.
3 (1856), 5 HL Cas 811 (HL); para. 16.15.
4 *Scott v Avery.*
5 *Lee v Showmen's Guild of Great Britain* [1952] 2 QB 329 at 342, [1952] 1 All ER 1175 at 1181, CA.

Appointment of arbitrators and umpires

2.42 The parties may name any person whom they wish to act as arbitrators or provide a method for his appointment, as by giving the power of appointment to the President of a relevant professional society. The type of arbitrator chosen depends on the type of case in question. Lawyers are appointed quite frequently, but in some cases a person with the relevant technical expertise, e.g. an accountant or a surveyor, is appointed.

Normally arbitration is conducted by a single arbitrator[1], but, if specific provision is made for the appointment of two arbitrators, they must immediately appoint an umpire. It is the umpire's duty to enter on the reference if the arbitrators are unable to agree[2]. The High Court has powers to appoint arbitrators and umpires in default of an appointment by the parties or arbitrators respectively[3]. It also has power to revoke the authority of an arbitrator or umpire on various grounds.

A judge of the Commercial Court may, if in all the circumstances he thinks fit, accept appointment as sole arbitrator or umpire in a case of a commercial character, provided the state of business in the High Court permits him to be made available[4].

---

1 Arbitration Act 1950, s.6.
2 *Ibid.*, s.8.
3 *Ibid.*, s.10.
4 Administration of Justice Act 1970, s.4.

Conduct of the proceedings
2.43 In the absence of contrary terms in the arbitration agreement, an arbitrator or umpire must follow the ordinary rules of English law in reaching his decision, and the normal rules of evidence apply.

2.44 An arbitrator or umpire may, and must if so directed by the High Court, state in the form of a special case for the opinion of the High Court:

a. any question of law arising in the course of arbitration proceedings;

b. an award (i.e. the arbitrator's decision) or any part of an award[1].

As we saw in para. 2.41, any restriction on the court's power to decide a question of law is void and, if the arbitrator or umpire refuses to state a case when required to do so, he can be compelled to do so by the High Court.

---

1 Arbitration Act 1950, s.21.

2.45 To be valid, the award must decide all the issues submitted to arbitration and not decide other issues. It may provide for the payment of money, direct costs to be paid[1] and order the specific performance of a contract (other than one relating to land or an interest in land)[2], unless the arbitration agreement is to the contrary. The award is final and binding on the parties and persons claiming through them, unless the arbitration agreement otherwise provides[3], and there is no right of appeal to the courts (other than the procedure of stating a special case mentioned above). However, the High Court has power to set aside an award or remit the case for re-consideration where the arbitrator has misconducted himself or the proceedings[4], where there is an error of fact or of law *on the face* of the award (or of a document forming part of it)[5], and in certain other circumstances.

---

1 Arbitration Act 1950, s.18.
2 *Ibid.,* s.15.
3 *Ibid.,* s.16.
4 *Ibid.,* ss.22 and 23.
5 *Giacomo Costa Fu Andrea v British Italian Trading Co Ltd* [1963] 1 QB 201, [1962] 2 All ER 53, CA.

Enforcement of an award

2.46 An award may, by leave of the High Court, be enforced in the same manner as a judgment or order of that court, and where leave is granted, judgment may be entered in terms of the award. If this is done, the award can be enforced in any way allowed in the case of a judgment. Otherwise, the award is enforced by bringing a court action on the award as a contractual debt.

Reference by statute

2.47 Numerous statutes provide for the reference of certain types of dispute to arbitration. In some cases, e.g. disputes involving building societies, the parties have an option to refer, in others reference is compulsory, e.g. disputes involving street works. The provisions of the Arbitration Act 1950 apply to statutory references, with certain exceptions, unless the particular statute otherwise provides. Thus, what we have said above concerning the appointment of arbitrators and umpires, the proceedings, and the enforcement of awards is generally applicable to a statutory reference.

Reference by order of the court

2.48 The High Court may refer any case within its jurisdiction, or any particular issue in such a case, to be *tried* by an Official Referee (a Circuit judge assigned for such business), a senior officer of the court, such as a Master, or, where the issue is of a technical nature requiring specialist knowledge, a Special Referee[1]. Such a reference can be made even against the wishes of the parties and is particularly likely to be made if:

a. the prolonged examination of documents or scientific or local examination is required; or

b. the examination of accounts is involved.

The award of the arbitrator is entered as a judgment in the court proceedings, and is binding as such. In certain circumstances an appeal lies to the Court of Appeal (Civil Division).

In addition, the High Court has a similar power to refer to the same persons as above any question in a cause or matter before it for *inquiry and report*. The report may be adopted wholly or partially by the court, and if so adopted is as binding as a judgment to the same effect[2].

The power of a county court to refer a case to arbitration has been discussed in para. 2.12. In addition, any question in a case before a county court may be referred for inquiry and report[3].

---

1 Administration of Justice Act 1956, s.15; Rules of the Supreme Court, 0.36.
2 *Ibid.*
3 County Courts Act 1959, s.93 (as amended by the Administration of Justice Act 1973, s.7); County Court Rules 1973.

2.49 References to arbitration by the courts must be distinguished from references to arbitration by agreement or under a statutory provision because they operate in the context of court proceedings rather than as an alternative to them.

THE LEGAL PROFESSION

Barristers

2.50 Barristers do not form partnerships but instead work together in sets of chambers sharing rent and other expenses. Their work comprises drafting legal documents and writing opinions on points of law as well as appearing as advocates. Barristers do not work directly for lay clients but may only accept work from solicitors. Most sets of chambers are in London in the Inns of Court but there are also chambers in many other major cities. A barrister of more than 10 years' standing may apply to be made a Queen's Counsel by the Queen on the Lord Chancellor's advice. The work of a Queen's Counsel is confined to the most important cases and chiefly involves advocacy.

Barristers are members of one of the four Inns of Court (Middle Temple, Inner Temple, Lincoln's Inn and Gray's Inn) but much of the central control of the profession is now vested in the Senate of the Inns of Court and the Bar, and the Bar as a profession is represented by the General Council of the Bar.

Solicitors

2.51 Unlike practising barristers, solicitors are normally members of a partnership or employed by a partnership. Solicitors act as legal advisers on commercial, family and personal matters; they convey land and draft wills, and they prepare cases involving litigation. In addition, solicitors can act as advocates, instead of a barrister, in various tribunals; magistrates' and county courts, and in the Crown Court (when it is hearing appeals from, or sentencing persons committed for sentence by, magistrates' courts). To adopt a medical analogy, a barrister is the 'consultant' and the solicitor the 'general practitioner'.

The Law Society is responsible for the solicitors branch of the legal profession, the Council of that society being the ultimate authority.

Legal executives

2.52 Legal executives are qualified legal assistants in solicitor's offices who, while working under the control and authority of a solicitor, possess a high degree of expertise in their chosen field. Their professional body is the Institute of Legal Executives which, like the other professional bodies, is responsible for admission to its numbers and holds examinations.

THE JURY

2.53 The only courts in which juries are found are the Crown Court and the High Court (12 jurors) and the county courts (eight jurors). The use of juries in civil cases is rare and the parties generally have no right to demand a jury; except that a jury must be ordered on the application of either party in cases of defamation, malicious prosecution and false imprisonment, or on the application of a party against whom fraud is charged, unless the court considers that the trial cannot conveniently be undertaken with a jury because, for instance, a prolonged examination of accounts or documents is necessary[1]. The only civil cases where a jury is common are defamation cases. Provided the accused has pleaded not guilty, a jury is always empanelled in trials on indictment in the Crown Court.

---

1 Administration of Justice (Miscellaneous Provisions) Act 1933, s.6; see *Rothermere v Times Newspapers Ltd* [1973] 1 All ER 1013, [1973] 1 WLR 448, CA.

2.54 A person is eligible for jury service if he or she is between the ages of 18 and 65, is included on the electoral register for parliamentary and local government elections, and has been resident in the United Kingdom, the Channel Islands or the Isle of Man for five years since the age of 13. There are certain exceptions. Some persons are ineligible for jury service, including judges, barristers and solicitors, police officers, clergymen and the mentally ill. Certain ex-prisoners are disqualified and persons such as peers, soldiers and doctors are excusable as of right[1].

---

1 Juries Act 1974, ss. 1 and 3, and Sched. 1.

2.55 The division of labour between judge and jury is that the judge rules on law, the jury on fact. The judge directs the jury as to the law and they apply it to the facts. Their discussions are in secret, they choose their own foreman and they give no reasons for their decisions. Their verdict in a civil case can be overturned by the Court of Appeal but only if no reasonable jury properly directed could have reached it. In his summing-up the judge may comment on the plausibility of the evidence and may give guidance as to what inferences may be drawn. Generally, the jury must reach a unanimous verdict but a majority of 10 (seven in the county courts) may be accepted after the jury have had a reasonable time in all the circumstances for deliberation; and there is a minimum time of two hours in the Crown Court[1]. In civil cases the parties can always consent to accept any majority verdict[2].

---

1 Juries Act 1974, s.17.
2 Recognised in s.17(5) of the Juries Act 1974.

LEGAL AID AND ADVICE

2.56 Although a litigant can conduct his case in person[1] or, in certain tribunals can be represented by another layman, such as a trade union official, most people, particularly in the superior courts, are legally represented. The legal aid and advice provisions are concerned not only with cases involving litigation but also with legal services in other cases. The relevant law is now governed by the Legal Aid Act 1974 and regulations thereunder. It should be noted that the financial limits mentioned below were correct at the time of going to press but are liable to amendment by regulation.

---

1 Under the Litigants in Person (Costs and Expenses) Act 1975, a litigant in person can recover costs in civil proceedings.

Legal advice and assistance[1]

2.57 This is often called the '£25 scheme'. The scheme allows a solicitor to give oral and written advice, write letters, negotiate settlements and so on but, basically, does not extend to representation in a court (as this is a matter for legal aid, below).

The financial limits of the scheme are strict. The applicant's maximum disposable income must not exceed £48 per week and his maximum disposable capital must not exceed £340. Disposable income is gross income less prescribed deductions in respect of maintenance of dependants, income tax, interest on loans, rent, rates and so on. If the applicant's disposable income exceeds £23 a week the scheme is contributory on a sliding scale. Advice and assistance is normally only available to the extent that the solicitor giving it considers the cost of giving it will not exceed £25. He must not exceed that limit without obtaining the approval of the Supplementary Benefits Commission or the Law Society.

---

1 Legal Aid Act 1974, ss. 1—5.

Civil legal aid[1]

2.58 Legal aid is available for legal representation and other costs of litigation in most civil proceedings before the courts. One exception is proceedings in respect of defamation. Legal aid is not available for arbitrations, nor for proceedings before most tribunals. Although the administration of civil legal aid is ultimately the Lord Chancellor's responsibility, its practical implementation lies with the Law Society, through its Legal Aid Committee.

Civil legal aid is available for any person whose disposable income does not exceed £2,400 a year but it may be refused if his disposable capital exceeds £1,600, and it appears that he could afford to proceed without legal aid. Unless his disposable income is below £760 a year and his disposable capital below £340, the applicant will be expected to contribute financially, on a sliding scale, to his legal costs. The applicant's means are investigated for the above purposes by the Supplementary Benefits Commission. Apart from satisfying the financial limits, an applicant must also get a legal aid certificate from a local certifying committee composed of lawyers, who decide whether the applicant has a reasonable chance of success, be it as a plaintiff or defendant. If a certificate is refused appeal can be made to an area committee.

---

1 Legal Aid Act 1974, ss. 6—10 *et passim.*

Criminal legal aid[1]

2.59 At each stage of criminal proceedings an accused or convicted person whose means are such that he cannot afford 'immediate' legal representation may be granted legal aid if it appears to the appropriate court to be desirable in the interests of justice to grant it. The only cases in which legal aid must be granted are either where a person is committed for trial on a charge of murder or where the prosecution appeals, or applies for leave to appeal, from the Court of Appeal to the House of Lords. In all other cases the decision lies within the discretion of the court to which application is made. However, any doubt about whether legal aid should or should not be granted must be resolved in the applicant's favour. An applicant will usually get legal aid if he is charged with a serious offence, even if he intends to plead guilty.

The court to whom application is made will often make a criminal legal aid order before a full investigation of the applicant's means has been conducted. The applicant is, however, required to give the court a written statement of his means. There is no upper income limit beyond which an applicant cannot be granted legal aid but he may well be required later to make a contribution to his legal costs. Questions concerning means may ultimately have to be determined by the Supplementary Benefits Commission.

---

1 Legal Aid Act 1974, ss.28—40.

2.60 Of course, the cost of all legal advice and aid is defrayed out of public monies.

Chapter 3
Sources of English Law

3.1   The direct means by which law is made or comes into existence constitute legal sources, while a literary source is simply the written material in which a legal source is recorded.

Legislation and judicial precedent are the principal legal sources of English law and the only other source, custom, is now of very little relevance. The courts must consciously look to these sources to determine what the law is and are bound to apply the rules which they create. The literary sources of legislation are the various publications of statutes and statutory instruments, and, of precedent, law reports and, to a lesser extent, certain books of authority.

LEGISLATION

3.2   Unlike many continental countries where, the law having been codified, the mass of law is legislation, our law is predominantly derived from judicial precedent. Leaving aside certain areas which have been codified, such as the law relating to the sale of goods and to partnership (by the Sale of Goods Act 1893 and the Partnership Act 1890), the body of law concerning private rights is essentially derived from judicial precedent with relatively few alterations made by statute. Normally, the purpose of statutory alteration or revision of this area of the law is to revise a legal rule which has become inappropriate in changing social circumstances and which, because of the operation of the doctrine of judicial precedent, is incapable of adaptation by the courts. The generation of law reform proposals has been greatly assisted since 1965 by the existence of the Law Commission, consisting of full-time Commissioners, assisted by a research staff. Under the Law Commission Act 1965 it is the duty of the Law Commission to keep under review all the law with a view to its systematic development and reform, including in particular the codification of such law, the elimination of anomalies, the repeal of obsolete and unnecessary enactments, the reduction in the number of separate enactments, and generally the simplification and modernisation of the law. A large number of Law Commission reports and draft Bills have been implemented by Act of Parliament.

Legislation plays a more important part in criminal law, mainly in defining most offences, and in the sphere of family law. Another notable of modern legislation can be put into the category of 'social legislation'. example is legislation concerning the revenue, for instance, the Finance Acts which implement the budget proposals. However, the great majority Such legislation is concerned essentially with regulating the day to day running of the social system rather than with creating criminal offences or rights and duties between individuals. In this area in particular much of the flesh is put on the bones of the relevant Act by delegated legislation. Examples of 'social legislation' are the Health and Safety at Work etc. Act 1974, Trade Union and Labour Relations Act 1974, the Landlord and Tenant Acts and the Rent Acts.

3.3 Sometimes a statute is described as a consolidating or codifying statute. Where a branch of statute law has evolved piecemeal, a consolidating statute may be passed, for the purpose of clarification, containing substantially the existing law in a consolidated form. An example of a recent consolidation Act is the Income and Corporation Taxes Act 1970. A consolidation Act only consolidates statute law: a codifying Act may codify both case law and statute law, a notable example being the Sale of Goods Act 1893. However, the object of both consolidation and codification is to simplify and clarify the existing law rather than to effect substantial alterations to it.

3.4 There are essentially three types of legislation: Acts of Parliament; subordinate legislation, which mainly consists of delegated legislation made by government Ministers, local authorities and other bodies under powers derived from Parliament, and the legislation of the European Communities. Subject to compliance with the overriding legislation of the European Communities, Parliament (which consists of the Queen, House of Lords and House of Commons) is sovereign, which means that it is not subject to any legal limits on its powers to create, alter and repeal English law. It also means that an Act of Parliament cannot be questioned in, or by, the courts; it has to be applied by them. In certain cases the validity of subordinate legislation and of most types of legislation of the European Communities can be challenged.

Acts of Parliament

3.5 While it is going through the Parliamentary process, and before it receives the Royal Assent, an Act is known as a Bill. Most Bills originate from government departments, having been drafted by Parliamentary draftsmen, and are introduced into either House of Parliament by a government Minister. However, although the opportunities are rather limited, a Bill may be introduced by an ordinary Member of Parliament (a Private Member's Bill). The Bills mentioned so far are Public Bills, i.e. Bills which when enacted will be general in their application. In addition, Private Bills — Bills of a local or personal nature — may be presented by local authorities, public corporations, companies or even individuals and are subject to a different Parliamentary procedure. A third type of Bill is the Hybrid Bill. A Hybrid Bill is one which is introduced as a Public Bill but which affects the private interests of particular bodies or individuals. Part of the Parliamentary procedure for a Hybrid Bill is similar to that for a Private Bill.

3.6 The 'official' copies of Acts of Parliament are printed by the Queen's Printer and are available for sale to the public as soon as an Act is passed, as are the annual volumes of Acts. The Incorporated Council for Law Reporting publish texts of Acts taken from the Queen's Printers' copies, as do certain commercial publishers who publish annual volumes of Acts of Parliament verbatim, as well as in unbound parts soon after the Act is passed, a leading series is *Halsbury's Statutes of England*.

Citation
3.7 Originally statutes were cited either by the place where Parliament met[1] or by their subject matter[2]. However, by the end of the fourteenth century statutes were cited by the date of the regnal year or years of the Parliamentary session in which the Act was passed, the regnal year being assessed from the monarch's accession, together with a chapter number which denoted the order in which it received the Royal Assent. Thus, the Sale of Goods Act 1893 is cited '56 and 57 Vict. c.71'. This system of citation does not apply to Acts passed after 1962. The Acts of Parliament Numbering and Citation Act 1962 provides that the Chapter numbers assigned to Acts of Parliament in and after 1963 shall refer to the calendar year, not the regnal year, in which they were passed, and such acts may be cited accordingly. Thus, the Misrepresentation Act 1967 is cited '1967, c.7'. Local and Personal Acts are cited according to the same rules, depending on whether they were passed before 1963 or not, except that the chapter numbers of Local Acts are put in small Roman numerals, e.g. c. ii, and of Personal Acts in italics, e.g. c. *2*.

Of course, the more usual way to cite an Act is by its short title. However, it was not until the Short Titles Act 1896 that Acts were given official short titles which were permitted as an alternative method of citation. That Act gave short titles *ex post facto* to about 2,000 previous statutes: subsequent Acts generally set out their short title in a section near the end.

---

1 E.g. Statute of Gloucester (1278).
2 E.g. Statute of Labourers (1349).

Commencement
3.8 An Act of Parliament comes into operation on the date on which it receives the Royal Assent unless, as frequently occurs, some other date is specified in the Act or is to be appointed either by Order in Council or by a government Minister by way of statutory instrument[1].

---

1 Act of Parliament (Commencement) Act 1793.

Repeal
3.9 A statute may be repealed expressly by a subsequent statute, or impliedly, by being inconsistent with it (although there is a presumption against implied repeal)[1]. Unless the contrary intention appears, repeal does not:

a. revive a previously repealed rule of law; or

b. affect existing rights and liabilities, or legal proceedings, civil or criminal[2].

No statute becomes obsolete through the passing of time, except for certain Acts usually of an experimental or transitional nature which are expressed to be operative only for a limited period. The most convenient way of finding out whether a statute has been wholly or partly repealed or amended is to look it up in the *Chronological Table of the Statutes* published annually by the Stationery Office. This covers the period from 1235 to the end of the year preceding publication. The companion work is the *Index to the Statutes in Force,* arranged alphabetically under subject headings and also published annually.

---

1 Para. 3.25.
2 Interpretation Act 1889, ss. 11(1) and 38(2).

Subordinate legislation

3.10 Various institutions, such as the Crown, Ministers, public corporations and local authorities have legislative powers. Such legislation is subordinate since it is made by bodies with limited powers and it is always subject to abrogation or amendment by Act of Parliament. Moreover, it may be required to be subject to Parliamentary scrutiny and, unlike an Act of Parliament, it may be held invalid in certain cases by the courts. Subordinate legislation can be of two types: delegated legislation and autonomic legislation.

Delegated legislation

3.11 Delegated legislation comprises the great bulk of subordinate legislation. Delegated legislation is legislation made by some executive body under powers delegated to it by Act of Parliament. An Act of Parliament often gives powers to some bodies such as the Queen in Council (in effect the Government), a Minister or a local authority or public corporation to make regulations and prescribe for their breach. There is a vast amount of delegated legislation — the number of pieces made annually being numbered in thousands, whereas the number of Public and Private Acts of Parliament a year rarely exceeds 150. Recent examples of an Act giving very wide powers of delegated legislation are the European Communities Act 1972[1] and the Consumer Credit Act 1974[2]. Delegated legislation made by the central executive may be required to be made by Order in Council made by the Queen in Council, otherwise it takes the form of regulations, rules or orders made by a Minister or government department. Generally, delegated legislation of these types must be made by Statutory Instrument (formerly Statutory Rules and Orders). Statutory Instruments are printed by the Queen's Printer and are available in the same way as Acts of Parliament. They are cited by calendar year and number and by a short title. For instance, the Consumer Credit (Termination of Licences) Regulations 1976 are cited *S.I.* 1976 *No.* 1002. A Statutory Instrument comes into effect when made unless, as is usual, it specifies a later date[3]. Unlike an Act of Parliament, it is a defence for a person charged with contravening a Statutory Instrument to prove that it had not been issued by the Stationery Office at the date of the alleged offence, unless it is proved that at that date reasonable steps had been taken to bring the purport of the instrument to the notice of the public, or of persons likely to be affected by it, or of the person charged[4].

---

1 Para. 3.32.
2 Chap. 23, *passim.*
3 *Johnson v Sargant & Sons* [1918] 1 KB 101.
4 Statutory Instruments Act 1946, s.3.

3.12 By the Statutory Orders (Special Procedure) Act 1945 and 1965, a special parliamentary procedure is provided where, but only where, the making and confirmation of orders is declared by Acts passed after the 1945 Act to be subject to 'special parliamentary procedure'. The object of this procedure, which involves opportunities to object to the order at a local inquiry and also by petition to Parliament, is to ensure maximum publicity and maximum parliamentary control. For most legal purposes these 'Special Procedure Orders' are Statutory Instruments. In relation to other Statutory Instruments parliamentary control is secured to some extent by requirements of 'laying' and of publications. Often the enabling statute will require the instrument to be laid before Parliament, in which case it must be so laid before it becomes into operation, and in addition an affirmative resolution by Parliament may be required to give it effect or it may be made subject to cancellation by a negative resolution of either House within 40 'sitting' days[1]. Closer parliamentary scrutiny of new Statutory Instruments is provided by the Joint Select Committee on Statutory Instruments which is composed of members of both Houses and reports to Parliament. Its terms of reference include consideration of every Statutory Instrument of a general character, various other Statutory Instruments which, pursuant to the parent Act, have been laid before Parliament subject to the negative or affirmative resolution procedure, and Special Procedure Orders, with a view to seeing whether the special attention of Parliament should be drawn to the instrument on one of a number of grounds, e.g. that is obscurely worded or appears to impose charges on the subject or on the public revenue or purports to have a retrospective effect unauthorised by the parent statute. The Select Committee is not concerned with the merits of delegated legislation.

Another type of delegated legislation is the byelaw. These are made by local authorities, public corporations and certain other bodies authorised by statute. Although general in operation, they are restricted to the locality or undertaking to which they apply. They are not made by Statutory Instrument.

---

1   Statutory Instruments Act 1946, ss. 4 and 5, as clarified by the Laying of Documents before Parliament (Interpretation) Act 1948.

3.13   All forms of delegated legislation are invalid if they are *ultra vires*, i.e. in excess of the powers conferred by the enabling statute on the rule-making body or made in breach of a mandatory part of the prescribed procedure concerning their making or, in the case of byelaws, on the additional grounds that they are unreasonable or excessively uncertain or repugnant to the general law. The invalidity of delegated legislation can either by challenged directly before the courts or, more commonly, is raised as a defence to an action which concerns the application of the delegated legislation.

3.14 The principal advantages of delegated legislation are:

a. Parliament has insufficient time to deal with details. The availability of delegated legislation enables Parliament to limit itself to settling the general policy of a measure, such as the Consumer Credit Act 1974, leaving a Minister to supply the detailed provisions in the form of regulations and orders.

b. Delegated legislation is eminently suitable in the case of provisions on technical matters which would be inappropriate for Parliamentary discussion.

c. In some cases, the power to make delegated legislation enables a Minister to deal speedily with urgent situations, such as an economic crisis or a strike in an essential industry.

d. The power to make delegated legislation is also useful in that, within the terms of the parent Act, it enables the application of an Act to be tailored to deal with contingencies which were not foreseen when the Act was passed.

3.15 On the other hand, delegated legislation is open to the following criticisms:

a. Parliament has neither the time nor the opportunity to supervise all delegated legislation effectively.

b. The detail which delegated legislation provides may be just as important as the general policy of the parent Act, yet Parliament cannot discuss its merits.

Autonomic legislation

3.16 Autonomic legislation is legislation made by the Crown or by autonomous associations within the State under powers not delegated by Parliament but which are recognised by the courts. Trade unions and professional associations are examples of autonomous associations in this context. The legislation of such autonomous associations is directly binding only on their members, though negatively it binds everyone since interference with it is wrongful: it is invalid if *ultra vires.* Autonomic legislation made by the Crown is made under the royal prerogative. The Crown has no power under the prerogative to alter the general law of the land[1] but it has a limited prerogative power to legislate for the colonies, the armed forces and the civil service. The prerogative comprises those independent powers left to the Crown by Parliament and, legislation outside the prerogative powers of the Crown will be held invalid by the courts.

---

1 *Case of Proclamations* (1611) 12 Co Rep 74.

Interpretation

3.17 Language being inherently capable of ambiguity and human affairs being capable of great diversity, the courts are often faced with the question of whether a particular matter or piece of conduct falls within the wording of a particular legislative provision. The exposition which follows is concerned with the interpretation of Public Acts of Parliament but, essentially, the same rules apply to the interpretation of other Acts of Parliament and of subordinate legislation. In interpreting statutes the courts are trying to discover Parliament's intentions and may be helped by statutory definitions:

a. The Interpretation Act 1889 provides a number of definitions which apply unless there is a contrary intention, express of implied, in a particular statute, e.g. 'unless the contrary intention appears, (a) words importing the masculine gender shall include females; and (b) words in the singular shall include the plural and words in the plural shall include the singular'[1]. Again, 'person' includes any body of persons corporate or unincorporate[2].

b. Many statutes contain an interpretation section towards their end, whose definitions apply throughout the Act unless a contrary intention, express or implied, appears in a particular context.

---

1 S.1(1).
2 S.19.

3.18 Judges vary in their basic approach to statutory interpretation. Some insist that statutes must be interpreted literally, however ridiculous the consequences: others that statutes may be given a liberal construction to arrive at a just and sensible solution, thereby avoiding any absurdity which strict adherence to the literal approach would produce. The former are said to apply the 'Literal Rule': the latter the 'Golden Rule' supplemented by the 'Mischief Rule'. Sometimes judges decide a case on the basis of the golden or mischief rules without advertence to the literal rule. Which rule is adopted in a particular case will depend on the personality of the judge. The result of all this is that it is never possible to tell in advance which approach will be adopted to the interpretation of a provision when the case gets to court. Essentially, the question of which approach is the better depends upon whether one believes judges should mechanically give effect to the literal meaning of statutory words, however absurd, or should have a creative part to play in securing a just and sensible result.

The Literal Rule

3.19 This rule states that Parliament's intention must be found by interpreting the words used in their ordinary, literal or grammatical sense. The literal rule breaks down, of course, in the face of an ambiguity, but provided there is no ambiguity the court cannot avoid giving the words their literal meaning even if the literal interpretation appears to lead to an undesirable or absurd result. In *IRC v Hinchy*[1], the House of Lords had to interpret the Income Tax Act 1952, s.25(3), which provided that a person who failed to deliver a correct income tax return should forfeit 'the sum of twenty pounds and treble the tax which he ought to be charged under this Act'. The House of Lords held that, in addition to the penalty of £20, a tax payer who had declared only part of his Post Office interest was liable to pay treble the whole tax chargeable for the year and not merely treble the tax on the undeclared income.

---

1 [1960] AC 748, [1960] 1 All ER 505, HL. The actual decision in this case was overruled by the Finance Act 1960, s.44, which amended the wording of the provision in question.

The Golden Rule

3.20 The golden rule can be used to modify the literal rule. It has been expressed as follows: 'it is a very useful rule in the construction of a statute to adhere to the ordinary meaning of the words used, and to grammatical construction, unless that is at variance with the intention of the legislature to be collected from the statute itself, or leads to any manifest absurdity or repugnance, in which case the language may be varied or modified so as to avoid such inconvenience, but no further'[1]. An example of the application of the golden rule is *Re Sigsworth*[2], where the rule was applied to prevent a son who had murdered his mother from being entitled to succeed to her intestate estate, although he was her sole issue and the relevant statute said that the residuary estate of an intestate should be divided among 'the issue', and made no express exception for the case of murder. Mention of the golden rule raises the question of how, where the literal rule gives rise to inconsistency or absurdity or repugnance, the construction of the statute can be modified to avoid this. This brings us to the mischief rule.

---

1 *Becke v Smith* (1836) 2 M & W 191 at 195.
2 [1935] Ch 89.

The Mischief Rule

3.21 This is often called the rule in *Heydon's case* since it was formulated there[1]. The rule is best paraphrased by the statement by Lord

Halsbury in *Eastman Photographic Co v Comptroller of Patents*. 'We are to see what was the law before the Act was passed, and what was the mischief or defect for which the law had not provided, what remedy Parliament appointed, and the reason of the remedy'[2]. A judge may go straight to the mischief rule in interpreting a statute on the basis that the statute was passed to remedy a mischief; alternatively, he may turn to the mischief rule after application of the literal rule has revealed an ambiguity, inconsistency between provisions, incompleteness or lack of clarity. An example of the application of the mischief rule is *Gorris v Scott*[3]. The plaintiff claimed in respect of the loss of his sheep which were washed overboard and drowned while the defendant was engaged in carrying them by sea. The loss was due to the fact that no pens had been provided and this was in breach of the duty imposed by a statute to provide pens for animals carried by sea. The plaintiff based his claim on the fact that loss had been caused by breach of the statutory duty but it was held that the purpose of the relevant provision was not to prevent loss overboard but to minimise the spread of contagious diseases. It therefore followed that the claim did not fall within the 'mischief' of the Act.

It must be clearly understood that the mischief rule is limited to giving effect to the words in the statute. It does not extend to reading words into it unless clear reason is found within the body of the Act itself: a judge cannot attribute to Parliament an intention which Parliament never had. For a judge to do so was condemned by Lord Simonds in *Magor and St. Mellons RDC v Newport Corpn*[4], as a 'naked usurpation of the legislative function under the thin disguise of interpretation'. His Lordship added that if a gap is disclosed the remedy lies in an amending Act.

---

1 (1584) 3 Co Rep 7a.
2 [1898] AC 571 at 573, HL.
3 (1874) LR 9 Exch 125.
4 [1952] AC 189 at 191, [1951] 2 All ER 839 at 841, HL.

3.22 The following rules and presumptions assist the court in the interpretation of the words in the statute and in the resolution of uncertainties and ambiguities.

Consideration of the whole enactment
3.23 Isolated words often bear a different meaning from their meaning in a particular context. In addition, consideration of the whole enactment, particularly of an interpretation section, assists in resolving apparent ambiguities, inconsistencies or redundancies in a particular provision. In this connection it is of obvious importance to know what parts of an Act may be regarded as intrinsic aids to interpretation.

a. *Long title and short title* These are part of the Act, but, in practice, the courts do not refer to the short title and only refer to the long title to resolve an ambiguity, in other words the long title is not allowed to restrict the clear meaning of the operative part. In *Re Groos*[1], it was held that s.3 of the Wills Act 1861 applied to the will of an alien, even though the long title read: 'An Act to amend the law with respect to wills of personal estates made by British subjects'.

b. *A preamble* is part of the Act. It appears at the beginning and sets out the background and purpose of the enactment. Modern statutes very rarely contain a preamble and the best known examples appear in earlier statutes. The preamble can only be looked at for guidance if the body of the Act is not clear and unambiguous[2].

c. *Punctuation, marginal notes, and headings* to a section or group of sections are inserted into a Bill by the Parliamentary draftsmen and can be altered any time up to Royal Assent. They are not debated by Parliament and are therefore not part of the Act with the result that they may only be looked at to determine the purpose, as opposed to the scope of the section[3], although it may be that headings have a wider use[4]. Even in their limited sphere of operation punctuation and marginal notes in particular carry little weight and cannot oust a meaning indicated by some part of the Act itself.

d. *Schedules*, which are used for instance to list repeals and set out transitional or more detailed provisions, are part of the Act, but they cannot affect the interpretation of a word in the body of the Act unless it is ambiguous or uncertain. Thus, in *Ellerman Lines Ltd v Murray*[5], the House of Lords, in interpreting an Act passed to give effect to a treaty, refused to look at the text of the treaty set out in a schedule because the words of the Act were unambiguous.

---

1 [1904] P 269.
2 *Powell v Kempton Park Racecourse Co Ltd* [1899] AC 143 at 157, HL.
3 *Director of Public Prosecutions v Schildkamp* [1971] AC 1, [1969] 3 All ER 1640, HL, *R v Kelt* [1978] 1 All ER 1099, CA.
4 *Director of Public Prosecutions v Schildkamp* [1971] AC 1 at 28, [1969] 3 All ER 1640 at 1656.
5 [1931] AC 126, HL.

3.24 The rule that the whole enactment must be considered is really part of the principle that words must be taken in their context. A word in itself does not have an absolute meaning: its meaning is relevant to its context (this statement is often described by the Latin tag *noscitur a sociis*). Another important example of this principle is the *ejusdem generis* (of the same class) rule. Enactments often list things forming a class to which a provision is to apply, following the list with some general words implying that some other similar things are intended to fall within the class. Whether something which is not specified in the list of things falls within the general words depends upon whether or not it is *ejusdem generis* as the specified things. In *Powell v Kempton Park Racecourse Co Ltd*[1], an Act prohibited the keeping of a 'house, office, room or other place' for betting with persons resorting thereto. The House of Lords held that Tattersall's Ring (an uncovered enclosure of a superior sort) at a racecourse was not *ejusdem generis* as the specified things, and was not therefore an 'other place' within the meaning of the Act since the specific words 'house, office, room' created a *genus* (class) of indoor places.

An allied doctrine is that of *expressio unius exclusio alterius*, i.e. the expression of one person or thing implies the exclusion of other persons or things of the same class which are not mentioned. Thus, in *Muir v Keay*[2], the word 'entertainment' in s.6 of the Refreshment Houses Act 1860, where the words were 'for public refreshment, resort and entertainment', was held to relate to bodily comfort in the accommodation provided and not to mental enjoyment, such as a theatrical or musical public 'entertainment'. In *R v Midland Rly Co*[3], an Act imposed a rate on houses, buildings, works, tenements and hereditaments but exempted 'land'. The latter was interpreted to mean land without houses, buildings, or works upon it, although in legal, as opposed to lay usage, 'land' would include houses, buildings and the like.

---

1 [1899] AC 143, HL. Also see *Brownsea Haven Properties Ltd v Poole Corp*, [1958] Ch 574, [1958] 1 All ER 205, CA.
2 (1875) LR 10 QB 594.
3 (1885) 4 E & B 958.

Presumptions
3.25 There are a number of presumptions as to the intentions of Parliament. These evidential presumptions are rebutted by express words or necessary implication from the subject matter in the Act itself.

a. *An Act applies to the United Kingdom* There is a presumption that an Act applies to the whole of the United Kingdom but not elsewhere. Acts frequently reveal a contrary intention by containing a section restricting their operation to one or more of the four home countries, or, in the case of a local Act, to a particular locality: on the other hand an extension of the application of an Act outside the United Kingdom is rarely provided for.

b. *Against retrospective effect of legislation affecting substantive rights*
This presumption is not concerned with when a statute comes into
operation but whether it affects factual situations which arose before
that date. The presumption is particularly strong where the statute
creates offences or tax obligations. An example of the rebuttal of the
presumption against retrospective effect is provided by an Act of
Indemnity which validates *ex post facto* a thing which was initially
invalid or illegal. It should be noted that an Act which alters rules of
evidence and procedure, as opposed to rules of substantive law, is
always retrospective — unless the contrary intention appears — because
the procedural and evidential rules applied by a court are those existing
at the time of hearing[1].

c. *Against alteration of the law* Parliament is presumed to know the
common law and not to intend to change it, with the result that, unless
the words of the statute unmistakably indicate that the common law is
changed, they must be interpreted so as not to alter it[2]. As part of the
presumption against alteration in the law there are certain more specific
presumptions: against the restriction of individual liberty; against
compulsory deprivation of property, at least without compensation;
and that there should be no criminal liability without fault (in this
context it may also be noted that the meaning of a doubtful expression
in a criminal statute is interpreted in favour of the accused)[3]. The
presumption against alteration of the law also applies in relation to
statute law. In particular, a consolidating Act is presumed not to
introduce a change in the law by a change of words[4].

d. *Against the Crown being bound* 'It is, of course, a settled rule', said
Denning, L.J., reading the judgment of the Court of Appeal in *Tamlin v
Hannaford*, 'that the Crown is not bound by a statute unless there can
be gathered from it an intention that the Crown should be bound'[5]. The
presumption also extends to servants of the Crown, in the course of
their duties, and to Crown property. However, statutes frequently
provide that they are to bind the Crown.

Other presumptions made in construing a statute are those against
implied repeal of earlier legislation by later, apparently inconsistent,
legislation (the earlier only being impliedly repealed if reconciliation is
logically impossible); against infringement of International Law; and
against ousting the jurisdiction of the courts.

---

1 *Craxfords (Ramsgate) Ltd v Williams and Steer Manufacturing Co Ltd* [1954]
   3 All ER 17.
2 *Leach v R* [1912] AC 305, HL.
3 *R v Chapman* [1931] 2 KB 606.
4 *Beswick v Beswick* [1968] AC 58, [1967] 2 All ER 1197, HL.
5 [1950] 1 KB 18 at 22, CA.

Extrinsic aids

3.26 While a court may look at the enactment as a whole it may not, unlike most continental courts, generally look at material outside the four walls of the Act to find Parliament's intention. It cannot, for instance, look at reports of the Parliamentary debates on the Bill which became the Act[1]. This may appear to fly in the face of common sense but it must be admitted that it might be difficult to determine a legislative intent from a two, or more, sided Parliamentary debate. However, the following extrinsic aids can be looked at for limited purposes:

a. *Dictionaries* can be consulted to ascertain the ordinary and natural meaning, for the purposes of the literal rule, of words which have no particular legal meaning[2].

b. *Reports of committees* containing proposals for legislation which have been presented to Parliament and resulted in the enactment in question can be looked at, for the purpose of the mischief rule, to discover the state of the pre-existing law and the mischief which the enactment was passed to remedy. A recent authority is the House of Lords discussion in *Black-Clawson International Ltd v Papierwerke Waldof-Aschaffenburg AG*[3], where their Lordships, in order to interpret s.8 of the Foreign Judgments (Reciprocal Enforcement) Act 1933, referred to the report of a committee which resulted in the passing of the Act to discover what the pre-existing law was understood to be and what its mischief was. Two of the five Lords of Appeal, Viscount Dilhorne and Lord Simon, went further and stated that it was permissible to look at such a report for a direct statement of what the resulting enactment means. This minority statement goes further than our courts have been prepared to go in the past and it remains to be seen whether they will now adopt it. Lord Reid and Lord Wilberforce disagreed with it expressly in *Black-Clawson*.

c. *Judicial precedent* The interpretation given by a court to a statutory provision or word may be binding in relation to *that* provision or word in *that* Act, in accordance with the principles of the doctrine of judicial precedent (paras. 3.35 to 3.47). Moreover, a judicial interpretation of a particular provision in one Act will be a similarly binding precedent in a subsequent one if they both deal with the same subject-matter, as where the latter is a consolidating Act.

---

1 *Assam Railways and Trading Co Ltd v IRC* [1935] AC 445, HL; *Davis v Johnson* [1978] 1 All ER 1132, HL.
2 *Re Ripon (Highfield) Housing Order 1938* [1939] 2 KB 838, [1939] 3 All ER 548, CA.
3 [1975] AC 591, [1975] 1 All ER 810, HL.

Acts giving effect to international conventions

3.27   Sometimes an Act of Parliament incorporates, and puts into domestic effect, an international convention. Conventions are apt to be more loosely worded than Acts of Parliament, and in *James Buchanan & Co Ltd v Babco Forwarding and Shipping (UK) Ltd*[1] the House of Lords held that a court must interpret the English text of an incorporated convention in a broad and sensible manner, appropriate for the interpretation of a convention, unconstrained by the technical rules of English law. Moreover, the majority of their Lordships held, if there is doubt about the true construction of the English text the court can look at an authorised text in a foreign language to resolve it.

1   [1978] AC 141, [1977] 3 All ER 1048, HL.

Legislation of the European Communities

3.28   This legislation is to be found in the Treaties of the Communities[1] and in regulations, directives and decisions of their organs. It is largely concerned with economic matters, such as agriculture, free trade, fair competition and transport regulation, but also deals with other matters such as immigration.

In discussing the types of legislation of the Communities a fundamental point must be emphasised at the outset: some rules of Community law are 'directly applicable' in the sense that they confer rights and duties on individuals and institutions which are enforceable in the courts of member states without being re-enacted by legislation in those states[2]. Moreover, the European Court[3] has stated on a number of occasions that no Parliament of a member state can legislate inconsistently with Community law. In addition the (United Kingdom) European Communities Act 1972, s.2(4), provides that any enactment of the United Kingdom Parliament passed or to be passed shall have effect subject to the directly applicable legislation of the Communities. One can assume that United Kingdom legislation is impliedly repealed by subsequent directly applicable legislation of the Communities to the extent that the two are irreconcilable. However, it remains to be seen whether United Kingdom legislation irreconcilable with previous directly applicable legislation of the Communities will be held void or not to apply by our courts, who are alone competent to decide. Whatever the answer, there is no doubt that in practice the obligations imposed by membership of the Communities will result in Parliament abstaining from legislation inconsistent with the legislation of the Communities.

1   E.g. the treaties establishing the European Economic Community, the European Coal and Steel Community and the European Atomic Energy Community, further treaties which merged the main institutions of the Communities, and

the Treaty of Accession (including the Act of Accession annexed to it) by which the United Kingdom acceded to the Communities.
2 For the incorporation of this in United Kingdom legislation, see European Communities Act 1972, s.2(1) and (4).
3 Para. 2.32.

Regulations

3.29 Certain provisions of the Treaties are directly applicable in the sense described above, but in the main directly applicable rules are contained in 'regulations', which have general application and are made by the Council of Ministers (a political body composed of foreign ministers) or the Commission (a supranational body composed of the highest officials) under the Treaties.

Directives and Decisions

3.30 Directives can be issued or decisions made by the Council or the Commission. Directives are directed to member states, who are obliged to implement them although they have a choice as to the form and methods of implementation. Decisions are addressed either to a member state or to an individual or institution. They are a formal method of enunciating administrative decisions effecting the policy of the Communities and are binding on the addressee.

3.31 While they bind their addressees, directives and decisions are not generally directly applicable in the courts of a member state and require implementation by the government or other parties to be applicable. However, the European Court has held that directives and decisions may be directly applicable without implementation in the member state concerned. An example is provided by Case 41/74: *Van Duyn v Home Office*[1], where the European Court held that a directive was of immediate binding effect so as to confer rights on the plaintiff even though the United Kingdom had not implemented that directive. Whether or not a directive or decision is directly applicable depends on an examination of the nature, general scheme and wording of its provisions to see whether they are capable of producing direct effects on their addressees[2]. In practice, very few directives or decisions are likely to be regarded as directly applicable.

1 [1975] Ch 358, [1975] 3 All ER 190, CJEC.
2 Case 9/70: *Franz Grad v Finanzant Traustein* [1971] CMLR 1, CJEC.

3.32 Regulations, directives and decisions are subject to review by the European Court. They can be held invalid on the grounds of lack of competence, or infringement of any essential procedural requirement or of the Treaties or of any rule of law concerning their application, or misuse of power[1].

Directives and decisions are implemented in the United Kingdom under powers delegated by s.2(2) of the European Communities Act 1972, as is the implementation in further detail of regulations made by the Council or Commission. Orders in Council and departmental regulations made under these powers can include any provision which might be made in an Act of Parliament[2]. This power to make delegated legislation is the widest given to the executive in modern times apart from times of war. The power must be exercised by way of Statutory Instrument and presumably such an instrument will be *ultra vires* if it is not related to the affairs of the Communities. There are a number of limits on this power of delegated legislation, for instance it cannot be used to impose taxation.

---

1   EEC Treaty, art. 173; Euratom Treaty, art. 146. Also see ECSC Treaty, art. 33.
2   European Communities Act 1972, s.2(4). Also see Sched. 2.

3.33   The literary source of regulations, directives and the principal decisions is the Official Journal of the European Communities, a huge work. It is usually as effective, and certainly quicker, to consult *Halsbury's Statutes of England* where regulations are set out in full and directives and decisions summarised.

Interpretation of the legislation of the European Communities
3.34   The drafting of the legislation of the Communities is quite unlike that of our legislation but, like the legislation of other European countries, is drafted in terms of broad principle, leaving the courts to supply the detail by giving effect to the general intention of the legislature. As an essential aid to this process, the regulations, directives and decisions mentioned above are required to state the reasons on which they are based and to refer to any proposals or opinions which were required to be obtained pursuant to the treaties[1]. These are usually incorporated into a preamble.

The result of this difference in drafting is that the interpretation of the legislation of the Communities, whether by the European Court or by an English Court[2], is not based on a slavish interpretation of the words or the grammatical structure of the sentences but on the purpose or intent of the legislation[3].

---

1   EEC Treaty, art. 190; Euratom Treaty, art. 162.
2   *H. P. Bulmer Ltd v J. Bollinger SA* [1974] Ch 401 at 425—6, [1974] 2 All ER 1226 at 1237—1238, CA.
3   *H. P. Bulmer Ltd v J. Bollinger SA;* Case 41/74: *Van Duyn v Home Office* [1975] Ch 357, [1975] 3 All ER 190, CJEC.

JUDICIAL PRECEDENT

3.35 This is the other important legal source and consists of the 'decisions' of courts made in the course of litigation. As will be seen, the 'decisions' of certain courts are more than just authoritative statements of the law since they can be binding (i.e. must be applied) in subsequent cases where the legally material facts are the same, whether or not the later court considers them to be correct or appropriate. Whether a particular statement of law made by a judge in one case is binding in a subsequent case depends partly on whether the statement formed the *ratio decidendi* (the reason of the decision) of the case or was merely an *obiter dictum* (something said by the way), and partly on the relative position of the two courts.

Ratio decidendi and obiter dictum

3.36 Only the *ratio decidendi* of a case can have binding effect. A judgment usually contains the following elements:

a. A statement of the facts found with an indication, express or implied, of which of them are material facts. (If a jury is employed these findings will be made by it, otherwise they will be made by the judge.)

b. Statements by the judge of the legal principles which apply to the legal issues raised by the material facts. Normally these statements are only made after a review of existing precedents and general legal principles.

c. The actual judgment, decree or order delivered by the judge after application of b. to a., e.g. that the defendant is liable coupled with an award of damages.

Part c. is binding only on the parties to the case and is not a precedent for the future, nor is part a. in itself. It is part b. of this process which constitutes the *ratio decidendi*.

3.37 Sometimes the statements of the applicable principle made by the judge may be wider than the material facts warrant — in such a case the *ratio* of the decision will be limited to that part of it which applies to the material facts and, to the extent that the statement is wider, it will be *obiter dictum*[1], to which we now turn. Apart from that just mentioned, there are two other types of *obiter dictum*.

First, a statement of legal principle is *obiter* if it relates to facts which were not found to exist in the case or, if found, were not material. Two famous cases provide good examples. In *Central London Property Trust Ltd v High Trees House Ltd* which we discuss later in this book[2],

Denning, J's, statement of promissory estoppel was *obiter* since it applied to a set of facts which were not found to exist in the case. Similarly, in *Rondel v Worsley*[3], the House of Lords expressed opinions that a barrister who was negligent when acting other than in connection with litigation might be held liable in tort and that a solicitor, when acting as an advocate, might be immune from such liability. Both statements were *obiter* since the case concerned the tortious liability of a barrister when acting as an advocate.

Secondly, a statement of legal principle which relates to some or all of the material facts but is not the basis of the courts decision, e.g. because it is given in a dissenting judgment or because another material fact prevents the principle applying, is also *obiter*. A leading example is *Hedley Byrne & Co Ltd v Heller & Partners Ltd*[4]. The House of Lords expressed the opinion that the maker of a statement owes a duty of care, in certain circumstances, to persons whom he may expect to rely upon that statement. This opinion was *obiter* because, although it was based on material facts found to exist in the case, the actual decision — that there was no breach of such a duty — was based on another material fact, that the maker of the statement had made it subject to a disclaimer of responsibility.

---

1 *Cassidy v Minister of Health* [1951] 2 KB 343, [1951] 1 All ER 574, CA.
2 [1947] KB 130, [1956] 1 All ER 256n.
3 [1969] 1 AC 191, [1967] 3 All ER 993, HL.
4 [1964] AC 465, [1963] 2 All ER 575, HL.

The hierarchy of the courts and judicial precedent

3.38 We saw in the previous chapter that the system of courts is a hierarchy. Essentially, one court is bound by the *ratio decidendi* of a case decided by another court if it is lower in the hierarchy than the latter and will not be bound by it if it is higher. Magistrates' courts and county courts are bound by the *rationes decidendi* in cases decided by High Court judges or the courts above such judges. A High Court judge is bound by the *rationes decidendi* of cases decided by the Court of Appeal and the House of Lords, and the Court of Appeal is bound by those of the House of Lords. This basic statement will be expanded by taking courts in turn, starting from the top of the hierarchy. For convenience, the word 'decision' will be used to indicate '*ratio decidendi*'.

The Court of Justice of the European Communities

3.39 As we said in paras. 2.33 and 2.34, the European Court is now the ultimate court in the following matters:

a. the interpretation of the EEC and the Euratom Treaties;

b. the validity and interpretation of the acts of the instutitions of the Communities;

c. the interpretation of the statutes of bodies established by an act of the Council of the Communities.

Consequently, *in these limited areas of jurisdiction* the decisions of the European Court bind all English Courts. Indeed, s.3(1) of the European Communities Act 1972 provides that any question as to the meaning or effect of any of the Treaties, or as to the validity, meaning or effect of any Community instrument, shall be treated as a question of law (and, if not referred to the European Court, be for determination in accordance with the principles laid down by, and any relevant decision of, the European Court).

The European Court does not observe a doctrine of binding precedent and does not regard itself as bound by its previous decisions[1], although it leans in favour of consistency with its previous decisions.

---

1 Case 28 — 30/62: *Da Costa en Schaake NV v Nederlands Belasting* administratie [1963] CMLR 224, CJEC.

The House of Lords

3.40 A decision of the House of Lords binds all courts inferior to it. Until 1966, a decision of the House of Lords also bound that House, a principle which was finally established at the end of the nineteenth century in *London Tramways Co Ltd v LCC*[1]. This meant that a legal principle might become unalterable by the House of Lords, in which case legislation was the only remedy if a change in the law was desired. In 1966, the House of Lords reversed this principle in an extra-judicial statement made by the Lord Chancellor (which has been regarded as having the force of law) declaring that it would not be bound by *its own* decisions where it appeared right to depart from them[2]. The declaration added that in this connection the House would bear in mind the danger of disturbing retrospectively the basis on which contracts, settlements of property and fiscal arrangements have been entered into and also the special need for certainty as to the criminal law. The declaration emphasised that it was not intended to apply elsewhere than in the House of Lords.

So far their Lordships have not made much use of their new-found freedom and have held that it is not enough that they should consider their previous decision was wrong; there must be an additional factor such as a change of circumstances on which the decision was based or that it is productive of manifest injustice[3]. The only cases in which the House of Lords has overruled one of its previous decisions are *British Railways Board v Herrington*[4], where it overruled its previous decision in *R. Addie & Sons (Collieries) Ltd v Dumbreck*[5] on the question of the extent of the duty of care owed to trespassers by an occupier of land, and *Miliangos v George Frank (Textiles) Ltd*[6], where it overruled its decision in *Re United Railways of Havana and Regla Warehouses*[7] that judgment must be given in sterling.

---

1   [1898] AC 375, HL.
2   [1966] 3 All ER 77.
3   *Fitzleet Estates Ltd v Cherry* [1977] 3 All ER 996, HL.
4   [1972] AC 877, [1972] 1 All ER 749, HL.
5   [1929] AC 358, HL.
6   [1976] AC 443, [1975] 3 All ER 801, HL.
7   [1961] AC 1007, [1960] 2 All ER 332, HL.

The Court of Appeal

3.41   The Civil Division of the Court of Appeal is bound by the decisions of the House of Lords. It is also bound by previous Court of Appeal decisions in either of its two Divisions[1]. This was settled by the Court of Appeal in *Young v Bristol Aeroplane Co Ltd*[2], but as was recognised in that case there are three exceptional circumstances where an earlier Court of Appeal decision is not binding on the Civil Division:

a. Where two of its previous decisions conflict; the decision not followed will be deemed to be overruled[3].

b. The Court must refuse to follow a previous decision of its own which, though not expressly overruled, is inconsistent with a later House of Lords decision.

c. The Court is not bound to follow its previous decision if that decision was given *per incuriam* (i.e. through lack of care), which will only occur where some relevant statute or binding precedent, which might have affected the decision, was overlooked or misunderstood by the court in the previous case: faulty reasoning alone is insufficient. Very few decisions have subsequently been found to be *per incuriam*[4]. While the *per incuriam* doctrine is also open to the House of Lords as a basis for rejecting one of its own previous decisions, the refusal of the Court of Appeal to follow the House of Lords decision in *Rookes v Barnard*[5], on the basis that it had been reached *per incuriam* because of two previous House of Lords decisions was rejected in extremely strong terms by the House of Lords on appeal in *Cassell & Co Ltd v Broome*[6].

---

1   And those of its predecessors: the Court of Exchequer Chamber and the Court of Appeal in Chancery, but not by the decisions of the now defunct Court of Criminal Appeal.
2   [1944] KB 718, [1944] 2 All ER 293, CA. The rule in *Young v Bristol Aeroplane* was recently re-affirmed by the House of Lords in *Davis v Johnson* [1978] 1 All ER 1132.

3   As happened in *Fisher v Ruislip-Northwood UDC and Middlesex County Council* [1945] KB 584, [1945] 2 All ER 458, CA.
4   A recent example is *Industrial Properties (Barton Hill) Ltd v Associated Electrical Industries Ltd* [1977] QB 580, [1977] 2 All ER 293, where the Court of Appeal (Civil Division) held that its decision in *Harrison v Wells,* [1967] 1 QB 263, [1966] 3 All ER 524, CA was made *per incuriam* because incomplete reference to a previous decision had led the court to misunderstand what had been decided.
5   [1964] AC 1129, 1 All ER 367, HL.
6   [1972] AC 1027, [1972] 1 All ER 801, HL.

3.42 The Criminal Division of the Court of Appeal is bound not only by House of Lords and Court of Appeal decisions but also by those of its predecessor, the Court of Criminal Appeal. However, in the case of decisions of the last two named courts there are exceptions:

a. The three exceptions mentioned in *Young v Bristol Aeroplane.*

b. When sitting as a 'full court', i.e. one constituted by more judges than usual, the Criminal Division has power to overrule a previous decision of itself or the Court of Criminal Appeal, on the grounds that the law has been 'misapplied or misunderstood'[1]. It appears that, contrary to previous practice, an earlier decision may be overruled even though it is not in the appellant's favour to do so[2].

1   *R v Taylor* [1950] 2 KB 368, [1950] 2 All ER 170; *R v Newsome and Brown* [1970] 2 QB 711, [1970] 3 All ER 455, CA.
2   *R v Newsome and Brown.*

Divisional Courts
3.43 Divisional Courts are bound by decisions of the House of Lords and of the Court of Appeal, except, apparently, a Court of Appeal decision which is *per incuriam,* in that a relevant decision of the House of Lords was not cited[1]. A Divisional Court is bound by its own previous decisions unless the *Young v Bristol Aeroplane* principles apply[2] or, probably, in criminal cases the law has been misapplied or misunderstood.

1   *R v Northumberland Compensation Tribunal, ex parte Shaw* [1952] 1 KB 338, [1952] 1 All ER 122, CA.
2   *Huddersfield Police Authority v Watson* [1947] KB 842, [1947] 2 All ER 193, DC.

High Court Judges
3.44 A High Court judge sitting at first instance is bound by the decisions of the courts mentioned above, but he is not bound by decisions of another High Court judge sitting at first instance, although

he will treat such a decision as strong persuasive authority and will only refuse to follow it if he is convinced that it is wrong, and with a clear statement of the reason for doing so[1]. There is good reason for this hesitation since a conflict of authority, which can be sorted out only by a higher court, will result from one judge 'disapproving' or 'not following' one of his brethren's decisions. Legal rulings made in the Crown Court by a High Court judge are presumably as authoritative as any other decision by a High Court judge.

---

1 *Re Hillas-Drake, National Provincial Bank v Liddell* [1944] Ch 235, [1944] 1 All ER 375.

Other courts

3.45 County courts, circuit judges and Recorders in the Crown Court, magistrates' courts and other inferior tribunals are bound by the decisions of all the courts mentioned in the previous paragraphs, and by those of High Court judges sitting alone. The decisions of one of these courts are not binding on another mainly because they are not reported.

Application of judicial precedents

3.46 The fact that a judicial precedent may be binding or merely persuasive in a subsequent case has already been touched on. It may also be noticed that a judicial precedent will become devoid of effect if it is overruled by a court competent to do so (i.e. one higher in the hierarchy). As opposed to overruling by statute[1], judicial overruling operates retrospectively, which may have the effect of disturbing financial interests or vested rights generally. For this reason the courts are reluctant to overrule a previous decision unless they consider it is clearly wrong.

Where a precedent is binding on the court that court must follow it unless that court can distinguish it on the facts. Suppose that the House of Lords has held that, if facts A and B exist principle X applies, and that a case is heard by a High Court judge at first instance where facts A and B exist as well as fact E, which did not exist in the House of Lords case. The judge may distinguish the House of Lord's case on its material facts and, consequently since that decision will not be binding in relation to the case before him, decide to apply some other principle or to apply principle X by analogy. Since the facts are never identical in any two cases there is wide scope for 'distinguishing'. However, a court inferior to that which gave the previous decision will not normally distinguish it on strained grounds.

---

1 Para. 3.9, b.

3.47 There are various types of persuasive precedents:

a. Those decisions of courts inferior in the hierarchy of courts to a court which subsequently hears a similar case. Into this category one can also put decisions of the Judicial Committee of the Privy Council on appeals from Commonwealth states, which do not bind English courts or the Privy Council itself. However, the Court of Appeal has held that if one of its previous decisions has been disapproved by the Privy Council it is at liberty to depart from it and apply the Privy Council decision[1].

b. Where otherwise binding precedent is distinguishable it will nevertheless have persuasive authority[2].

c. *Obiter dicta*, the persuasiveness of which depends on the seniority of the court or prestige of the judge by whom the words were uttered and the relative position of that court and a subsequent court. One of the most significant examples is the 'neighbour principle' expounded by Lord Atkin in 1932 in *Donoghue v Stevenson*[3], which was much wider than the actual case required but has become the basis of the modern tort of negligence and has been applied in numerous cases since.

d. Decisions of Irish, Scottish, Commonwealth and United States courts, which decisions are being referred to increasingly by our courts.

---

1 *Doughty v Turner Manufacturing Co Ltd* [1964] QB 518, [1964] 1 All ER 98, CA; *Worcester Works Finance Ltd v Cooden Engineering Co Ltd* [1972] 1 QB 210, [1971] 3 All ER 708, CA.
2 Especially if it is a House of Lords decision: *Re House Property and Investment Co* [1954] Ch 576, [1953] 2 All ER 1525.
3 [1932] AC 562, HL.

General comments

3.48 Essentially, judicial decisions are declaratory of the common law, merely applying existing law to new fact situations. However, where there is no relevant statute or judicial precedent on a particular point, as still happens occasionally, a judge has to decide the case in accordance with general principles and his decision becomes the original source of a new rule since he is making law rather than applying it.

3.49 The advantages of the system of judicial precedent are its precision and detail, and consequent certainty of application, and in these respects it is far superior to a code or statute which cannot hope to anticipate the innumerable factual situations which can arise in a given area of law. It is sometimes said that the system also has the advantage of flexibility in that outmoded or unsound decisions can be overruled or distinguished. Too much should not be made of this since overruling may be difficult, if not impossible, given the relationship of the courts in question. There is also the danger of illogical or over-subtle distinctions being drawn to avoid hardship in a particular case, but increasing the complexity of the law. Moreover, the vast mass of reported cases can make discovering the law an arduous task and cause a precedent to be overlooked.

Literary sources of judicial precedent

3.50 The most important of these are of course the law reports. A law report must be differentiated from a court record which simply contains the name of the parties, the pleadings, the main facts and the decision, decree or order of the court. Apart from containing most of these things, a law report also contains the judgment of the court which includes the reasoning on which the result has based.

It may appear surprising that there is no official series of law reports. By no means all cases in the superior courts are reported: only those of legal interest. Law reports may be divided roughly into those published from the time of Henry VIII to 1865, and those published subsequently. Before Henry VIII's time there were the Year Books dating from the time of Edward I, which contained notes on the argument, exchanges between bench and bar and rulings on points of law in cases. The publication of law reports began in about 1535. They were usually published under the names of the reporter and, initially, were little more detailed than the Year Books but gradually developed until they came to resemble the modern law report. Altogether there were some hundreds of different series. Most, but not all, of them have been reprinted in a series known as the English Reports. These 'nominate reports', as they are sometimes called, vary a good deal in quality. However, the reports of Coke, often simply referred to as 'The Reports', Dyer, Plowden, Burroughs and certain others are regarded as particularly outstanding and authoritative. The name of the report or reporter is traditionally cited in abbreviated form in footnote references, e.g. Co Rep (Coke), Burr (Burroughs), B & Ald (Barnewell and Alderson) and Term Rep (Term Reports).

In 1865 the semi-official 'Law Reports' commenced. One or more volumes is published annually under each of the following titles 'QB' (covering cases decided in the Queen's Bench Division or by the Court of Appeal on appeals therefrom of from a county court), 'Ch' (covering cases decided in the Chancery Division or by the Court of Appeal on appeal therefrom), 'Fam'[1] (covering cases decided in the Family Division or by the Court of Appeal therefrom or from a county court in family matters) and 'AC' (covering decisions of the House of Lords and Privy Council). Since 1952, many cases appearing in the Law Reports have appeared previously, soon after judgment has been given, in the Weekly Law Reports published by the same organisation, the Incorporated Council of Law Reporting, as do some cases not subsequently published in the Law Reports. The difference between the two series are that the Law Reports contain a summary of the arguments of counsel.

Although the Law Reports superseded most of the series of private reports there are still a number of commercially owned reports. The All England Reports, a weekly publication, are a general series of reports, while others, such as Lloyd's Law Reports, which deal with commercial cases, are more specialised. The All England Reports commenced publication in 1936 and subsequently superseded two other series, the Law Times Reports and the Law Journal Reports. The citation of law reports is a somewhat complex matter, outside the scope of this book, and the inquiring student is referred to *Where to Look for Your Law*, reprinted, to Osborn's *Concise Law Dictionary*, or to any volume of the *English and Empire Digest* or Stroud's *Judicial Dictionary*.

Cases decided by the European Court may be found in the Offical Reports of the Court and in the Common Market Law Reports. They are occasionally reported in the series of reports referred to in the last two paragraphs.

Law reports in this country are made by a barrister and this is necessarily so since a case can only be cited to a court if it is vouched for by a barrister who was present in court when judgment was delivered. Provided there is such vouchsafing, and this may be on the part of the judge if he recollects a case from his days at the Bar, a decision can be relied on even though it is not reported. Reliance, however, on cases which have not been reported is extremely rare.

---

1 Until 1972 the citation was 'P' since what is now the Family Division was known as the Probate, Divorce and Admiralty Division until its name, and jurisdiction, were changed.

3.51 Mention can be conveniently made at this stage of a secondary literary source, certain 'books of authority'. On the Continent the writings of legal authors form an important source of law. In England, in accordance with the traditional approach that the common law is to be found in judicial decisions, the works of writers are of no official effect, except for books of authority. These are books of some antiquity by authors of great eminence which are regarded as being persuasive authority of the common law as it was then they were written and of the present law if it is not shown to have changed. Generally, these do not contain reports of cases but state principles instead. Perhaps the best known books of authority are Coke's *Institutes,* written in the seventeenth century, and Blackstone's *Commentaries* of the eighteenth century. While the works of modern authors are in no way authoritative the courts are increasingly being referred to them for guidance on the correct interpretation of the law.

CUSTOM

3.52 In Anglo-Saxon times, custom, in the sense of patterns of behaviour recognised and enforced by the state, was the principle source of law. However, general customs, i.e. customs universally observed throughout the land, have either fallen into desuetude or become absorbed into judicial precedent or statute. In this sense it may be noted that at one time under the declaratory theory of judicial precedent, judges merely discovered the general customs of the realm and applied them in their decisions. A process of absorption has also occurred in relation to the general customs of merchants which were assimilated by our courts in the seventeenth and eighteenth centuries and developed into a mercantile law as we now know it. On the other hand, local customs, i.e. customs operative in a particular locality or among a particular group of people in a particular locality, are even now occasionally recognised by the courts as establishing a local 'law' for the locality in question at variance with the general law of the land, although they must not be contrary to statute or to a fundamental principle of the common law. Local customs are largely to be found in rights of way and common. Recognition of a local custom depends on a number of conditions being satisfied, the most important of which are that the alleged custom must:

a. Have existed since 'time immemorial', which, theoretically, it will only do if it goes back to 1189 (for reasons of historical accident).

b. Have been continuous. The custom must have been in existence continuously. This means that the right to exercise it must not have been interrupted; but the fact that the right has not actually been exercised for a period of time, even 100 years in one case[1], does not negative the existence of a local custom (although if the evidence of custom is dubious it will go far to negative any customary right).

c. Not be unreasonable[2].

d. Be certain, in other words the right claimed must be certain in nature and scope and prove to adhere to a defined locality or group of people.

e. Be recognised as compulsory[3].

The first condition is not as strict as may appear since the plaintiff will succeed in proving it if he can prove that the practice in question has existed in the locality for a substantial time: the oldest local inhabitant is often called as a witness in this context. If the plaintiff proves this, existence since 1189 will be presumed[4], provided, of course, that such a practice was possible in 1189. In *Simpson v Wells*[5] a person who was charged with obstructing a public footway with his refreshment stall pleaded that he did so by virtue of a custom existing at a 'statute sessions', a fair held for hiring servants. His defence failed because statute sessions were first introduced by a fourteenth century statute, so that the custom could not have existed before then.

---

1   *New Windsor Corpn v Mellor* [1975] Ch 380, [1975] 3 All ER 44, CA.
2   *Wolstanton Ltd and A-G of Duchy of Lancaster v Newcastle-under-Lyme Corpn* [1940] AC 860, [1940] 3 All ER 101, HL.
3   Blackstone's Commentaries: 'a custom that all the inhabitants shall be rated towards the maintenance of a bridge will be good, but a custom that every man is to contribute thereto at his own pleasure is idle and absurd, and indeed not custom at all'.
4   *Mercer v Denne* [1905] 2 Ch 538 at 577, CA.
5   (1872) LR 7 QB 214.

Chapter 4
Persons and Property

PERSONS

4.1 English law applies to people but it also applies to companies, partnerships, clubs, trustees, trade unions and the Crown. People are natural legal persons, companies are artificial legal persons; the other bodies mentioned above, except the Crown, can be described generally as unincorporated associations. We must consider the nature of some of these persons and bodies and then consider nationality, domicile and residence[1], which may be relevant to the application of English law to such persons or bodies.

---

1 Paras. 4.18–4.27.

Natural legal persons

4.2 Human beings are, of course, potentially the subjects of any rule of English law. A particular rule may be inapplicable to people, for example, corporation tax is only payable by companies, or inappropriate for all but particular people, for example, only employers can be subject to the statutory provision requiring them to give their employees written particulars of their terms of employment. Anyone can of course become an employer and thus be subject to that statutory provision but there is one category of natural legal persons who are subject to special provisions: minors. People under 10 cannot be convicted of a crime, those under 16 cannot marry, and until they are 18 they have limited contractual capacity.

Not every person or dispute is subject to English law. The English courts will not waste their time in hearing actions relating to people against whom they could not enforce their judgments[1]. The absence of a person from this country does not necessarily mean that the judgment of an English court is unenforceable. Even if a judgment is enforceable, an English oourt may only hear an action if it has the capacity (i.e. jurisdiction) to do so. Such capacity may be conferred by statute or the common law.

People who apparently fall within the jurisdiction of the English courts may be immune from process. The most obvious immunity is that granted to diplomats. Diplomats are not subject to English criminal law nor can they be used in the civil courts except in certain cases, such as, actions relating to land in the United Kingdom which they own in a personal capacity[2]. This immunity is recognised by countries other than the United Kingdom.

---

1   *Richard West & Partners Inverness Ltd v Dick* [1969] 2 Ch at 443, [1969] 1 All ER 143, CA.
2   Diplomatic Privileges Act 1964.

Artificial legal persons

Legal status
4.3   A company, which is an artificial legal person, may be formed in England in any one of three ways:

a. by registration under the Companies Acts 1948—1976 (registered companies); or

b. by Private Act of Parliament (statutory companies); or

c. by Royal Charter (chartered companies).

Registered companies, which are comparatively cheap and easy to form, are the most common. There were 43,428 registered companies formed in the year ending December 1975, and there are in total 638,511 registered companies in England and Wales. All three types of company are associations of people who have amalgamated their ideas or resources to pursue some common lawful purpose. Companies may be formed for any purpose which their progenitors or promoters choose but trading bodies will usually be in registered form. Statutory companies are often specialised trading bodies, for example, Building and Friendly Societies and Insurance Companies. Chartered companies are typically charitable or quasi-charitable associations, although some famous trading companies have been incorporated by Royal Charter, for example, the East India Co and the Hudson Bay Co.

4.4   Other associations of people may pursue some common purpose — trade unions, clubs and partnerships are examples — but companies can be distinguished from other associations in that the company is itself a legal person totally distinct from its shareholders (who are also called members) and employees. Companies are artificial legal persons and when a statute refers to a person then *prima facie* it means people and companies. Even if a company is totally dominated by one shareholder the company and that shareholder are distinct legal persons. This was first established in *Salomon v Salomon & Co*[1], in which the validity of a secured debt contracted by the company in favour of Salomon was contested in the winding-up of the company. The House of Lords said that even though the company was formed to take over Salomon's existing business, and even though he held 20,001 of the 20,007 shares which had been issued by the company, the company and Salomon were distinct legal beings: they could not be regarded as synonymous. Lord MacNaghten stated firmly, 'the company is at law a different person from the subscribers to the memorandum [i.e. the first shareholders]; and, though it may be that after incorporation the business is precisely the same as it was before . . . the company is not the agent of the subscribers or trustee for them.' In *Lee v Lee's Air Farming Ltd*[2], where Lee, who was founder, principal shareholder, managing director, and chief pilot of a company, had been killed while engaged on the business of the company, the Privy Council was still able to find that Lee and the company were distinct legal personalities. Because they were different people in law, Lee could enter into a contract of employment with the company and his widow could therefore claim compensation under a government scheme. Had there been no contract of employment her claim would have failed.

---

1 [1897] AC 22, HL.
2 [1961] AC 12, [1960] 3 All ER 420, PC.

Some consequences of the separate legal identities of the company and its members
4.5

a. The company can sue and be sued in its own name.

b. The company can make contracts on its own behalf[1] and the members cannot claim the benefit nor be subject to the burdens of such contracts[2].

c. The company can own property in its own right and the members have no direct interest in the property of the company. Because the members do not own the property of the company, but only shares in the company, they cannot pledge or insure such property. In *Macaura v Northern Assurance Co*[3], the plaintiff, who was the principal shareholder in a company he had formed to take over his timber estate, was unable to recover on an insurance policy which he had taken out on the timber prior to the incorporation of the company, when the timber was destroyed by fire. The death of a member has no effect on the company or its property. Indeed a company must be formally wound up (i.e. dissolved) even if all the shareholders are dead.

d. While the company is operational its debts are not the responsibility of the members. However, if the company is wound up and the company was an unlimited company the members are personally liable for the debts of the company; because of this, the majority of companies are limited. On the winding-up of a limited liability company the members are only liable to pay the nominal value of their shares (if it is a company limited by shares) insofar as this has not been paid already, or a pre-arranged fixed sum (if the company is limited by guarantee), towards the discharge of the company's debts. In the year ending December 1975 40,130 companies were formed with limited liability and 241 with unlimited liability.

---

1 Paras. 4.8—4.12.
2 This is merely the effect of the doctrine of privity, paras. 6.19—6.30.
3 [1925] AC 619, HL.

Lifting the veil
4.6 There are some circumstances in which the court will ignore the separate legal personality of the company and find the members responsible for the actions of the company. This is called lifting or piercing the veil, the veil being the veil of incorporation which usually hides the members from view. This disregard of corporate legal status may be required by statute, or in exceptional cases, be decreed by the courts. It is not certain when the courts will choose to lift the veil, but we have listed some illustrations of when they have done so, as well as some of the statutory provisions:

a. Where the number of members falls below the legally prescribed minimum, the members are personally liable for the debts of the company contracted during the period when there are too few members[1].

b. Some tax statutes permit the Inland Revenue to ignore the existence of a company[2].

c. If, on winding-up, it appears that the business of the company has been carried on with intent to defraud creditors, members who are party to the fraud will be personally liable for the debts of the company[3].

d. Companies which are part of a group or subsidiaries of another company may be required to produce not merely their own accounts but also group accounts so that the financial position of the individual companies can be seen in context[4].

e. If the company is a mere sham, formed only to promote a fraudulent design, then the courts may treat the company as the *alter ego* of (i.e. as being synonymous with) the members, and a court order will be made against the company and the members. In *Jones v Lipman*[5], for example, where a vendor of property sought to avoid performance of a binding contract of sale by conveying it to a company he had formed, both the vendor and the company were ordered to perform the contract.

f. If the facts clearly reveal it to be the case, the company can be regarded as the agent of its members.

g. If a case involves an element of public policy, the courts may be more prepared to cast aside the corporate veil. In *Daimler Co Ltd v Continental Tyre & Rubber Co (Gt Britain) Ltd*[6], the question before the House of Lords turned on whether a company registered in Great Britain was an alien enemy. Looking behind the corporate veil revealed that the shareholders and controllers of the company were German and the company was therefore an alien enemy.

1　Companies Act 1948, s.31.
2　See, for example, legislation on close companies.
3　Companies Act 1948, s.322.
4　*Ibid.,* ss.150—153.
5　[1962] 1 All ER 442, [1962] 1 WLR 832.
6　[1916] 2 AC 307, HL.

4.7　Two areas which, while not strictly cases of lifting the veil are illustrations of the fact that a court may look at the realities of a corporate structure as well as the theoretical position, are criminal cases and cases where there is a petition for winding-up under s.222(f) of the Companies Act 1948. It is difficult to convict a company of a criminal offence when the offence requires a particular mental state, for example, intention or recklessness. However, the courts are prepared to find the acts and mental state of a senior official of the company to be the acts and mental state of the company, if the company and natural person are sufficiently closely identified[1]. If a petition for a winding-up is presented under s.222(f), on the basis that it is fair and reasonable to do so, the court may have regard to the structure and history of the company. If the company, though in corporate form, is essentially a partnership and the relationship of the member who wishes the company to be wound up with his fellow members is so bad that, if it were a partnership, the partnership would be dissolved the court will take note of this relationship and order the company to be wound up[2].

1　*Tesco Supermarkets Ltd v Nattrass* [1972] AC 153, [1971] 2 All ER 127, HL.
2　*Ebrahimi v Westbourne Galleries Ltd* [1973] AC 360, [1972] 2 All ER 492, HL.

Contractual capacity

4.8 A company is a legal person, but it does not have the contractual capacity of a natural person. Natural legal persons, with the exception of infants, mental patients and drunkards[1], have the capacity to make any contract, but companies, with the exception of chartered companies, which do have the capacity of natural legal persons[2], do not. The contractual capacity of registered and statutory companies is limited by the memorandum of association and the creating statute respectively.

---

1 Chap. 16.
2 *Sutton's Hospital Case* (1612) 10 Co Rep 23a; *Pharmaceutical Society of Great Britain v Dickinson* [1970] AC 403, [1968] 2 All ER 686, HL.

4.9 When a registered company is created the people forming the company are required to lodge two documents with the Registrar of Companies at Companies House in Cardiff — the Memorandum of Association and the Articles of Association. These documents are available for public inspection[1]. The memorandum of association must state certain specific things including the objects of the company[2] (i.e. the purposes for which the company was formed and the aims and business it intends to pursue). This provision in the memorandum, the objects clause, defines exclusively what a company may do and for what purposes it can make contracts. If a company enters into a contract which is not authorised, expressly or impliedly, by the objects clause such contract is *ultra vires* (beyond the powers of the company) and unenforceable. If a company is formed to manufacture railway rolling stock, it cannot build railways; and if it attempts to do so, any contracts entered into to promote or carry out the building of railways are beyond the powers of the company and unenforceable[3]. A company has the power to make contracts expressly authorised by its objects clause but contracts impliedly authorised by the objects clause will also be enforceable. A company has an implied power to engage in activities which are reasonably incidental to the express objects of the company if they are for the benefit of the company. In *Deuchar v Gaslight & Coke Co*[4], a company, which had an express power to transform residuals remaining after the manufacture of their principal product into a marketable state, had implied power to manufacture the reagent required to effect the transformations. They would also have had an implied power to buy the reagent, and a contract for the purchase of the reagent would have been impliedly authorised and therefore enforceable.

Because objects clauses are contained in a document open to public inspection everyone is deemed to have notice of them. Since very few people actually consult the object clause of a company with which they intend to contract, it is extremely easy to enter unknowingly into an *ultra vires* contract. This can work injustice. In *Ashbury Railway Carriage & Iron Co v Riche*[5], Riche sued the company for breach of a contract of employment. The contract employed Riche to supervise the building of a railway in Belgium. The company was not authorised to build railways and abandoned the project. The House of Lords rejected Riche's claim, saying that the company had no power to make contracts relating to the pursuance of an unauthorised purpose. The contract was *ultra vires*, as Riche should have known, because he was deemed to have knowledge of the objects clause of the company, and the contract could not be rendered enforceable by ratification by the shareholders. Therefore, if a person intends to enter into a contract with a company he should check whether the contract is within the contractual capacity of the company as enunciated in the objects clause, which procedure is clearly impractical.

---

1 Companies Act 1948, ss. 1 and 4.
2 *Ibid.*, s.2.
3 *Ashbury Railway Carriage and Iron Co Ltd v Riche* (1875) LR 7 HL 653, HL.
4 [1925] AC 691, HL.
5 (1875) LR 7 HL 653, HL.

4.10 Attempts to mitigate the effects of *ultra vires* have been made by the courts, by companies themselves and most recently by statute. First, the courts have held that if a contract is apparently authorised by the objects clause, but is in fact *ultra vires* because of the use the company intends to make of the contract, then the company cannot enforce the contract but the other contracting party can. However, the other contracting party can only enforce the contract if he does not know of the intended *ultra vires* use of the contract[1]. For example, if a company, which is authorised to borrow money to develop its business, borrows money, this does not appear, so far as the lender can tell, to be an *ultra vires* contract. But if the company intends to use this money for an *ultra vires* purpose then it could not enforce the contract of loan though the lender could[2] (i.e. he could recover principal and interest). Companies sought to mitigate the effects of *ultra vires* by drafting objects clauses of immense length which contained many clauses and stated that every clause was an object, hoping thereby to authorise every conceivable purpose and contract they undertook. Lengthy objects clauses received reluctant approval from the House of Lords in *Cotman v Brougham*[3], but the effectiveness of stating that all sub-clauses of the object clause are to be regarded as independent objects was doubted in *Re Introductions Ltd*[4]. In the *Introductions* case the Court of Appeal distinguished between objects and mere powers, mere powers could only be validly exercised in pursuance of an object. In this case the company had borrowed money not to expand their authorised business of showing visitors around Great Britain, but to set up a pig farm. The loan was held *ultra vires* despite a sub-clause in the objects clause permitting the company to borrow money and another sub-clause saying that all sub-clauses of the objects clause were independent objects. The Court of Appeal considered that borrowing money was a mere power and could only authorise borrowings designed to promote the objects of the company. A device which has been approved in *Bell Houses Ltd v City Wall Properties Ltd*[5] is that of including a sub-clause in the objects clause authorising the company to make any contract which, in the honest opinion of the directors, would benefit the company. This is limited, however, to situations where the company wished to make a contract not otherwise authorised by the objects clause without abandoning their usual authorised business. This decision of the Court of Appeal in *Bell Houses Ltd v City Wall Properties Ltd* seems a useful way of evading *ultra vires*, at least where the company can show it is still pursuing its authorised business as well.

---

1   *Re Jon Beauforte (London) Ltd* [1953] Ch 131, [1953] 1 All ER 634.
2   *Re Introductions Ltd* [1970] Ch 199, [1969] 1 All ER 887, CA, though in this case the bank knew of the *ultra vires* purpose and were unable to enforce their contract.
3   [1918] AC 514, HL.
4   [1970] Ch 199, [1969] 1 All ER 887, CA.
5   *Bell Houses Ltd v City Wall Properties Ltd* [1966] 2 QB 656, [1966] 2 All ER 674, CA.

4.11   The most important attack on the rigours of *ultra vires* is contained in s.9 of the European Communities Act 1972. This section is of immense importance for those dealing with the contractual capacity of companies but its drafting is far from ideal. The section provides that an *ultra vires* contract shall be enforceable *against* (not by) the company by the other party to that contract if certain conditions are satisfied. These conditions, which the other party must prove exist, are:

a. That he acted in good faith; this will be presumed unless the company can prove lack of good faith. Knowing that the company lacked capacity to make the contract would probably be a lack of good faith, and

b. That he was 'dealing' with the company. Therefore, non-trading contracts may not be enforceable; and

c. That the transaction which it is sought to enforce has been 'decided on by the directors'. It is not clear whether this means 'decided on' by all, or by a majority of, the directors, or whether the decision must have been taken at a formal board meeting. Nor is it certain if the particular contract has to have been decided on by the directors or if it is enough for a change of policy, which the contract seeks to implement, to be decided on by the directors.

Despite these criticisms s.9 will render enforceable many *ultra vires* contracts.

4.12 If s.9 does not apply in a particular case there are other remedies which a party to an *ultra vires* contract might seek to pursue.

a. *Tracing* If the company still has assets transferred under an *ultra vires* contract, the person who supplied the goods can recover them (though he could not sue for their price) even, sometimes, where they have been mixed with similar assets from other sources[1].

b. *Subrogation* Insofar as money borrowed under an *ultra vires* contract is used to discharge valid, enforceable debts of the company, the lender can be subrogated to, i.e. put in the position of, the discharged creditor. However, a lender who is so subrogated does not acquire any preferential rights to repayment which the discharged creditor may have had[2].

c. *Quasi-contract*[3] A party who provided services for a company under an *ultra vires* contract may be able to sue on a *quantum meruit*[4]. An action for money had and received can also be sustained[5].

Statutory companies are also subject to the *ultra vires* doctrine but their contractual capacity is determined by reference to the Act of Parliament which created the company and not the objects clause.

A registered company is able to alter is objects clause for any of the reasons specified in s.5 of the Companies Act 1948 if the alteration is approved by a three-quarters majority of members present and voting at the meeting. If 15 per cent of the shareholders object to the alterations they can petition the court to cancel the alteration.

---

1 *Sinclair v Brougham* [1914] AC 398, HL.
2 *Re Wrexham, Mold and Connah's Quay Rly Co* [1899] 1 Ch 440, CA.
3 For quasi-contract generally see Chap. 17.
4 *Craven Ellis v Canons Ltd* [1936] 2 KB 403, [1936] 2 All ER 1066.
5 *Brougham v Dwyer* (1913) 108 LT 504, DC.

Unincorporated associations

4.13 It may come as no surprise to the reader to learn that any association which is not in corporate form is an unincorporated association. Unincorporated associations are many and varied. They may be large or small, transient or well established, profit-making or charitable, open to all or with restricted membership. They all differ from companies, which are equally varied, in that they do not possess a legal personality separate and distinct from their members. Many unincorporated associatioñs, particularly partnerships, resemble companies in what they do, yet lack the advantages of separate legal personality.

Trade unions

4.14 Trade unions are not allowed to become, nor are they to be regarded as, a body corporate[1]. However, many of the benefits of incorporation have been bestowed on them by statute: trade unions can make contracts on their own behalf; their property is vested in trustees who hold it for the benefit of the trade union, and members of trade unions have no legal interest in the property of their unions; they can sue and be sued in their own name; and judgments are enforceable against union property and not the property of members. Trade unions, like companies, are required to keep proper accounts and send a copy of their annual return to the Registrar of Friendly Societies, where it is available for public inspection. Trade unions have an immunity not conferred on individuals, companies or other unincorporated associations in that they cannot be sued for torts committed in furtherance of a trade dispute[2]. They may also make agreements in restraint of trade if such agreements relate to the regulation of relations between employers and workers[3]. A member of a trade union can sue the union as if it was a distinct legal entity even though technically the trade union is not a legal person[4].

The contractual capacity of trade unions is determined by reference to the union rules, and the *ultra vires* doctrine (but not s.9 of the European Communities Act 1972) can apply.

---

1 Trade Union and Labour Relations Act 1974, s.2.
2 *Ibid.*, s.13.
3 *Ibid.*, s.2.
4 For example, *Bonsor v Musicians Union* [1956] AC 104, [1955] 3 All ER 518, HL.

Partnerships

4.15 A partnership will usually be governed by the rules laid down in the Partnership Act 1890, but it is possible to create limited partnerships and they are governed by the Limited Partnership Act 1907. The limited partnership, which is a partnership with some of the characteristics of a limited liability company, is not very popular in the United Kingdom, though much used in continental Europe.

Section 1 of the Partnership Act 1890 defines a partnership as 'the relation existing between two or more persons carrying on a business in common with a view to profit'. Because the partners and the partnership are not separate legal entities, unlike shareholders and the company in which they hold shares, a partner is liable for the debts and liabilities of the partnership[1]. Conversely, the partners do have a legal interest in the assets of the partnership[2]. Shares in a company may be bought and sold, shares in a partnership are not transferable[3]. The death of shareholders leaves the company unaffected, the death of a partner technically terminates the partnership though the remaining partners may agree to carry on the partnership[4]. A partnership can usually sue and be sued in its own name[5].

The maximum number of partners permissible for a partnership is 20[6], unless the partnership is one of solicitors, certain accountants[7], estate agents and certain other professional men, when this number may be exceeded[8].

A limited partnership is a partnership where one or more partners has only a limited liability for the debts of the partnership. Every limited partnership must have at least one general partner[9] (i.e. with full liability for debts) and any limited partner who is active in the affairs of the partnership becomes a general partner[10]. The limited partnership is only suitable for those who wish to invest money in a partnership but take no part in its running; their lack of popularity seems hardly surprising.

It is unusual to find large businesses run as partnerships and, while there are advantages over companies in that there is less publicity for the affairs of the partnership, and perhaps less tax to be paid, these benefits will probably be outweighed by the advantages of limited liability and tax saving once profits reach a certain size.

In making contracts, a partnership has to work through agents, usually the partners, but since the partnership is not a separate legal entity there is no equivalent to the object clause of a company. In theory, a partnership can make any contract it wishes. Whether a contract entered into by a partner binds his fellow partners depends on the usual rules of agency[11], with the additional rule that any contract entered into by a partner which would be within the usual practice of the partnership will bind his fellow partners[12].

---

1 Partnership Act 1890, s.9.
2 *Ibid.*, s.20.
3 *Ibid.*, s.24.
4 *Ibid.*, s.33.
5 Under various rules of the Supreme Court.
6 Companies Act 1948, s.434.
7 Those qualified within Companies Act 1948, s.161.
8 Companies Act 1967, ss.119–121.
9 Limited Partnership Act 1907, s.4.
10 *Ibid.*, s.6.
11 Chap. 18.
12 Partnership Act 1890, s.5.

Clubs and Societies

4.16 A club may regulate its own internal management by contract between the members but it does not have legal personality distinct from its members. Clubs and societies usually arrange to have their property held on trust for the benefit of the club so that such property is distinct from the property of members, but all the members could, subject to club rules, call for the dissolution of the trust and then the property would be divided in accordance with the rules of the club or society. Legal actions can be brought by or against the committee and it may be possible for a member to sue the club (rather than the committee), but this can be very difficult.

If a club or society is carried on with a view to gain it must register as a company if membership exceeds 20[1], and many clubs choose to operate in corporate form.

The contractual capacity of a club is technically that of a natural legal person but, since a club can only make contracts via an agent, whether a particular contract binds a club and who is liable on it depends on the rules of the club and agency principles.

---

1 Companies Act 1948, s.434.

The Crown

4.17 Because of the principle of sovereign immunity the Crown originally could not be made a party to court action, although Crown servants could be sued in their personal capacity. This is important because the Crown includes not only the British sovereign but also government departments and the armed forces. Thus, if prior to 1947 you had been knocked down by a tank or the car of the Prime Minister as he rushed to a Cabinet meeting, or you had been supplied with defective goods under a contract of sale with the Minister for Supply, you had no redress against the army or government department. However, since 1947[1], the Crown, but not the sovereign, may generally be sued in contract or tort although, if it declines to meet an award of damages or refuses to comply with a court order, judgment cannot be enforced against it. The Crown may still be able to refuse to give evidence in a particular case if such evidence, if revealed, would be prejudicial to the interests of the state.

---

1 Crown Proceedings Act 1947.

Nationality

4.18 Nationality is a legal status, and in the United Kingdom the law relating to nationality and its legal effects is uniform in England and

Wales, Scotland and Northern Ireland. A person's nationality is important in a number of ways in the spheres of criminal law and constitutional law. For instance, a person's nationality is a crucial determinant in the application of United Kingdom law relating to immigration and deportation, just as it is in relation to civic rights and duties, such as the right to vote and the liability to jury service.

The law of the United Kingdom distinguishes between the following classes of persons:

a. *Citizens of the United Kingdom and Colonies* Obviously, these citizens are accorded the full range of civic rights and duties, subject to age qualifications and the like. Historically, all citizens of the United Kingdom and Colonies were free from immigration controls and liability to deportation but, since the Immigration Act 1971, this is now only true in the case of citizens who are 'patrials'. A citizen is a patrial if —

i. he was born, adopted, naturalised or registered as a citizen in the United Kingdom or Channel Islands or Isle of Man; or

ii. his parent had United Kingdom citizenship at the time of his birth or adoption, provided that either the parent had acquired citizenship in the United Kingdom or the Islands or the parent had been born to or adopted by a citizen parent who at that time had citizenship acquired in the United Kingdom or the Islands: or

iii. he has at any time been settled in the United Kingdom and Islands and had at that time been ordinarily resident there for the last five years or more[1].

b. *Citizens of Commonwealth countries* Along with citizens of the United Kingdom and Colonies, these citizens possess the status of British subjects (or Commonwealth citizens) under United Kingdom law[2]. All British subjects have the same civic rights and duties under United Kingdom law. Like citizens of the United Kingdom and Colonies, other British subjects are only free from United Kingdom immigration controls and liability to deportation if they are patrials or the wives of patrials. A Commonwealth citizen is a patrial if he is a person born to or adopted by a parent who at the time of the birth or adoption had citizenship of the United Kingdom and Colonies by birth in the United Kingdom or the Islands[3].

c. *Citizens of the Republic of Ireland* These citizens are neither British subjects nor aliens under United Kingdom law[4]. Apart from Northern Ireland, where the emergency conditions have necessitated special provisions, Irish citizens are not subject to immigration controls in relation to the rest of the United Kingdom. However, the Home Secretary does have power to refuse entry to an Irish citizen if he deems it conducive to the public good in the interests of national security, and Irish citizens are liable to deportation[5]. Irish citizens have the right to vote in elections in the United Kingdom.

d. *British protected persons* These persons are inhabitants of British protected states and protectorates, or of a former protectorate if they have been allowed to retain that status instead of opting for local citizenship. They are neither British subjects nor aliens[6]. They are liable to immigration controls and deportation, and do not possess civic rights and duties.

e. *Aliens* Aliens do not have any civic rights or duties under United Kingdom law. In relation to immigration and deportation, aliens other than EEC nationals are liable to immigration controls and deportation, but EEC nationals, are in a special position and are either subject to no immigration controls (in the case of a migrant worker) or more limited controls[7]. Deportation of an EEC national is only possible in accordance with EEC law.

---

1   Immigration Act 1971, ss. 1 and 2.
2   British Nationality Act 1948, s.1.
3   Immigration Act 1971, ss. 1 and 2.
4   British Nationality Act 1948, ss. 2 and 32; Ireland Act 1949, s.2.
5   Immigration Act 1971, s.3.
6   British Nationality Act 1948, s.32.
7   EEC Treaty, arts. 3(c), 48–58 and regulations and directives thereunder.

4.19   The rules regulating the acquisition of citizenship (i.e. nationality) of the United Kingdom and Colonies are provided by the British Nationality Act 1948, as amended. Citizenship of the United Kingdom and Colonies can be acquired in the following ways:

a. *By birth* As a general rule, anyone born within the United Kingdom and Colonies automatically acquires citizenship, whatever the nationality of his or her parents. The only exception of practical importance is where the father is a diplomat who is not a citizen of the United Kingdom and Colonies[1].

b. *By descent* Anyone born outside the United Kingdom and Colonies, whose father is a citizen of the United Kingdom and Colonies by birth at that time, automatically acquires citizenship[2]. On the other hand, if the father is only a citizen by descent, the child only acquires citizenship by descent if his birth is registered at a United Kingdom consulate within one year, or if his father is employed in Crown service under the United Kingdom Government at the time of birth, or in certain other circumstances[3].

c. *By naturalisation* Aliens and British protected persons of full age and capacity may apply to the Home Secretary for naturalisation. An alien applicant must:
  i. have resided in the United Kingdom, or been in Crown service, continuously for the preceding 12 months, and resided in the United Kingdom or Colonies for four years of the seven before that;
  ii. be of good character;
  iii. have a sufficient knowledge of the English language;
  iv. intend to remain resident in the United Kingdom or a colony or protectorate, or to continue in Crown service under the United Kingdom government or in certain other types of service[4].

The requirements for an applicant who is a British protected person are the same, except that requirement i. is replaced by a requirement that the applicant must have been ordinarily resident in the United Kingdom or in Crown service under the United Kingdom Government in the United Kingdom throughout the previous five years[5]. The Home Secretary has a discretion as to whether to make a naturalisation order.

d. *By registration* A woman who has married a citizen of the United Kingdom and Colonies is entitled as of right to be registered as such a citizen on application to the Home Secretary, as is a 'patrial' citizen of full age and capacity of a Commonwealth country provided he or she has been ordinarily resident in the United Kingdom, or engaged in Crown service under the United Kingdom Government in the United Kingdom or in certain other types of service in the United Kingdom, throughout the five years preceding the application, and has a close connection with the United Kingdom[6]. Non-patrial Commonwealth citizens and citizens of the Irish Republic may apply to the Home Secretary for the discretionary grant of registration subject to requirements similar to those relating to applications for naturalisation by British protected persons and to the additional requirement of a close connection with the United Kingdom and Colonies[7].

1 British Nationality Act 1948, s.4. An alien who is adopted by a citizen of the UK or Colonies or, in the case of a joint adoption, whose adoptive father is such a citizen, becomes a citizen of the UK or Colonies as from the date of the adoption: Adoption Act 1976, s.40.
2 British Nationality Act 1948, s.5.
3 *Ibid.*
4 *Ibid.*, s.10 and Sched. 2.
5 *Ibid.*, s.10 and Sched. 2; Commonwealth Immigrants Act 1962, s.12.
6 British Nationality Act 1948, s.5A(1) (inserted by the Immigration Act 1971, Sched. 1).
7 *Ibid.*, s.5A(2) (inserted by Immigration Act 1971, Sched. 1).

4.20 A person who has acquired citizenship by naturalisation or registration may be deprived of it by the Home Secretary if the naturalisation or registration was procured by misrepresentation or concealment of a material fact, or (in the case of naturalisation only) if he has shown himself disloyal to Her Majesty or has been sentenced to not less than 12 months' imprisonment within five years of naturalisation, unless deprivation would render him stateless[1]. If any citizen of full age and capacity also has the nationality of any other country he may renounce his citizenship of the United Kingdom and Colonies by making a declaration to that effect which becomes operative when registered by the Home Secretary. The Home Secretary may only refuse registration of a declaration if this country is at war and the applicant is a national of a country outside the Commonwealth[2].

---

1 British Nationality Act 1948, s.20.
2 *Ibid.*, s.19.

Domicile

4.21 In English law the law of the domicile (*lex domicilii*) governs, or is influential in, many questions concerning the personal and proprietary relationships of members of a family. For example, capacity to marry is governed by the law of each party's antenuptial domicile and capacity to make a will of movable property is governed by the law of the testator's domicile. In Scotland and other Commonwealth countries the personal law is the law of the domicile, but in most European countries it is the law of the nationality.

Domicile is wholly unconnected with nationality. Originally, domicile meant one's personal home but it has now become a legal concept used for establishing a connection for the determination of questions of the type just mentioned between an individual and the legal system of the territory with which he either has or is deemed to have the closest connection.

The classical view is that a person can only be domiciled in a place which has a separate system of law. Thus, a person may be domiciled in England or Scotland (which have separate legal systems), but not in the United Kingdom, and he may be domiciled in one of these two countries even though he is not a citizen of the United Kingdom and Colonies[1].

---

1 In a number of federal countries, however, some legal rules are governed by federal law and some by state or provincial law. The result is that a person can be domiciled in the federal country for some legal purposes, although domiciled in a particular state or province for others.

4.22 There are four basic principles of the theory of domicile in English law:

a. *No person can be without a domicile*[1] This is ensured by the rules governing the acquisition and loss of domicile which we discuss in para. 4.23. The basis of this principle is the need to connect every person with a system of law by which a number of his legal relationships may be regulated. The same basis underlies the second principle which we now mention.

b. *No person can have more than one domicile at the same time*[2] A multiplicity of domiciles would cause obvious difficulties.

c. *An existing domicile is presumed to continue* until it is proved that a new domicile has been acquired[3]. This principle is a corollary of the need to provide a domicile for every person at all times.

d. *The question where a person is domiciled is generally determined by English courts solely in accordance with English law*[4].

---

1   *Udny v Udny* (1869) LR 1 Sc & Div 441.
2   *Ibid.*
3   *Ramsay v Liverpool Royal Infirmary* [1930] AC 588, HL.
4   *Re Annesley* [1926] Ch 692.

4.23 In English law there are three types of domicile of natural persons: of origin, of choice and of dependence.

Domicile of origin This is the type of domicile which is assigned by law to every person at birth and continues to operate throughout his life unless he acquires another domicile, whether of choice or dependence[1]. If a person acquires another domicile but subsequently loses it, and does not acquire a new one simultaneously, his domicile of origin automatically revives[2]. The domicile of origin of a legitimate child is the same as his father's domicile at the time of the child's birth[3]. On the other hand, an illegitimate child takes his mother's domicile at the time of his birth as his domicile of origin[3].

Domicile of choice A person aged 16 or over may acquire a domicile of choice[4]. A domicile of choice can only be acquired by residence in another country coupled with the intention, formed independently of external pressures, of remaining there permanently or, at least, for an unlimited time[5]. Thus, an intention to change a domicile does not have that result if there is no residence in the new country[6]. Conversely, residence in a new country cannot result in the acquisition of a domicile of choice there if the necessary intention does not exist[7]. A domicile of choice is lost by giving up residence in the country *and* abandoning the intention of residing ther permanently or for an unlimited time[8]. It is not necessary to prove a positive intention not to return: it is sufficient merely to prove the absence of an intention to continue to reside[9].

Domicile of dependence This type of domicile is conferred by operation of law on children under the age of 16 and, in certain cases, on the mentally disordered.

If the father of a legitimate child under 16 acquires a new domicile the child automatically receives that domicile as a domicile of dependence. Similarly, if the mother of an illegitimate child under 16 takes a new domicile the child receives it as a domicile of dependence[10]. Special rules apply, in the case of *legitimate* children only, where the parents are separated or after the death of one parent:

a. If the child of separated parents is living with his father, his domicile changes with that of the father.

b. If the child of separated parents is not living with the father, the child receives any domicile acquired by the mother provided i. he then has his home with her and has no home with his father *or* ii. he has at any time had her domicile under i. and has not since had a home with his father[11].

c. The death of the mother does not affect the domicile of the child, which (since the child is legitimate) will continue to be the same as the father's, except that, where the parents were separated and the child has received his mother's domicile under b. above, he will continue to possess his mother's last domicile after her death if he has not subsequently had a home with his father.

d. A child acquires the domicile of his mother on the death of his father and his domicile will *prima facie* change with that of his mother[12]. However, the child's acquisition of a new dependent domicile on a change of domicile by the mother is not automatic, instead the mother has a *power* to change the child's domicile. The power must be exercised for the child's welfare, otherwise no change of his domicile will occur, nor of course will there be a change if the power is not exercised[13].

After the death of both parents (or of the mother of an illegitimate child) the child's domicile cannot be changed until he acquires the capacity to acquire a domicile of choice.

A mentally disordered person who is unable to form the necessary intention to acquire or lose a domicile cannot acquire a domicile of choice and, with one exception, retains the domicile which he had when he became insane[14]. The one exception is that if a child becomes insane and remains so after reaching 16, his domicile continues to change with that of the appropriate parent[15].

Prior to 1 January 1974, a married woman took her husband's

domicile on marriage, and any domicile subsequently acquired by him, as a domicile of dependence[16]. She was incapable of acquiring a separate domicile even though the spouses separated[17]. The law was changed by s.1 of the Domicile and Matrimonial Proceedings Act 1973. This abolished the wife's dependent domicile and provided that, as from 1 January 1974, a married woman has full capacity to acquire a domicile of choice. A woman married before 1 January 1974, who then had her husband's domicile by dependence, is treated as retaining that domicile (as a domicile of choice, if it was not her domicile of origin) until she acquires another.

1 *Bell v Kennedy* (1868) LR 1 Sc & Div 307.
2 *Udny v Udny* (1869) LR 1 Sc & Div 441.
3 *Ibid.*, at 457.
4 Domicile and Matrimonial Proceedings Act 1973, s.3. S.3 also provides that a child under 16 who is validly married can also acquire a domicile of choice. This cannot apply to a child domiciled in England because under English law, which, as the law of the domicile, governs his capacity to marry, he cannot marry under the age of 16. The provision can only apply to a child under 16 who is domiciled abroad and is validly married by his law of the domicile: he can now acquire a domicile of choice by English law.
5 *Bell v Kennedy* (1868) LR 1 Sc & Div 307; *Re Fuld, Hartley v Fuld* [1968] P675, [1965] 3 All ER 776.
6 *Harrison v Harrison* [1953] 1 WLR 865.
7 *Ramsay v Liverpool Royal Infirmary* [1930] AC 588, HL.
8 *Udny v Udny* (1869) LR 1 Sc & Div 441 at 450.
9 *Re Flynn* [1968] 1 All ER 49 at 58; *Qureshi v Qureshi* [1972] Fam 173 at 191, [1971] 1 All ER 325 at 328.
10 *Henderson v Henderson* [1967] P 77, [1965] 1 All ER 179; the age limit of 16 results from s.3 of the Domicile and Matrimonial Proceedings Act 1973. A child under 16 but validly married cannot acquire a domicile of dependence. See note 4. An adopted child takes by adoption the domicile of his adoptive parents or, in the case of a joint adoption, of his adoptive father.
11 Domicile and Matrimonial Proceedings Act 1973, s.4.
12 *Potinger v Wightman* (1817) 3 Mer 67.
13 *Re Beaumont* [1893] 3 Ch 490.
14 *Urquhart v Butterfield* (1887) 37 Ch D 357.
15 *Sharpe v Crispin* (1869) LR 1 P & D 611.
16 *Harvey v Farnie* (1882) 8 App Cas 43, HL.
17 *Dolphin v Robins* (1859) 7 HL Cas 390.

4.24 So far we have only been concerned with the domicile of individuals. A corporation is domiciled in its place of incorporation and it cannot change that domicile[1]. The significance of a corporation's domicile is that it is the law of the domicile which determines whether a so-called corporation possesses corporate personality, whether it has been amalgamated with another corporation, or whether it has been dissolved, and which regulates it and its affairs. In addition, the domicile of a corporation, like that of an individual is relevant for certain taxation purposes.

1 *Gasque v IRC* [1940] 2 KB 80.

Residence and ordinary residence

4.25 These concepts are relevant mainly in relation to taxation, but in that context they are more important than nationality or domicile. For example, under United Kingdom legislation an individual is chargeable to tax in the United Kingdom on business and trade profits earned overseas if he is resident in this country[1].

---

1 Income and Corporation Taxes Act 1970, s.108.

4.26 *Residence of individuals* Residence and ordinary residence are not defined in the Taxes Acts though there are statutory guidelines[1]. Whether a person is resident or ordinarily resident in the United Kingdom is a question of fact to be determined by the courts[2]. Ordinary residence seems to mean habitual residence and therefore the vital question is usually whether an individual is or is not resident in this country. If there is residence which is habitual, temporary absences abroad will not prevent such residence being ordinary residence[3]. Indeed, an individual can be ordinarily resident in this country in a tax year when he is not present at all, providing such absence is sandwiched between years of physical presence and residence.

In determining if an individual is resident in this country, s.51 of the Income and Corporation Taxes Act 1970 provides some guidance. This section says that an individual who is present in this country for a temporary purpose, with no intention of residing here, and who is physically present for less than six months in a tax year will not be regarded as a resident. However, physical presence in the United Kingdom, even if for a period of less than six months, will suffice to render a person a British resident provided that such presence is accompanied by an intention to reside here. If s.51 does not provide an answer, the courts take into account such factors as whether the individual has a home here, whether they have lived here, why visits are made to this country and how frequent and regular are such visits. Having a home in this country can be regarded as fairly conclusive in determining residence, even if the individual has another home abroad or makes very infrequent visits to this country (providing there are some)[4]. If an individual has no home in this country, he may still be resident here if he is present in this country during a tax year, particularly if the individual had a home here at one time[5]. In *Levene v IRC*[6], a British citizen who left this country in 1919 for health reasons, intending to live abroad, but who made visits here for up to five months to see friends and advisers until 1925, was found to be resident and ordinarily resident in this country for those six years.

While having a home in this country is a most persuasive factor in determining residence, there is a statutory provision which affects the issue. Section 50 of the Income and Corporation Taxes Act 1970 provides that people having a home here are not to be regarded as residents merely by virtue of having a home if they are working in a trade, job or profession which is performed almost entirely outside the United Kingdom. If there are factors other than home ownership which tend to establish than an individual is resident in the United Kingdom while working abroad, s.50 is inoperative.

United Kingdom residence and ordinary residence once acquired, are extremely difficult to lose[7].

---

1 Income and Corporation Taxes Act 1970, ss.49—51.
2 *IRC v Lysaght* [1928] AC 234, HL.
3 Income and Corporation Taxes Act 1970, s.49.
4 *Lloyd v Sulley* (1884) 2 TC 37, HL.
5 *IRC v Lysaght* [1928] AC 234, HL.
6 [1928] AC 217, HL.
7 Consider *Miesagaes v IRC* (1957) 37 TC 493, CA, where a taxpayer who was at school in England was found to be ordinarily resident here.

4.27 *Residence of companies and partnerships* The place where trading bodies have been created, or where they carry on their business is not necessarily their place of residence. The residence of companies and partnerships is determined by reference to the place of central control and management of the organisation[1]. Normally, control and management is vested in the directors or partners, but if control is in fact exercised by another person or persons then their place of residence constitutes the residence of the organisation.

---

1 *Unit Construction Co Ltd v Bullock* [1960] AC 351, [1959] 3 All ER 831, HL.

PROPERTY

Legal and equitable interests

4.28 Property, be it real or personal[1], can be the subject of legal and equitable interests. Such interests may be concurrent, and legal and equitable interests in property may be held by different people. For example, A may own an estate (which is a legal interest) in Blackacre, a plot of land, which is let to B, who thereby also has a legal interest in it, and, if B sub-lets it to C by means of an informal lease for six years, C may have an equitable interest in the plot of land if the equitable doctrine of part performance is satisfied[1]. Another example of the separation of legal and equitable interests is afforded by the trust. The trust is a device whereby the trustees hold property, real or personal, to which they have the legal title, for the benefit of the beneficiaries who have an equitable interest in that property. In law, the trustees own the property and can do what they like with it, but equity requires them to use the property as specified by the trust and they are accountable to the beneficiaries for their dealings with the property.

Legal interests are rights *in rem* (rights affecting the property itself) and can be enforced against anyone attempting to intermeddle with the property. Equitable interests are rights *in personam* (rights enforceable against certain persons who have the property, but not attached to the property itself). The distinction between rights *in rem* and *in personam* is relevant in relation to the purchaser for value without notice.

---

1   Paras. 7.17 and 7.18.

Purchasers for value without notice

4.29   Legal rights and interests bind everyone, whether or not they know of the existence of such rights and interests. For example, if the owner of land grants you a legal lease of that land, your lease is binding on a subsequent purchaser of the land, even if he foolishly neglected to inquire whether the land was subject to a prior legal claim or not.

However, equitable rights and interests in land are vulnerable in that while they bind persons who take subsequent equitable interests in that land they do not bind *bona fide* purchasers of the legal estate for value without notice of the prior equitable interest. *Bona fide* means that the person seeking to ignore an equitable interest must not have acted fraudulently or in bad faith. A purchaser, who can include someone taking a mortgage or lease of the land, must give money or money's worth[1] and purchase a legal interest in the property. Furthermore, to escape being bound by a prior equitable interest, the purchaser must not have notice of the existence of the equitable interest. The burden of proving that he is *bona fide* purchaser etc. is on the party seeking to defeat the equitable interest.

If there is notice of the equitable interest, that interest will bind the subsequent purchaser. Notice may be actual, constructive or imputed. Actual notice means what it suggests, that the purchaser in fact knew of the prior equitable right, but this has been modified by statute in relation to interests in land. Certain equitable interests in land must be registered in the Land Charges Register if they are to bind a subsequent purchaser. Failure to register renders the equitable right void[2] and therefore not binding on a purchaser for money or money's worth of the legal estate, even if he had actual notice of their existence. Conversely, registration of such interests in the Land Charges Register is actual notice to all the world of their existence and therefore registration of such an interest means that no one can be a purchaser for value without notice. However, not all equitable interests are registrable.

Constructive notice means that a purchaser who did not actually know of an equitable interest (being a non-registrable interest) will be deemed to have notice of the interest if they ought to have known about it. If a purchaser could defeat equitable interests by declining to inquire whether any interest existed, equitable interests would be sadly unprotected. Therefore, purchasers are required to show due diligence in seeking out equitable interests and must certainly inspect any land to be purchased. Failure to exercise due diligence means the purchaser will be fixed with constructive notice of any equitable interests which diligence would have revealed.

Imputed notice merely means that the actual or constructive notice of an authorised agent of the purchaser is imputed to the purchaser.

Any successor of a *bona fide* purchaser for value without notice also takes free of equitable interests, even if he knew of their existence.

Some non-registrable equitable interests in land are 'over-reached' when the land is purchased, whether by the purchaser without notice or not[3]. Such interests are not destroyed but they are no longer attached to the land, but to the purchase money paid for the land and the purchaser takes the land unencumbered.

---

1 Money's worth includes non-monetary consideration (in the contractual sense), and the satisfaction of an existing debt and 'marriage' (a promise made in consideration of a future marriage is a promise made for value as regards the future spouses and any children they may have).
2 Land Charges Act 1972, s.4.
3 Law of Property Act 1925, s.2; Settled Land Act 1925, ss. 18, 72 and 75.

Part II
The Law of Contract

Part II

The Law of Contract

Chapter 5
Agreement

5.1 In this part of the book we adopt the following order. In this chapter and in Chapters 6 and 7 we outline those basic elements of the law of contract which relate to the existence of an enforceable contract. In the following five chapters (Chapters 8–12) we deal with contractual obligations, with how they are discharged, and with the remedies available if they are broken. Sometimes a contract, which would otherwise be enforceable, is invalidated or liable to be set aside because of mistake, misrepresentation, illegality, the incapacity of a party or certain other factors. We deal with these matters in Chapters 13–16. The last three chapters in this Part are concerned with the law of quasi-contract (otherwise known as the law of restitution) with particular emphasis on its application to contracts, with the assignment of contractual rights and with the law relating to agency.

5.2 All contracts, if they are to be valid, have to be formed in the same way.

a. There must be a valid offer and acceptance;

b. the parties must have intended their agreement to be legally binding; and

c. the contract must be supported by consideration or be under seal.

We commence with the basic requirement of any contract: agreement between the parties.

A contract can usually be made orally, or in writing, or by deed, although some contracts have to be in a particular form to be enforceable[1]. Any contract which complies with the three requirements listed above, and which does not contain a vitiating element[2], is legally binding. While an oral contract is normally as binding as a written contract, there are obvious advantages in reducing a contract to writing.

Contracts may be either bilateral, whereby one party promises to do something and the other party promises to do something in return (i.e. an exchange of promises), or unilateral, whereby one party promises to do something in return for the action or inaction of another, such as a reward for the finding of a lost dog as payment.

It is necessary to consider what is an offer, what constitutes an acceptance, how that acceptance is conveyed to the offeror and how an offer can be terminated.

1 Chap. 7.
2 Chaps. 13–16.

Offer

5.3 Where one person (the offeror) makes an unequivocal offer to another person (the offeree) who firmly accepts that offer an agreement is made which is prima facie a contract.

Whether an unequivocal offer is made during the course of negotiations is for the courts to decide. Something which appears to be an unequivocal offer will usually be an offer, although certain decided cases have determined that statements which might otherwise be thought to be unequivocal offers are not offers but invitations to treat. Also, inquiries and replies to inquiries are not offers though sometimes they may resemble them. In *Harvey v Facey*[1], one party inquired the lowest acceptable price for certain land, the other party telegraphed his lowest acceptable price. This was not an offer but merely the reply to the inquiry.

An offer may be made to a specific person, to a group of people or to the world at large[2]. An offer to a specific person cannot be accepted by anyone except that person[3].

We turn now to some specific examples where something that appears to be an offer is not an offer in law.

1 [1893] AC 552, PC.
2 *Carlill v Carbolic Smoke Ball Co* [1893] 1 QB 256, CA.
3 *Cundy v Lindsay* (1878) 3 App Cas 459, HL.

Invitation to treat

5.4 An invitation to treat is a starting point for contractual negotiations and precedes the making of an offer. In *Fisher v Bell*[1], a shopkeeper was charged with offering for sale a flick knife which was on display in his shop window[2]. The Divisional Court held that the display of goods in a shop window was not an offer to sell but an invitation to treat; it was for customers to make the offer. The rationale behind this decision is that a shop is a place for negotiation over the terms of a contract, including the price, and that the shopkeeper invites customers to make him an offer which he can accept or reject as he pleases. This is an unrealistic view of how shops operate today. Circulars sent to potential customers are also invitations to treat for the supply of goods and not offers[3].

An area of difficulty which has arisen since the Second World War concerns self-service shops. The display of goods could be regarded as an offer to sell or as an invitation to treat. If it is an invitation to treat it is not immediately obvious when the offer to buy is made. It could be when the goods are picked up, or when they are put in a basket, or when the customer approaches the point of payment or when they are actually presented for payment. In *Pharmaceutical Society of Great Britain v Boots Cash Chemist (Southern) Ltd*[4], statute required certain drugs to be sold only under the supervision of a qualified pharmacist. A pharmacist was at the cash desk but if the sale of drugs was made before a customer reached it the statute would have been broken. The Court of Appeal had no hesitation in finding that the display of goods was only an invitation to treat and that the contract was concluded at the place of payment and so Boots were not in breach of the statute. The Court did not determine when the offer was made.

Whether running a bus is an offer or merely an invitation to treat has, surprisingly, never been determined but obiter dicta would seem to suggest that it is an offer which the passenger accepts on boarding the bus even before any money is proffered or destination indicated[5].

---

1 [1961] 1 QB 394, [1960] 3 All ER 731, DC.
2 Contrary to the Restriction of Offensive Weapons Act 1959, now the Restriction of Offensive Weapons Act 1961 which reverses the decision in the case.
3 *Grainger & Son v Gough* [1896] AC 325, HL.
4 [1953] 1 QB 401, [1953] 1 All ER 482, CA.
5 *Wilkie v London Passenger Transport Board* [1947] 1 All ER 258, CA.

Advertisements

5.5 Advertisements of goods for sale are not necessarily offers to sell, some advertisements are merely invitations to treat. Whether an advertisement is an offer is a question of intention. Advertisements of rewards are normally offers since the party who offers the reward does not intend any further negotiation to take place. However, the advertising of an auction is not an offer; instead, those who bid at auction make an offer which the auctioneers are free to accept or reject, and an offer can be withdrawn at any time before the auctioneer accepts. Because advertisement of an auction is merely a declaration of an intention to hold the auction, potential buyers have no claim against the auctioneers if they fail to hold the auction[1].

The famous case of *Carlill v Carbolic Smoke Ball Co*[2] is an illustration of where the courts were able to find that an advertisement constituted an offer. In this case the defendants advertised that they would pay £100 to anyone contracting influenza after using their product in a specified manner. The plaintiff duly used her smoke ball but succumbed to influenza and claimed £100. Among the numerous defences pleaded unsuccessfully by the defendants was that their advertisement was not an offer but a mere invitation to treat.

1 *Harris v Nickerson* (1873) LR 8 QB 286.
2 [1893] 1 QB 256, CA.

Tenders

5.6 An announcement that the provision of goods or services is open to tender is not an offer but only an invitation to treat. Consequently, a person who submits a tender makes an offer. This offer may be accepted or rejected by the person seeking tenders[1].

In *Spencer v Harding*[2], the defendant issued a circular offering by tender the stock in trade of X. This was held not to be an offer. Thus, the defendant was not required to sell the goods to the plaintiff who had submitted the highest bid.

1 For acceptance of tenders see para. 5.10.
2 (1870) LR 5 CP 561.

Acceptance

5.7 To convert an offer into a contract the offeree must make an effective acceptance of the offer and also, usually, communicate this decision to the offeror. An acceptance may be express or based on the conduct of the offeree. A contract may arise during the course of long and complicated negotiations and it is then difficult for the court to determine the exact moment when the contract arose. In such cases no formal statement constituting an offer or acceptance may have been made. If this is so, the conduct of the parties and all their actions and statements will be considered by the court to see whether the parties intended to contract and, if there is a contract, when they contracted.

The nature of acceptance

5.8 It should come as no surprise to anyone to learn that one cannot accept an offer of which one is ignorant. This is important in the case where A offers a reward for the performance of a particular action, e.g. finding his lost dog. If B, who is ignorant of the offer, finds the dog, his action cannot constitute an acceptance of the offer and he cannot claim the reward successfully[1]. Moreover, if someone who knows of the offer performs the specified action for reasons entirely unconnected with that offer, there is no acceptance[2]. But, if his conduct is motivated partly by the offer and partly by other reasons there is a valid acceptance[3].

A related point is that if two offers which are identical in terms cross in the post there can be no contract. The courts will not construe one offer as the offer and the other offer as the acceptance[4]. The practical basis for such a view would seem to be that neither party would know if he was bound, although if the terms of the offers were identical the parties would surely have no objection to being bound.

Another basic rule relating to acceptance is that the acceptance should be an unequivocal agreement to the terms proposed in the offer. If an offeree who purports to accept the offer seeks to introduce entirely new terms in his acceptance, this is a counter offer, and not an acceptance. For example, an offeree cannot agree to accept half the quantity of goods offered by the offeror, even on the same terms as would have applied to the full quantity[5].

In *Hyde v Wrench*[6], the defendant offered to sell property to the plaintiff for £1,000. The plaintiff 'agreed' to buy the property for £950 and when this was rejected the plaintiff purported to accept the original offer of £1,000. The Master of the Rolls rejected the plaintiff's claim finding that his purported acceptance for £950 was a counter offer which destroyed the original offer. Not every inquiry by the offeree will be regarded as a counter offer, some inquiries are merely seeking information and even if answered negatively by the offeror do not destroy the offer. An example is *Stevenson v MacLean*[7]. The defendant offered to sell iron to the plaintiffs at 40 shillings a ton with immediate delivery. The plaintiffs asked the defendant by telegram if he would sell at the same price if delivery was staggered over two months. On receiving no reply, the plaintiffs accepted the original offer but the defendant failed to deliver and claimed the telegram was a counter offer. The court rejected the defendant's claim and held that the telegram was a mere request for information and not a new offer so the original offer could still be accepted.

1   *R v Clarke* (1927) 40 CLR 227.
2   *Ibid.*
3   *Williams v Carwardine* (1833) 5 C & P 566.

4   *Tinn v Hoffmann & Co* (1873) 29 LT 271.
5   *Ibid.*
6   (1840) 3 Beav 334.
7   (1880) 5 QBD 346.

5.9   An offer can be accepted by an oral or written statement by the offeree. An acceptance may also be based on conduct. For instance, a cover note issued by an insurance company is an offer to insure which would be accepted by using a car in reliance on it[1]. A more complicated case of acceptance by conduct is that of *Brogden v Metropolitan Rly Co*[2], in which Brogden was sued for failing to deliver coal. Brogden regularly supplied the company with coal and they decided to draw up an agreement for such supply. A draft agreement was submitted to Brogden with a blank space for the name of a mutually agreeable arbitrator, and this constituted the offer. Brogden filled in the name of an arbitrator, marked the agreement 'approved' and returned it to the agent of the company who put it in a drawer where it remained. Brogden's action was not an acceptance but a counter offer[3], because the company had to consider whether to accept his choice of arbitrator. The parties bought and sold coal in accordance with the terms of the draft agreement. Subsequently Brogden refused to supply more coal and claimed there was no binding contract for its supply. The House of Lords inferred from the conduct of the parties, the buying and selling of coal on terms exactly the same as those in the draft contract, that a contract had been concluded, which came into effect with the first order of coal by the company. The House of Lords stressed that mere verbal acquiescence by the parties that the contract should exist would not have sufficed: it was their actions that completed the contract.

---

1   *Taylor v Allon* [1966] 1 QB 304, [1965] 1 All ER 557.
2   (1877) 2 App Cas 666, HL.
3   Para. 5.8.

5.10   The acceptance of tenders illustrates another aspect of acceptance. Tenders can be in two forms.

a. Where people are invited to tender, for example, by a local authority, for the supply of specified goods or services over a given period, a contract for the supply of those goods or services is constituted when a person's tender (offer) is accepted.

b. However, if people are invited to tender for the supply of such goods and services as may be required over a given period, a contract is not immediately concluded with the successful tenderer. Instead, his offer is treated as a standing offer and each time an order is placed this constitutes acceptance of the standing offer and there is a contract for the goods or services ordered. Because the person making the successful tender has no definite contract, he can revoke his offer before any particular order is placed, and the person who invited tenders need never place an order[1].

---

1 *Great Northern Rly Co v Witham* (1873) LR 9 CP 16.

Communication of acceptance

5.11 If an offer has been made and it has been accepted, there is no legally binding contract until that acceptance has been communicated, or made manifest if acceptance is by conduct[1]. The reason for this is practical: if the offeror is not told his offer has been accepted he does not know whether he has made a contract or can make offers to others.

Communication of acceptance usually requires actual communication so that an oral acceptance which is drowned by a passing aeroplane or inaudible because of interference on the telephone is not a valid communication[2]. Telex messages are regarded as instantaneous communications and are subject to the same principles as oral communications[2]. However, if an oral or telex acceptance does not reach the offeror and the party accepting does not realise this, there may be a valid communication of acceptance. But this will only be the case where the offeror realises he has missed some of what the offeree is seeking to communicate and does not attempt to discover what he has missed.

Acceptance may also be communicated by an authorised agent to an authorised agent[3].

---

1 Para. 5.9.
2 *Entores v Miles Far East Corpn* [1955] 2 QB 327, [1955] 2 All ER 493, CA.
3 Paras. 18.32—18.38.

5.12 The offeror may dispense, expressly or impliedly, with the need to communicate acceptance by the terms of the offer. In *Carlill v Carbolic Smoke Ball Co*[1], the vendors of a product argued that a user of the product, who claimed a reward which they had offered to anyone catching influenza after using the product, should have told them of her acceptance of their offer of a reward. The vendors' claim was rejected, since it was clear they had not intended every purchaser of the product to write to them formally accepting the offer of a reward if illness was not avoided.

---

1 [1893] 1 QB 256, CA.

5.13 While communication of acceptance can be dispensed with by the offeror he cannot frame his offer in such terms that a contract is presumed to occur unless non-acceptance is communicated: silence cannot be acceptance. In *Felthouse v Bindley*[1], the plaintiff offered to buy X's horse and said he would presume his offer to be accepted unless he heard to the contrary. X did not reply. The horse was sold by the defendant, an auctioneer, to another and the plaintiff sued. It was held that no contract had been formed: the plaintiff was not entitled to presume acceptance unless he heard to the contrary.

1   (1862) 11 CB NS 869.

5.14 While some offers dispense with communication of acceptance, others require a particular form of acceptance to be employed. The attitude of the courts seems to be that an acceptance made in some other way than that prescribed can be effective as long as it is as advantageous to the offeror as the prescribed method[1]. In *Manchester Diocesan Council for Education v Commercial & General Investments Ltd*[2], the defendant offered to buy property which the plaintiffs were selling by tender. The terms of the tender said that acceptance of offers would be sent to the address specified by the offeror. It was held that a reply in fact sent to the defendant's surveyor was a valid acceptance[2]. Even if the offer does not prescribe a method of acceptance, the acceptance should be made in a way consistent with the offer. Thus, telegram offers should be accepted by telegram or some equally speedy method.

1   This seems to be true even if the offer says reply by specified method *only*; see *Compagnie de Commerce et Commission SARL v Parkinson Stove Co Ltd* [1953] 2 Lloyd's Rep 487, CA.
2   [1969] 3 All ER 1593, [1970] 1 WLR 241.

5.15 To the general rule that acceptance must be actually communicated to be effective there is an exception. It is that a posted acceptance is communicated when it is posted, not when it arrives. This was first established in *Adams v Lindsell*[1], where a letter of acceptance was posted the day that a postal offer to sell wool was received. The acceptance arrived two days later than expected and, after it had been posted but before it arrived, the offeror sold the wool to another. It was held that a contract was complete as soon as the letter was posted. This rule is an exception to the general law and the offeror can exclude the special postal acceptance rule in his offer by specifying that acceptance must be *actually* communicated to him[2]. In addition, the postal acceptance rule will be disregarded, and the usual rule prevails, if it leads to 'manifest inconvenience or absurdity'[3]. But if the postal acceptance rule does prevail (and it would seem to apply to telegrams as well as letters), a posted acceptance is a communicated acceptance even if the letter fails to arrive. The justification for this special rule for postal acceptances seems to be that the offeror, by expressly or impliedly (e.g. by making the offer by post) allowing an acceptance to be made by post, must stand the risk of failures of the postal system. However, if a postal acceptance goes astray because of the negligence of the offeree, as where he wrongly addresses the letter, there seems no reason why the court should not decide the acceptance to be communicated at whatever time is least advantageous to the negligent offeree.

1 (1818) 1 B & Ald 681.
2 For a recent example see *Holwell Securities Ltd v Hughes* [1974] 1 All ER 161, [1974] 1 WLR 155, CA.
3 *Ibid.*

5.16 If an acceptance made by letter is communicated when it is posted, then, logically, an attempt to withdraw the offer after the acceptance has been posted should be ineffective since the contract has been concluded. There are no English cases which support this view though the principle stated is consistent with American cases. The Scottish case of *Countess of Dunmore v Alexander*[1] has been cited as authority for the view that if a revocation is communicated before a postal acceptance arrives the revocation is effective. However, the facts of this case are somewhat obscure and it is by no means certain that the acceptance was communicated before the withdrawal of the offer.

1 (1830) 9 Sh (Ct of Sess) 190.

Termination of offers

5.17 An offer may be terminated in several ways: by revocation, by lapse of time and by death.

Revocation

5.18 At any time until acceptance by the offeree, the offeror can withdraw his offer. The fact that the offeror has given the offeree time to make up his mind does not mean the offeror is required to keep the offer open for that length of time. In *Routledge v Grant*[1], reply to an offer was required within six weeks but this did not mean the offeror could not withdraw the offer within the six week period.

There is an exception to the rule that the offer need not be kept open for a specified period. This is where there is a separate contract whereby the offeror contracts to keep the offer open for a given time. If there is such a contract the offer can be accepted at any time within the specified period. An example of such a contract is the granting of an option.

If an offer is revoked before acceptance, the revocation only becomes effective when it is communicated to the offeree. In *Byrne v Van Tienhoven*[2], the parties were in Cardiff and New York respectively. The plaintiffs accepted an offer made by letter the day the offer was received. However, between the dispatch of the offer and its arrival, a letter revoking the offer was sent, which arrived after the acceptance was communicated. The plaintiffs sued the defendants for non-delivery and the defendants alleged that the offer had been revoked. The court found that the offer was only revoked when it arrived at the plaintiffs' establishment. There is no parallel rule to that which treats a posted acceptance as a communicated acceptance, a revocation must be actually communicated.

Communication of revocation may be indirect in that if the offeree hears from a reliable source that the offer has been withdrawn the courts will regard this as an effective revocation[3]. The difficulty inherent in this is that it is difficult to know what constitutes a reliable source.

1   (1828) 4 Bing 653.
2   (1880) 5 CPD 344.
3   *Dickinson v Dodds* (1876) 2 Ch D 463, CA.

5.19   Particular difficulty has arisen over the revocation of the type of offer whereby A promises to pay B if B does something. A typical example of such a situation is a reward for the return of lost property. If such an offer has been made, can it be revoked when the offeree has begun performance but before it is completed? In other words, if the offeree is seen by the offeror leading the lost dog, can the offeror rush out and revoke the offer? It seems probable that once acceptance has commenced the contract is complete and the offer cannot be withdrawn — there are dicta to this effect in *Offord v Davies*[1] and the decision in *Errington v Errington*[2] supports this view. In *Errington v Errington*, a father purchased a house, partially by means of a mortgage, and allowed his daughter and her husband to live in it. The daughter and her husband paid the mortgage instalments in response to the offer of the father that, if they did so, he would give them the house when it was paid for. This offer could not, said the Court of Appeal, be revoked by the executors of the father once the daughter and her husband had begun performance of the act specified in the offer.

A compromise between finding no acceptance until the act requested is completed and finding acceptance as soon as the act is begun would be to allow recovery for work actually done on a *quantum meruit*[3].

1   (1862) 12 CB NS 748.
2   [1952] 1 KB 290, [1952] 1 All ER 149, CA.
3   Para. 17.8.

Lapse of time

5.20 The courts may find that an offer could only reasonably be expected to be open for a limited period. Whether the offer has lapsed will depend on the facts of the case and there is no specified period after which offers are deemed to lapse. In *Ramsgate Victoria Hotel Co v Montefiore*[1], an offer to buy shares which was made in June could not be accepted in November since the offer had lapsed.

---

1   (1866) LR 1 Ex 109.

Death

5.21 Death after an offer has been accepted cannot affect the validity of a contract though it may render performance impossible. There are however cases where either the offeror or the offeree dies before the offer is accepted. If the offeror dies the offer does not seem to terminate automatically, except where the offer is clearly of such a type that it must end on death, e.g. an offer to be cook for X, however, the offeree cannot accept the offer once he knows of the death of the offeror[1]. The cases show that an offer to guarantee the debts of a third party over a given period does not terminate on the death of the offeror. In such cases there may be more than one acceptance in that every time the third party incurs a debt the offer to guarantee is accepted. It is not clear if the same rule applies if the offer is only capable of a single acceptance, e.g. an offer to sell a horse.

The effects of the death of the offeree have not been decided conclusively but contraindicated dicta suggest that the offer lapses. In *Reynolds v Atherton*[2], it was suggested that an offer being made to a living person cannot survive his death and be accepted by someone else. This may be an illustration of the basic rule that an offer made to A cannot be accepted by B but if an offer is made to A or B there seems no reason why the death of B should prevent A's acceptance of it.

---

1   *Bradbury v Morgan* (1862) 1 H & C 249; *Coulthart v Clementson* (1879) 5 QBD 42.
2   (1921) 125 LT 690, CA; affd. by the House of Lords who did not comment on this point.

Special cases

5.22 There are some situations where there is a contract but it is impossible to find offer and acceptance in the strict sense. This may arise where several parties agree with X that they will be bound by certain terms. In such a case the parties may have entered into a contract not merely with X but with each other. In *Clarke v Dunraven*[1], competitors wrote to the secretary of a yacht club agreeing to be bound by certain rules during a yacht race. The House of Lords held a contract to exist between the competitors with the result that a competitor whose yacht was damaged was able to recover damages in accordance with that contract. It cannot really be pretended that there was an offer and acceptance in the traditional sense between the competitors.

---

1 [1897] AC 59, HL.

Uncertain, inconclusive and conditional agreements

5.23 Here we are concerned with cases where, although there is offer and acceptance, there may not be a legally binding contract because the agreement is uncertain in its terms, or is merely an agreement to agree in the future, or is subject to the operation of a condition.

Uncertainty

5.24 A contract may be uncertain in that the meaning of particular terms is unclear or in that the agreement lacks some of its vital terms because matters are left open for further negotiation. The latter is an agreement to agree.

Where particular terms are not subject to further negotiation but are vague or unclear the courts will try to divine the intention of the parties and find a contract, but if such intention cannot be discovered the agreement is not a legally binding contract and cannot be enforced[1]. Terms which have been held to be unclear include 'subject to war clause' when there is no universally accepted war clause[2], and, in *Scammell v Ouston*[1], 'purchase on hire-purchase terms', there being more than one form of hire-purchase. If uncertainty cannot be resolved by reference to the intention of the parties, the courts may be able to dispel uncertainty by reference to the practices and usages of a particular trade or profession to which the parties belong or the previous dealings of the parties. In *Hillas & Co Ltd v Arcos Ltd*[3], the parties had entered into a contract for the sale and purchase of timber in 1930. This contract contained an option to buy 100,000 standards of timber in 1931 but the size and quality of the timber were not specified. The House of Lords refused to find the agreement unenforceable, clarifying any uncertainties by reference to the previous dealings of the parties and usual practice in the timber trade. The judgment of the House is permeated by the view that the courts ought to strive to give effect to business arrangements and not zealously demand absolute certainty of all terms.

---

1 *Scammell v Ouston* [1941] AC 251, [1941] 1 All ER 14, HL.
2 *Bishop and Baxter Ltd v Anglo-Eastern Trading and Industrial Co Ltd* [1944] KB 12, [1943] 2 All ER 598, CA.
3 [1932] 147 LT 503, HL.

5.25 Sometimes it may be possible to ignore uncertainty in an agreement. This can be done, for instance, where the uncertainty relates to what is a meaningless term. In *Nicolene Ltd v Simmonds*[1], the agreement contained the phrase 'I assume the usual conditions of acceptance apply'. There were no usual conditions of acceptance, but the Court of Appeal said the phrase was meaningless and since it did not relate to an important term or part of the contract it could be ignored. A distinction must be drawn between meaningless phrases and phrases which denote that terms are still to be agreed. A phrase is unlikely to be considered meaningless and thus capable of being ignored if it concerns an important term of the contract. For example, in *Scammell v Ouston*[2], the court would have been most unlikely to regard as uncertain but meaningless a term relating to payment.

If there is a contract, assistance in resolving uncertainties may be found in s.8(2) of the Sale of Goods Act 1893. The section provides that if an agreement for the sale of goods does not specify a price for goods then a reasonable price will be payable. Further, if a concluded agreement is uncertain in that the price has not been fixed it may be possible to claim reasonable remuneration by bringing a *quantum meruit* action[3].

---

1 [1953] QB 543, [1953] 1 All ER 822, CA.
2 [1941] AC 251, [1941] 1 All ER 14, HL.
3 See further para. 17.8.

Agreement to agree

5.26 If some terms of an agreement are open to further negotiation there is no concluded contract. If contract for the sale of goods leaves the price to be fixed by subsequent agreement between the parties, there is merely an agreement to agree. In *May and Butcher Ltd v R*[1], the price of surplus tentage which was being sold by a government department to the plaintiffs was such as 'shall be agreed upon from time to time between the government department and the purchasers'. The House of Lords found that because a vital term was left open for future negotiation the agreement was not a legally binding contract.

However, in *Foley v Classique Coaches Ltd*[2], the Court of Appeal found an agreement containing the words 'price to be agreed by the parties' to be a binding contract. The court felt able to distinguish *May and Butcher Ltd v R*[1] on two grounds. First, on the basis that the parties had acted on the agreement for three years and their implied belief that they had been contractually bound during that period must be given effect, and, secondly, because in the absence of agreement on price it was to be determined by arbitration. If an agreement appears to be merely an agreement to agree but the agreement itself provides a method of resolving lack of agreement then, certainly as regards apparently uncertain terms relating to price and perhaps in all cases, the contract will be binding. In *Campbell v Edwards*[3], doubts on the validity of this view were rejected by the Court of Appeal. In this case a contract which provided that the surrender value of a lease was to be determined by a surveyor was found to be a perfectly binding contract. If the contract does not provide a method of determining disputes about terms which are still to be agreed, the agreement is not a binding contract. In such cases, there can be no question of implying reasonable terms, e.g. as to price, into the agreement in order to make it a legally binding contract.

---

1   [1934] 2 KB 17 n, HL.
2   [1934] 2 KB 1, CA.
3   [1976] 1 All ER 785, [1976] 1 WLR 403, CA.

Operation of a condition

5.27   An agreement which appears to be a legally binding contract may never come into operation because it is subject to a condition precedent which is not satisfied[1]. An example is afforded by *Pym v Campbell*[2]. In this case an agreement to purchase a share in an invention was subject to the condition precedent that the invention be approved by X. X failed to approve and thus no binding agreement to buy came into existence. It is not certain what, if any, is the legal effect of an agreement subject to a condition precedent[3]. Since there is no binding contract it might be thought that either party could withdraw from the agreement with impunity. However, the courts seem to regard the effect of such an agreement as a matter of construction. On its true construction, the effect of an agreement subject to a condition precedent may be that neither party can withdraw until it is clear whether the condition will be satisfied[4]. Alternatively, the effect of such an agreement may be that one party must do his best to fulfil the condition[5] or, at least, not obstruct its fulfilment[6]. Other conditions precedent, it has been decided, impose no obligations on the parties. For example, it is usual in sale of land to make agreements 'subject to contract'. Such agreements are not legally binding nor are the parties required to try to ensure a contract is concluded[7]. Phrases similar to 'subject to contract' have the same effect.

---

1 For a different type of condition precedent see para. 10.14.
2 (1856) 6 E & B 370.
3 In *Pym v Campbell* the court said there was no agreement at all.
4 *Smith v Butler* [1900] 1 QB 694, CA. In *Smallman v Smallman* [1972] Fam 25, [1971] 3 All ER 717, CA, a buyer, who withdrew from an agreement to purchase which was subject to a condition precedent before it was clear whether the condition was satisfied, was unable to recover the deposit he had paid.
5 *Marten v Whale* [1917] 2 KB 480, CA.
6 *Mackay v Dick* (1881) 6 App Cas 251, HL.
7 *Winn v Bull* (1877) 7 Ch D 29.

5.28 An agreement may also be subject to the operation of a condition subsequent. In such cases an agreement will be a binding contract unless and until the condition occurs. In *Head v Tattersall*[1], a contract for the sale of a horse was subject to the condition subsequent that, if the contractual description, the horse could be returned and the contract terminated. The purchaser was able to return the horse, even though it had been injured, when he found it did not meet the contractual description.

---

1 (1871) LR 7 Exch 7.

Chapter 6
Consideration and Privity

6.1 An agreement which complies with the rules specified in the previous chapter will constitute a binding contract, provided it is supported by consideration and the parties intended to enter into a legally binding contract. If a binding contract has been formed only those persons who are parties to the contract can sue or be sued on it. Even if a person has provided consideration, or a contract is expressly intended to confer a benefit or burden on him, he cannot sue or be sued if he is not a party to the contract: this is the doctrine of privity.

Intention to create legal relations

6.2 If there is offer and acceptance and consideration there is in fact usually an intention to create legal relations, although the parties to an agreement rarely state this intention expressly. If the parties do not wish their agreement to be legally binding, they may expressly state this and the courts will give effect to their intention. In the absence of an express indication of intention, the courts rely on two presumptions in deciding whether there was an intention to create legal relations, both of which can be rebutted expressly or impliedly by the parties:

a. parties to social, domestic and family arrangements do not intend to be legally bound[1]; and

b. parties to business and commercial agreements expect their agreements to be legally binding.

An example of the first type of arrangement is an agreement to give lifts to work, even if it is on an organised basis and involves payment to the car owners for their petrol[2]. While arrangements made within the family or household are presumed not to be intended to be legally binding, the nature of the agreement may clearly indicate the parties intended a particular arrangement to be binding. In *Simpkins v Pays*[3], three members of the same household submitted a joint entry to a competition on the basis that they would share any winnings. This arrangement was binding on the parties.

If there is a business arrangement it is extremely difficult to rebut the presumption that the arrangement is to be legally binding, other than by clear words. A leading illustration is *Rose and Frank Co v J. R. Crompton & Bros Ltd*[4], in which the defendants appointed the plaintiffs their agents to sell their products in America under an agreement which contained an 'honour clause', i.e. a clause which said the agreement was merely recording the intention of the parties and was binding in honour only and not in law. The plaintiffs sued for alleged breach of contract. The Court of Appeal and House of Lords found that the honour clause was a clearly expressed intention that the agreement was not to be legally binding and the court would give effect to this intention. However, in *Esso Petroleum Ltd v Customs and Excise Comrs*[5], a promotion scheme organised by the company involved giving a free World Cup coin to any motorist who purchased four gallons of petrol. The House of Lords found that while the scheme stressed that the coins were free, and even though the scheme was for advertising purposes, there was a contract to supply coins to any motorist buying the requisite number of gallons. Had the company failed to supply a coin to a motorist he could have sued the company. This case illustrates the difficulty of rebutting the presumption of 'intention to create legal relations' other than by the use of clear words.

But even where the presumption is rebutted by clear words, this does not prevent the subsequent conduct of the parties to the agreement constituting a binding contract. In *Rose and Frank Co v J. R. Crompton Bros Ltd*, the parties to the agency agreement ordered and supplied goods for sale in America. It was held that these orders and acceptances were binding contracts even though the agency contract was not.

An important statutory exception to the presumption that business and commercial dealings are intended to be legally binding is contained in s.18 of the Trade Union and Labour Relations Act 1974, which provides that collective agreements between employees and trade unions are presumed not to be legally binding unless they are made in writing and expressly state that the agreement is to be legally binding.

---

1 *Balfour v Balfour* [1919] 2 KB 571, CA.
2 *Coward v Motor Insurers Bureau* [1963] 1 QB 259, [1962] 1 All ER 531, CA.
3 [1955] 3 All ER 10, [1955] 1 WLR 975.
4 [1925] AC 445, HL.
5 [1976] 1 All ER 117, [1976] 1 WLR 1, HL.

CONSIDERATION

6.3 Agreements not made under seal[1] must be supported by consideration if they are to be enforceable, and a person who wishes to enforce a contract must show that he himself provided consideration. It is in the requirement of consideration that English law recognises the idea that a contract is a bargain. If you wish to receive the benefit of the contract you must do something to earn that benefit, either by promising to do something or actually doing something. If a person does something at the request of another, e.g. finding a lost dog or refraining from smoking in return for the promise of a reward, he thereby not only accepts the offer of a reward but also provides consideration and the contract is known as a unilateral contract. If a party to an agreement promises to do something in response to a promise by the other, as where X promises to pay for goods to be supplied by Y, he thereby provides consideration, and the contract is known as a bilateral contract. Consideration has been defined in terms of benefit to the promisor and detriment to the promisee[2], and certainly if there is either a benefit or a detriment to the appropriate party that is good consideration. But this definition has been criticized and some cases cannot be explained in terms of benefit and detriment. A more modern view of consideration is that each party's action or forbearance, promised or actual, is the price for which the other's is bought, and without that price there would be no bargain[3].

---

1 Para. 7.4.
2 *Currie v Misa* (1875) LR 10 Exch 153.
3 *Dunlop Pneumatic Tyre Co Ltd v Selfridge & Co Ltd* [1915] AC 847 at 855.

6.4 Consideration may be 'executed', i.e. an act done in response to a promise by the other party to the agreement, for example, finding and returning the lost dog for whose return a reward was promised. Alternatively, it may be 'executory', i.e. a promise of action in response to a promise of the other party, for example, to pay for goods which are to be made by the other party. The concept of executory consideration illustrates the difficulty of the benefit and detriment theory of consideration. When no one has done anything and there are merely promises there is no benefit or detriment to anyone, but it is possible to say that the price of one party's promise was the promise made by the other party. Both executed and executory consideration are good consideration in law, unlike past consideration.

The fact that past consideration is not good consideration illustrates the idea that consideration is the price of a promise. In *Re McArdle*[1], work was done on a family house by X. Her relations then promised to reimburse the cost to her of this work but failed to keep their promise. X sued but failed in her claim for the promised sum because she had provided no consideration for the promise to pay, since the action which she alleged constituted consideration pre-dated the promise by the relatives. The motive for the promise was to reimburse for work done but since the work was not done at the request of the relatives and it was complete before the promise was made, it was past consideration and thus not good consideration. It would be wrong to think that all actions preceding a promise constitute past consideration. If an action is done at the request of another and the action is such that there is a clear expectation that it will be paid for, then the action is good consideration for any claim for payment[2]. The action which raises the expectation may be followed by a promise to pay, if this is so, then the promise quantifies the amount due to the party who performed the requested act. If there is no subsequent promise then the amount due is determined on a *quantum meruit* basis. What transforms apparently past consideration into good consideration is the fact that the action is in response to a request which raises an expectation of payment. The requested action is the price of the implied promise to pay. In the case of *Re McArdle*[3] there was no prior request or expectation of payment. However, in *Re Casey's Patents, Stewart v Casey*[4], the plaintiffs wrote to Casey saying that 'in consideration of your services as practical manager' they would give him a one-third share in certain patents. This promise was fulfilled but subsequently the plaintiffs sought to recover the patents, claiming Casey had given no consideration for their promise. The Court of Appeal rejected the argument of the plaintiffs, saying that Casey's services as manager clearly raised an implication that they would be paid for and the subsequent promise of payment (by the gift of patents) was enforceable. The court gave two alternative explanations for its decision:

a. because of the implication that payment would be forthcoming the consideration was not past consideration merely because it pre-dated the promise; or

b. because of the implication that payment would be forthcoming the party providing the services could pursue a *quantum meruit* claim[5].

In certain cases consideration which is genuinely past consideration, is good consideration in law. One such case is that of cheques and other bills of exchange. The Bills of Exchange Act 1882 provides that valuable consideration may be constituted by an 'antecedent debt or liability' i.e. by past consideration[6].

---

1   [1951] Ch 669, [1951] 1 All ER 905, CA.
2   *Lampleigh v Braithwait* (1615) Hob 105.
3   [1951] Ch 669, [1951] 1 All ER 905, CA.
4   [1892] 1 Ch 104, CA.
5   Para. 17.8.
6   S.27; see further para. 24.12.

6.5 In determining whether a contract is supported by consideration the courts have regard to two factors.

a. consideration must have some value but need not be adequate; and

b. consideration must be real and sufficient, i.e. what is alleged to be consideration must be an action or promise which the law recognises as capable of being consideration.

Adequacy

6.6 Providing that the alleged consideration has some economic value the courts will not question its adequacy. If the parties to the agreement consider the consideration to be adequate the courts will not intervene even if one party is apparently making a very good bargain and the other is not. In *Mountford v Scott*[1], £1 was paid for an option to purchase a house and this was found to be good consideration. Money is always considered to have an economic value and the fact that the amount was small was irrelevant. In *Chappell & Co Ltd v Nestlé Co Ltd*[2], customers were invited to send for a record, enclosing 1s 6d, and three wrappers from the defendant's chocolate bars. The House of Lords found that while the wrappers might have little intrinsic value (they were indeed thrown away on their receipt), they formed part of the consideration provided by purchasers of the record. There are other examples which illustrate that the courts will not question the adequacy of consideration.

---

1 [1975] 1 All ER 198, [1975] 2 WLR 114, CA.
2 [1960] AC 87, [1959] 2 All ER 701, HL.

Forbearance to sue

6.7 If a person who could sue another agrees not to pursue his claim, that constitutes good consideration for a promise by the other person. There is in fact a benefit to the person not sued and a detriment to the party who could sue. It might be thought that agreeing to abandon an invalid claim[1] cannot be good consideration. However, the abandonment of an invalid claim will be good consideration if the party abandoning the claim can show that he genuinely believed the claim had some chance of success[2] and that he was not concealing from the other party facts that would constitute a defence to the claim[3]. The argument is that abandoning a doubtful claim saves the parties from the uncertainties of litigation and its attendant expense.

The same principles apply where there is no actual agreement not to sue but the potential plaintiff in fact refrains from pursuing a claim, provided the forbearance would not have been displayed but for the promise of the potential defendant[4].

---

1 For example in *Poteliakhoff v Teakle* [1938] 2 KB 816, [1938] 3 All ER 686, CA, an agreement not to sue on unenforceable gaming debts was not good consideration for a promise by the debtor.
2 *Horton v Horton (No. 2)* [1961] 1 QB 215, [1960] 3 All ER 649, CA.
3 *Miles v New Zealand Alford Estate Co* (1886) 32 Ch D 266.
4 *Alliance Bank Ltd v Broom* (1864) 2 Dr & Sm 289.

Gratuitous services

6.8 If a person voluntarily undertakes to do something for another there is no apparent consideration and if the service is performed defectively no contractual claim can be maintained. There may, of course, be a claim in tort. However, in some cases, the courts have found consideration, despite its apparent absence, and allowed a contractual claim. If the courts paid the slightest heed to the view that consideration must be adequate the following case would clearly have been decided differently.

In *Gore v Van der Lann*[1], the plaintiff was injured while boarding a bus and sued the conductor. The plaintiff was travelling on a free bus pass which contained an exemption clause. By statute the clause was invalid if contained in a contract of carriage. The Court of Appeal found she was travelling under such a contract based on the terms of the pass, the consideration she provided being 'a detriment in return for the advantages gained'.

---

1 [1967] 2 QB 31, [1967] 1 All ER 360, CA.

Bailment

6.9 Bailment is a transfer of possession of goods on condition that they will eventually be restored to the owner, e.g. pawning articles, leaving them in a left luggage office or lending them to a person. The very fact that there is a bailment gives rise to certain duties on the part of the bailee even if there is no consideration given by the owner. If the owner seeks to impose duties above those imposed by law on the bailee he can do so in a contract of bailment. The consideration which the courts require to support a contract of bailment is extremely slight: indeed in some cases it is difficult to find any consideration[1].

---

1 *Bainbridge v Firmstone* (1838) 8 Ad & El 743.

Sufficiency

6.10 In certain cases the law will not recognise an action or promise as capable of constituting good consideration. Some actions and promises which are recognised as capable of constituting consideration cannot be satisfactorily explained in terms of benefit and detriment, which supports the view that this definition of consideration is no longer acceptable.

Performance of an existing duty imposed by law

6.11 The law imposes obligations on all people, and it is necessary to decide if performing or promising to perform such an obligation can also be good consideration for a contractual promise of another. The basic position was stated in *Collins v Godefroy*[1], in which the plaintiff gave evidence at the defendant's trial in response to a promise of payment. When he sued for the payment, it was held that he could not succeed because he had provided no consideration since he was obliged by law to give evidence.

But, if the court can discover that the party seeking to show that he provided consideration did more than was required by law, that can constitute good consideration. Since consideration need not be adequate it does not matter that what is done exceeds the legal requirements only slightly. This may be demonstrated by two cases. In *Glasbrook Bros v Glamorgan County Council*[2], the company requested greater protection for their mine during a strike than the police thought necessary and offered to pay for the increased police presence. The company later refused to pay, claiming that, since the police were under a legal duty to protect property, they had provided no consideration for the promise of payment by the company. The House of Lords held that the company was obliged to pay because, while the police were required to guard the mine, they were free to choose the form of protection, and in this case they had provided more protection than they thought necessary at the request of the company. In *Ward v Byham*[3], the father of an illegitimate child promised to pay its mother £1 a week for its maintenance if she looked after it, kept it well and happy, and allowed it to choose which parent it wished to live with. When the payments stopped and the mother sued the father, he alleged that since the mother of an illegitimate child is required by statute to maintain it she had provided no consideration for his promise. The Court of Appeal managed to discover that the mother had done more than her legal duty and thus provided consideration for the promise, in that as well as maintaining the child she had agreed to keep it well and happy and allow it to choose with which parent to live.

---

1 (1831) 1 B & Ad 950.
2 [1925] AC 270, HL.
3 [1956] 2 All ER 318, [1956] 1 WLR 496, CA.

Performance of an existing contractual duty owed to the other party
6.12 If a person is under a contractual duty to do something, a promise to perform it cannot be good consideration for another promise by the person to whom the contractual duty is already owed. In *Stilk v Myrick*[1], the crew of a ship were paid a lump sum for a voyage including all normal emergencies. During the voyage two of the crew deserted and the captain promised to pay the wages of the deserters to the rest of the crew if they would continue the voyage short-handed. Once returned to England, the extra wages were not paid and the seamen sued. Their claim failed, the court finding they had provided no consideration since they were required to cope with normal emergencies by their existing contracts. Desertion or death of fellow crew members was a normal emergency so they had done no more than they had contracted to do. But the court stressed that, if they had promised to do more than they were obliged to do by their existing contracts, that would have been good consideration. For example, if they had promised to face exceptional hazards that would have been good consideration for the promise of their employer[2].

---

1 (1809) 2 Camp 317.
2 Cf. *Hartley v Ponsonby* (1857) 7 E & B 872.

6.13 *Debts at common law* Particular difficulty has arisen over debts. If A is under a contractual obligation to pay B and B agrees to forego part of the debt, A has provided no consideration for B's promise and B can subsequently sue for the remainder of the debt. In *Foakes v Beer*[1], Mrs. Beer was owed money under a judgment debt by Dr. Foakes. She agreed to accept payment by instalments but the agreement did not refer to the question of interest, which is payable on a judgment debt. Dr. Foakes paid the debt and, when Mrs. Beer sued for the interest, Dr. Foakes pleaded the agreement whereby Mrs. Beer had agreed to bring no further action on the judgment. Mrs. Beer contended successfully that there was no consideration for her promise. Dr. Foakes owed her money and agreeing to pay it by instalments could not be consideration for a promise by her to take no further action. He was merely doing what he was obliged to do. The House of Lords regretted that this decision must be reached but considered themselves bound by previous cases. One of their Lordships thought that since prompt part-payment of a debt could be more beneficial than full payment over a lengthy period such part-payment should be good consideration for a promise to remit the rest of the debt, but felt constrained to agree with the rest of the House.

There are exceptions to the rule that part payment of a debt is no consideration for a promise to remit the rest of the debt. In *Pinnel's Case*[2], for instance, it was said that early payment of part of a debt, or part-payment at another place than that specified for payment, or payment in kind, even if the value of the goods is less than the debt, is good consideration for a promise to forego the remainder of the debt. Thus, if A owes B £100 payable on 1 January 2001 at Reading and B accepts either £1 on 31 December or £1 at Oxford on the correct day, or a rose or a scarf on the correct day, then the debt is validly discharged[3]. It used to be thought that a part payment by cheque was good consideration for a promise to remit a debt payable in cash. This has been rejected by the Court of Appeal who decided that nowadays there is no effective difference between cash and a cheque which is honoured[4].

---

1 (1884) 9 App Cas 605, HL.
2 E.g. *Pinnel's Case* (1602) 5 Co Rep 117a, which established the basic rule regretted by the House of Lords in *Foakes v Beer* (1884) 9 App Cas 605.
3 For other exceptions see para. 6.16.
4 *D. and C. Builders Ltd v Rees* [1966] 2 QB 617, [1965] 3 All ER 837, CA.

6.14 *Debts in equity* Apart from these exceptions it appeared that a debtor who paid part of a debt and believed that the creditor agreed to remit the remainder of the debt had no defence if that creditor sought to recover the amount foregone. However, in 1947 Denning, J, (as he was then) called upon equity to aid the debtor. In *Central London Property Trust Ltd v High Trees House Ltd*[1], the plaintiffs let a block of flats to the defendants in 1937 for 99 years at a rent of £2,500 per year. The defendants intended to sub-let the flats, but because of the war found they had many vacant flats and could not pay the rent out of profits. The plaintiffs agreed to accept a reduced rent of £1,250, which was paid quarterly from 1941 until September 1945, by which time all the flats were let. The plaintiffs demanded full rent from September 1945 and claimed the amount of rent underpaid during the previous quarter. The defendants had provided no consideration for the promise by the plaintiffs to remit the rent. Denning, J, found that, while the common law provided no defence, equity did. The judge, drawing on little known cases, said that where one party gave a promise which he intended should be acted on, and which was acted on, that promise must be honoured. In this case the plaintiffs had promised to reduce the rent, they knew the defendants would act on this and the defendants did so act, therefore the rent underpaid in the past could not be demanded by the plaintiffs since this would be inequitable. However, the judge found that the promise was intended to apply only while certain conditions prevailed. These conditions were the difficulties of finding tenants because of the war, and when this condition no longer applied the promise to remit part of the rent ceased to bind the plaintiffs. The judge also suggested that a promise of this type might be terminated by notice. This case illustrates the equitable doctrine known as promissory or quasi-estoppel[2] which applies to promises to remit debts and also promises not to enforce other contractual terms[3].

---

1 [1947] KB 130, [1956] 1 All ER 256n.
2 Estoppel (as opposed to promissory estoppel) is a legal doctrine whereby if a person misrepresents an existing fact and intends this misrepresentation to be acted on and it is acted on he cannot subsequently deny the truth of that fact. The doctrine was inapplicable in the *High Trees* case because the representation was as to the future not an existing fact.
3 Para. 6.34.

6.15 The boundaries of promissory estoppel were uncertain in 1947, but it was soon established that the doctrine could only be used as a defence to an action and not to found an action. In *Combe v Combe*[1], a husband agreed, informally, to pay his divorced wife maintenance. He failed to pay the promised sum and she sued him. She had provided no consideration for her husband's promise and therefore based her claim on the fact that she had acted on the promise by not seeking an order for maintenance from the court. The Court of Appeal rejected her claim saying that promissory estoppel was a shield, i.e. a defence, and not a sword.

The cases on estoppel show that an estoppel may be founded on the conduct as well as the statements of a party and promissory estoppel can also be based on conduct, if that conduct is acted on, and the other requirements of promissory estoppel are satisfied.

A problem which arises in determining the scope of promissory estoppel is that it is not certain whether the party who relies on the promise must act on it to his detriment, or whether it is sufficient for him simply to rely on it[2]. Certainly there was no detriment in *High Trees* itself and it is thought that mere reliance would suffice. The idea of detriment appears to be borrowed from the common law.

It is clear that promissory estoppel will only operate if it would be inequitable to allow the promisor to enforce his contractual rights. If the promisee is deserving of no sympathy, and justice and equity are on the side of the party seeking to enforce his contractual rights, promissory estoppel will provide no defence for the promisee. In *D. and C. Builders Ltd v Rees*[3], the plaintiffs were owed £482 by the defendant who knew they were in desperate need of money to stave off bankruptcy. The defendant offered the plaintiffs £300 in settlement of the debt saying that if they refused they would get nothing. The plaintiffs accepted the £300 reluctantly and sued for the balance. The Court of Appeal refused to allow the defendant to rely on promissory estoppel: his conduct had been inequitable and therefore he was not deserving of equitable aid.

The principal area of controversy surrounding promissory estoppel is the effect of the doctrine. In *High Trees*, the judge found that the promise not to seek full rent only operated while the conditions contemplated by the parties (lack of tenants) prevailed, i.e. the effect of the promise was only to suspend contractual rights. But if the contractual payment was not periodic (as rent is) but a single payment, or if the promise was not to enforce some other term, the effect of the doctrine is uncertain. Promissory estoppel could either have the effect of suspending contractual rights or the effect of abrogating contractual rights completely. If the doctrine merely suspends rights until they are re-activated by notice a further problem arises. It is uncertain whether such re-activation is retrospective in effect or whether it re-activates contractual rights only for the future. The House of Lords discussed the question in *Tool Metal Manufacturing Co Ltd v Tungsten Electric Co Ltd*[4], and found that if equity had intervened that equitable intervention had been terminated by notice. The House, while not called upon to discuss the principle of promissory estoppel, said that its effect, if any, was merely suspensory and not abrogatory. If the effect is suspensory then it can be terminated by adequate notice and any debts owing are revived. But apparently if the contractual obligation which is re-activated by notice is of a periodic type e.g. rent, that contractual obligation is re-activated only for the future and not retrospectively.

Promissory estoppel is closely linked with the doctrine of waiver of contractual terms and accord and satisfaction, which we mention later[5].

---

1   [1951] 2 KB 215, [1951] 1 All ER 767, CA.
2   In fact in many cases of estoppel and promissory estoppel there is detriment anyway.
3   [1966] 2 QB 617, [1965] 3 All ER 837, CA.
4   [1955] 2 All ER 657, [1955] 1 WLR 761, HL.
5   Para. 6.32—6.34 and 6.36.

Compositions with creditors

6.16   There are two somewhat anomalous areas where performance of an existing contractual duty can amount to consideration. Both areas concern debts. Firstly, where a debtor makes an arrangement with all his creditors that they will all be paid a given percentage of what they are owed, no creditor can recover more than that given percentage. There is no logical explanation of why this arrangement with creditors is legally binding since there is no consideration in the usual sense. Secondly, when a third party discharges part of a debt, that is a valid discharge of the whole debt[1]. While this can be understood where any attempt to recover the remainder of the debt would be fraudulent, e.g. where the partial discharge was made on the strict understanding that the rest of the debt would be remitted[2], the principle extends to cases where there is no fraud.

---

1 *Welby v Drake* (1825) 1 C & P 557.
2 *Hirachand Punamchand v Temple* [1911] 2 KB 330, CA.

Performance of an existing contractual duty owed to a third party
6.17 If a party to a contract is obliged to perform some action it might be thought that a promise to perform or the performance of that action cannot be good consideration for a promise by a third party But the cases would seem to suggest that the opposite is true. Two nineteenth century decisions permitted the discharge of a pre-existing contractual obligation to constitute consideration for another contract. Neither case is entirely free from difficulty. In *Scotson v Pegg*[1], the plaintiff had contracted to deliver coal to X, or wherever X ordered it to be delivered. X sold the coal to the defendants and told the plaintiff to deliver it to them. The defendants then agreed with the plaintiff that if he delivered the coal they would unload it at a given rate. The defendant failed to unload at this rate and when sued argued that the plaintiff had provided no consideration for their promise. The court found for the plaintiff but for reasons which are far from clear. In *Chichester v Cobb*[2], the defendant promised one of the plaintiffs (who were engaged) that, in consideration of their marriage and once all their arrangements were complete, he would pay her £300. The defendant failed to pay the £300 and the plaintiffs sued successfully for the money. The judge held there was consideration for the defendant's promise without specifying what it was.

The principle which is gleaned from these cases, that discharge of a pre-existing contractual duty owed to a third party can be good consideration for another's promise, was approved recently by the Privy Council in *New Zealand Shipping Co Ltd v A. M. Satterthwaite & Co Ltd*[3]. In this case, consideration for a promise consisted of unloading a ship which the party in question was already bound to unload under a contract with a third party. It is thought that the principle involved in these cases only extends to cases where the consideration has been

119

provided and not to those where there is only a promise to provide consideration, i.e. where consideration is executed and not executory.

---

1   (1861) 6 H & N 295.
2   (1866) 14 LT 433.
3   [1975] AC 154, [1974] 1 All ER 1015, PC.

Consideration must move from the promisee

6.18 It is not sufficient that there is consideration in the abstract: it is also necessary for a person who wishes to enforce a promise to show that he provided consideration. This bears a strong resemblance to the doctrine or privity of contract which states that a person who is not party to a contract cannot sue on it. In some early cases claims failed either on the basis that the party seeking to enforce the contract had provided no consideration or because he was not a party to the agreement[1]. But later cases have shown that consideration and privity are two separate requirements and not two facets of the same rule[2]. In many cases it is not necessary to decide on which basis a claim fails but if, as it seems, the rules are separate it is not sufficient to be a party to an agreement to enforce it, consideration must also be provided[3].

---

1   *Price v Easton* (1833) 4 B & Ad 433.
2   For example *Dunlop Pneumatic Tyre Co Ltd v Selfridge & Co Ltd* [1915] AC 847, HL.
3   There are cases which suggest that consideration in general and not moving specifically from the promise might suffice, see para. 6.23.

PRIVITY OF CONTRACT

6.19 It is apparently a distinct rule of English law that only those persons who are parties to a contract may sue and be sued on that contract, subject to certain recognised exceptions. There are two consequences of the doctrine: a person not a party to a contract is not entitled to enforce the contract, even apparently if it was intended to benefit him and he provided consideration; and a contract cannot impose obligations on a stranger to it. Suggested reasons for the doctrine are: a. that mere donees should not be able to enforce a contract (but the doctrine operates even against those who provide consideration); and b. that the parties to the contract should not have their freedom to vary it restricted by the existence of third party rights. There seems more justification for refusing to allow a contract to impose a burden on a third party than in denying the benefit of a contract to a third party whom the contract sought to benefit.

Established exceptions

6.20 There are certain established exceptions to the doctrine of privity of contract. If an agent enters into an authorised contract with a third party on behalf of his principal, there is a contract between the principal and the third party[1]. It is possible to assign rights under a contract[2]. A third party can sue on a bill of exchange or cheque[3]. Beneficiaries under certain contracts of insurance have a statutory right to claim the benefit of the contract of insurance even if they are not parties to the contract. For example, a spouse can take the benefit of a contract of life insurance entered into by the other spouse[4].

Another possible exception to the doctrine of privity spawned by commercial necessity concerns bankers commercial credits. It is clearly a risk for businessmen to despatch goods to sellers of whom they know nothing because they may never be paid or payment, if it depends on delivery, may be long delayed. To alleviate these difficulties it is common for sellers to require buyers to open an irrevocable letter of credit in their favour. A buyer will arrange this with his bank (he will reimburse the bank and usually a fee is also payable) and the bank will pay the seller as soon as delivery commences. The bank protects its interests by taking the shipping documents as security[5]. It can be argued that the seller is not party to the agreement between the buyer and his bank about payment and that if the bank fails to pay the buyer the seller would have no remedy against the bank. The seller might also be met by the argument that he had provided no consideration for the arrangement of the buyer and his bank. There are dicta to the effect that a well established commercial system should not be upset by a strict application of the rules of contract[6]. The court may indeed find consideration between the seller and the buyer's bank if the seller acted upon the faith of the letter of credit[7], but the bank may be bound even before the seller begins to act on the faith of the letter of credit[8].

The requirements of land law have also necessitated some modifications of the strict rules of privity. The benefits and burdens of covenants in leases are transferred to successors in title of the landlord and tenant, despite the absence of privity, if the covenants affect the land[9]. Indeed, even on the sale of property it is common to insert in the contract of sale covenants governing the use of the land. These covenants may bind subsequent purchasers and occupiers of the land if they are negative in nature, providing that the subsequent occupier is not a bona fide purchaser for value without notice[10] and that the person claiming the benefit of the covenant has land capable of benefiting by its enforcement[11].

---

1 Chap. 18.
2 Chap. 19.

3 Bills of Exchange Act 1882, s.29.
4 Married Women's Property Act 1882, s.11. Also see Chap. 24.
5 For an analysis of the system of commercial credits see *Trans Trust S.P.R.L. v Danubian Trading Co Ltd* [1952] 2 QB 297 at 304, [1952] 1 All ER 570, CA.
6 *United Dominions Trust v Kirkwood* [1966] 2 QB 431, [1966] 1 All ER 968, CA.
7 *Urquhart Lindsay & Co Ltd v Eastern Bank Ltd* [1922] 1 KB 318.
8 For example, it has been suggested that the bank is bound as soon as it informs the seller that an irrevocable credit has been established, *Commercial Banking Co of Sydney Ltd v Jalsard Pty Ltd* [1973] AC 279, PC.
9 Law of Property Act 1925, ss. 78, 79 and ss. 141, 142.
10 Para. 4.29.
11 *Tulk v Moxhay* (1848) 2 Ph 774.

6.21 The above situations are exceptions or possible exceptions to the doctrine of privity. It may also be possible to outflank the rule. If a collateral contract can be found, a person not a party to the principal contract can sue on the collateral contract. In *Shanklin Pier Ltd v Detel Products Ltd*[1], the plaintiffs employed contractors to paint their pier and instructed them to buy and use the defendants' paint. The defendants had told the plaintiffs the paint would last for seven to 10 years, but it lasted for only three months. The judge found that while the plaintiffs could not sue on the contract of sale, to which they were not parties, they could sue on a collateral contract between them and the defendants which contained a promise — that the paint would last seven to 10 years. The plaintiffs had provided consideration for the collateral contract by requiring their contractors to use the defendants' paint. Similarly, in *Andrews v Hopkinson*[2], the plaintiff entered into a contract of hire-purchase with a finance company for a car after the car dealer had misrepresented that she was a 'good little bus'. It was held that the dealer was liable under a collateral contract between himself and the plaintiff[3].

1 [1951] 2 KB 8541, [1951] 2 All ER 471, CA.
2 [1957] 1 QB 229, [1956] 3 All ER 422.
3 See now Consumer Credit Act 1974, s.56 for a possible claim against the finance company, para. 23.32.

6.22 Apart from these recognised exceptions there have been other attempts to evade the doctrine of privity and to confer benefits or impose burdens on strangers to a contract.

Benefits

Enforcement by the party intended to benefit
6.23 Prior to *Tweddle v Atkinson*[1] it was possible to confer a benefit on a person if there was some family relationship between the intended

beneficiary and one of the contracting parties. However, in *Tweddle v Atkinson*, a contract between the plaintiff's father and X for the benefit of the plaintiff was regarded as unenforceable by the plaintiff. It may be possible to confer a benefit on someone not really involved in a contract by making him a party to the agreement even if in name only. Unfortunately, the party whom this is intended to benefit may be unable to show that he provided any consideration. The High Court of Australia suggested a circumvention of this difficulty obiter in *Coulls v Bagot's Executor and Trustee Co Ltd*[2], where a contract for the right to quarry a mine made all royalties payable to X, who granted the right, and his wife. The High Court of Australia held that the wife could have been entitled to the royalties after her husband's death because she was a party to the contract, even though she had provided no consideration, since the promise was supported by consideration. The English courts do not yet seem ready to follow the Australian approach.

1   (1861) 1 B & S 393.
2   [1967] ALR 385.

6.24   Some judges have constructed an argument, intended to defeat the doctrine of privity, based on the Law of Property Act 1925, s.56. They argue that the section abolished the doctrine of privity and allowed intended beneficiaries of contracts not named as parties to that contract to enforce the agreement[1]. This view was rejected by the House of Lords in *Beswick v Beswick*[2], and s.56 has effectively been limited to cases involving land where the contract, while not naming the third party, is intended to be made with him as well as benefiting him.

1   *Beswick v Beswick* [1966] Ch 538, [1966] 3 All ER 1, CA; *Drive Yourself Hire Co (London) Ltd v Strutt* [1954] 1 QB 250, [1953] 2 All ER 1475, CA.
2   [1968] AC 58, [1967] 2 All ER 1197, HL.

6.25   The most effective evasion of privity other than those discussed in paras. 6.20 and 6.21 is the use of a trust. The subject-matter of a trust is normally tangible property, but when used in this context the subject-matter of the trust is the promise given by one party to a contract to the other party that he will benefit a third party. In equity, if a trust of a promise can be discovered, the courts will enforce an agreement for the benefit of the third party; he is regarded as a beneficiary and the party contracting for his benefit as a trustee. In *Lloyd's v Harper*[1], Lush, LJ, said that, 'when a contract is made with A for the benefit of B, A can sue on the contract for the benefit of B and recover all that B could have recovered if the contract had been made by B himself'. In this case creditors of a Lloyd's underwriter sought to sue the guarantor of that underwriter on the contract of guarantee. The contract was with Lloyd's, not the creditors, but the Court of Appeal held Lloyd's could recover on behalf of the creditors, and not merely for their own loss. The difficulty with using the trust concept to defeat the doctrine of privity is that it is not certain when it will apply, and the type of trust recognised by these cases cannot be regarded as the usual type of trust which is subject to strict rules clearly inapplicable here. *Lloyd's v Harper* allowed the trustee to recover for the third party, it did not give a right to sue to the third party. However, it seems that if the third party wishes to sue he can do so by joining as co-plaintiff the party to the contract who was hoping to benefit him[2]. If the trustee pursues a claim for the beneficiary any damages are payable to the beneficiary. If the trustee refuses to sue either alone or as co-plaintiff there seems no reason why he should not be joined as co-defendant in an action by the third party beneficiary.

Although no formal words are required, an intention to create a trust, not merely an intention to benefit a third party, must exist, and this is the principal reason why the application of the trust concept is uncertain. The courts generally seem reluctant to use the trust concept to circumvent the doctrine of privity. Some cases illustrate the difficulties of determining if there is the necessary intention to create a trust. In *Re Flavell, Murray v Flavell*[3], the terms of a partnership (the contract) provided that the executors of a deceased partner should be paid a certain sum for his widow. The executors were held to be trustees for the widow. However, in *Re Schebsman*[4], a contract between Schebsman and X Ltd, that in certain circumstances his wife and daughter should be paid a lump sum, was held not to create a trust. The Court of Appeal was influenced by the fact that Schebsman and the company might have wished to vary the agreement which would have been impossible had the contract created a trust. Finally, in *Green v Russell*[5], a contract of insurance between Russell and an insurance company made certain sums payable if any of his employees died. Green, an employee, died and the Court of Appeal found there was no trust of the sum due under the contract of insurance. *Beswick v Beswick*[6], the most important recent case on privity of contract does not discuss trusts and so this attempt to outflank privity seems to have been limited by the courts.

---

1   (1880) 16 Ch D 290, CA.
2   *Les Affréteur Réunis SA v Leopold Walford London Ltd* [1919] AC 801, HL.
3   (1883), 25 Ch D 89, CA.
4   [1944] Ch 83, [1943] 2 All ER 768, CA.
5   [1959] 2 QB 226, [1959] 2 All ER 525, CA.
6   [1968] AC 58, [1967] 2 All ER 1197, HL.

Enforcement by a party to the contract

6.26 The party who intended to confer the benefit on the third party may be prepared to sue if the other party to the agreement does not carry out his contractual obligations. The usual remedies for failure to perform contractual obligations are available, but there are severe difficulties if the contract was intended to benefit not the plaintiff but a third party. For example, if A and B agreed that in consideration of A agreeing to do something B would pay C £100, A could not sue for that £100 to be paid to him. That is not enforcing the contract but rewriting it and unacceptable, even though B had effectively agreed to pay £100 for the specified act. An order of specific performance may be granted or damages awarded[1]. The use of specific performance is illustrated by *Beswick v Beswick*[2]. In this case, in consideration of Peter Beswick transferring his business to his nephew, the nephew agreed to pay his uncle a pension and, after his death, a weekly annuity to his widow. The nephew paid his uncle the pension but only one payment of the annuity was made. The widow, as administratix of her husband's estate, successfully sued her nephew for specific performance of the contract to pay the annuity, although the House of Lords implied that she would not have succeeded if she had sued merely as the intended recipient. Thus, if specific performance of a contract can be ordered, a party to a contract or his personal representative can ensure enforcement of the contract for the benefit of a third party. However, the courts will not always order specific performance, it is a discretionary remedy.

The converse of specific performance, whereby a contract is enforced by the court, is an injunction whereby an action is required to cease. An injunction may be awarded to restrain a breach of contract adversely affecting a third party at the suit of a contracting party. However, if the breach of contract consists of pursuing a legal claim against the third party, such an action cannot be restrained by injunction[3], though a stay of the proceedings may be ordered if the contract embodied the promise not to sue the third party *and* the party seeking to stay the proceedings has a sufficient interest in the cesser of the action[4]. Indeed, in *Snelling v John G. Snelling Ltd*[5], where the defendant had no apparent interest in the cesser of proceedings. A stay was granted because all the relevant parties were before the court.

---

1   For remedies in general see Chap. 12.
2   [1968] AC 58, [1967] 2 All ER 1197, HL.
3   Supreme Court of Judicature (Consolidation) Act 1925, s.41.
4   *Gore v Van Der Lann* [1967] 2 QB 31, [1967] 1 All ER 360, CA.
5   [1973] QB 87, [1972] 1 All ER 79.

6.27 The House of Lords in *Beswick v Beswick*[1] also discussed the question of damages and concluded that a contracting party could only sue for his loss and not for the loss suffered by the third party so that damages might only be nominal. Certainly, in *Beswick v Beswick*, damages would have been nominal because the husband's estate suffered no loss when the widow was not paid her annuity. Had the husband's estate suffered loss, e.g. if the widow had been able to pursue a claim against the estate because she was deprived of her annuity, damages might have been substantial. However, in *Jackson v Horizon Holidays Ltd*[2], the Court of Appeal took a wider view. The plaintiff entered into a contract with a holiday firm for a holiday for his family and himself in Ceylon. The holiday was a disaster. The plaintiff was able to recover substantial damages not merely for himself but also for his family, although the court gave no explanation of how damages were to be assessed. A further problem with damages is that the successful litigant may refuse to pay them to the third party whom the contract intended to benefit. If this occurs it seems the third party has no remedy against the litigant. Equally the third party cannot require a party to the contract to sue on that contract[3].

If it happens that an award of damages or an order of specific performance results in money being paid directly to the third party, and not to a party to the contract, the third party can keep the money if this is in accordance with the term of the contract.

---

1 [1968] AC 58, [1967] 2 All ER 1197, HL.
2 [1975] 3 All ER 92, [1975] 1 WLR 1468, CA.
3 *Beswick v Beswick* [1968] AC 58, [1967] 2 All ER 1197, HL.

Burdens

6.28 If the person intended to benefit from a contract has no direct right to enforce that contract then equally it should not be possible to impose a contractual burden on a third party. The doctrine of privity by land law[1] and the modifications developed by land law have been extended to create two further exceptions so that:

a. it may be possible to impose restrictions on the use of certain chattels; and

b. it is possible for the *maximum* resale price of goods to be fixed by their supplier[2].

---

1 Para. 6.20.
2 For the position where there is an attempt to fix a minimum resale price, see para. 15.43.

Restrictions on the use of chattels

6.29 In *De Mattos v Gibson*[1], X, the owner of a ship chartered her to the plaintiff, but subsequently mortgaged the ship to the defendant. The plaintiff alleged that the defendant was intending to sell the ship in disregard of his contractual rights and sought an interlocutory injunction to restrain this. An injunction was granted, and the case is authority for the principle that contractual obligations attaching to chattels can bind third parties who have notice of those existing contractual rights when they acquire the chattel. This principle is based on a dictum of Knight Bruce LJ, who gave no authority for the existence of such a principle. The dictum of Knight Bruce LJ is to the effect that if a person acquires property from another knowing that that property is subject to a binding contract giving a third party a right to use that property for a particular purpose, the acquiror cannot use the property in such a way that it interferes with the existing contractual rights. The principle enunciated in this case has received approval in the Privy Council[2] but it was strongly doubted in *Port Line Ltd v Ben Line Steamers Ltd*[3]. In *Port Line Ltd v Ben Line Steamers Ltd*, a ship under charter to the plaintiffs was sold to the defendants who knew of the charter but not its terms. The ship was requisitioned because of the Suez crisis and compensation was paid to the defendants. This compensation was claimed by the plaintiffs who based their claim on their charter party. Diplock J, rejecting the plaintiffs claim, thought that the principle based on *De Mattos v Gibson* did not exist; or if it did exist it applied only to allow the granting of an injunction to restrain a breach of contract (and not to a claim for damages or compensation), and then only if the purchaser knew not only that there was a contract relating to the chattel but also the terms of that contract.

Since other cases have sought to limit the principle in *De Mattos v Gibson* to ships under charter (and perhaps by analogy aircraft)[4], the principle, if it exists at all, is severely limited.

---

1 (1858) 4 De G & J 276, CA.
2 *Lord Strathcona SS Co v Dominion Coal Co* [1926] AC 108, PC.
3 [1958] 2 QB 146, [1958] 1 All ER 787.
4 *Clore v Theatrical Properties Ltd* [1936] 3 All ER 483, CA.

Restrictions on price

6.30 Prior to 1956 a contract of sale which fixed the resale price of goods could not, because of the doctrine of privity, bind a third party who could sell any goods he acquired for whatever price he desired. Under s.26 of the Resale Prices Act 1976, a supplier who sells goods under a contract which provides a *maximum* resale price can enforce that price against anyone not party to the contract who acquires the goods for resale with notice of that maximum resale price. Any attempt to fix a minimum price is void by virtue of s.9 of the Resale Prices Act 1976 unless the goods are exempt from the operation of the 1976 Act[1].

---

1 Paras. 15.42–15.45.

CONSIDERATION: DISCHARGE AND VARIATION

6.31 We have seen that consideration is necessary for the formation of contracts, and that a promise by the creditor to remit a debt is not binding without the provision of consideration by the debtor. We will now discuss whether consideration is necessary when the parties agree to terminate or vary their contract before the contract is completely performed. Discharge and variation may arise either where both parties still have contractual obligations to perform, i.e. there is executory consideration on both sides, or where one party still has contractual obligations to perform but the other party has completed his performance of the contract. Apart from the question of whether consideration is necessary to effect a binding discharge or variation, it is also necessary to discuss whether the agreement which purports to discharge or vary the contract must be made in any particular form.

We discuss other methods of discharge of contracts in later chapters[1].

---

1 Discharge by performance, by breach and frustration: Chaps. 9, 10 and 11.

Mutual discharge

Common law

6.32 An agreement to discharge a contract must be supported by consideration. However, if both parties still have contractual obligations to perform, any agreement to discharge the contract relieves both parties from further performance of it. In such a case, both parties have provided consideration, for each party promises not to require further performance of contractual obligations by the other party in return for being absolved from further performance.

If there is an agreement to vary rather than discharge a contract[1], the cases show that the agreement must also be supported by consideration and consideration must be provided by the party seeking to enforce the variation. If A agrees to vary the contractual obligations of B, A has provided consideration and could enforce the variation but B has not necessarily done so and, without providing consideration, could not enforce the variation, nor plead it as a defence at law if A sought to rely on the original contract. The agreement may, in fact, be supported by consideration emanating from both parties and, if this is the case, then either party can, of course, enforce the variation. If a variation could benefit either party then both parties provide consideration[2]. The examples discussed in *Pinnel's Case*[3] are variations where both parties provide consideration: the creditor by accepting less than he is owed, and the debtor by providing some benefit to the creditor at the creditor's request, for example, by paying a lesser sum before the date due for payment or by paying in kind. The cases where one party agrees to remit part of a debt, or vary another contractual term, for the benefit of the other party, without any benefit or potential benefit to himself are cases where the party agreeing to the remission or variation is the only party to provide consideration and he can rely on the original agreement or the varied agreement as he desires[4]. If an agreement appears to be capable of benefiting either or both parties, but it is in fact intended to benefit one party only, then that party has provided no consideration and cannot enforce the variation[5].

---

1 For cases distinguishing between agreements to discharge and agreements to vary see para. 6.35.
2 For example, if altering the currency under which payment is to be made means that either party could gain by the substitution of a new currency. See *W. J. Alan & Co Ltd v El Nasr Export and Import Co* [1972] 2 QB 189, [1972] 2 All ER 127, CA.
3 Para. 6.13.
4 For example, *Foakes v Beer* (1884) 9 App Cas 605, HL; para. 6.13.
5 *Vanbergen v St. Edmund's Properties Ltd* [1933] 2 KB 233, CA.

6.33 Because a variation may not be enforceable for lack of consideration or because it has been made in an incorrect form[1], the law has developed another type of alteration of contract — the waiver. A waiver can take effect even if unsupported by consideration by the party seeking to enforce the waiver and even if in the incorrect form for a variation. Whether an alteration of contract is a variation or waiver is said to be a question of intention; but in fact there is no rational distinction between waiver and variation, and the theoretical basis of waivers is extremely uncertain. It is said that a variation alters the terms of the contract while a waiver alters the effect of the original terms of the contract but that begs the question of when an alteration is a variation. Probably, the common rules on waiver will now be subsumed under the equitable provisions mentioned in the next paragraph. However, the following effects of a waiver at common law have been revealed by the cases:

a. The waiver binds the party who sought its operation. Therefore, in *Levey & Co v Goldberg*[2], when a buyer of goods sued for non-delivery by the contractual date, the seller had a defence in that the buyer had himself requested that delivery be postponed until after that date.

b. The waiver binds the party who granted it[3], at least until he has given reasonable notice that the waiver is withdrawn and that the original contract is revived, if this is possible. If, for example one party to a contract agreed to waive the contractual method of payment he could give notice that payment was to be made as specified in the contract but not, surely, if payment had been made under the method permitted by the waiver and the money had been lost.

---

1 For form see para. 6.35.
2 [1922] 1 KB 688.
3 *Hartley v Hymans* [1920] 3 KB 475.

Equity

6.34 Because of the difficulty of establishing a valid variation at law, and the unsatisfactory nature of waiver at law (particularly the difficulty of distinguishing between variation and waiver), equity developed a parallel remedy when a contract had been altered which is an application of promissory estoppel, which we have discussed in relation to debts[1].

If one party to a contract represents by words or by conduct that he will not enforce his contractual rights and the other party to the contract acts on this representation[2], the party making that representation will not be permitted to go back on that representation unless it would be equitable for him to do so — which will be rare[2].

The case which is thought of as the foundation of the equitable jurisdiction, and which was relied on in *Central London Property Trust Ltd v High Trees House Ltd*[3], is *Hughes v Metropolitan Rly Co*[4]. In this case, a landlord gave his tenant, who was obliged by the lease to repair the demised premises, notice to effect repairs. Failure to comply with this notice would have allowed the landlord to terminate the lease. The parties then entered into negotiations for the sale and purchase of the lease, and, when these negotiations proved abortive, the landlord sought to forfeit the lease for failure to repair. The House of Lords denied the right to forfeit. The landlord had led the tenant to believe that he would not enforce his right to forfeit for failure to repair with the result that the tenant had not carried out the repairs, and it would be inequitable to allow the landlord to rely on his strict contractual rights. The conclusion was that the landlord should have given the tenant a further six months notice from the date when negotiations ended. This case clearly establishes that the party to whom representations are made must act on the representation, that the effect of the representation is only supensory, and that the original contract can be revived by reasonable notice[5]. That a representation giving rise to an equitable intervention gives rise to no new legal rights, but only provides a defence, was established by *Combe v Combe*[6].

---

1 Para. 6.14.
2 For whether the action must involve detriment see para. 6.15. But see for example *D. and C. Builders v Rees* [1966] 2 QB 617, [1965] 3 All ER 837, CA.
3 [1947] KB 130, [1956] 1 All ER 256n.
4 (1877) 2 App Cas 439, HL.
5 See also, *Tool Metal Manufacturing Co Ltd v Tungsten Electric Co Ltd* [1955] 2 All ER 657, HL.
6 [1951] 2 KB 215, [1951] 1 All ER 767, CA.

Form

6.35 If a contract is discharged by an agreement supported by consideration from both parties, the agreement is binding whatever form it is in. For example, a contract by deed can be discharged by deed or in writing or orally[1]. But variations are not so straightforward. If the contract which is alleged to have been varied had to be made in writing or evidenced in writing, e.g. a contract for the disposition of land, then the variation must be in writing or evidenced in writing[2] and oral variation is ineffective (unless the courts can construe the variation as a waiver or equity intervenes). However, what the parties choose to call a variation may be regarded by the courts as a discharge of the original contract and the substitution of a new one. If this is the case, the informal 'variation' is effective to discharge the original contract, though whether the new agreement is enforceable or not depends on whether it satisfies the rules for the creation of a binding contract[3]. If an alteration of a contract is merely an ineffective variation it does not affect the validity of the original contract[4].

Whether an alteration is to be regarded as a variation or as a discharge and substitution may be expressly stated by the parties or implied from the nature of the alteration. An alteration will rescind a contract by implication only if it is entirely inconsistent with the original contract. The inconsistency must go to 'the very root of the contract' if it is to be an implied rescission[5]. An example of an implied rescission occurred in *Morris v Baron & Co*[6], in which a contract for the sale of blue serge, which at the time had to be evidenced in writing, was effectively rescinded by an agreement compromising a dispute about the goods and varying the amount to be sold. Alterations which have been found not to be inconsistent with the original contract are changing the place of delivery of a shipment of tea (this was an alteration of one term out of seven in the contract)[7], and varying the rate of interest of a loan[8].

---

1 *Berry v Berry* [1929] 2 KB 316.
2 *Goss v Lord Nugent* (1833) 5 B & Ad 58.

3   So that, if the subject matter of the new contract was land, the contract might well have to be in writing or evidenced in writing. See paras. 7.10–7.16.
4   *United Dominions Corpn (Jamaica) Ltd v Shoucair* [1969] 1 AC 340, [1968] 2 All ER 904, PC.
5   *British and Benningtons Ltd v North Western Cachar Tea Co Ltd* [1923] AC 48, HL.
6   [1918] AC 1, HL.
7   *British and Benningtons Ltd v North Western Cachar Tea Co Ltd* [1923] AC 48, HL.
8   *United Dominions Corporation (Jamaica) Ltd v Shoucair* [1969] 1 AC 340, [1968] 2 All ER 904, PC.

Unilateral discharge

6.36   If the parties agree to discharge their contract the agreement must be supported by consideration. No difficulty arises when both parties still have contractual obligations to perform. However, where one party has performed all his contractual obligations prior to the agreement his promise to release the other party from further performance does not bind him unless that other party provides consideration. Unilateral discharge by agreement is also known as accord (agreement to discharge) and satisfaction (consideration for that agreement).

There is one exception to the rule that a promise to discharge a contract must be supported by consideration. Section 62 of the Bills of Exchange Act 1882 states that the holder of a bill of exchange or promissory note which has matured can discharge the bill or note by renouncing his rights absolutely and unconditionally in writing. Writing may be dispensed with if the bill or note is delivered to the debtor.

Apart from the exception mentioned above accord without satisfaction is ineffective to discharge a contract. Satisfaction usually consists of doing something in return for the promise to rescind, but the satisfaction which is offered might be a promise to do something. If so, it is necessary to decide if the original contract is discharged from the moment of the accord or only when the promise, which is the alleged satisfaction, has been translated into action. It is a question of construction. If the accord can be construed to mean that a promise to do something is satisfaction then the original contract is discharged from the making of the accord. If, however, the accord means that *performance* of a promise to do something is satisfaction then the original contract can only be discharged when the promise is performed. The meaning of the accord is a question of fact in every case. In *Elton Cop Dyeing Co Ltd v Robert Broadbent & Son Ltd*[2], buyers of machinery sued the suppliers for damages. An agreement was made by which the buyer withdrew his claim and the seller agreed to repair the machines partly at his own expense. The buyer then attempted to sue on the original contract of sale but failed, the Court of Appeal finding an accord which on its true construction was supported by consideration, viz. the promise to repair the machines.

---

1 See para. 6.32.
2 (1919) 89 LJKB 186, CA.

Chapter 7
Form

7.1 With the exception of the contracts mentioned hereafter English law does not require a contract to be in writing in order to be valid and enforceable.

CONTRACTS WHICH MUST BE UNDER SEAL OR IN WRITING

Contracts which must be under seal

Leases for three years or more

7.2 These are void at law and pass no legal estate unless made under seal[1]. However, such a lease not made under seal can take effect as a contract to grant a lease[2], which can be specifically enforced provided it is evidenced in writing[3] or supported by a sufficient act of part performance[4], and will create the same rights as a lease between the parties for many purposes.

---

1 Law of Property Act 1925, ss. 52 and 54. A lease for less than three years which does not take effect in possession or is not for the best rent reasonably obtainable must also be under seal, *ibid.*
2 *Walsh v Lonsdale* (1882) 21 Ch D 9, CA.
3 Para. 7.10.
4 Paras. 7.17—7.18.

Contracts in which there is no consideration

7.3 If there is no consideration for the promise made by one party to the other the contract is invalid unless made under seal[1]. A common example of such a contract under seal is a covenant for the gratuitous payment of a sum to a charity over a seven year period, whereby the charity is enabled to claim the income tax paid by the donor in addition to the covenanted sum.

---

1 *Rann v Hughes* (1778) 1 Term Rep 350n.

7.4 A contract under seal is a contract which is made by deed. A deed is a written document which has been signed and sealed (normally by attaching a red circular adhesive wafer to it) by the person executing it. The execution of a deed also requires it to have been 'delivered'. However, a deed is regarded as delivered if the person making it intends unconditionally to be bound by it: physical delivery of it to the other party is no longer required and a deed may be delivered even though it remains in the custody of its maker.

A contract under seal is known as a contract by specialty: all other contracts, whether written or not, are known as simple contracts.

Contracts which must be in writing

7.5 Some contracts such as those below are invalid or unenforceable unless they are in writing:

a. *Bills of exchange and promissory notes*[1] However, an oral agreement to the same effect is a valid contract, although it will not have the same legal and commercial characteristics.

b. *Contracts of marine insurance* Such a contract is 'inadmissable in evidence' unless it is embodied in a marine policy signed by the insurer and specifying the name of the assured, or of some person who effects the insurance on his behalf[2].

c. *Regulated agreements under the Consumer Credit Act 1974* Consumer credit agreements and consumer hire agreements which are not executed in writing in the manner required by the Act of 1974 are enforceable against the debtor or hirer only on an order of the court[3].

In addition, there are a number of transactions, closely connected with or involving contracts, where writing is essential. For example, a bill of sale is only valid if it is in writing in the prescribed statutory form[4]; an acknowledgement of a statute-barred debt must be written in order to start time running again under the Limitation Act 1939[5], and the transfer of a British registered ship, or of a share in it, must be in writing[6].

---

1 Bills of Exchange Act 1882, ss. 3, 17, 73 and 83.
2 Marine Insurance Act 1906, ss. 22—24.

3 Consumer Credit Act 1974, s.65. Para. 23.26.
4 Bills of Sale Act 1878 (Amendment) Act 1882, s.9.
5 Limitation Act 1939, s.24. Para. 12.31.
6 Merchant Shipping Act 1894, s.24.

CONTRACTS WHICH MUST BE EVIDENCED IN WRITING

7.6 Contracts of guarantee and contracts for the sale or other disposition of land or an interest in land do not have to be written but merely be evidenced in writing before they can be enforced in legal proceedings.

Contracts of guarantee

7.7 By s.4 of the Statute of Frauds (1677), no action can be brought on a promise to answer for the debt, default or miscarriage of another (i.e. a guarantee) unless the agreement, or some memorandum or note thereof, is in writing and signed by the party to be charged or some other person lawfully authorised by him. The nature of the required written evidence, and the effects of non-compliance with s.4, are discussed in paras. 7.11 to 7.16. For the present we devote ourselves to the nature of a contract of guarantee.

7.8 A contract of guarantee must be sharply distinguished from one of indemnity because s.4 only applies to guarantees, whether of contractual or tortious liability[1], so that an oral contract of indemnity is enforceable. The distinction between a guarantee and an indemnity is a fine one but the two terms can be expressed as follows:

A will *guarantee* B's debt to C if he makes himself liable to pay it if B fails to pay. Here A has assumed a liability subsidiary to that of B, which continues as the primary liability.

A will *indemnify* C if he assumes primary liability to pay B's debt in any event. Here A has assumed a sole liability to C, B's liability being discharged or never arising.

As these two statements imply, for a promise to constitute a guarantee, and therefore to be required to be evidenced in writing to be enforceable, the following criteria must be satisfied:

a. Three parties must be involved: a creditor, a principal debtor (whose liability may be actual or prospective) and the promisor, who undertakes to discharge the principal debtor's liability if the latter fails to do so himself. If there never has been a person who can be described as the principal debtor a contract cannot be one of guarantee, as is shown by *Lakeman v Mountstephen*[2]. The plaintiff, a builder, was asked by the defendant, the chairman of the Brixham Local Board of Health whether he would connect certain drains to a sewer which he had laid. The plaintiff said he would do so if the defendant or the Board would become responsible for payment. The defendant replied: 'Go on, Mountstephen, and do the work, I will see you paid'. When sued on his promise, the defendant pleaded that it was a promise to guarantee the debt of another (the Board) and, not being evidenced in writing, was unenforceable. The House of Lords rejected this defence because the defendant's promise was an undertaking of sole liability, the Board never having been liable to the plaintiff, so that the contract between the plaintiff and defendant was not one of guarantee and did not have to be evidenced in writing.

Unlike a guarantee only two parties need be concerned in a contract of indemnity. Thus, if A agrees to keep B immune from loss through some cause extraneous to A, such as fire or flood, or attributable to him, the contract will be one of indemnity and need not be evidenced in writing to be enforceable.

b. To be a guarantee, the principal debtor must continue to have the primary liability towards the creditor, *the promisor being liable only in the event of his default*. Thus, if the effect of the promisor's undertaking is to determine the principal debtor's debt and substitute the indebtedness of the promisor the contract is one of indemnity, not of guarantee. An example is provided by *Goodman v Chase*[3]. The plaintiffs had been awarded damages in legal proceedings against X. X was subsequently arrested for failure to satisfy the judgment but the plaintiffs consented to his release when the defendant, X's father-in-law, promised to pay the debt in return. It was held that since the defendant's promise had discharged X's debt and substituted his own indebtedness his promise was one of indemnity.

The fact that a guarantor's liability is secondary to that of the principal debtor's continuing liability, whereas a promise to indemnify creates a primary liability in the promisor is well illustrated by the following dictum in *Birkmyr v Darnell*[4]:

'If two come to a shop, and one buys, and the other to gain him credit, promises the seller *"If he does not pay you, I will"*, this is a collateral undertaking, and unenforceable without writing, by the Statute of Frauds: but if he says, *"Let him have the goods, I will be your paymaster"*, or *"I will see you paid"* this is an undertaking as for himself, and he shall be intended to be the very buyer, and the other to act but as his servant.'

The requirement for a guarantee that the promisor must undertake to be liable to pay only of the principal debtor fails to do so is crucial. Thus, if the promisor has assumed liability to pay in any event, the transaction cannot be one of guarantee even though the principal debtor still remains obliged to pay. This is shown by *Guild & Co v*

Conrad[5], which also demonstrates that it is the effect, not the words, of the promise which is important. The plaintiff accepted a batch of bills of exchange drawn on him by a firm of Demerara merchants after he had been orally promised by the defendant that 'If you accept these bills I will guarantee them'. The Court of Appeal held that, despite the defendant's use of the word 'guarantee', his promise was one of indemnity because, notwithstanding that the Demerara merchants' liability under the bills continued, the defendant had promised to put the plaintiff into funds in any event, regardless of whether the merchants defaulted in payment. Since the promise was one of indemnity it was irrelevant that it was oral.

---

1   *Kirkham v Marter* (1819) 2 B & Ald 613.
2   (1874) LR 7 HL 17, HL.
3   (1818) 1 B & Ald 297.
4   (1704) 1 Salk 27 at 28.
5   [1894] 2 QB 885, CA.

7.9   Even where the above criteria are satisfied, and the promisor's undertaking consequently a guarantee, it is nevertheless not affected by s.4 of the Statute of Frauds unless the promisor has made his promise direct to the creditor (and not to the debtor or some other person)[1] and unless the promisor's assumption of a secondary liability is the sole object of the transaction between him and the creditor. Hence, s.4 does not apply:

a. Where the promise made is incidental to a larger transaction between the promisor and the creditor. In *Sutton & Co v Grey*[2], the defendant orally agreed to introduce clients to the plaintiffs, a firm of stock-brokers. He was to receive half the commission earned by the plaintiffs on transactions for such clients and to pay the plaintiffs half of any loss caused by the default of such clients. Despite being oral, this last promise, although in essence a guarantee, was held enforceable because it formed part of a larger transaction. Similarly, if A appoints B as his *del credere* agent (an agent who guarantees payment in the event of non-payment by the customers whom he introduces to his principal), B's promise to pay if the customers default need not be evidenced in writing because it is incidental to a larger transaction[3].

b. Where the main purpose of the promisor in giving his promise is to acquire or retain property, and the guarantee is given by him to relieve the property from a charge or encumbrance, existing in favour of another, it is not caught by s.4. Thus, if A buys goods from B which are subject to a lien[4] in favour of C, and in order to discharge the lien A promises C to pay B's debt if B does not do so, his promise (guarantee) need not be evidenced in writing[5].

However, this exception does not apply where the promisor's interest is a purely personal one: he must have a proprietary interest in the property in question. Thus, if a large shareholder in a company orally promises to guarantee the company's debts in order to prevent its goods being taken in execution, the case does not fall within the exception because he has no legal interest in, or charge on, the goods, his interest in the company being a contractual and therefore purely personal one, and since his promise is oral it is unenforceable[6].

Neither of these exceptions appears in s.4 of the Statute of Frauds but are judicial glosses on it. They, and the other intricate rules which have been developed concerning what is and what is not a promise governed by the section, have resulted from the courts' reluctance to see agreements rendered unenforceable for lack of written evidence. The resulting complexity and limited extent of the section prompt us to ask whether the section is worth retention at all or, if protection of guarantors is necessary, whether it should not be extended without exception to all guarantees and indemnities.

---

1 *Eastwood v Kenyon* (1840) 11 Ad & El 438; *Reader v Kingham* (1862) 13 CB NS 344.
2 [1894] 1 QB 285, CA.
3 *Couturier v Hastie* (1852) 8 Exch 40 at 56.
4 A lien is a right by which a person is entitled to obtain satisfaction for a debt by retaining property belonging to the person indebted to him.
5 *Fitzgerald v Dressler* (1859) 7 CB NS 374.
6 *Harburg India Rubber Comb Co v Martin* [1902] 1 KB 778, CA.

Contracts for the sale or other disposition of land or any interest in land

7.10 This class of contract, which was formerly governed by s.4 of the Statute of Frauds, is now regulated by s.40(1) of the Law of Property Act 1925. Section 40(1) provides:

'No action may be brought upon any contract for the sale or other disposition of land or any interest in land, unless the agreement upon which such action is brought, or some memorandum or note thereof is in writing, and signed by the party to be charged or by some other person thereunto by him lawfully authorised.'

The section is comprehensive. It applies to a contract for any disposition of *any interest in land*, whether by sale, mortgage, lease or otherwise. The expression 'any interest in land' is widely defined and includes sporting rights and *fructus naturales* (things which are the natural, rather than cultivated, produce of the soil, such as grass and even planted trees and their fruit) unless they are to be severed by the vendor or the contract binds the purchaser to sever them at once[1].

---

1 *Smith v Surman* (1829) 9 B & C 561; *Marshall v Green* (1875) 1 CPD 35.

Formal requirements of s.4 of the Statute of Frauds and of s.40(1) of the Law of Property Act 1925

7.11 Both sections require that the agreement, or some memorandum or note thereof, shall be in writing and signed by the party to be charged or by some person lawfully authorised by him for that purpose. If the contract is in writing no difficulty arises. However, whether there is written evidence sufficient to constitute a signed memorandum or note (which can come into existence at any time before action is brought to enforce the contract) is a somewhat complex question because, although the sections do not specify the form and contents of a signed memorandum or note, the following rules have been laid down by the judges:

Contents of the 'memorandum or note'
7.12
a. The memorandum or note must name the parties to the contract or so describe them that they can be identified with certainty[1].

b. The memorandum or note must describe the whole subject-matter[2] but may sufficiently describe it although it has to be supplemented by extrinsic evidence. In *Plant v Bourne*[3], for instance, a memorandum recording the sale of '24 acres of land, freehold, and all appurtenances thereto at Totmonslow, in the parish of Draycott, in the county of Stafford' was held sufficient on proof that the vendor had no other land there.

c. The memorandum or note must accurately set out the material terms of the oral contract and if it differs in a material term it will not be a memorandum or note of the contract and the plaintiff will not be able to rely on it[4]. However, if the memorandum or note merely omits a term which is for the *exclusive benefit of the plaintiff* then, but only then[5], the plaintiff can waive the term and enforce the contract without it[6]. Similarly, if the omitted term is for the *exclusive benefit of the defendant* the plaintiff can enforce the contract if he agrees to perform that term[7]. Thus, in *Scott v Bradley*[8], where the written memorandum of a contract for the sale of land failed to state that one of its terms was that the purchaser would pay half the legal costs of the vendor, it was held that, on submitting to pay half the legal costs, the purchaser could rely on the memorandum and was entitled to specific performance of the contract of sale.

d. The memorandum or note of a contract for the disposition of any interest in land must state the consideration[9], but a memorandum or note of a contract of guarantee need not do so[10].

---

1 *Williams v Jordan* (1877) 6 Ch D 517; *Rossiter v Miller* (1878) 3 App Cas 1124, HL.
2 *Burgess v Cox* [1951] Ch 383, [1950] 2 All ER 1212.
3 [1897] 2 Ch 281, CA.
4 *Beckett v Nurse* [1948] 1 KB 535, [1948] 1 All ER 81, CA.
5 *Hawkins v Price* [1947] Ch 645, [1947] 1 All ER 689.
6 *North v Loomes* [1919] 1 Ch 378.
7 *Martin v. Pycroft* (1852) 2 De G & G 285; *Scott v Bradley* [1971] Ch 850, [1971] 1 All ER 583.
8 [1971] Ch 850, [1971] 1 All ER 583.
9 *Laythoarp v Bryant* (1836) 2 Bing NC 735 at 742.
10 Mercantile Law Amendment Act 1856, s.3.

Signature

7.13 The document must be signed by the party to be charged or by his agent lawfully authorised to sign for him. The extent of an agent's authority is determined by agreement or trade usage.

The sections do not require signature by both parties or their agents, merely signature by the party to be charged, i.e. the party against whom it is sought to enforce the contract, or his agent[1]. Thus, where there is a contract between A and B, and B alone has signed a memorandum or note of it A can enforce the contract against B, but B cannot enforce it against A.

The word 'signed' has been liberally interpreted. Provided the name, or even the initials, of the party to be charged appears in some part of the memorandum or note in some form, whether in handwriting, stamp, print or otherwise, there will be a sufficient signature, if that party has shown in some way that he recognises the whole document as a record of the contract[2] Thus, a memorandum in the handwriting of A, the person to be charged, which began 'I, A, agree' without any other signature, was held in *Knight v Crockford*[3] to have been sufficiently signed on the ground that by his writing A had shown that he recognised the existence of the contract mentioned in the document. However, unless there is such a recognition the mere fact that a party's name appears in the document does not make it signed by him[4].

---

1 *Laythoarp v Bryant* (1836) 2 Bing NC 735.
2 *Halley v O'Brien* [1920] 1 IR 330 at 339, CA; *Leeman v Stocks* [1951] Ch 941, [1951] 1 All ER 1043.
3 (1794) 1 Esp 190.
4 *Hubert v Treherne* (1842) 3 Man & G 743.

Purpose for which document prepared irrelevant
7.14 It is irrelevant that the document was never intended to serve as a note or memorandum but was prepared for some entirely different purpose. In *Cohen v Roche*[1], for instance, a note in the auctioneer's book was held to be an effective memorandum, and so was a letter to a third party in *Moore v Hart*[2]. Moreover, a written offer signed by the defendant and orally accepted by the plaintiff is a sufficient memorandum, even though the contract does not come into existence until after the offer has been accepted[3]. In addition, a letter repudiating liability under an alleged contract is a sufficient memorandum of the contract if it constitutes an unambiguous recognition of the existence of the contract and of its terms and merely denies liability under it, but not if it denies the contract was made on the terms alleged[4]. For the same reason a memorandum stating that an agreement is 'subject to contract' does not constitute a sufficient memorandum because these words amount to a denial of the existence of a contract[5].

1 *Cohen v Roche* [1927] 1 KB 169.
2 *Moore v Hart* (1682) 1 Vern 110 at 201.
3 *Reuss v Picksley* (1866) LR 1 Exch 342.
4 *Thirkell v Cambi* [1919] 2 KB 590, CA.
5 *Tiverton Estates Ltd v Wearwell Ltd* [1975] Ch 146, [1974] 1 All ER 209, CA.

Joinder of documents
7.15 A memorandum or note may consist of various documents, each in themselves insufficient, so long as there is some internal reference between them. A plaintiff who wishes to rely on a memorandum or note allegedly constituted by more than one document must prove:
a. the existence of a document signed by the defendant (the party to be charged);
b. a reference in the *signed document,* express or implied, to some other document(s) or transaction. Where any such reference can be spelt out of the signed document, then oral evidence can be given to identify the other document(s) referred to, or, as the case may be, to explain the other transaction, and to identify any document relating to it;
c. that a sufficient memorandum or note is constituted when the signed document and the other document(s) which has been revealed are read together[1].

Where two documents are *both signed* then, even though neither expressly or impliedly refers to the other or to another transaction, they can be joined so as to form a memorandum if, on placing them side by side, it is obvious without the aid of oral evidence that they are connected[2].

1 *Timmins v Moreland Street Property Co Ltd* [1958] Ch 110 at 120, [1957] 3 All ER 265 at 276, CA.
2 *Studds v Watson* (1884) 28 Ch D 305; cf. *Timmins v Moreland Street Property Co Ltd* [1958] Ch 110, [1957] 3 All ER 265, CA.

Effect of non-compliance

7.16 The effect of non-compliance with the requirements of s.4 of the Statute of Frauds and of s.40 of the Law of Property Act 1925 is not to make the contract void or voidable. It merely makes it unenforceable by action against a party who has not signed a sufficient memorandum or note, unless, and until, he has signed such a memorandum or note, because the agreement is incapable of proof[1]. Thus, a plaintiff is caught by the statutory provisions whenever he has to rely on an oral or insufficiently evidenced contract of guarantee or for the disposition of any interest in land, even though he is not directly claiming damages for its breach[2].

Admittedly, in depriving a party of his right to enforce the contract by an action, the sections deprive him of what is usually his most important right. Nevertheless, since the contract is valid and subsisting, a transferee of money, or property transferred under the contract obtains a good title to it and the contract can be enforced in any way other than by action. Thus, if a purchaser pays a cash deposit to the vendor under an oral contract for the sale of land, the vendor can keep that deposit if the purchaser defaults and, if sued for its recovery, can plead the oral contract as a defence[3].

---

1 *Maddison v Alderson* (1883) 8 App Cas 467, esp 488, HL.
2 *Delaney v T. P. Smith Ltd* [1946] KB 393, [1946] 2 All ER 23, CA.
3 *Thomas v Brown* (1876) 1 QBD 714; *Monnickendam v Leanse* (1923) 39 TLR 445.

Part performance

7.17 Under the equitable doctrine of part performance the courts allow the terms of an oral, or insufficiently evidenced, contract for the disposition of any interest in land to be proved by oral evidence if the party seeking to enforce the contract has done acts in part performance of his obligations under it[1]. If the strict rules of part performance are satisfied, a contract whose terms have been proved by the oral evidence admitted is enforceable in equity in favour of the party who has partly performed it. Nevertheless, a contract which is enforceable under the doctrine of part performance is not in as good a position as one properly evidenced in writing. A contract merely supported by part performance may be enforced in equity by an order of specific performance[2] if the case is a proper one, but that lies *in the discretion* of the court and no damages can be awarded if specific performance could not, or would not, be awarded. On the other hand, a contract properly evidenced in

143

writing is enforceable at law and the plaintiff is *entitled* to damages, the equitable remedy of specific performance also being available to him at the court's discretion.

---

1 *Brough v Nettleton* [1921] 2 Ch 25.
2 Paras. 12.18–12.20.

7.18 The doctrine of part performance is expressly recognised by s.40(2) of the Law of Property Act 1925. Four conditions, recognised in *Chapronière v Lambert*[1], must be satisfied to bring the doctrine into operation:

a. *The acts in question, taken together, must be referable to the alleged contract* The acts in question must be such as *must* be referred to some contract concerning the land[2] and may be referred to the alleged one: they must be such that they prove the existence of some contract concerning the land and are consistent with the contract alleged[3]. In other words, the acts of part performance must point to the existence of some contract concerning the land and not be inconsistent with the contract alleged, the plaintiff having to prove that they do so on the balance of probabilities[4]. At one time the test was thought to be stricter, requiring the acts to point to the contract alleged and have no other explanation[5], but modern cases[3] show that this is not so.

A good example of the operation of the present requirement is provided by *Wakeham v Mackenzie*[6]. B, a widower of 72 who was in poor health, orally agreed with the plaintiff, a widow of 67, that, if she would give up her council flat, move into his house and look after him and the house without wages, and pay her share for food and coal, he would leave his house to her in his will. The plaintiff observed all her obligations under the oral contract but B left her nothing in his will. The plaintiff was awarded specific performance of the oral contract. Her acts of giving up her flat, moving into a new home, looking after B and his house and contributing towards food and fuel were necessarily referable to some contract and were not inconsistent with the contract which she alleged. The same decision was reached in *Steadman v Steadman*[7]. After the breakdown of their marriage the parties made an oral contract whereby: the wife was to transfer her interest in the matrimonial home to the husband for £1,500; the wife would agree to the discharge of a magistrates' maintenance order in her favour; the husband would pay her £100 in part discharge of arrears under the order, and the wife would consent to the discharge of the balance. The agreement was revealed to the magistrates, who approved the relevant part of it. The husband then paid the £100 to the wife and his solicitors then prepared and sent a form of transfer of the wife's interest in the house, but she refused to sign it and claimed that, being oral, the contract referred to above was unenforceable under s.40 of the Law of Property Act 1925. The House of Lords ordered specific performance of the contract, holding that the payment of the £100, together with the announcement of the agreement to the magistrates and the preparation and sending of the form of transfer, amounted to sufficient acts of part performance by the husband because the acts were such as to indicate that they had been carried out by him in reliance on a contract with the wife and were not inconsistent with the contract alleged.

b. *Fraud on the part of the defendant* The plaintiff must have been induced, or allowed, to alter his position in reliance on the contract, so that it would be a fraud on the part of the defendant to take advantage of the contract not being sufficiently evidenced in writing[8]. In *Rawlinson v Ames*[9], the defendant agreed to take a lease of a flat from the plaintiff but the agreement was insufficiently evidenced in writing. At the defendant's request the plaintiff carried out alterations to the flat, but the defendant refused to take the lease. It was held that, as the plaintiff had materially changed her position for the worse in carrying out her part of the contract, it would be a fraud in the defendant to take advantage of the contract not being sufficiently evidenced in writing. The other conditions of part performance also being satisfied, the plaintiff was granted a decree of specific performance.

It was formerly thought that a result of the present condition was that the payment of money could never be a sufficient act of part performance by the payer because he could recover his payment if the payee refused to perform the contract, so that there would be no fraud on the part of the payee in setting up the defence of non-compliance with s.40. However, the House of Lords decision in *Steadman v Steadman* clearly establishes that there is no general rule that the payment of money cannot be a sufficient act of part performance. Nevertheless, a payment alone will frequently not suffice since it will normally be equivocal so that condition will not be satisfied. On the other hand, as the decision in *Steadman v Steadman* shows, the payment of money, together with other acts by the plaintiff, may be highly indicative of a contract.

c. *Contract must be specifically enforceable* The contract to which the acts of part performance refer must be of a type of which the court can direct specific performance[10]. The availability of specific performance is subject to certain general rules, which we mention in para. 12.18, and if specific performance is not available under them the doctrine of part performance cannot be relied on. Contracts of guarantee are never specifically enforceable and this is why the doctrine of part performance does not apply to them.

d. *Proper evidence* There must be proper evidence, whether written or oral, of the existence and terms of the contract which is let in by the acts of part performance[11]. In other words, acts of part performance having been proved and evidence having been admitted in consequence, that evidence must show that a contract has been concluded and what its terms are: if the evidence does not do so the doctrine of part performance cannot be relied on.

---

1 [1917] 2 Ch 356 at 361, CA.
2 *Re Gonin* [1977] 2 All ER 720, [1977] 3 WLR 379.
3 *Kingswood Estate Co Ltd v Anderson* [1963] 2 QB 169, [1962] 3 All ER 593, CA; *Wakeham v Mackenzie* [1968] 2 All ER 783, [1968] 1 WLR 1175; *Steadman v Steadman* [1976] AC 536, [1974] 2 All ER 977, HL.
4 *Steadman v Steadman* [1974] 2 All ER 977 at 1000.
5 *Maddison v Alderson* (1883) 8 App Cas 467, HL; *Chapr. onière v Lambert* [1917] 2 Ch 356, CA.
6 [1968] 2 All ER 783, [1968] 1 WLR 1175.
7 [1976] AC 536, [1974] 2 All ER 977, HL.
8 *Caton v Caton* (1865) LR 1 Ch App 137 at 148 (affd (1867) LR 2 HL 127).
9 [1925] Ch 96.
10 *McManus v Cooke* (1887) 35 Ch D 681 at 697.
11 *Kingswood Estates Co Ltd v Anderson* [1963] 2 QB 169, [1962] 3 All ER 593, CA.

Chapter 8
Contractual Terms

8.1 The terms of a contract may be express or implied.

EXPRESS TERMS

8.2 Clearly, the ascertainment of its express terms is facilitated when the contract has been reduced to writing, particularly because under the 'parol evidence'[1] rule oral or other evidence extrinsic to the document is not admissible generally to add to, vary, or contradict the terms of the written agreement[2]. However, this rule is not as harsh as might be supposed because in a number of cases extrinsic evidence is admissible, either as an exception to the parol evidence rule or because the circumstances fall outside its bounds. The following can be mentioned as examples.

---

1 Parol evidence of a written document means extrinsic evidence, whether oral or otherwise: Jowitt's *Dictionary of English Law*.
2 *Jacobs v Batavia and General Plantations Trust Ltd* [1924] 1 Ch 287 at 295.

Implied terms
8.3 The fact that a contract has been reduced into writing does not prevent extrinsic evidence being given to support or rebut the implication of a term into it[1] under rules which are discussed shortly.

---

1 *Burges v Wickham* (1863) 3 B & S 669; *Gillespie Bros & Co v Cheney, Eggar & Co* [1896] 2 QB 59.

Conditions precedent
8.4 Extrinsic evidence is admissable to show that, although a written contract appears absolute on its face, it was not intended that a binding contract should be created (or that, although there was an immediate

binding contract, a party's obligation to perform would not arise) until the occurrence of a particular event, such as a surveyor's report or the availability of finance. For example, in *Pym v Campbell*[1], a signed document stated that the defendants had agreed to buy a share in the plaintiff's invention. It was held that oral evidence could be admitted to show that the document had been signed subject to the condition that there would not be a binding contract until a third party had approved the invention. The reason given was that the evidence did not purport to vary the terms of the written agreement but to show that there was not a binding contract.

---

1   (1856) 6 E & B 370.

Invalidating factors
8.5   Extrinsic evidence of a factor, such as mistake or misrepresentation which invalidates the written contract is, of course, admissible.

Written contract not the whole contract
8.6   While a document which looks like a contract is presumed to include all the terms of the contract, this presumption is rebutted by evidence that the parties did not intend all the terms of their contract to be contained in the document[1]. If the presumption is rebutted, extrinsic evidence is admissible to prove the other terms of the contract. An example is provided by the case of *J. Evans & Son (Portsmouth) Ltd v Andrea Merzario Ltd*, which is discussed in para. 8.11.

---

1   *Gillespie Bros & Co v Cheney, Eggar & Co* [1896] 2 QB 59 at 62.

Collateral contracts
8.7   The parol evidence rule will also be circumvented if the court finds that the parties have made two contracts, the main written one and an oral one collateral to it. An example is provided by *Birch v Paramount Estates Ltd*[1], where the defendants, who were developing a housing estate, offered a house they were then building to the plaintiff, stating orally that it would be as good as the show house. Subsequently, the plaintiff agreed to buy the house but the written contract of sale made no reference to this statement. The completed house was not as good as the show house. The Court of Appeal held that there was an oral contract, to the effect that the house would be as good· as the show house, collateral to the contract of sale and upheld the award of damages for its breach.

In essence, a collateral contract exists where A promises B something in return for B making the main contract. A's promise must have been intended by the parties to be legally binding and to take effect as a collateral contract, and not merely as a term of the main contract, and it must be supported by separate consideration, although this may simply be B's making of the main contract[2]. Provided these requirements are satisfied a collateral contract will be valid and enforceable even though it conflicts with a term in the main contract. This is shown by *City and Westminster Properties (1934) Ltd v Mudd*[3]. In 1941 the defendant became the tenant of a lock-up shop for three years. He was allowed by the landlords, the plaintiffs, to sleep in the shop. In 1944 a second lease for three years was granted to the defendant. In 1947, during negotiations for a new lease, the plaintiffs inserted in the draft lease a clause restricting the use of the premises to trade purposes only. The defendant objected and was told by the plaintiff's agent that, if he accepted the new lease as it stood, the plaintiffs would not object to him residing on the premises. In consequence the defendant signed the lease. Later, the plaintiffs sought to forfeit the lease for breach of the covenant only to use the premises for trade purposes. It was held that the defendant could plead the collateral contract as a defence to a charge of breach of the main contract, the lease.

---

1   (1956) 168 Estates Gazette 396, CA.
2   *Heilbut, Symons & Co v Buckleton* [1913] AC 30, HL.
3   [1959] Ch 129, [1958] 2 All ER 733.

Contractual terms and mere representations

8.8   Where contractual terms are oral they must be proved by the evidence of the parties and other witnesses in the event of a dispute. A particular difficulty in this context is whether a written or oral statement which is made in contractual negotiations and not explicitly referred to at the time the contract is made is nevertheless a term of the contract instead of being a mere representation. The present issue can be exemplified as follows. At the time the contract was made A may simply have said to B: 'I offer you £1,000 for the car' to which B replied 'I accept'. These two sentences will probably be the culmination of previous, and perhaps lengthy, negotiations between the parties during which B will have given A a number of assurances as to the condition of the car, its mileage and so on. Whether these pre-contractual statements are contractual terms or undertakings, or simply mere representation, is of great importance for the following reason. Breach of a contractual term results in liability in damages, and certain other remedies for breach of contract may also be available to the 'injured party'. On the other hand, if a mere representation turns out to be false there can be no liability for breach of contract, although it *may* be possible for the misrepresentee to have the contract set aside (rescinded) for misrepresentation; and he can recover damages for misrepresentation provided the misrepresentation was made fraudulently or negligently. We discuss the subject of misrepresentation in Chapter 15 and for the present we are concerned with the question of how it is ascertained whether a pre-contractual statement has become a contractual term.

8.9 A representation will be a contractual term if the parties intended that the representor was making a binding promise as to it[1]. Whether the parties did so intend can only be deduced from all the evidence. If an intelligent bystander would infer from the words and behaviour of the parties that a binding promise was intended that will suffice[1]. In approaching the question of the parties' intentions the courts take into account factors such as the following.

---

1 *Oscar Chess Ltd v Williams* [1957] 1 All ER 325 at 327—328.

Execution of a written contract
8.10 If the representation was followed by a written contract in which it does not appear it will probably, but not necessarily, be regarded as a mere representation[1] since, because of the parol evidence rule, it can only take effect as a contractual term if the court finds that the parties intended that the contract should not be contained wholly in the written document or that the representation should form part of a collateral contract. An example of a case where a pre-contractual representation was found to be a contractual term despite the subsequent execution of a written contract is *J. Evans & Son (Portsmouth) Ltd v Andrea Merzario Ltd*, which is discussed in the next paragraph.

---

1 *Heilbut, Symons & Co v Buckleton* [1930] AC 30 at 50; *Oscar Chess Ltd v Williams* [1957] 1 All ER 325 at 329.

The importance of the representation
8.11 The more important the subject-matter of the representation the more likely it is that the parties intended a binding promise concerning it. In particular, if the representation was so important that without it the representee would not have made the contract, the court is very likely to hold that it is a contractual term. In *J. Evans & Son (Portsmouth) Ltd v Andrea Merzario Ltd*[1], the plaintiffs brought some machines from an Italian company. They had previously employed the defendants to arrange transport and the machinery had always been packed in crates or trailers and carried under deck. On this occasion the defendants' representative told the plaintiffs' that it was proposed that the machinery should be packed in containers. The plaintiffs' representative replied that if containers were used they must be stowed under, and not on,

deck in case the machinery rusted. He was assured by the defendants' representative that this would be done but this oral assurance was not included in the written agreement subsequently made between the plaintiffs and the defendants. In fact, the containers were carried on deck and two fell into the sea. In the Court of Appeal, Roskill and Geoffrey Lane LJJ held that the oral assurance had become a term of the contract between the parties, which was not wholly written, and that the plaintiff could recover damages for its breach. Roskill, LJ, stated that in the light of the totality of the evidence it was clear that the plaintiffs had only agreed to contract with the defendants on the basis that the containers were stowed under deck, and therefore the defendants' assurance concerning this had become a contractual term. Similarly, in *Bannerman v White*[2] a representation that sulphur had not been used in the treatment of hops was found to have become a term of the subsequent contract. It related to a matter of great importance and the buyer would not have made the contract without it.

1 [1976] 2 All ER 930, [1976] 1 WLR 1078, CA.
2 (1861) 10 CB NS 844.

Invitation to verify

8.12 If a seller invites the buyer to check his representation it is very unlikely to be regarded as a contractual term. In *Ecay v Godfrey*[1], for instance, the seller of a boat said that it was sound but advised a survey. It was held that this advice negatived any intention that the representation should be a contractual term. Conversely, if the seller assures the buyer that it is not necessary to verify the representation since he can take the seller's word for it, the representation is likely to be found to be intended to be a term of the resulting contract if the buyer contracts in reliance on it. In *Schawel v Reade*[2], the plaintiff, who required a stallion for stud purposes, went to the defendant's stables to inspect a horse. While he was inspecting it the defendant said: 'You need not look for anything: the horse is perfectly sound. If there was anything the matter with the horse I would tell you'. The plaintiff thereupon ended his inspection and a price was agreed upon a few days later, the plaintiff relying on the defendant's statement. The House of Lords held that the jury's finding that the defendant's statement was a contractual term was correct.

1 (1947) 80 LL L REP 286.
2 [1913] 2 IR 64, HL. Cf. *Hopkins v Tanqueray* (1854) 15 CB 130.

Statements of fact, of opinion or as to the future

8.13 A statement of fact is more likely to be construed as intended to have contractual effect than a statement of opinion or as to future facts (e.g. a forecast)[1]. A promise about something which is or should be within the promisor's control is very likely to be construed as a contractual term[2].

---

1 *Esso Petroleum Co Ltd v Mardon* [1976] 2 All ER 5 at 20.
2 *Oscar Chess Ltd v Williams* [1957] 1 All ER 325 at 329.

Ability of the parties to ascertain the accuracy of the statement
8.14 If the representor had a special skill or knowledge, or was otherwise in a better position than the representee to ascertain the truth of the representation, this strongly suggests that the representation was intended to be a contractual term, and *vice versa*. An example is provided by *Dick Bentley (Productions) Ltd v Harold Smith (Motors) Ltd*[1]. The plaintiff purchased a Bentley car from the defendants in reliance on their statement that the car had been fitted with a new engine and gear box and had done only 20,000 miles since then. The representation as to mileage, although honestly made, was untrue. The Court of Appeal held that the representation had become one of the terms of the contract because it had been made by a dealer who was in a position to know or find out the car's history, and it could therefore be inferred that the representation was intended to have contractual effect. The Court distinguished its previous decision in *Oscar Chess Ltd v Williams*[2]. There, Williams, a private person, represented in negotiations for the part-exchange of his Morris car that it was a 1948 model. This representation was based on the logbook which had been falsified by a person unknown. The representation was held not to have become a contractual term on the ground that the seller had no special knowledge as to the car's age, while the other party, who were car dealers, were in at least as good a position to ascertain whether the representation was true.

---

1 [1965] 2 All ER 65, [1965] 1 WLR 623, CA. Cf. *Gilchester Properties Ltd v Gomm* [1948] 1 All ER 493.
2 [1957] 1 All ER 325, [1957] 1 WLR 370, CA.

8.15 It must be emphasised that the factors mentioned above are only guides, not decisive tests or the only factors, to determining the parties' intentions[1]. Sometimes they can be self-contradictory.

On many occasions judges, having found that the parties intended a pre-contractual representation to have contractual effect, have found that it has taken effect under a collateral contract rather than as a term of the main contract.

---

1 *Heilbut, Symons & Co v Buckleton* [1914] AC 30, HL.

IMPLIED TERMS

8.16 In addition to its express terms, the contract may contain certain terms implied by custom or by statute or by the courts.

Terms implied by custom

8.17 Terms may be implied by the custom of a particular locality, as in *Hutton v Warren*[1], or by the usage of a particular trade, as in *Harley & Co v Nagata*[2]. Although the terms are often used interchangeably, 'usage' differs from 'custom' in that it need not be ancient, but like custom it must be reasonable and certain in the sense that it is clearly established[3]. In *Hutton v Warren*, where a local custom was proved that a tenant was obliged to farm according to a certain course of husbandry for the whole of his tenancy and, on quitting, was entitled to a fair allowance for seeds and labour on the arable land, it was held that a term to this effect was implied in the lease. In *Harley & Co v Nagata*, it was held that, in the case of a time charterparty, a usage that the commission of a broker who negotiated the charterparty should be paid out of the hire that was earned, and should not be payable unless hire was in fact earned, was an implied term of the charterparty. Similarly, in *Cunliffe-Owen v Teather & Greenwood*[4], a usage of the Stock Exchange was held to be an implied term of an option to sell shares at a future date.

A customary term cannot be implied if the express wording of the contract shows that the parties had a contrary intention. This is shown by *Les Affréteurs Réunis SA v Leopold Walford (London) Ltd*[5]. Walford acted as a broker in effecting the charter of a ship. Before the charterparty could be operated, and therefore before any hire could be earned, the French government requisitioned the ship. The charterparty provided that commission should be payable to Walford 'on signing this charter (ship lost or not lost)'. The House of Lords held that Walford could recover his commission because the commercial usage referred to above (commission payable only in respect of hire earned) could have no application since it was inconsistent with the express terms of the charterparty.

---

1 (1836) 1 M & W 466. For the requirements of a valid local custom, see para. 3.52.
2 (1917) 23 Com Cas 121.
3 *Cunliffe-Owen v Teather and Greenwood* [1967] 3 All ER 561 at 572.
4 [1967] 3 All ER 561, [1967] 1 WLR 1421.
5 [1919] AC 801, HL.

Terms implied by statutes

8.18 Certain terms, which were originally implied by trade custom, are implied into contracts of marine insurance and for the sale of goods by the Marine Insurance Act 1906 and the Sale of Goods Act 1893[1] respectively. In addition, since the Hire-Purchase Act 1938 certain terms have been implied by statute into hire-purchase contracts, such terms now being implied by the Supply of Goods (Implied Terms) Act 1973[1], which applies to all hire-purchase contracts.

These statutorily implied terms can be illustrated by reference to some of the terms implied by the Sale of Goods Act 1893. Section 12(1)(a) of the Act provides that there is an implied condition on the part of a seller of goods that he has a right to sell them. Section 12(1)(b) provides, inter alia, that there is an implied warranty that the goods are free, and will remain free until the property passes, from any charge or encumbrance not known or disclosed to the buyer before the contract is made. Section 14(2) provides that where the seller sells goods in the course of a business there is generally an implied condition that the goods supplied under the contract are of merchantable quality (i.e. as fit for the purpose or purposes for which goods of that kind are commonly bought as it is reasonable to expect). Section 14(3) provides that where the seller sells goods in the course of a business and the buyer expressly or impliedly makes known to him any particular purpose for which the goods are being bought there is generally an implied condition that the goods supplied are reasonably fit for that purpose.

---

1 As amended.

Terms implied by the courts

8.19 In *Liverpool City Council v Irwin*[1], the House of Lords recognised that terms could be implied by the courts in two distinct situations: a. where the term was a legal incident of the kind of contract in question, and b. where it was necessary to give 'business efficacy' to the particular contract.

---

1 [1977] AC 239, [1976] 2 All ER 39, HL.

Implication of a term which is a legal incident of the type of contract in question

8.20 When a court implies this type of term for the first time it lays down a general rule for contracts of the same type, e.g. employment contracts and contracts of hire, so that the term will be implied in subsequent cases concerning that type of contract[1], subject to the rules of precedent, unless it is inconsistent with the express terms of the contract or the contract excludes it[2]. In implying a term of the present type, the court is not trying to put the parties' intentions, actual or presumed, into effect but is imposing an obligation on one party or the other[3]. In deciding whether to make such an implication the courts take into account the reasonableness of the suggested term and whether it is called for by the nature of the subject-matter of the type of contract in question[4].

---

1 *Lister v Romford Ice & Cold Storage Co Ltd* [1957] AC 555 at 576; *Liverpool City Council v Irwin* [1976] 2 All ER 39 at 46; *Shell UK Ltd v Lostock Garages Ltd* [1977] 1 All ER 481 at 487.
2 *Lynch v Thorne* [1956] 1 All ER 744, [1956] 1 WLR 303, CA
3 *Shell UK Ltd v Lostock Garages Ltd* [1977] 1 All ER 481 at 487.
4 *Liverpool City Council v Irwin* [1977] AC 239, [1976] 2 All ER 39, HL.

8.21 It is only possible here to refer to a few of the terms implied into contracts under the present heading. In contracts of employment a number of obligations on the employee are implied, for instance: to faithfully serve his employer[1]; not to act against his employer's interests[2]; to use reasonable care and skill in performing his duties[3]; and to indemnify his employer against any liability incurred by the employer as a result of his wrongful acts[4]. Reciprocal terms are implied in the employee's favour, the employer being obliged, for instance, not to require the employee to do any unlawful act[5], and to use due care to provide safe premises and a safe system of work[6].

The courts have held that there is an implied term in contracts for work and materials that the materials used are reasonably fit for their purpose[7], and that in contracts of hire there is an implied term that the chattel bailed is as fit for the hirer's purpose as reasonable skill and care can make it. In *Reed v Dean*[8], the plaintiff hired the defendant's cabin cruiser for a holiday on the Thames. Two hours after he set off the boat caught fire from an unexplained cause. The fire-fighting equipment on board was out of order and the plaintiff was injured and lost his personal belongings on board. The defendant was held liable for failing to make the boat as fit for the purpose of hiring as reasonable skill and care could make it.

Another example of an implied condition of the present type is provided by the decision of the House of Lords in *Liverpool City Council v Irwin*[9], where it was held that, where parts of a building have been let to different tenants (the case concerned a high rise block of flats) and essential rights of access over parts of the building, such as stairs, retained by the landlord have been granted to the individual tenants, a term could be implied in the tenancy agreement that the landlord will take reasonable care to keep them reasonably safe and reasonably fit for use by tenants, their families and their visitors.

1 *Hivac Ltd v Park Royal Scientific Instruments Ltd* [1946] Ch 169, [1946] 1 All ER 350, CA.
2 *Wessex Dairies Ltd v Smith* [1935] 2 KB 80, CA.
3 *Lister v Romford Ice and Cold Storage Co Ltd* [1957] AC 555, [1957] 1 All ER 125, HL.
4 *Ibid.*
5 *Gregory v Ford* [1951] 1 All ER 121.
6 *Lister v Romford Ice and Cold Storage Co Ltd,* supra.
7 *G. H. Myers & Co v Brent Cross Service Co* [1934] 1 KB 46.
8 [1949] 1 KB 188.
9 [1977] AC 239, [1976] 2 All ER 39, HL.

Implication to give business efficacy

8.22 The implication of a term under this heading is less common and can only be made when it is necessary in the particular circumstances to imply a term to give business efficacy to the contract and make it a workable agreement in such manner as the parties would clearly have done if they had applied their minds to the contingency which has arisen. This power of judicial implication was recognised in *The Moorcock*[1], which concerned a contract permitting the plaintiff to unload his ship at the defendants' jetty. A warranty on the part of the defendants was implied into the contract that the river bed was, so far as reasonable care could provide, in a condition which would not damage the ship when she grounded at low tide, as both parties realised she would. Bowen, LJ, stated that where the parties had not dealt with the burden of a particular peril a court could imply a term which would give such efficacy to the contract as both parties must have intended it to have.

The test which the courts apply in deciding whether to imply a term to give the contract business efficacy is a strict one. A term cannot be implied unless it is *necessary* to give business efficacy to the contract and can be formulated with a *sufficient degree of precision*: it is not enough that it is reasonable in all the circumstances to imply the term[2]. A classic statement of the test is that of Scrutton, LJ, in *Reigate v Union Manufacturing Co (Ramsbottom) Ltd*[3]: 'A term can only be implied if it is necessary in the business sense to give efficacy to the contract, i.e. if it is such a term that if at the time the contract was being negotiated someone had said to the parties: "What will happen in such a case?" they would both have replied: "Of course so and so will happen; we did not trouble to say that; it is too clear".'

1 (1889) 14 PD 64, CA.
2 *Liverpool City Council v Irwin* [1977] AC 239, [1976] 2 All ER 39, HL.

Shell UK Ltd v Lostock Garages Ltd [1977] 1 All ER 481, [1976] 1 WLR 1187, CA.
3   [1918] 1 KB 592 at 605. Also see *Shirlaw v Southern Foundries (1926) Ltd* [1939] 2 KB 206 at 227, [1939] 2 All ER 113 at 124.

8.23   Pursuant to these principles, the courts have, for instance, refused to imply terms in the following cases: where tariff booklets were supplied free to a hotel in consideration of its proprietors undertaking to circulate or display them for a specified period, a term to the effect that the proprietors' obligation should cease if the business was sold was not implied[1]; where a petrol company subsidised two neighbouring filling stations during a price cutting war, a term to the effect that it would not abnormally discriminate against the plaintiff's filling station in favour of competitors was not implied into a contract for the exclusive supply of petrol by the petrol company to the plaintiff[2]; where a variety artiste's clothes were stolen from his dressing room during rehearsals, a term was not implied into the contract between him and the theatrical producer that the latter would take reasonable care to ensure that the artiste's effects were not stolen[3].

In contrast, the courts have, for example, implied a term: into international contracts of sale, with respect to the responsibility of a party to obtain a necessary export or import licence[4]; into a contract for a Turkish bath, that the couches for reclining on were free from vermin[5]; into a contract between a driving school and its client, that any car provided under the contract would be covered by insurance[6]; and into a contract for the laying of a carpet, that it should be done in a proper and workmanlike manner[7]. In addition, the courts have generally held that a term is necessarily implied in any contract that neither party shall prevent the other from performing it[8].

Since the implication of a term under *The Moorcock* principle is always dependent on the particular circumstances of the case, the implication of a term under it does not lay down a general rule for the future.

---

1   *General Publicity Services Ltd v Best's Brewery Co Ltd* [1951] 2 TLR 875, CA.
2   *Shell UK Ltd v Lostock Garages Ltd* [1977] 1 All ER 481, [1976] 1 WLR 1187, CA.
3   *Deyong v Shenburn* [1946] KB 227, [1946] 1 All ER 226, CA.
4   *H O Brandt & Co v H N Morris & Co Ltd* [1917] 2 KB 784, CA.
5   *Silverman v Imperial London Hotels Ltd* (1927) 137 LT 57.
6   *British School of Motoring Ltd v Simms* [1971] 1 All ER 317.
7   *Kimber v William Willett Ltd* [1947] KB 570, [1947] 1 All ER 361, CA.
8   *William Cory & Son Ltd v London Corp* [1951] 2 KB 476 at 484, [1951] 2 All ER 85 at 88.

8.24   So far our discussion of the law of contract has concentrated on the formation and enforceability of a contract. In the next three chapters we shall be concerned principally with how a contract is discharged. The discharge of a contract generally means that both parties are freed from their contractual obligations. Sometimes, however, a contract is discharged in relation to one party, but not in relation to the other, in which case the latter becomes liable to an action for damages.

A contract can be discharged in four ways:

by agreement (which we discussed in paras. 6.32 and 6.36);
by performance;
by breach;
by frustration.

Chapter 9
Discharge by Performance

9.1 A contract is normally discharged by both parties performing their obligations under it, both parties being released from further liability thereby. If only one party performs his contractual obligations he alone is discharged and he acquires a right of action against the other for breach of contract, a subject which we discuss in the next chapter. Special rules govern the discharge of a party who has unsuccessfully tendered performance or whose obligations are performed for him by another.

PERFORMANCE

9.2 For a party to be discharged by performance he must have precisely performed all his obligations under the contract. Thus, to decide whether a party is discharged by performance, one must first ascertain and construe the terms of the contract, express and implied, to see what his contractual obligations were, and then look at what has happened to see whether what he has done precisely corresponds with those obligations. The requirement of precise performance is a strict one and, if it is not met, it is irrelevant that the performance effected is commercially no less valuable than that which was promised. In *Arcos Ltd v E. A. Ronaasen & Son*[1], the plaintiffs contracted to supply the defendants with a certain quantity of timber which, as they knew, was to be used for constructing cement barrels. The contract specified that the timber should be half an inch thick but when it was delivered the defendants discovered that 95 per cent of it was over half an inch thick, although none of it exceeded three quarters of an inch in thickness. It was still perfectly possible for the defendants to use all the wood, as it had been delivered, for the construction of cement barrels but the House of Lords held that they were entitled to reject the whole consignment since the plaintiffs had not performed a contractual obligation[2]. Lord Atkin stated, *obiter*, that only if a deviation from the terms of the contract was 'microscopic' could the contract be taken to have been correctly performed. An example of this is provided by *Shipton, Anderson & Co v Weil Bros & Co*[3], where a contract requiring the delivery of 4,950 tons of wheat was held to have been performed by the seller although he had delivered 4,950 tons 55 lbs.

Generally, no demand for performance is necessary to render an obligation to perform operative[4]. Thus, a debtor is bound to seek out his creditor and pay him[5].

---

1 [1933] AC 470, HL.
2 The contractual obligation broken was that implied by the Sale of Goods Act 1893, s.13(1), viz. that in a sale of goods by description the goods must correspond with that description. See para. 22.47.
3 [1912] 1 KB 574.
4 A demand will be necessary if there is an express agreement or trade usage requiring it.
5 *Walton v Mascall* (1844) 13 M & W 452.

Payment

9.3 Where the obligation of one party to the other consists in the payment of a sum of money the contract is discharged by the payment of that sum. Payment should, primarily, be made in legal tender[1] but may, with the consent of the creditor, be made by cheque or other negotiable instrument.

---

1 Para. 9.13, a.

9.4 Where a cheque or other negotiable instrument is given in payment its effect may be to absolutely discharge or only conditionally discharge the debtor. The discharge will be *absolute* if the creditor promises expressly or impliedly, in accepting the cheque, to discharge the debtor from his existing obligations. If this occurs the creditor loses his right of action on the original contract but can sue on his rights under the instrument if it is dishonoured[1]. However, the presumption is that the creditor only accepts a cheque as a *conditional* discharge, so that the debtor is not discharged unless, and until, the instrument is honoured and, if it is dishonoured, may be sued on the original contract or on the dishonoured instrument[2].

---

1 *Sard v Rhodes* (1836) 1 M & W 153.
2 *Sayer v Wagstaff* (1844) 5 Beav 415; *Re Romer and Haslam* [1893] 2 QB 286, CA.

9.5 If the creditor requests payment through the post, the payment will be deemed to have been duly made even though it is lost in transit after being posted[1], unless it was sent in a manner inappropriate to the amount in question (e.g. sending a substantial sum in cash)[2]. A request for postal payment may be express or implied, but the mere fact that remittances have been posted over a number of years without any objection by the creditor does not raise such an implication[3].

---

1 *Thairlwall v Great Northern Rly Co* [1910] 2 KB 509, DC.
2 *Mitchell-Henry v Norwich Union Life Insurance Society* [1918] 2 KB 67, CA.
3 *Pennington v Crossley & Son* (1897) 77 LT 43, CA.

Proof of payment

9.6 It is commonly, but mistakenly, believed that payment of a debt can only be proved by producing a written receipt. In fact, payment may be proved by any evidence from which payment may be inferred[1]. In particular, s.3 of the Cheques Act 1957 provides that an unindorsed cheque which appears to have been paid by the banker on whom it is drawn shall be evidence of the receipt by the payee of the sum payable on the cheque.

A debtor is not entitled to insist on a receipt when paying a debt and if he does obtain a receipt it is only prima facie, not conclusive, evidence that a debt has been paid[2]. Therefore, it is always possible for the person who has given the receipt to show either that he has not received payment or that the receipt was given by mistake[3], or obtained by fraud[4], or that it was given on certain terms or in respect of a particular matter[5].

---

1 *Eyles v Ellis* (1827) 4 Bing 112.
2 *Wilson v Keating* (1859) 27 Beav 121.
3 *Cesarini v Ronzani* (1858) 1 F & F 339.
4 *Skaife v Jackson* (1824) 3 B & C 421.
5 *Re W. W. Duncan & Co* [1905] 1 Ch 307.

Appropriation of payments

9.7 We are concerned here with the case where a debtor who owes two or more debts to the same creditor makes a payment which is insufficient to discharge the whole of his indebtedness to that creditor. In some cases it may be of vital importance to know to which of the debts payment relates (or, to use technical language, is appropriated). Suppose that X owes Y two debts, one of which is unenforceable for some reason and the other not, and X pays Y a sum which is insufficient to cover both debts. If it is permissible for Y to appropriate the payment to the unenforceable debt, he will thereby have succeeded in getting an unenforceable debt paid, leaving the other debt still payable. Similarly, if one debt is guaranteed or secured and the other is not, it will be of advantage to Y if it is permissible for him to appropriate the payment to the unsecured debt, because he can enforce his guarantee or security to obtain payment of the other.

The following three rules govern the appropriation of payments.

Appropriation by the debtor
9.8 The debtor may appropriate his payment to a particular debt or debts, *provided he does so at the time of payment*. The debtor's intention to appropriate payments in a particular way must either expressly be communicated to the creditor or be capable of being inferred from the circumstances of the case as known to both parties[1]. Thus, if a debtor who owes a creditor two debts makes a payment denying the existence of one of them, an appropriation to the debt which is not denied can be inferred[2]. Similarly, if he makes a payment which exactly corresponds to the amount owing under one of the debts, an appropriation to that debt can be inferred[3]. The debtor must appropriate at the time of payment and if he does so the creditor is bound, assuming he accepts the payment, to apply it in the manner directed by the creditor[4]. Therefore, if the creditor does not agree with the debtor's appropriation, he must refuse to accept payment, and stand upon his legal rights[5].

---

1 *Leeson v Leeson* [1936] 2 KB 156, [1936] 2 All ER 133, CA.
2 *Burn v Boulton* (1846) 2 CB 476.
3 *Marryatts v White* (1817) 2 Stark 101.
4 *Peters v Anderson* (1814) 5 Taunt 596; *Croft v Lumley* (1858) 5 E & B 648.
5 *Croft v Lumley* (1858) 5 E & B 648.

Appropriation by the creditor
9.9 *In the absence of an appropriation by the debtor,* the creditor may appropriate the payment as he chooses, *at any time*. The creditor's choice of appropriation need not be made in express terms: it may be declared by bringing an action on a debt to which he has decided not to appropriate the payment or in any other way which indicates his choice of appropriation[1]. Moreover, until he has declared his appropriation to the debtor he may alter it[2].

Unlike an appropriation by the debtor, an appropriation by the creditor can be made at any time before he finally exercises his right of appropriation or something has happened which would make it inequitable for him to exercise it[3]. Thus, it was held in *Seymour v Pickett*[4] that a creditor who had been owed two debts could make his appropriation for the first time in the witness box. If he wishes, the creditor may appropriate the payment to a debt which, though valid, is unenforceable, because it is statute barred, or because the contract should have been evidenced in writing, or for some other reason. In *Seymour v Pickett*, for example, the plaintiff creditor was an unregistered dentist who, by statute, could not recover any fee for performing dental surgery (although the debt was not an illegal one), but could recover the price of material supplied. The plaintiff treated the defendant and the bill came to £45, £24 for services and £21 for material, including a bridge and gold fillings. The defendant gave the plaintiff two cheques, one for £20 and the other, which was post-dated, for £25, without appropriating either. The latter was dishonoured, the defendant having stopped payment of it by his bank. In an action by the plaintiff it was held that he could appropriate the £20 to the payment of his professional fees, and had done so by a declaration in the witness box, and therefore could recover the £21 relating to materials supplied which thus remained unpaid. On the other hand, the creditor cannot appropriate payment to an illegal debt[5] or to a 'debt' under a void contract[6].

It should be noted that in many cases where money is owed under agreements regulated by the Consumer Credit Act 1974, e.g. hire-purchase agreements, the creditor has no right of appropriation. We consider the position under the Consumer Credit Act in para. 23.35.

---

1 *The Mecca* [1897] AC 286, HL.
2 *Simson v Ingham* (1823) 2 B & C 65.
3 *The Mecca* [1897] AC 286, HL; *Seymour v Pickett* [1905] 1 KB 715, CA.
4 [1905] 1 KB 715, CA.
5 *Wright v Laing* (1824) 3 B & C 165.
6 *Keeping v Broom* (1895) 11 TLR 595.

Payments into a current account
9.10 A special rule, the rule in *Clayton's Case*[1], applies to payments into a current account. This rule of convenience, based on so-called presumed intention, is that each payment into a current account is appropriated to the earliest debt which is not statute-barred[2]. The rule is limited to cases where there is a current account, i.e. an unbroken account between the parties into which all receipts and payments out are carried in order of date, so that all sums paid in form a blended fund[3], such as a current account at a bank, or a current account between traders 'for goods supplied and work done rendered periodically with a balance carried forward'[4]. The rule does not apply where there is no unbroken account, but merely an account containing distinct and separate debts[5].

Since the rule is based on presumed intention it is excluded if the parties otherwise agree, or a contrary intention appears from the circumstances[6]. It is insufficient, however, simply to show that a bank refused to allow cheques to be drawn on an overdrawn account unless credits of an equivalent amount were paid in. The rule will not be excluded if such credits are paid in, and they will therefore go in reduction of the oldest debts and not in offsetting newly drawn cheques.

Despite the rule, the balance owed on an unbroken account is a single and undivided debt, and for that reason payment constitutes part payment of that debt within the meaning of the Limitation Act 1939 and revives the whole outstanding balance[7].

---

1 *Devaynes v Noble: Clayton's Case* (1816) 1 Mer 572.
2 *Re Sherry* (1884) 25 Ch D 692 at 702; *Nash v Hodgson* (1855) 6 De G M & G 474.
3 *Hooper v Keay* (1871) 1 QBD 178.
4 *Albemarle Supply Co Ltd v Hind & Co* [1928] 1 KB 307 at 319.
5 *The Mecca* [1897] AC 286, HL.
6 *The Mecca*; *Mutton v Peat* [1899] 2 Ch 556 (reversed on the facts, [1900] 2 Ch 79, CA).
7 *Re Footman, Bower & Co Ltd* [1961] Ch 443, [1961] 2 All ER 161.

TENDER OF PERFORMANCE

9.11 If a party makes a valid tender (i.e. offer) of performance of his contractual obligations and the other party refuses to accept performance, the party making the tender is freed from liability for non-performance of those obligations, provided that the tender is made under such circumstances that the other party has a reasonable opportunity of examining the performance tendered, e.g. the goods tendered, in order to ascertain that it conforms with the contract[1].

---

1 *Startup v Macdonald* (1843) 6 Man & G 593 at 610. Also see Sale of Goods Act 1893, ss. 29 and 34; para. 22.65.

Tender of payment

9.12 If a party makes a valid tender of payment of money which he owes but the other party refuses to accept it, this does not discharge his debt but there is no obligation to make a further tender. If an action is brought for non-payment against a party who has tendered unsuccessfully, all he has to do is to pay the money into court, whereupon, if he has pleaded and proved a valid tender:

a. the costs of the action must be borne by the other party[1];

b. a claim for interest on the debt subsequent to the rejection of the tender is barred[2];

c. a right of lien is generally extinguished[3]; and

d. he is not liable for his non-performance;

so that a creditor who refuses a valid tender of payment eventually can obtain nothing but the money originally tendered to him and a debtor who has validly tendered payment is not prejudiced by a refusal to accept it.

---

1 *Griffiths v Ystradyfodwg School Board* (1890) 24 QBD 307.
2 *Norton v Ellam* (1837) 2 M & W 461.
3 A lien is a right by which a person is entitled to obtain satisfaction for a debt by retaining property belonging to the person indebted to him.

9.13 A valid tender requires the following:

a. The money must be actually produced[1]: it is not enough for the debtor to offer to pay and simply put his hand in his pocket[2]. The sole exception to the requirement of production is where the creditor expressly or impliedly dispenses with it[3]. The creditor will impliedly dispense with the need for production if, when the debtor tells him that he has come to pay a specified amount, the creditor says it is too late or otherwise indicates that he will not accept the money[4].

b. The tender must be in legal currency: a creditor is not obliged to accept a cheque or other negotiable instrument or payment in currency which is not legal tender[5]. By the Currency and Bank Notes Act 1954 and the Coinage Act 1971 legal tender is as follows:

   i. Bank of England notes, to any amount;
   ii. gold coins of the Mint, to any amount;
   iii. silver and cupro-nickel coins of the Mint of more than 10p, up to £10;
   iv. silver and cupro-nickel coins of the Mint of not more than 10p, up to £5;
   v. bronze coins, up to 20p.

c. If the amount tendered is greater than the debt due the tender is invalid if the creditor is required to give change[6]. However, a tender of an excess payment will be valid if, though change is requested, the creditor refuses the tender for some other reason[7], or if the debtor is happy for the creditor to keep the excess amount[8].

d. The tender must not be made on any condition. Thus, in *Finch v Miller*[9], it was held that a tender made on condition that a receipt for a full discharge be given was invalid. On the other hand, a valid tender may be made under protest so as to reserve the right of the debtor to dispute the amount, provided it does not impose conditions on the creditor[10].

e. Where a debt is expressly made payable on a particular day, a tender made after that date is not strictly a valid tender. However, provided it is made before the commencement of an action for the recovery of the debt it will, generally, have the same effect as a valid tender[11].

f. The tender must be in exact accordance with any other special terms of the contract, e.g. as to place of payment.

---

1 *Thomas v Evans* (1808) 10 East 101.
2 *Finch v Brook* (1834) 1 Bing NC 253.
3 *Farquharson v Pearl Insurance Co Ltd* [1937] 3 All ER 124.
4 *Ibid.*
5 *Blumberg v Life Interests and Reversionary Securities Corpn* [1897] 1 Ch 171 (upheld on appeal [1898] 1 Ch 27, CA).
6 *Robinson v Cook* (1815) 6 Taunt 336.
7 *Bevans v Rees* (1839) 5 M & W 306.
8 *Wade's Case* (1601) 5 Co Rep 114a.
9 (1848) 5 CB 428.
10 *Greenwood v Sutcliffe* [1892] 1 Ch 1, CA.
11 *Briggs v Calverly* (1800) 8 Term Rep 629.

Tender of acts

9.14 Where a party is obliged to perform some act, other than the payment of something, he will make a valid tender of performance if he attempts to perform the act in precise accordance with the terms of the contract. In the case of a contract for the sale of goods, the tender of them must be made at a reasonable hour[1].

If a party (A) makes a valid tender of an act, but the other (B) refuses to accept the tendered performance, A is entitled to maintain an action for breach of contract[2]. Moreover, if B's refusal is absolute and unqualified it will constitute a repudiation of the contract, in which case A will also be entitled to treat the repudiation as discharging him from his obligation to perform the contract[3]. In the case of contracts for the sale of goods these rules have been given statutory effect by the Sale of Goods Act 1893, s.37, which we discuss in para. 22.82.

An invalid tender does not as a rule prevent the party who made it from subsequently making a valid tender[4]. However, it may be impossible to make a subsequent, valid tender simply because performance had to be made on a particular day and that day is now past.

Again, if the invalid tender amounts to a repudiation of the contract and this is treated by the other party as discharging his obligations under the contract, a subsequent tender cannot be valid.

1   Sale of Goods Act 1893, s.29, para. 22.65.
2   *Startup v Macdonald* (1843) 6 Man & G 593.
3   Para. 10.10.
4   *Tetley v Shand* (1871) 25 LT 658.

TIME FOR PERFORMANCE

9.15   When a contract does not stipulate a time within which a party's contractual obligations must be performed, they must be performed within a reasonable time[1].

1   *Postlethwaite v Freeland* (1880) 5 App Cas 599, HL; Sale of Goods Act 1893, s.29; para. 22.65.

9.16   When a time is stipulated for performance of a party's obligations by the contract, the question arises whether time is 'of the essence of the contract'. If it is, a failure on his part to perform in the stipulated time not only constitutes a breach of contract entitling the other party to maintain an action for damages but also a repudiation of the contract, which the other party can accept as discharging him from his contractual obligations[1].

1   Paras. 10.3–10.8.

9.17   Before the Judicature Act 1873, common law and equity had different rules about when time was of the essence of a contract, but since that Act the equitable rules prevail[1], with the result that time is not of the essence unless it falls within one of the following three categories where equity treated it as of the essence:

a. Where the contract expressly states that stipulations as to time must be strictly complied with. In *Harold Wood Brick Co Ltd v Ferris*[2], for instance, a stipulation that the purchase of a brickfield should be completed by 31 August which added that 'the purchase shall in any event be completed not later than 15 September' was held to make time (15 September) the essence of the contract.

b. Where the stipulation does not make time of the essence of the contract, a party who has been subjected to unreasonable delay by the other can make time of the essence by giving him a notice fixing a reasonable time for performance[3].

c. Where the nature of the contract or of its subject-matter, or the circumstances surrounding it, require precise compliance with a stipulation as to time, time must be taken to be of the essence of the contract. An example of a contract where time is normally of the essence under this heading is a contract of a commercial nature. Thus, a stipulation as to the time for the delivery of goods in a sale of goods contract is presumptively of the essence of the contract[4]. However, s.10 of the Sale of Goods Act 1893 provides that a term as to the time of *payment* for goods is deemed not to be of the essence of the contract, unless the contrary intention appears from the contract.

When time is of the essence of a contract the requirement of punctual performance can be waived by extending the time for performance: the end of the extension becoming the new 'essential' time of performance[5].

Even if time is not of the essence, a party who fails to perform within the stipulated time because of his negligence or wilful default is liable in damages[6].

---

1 Law of Property Act 1925, s.41.
2 [1935] 2 KB 198, CA.
3 *Stickney v Keeble* [1915] AC 386, HL.
4 *Reuter, Hufeland & Co v Sala & Co* (1879) 4 CPD 239, CA.
5 *Barclay v Messenger* (1874) 43 LJ Ch 449. Withdrawal of a waiver is discussed in para. 6.33b.
6 *Jones v Gardiner* [1902] 1 Ch 191.

PERFORMANCE BY A THIRD PARTY

9.18 In some cases performance of a contractual obligation by a third party can discharge it. Different rules apply depending on whether or not the person to whom the obligation is owed agrees to accept performance by a third party.

Performance by a third party with creditor's consent

9.19 Payment of a debt (or, presumably, the performance of any other type of obligation) by a third party with the creditor's consent is not sufficient to discharge it unless it is made by him as agent for, and on behalf of, the debtor and with the debtor's prior authority or subsequent ratification (which can even be given at the trial of an action to enforce the debt against him)[1]. If this test is not satisfied the debt is not discharged and therefore remains enforceable against the debtor. In *Smith v Cox*[2], S was R's tenant and C, an estate agent, was

R's agent to collect the rent. S owed £260 arrears of rent, but C, knowing that R was old and poor, and largely dependent on the rent of the house, had, as the rent became due, sent her out of his own pocket a sum equivalent to the rent owing, trusting to recoup himself out of the rent when it was paid by S. When he failed to obtain the rent C distrained and recovered the arrears less a deduction for repairs. S sued C, arguing that the distress was unlawful because R had been paid by C and his (S's) liability had been discharged thereby. He admitted that the payments were made without his knowledge and not at his request. It was held that S had not been discharged, and therefore the distress was lawful, because the payments had not been made by C as agent for, and on behalf of, S, nor with his authority or subsequent ratification.

Provided the above test is satisfied the contract is discharged even though the third party's performance which is accepted by the creditor differs from that required by the contract. In *Hirachand Punamchand v Temple*[3], for instance, a debt was held to be discharged when the creditor accepted a smaller sum from the debtor's father in full settlement, with the result that the creditor's action against the debtor for the balance was dismissed.

---

1 *Simpson v Eggington* (1855) 10 Exch 845.
2 [1940] 2 KB 558, [1940] 3 All ER 546.
3 [1911] 2 KB 330, CA.

Performance by a third party without creditor's consent

9.20 Even though the creditor does not consent to performance by a third party, it is permissible for the debtor to get a third party to precisely perform his contractual obligation, and hence secure his discharge, provided it can be properly inferred from the terms of the contract, its subject-matter and surrounding circumstances that it is a matter of indifference whether the performance is by the debtor or his nominee. This inference is easily made in the case of a debt since if full payment is made in cash it is normally a matter of indifference to the creditor that it is paid by someone other than the debtor. The inference has also been drawn in the case of other types of obligation, as is shown by *British Waggon Co v Lea & Co*[1]. The Parkgate Waggon Co had contracted to let a number of railway wagons to the defendants and to keep them in repair. The Parkgate Waggon Co went into liquidation and assigned both the benefit of, and the liabilities under, the contract to the plaintiffs. The defendants claimed to treat the contract as at an end and refused to accept performance by the plaintiffs. It was held that the contract could be validly performed by the plaintiffs since it was a matter of indifference to the defendants who kept the wagons in repair — it being 'work which any ordinary workman conversant with the business could execute' — so long as the work was done efficiently by someone.

On the other hand the inference that vicarious performance is permissible will not be drawn where the contract expressly or impliedly provides that it must be performed personally by the debtor. Thus, a contract performed without the creditor's consent by a third party will not discharge the debtor's liability if the contract is of such a nature that the creditor was relying on some personal skill or other personal qualification of the debtor. Thus, it has been held that personal care and skill is an ingredient of a contract by a warehouseman to store furniture[2]. A fortiori, obligations under a contract of employment are normally personal to the parties.

---

1   (1880) 5 QBD 149.
2   *Edwards v Newland & Co* [1950] 2 KB 534, [1950] 1 All ER 1072, CA.

9.21   Where performance by a third party without the creditor's consent is permissible, the debtor nevertheless remains liable on the contract for performance and can be sued for non-performance or defective performance[1]. The third party is not liable on the contract, but if he performs the contract negligently he may be liable in tort.

---

1   *Stewart v Reavell's Garage* [1952] 2 QB 545, [1952] 1 All ER 1191.

Chapter 10
Breach

10.1 Breach of contract occurs where a party does not perform his contractual obligations precisely, in the sense discussed in para. 9.2, and this failure is without lawful excuse. Thus, a breach will occur where a party without lawful excuse refuses to perform his contractual obligations, or simply fails to perform them, or incapacitates himself from performing them, or performs them defectively. Thus, to decide whether a party is in breach of contract, one must first ascertain and construe the terms of the contract, express and implied, to see what his contractual obligations were, and then look at what has happened to see whether he has failed without lawful excuse to perform those obligations precisely.

A person has a lawful excuse for failing to perform his contractual obligations precisely in the following cases:

a. if the contract has been discharged by frustration, a matter which we discuss in the next chapter;

b. if there is impossibility of performance less than frustration; for instance, a temporary illness preventing an employee working provides a lawful excuse for his failure to work during the period of the illness[1];

c. if he has validly tendered performance of his obligations in accordance with the rules set out in paras. 9.11 to 9.14, but this has been rejected by the other party;

d. if the other party has made it impossible for him to perform his obligations.

---

1 *Poussard v Spiers and Pond* (1876) 1 QBD 410.

10.2 Subject to a valid exemption clause to the contrary, whenever a party to the contract is in breach of contract, the injured party may always claim damages, either by an action of his own, or by way of a counter-claim in an action brought against him by the defaulting party, and even where no actual loss or damage to the injured party can be proved, nominal damages will be awarded. Furthermore, the injured party may be entitled, additionally or instead, to claim specific performance or an injunction. We discuss the question of remedies in Chapter 12.

In addition, if the breach constitutes a repudiatory breach of contract the injured party has the right to treat the contract as discharged. If he elects to do so, he is said to rescind the contract for breach.

Before we proceed to discuss the question of discharge by repudiatory breach, we wish to point out that a party is also entitled to rescind in a case where there would have been a repudiatory breach but for the fact that the other party's failure to perform was due to impossibility less than frustration[1].

---

1 *Poussard v Spiers and Pond* (1876) 1 QBD 410.

RESCISSION FOR BREACH

Option to rescind or affirm

10.3 A repudiatory breach does not automatically discharge the contract. Instead, the injured party has an option to rescind the contract or to affirm it.

Rescission

10.4 The injured party will rescind the contract if he notifies the defaulting party that he regards himself as discharged by the repudiatory breach. Thus, the contract will be rescinded if the injured party refuses to accept defective performance or refuses to accept further performance or simply refuses to perform his own contractual obligations. If the injured party elects to rescind the contract, his contractual obligations which are not yet due for performance are discharged with the result that, for instance, he is not bound to accept or pay for further performance[1]. Thus, an injured party who has rescinded the contract for breach can resist successfully any action brought for failing to perform an obligation which is due thereafter. In addition, an injured party who has rescinded may be entitled:

a. to refuse to pay for partial or defective performance already received by him (see paras. 10.14 and 10.15); or

b. to reclaim any money which he has paid to the defaulting party if he can reject the defective performance or if certain other circumstances exist (see para. 17.7,b.).

---

1 *General Billposting Co Ltd v Atkinson* [1909] AC 118, HL.

10.5 The defaulting party's position is as follows. He remains liable to perform any obligations which are due at the time of the election to rescind, and can be sued for damages for the repudiatory breach, or any other breach committed before the injured party's election. On the other hand, the defaulting party's obligations which are not due for performance at the time of the election are discharged but he can, nevertheless, be sued for damages for any loss suffered by the injured party as the result of his repudiatory breach[1].

---

1 *R. V. Ward Ltd v Bignall* [1967] 1 QB 534, [1967] 2 All ER 449, CA; *Moschi v Lep Air Services Ltd* [1973] AC 331, [1972] 2 All ER 393, HL.

10.6 It may be added that if the injured party has started to perform his contractual obligations but is unjustifiably prevented from completing them by the other party, he can bring an action for reasonable remuneration. This is called suing on a *quantum meruit*[1].

---

1 Para. 12.17.

10.7 Rescission does not necessarily extinguish the contract completely in relation to obligations whose performance is due after the time of the election to rescind, since obligations relating to matters such as arbitration or jurisdiction may continue in existence if it was the intention of the parties, when they made the contract, that this should be so[1]. In addition, the parties' future obligations under the contract are still relevant in that they must be referred to in assessing the damages due from the party in default. The fact that, unlike rescission for misrepresentation[2], rescission for breach does not terminate the contract as if it had never been made means that it is not barred by impossibility of restoring the parties to their former position.

---

1 *Heyman v Darwins Ltd* [1942] AC 356, [1942] 1 All ER 337, HL.
2 Para. 15.9.

Affirmation

10.8 The injured party will affirm the contract if, with full knowledge of the facts, he treats it as still in existence, as where he decides to keep the defective goods delivered or, if the defaulting party has not completed performance, where he calls on him to perform.

If the injured party elects to affirm, the contract remains in force, so that both parties are bound to continue performing any outstanding contractual obligations. Each party retains the right to sue for past or future breaches. Thus, if a seller of goods affirms the contract after a repudiatory breach by the buyer, the seller remains liable to deliver possession of the goods to the buyer and the buyer remains liable to accept delivery of the goods and pay the contract price[1]. Another example is provided by *Bentsen v Taylor, Sons & Co*[2], where a charterparty described the ship as 'now sailed or about to sail' from a port to the United Kingdom. In fact, she did not sail for another month. This constituted a repudiatory breach of contract[3] but, instead of electing to rescind the contract, the charterers intimated to the shipowner that he was still bound to send the ship to the port of loading and that they, the charterers, would load her there, thereby affirming the contract. When the ship arrived, the charterers refused to load her. The Court of Appeal held that, since the contract had been affirmed, the shipowner was entitled to payment of freight, subject to a set-off for the charterers for damages for the breach of contract referred to above.

---

1 *R. V. Ward Ltd v Bignall* [1967] 1 QB 534, [1967] 2 All ER 449, CA.
2 [1893] 2 QB 274, CA.
3 Because the term broken was a condition, see paras. 10.18–10.20.

Cases where there is no option to rescind or affirm

10.9 The injured party is not entitled to affirm where continued performance by him depends on the co-operation of the defaulting party and this is refused[1]. The result in such a case is that the contract is automatically discharged by a repudiatory breach. Thus, if an employer wrongfully dismisses an employee, this automatically terminates the contract of employment and the employee must sue for damages for breach of contract[2].

On the other hand, if the broken contract is contained in a lease and is inseparable from it, the injured party does not have the option to rescind the lease or the contract[3]. Another case where he does not have the option to rescind is discussed in para. 22.40,b.

---

1 *White and Carter (Councils) Ltd v McGregor* [1962] AC 413 at 430, 432 and 439.

2   *Denmark Productions Ltd v Boscobel Productions Ltd* [1969] 1 QB 699, [1968] 3 All ER 513, CA.
3   *Total Oil (Great Britain) Ltd v Thompson Garages (Biggin Hill) Ltd* [1972] 1 QB 318, [1971] 3 All ER 1226, CA.

Types of repudiatory breach

Renunciation

10.10   Where one party renounces his contractual obligations the other party is entitled to rescind the contract. A party is said to renounce his contractual obligations if he has evinced an intention no longer to be bound by the contract[1]. Such an intention is easily established where there has been an express and unequivocal refusal to perform. Thus, if an employee unqualifiedly refuses to carry out his duties his employer is entitled to dismiss him (i.e. rescind the contract of employment)[2]. Another example of renunciation by express refusal is *Hochster v De La Tour*, which is dealt with in para. 10.12. However, express refusal is not essential; an intent no longer to be bound by the contract can also be implied by the words or conduct of a party. The actual intention of the party is not decisive in such a case since the test is whether his words and conduct were such as to lead a reasonable person to believe that he did not intend to be bound by the contract[3].

---

1   *Mersey Steel and Iron Co v Naylor, Benzon and Co* (1884) 9 App Cas 434, HL; para. 22.71.
2   *Gorse v Durham County Council* [1971] 2 All ER 666, [1971] 1 WLR 775.
3   *Ross T. Smyth & Co Ltd v Bailey & Son & Co* [1940] 3 All ER 60 at 72.

Incapacitation

10.11   Even though he has not evinced an intention not to be bound by the contract, a party who, *by his own act or default* incapacitates himself from performing his contractual obligations, is treated as if he had refused to perform them. As Devlins J, said in *Universal Cargo Carriers Corpn v Citati*[1], 'To say "I would like to but cannot" negatives intent to perform as much as "I will not" '. Where a party has incapacitated himself from performing, it is no defence to show that he might be able to recover the capacity to perform[2]. As *Lovelock v Franklyn*, which is dealt with in the next paragraph, shows, one example of a case where a party has made performance of his obligations impossible is where A has contracted to sell a specific thing to B but then sells it to C.

---

1   [1957] 2 QB 401 at 437, [1957] 2 All ER 70 at 85.
2   *Omnium D'Enterprises v Sutherland* [1919] 1 KB 618, CA.

10.12 Renunciation or incapacitation may take place not only in the course of performance but also before either party is entitled to demand performance by the other of his obligations – a situation which is normally described as 'anticipatory breach'. If a party commits an anticipatory breach the injured party can accept the breach as discharging the contract (i.e. rescind) and bring an action for damages for breach of contract or a *quantum meruit* action immediately: he does not have to wait for the time of performance to become due. A leading authority is *Hochster v De La Tour*[1]. The defendant agreed to employ the plaintiff as a courier from 1 June 1852. On 11 May, the defendant informed the plaintiff that his services would no longer be required. The plaintiff brought an action for damages before 1 June and succeeded. Another example is provided by *Lovelock v Franklyn*[2], where the defendant agreed to assign his interest in a lease to the plaintiff for £140. Before the agreed date of performance arrived, the defendant assigned his interest to another person. It was held that the plaintiff could bring an action for damages immediately: he did not have to wait for the time of performance to arrive.

If the injured party decides to rescind for anticipatory breach the other party is not permitted to withdraw his renunciation and seek to perform his contractual obligations[3].

---

1 (1853) 2 E & B 678.
2 (1846) 2 QB 371.
3 *Xenos v Danube and Black Sea Rly Co* (1863) 14 CB NS 325.

10.13 As in the other situations where a party can rescind for the other's failure to perform, a contract is not automatically discharged by anticipatory breach; instead the injured party has an election to rescind or affirm the contract. If he refuses to accept the renunciation as discharging the contract and continues to insist on performance he will affirm it. When a contract is affirmed after anticipatory breach the effects are as follows:

a. The injured party loses his right to bring an action for damages for anticipatory breach.

b. The contract remains in force. Each party remains liable to perform his obligations when they become due and will be liable if he fails to perform then. Thus, the party who committed the anticipatory breach is given an opportunity to perform his obligations and only if he fails to do so will he be liable. The contract remains in existence at the risk of both parties so that if the party who has affirmed after anticipatory breach subsequently commits a breach of contract he will be liable and either party can take advantage of any supervening circumstance which would justify him in declining to perform[1].

c. As opposed to the case where the injured party immediately sues for damages for anticipatory breach, a party who affirms is under no duty to mitigate his damages before performance is due[2] with the result that he may recover larger damages in the event of ultimate non-performance by the other.

---

1 *Frost v Knight* (1872) LR 7 Exch 111 at 112; *White and Carter (Councils) Ltd v McGregor* [1962] AC 413, [1961] 3 All ER 1178, HL.
2 *White and Carter (Councils) Ltd v McGregor;* para. 12.10, b.

Failure to perform an entire obligation

10.14 An entire obligation is one whose complete and precise performance is a condition precedent[1] (i.e. a pre-condition) of the performance by the other party of his obligations. A particular obligation may be entire:

a. *By statute* For instance, in contracts for the sale of goods the obligation to deliver the *quantity* specified in the contract is entire[2].

b. *By express agreement between the parties.*

c. *By implication* This occurs where, on the true construction of the contract, the parties intended that complete and precise performance by a party of a particular obligation should be a pre-condition of performance by the other party of his obligations. The cases show that, if B is to pay a lump sum for A's work *after* it has been completed, A's obligation to do the work is impliedly entire[3]. Because of the harsh consequences of finding an obligation to be entire, the courts lean against construing a contract so as to require complete performance of an obligation before the other party's obligations become operative[4]. Thus, if a lump sum is payable for work, but the contract does not say when it is payable, the court is likely to construe the obligation as not being entire but severable[5].

If a party does not completely and precisely perform an entire obligation, the injured party can rescind the contract and the defaulting party cannot claim any performance by him. This is exemplified by *Sumpter v Hedges*[6], where the plaintiff agreed to build two houses and a stable on the defendant's land for a lump sum of £565. The plaintiff did part of the work to the value of about £333 and then abandoned the contract because of lack of money. It was held that the plaintiff's obligation to build the two houses and a stable was entire and, having failed to do so, he could not recover the contract price nor reasonable remuneration for the work done.

---

1 The present type of 'condition precedent' must be distinguished from that discussed in para. 5.27, which arises where the parties make an agreement subject to some contingent future event on the basis that no immediate

binding contract shall exist until the contingency occurs. The present type of 'condition precedent' does not negative the immediate existence of a binding contract but suspends the liability of one party to perform his obligations until the other party has performed something which he has promised (and is therefore obliged) to do.

2 Sale of Goods Act 1893, s.30.
3 E.g. *H. Dakin & Co Ltd v Lee* [1916] 1 KB 566, CA.
4 *Roberts v Havelock* (1832) 3 B & Ad 404.
5 *Ibid.* Severable obligations are discussed in para. 10.17.
6 [1898] 1 QB 673, CA.

10.15 There are three exceptions to the rule that a party who has not completely and precisely performed an entire obligation cannot recover in respect of any partial performance:

Acceptance of partial performance of entire obligation A claim to remuneration may be made by a party who has incompletely performed an entire obligation if the other party has accepted such partial performance *voluntarily*. Such acceptance gives rise to an inference that there is a fresh agreement by the parties that payment of a reasonable sum or pro rata be made for the work already done or the goods supplied under the original contract[1].

Since the right of recovery depends on the inference of a fresh agreement, it is essential that the party from whom payment is demanded has not just received a benefit but has voluntarily accepted it. He must have had an opportunity, at the time when it became clear that there would not be complete performance of the entire obligation, to accept or reject the partial or defective performance. Thus, in *Sumpter v Hedges*[2], it was held that the builder could not recover reasonable remuneration for the work done because the defendant had no option but to accept the partial performance, viz. the partly erected buildings.

Unjustifiable prevention of performance If the party to whom the entire obligation is owed unjustifiably prevents performance of it, e.g. by stating that he will not accept performance, this will normally constitute a repudiatory breach of contract[3]. If the other party elects to rescind the contract, he can recover reasonable remuneration for his partial performance by a *quantum meruit* claim, or, whether he elects to rescind or not, recover damages for breach of contract.

Frustration As we show in paras. 11.13–11.17, if the contract is discharged by frustration before an entire obligation has been performed, a party who has partly performed it may be able to recover remuneration.

1 *Christy v Row* (1808) 1 Taunt 300; *Sumpter v Hedges* [1898] 1 QB 673 at 674; Sale of Goods Act 1893, s.30.
2 [1898] 1 QB 673.

3 Because the courts are usually ready to imply a term that neither party shall prevent the other from performing his contractual obligations (see para. 8.23), and this term is regarded as a condition (thereby entitling rescission for its breach, para. 10.19).

10.16 *It is important to retain a sense of proportion about entire obligations because they are the exception rather than the rule, as we now propose to demonstrate.*

Although a contract containing an entire obligation is known as an entire contract this is usually something of a misnomer because a contract usually comprises a complex of obligations and, even though one of a party's obligations is entire, the rest may not be. Thus, if A agrees to build a house for B for a lump sum payable on completion, his obligation to build the house is impliedly entire, but his other obligations as to time of performance, quality of work etc. are not entire, unless, very exceptionally, the contract expressly provides that precise performance of them is a pre-condition of payment[1]. Similarly, if C agrees to sell goods to D, his obligation to deliver the correct quantity is entire by statute, but his other obligations as to the quality of the goods and so on are not normally entire. It follows that, if A builds the house but does so defectively or if C delivers the goods but they are defective, B and D are not entitled to rescind the contract for breach of an entire obligation, no such obligation having been broken; nor, unless the obligation broken is sufficiently important or the effects of its breach sufficiently serious, can they rescind under the ground which we discuss next (paras. 10.18–10.22). If the contract cannot be rescinded, A and C are entitled to their contractual payment, subject to a set-off or counter-claim in favour of B and D. In *H. Dakin & Co Ltd v Lee*[2], the plaintiff builders agreed to repair the defendant's house for £264, payable on completion, in accordance with a specification. They did the repairs but these were defective in three ways: a. only two feet of concrete had been put in in underpinning a wall, whereas four feet had been specified; b. four inch iron columns had been fitted in a bay window, instead of five inch ones; c. certain joists in the bay window had not been bolted together in the manner specified. These defects were relatively unimportant. The Court of Appeal held that the plaintiff builders were entitled to recover the £264, less a reduction in respect of the defective work.

---

1 *Eshelby v Federated European Bank Ltd* [1932] 1 KB 423, CA.
2 [1916] 1 KB 566, CA. Also see *Hoenig v Isaacs* [1952] 2 All ER 176, CA; cf. *Bolton v Mahadeva* [1972] 2 All ER 1322, [1972] 1 WLR 1009, CA.

10.17 *Severable obligations* It would be wrong to think that an obligation to build or do some other thing is always an entire obligation. It is only so if the parties expressly or impliedly agree to the effect, or statute provides, that complete performance of the obligation is a pre-condition of the other party's obligations becoming operative. Otherwise an obligation to do something is known as a 'severable' obligation, and the contract containing it as a severable contract. A clear example of a severable obligation is where the contract provides that payment is due from time to time as specified instalments of the other party's obligation are rendered. In such a case, the latter's obligation to do the work etc. is severable, and so is it if payment is at a fixed rate per item or instalment even though payment is not due until after performance has been completed. Partial or defective performance of a severable obligation gives the injured party a right of action in damages but it does not entitle him to rescind the contract unless it amounts to a renunciation or falls within the next ground of rescission which we discuss. The defaulting party is entitled to recover payment at the stipulated rate for each item or instalment which he has provided, subject to a set-off or counter-claim for damages for breach. In *Taylor v Laird*[1], for instance, it was held that a person, who had agreed to skipper a steamer on an exploration and trading voyage up the River Niger at a pay of £50 per month but who abandoned the job before the voyage was completed, was entitled to his salary as each month's service was completed and therefore could recover the month's salary outstanding. Similarly, where a contract provides for the supply of 3,000 tons of coal to be delivered in equal monthly instalments over 12 months at £x per ton, the supplier's obligation to deliver is severable so that, if he abandons the contract after four instalments, he is entitled to payment at the contractual rate for those instalments[2].

---

1 (1856) 1 H & N 266.
2 *Jackson v Rotax Motor and Cycle Co* [1910] 2 KB 937.

Failure to fulfil an obligation which is not an entire obligation
10.18 Failure to fulfil an obligation which is not an entire obligation is the most common type of breach of contract. Unless the party in default has a lawful excuse the injured party can, of course, recover damages for breach of contract but, leaving aside rescission for renunciation or incapacitation, he can only rescind for failure to perform an obligation which is not an entire obligation in two cases:

where it involves breach of a term of the contract which is a condition;

where it involves breach of an 'intermediate term' and the effect of the breach deprives the injured party of substantially the whole benefit of the contract.

10.19 *Breach of condition* Some contractual terms can be classified as conditions, others as warranties. A condition is a statement of fact, or a promise, which forms an *essential* term of the contract[1], or, as it is sometimes put, one which goes to the root of the contract. If the statement is not true, or the promise is not fulfilled, the injured party may[2] rescind the contract for breach of condition, as well as claiming damages[3]. In this context the word 'condition' is used in yet another sense. It does not bear its orthodox meaning, discussed in para. 10.14, of an event by which an obligation is suspended or cancelled but is used to describe a particular type of contractual term. It is certainly an odd word to use for this purpose.

A warranty is a contractual term concerning a less important or subsidiary statement of fact or promise[4]. If a warranty is broken this does not entitle the other party to rescind. It simply entitles him to sue for damages or make a set-off and the party in breach is entitled to the contractual price less the damages or set-off[5].

In the case of sales of goods these distinctions have been given statutory effect by the Sale of Goods Act 1893[6].

---

1 *Heyworth v Hutchinson* (1867) LR 2 QB 447 at 451.
2 Unless the failure in performance is microscopic, para. 9.2.
3 In relation to contracts for the sale of goods this rule is given statutory effect by the Sale of Goods Act 1893, s.11(1)(b).
4 *Oscar Chess Ltd v Williams* [1957] 1 All ER 325 at 328, CA; Sale of Goods Act 1893, s.11(1)(h).
5 *Gilbert-Ash (Northern) Ltd v Modern Engineering (Bristol) Ltd* [1974] AC 689, [1973] 3 All ER 195, HL; Sale of Goods Act 1893, s.53(1)(a).
6 Ss. 11(1)(b) and 62(1).

10.20 The classification of a term depends on the following considerations:

a. Sometimes statute provides that particular terms are conditions or warranties, e.g. the implied conditions and implied warranties under the Sale of Goods Act 1893[1].

b. In other cases a term which has been classified as a condition in judicial decisions will be so classified thereafter[2].

c. In the absence of classification by statute or case authority, a court has to decide whether the broken term is a condition or warranty (if either) by ascertaining the intention of the parties. The parties' intentions are particularly important and it is open to them to agree that what is a condition according to a previous judicial decision shall be a warranty in their contract, and vice versa. Because of the drastic consequences, the courts should lean against construing a term as a condition[3].

The approach of the courts is as follows:

First, the court must seek to ascertain the intention of the parties as expressed in the contract. If the wording clearly reveals that the parties intended that any breach of the term should give rise to a right to rescind, that term will be regarded as a condition. But if the parties clearly did not so intend, the term will not be regarded as a condition even though it is described as a 'condition' in the contract. This is shown by *Schuler AG v Wickman Machine Tool Sales Ltd*[4]. A four year distributorship agreement provided that the distributor should visit six named customers every week. The agreement described this provision as a 'condition'. The House of Lords held that the contract could not be rescinded simply because of breach of this 'condition'. Its reasoning was that the parties could not have intended a mere failure to make one visit to result in a right to rescind. It thought that more probably 'condition' had been used simply to mean 'term'.

Secondly, if the wording of the contract does not indicate the parties' intentions, the court must ascertain them by inference from the subject-matter of the contract. If, in the context of the whole contract, the term was so important that a party would *always* want to rescind if it was broken it will be regarded as a condition. An example is *Behn v Burness*[5], where one term of a charterparty was that the ship was 'now in the port of Amsterdam': the ship was not then there. The statement was held to be a condition because of the commercial importance attached to such a statement. On the other hand, a term in a charterparty that a ship is seaworthy has not been construed as a condition because it can be broken in a number of ways, in some of which the parties would clearly not intend that the charterer should be entitled to rescind[6].

---

1 Paras. 8.18 and 22.42–22.60.
2 *The Mihalis Angelos* [1971] 1 QB 164, [1970] 3 All ER 125, CA.
3 *The Hansa Nord* [1975] 3 All ER 739 at 755, CA.
4 [1974] AC 235, [1973] 2 All ER 39, HL.
5 (1862) 3 B & S 751.
6 *Hong Kong Fir Shipping Co Ltd v Kawasaki Kisen Kaisha Ltd* [1962] 2 QB 26, [1962] 1 All ER 474, CA.

10.21 *Breach of an intermediate term* If the term broken is not a condition, it must not be assumed that it is a warranty for which the only remedy is damages, unless statute or a judicial decision compels such a classification. Instead it must be asked whether the term is an intermediate term, i.e. a term which cannot be classified as a condition or a warranty, and, if so, whether the nature and effect of its breach is such as to deprive the injured party of substantially the whole benefit which it was intended that he should obtain under the contract[1]. If it is, the injured party is entitled to rescind, as well as claiming. In applying this test, account must be taken not only of the actual consequences of the breach but also of those whose occurrence is reasonably foreseeable[2]. Regard must also be had to the quantitative ratio between the breach and the contract as a whole[3].

A leading authority for the present doctrine is *Hong Kong Fir Shipping Co Ltd v Kawasaki Kisen Kaisha Ltd*[4]. The plaintiffs chartered a ship to the defendants for 24 months. The ship was old and needed to be maintained by an adequate and competent engine room crew but the plaintiffs did not provide such a crew and thereby were in breach of a term of the charterparty to provide a ship 'in every way fitted for ordinary cargo service'. Because of the incompetence and inadequacy of the engine room crew there were many serious mechanical breakdowns. In the first seven months of the charter, the ship was only at sea for eight and a half weeks, the rest of the time being spent in breakdowns and repairs. After the seven months had elapsed the ship was finally made seaworthy. In the meantime, however, the defendants had purported to rescind the charterparty and the plaintiffs sued for breach of contract and claimed damages for wrongful rescission. The defendants pleaded that the seaworthiness clause was a condition of the contract, and that therefore they could rescind for breach of it. Having held that the clause was not a condition for the reason set out at the end of para. 10.20, the Court of Appeal held that the effect of the plaintiffs' breach of the clause was not sufficiently serious to justify the defendants in rescinding. One reason which it particularly relied on was the fact that after the repairs the ship was still available for 17 of the original 24 months. The defendants' rescission had therefore been wrongful.

The same decision was reached in *The Hansa Nord*[5]. Citrus pulp pellets were sold by a German company to a Dutch company, delivery to be made in Rotterdam. The contract included a term that shipment was to be made in good condition. Some of the pellets arrived damaged. The buyers rejected the whole consignment (i.e. rescinded the contract) and the goods were sold by the order of a Dutch court to a third person. Subsequently they were re-sold at one-third the original contract price to the original buyers who then used the whole consignment for a purpose (cattle food) similar to that for which they had originally bought it (animal feed) – though at a lower rate of inclusion in the case of the damaged pellets. The Court of Appeal held that the 'shipment in good condition' term was not a condition of the contract because it could not have been intended that any breach of it should entitle the buyers to rescind[6]. The Court then turned to the present doctrine and held that the buyers were not entitled to rescind under it because, particularly in the light of the subsequent events, the effect of the breach was not sufficiently serious to justify rescission. Thus, the buyers were only entitled to damages and could not treat themselves as discharged from their obligation to accept the pellets and pay the contract price.

1 *Hong Kong For Shipping Co Ltd v Kawasaki Kisen Kaisha Ltd* [1962] 2 QB 26 at 70.
2 *Ibid.*, at 64.
3 *Ibid.; Maple Flock Co Ltd v Universal Furniture Products (Wembley) Ltd* [1934] 1 KB 148, CA; para. 22.71.
4 [1962] 2 QB 26, [1962] 1 All ER 474, CA.
5 [1975] 3 All ER 739, [1976] QB 44, CA.
6 The Court also held that there was no breach of the implied condition of merchantable quality under the Sale of Goods Act 1893, s.14(2); see paras. 22.49–22.54.

10.22   These two cases can be contrasted with *Aerial Advertising Co v Batchelors Peas Ltd (Manchester)*[1]. The plaintiffs agreed to conduct an aerial advertising campaign for the defendants. One term of the contract was that the pilot of the aeroplane should telephone the defendants each day and obtain their approval for what he proposed to do. On Armistice Day 1937, the pilot, in breach of this term, failed to contact the defendants and flew over Salford during the two minutes' silence. The aeroplane was towing a banner saying 'Eat Batchelors Peas'. Of course, the term broken was not a condition since breach of it might well only have had trivial consequences, so that the parties could not have intended that its breach should always entitle the defendants to rescind. However, the effect of the particular breach was disastrous since it aroused public hostility towards the defendants and their products. It was held that the defendants were entitled to rescind the contract and therefore the plaintiffs' claim for payment for advertising already done under the contract was dismissed.

1 [1938] 2 All ER 788.

EXEMPTION CLAUSES

10.23   A contract may contain an exemption clause, i.e. a clause purporting to exclude or restrict one of the parties' liability for breach of contract, or some other liability, such as for the tort of negligence, or both. Because exemption clauses could operate very unfairly in the case of standard form contracts, where one party has no real option but to accept the terms offered by the other, a number of restrictive rules have been applied to exemption clauses by the courts and, more important, statutory limitations on the validity of many exemption clauses have been introduced.

10.24   Before a defendant can rely on an exemption clause in his favour he must show that it is a term of the contract and that, as a matter of construction, it covers the damage in question. We will look at these matters, as well as certain general limitations on the application of exemption clauses, before turning to the crucial question of their validity.

Term of the contract

10.25   The determination of whether what purports to be an exemption clause is a term of the contract depends very much on whether the clause is contained in a signed contractual document or not. If it is, it is a contractual term even though the person who signed the document was unaware of it, e.g. because he had not read it[1].

---

1   *L'Estrange v Graucob* [1934] 2 KB 394, CA. For an exception, see para. 10.34.

10.26   In other cases, e.g. where the clause is printed on a ticket or a notice, the clause will only be a contractual term if adequate notice of it is given. The following rules apply in this connection.

Notice must be given before or at the time of the contract
10.27   The exemption clause is ineffective unless it was brought to the party's notice before or at the time the contract was made. This is shown by *Olley v Marlborough Court Ltd*[1]. The plaintiff and her husband were accepted as guests at a hotel. They paid for a week in advance and went to their room, on the wall of which was a notice exempting the hotel proprietors from liability for the loss or theft of property. Due to the negligence of the hotel staff, property was stolen from the plaintiff's room. The Court of Appeal held that the hotel was not protected by the exemption clause because the contract had been made before the exemption clause was communicated so that it formed no part of the contract.

There is an exception to the present rule. If there have been previous dealings between the parties on the basis of documents incorporating similar terms exempting liability, then, provided those dealings have been of a consistent nature[2], the court may imply the exemption clause into a particular contract where express notice is given too late. In *J. Spurling Ltd v Bradshaw*[3], the defendant had dealt with the plaintiff warehousemen for many years. He delivered barrels of orange juice to them for storage. Later he received a document from them which acknowledged receipt and referred to clauses on its back, one of which excluded the plaintiffs from any liability for loss of damage occasioned by their negligence. Later, the defendant refused to pay the storage charges because the barrels were empty on collection. He was sued for these charges and counter-claimed for negligence. The Court of Appeal held that the exemption clause was incorporated into the contract, and the defendant was bound by it because in previous dealings he had often received a document containing the clause, although he had never read it.

1   [1949] 1 KB 532, [1949] 1 All ER 127, CA.
2   *McCutcheon v David MacBrayne Ltd* [1964] 1 All ER 430, [1964] 1 WLR 125, HL.
3   [1956] 2 All ER 121, [1956] 1 WLR 461, CA.

The notice must be contained in a contractual document
10.28   An exemption clause is ineffective if it, or notice of it, is contained in a document which a reasonable person would not assume to contain contractual terms. Thus, in *Chapelton v Barry UDC*[1], it was held that an exemption clause contained in a ticket for a deck chair on a beach was ineffective because no reasonable person would expect the ticket to be more than a receipt: he would not assume it contained contractual terms. The same decision was reached concerning a cheque book cover in *Burnett v Westminster Bank Ltd*[2].

1   [1940] 1 KB 532, [1940] 1 All ER 356, CA.
2   [1966] 1 QB 742, [1965] 3 All ER 81.

Reasonable notice of the exemption clause must be given
10.29   A leading authority is *Parker v South Eastern Rly Co*[1]. The plaintiff left his bag at a station cloakroom. He received a ticket which said on its face: 'See back'. On the back were a number of terms, one of which limited the railway company's liability to £10 per package. The plaintiff's bag was lost and he claimed its value of £24 10s. It was held that the plaintiff was bound by the exemption clause, even though he had not read it, because the railway company had given reasonable notice of its existence. Notice can be reasonable even though it involves reference to other documents or to a notice[2]. The test laid down in *Parker v South Eastern Rly Co* is objective and if reasonable notice has been given it is irrelevant that the party affected by the exemption clause was blind or illiterate or otherwise unable to comprehend its meaning[3].

1   (1877) 2 CPD 416, CA.
2   *Watkins v Rymill* (1883) 10 QBD 178; *Thompson v London, Midland and Scottish Rly Co* [1930] 1 KB 41, CA.
3   *Thompson v London, Midland and Scottish Rly Co* [1930] 1 KB 41, CA.

Construction

10.30 If an exemption clause is a term of the contract the next question is whether it applies to the loss or damage in question. We set out below certain rules of construction which are applied to exemption clauses by the courts and which tend to favour the party affected by such a clause.

Liability can only be excluded or restricted by clear words
10.31 The liability in question must be precisely covered by the exemption clause relied on. In *Andrews Bros (Bournemouth) Ltd v Singer & Co Ltd*[1], the plaintiffs entered into a contract to buy 'new Singer cars' from the defendants. One of the cars delivered by the defendants was not a new car, having run a considerable mileage. A clause in the contract exempted the defendants from liability for breach of all 'conditions, warranties and liabilities *implied* by common law, statute or otherwise' but the Court of Appeal held that this did not protect the defendants against liability for breach of an *express* term. A similar decision was reached in *Wallis, Son and Wells v Pratt and Haynes*[2]. The defendants sold by sample to the plaintiffs seed described as 'common English sainfoin'. The contract stated that the defendants gave 'no *warranty* express or implied' as to any matter concerning the seed. The seed turned out to be the inferior and cheaper 'giant sainfoin'. The House of Lords held that the exemption clause did not apply because there had been a breach of the *condition* implied by s.13 of the Sale of Goods Act 1893 (that goods sold by description correspond with it) and the clause did not purport to exclude liability for breach of condition.

---

1 [1934] 1 KB 17, CA.
2 [1911] AC 394, HL.

All ambiguities in the exemption clause are construed against the party relying on it
10.32 This is in accordance with the rule normally applied in the construction of contracts[1].

---

1 *Houghton v Trafalgar Insurance Co* [1954] 1 QB 247, [1953] 2 All ER 1409, CA.

Exclusion of tortious liability
10.33 Sometimes an exemption clause is drafted in terms sufficiently wide to exclude a party's liability in tort (usually for negligence) as well as any contractual liability. If the clause clearly purports to exclude all liability, effect must be given to it[1] (subject to the general rules as to

the validity of exemption clauses), but if the clause is not so clearly drafted but could exclude tortious as well as any contractual liability the law is as follows:

Where liability can be based on some ground other than negligence, the clause is normally construed as being confined to loss occurring through that other cause[2]. Accordingly, where a party can be made liable either in the tort of negligence or for breach of a particular contractual obligation, liability for which is strict, the clause will normally be construed as only applying to the latter ground and not as exempting him from liability for negligence as well. A leading example is *White v John Warwick & Co Ltd*[3]. The plaintiff hired a bicycle from the defendants. While he was riding it the saddle tilted forward and he was injured. The contract of hire stated: 'nothing in this agreement shall render the owners liable for any personal injury'. The Court of Appeal held that the defendants were liable in negligence. Its reason was that, in the absence of the exemption clause, the defendants would have been liable for breach of contract in supplying a defective bicycle irrespective of negligence and the operation of the clause had to be restricted to that stricter liability.

Where liability can be based on negligence and nothing else, the exemption clause will normally be construed as extending to that head of damage, because if it were not so construed it would lack subject-matter[4]. This is shown by *Alderslade v Hendon Laundry Ltd*[5]. The defendants contracted to launder the plaintiff's handkerchief's, the contract limiting their liability 'for lost or damaged articles' to 20 times the laundering charge. The handkerchiefs were lost through the defendants' negligence. The Court of Appeal held that the only way in which the defendants could be made liable for the loss of the handkerchiefs would be if they could be shown to have been guilty of negligence. It held that the exemption clause applied to limit the defendants' liability for negligence because otherwise the clause would be left without any content at all.

Both these rules are only rules of construction and, although they will normally be adopted, the court is free to construe the clause in another way if, on its wording or other evidence, it considers that the parties had some other intention[6].

---

1   *Joseph Travers & Sons Ltd v Cooper* [1915] 1 KB 73.
2   *Alderslade v Hendon Laundry Ltd* [1945] KB 189 at 192.
3   [1953] 2 All ER 1021, CA.
4   *Alderslade v Hendon Laundry Ltd* [1945] KB 189 at 192; *Hollier v Rambler Motors (AMC) Ltd* [1972] 2 QB 71, [1972] 1 All ER 399, CA.
5   [1945] KB 189, [1945] 1 All ER 244, CA.
6   *J. Archdale Ltd v Comservices Ltd* [1954] 1 All ER 210, [1954] 1 WLR 459, CA; *Hollier v Rambler Motors (AMC) Ltd* [1972] 2 QB 71, [1972] 1 All ER 399, CA.

General limitations on the application of an exemption clause

Misrepresentation

10.34 If the party favoured by the exemption clause induced the other party to accept it by misrepresenting its contents or effect he cannot rely on it, even though the contract was signed by the other party and even though his misrepresentation was innocent. In *Curtis v Chemical Cleaning and Dyeing Co Ltd*[1], the plaintiff took a dress to the defendants' shop for cleaning. The dress was trimmed with beads and sequins. The plaintiff was asked to sign a receipt exempting the defendants from all liability for any damage to articles cleaned. The plaintiff asked why her signature was required and was told that the receipt exempted the defendants from liability for damage to the sequins and beads. When the dress was returned it was badly stained. It was held that the defendants were not protected by the clause because through their employee they had innocently induced the plaintiff to believe that the clause only referred to the beads and sequins.

---

1 [1951] 1 KB 805, [1951] 1 All ER 631, CA.

Inconsistent undertakings

10.35 If, at or before the time the contract was made, the party favoured by the exemption clause gives an undertaking which is inconsistent with it, the exemption clause is rendered ineffective to the extent that it is inconsistent with the undertaking, even though the undertaking does not form part of the contract or of a contract collateral to it. In *Mendelssohn v Normand Ltd*[1], the plaintiff left his car in the defendants' garage on terms contained in a ticket, one of which was that the defendants would not accept any responsibility for any loss sustained by the vehicle or its contents, however caused. The car contained valuables and the plaintiff wanted to lock it but the attendant told him that this was not permissible. The plaintiff told the attendant about the valuables and the attendant promised to lock the car after he had moved it. On his return the plaintiff discovered that the valuables had been stolen. The Court of Appeal held that the defendants were not protected by the exemption clause because their employee had in effect promised to see that the valuables were safe and this oral undertaking took priority over the exemption clause.

---

1 [1970] 1 QB 177, [1969] 2 All ER 1215, CA. Also see *J. Evans & Son (Portsmouth) Ltd v Andrea Merzario Ltd* [1976] 2 All ER 930, [1976] 1 WLR 1078, CA.

Third party generally not protected by an exemption clause

10.36 As part of the doctrine of privity of contract[1] a person who is not a party to a contract containing an exemption clause is generally not protected by the clause, even though it purports to have this effect. In *Cosgrove v Horsfall*[2], the Court of Appeal held that a clause in a free bus pass exempting the London Passenger Transport Board and its servants from liability for injury was ineffective to protect the servants from liability in tort for negligence since they were not parties to the contract between the Board and the pass-holder. This decision was approved by the House of Lords in *Scruttons Ltd v Midland Silicones Ltd*[3], although the clause in that case did not expressly purport to exclude the liability of the third parties in question. A drum containing chemicals was shipped from New York to London. It was consigned to the plaintiffs under a bill of lading which restricted the carrier's liability to $500 (then about £180). While the drum was being handled by the defendants, who were stevedors employed by the carriers, it was damaged through the defendants' negligence: the damage amounted to £593. The contract between the *carriers* and the defendants stated that the defendants should have the benefit of the exemption clause in the bill of lading but the majority of the House of Lords held that the defendants could not limit their liability for negligence by relying on the exemption clause because they were not parties to the bill of lading. These two decisions show that it will sometimes be possible to circumvent an exemption clause by bringing proceedings against an employee or sub-contractor on the ground of his negligence. This may be desirable in the case of a standard form contract, particularly because the employee will usually be re-imbursed by his employer for, and a sub-contractor insured against, any damages awarded. However, the reliance on the technical rule of privity of contract is harder to justify in the case of a freely negotiated contract in which one party has agreed to assume the risk of damage, particularly where the contract purports to exempt an employee or sub-contractor of the other party.

---

1 Para. 6.19.
2 (1945) 175 LT 334, CA.
3 [1962] AC 446, [1962] 1 All ER 1, HL.

10.37 The position is different where one of the parties, whom we will call A, contracts with B as agent for the third person. In that case the third person is brought into contractual relations with B on terms of the exemption clause provisions in the main contract and is protected by the clause. This was recognised by the Privy Council in *New Zealand Shipping Co Ltd v A. N. Satterthwaite & Co Ltd*[1], which shows that there are four prerequisites for the validity of such an agency contract:

a. the contract must make it clear that the third person is intended to be protected by the exemption clause;

b. the contract must make it clear that A, in addition to contracting for the exemption clause on his own behalf, is also contracting as agent for the third person that these provisions should apply to the third person;

c. A must have authority from the third person to do that (or the third person can subsequently ratify the contract provided he was identifiable at the time it was made²); and

d. the third person must have provided consideration for the promise as to exemption made to him, through A as his agent, by B.

In the *New Zealand Shipping Co* case the Privy Council explained how the third person can provide consideration for B's promise as to exemption. The main contract brings into existence a bargain initially unilateral but capable of becoming mutual, between B and the third person, made through A as agent. This will become a full contract when the third person performs services under the main contract. The performance of these services for the benefit of B is the consideration for the agreement by B that the third person should have the benefit of the exemption clause contained in the contract.

Nevertheless, the *New Zealand Shipping Co* case is of limited effect because:

a. Consideration can only be furnished if the third person does something after the main contract has been made. If he has already performed his services there can be no unilateral contract of the above type and he will not have furnished the consideration necessary to make enforceable any promise as to exemption.

b. Presumably, the third person cannot be said to accept the offer of a unilateral contract unless he knows of the main contract. In the *New Zealand Shipping Co* case this appears to have been the case since the agent (A) was a subsidiary of the third person.

---

1 [1975] AC 154, [1974] 1 All ER 1015, PC.
2 Para. 18.10.

Third party not bound by an exemption clause

10.38 Because of the doctrine of privity of contract a third party cannot be deprived of his right to sue in tort by an exemption clause contained in a contract between others, even though it purports to have that effect. An authority is *Haseldine v C. A. Daw Ltd*¹. The owners of a block of flats employed the defendants to repair a lift in the block. The defendants repaired the lift negligently and the plaintiff was injured when the lift fell to the bottom of the lift shaft. The defendants were held liable to the plaintiff, it being irrelevant that the contract between the defendants and the owners of the block purported to exempt the defendants from liability for personal injury.

1   [1941] 2 KB 343, [1941] 3 All ER 156, CA.

10.39   The above rule can be avoided in the following cases:

a. If one of the parties to a contract containing an exemption clause in favour of the other contracted as agent for a third person that person is bound by the clause.

b. It may be that in the following situation a person is bound by an exemption clause contained in a contract between others. It sometimes happens where T has handed goods to A for repair or cleaning that A sub-contracts the work to B. If the contract between A and B contains an exemption clause in favour of B it will not bind T under the law of contract, as we have just seen, and he will be able to sue B in the tort of negligence should B carry out the sub-contracted work negligently. However, T will not have the right to sue B if he can be said to have voluntarily assumed the risk of loss or damage because voluntary assumption of risk is a defence to a charge of negligence. There is persuasive authority that T in the above situation would be barred by the defence of voluntary assumption of risk if he had expressly or impliedly consented to A making the sub-contract with B on terms usual in the trade, these terms including the exemption clause in question[1].

1   *Morris v C. W. Martin & Sons Ltd* [1966] 1 QB 716 at 728.

Validity

10.40   The Unfair Contract Terms Act 1977, which came into force on 1 February 1978 and does not apply to contracts made before that date[1], contains a number of provisions which greatly limit the extent to which it is possible to exclude or restrict liability for negligence or for breach of contract which arises *in the course of business*[2]. In this Act, 'business' includes a profession and the activities of any government department or public or local authority[3]. Although the Act uses the words 'contract term', we propose generally to use the more familiar expression 'exemption clause'.

1   Unfair Contract Terms Act 1977, s.31(2).
2   *Ibid.*, s.1(3).
3   *Ibid.*, s.14.

Avoidance of liability for negligence or breach of contract

10.41 *Liability for negligence* Section 2(1) of the Act provides that an exemption clause purporting to exclude or restrict a person's liability for death or personal injury (including any disease or impairment of physical or mental condition) resulting from negligence is of no effect.

In the case of other loss or damage, s.2(2) provides that such exclusion or restriction of liability for negligence is only valid in so far as the clause satisfies the 'requirement of reasonableness'.

These provisions do not extend to a contract of employment, except in favour of the employee[1].

'Negligence' in this context means the breach —

a. of any obligation, arising from the express or implied terms of a contract, to take reasonable care or exercise reasonable skill in the performance of the contract; or

b. of any common law duty to take reasonable care or exercise reasonable skill; or

c. of the common duty of care imposed by the Occupiers' Liability Act 1957[2].

1 Unfair Contract Terms Act 1977, Sched. 1.
2 *Ibid.*, s.1(1).

10.42 *Liability arising in contract* Section 3 lays down special rules which apply *as between the contracting parties where one of them deals as consumer or on the other's written standard terms of business*[1]. In the present context, a party to a contract 'deals as consumer' in relation to another party if he neither makes the contract in the course of a business nor holds himself out as doing so, and the other party does make the contract in the course of a business[2]. It provides that, *as against the party dealing as consumer etc.,* the other party cannot by reference to any contract term —

a. exclude or restrict his liability for breach of contract; or

b. claim to be entitled —

  i. to render a contractual performance substantially different from that which was reasonably expected of him, or

  ii. in respect of the whole or any part of his contractual obligation, to render no performance at all,

except in so far as the contract term satisfies the 'requirement of reasonableness'. This provision is widely drawn: under b.ii., for instance, a term excusing non-performance or entitling a party to cancel the contract may be held invalid.

1 Unfair Contract Terms Act 1977, s.3(1).
2 *Ibid.*, s.12(1). It is for those claiming that a party does not deal as a consumer to show that he does not.

10.43 *Unreasonable indemnity clauses* Contracts often contain terms requiring one party to indemnify the other against liability incurred by that other in performing the contract. Section 4(1) makes such an indemnity clause void *as against a consumer* unless reasonable. It states that a person dealing as consumer cannot by reference to any contract term be made to indemnify another person (whether a party to the contract or not) in respect of liability that may be incurred by the other for negligence or breach of contract, *except in so far as the contract term satisfies the 'requirement of reasonableness'*. This provision applies whether the liability in question is that of the person to be indemnified or is incurred by him vicariously, and whether that liability is to the person dealing as consumer or to someone else[1].

---

1 Unfair Contract Terms Act 1977, s.4(2).

10.44 *Excepted agreements* Sections 2 to 4 do not extend to –

a. any contract of insurance;

b. any contract so far as it relates to the creation, transfer or termination of an interest in land or of any right or interest in any patent, trade mark, copyright, registered design or other intellectual property;

c. any contract so far as it relates –
   i. to the formation or dissolution of a company (which means any body corporate or unincorporated association and includes a partnership), or
   ii. to its constitution or the rights or obligations of its corporators or members;

d. any contract so far as it relates to the creation or transfer of securities or of any right or interest in securities.

Section 2(1) extends –

a. to any charterparty of a ship or hovercraft; and

b. to any contract of marine salvage or towage or for the carriage of goods by ship or hovercraft;

but subject to this ss. 2–4 do not extend to any such contract, *except in favour of a person dealing as a consumer*.

Where goods are carried by ship or hovercraft in pursuance of a contract which either –

a. specifies that as the means of carriage over part of the journey to be covered, or

b. makes no provision as to the means of carriage and does not exclude that means, then ss. 2(2), 3 and 4 do not, *except in favour of a person dealing as consumer,* extend to the contract as it operates for and in relation to the carriage of goods by that means.

---

1   Unfair Contract Terms Act 1977, Sched. 1.

10.45   *The 'requirement of reasonableness'* In relation to an exemption clause the requirement of reasonableness is that the clause shall have been a fair and reasonable one to be included having regard to the circumstances which were, or ought reasonably to have been, known or in the contemplation of the parties when the contract was made[1]. Where a party seeks to restrict liability to a specified sum in reliance on an exemption clause, then, in determining whether the clause satisfies the requirement of reasonableness, regard must be had in particular to—

a. the resources which that party could expect to be available to him for the purpose of meeting the liability should it arise; and

b. how far it was open to him to cover himself by insurance[2].

It is for the party claiming that an exemption clause satisfies the requirement of reasonableness to show that it does[3].

---

1   Unfair Contract Terms Act 1977, s.11(1).
2   *Ibid.,* s.11(4).
3   *Ibid.,* s.11(5).

10.46   *Avoidance of liability arising from sale or supply of goods* Sections 6 and 7 contain additional provisions dealing with attempts to avoid liability where the ownership or possession of goods has passed.

10.47   *Sale and hire-purchase* By s.6(1) of the Act of 1977, an exemption clause purporting to exclude or restrict liability for breach of the obligations arising from —

a. the Sale of Goods Act 1893, s.12 (seller's implied undertakings as to title etc.)[1];

b. the Supply of Goods (Implied Terms) Act 1973, s.8 (the corresponding things in relation to hire-purchase),

is of no effect.

Section 6(2) provides that, *as against a person dealing as consumer,* an exemption clause purporting to exclude or restrict liability for breach of the obligations arising from —

a. the Sale of Goods Act 1893, ss. 13, 14 or 15 (seller's implied undertakings as to conformity of goods with description or sample, or as to their quality or fitness for a particular purpose)[2];

b. the Supply of Goods (Implied Terms) Act 1973, ss. 9, 10 or 11 (the corresponding things in relation to hire-purchase),

is of no effect. It must be emphasised that this provision is limited to the implied terms specified. The validity of a clause excluding or restricting liability for breach of any express term will depend on the application of the principles which we have mentioned in para. 10.42. Unlike s.6(1), s.6(2) only vitiates the exemption clause as against a person dealing as consumer. The definition of such a person is rather different from that which applies in s.3. In the present context, a party to a contract 'deals as consumer' in relation to another party if –

a. he neither makes the contract in the course of a business nor holds himself out as doing so; and

b. the other party does make the contract in the course of a business; and

c. the goods passing under or in pursuance of the contract are of a type ordinarily supplied for private use or consumption[3].

A buyer at an auction or by competitive tender is never regarded as dealing as consumer[4]. Where a party does not deal as consumer s.6(3) is the operative provision.

Section 6(3) provides that, *as against a person dealing otherwise than as consumer,* a clause purporting to exclude or restrict liability for breach of the obligations arising from the Sale of Goods Act 1893, ss. 13–15, is of no effect *except in so far as the term satisfies the 'requirement of reasonableness'.*

The provisions of s.6 (1) and (3) are exceptional in that they are not limited to liabilities arising in the course of business. Section 6 replaces substantially similar provisions introduced by the Supply of Goods (Implied Terms) Act 1973.

---

1 These terms are fully described in paras. 22.43–22.46.
2 These terms are fully described in paras. 22.47–22.60.
3 Unfair Contract Terms Act 1977, s.12(1).
4 *Ibid.,* s.12(2).

10.48 *Miscellaneous contracts under which the ownership or possession of goods passes* Section 7 of the Act of 1977 deals with contract terms excluding or restricting liability for breach of obligations implied at common law into contracts such as those of hire or exchange or for work and materials (provided ownership or possession of the materials used passes from one person to another). Section 7 applies to these contracts a regime which is broadly similar to that just mentioned in relation to sale of goods and hire-purchase.

Section 7(2) provides that, *as against a person dealing as consumer* (in the same sense as in sale of goods and hire-purchase), an exemption clause purporting to exclude or restrict liability in respect of the goods' correspondence with description or sample, or their quality or fitness for any particular purpose, is of no effect.

On the other hand, *as against a person dealing otherwise than as consumer*, s.7(3) provides that such liability can be excluded or restricted by reference to such a clause, but *only in so far as the term satisfies the 'requirement of reasonableness'*.

In any case, by s.7(4), liability in respect of —

a. the right to transfer ownership of the goods, or give possession; or

b. the assurance of quiet possession to a person taking goods in pursuance of the contract,

cannot be excluded or restricted by reference to any such clause, *except in so far as the term satisfies the 'requirement of reasonableness'*.

10.49 *The 'requirement of reasonableness' in relation to ss. 6 and 7* The provisions which we mentioned in para. 10.45 concerning the requirement of reasonableness also apply where that requirement is relevant under ss. 6 and 7. However, in addition, in determining for the purposes of these two sections whether a contract term satisfies the requirement of reasonableness, regard must be had in particular to the guidelines specified in Sched. 2 of the Act[1], viz.:

a. the strength of the bargaining positions of the parties relative to each other;

b. whether the customer received an inducement to agree to the term, or in accepting it had an opportunity of entering into a similar contract with other persons, but without having to accept a similar term;

c. where the term excludes or restricts any relevant liability if some condition is not complied with, whether it was reasonable at the time of the contract to expect that compliance with that condition would be practicable;

d. whether the goods were manufactured, processed or adapted to the special order of the customer;

e. whether the customer knew or ought reasonably to have known of the existence and extent of the term (e.g. because it was in small print or was unlikely to be read in full by the customer). We saw in para. 10.25 that an exemption clause may be a term of the contract even though the customer was unaware of it, especially if he has signed a contractual document containing it. This provision enables the court to hold an exemption clause which is undoubtedly a term of the contract unreasonable, and therefore invalid, because, for instance, the customer could not reasonably have known of its existence.

---

1 Unfair Contract Terms Act 1977, s.11(2).

General

10.50 *International supply contracts* The limits mentioned above on the exclusion or restriction of liability by an exemption clause do not apply to liability arising under international supply contracts[1].

An 'international supply contract' means a contract of sale of goods or a contract under which the possession or ownership of goods passes, which is made by parties whose places of business are in different States, provided:

a. the goods are, at the time of the conclusion of the contract, in the course of carriage, or will be carried, from one State to another; or

b. the offer and acceptance were effected in different States; or

c. the contract provides for the goods to be delivered to a State other than that within whose territory the offer and acceptance were effected[2].

---

1 Unfair Contract Terms Act 1977, s.26(1) and (2).
2 *Ibid.*, s.26(3) and (4).

10.51 *Evasion by means of a secondary contract* A person is not bound by any contract term prejudicing or taking away rights of his which arise under, or in connection with the performance of, another contract, so far as those rights extend to the enforcement of another's liability which the Act of 1977 prevents that other from excluding or restricting[1].

---

1 Unfair Contract Terms Act 1977, s.10.

10.52 *Varieties of exemption clauses* As we have shown, the Act repeatedly refers to the 'exclusion or restriction of liability'. These words are given a wide interpretation by s.13(1) which provides that to the extent that the provisions mentioned prevent the exclusion or restriction of any liability they also prevent:

a. making the liability or its enforcement subject to restrictive or onerous conditions (e.g. a term requiring 14 days notice of loss);

b. excluding or restricting any right or remedy in respect of the liability, or subjecting a person to any prejudice in consequence of his pursuing any such right or remedy;

c. excluding or restricting rules of evidence or procedure (e.g. a term that failure to complain within 14 days is deemed to be conclusive evidence of proper performance of the contract);

and (to that extent) ss. 2 and 6 and 7 also prevent excluding or restricting liability by reference to terms (and notices) which exclude or restrict the relevant obligation or duty.

Fundamental breach

10.53 If an exemption clause is not invalidated by the Unfair Contract Terms Act 1977, it may nevertheless not protect the party favoured by it if he has committed a fundamental breach of contract.

Before the House of Lords' decision in *Suisse Atlantique Société D'Armement Maritime SA v NV Rotterdamsche Kolen Centrale*[1] the courts had generally taken the view that there was a substantive rule of law whereby an exemption clause, however widely drafted, could not exclude or limit liability for a fundamental breach of contract[2]. This rule operated irrespective of the parties' intentions.

In *Suisse Atlantique,* the House of Lords rejected the rule of law approach and held that whether an exemption clause applied in the event of a fundamental breach depended on the *construction* of the clause to determine whether the parties had intended it to apply in the event of the fundamental breach in question. Not surprisingly, the more serious the breach the less likely the court is to hold that the exemption clause applies to it. Moreover, there seems to be a presumption that the parties did not contemplate the exemption clause applying to a fundamental breach so that it will not apply unless clearly and unambiguously expressed to do so[3].

In *Suisse Atlantique*, the plaintiffs chartered a ship to the defendants in December 1956 for two years' consecutive voyages. The defendants agreed to load and discharge cargo at specified rates and, in the event of any delay in doing so, to pay the plaintiffs $1,000 a day as demurrage (i.e. agreed damages). Lengthy delays occurred for which the plaintiffs alleged the defendants were responsible but they nevertheless allowed the defendants to continue to have the use of the ship for the rest of the charterparty. At the end of the period they sued the defendants for damages in excess of the demurrage provision. The House of Lords held that the plaintiffs could not recover this additional amount because:

a. The demurrage clause was not an exemption clause but an agreed damages provision[4], and was binding.

b. Even if the demurrage clause had been an exemption clause, and assuming the breaches were fundamental breaches, the clause, on its true construction, covered the breaches in question.

The opinions in the House of Lords on the effect of fundamental breach on an exemption clause were obiter, but are entitled to the highest respect in the lower courts.

---

1 [1967] 1 AC 361, [1966] 2 All ER 61, HL.
2 One example is *Karsales (Harrow) Ltd v Wallis* [1956] 2 All ER 866, [1956] 1 WLR 936, CA.
3 This view was adopted in, for instance, *Wathes (Western) Ltd v Austins (Menswear) Ltd* [1976] 1 Lloyd's Rep 14, CA.
4 Paras. 12.12 and 12.13.

The nature of a fundamental breach

10.54 The approach laid down in *Suisse Atlantique* is limited to what is generally described as 'fundamental breach'. It is clearly established that a person who supplies something essentially different from what he has contracted to supply is in fundamental breach of contract, his complete non-performance constituting a breach of a fundamental term (or obligation). There will be such a breach, for example, if a person who has contracted to supply mahogany logs supplies pine logs[1]. Again, there is a weight of authority that it is a fundamental breach of a charterparty for the ship owner to deviate from the stipulated or normal route without lawful excuse[2]; for a warehouseman to store goods in a place other than that agreed upon[3]; and for a person such as a carrier or cleaner of goods to deliver them to another by way of unauthorised sub-contracting[4]. There will also be a fundamental breach if the *effect* of a breach of contract is to make 'performance *totally different* from that which the contract contemplates'[5].

There is authority that, in addition to these clearly established rules, any other breach of contract is fundamental if it 'entitles the innocent party to treat it as repudiatory and to rescind the contract', in other words, that 'fundamental breach' includes any breach which entitles a party to elect to rescind the contract for breach. This extended meaning to the term 'fundamental breach' was supported by at least two of their Lordships in *Suisse Atlantique* and has been adopted in a number of subsequent decisions[6]. Of course, the less serious a fundamental breach is the more likely the court is to construe the exemption clause as applying to it, and the same is true if the breach is negligent or inadvertent rather than deliberate.

A special rule applies to a bailment contract: if the bailor pleads fundamental breach, the bailee must disprove it[7].

---

1 *Smeaton, Hanscomb & Co v Sassoon I: Setty & Co* [1953] 2 All ER 1471, [1954] 1 WLR 1468.

2   J. Thorley Ltd v Orchis SS Co Ltd [1907] 1 KB 660.
3   Woolf v Collis Removal Services [1948] 1 KB 11, [1947] 2 All ER 260, CA.
4   Davies v Collins [1945] 1 All ER 247.
5   Suisse Atlantique [1967] 1 AC 361 at 393.
6   E.g. Kenyon, Son & Craven Ltd v Baxter Hoare Ltd [1971] 2 All ER 708,
    [1971] 1 WLR 519; J. Evans & Son (Portsmouth) Ltd v Andrea Merzario Ltd
    [1976] 2 All ER 930, [1976] 1 WLR 1078, CA.
7   Levison v Patent Steam Carpet Cleaning Co Ltd [1978] 1 QB 69, [1977]
    3 All ER 498, CA.

Affirmation or rescission

10.55   If a fundamental breach is committed by one party it does not
automatically discharge the contract but gives the other party an option to
affirm or rescind the contract. This option results from the ordinary rules
governing repudiatory breach which we discussed in paras. 10.3–10.22.

10.56   *Affirmation*   If the party not in breach affirms the contract
this precludes him from subsequently treating it as repudiated (i.e. as
no longer binding on him) but he is still entitled to sue for damages,
unless, of course, the exemption clause on its true construction covers
the fundamental breach in question. This is shown by *Wathes (Western)
Ltd v Austins (Menswear) Ltd*[1]. The plaintiffs agreed to supply and
install an air-conditioning plant in the defendants' shop for £1,338.
The contract contained the following exemption clause: '*Consequential
damages*. The company [i.e. the plaintiffs] shall be under no liability
for any consequential loss, damage, claim or liabilities of any kind from
any cause whatsoever'. The plant was installed in December 1970 but
the defendants refused to pay for it on the ground that its outdoor
condensing unit was too noisy when working at speed in warm weather
and created a substantial nuisance to J Ltd, the owners of the shop
next door. In August 1971, J Ltd issued a writ for nuisance against the
defendants and they had to pay for a screen to be erected, as well as
legal costs and compensation to J Ltd. In an action by the plaintiffs for
the contractual price, the defendants counter-claimed successfully for
£1,323, representing the expense to which they had been put. The
Court of Appeal held that the plaintiffs were in fundamental breach
of contract since the breach had become fundamental some time in
May 1971, at the earliest, because by then its effect — the nuisance —
had become actual and serious, and was likely to continue and result in
legal liability on the part of the defendants to J Ltd. The Court went on
to hold that clearly the defendants had affirmed the contract after the
fundamental breach but that the exemption clause did not prevent them
succeeding on the counter-claim for damages because, on its true construction, the clause did not apply to the fundamental breach in question.

---

1   [1976] 1 Lloyd's Rep 15.

10.57 *Rescission* In principle, if the party not in breach elects to rescind the contract for fundamental breach the rescission does not have retrospective effect but only discharges future rights and obligations under the contract, the contract remaining alive for certain purposes, such as the assessment of damages, as we stated in para. 10.7. This being so, the court, in principle, should always take account of an exemption clause in the rescinded contract which on its true construction was intended to exclude or restrict liability for the fundamental breach in question.

The statement of principle contained in the previous paragraph is contradicted by the speeches of two of their Lordships, Lords Reid and Upjohn, in *Suisse Atlantique* and by the decision of the Court of Appeal in *Harbutt's 'Plasticine' Ltd v Wayne Tank and Pump Co Ltd*[1], to the effect that the discharge of a contract for fundamental breach extinguishes the whole contract, including an exemption clause, and that therefore damages can be recovered despite the fact that on its true construction the clause covers the breach. In *Harbutt's 'Plasticine'*, the defendants agreed with the plaintiffs to design and install piping in the plaintiffs' factory. They installed plastic pipes which were totally unsuitable for their purpose of containing molten material with the result that when used the pipes burst and the factory burnt down. When sued for damages amounting to £143,000, the defendants relied on an exemption clause limiting its liability to £2,330. Widgery and Cross, LJJ, held that on its true construction the clause covered the fundamental breach in question, and that the plaintiffs must be taken to have rescinded the contract because they had no sensible alternative but to treat it as discharged since the consequences of the defendants' breach rendered further performance of the contract impossible. The Lords Justices (along with Lord Denning, MR, who took the unorthodox view that, since the effect of the breach was to make further performance impossible, the contract had been discharged *automatically*) then proceeded to hold that the discharge of the contract extinguished the whole contract, including the exemption clause, and therefore the defendants were not entitled to limit their liability by reference to it.

In *Kenyon, Son and Craven Ltd v Baxter Hoare Ltd*[2], Donaldson, J, gave a restricted interpretation to the Court of Appeal's decision on the effect of a fundamental breach. He held that it only applied where the fundamental breach consisted of a 'performance totally different from that which the contract contemplates'. Outside this type of fundamental breach it was a question of construction whether the exemption clause was intended to apply to the particular fundamental breach.

---

1   [1970] 1 QB 447, [1970] 1 All ER 225, CA.
2   [1971] 2 All ER 708, [1971] 1 WLR 519.

10.58 The uncertainty surrounding the effect of rescission for fundamental breach on an exemption clause which on its true construction excludes or limits a party's liability for the loss or liability in question has been removed in relation to an exemption clause which has to satisfy the requirement of reasonableness under the Unfair Contract Terms Act 1977. Section 9(1) of that Act provides that, where for reliance upon it an exemption clause has to satisfy the requirement of reasonableness, it may be found to do so and be given effect notwithstanding that the contract has been discharged in consequence of its breach. This prevents the argument succeeding that, following the *Harbutt's* case, if a contract was discharged as the result of a fundamental breach, an exemption clause of the above type would not have applied even though the court considered that the requirement of reasonableness was satisfied. For the avoidance of doubt, s.9(2) adds that if the broken contract is nevertheless affirmed by the party entitled to treat it as repudiated, this does not of itself exclude the requirement of reasonableness in relation to any exemption clause.

Unfortunately, in cases not covered by s.9, the uncertainty remains. The approach taken in *Harbutt's 'Plasticine'* certainly seems to be out of line with the overall theme in *Suisse Atlantique*, that the applicability of an exemption clause to a fundamental breach is a question of construction. The apparent conflict between the two decisions can only be settled by the House of Lords.

10.59 What has been said above concerning the effect of fundamental breach only applies to exemption clauses and not to clauses which on their true construction do not exclude or restrict liability for breach of a particular obligation but are part of that obligation[1].

---

1 *The Angelia* [1973] 2 All ER 144, [1973] 1 WLR 210.

Fair Trading Act 1973

10.60 By Part II of the Act the Secretary of State for Prices and Consumer Protection, a Minister or the Director-General of Fair Trading (hereafter referred to as 'the Director') can refer to the Consumer Protection Advisory Committee the question whether a particular trade practice adversely affects the economic interests of consumers in the United Kingdom. A consumer trade practice is a practice carried on in connection with the supply of goods or services to consumers and which relates, inter alia, to the terms or conditions on which goods or services are supplied. If the Director considers that a consumer trade practice has or is likely to have the effect of making the terms or conditions of consumer transactions 'so adverse to consumers as to be inequitable' his reference to the Committee may propose recommendations to the Secretary of State to make an order in respect of that practice. In the light of this report the Secretary of State may make an order by statutory instrument prohibiting the particular consumer trade practice. Breach of such an order is a criminal offence, although a contract containing a prohibited exemption clause or other consumer trade practice is not rendered void or unenforceable thereby.

Part III of the Fair Trading Act also enables the Director to take action against a person carrying on a business who has persisted in a course of conduct which is detrimental to the interests of consumers in the United Kingdom and which is 'regarded as unfair to them'. If the Director fails to get a satisfactory written assurance that the conduct will cease, or if an assurance given is broken, he can start proceedings before the Restrictive Practices Court, which can make an order directing the person concerned to refrain from the course of conduct in question. Breach of such an order is punishable as contempt of court. Inter alia, a course of conduct is deemed to be unfair to consumers if it consists of contravention of an enactment imposing prohibitions enforceable by criminal proceedings. The effect of this provision seems to be that exemption clauses, and other consumer trade practices, prohibited under delegated legislation made under the power mentioned in the previous paragraph are subject to the present procedure.

Chapter 11
Discharge by Frustration

11.1 Under the doctrine of frustration a contract is automatically discharged if, subsequent to its formation and without any fault on the part of either party, a change of circumstances makes performance of it impossible or illegal, or otherwise frustrates it.

Scope

11.2 A contract is frustrated if, *subsequent to its formation*:
property essential to its performance is destroyed or becomes unavailable; or
a fundamental change of circumstances occurs; or
a party to a contract of a personal nature dies or is otherwise incapacitated from performing it; or
performance of it is rendered illegal; or
a basic assumption on which the parties contracted is destroyed.
The doctrine of frustration does not apply to cases where one of these circumstances existed at the time the contract was made: there the legal position must be answered by reference to the law relating to mistake[1] and illegal contracts[2]. In addition, a contract is not discharged by frustration simply because a subsequent event makes its performance more costly or difficult than envisaged when the contract was made. This is shown by *Davis Contractors Ltd v Fareham UDC*[3]. In 1946, the contractors entered into a contract with the council to build 78 houses for the fixed sum of £94,000. Owing to an unexpected shortage of skilled labour and of certain materials the contract took 22 months to complete instead of the anticipated eight months and cost £115,000. The contractors contended that the contract had been frustrated by the long delay and that they were entitled to a sum in excess of the contract price on a *quantum meruit* basis (i.e. reasonable recompense

205

for the benefit which they had conferred). The House of Lords disagreed, holding that the mere fact that unforeseen circumstances had delayed the performance of the contract and made it more costly to perform did not discharge the contract.

---

1 Paras. 13.2–13.10.
2 Paras. 15.46–15.64.
3 [1956] AC 696, [1956] 2 All ER 145, HL.

Supervening destruction or unavailability of property

11.3 A contract is discharged by frustration if performance of it is rendered impossible by the subsequent destruction or unavailability of a specific thing contemplated by the contract as essential to its performance. A leading authority is *Taylor v Caldwell*[1]. The defendants agreed to hire a music hall and gardens to the plaintiffs on specified days for the purpose of concerts. Before the first of the specified days, the music hall was destroyed by fire without the fault of either party. The defendants were held not liable for breach of contract because performance of the contract had become impossible through the destruction of the hall and they were not at fault. The contract was therefore frustrated and both parties discharged from their contractual obligations.

The subsequent unavailability of property will frustrate a contract if it renders performance of the contract in accordance with its terms impossible. This is shown by *Nickoll and Knight v Ashton, Edridge & Co*[2]. The defendants sold the plaintiffs a cargo of cotton seed to be shipped 'per steamship *Orlando* during the month of January'. Before the time for shipping arrived, the ship was so damaged by stranding as to be unable to load in January. It was held that the contract was discharged by frustration.

In order that a contract be frustrated under the present heading, the thing which has been destroyed or is otherwise unavailable must have been expressly or impliedly required by the contract for its performance. This point is well illustrated by *Tsakiroglou & Co Ltd v Noblee Thorl GmbH*[3], which concerned a contract for the sale of groundnuts which were to be shipped from the Sudan to Hamburg during November or December 1956. Both parties contemplated that the ship would proceed via the Suez Canal but this was not stated in the contract. On 2 November 1956, the Canal was closed (and remained so for five months). The House of Lords held that the unavailability of the Canal did not frustrate the contract, one of its reasons being that there was no express provision in the contract for shipping via the Canal nor could a provision be implied to that effect because the route was immaterial to the buyers. A fortiori, unavailability of a thing does not frustrate the contract if it merely affects the method of performance contemplated by one of the parties[4]. In *Nickoll and Knight v Ashton, Edridge & Co*, for instance, the contract would not have been frustrated if, instead of the name of the ship on which the cargo was to be loaded being stated in the contract, the defendant sellers had merely intended to load on that ship.

---

1   (1863) 3 B & S 826.
2   [1901] 2 KB 126.
3   [1962] AC 93, [1961] 2 All ER 179, HL.
4   *Blackburn Bobbin Co v T. W. Allen & Sons* [1918] 2 KB 467, CA.

Fundamental change of circumstances

11.4   A contract is frustrated if an event occurs of such gravity that, although technically the contract could still be performed, it would be the performance of a fundamentally different contract from that contemplated. Where the event causes delay in performing the contract, the decision whether it frustrates it or not must be decided in the light of the probable duration of the delay at its inception[1].

In *Jackson v Union Marine Insurance Co Ltd*[2], a ship was chartered to sail from Liverpool to Newport and there to load rails and then sail to San Francisco with them. She ran aground *en route* to Newport on 3 January and was not re-floated until 18 February, repairs not being completed until August. It was held that the charterparty had been discharged by frustration because it was found as a fact that the particular voyage contemplated by the parties had become impossible through the ship's temporary unavailability; that a voyage undertaken after the ship had been repaired would have been a different voyage — a voyage for which the shipowner had not contracted and for which the charterers had not the cargo, a voyage as different as though it had been described as intended to be a spring voyage, while the one after repair would be an autumn voyage. A similar decision was reached in *Metropolitan Water Board v Dick, Kerr & Co Ltd*[3]. The company contracted with the Board to construct a reservoir within six years, subject to a proviso that time could be extended if delay was caused by difficulties, impediments or obstructions. After two years had elapsed the Minister of Munitions, acting under statutory powers, required the company to stop work on the contract and remove and sell their plant. The House of Lords held that the interruption created by the prohibition was of such a nature and duration that the contract, if resumed, would in effect be radically different from that originally made. Therefore it was frustrated.

These cases can be contrasted with *Tsakiroglou & Co Ltd v Noblee Thorl GmbH*. In that case, the House of Lords held that the contract was not frustrated by the closure of the Suez Canal because a voyage round the Cape of Good Hope would not be commercially or fundamentally different from shipping via the Canal, albeit it was more expensive for the sellers.

---

1 *Bank Line Ltd v Arthur Capel & Co* [1919] AC 435 at 454.
2 (1874) LR 10 CP 125.
3 [1918] AC 119, HL.

Death or other personal incapacity
11.5 A contract of employment, or any other contract which can only be performed by a party personally, e.g. a contract to paint a portrait, is discharged by frustration if that party dies[1] or is otherwise rendered permanently incapable of performing it.

If a person becomes temporarily incapable of performing such a contract it may be discharged. Normally, whether or not the temporary incapacity frustrates the contract depends on whether, in the light of the probable duration of the incapacity at its inception, performance after it has ceased would be fundamentally different from what was envisaged by the contract and in effect be the substitution of a new contract. In *Morgan v Manser*[2], the defendant, a comedian, entered into a contract with the plaintiff in 1938 whereby he engaged the plaintiff's services as manager for 10 years. In 1940, the defendant was called up and was not demobilised until 1946. It was held that the contract was discharged by frustration in 1940 since it was then likely that the defendant would have to remain in the forces for a very long time. Similarly, if the duration of an employee's illness is likely to be so lengthy as to make performance of a contract of employment for a specified period fundamentally different from that undertaken by him and accepted by his employer the contract will be discharged by frustration, and so, a fortiori, will a contract to perform at a concert on a specified day by an illness of short duration[3]. Conversely, a contract of a personal nature for a specified duration is not frustrated by the illness of a party where this is likely to be of short duration: further performance after the party becomes available again will not be the performance of a fundamentally different contract.

---

1 *Stubbs v Holywell Rly Co Ltd* (1867) LR 2 Exch 311.
2 [1948] 1 KB 184, [1947] 2 All ER 666.
3 *Robinson v Davison* (1871) LR 6 Exch 269.

11.6 The situation is more complicated where (as in the majority of cases) employment is carried on on a weekly or monthly basis. The question of frustration often arises here where an employee who has been ill is not given his job back and when he brings proceedings for unfair dismissal is met by the defence that his contract of employment had already been terminated by a frustrating event, i.e. his illness. In this context, recent cases show that the question of frustration is to be judged not in the light of the probable duration of the illness at its inception but on the basis of whether in the light of the situation before the material time (normally, the time of the alleged dismissal) further performance of the employee's future obligations would be fundamentally different from what was envisaged by the contract. The judges have laid down a number of factors to be considered *cumulatively* in answering this test, such as:

a. the terms of the contract, including provisions as to sick pay (where there is a provision for sick pay there is a presumption against frustration if the employee appears likely to return during the period of its payment);

b. how long the employment was likely to last in the absence of sickness;

c. the nature of the employment (for example, in the case of a 'key worker', the need to engage a replacement);

d. the nature of the illness, and how long it has already continued;

e. the period of past employment[1];

f. whether the time has arrived when the employer can no longer reasonably be expected to keep the sick employee's job open for him; and

g. the acts or omissions of the employer (e.g. that the employer had not thought it right to dismiss the absent employee, the reasons for this are *one* of the relevant *factors*)[2].

---

1 *Marshall v Harland and Wolff Ltd* [1972] 2 All ER 715, [1972] 1 WLR 899.
2 *Egg Stores (Stamford Hill) Ltd v Leibovici* [1976] IRLR 376; *Hart v A. R. Marshall & Son (Bulwell) Ltd* [1977] IRLR 51.

Supervening illegality
11.7 A change in the law or in the circumstances may make performance of the contract illegal. If the change is such as to make it impossible to perform the contract legally it is discharged by frustration. In *White and Carter Ltd v Carbis Bay Garage Ltd*[1], for instance, it was held that a contract made in 1939 to display advertisements for three years was frustrated by wartime Defence Regulations prohibiting advertisements of the type in question. On the other hand, in *Cricklewood Property and Investment Trust Ltd v Leighton's Investment Trust Ltd*[2], the House of Lords held that, even if the doctrine of frustration applied to leases, a 99 year building lease was not frustrated

by Defence Regulations prohibiting building for only a small part of that term: performance had merely been suspended, not made impossible.

---

1   [1941] 2 All ER 633, CA.
2   [1945] AC 221, [1945] 1 All ER 252, HL.

Supervening destruction of a basic assumption on which the parties contracted

11.8   A contract is discharged by frustration if, although it is physically and legally possible for each party to perform his obligations under the contract, a change of circumstances has destroyed a *basic assumption* on which *the parties* contracted. In *Krell v Henry*[1], the defendant agreed to hire a flat in Pall Mall from the plaintiff for 26 and 27 June, 1902, one one of which days Edward VII was to be crowned. To the plaintiff's knowledge, the defendant hired the flat in order to view the Coronation processions, but this was not mentioned in their written contract. The processions were cancelled because of the King's illness. The Court of Appeal held that a view of the processions was not simply the purpose of the defendant in hiring the flat but the basis of the contract for both parties, and that since the cancellation of the processions prevented this being achieved the contract was frustrated.

It is not enough that the purpose of one party in making the contract cannot be fulfilled, the basis on which both parties contracted must have been destroyed. This is shown by *Herne Bay Steamboat Co v Hutton*[2], which also reveals the difficulty in drawing the distinction. The defendant chartered a ship from the plaintiffs for 28 and 29 June, 1902, on one of which days Edward VII was to be crowned. To the the Coronation naval review at Spithead and to cruise round the Fleet. The review was cancelled, but the Fleet remained. The Court of Appeal held that the charterparty was not frustrated because the holding of the review was not the basis on which both parties had contracted and it was irrelevant that the purpose of the defendant was defeated.

---

1   [1903] 2 KB 704, CA.
2   [1903] 2 KB 683, CA.

Limits

Express provision for frustrating event

11.9   The doctrine of frustration does not apply if the parties have made provision to deal with the frustrating event which has occurred. There is one exception: a contract is frustrated by supervening illegality despite an express provision to the contrary[1].

A provision concerned with the effect of a possible future event is narrowly construed and unless on its true construction it covers the frustrating event in question the doctrine of frustration is not ousted. This is shown by *Metropolitan Water Board v Dick, Kerr & Co Ltd*[2], where the contract for the reservoir provided that in the event of delays 'however caused' the contractors were to be given an extension of time. The House of Lords held that this provision did not prevent the doctrine of frustration applying because it did not cover the particular event which had occurred. Although the event was literally within the provision, the provision could be construed as limited to temporary difficulties, such as shortage of supplies, and not as extending to events which fundamentally altered the nature of the contract and which could not have been in the parties' contemplation when they made the contract.

---

1 *Ertel Bieber & Co v Rio Tinto Co Ltd* [1918] AC 260, HL.
2 [1918] AC 119, HL.

Foreseen and foreseeable events

11.10 If, by reason of special knowledge, the risk of the particular frustrating event was foreseen or foreseeable by only *one* party the doctrine of frustration cannot apply. It is up to that party to provide against the risk of that event, and if he fails to do so and cannot perform the contract he is liable for breach[1].

On the other hand, where the risk of the frustrating event was foreseen or foreseeable by both parties, but they did not make provision to deal with it, the doctrine of frustration can apply[2]. In each case, however, it is a question of construction whether the failure to make provision for the event means that each party took the risk of it rendering contractual performance impossible or whether, in the absence of any such intention, the doctrine of frustration should apply to discharge the contract[3].

---

1 *Walton Harvey Ltd v Walker and Homfrays Ltd* [1931] 1 Ch 274, CA.
2 *W. J. Tatem Ltd v Gamboa* [1939] 1 KB 132, [1938] 3 All ER 135; *The Eugenia* [1964] 2 QB 226, [1964] 1 All ER 161, CA.
3 *Chandler Bros Ltd v Boswell* [1936] 3 All ER 179, CA; *The Eugenia* [1964] 2 QB 226, [1964] 1 All ER 161, CA.

Fault of a party

11.11 The doctrine of frustration can only apply if the frustrating event occurred without any fault of either party. The onus of proving fault is on the party alleging it[1], and if it is proved it will generally give rise to liability for breach of contract. A deliberate election to pursue a course of conduct which renders performance of the contract impossible is clearly established as fault in this context. In *Maritime National Fish Ltd v Ocean Trawlers Ltd*[2], the plaintiffs chartered to the defendants a trawler fitted with an otter trawl. Both parties knew that use of an otter trawl without a licence from a Minister was illegal. Later, the defendants applied for licences for five trawlers which they were operating, including the plaintiffs'. They were only granted three licences and were asked to specify the three trawlers which they wished to have licenced. The defendants named three trawlers other than the plaintiffs'. They then claimed that they were no longer bound by the charterparty because it had been frustrated. The Privy Council held that the frustration was due to the defendants' deliberate act in not specifying the plaintiffs' trawler for a licence and therefore the doctrine of frustration did not apply and, the charterparty not having been discharged by frustration, the plaintiffs could recover the hire under it.

It has not yet been decided whether a negligent, as opposed to deliberate, act rendering performance of the contract impossible constitutes sufficient fault to render the doctrine of frustration inapplicable.

1   *The Kingswood* [1942] AC 154, [1941] 2 All ER 165, HL.
2   [1935] AC 524, PC.

Leases

11.12   There is authority binding on the Court of Appeal and lower courts that the doctrine of frustration does not apply to leases[1] but the point has not been settled finally because the House of Lords was evenly split on the matter in *Cricklewood Property and Investment Trust Ltd v Leighton's Investment Trust Ltd*[2].

In contrast, particular covenants in a lease can be discharged by frustration[3], and so, probably, can agreements for a lease[4] or for the sale of land in exceptional cases.

1   *Denman v Brise* [1949] 1 KB 22, [1948] 2 All ER 141.
2   [1945] AC 221, [1945] 1 All ER 252, HL.
3   *Baily v De Crespigny* (1869) LR 4 QB 180.
4   *Rom Securities Ltd v Rogers (Holdings) Ltd* (1967) 205 Estates Gazette 427.

Effect

11.13   Frustration does not merely make the contract voidable at the election of a party: the frustrating event *automatically* discharges the contract[1]. Where a contract is severable[2], part may be discharged by frustration and part remain in force[3]. Leaving aside the complicated question of the effect of frustration on money paid or payable under the contract, the effect of frustration on other obligations under the contract is governed by the common law and is as follows: the discharge of a contract by frustration releases both parties from further performance of any such obligations due after the frustrating event[4] but not from any such obligations due before that time, which remain enforceable[5].

Turning to the effect of frustration on money paid or payable under the contract, the position is as follows:

---

1 *Hirji Mulji v Cheong Yue SS Co Ltd* [1926] AC 497, PC.
2 Para. 10.17.
3 *Denny, Mott and Dickson Ltd v James B. Fraser & Co Ltd* [1944] AC 265 at 278–280.
4 *Chandler v Webster* [1904] 1 KB 493, CA. Despite the fact that frustration discharges a contract as to the future, an arbitration clause may remain in force, *Heyman v Darwins Ltd* [1942] AC 356, [1942] 1 All ER 337, HL.
5 *Ibid.*

Money paid or payable under the contract before the occurrence of the frustrating event

11.14 At common law the original position was that an obligation to pay money due before the frustrating event remained enforceable and money paid under the contract before that event was irrecoverable[1]. However, in 1942 in *Fibrosa Spolka Akcyjna v Fairbairn Lawson Combe Barbour Ltd*[2], the House of Lords held, in a case where money payable in advance for machinery had been paid but the contract had been frustrated before any of the machinery had been delivered, that the money could be recovered in quasi-contract on the ground of a total failure of consideration, in the sense that the buyers had got nothing of what they had bargained for.

Nevertheless, the decision in the *Fibrosa* case left the law unjust in two ways:

a. The decision only permitted recovery if there had been a total failure of consideration. This could be unjust to the payer of the money because, if he had received any part, however small, of the contractual performance, he could not recover a penny of what he had paid.

b. The decision could also be unjust to a payee who was ordered to return a pre-payment because he might have incurred expenses in seeking to perform the contract.

---

1 *Chandler v Webster* [1904] 1 KB 493, CA.
2 [1943] AC 32, [1942] 2 All ER 122, HL.

11.15   These injustices were removed by the Law Reform (Frustrated Contracts) Act 1943. Section 1(2) of the Act provides:

a. All sums *payable* under the contract *before* the frustrating event *cease to be payable* whether or not there has been a total failure of consideration.

b. All sums *paid* under the contract *before* the frustrating event are *recoverable* whether or not there has been a total failure of consideration.

c. The court has a discretionary power to allow the payee to set off against the sums so paid or payable a sum not exceeding the value of the expenses he has incurred before the frustrating event in, or for the purpose of, the performance of the contract.

If the court exercises this power it allows the payee to retain the amount stipulated by it (if he has been paid) or to recover the stipulated amount (if the money was payable but not paid). The stipulated amount, which may include an element in respect of overhead expenses and of any work or services performed personally by the payee[1], cannot exceed the sums paid or payable to him. The following illustrates the operation of these provisions. X contracts with Y to manufacture and deliver certain machinery by 1 March for £5,000, £1,000 to be paid on 1 January and the balance on delivery. The contract is discharged by frustration on 1 February before the machinery is delivered but after X has incurred expenses of £500 in making the machinery. Pursuant to s.1(2), Y need not pay the £1,000 if he has not paid it before 1 February or, if he has, he can recover the £1,000, but the court may order Y to pay X up to £500 for his expenses or may allow X to retain up to £500, as the case may be.

1   Law Reform (Frustrated Contracts) Act 1943, s.1(4).

Money payable under the contract after the occurrence of the frustrating event

11.16   Such money is not recoverable by the person to whom it was due, in accordance with the rule that frustration releases both parties from performing any contractual obligation due after the frustrating event. Thus, in *Krell v Henry*[1], it was held that the owner of the flat could not recover a sum payable for the hire of the flat because it was not due until a date after the processions had been cancelled (the frustrating event).

1   [1903] 2 KB 704, CA.

Compensation for valuable benefit obtained

11.17 At common law a party who had benefited another by partly performing the contract before it was frustrated could not recover compensation for this[1]. This rule was particularly harsh where payment was not due to him until after the occurrence of the frustrating event because where money was paid or payable before that time he could retain or recover it, as the case might be.

Section 1(3) of the Law Reform (Frustrated Contracts) Act 1943 now makes compensation available to either party for a valuable benefit conferred on the other. It provides that where a party to a frustrated contract has, by reason of anything done by any other party in, or for the purpose of, the performance of the contract, obtained a valuable benefit before the frustrating event (other than the payment of money), that other party may recover from him such sum, if any, as the court considers just, having regard to all the circumstances of the case. In assessing the amount of compensation the court is required to take particular account of the expenses incurred by the benefited party before the contract was frustrated, including any sums paid or payable by him to another party under the contract and retained or recoverable by that other party under s.1(2)[2]. The court must also have regard to the effect in relation to the benefit of the circumstances giving rise to the frustration[3].

The operation of the Act of 1943 can be illustrated as follows: A, a jobbing decorator, contracts with B to paint the outside of B's house for £300, £100 to be paid on 1 September and the rest on completion. B pays A the £100 on 1 September. After A has painted most of the house the contract is frustrated, A having been seriously incapacitated in a car crash. Under s.1(2), A must return the £100 to B, unless and to the extent that the court exercises its discretion to allow A to retain some or all of it. Suppose his expenses were £50 and the court allows him to retain this — only £50 will be recoverable by B. The obligation as to the further £200 is, of course, discharged by frustration and A cannot claim this from B. However, as A has conferred a valuable benefit on B before the frustrating event, s.1(3) comes into play. Suppose that the benefit conferred on B is worth £175. The court can order B to pay A for that benefit, but in assessing the compensation payable under s.1(3) the court must take into account what it has allowed A to retain under s.1(2).

---

1 *Appleby v Myers* (1867) LR 2 CP 651.
2 Law Reform (Frustrated Contracts) Act 1943, s.1(3)(a).
3 *Ibid.*, s.1(3)(b).

Application of the Law Reform (Frustrated Contracts) Act 1943

11.18 Where a contract to which the Act applies is severable, e.g. a contract to work for a year at £400 a month[1], and a severable part of it is wholly performed before the frustrating event, or wholly performed except in respect of payment of sums which are or can be ascertained under the contract, that part is to be treated as if it were a separate contract and had not been frustrated, and the Act is only applicable to the remainder of the contract[2]. The result is that, if the employee under the above contract works for two months and two weeks and then dies before any salary has been paid, his executors can recover the two months' salary owing to him (each month being treated as a separate contract) *plus* compensation under s.1(3) of the Act for any valuable benefit conferred by the deceased on the employer during the remaining two weeks.

The Act applies to contracts to which the Crown is a party[3].

The Act does not apply to the extent that it is inconsistent with a provision in the contract[4].

The Act does not apply to the following types of contract:

a. Any charterparty, except a time charterparty (i.e. one for a definite period) or a charterparty by way of demise (i.e. one where temporary ownership of the ship is passed to the charterer), nor does it apply to any contract (other than a charterparty) for the carriage of goods by sea[5]. Where the Act does not apply freight paid in advance is not recoverable even though completion of the voyage is frustrated.

b. A contract of insurance[6]. Generally, a premium is not returnable once the risk has attached.

c. A contract to which s.7 of the Sale of Goods Act 1893 applies, or any other contract for the sale or for the sale and delivery of specific goods, where the contract is frustrated by reason of the fact that the goods have *perished*[7]. In such a case the loss is borne by the party who is carrying the risk at the time, a matter which we discuss in paras. 22.26 and 22.27.

---

1 Para. 10.17.
2 S.2(4).
3 S.2(2).
4 S.2(3).
5 S.2(5)(a).
6 S.2(5)(b).
7 S.2(5)(c). For the meaning of 'specific goods' and 'perished', see paras. 22.10 and 22.23.

Chapter 12
Remedies for Breach of Contract

12.1 In the event of a breach of contract, the injured party may have one or more of the following remedies:

a. In the case of a serious breach, he may rescind the contract for breach, i.e. accept the breach as discharging the contract, thereby discharging him from any obligation to perform the contract further. If the injured party elects to rescind for breach, he may also bring an action for damages. We have already discussed rescission for breach in detail in paras. 10.3 to 10.22.

b. In any case, the injured party may bring an action for damages for breach.

c. Where he has performed part of his own obligations, he may sue in quasi-contract on a *quantum meruit* for the value of what he has done if he rescinds the contract for breach.

d. If he has paid the contractual price, but the other party has totally failed to perform his side of the contract, the injured party must sue in quasi-contract (a matter which we discuss in Chapter 17) for the return of the money paid if he rescinds the contract for breach.

e. In appropriate cases, he may seek a decree of specific performance or an injunction.

DAMAGES

12.2 Damages for breach of contract are not awarded as punishment (with the result that the amount awarded is not affected by the manner of the breach or the motive behind it[1]) but are compensatory. Their object is to put the party not in breach into the same position, so far as money can do it, as if the contract had been performed, or in other words, to compensate him for loss of the bargain[2]. This means that where that party has not suffered any loss as a result of the breach the damages recoverable by him will be purely nominal (usually £2.00). Subject to the rules of remoteness, a plaintiff can recover not merely for financial loss resulting from the breach of contract, but also for personal injury, injury to property, inconvenience or discomfort[3], or disappointment, distress or upset resulting from the breach. In *Jarvis v Swan Tours Ltd*[4], for instance, the plaintiff booked a 15 day winter sports holiday with the defendants. He did so on the faith of the defendants' brochure, which described the holiday as a house party and promised a number of entertainments, including excellent ski-ing, a yodeller evening, a bar, and afternoon tea and cakes. In the first week there were 13 guests; in the second the plaintiff was entirely alone. The entertainments fell far short of the promised standard. The Court of Appeal held that the plaintiff was entitled to damages for mental distress and disappointment for loss of enjoyment caused by the breach of contract. *Cox v Philips Industries*[5] shows that damages for emotional distress brought about by breach of contract can be awarded even though the subject-matter of the contract did not involve the giving of pleasure or enjoyment, unlike a contract to provide a holiday. In that case an employee who had suffered emotional distress by being demoted in breach of his contract of employment was awarded damages for that distress.

---

1 *Addis v Gramophone Co* [1909] AC 488, HL.
2 *Wertheim v Chicoutimi Pulp Co* [1911] AC 301, PC.
3 *Hobbs v London and South Western Rly Co* (1875) LR 10 QB 111.
4 [1973] QB 233, [1973] 3 All ER 71, CA.
5 [1976] 3 All ER 161, [1976] 1 WLR 638.

Remoteness of damage

12.3 In order to succeed in his action for damages, the plaintiff must, of course, prove that the loss which he has suffered was caused by the defendant's breach of contract[1]. But such proof is not in itself enough to entitle him to damages for that loss, because a defendant will only be liable for it if it was not too 'remote'. Whether or not loss suffered is too remote is determined by applying the rule in *Hadley v Baxendale*[2] (as explained in *Victoria Laundry (Windsor) Ltd v Newman Industries Ltd*[3] and *The Heron II*[4]).

The rule, as explained, provides that damage is not too remote if one of the two following sub-rules is satisfied:

a. if the loss arises naturally, i.e. according to the usual course of things, from the breach of contract as the probable result of it; or

b. if the loss could reasonably be supposed to have been in the contemplation of the parties, when they made the contract, as the probable result of the breach of it.

Sub-rule a. deals with 'normal' damage which arises in the ordinary course of events, while sub-rule b. deals with 'abnormal' damage which arises from special circumstances.

---

1 *Weld-Blundell v Stephens* [1920] AC 956, HL.
2 (1854) 23 LJ Exch 179.
3 [1949] 2 KB 528, [1949] 1 All ER 997, CA.
4 [1969] AC 350, [1967] 3 All ER 686, HL.

12.4 In the light of subsequent cases, a number of things can be said about both sub-rules. First, the plaintiff can only recover for such loss as was, *at the time of the contract,* within the reasonable contemplation of the parties as the probable result of its breach, *had they had their attention drawn to the possibility of the breach which has in fact occurred*[1]. Secondly, what was within the parties' reasonable contemplation depends on the knowledge 'possessed' by them at that time. For this purpose, knowledge 'possessed' is of two kinds: one imputed, the other actual. Under sub-rule a., everyone is taken to know (i.e. knowledge is imputed) the 'ordinary course of things' and, consequently, what loss is the probable result of a breach of contract in that ordinary course. In addition, 'knowledge possessed' may, in a particular case, include knowledge which the guilty party (and the other party) actually possess of special circumstances outside the ordinary course of things, of such a kind that the breach in these special circumstances would be liable to cause more loss. Such a case attracts sub-rule b. so as to make the additional loss recoverable[2]. Thirdly, provided the *type* of loss caused by a breach of contract was within the reasonable contemplation of the parties when the contract was made, the loss is not too remote and damages can therefore be recovered for it even though its *extent* was much greater than could have been reasonably contemplated[3].

---

1 *H. Parsons (Livestock) Ltd v Uttley Ingham & Co Ltd* [1978] 1 All ER 525, CA.
2 *Victoria Laundry (Windsor) Ltd v Newman Industries Ltd* [1949] 2 KB 528, [1949] 1 All ER 997, CA.
3 *Wroth v Tyler* [1974] Ch 30, [1973] 1 All ER 897; *H. Parsons (Livestock) Ltd v Uttley Ingham & Co Ltd* [1978] 1 All ER 525, CA.

12.5 The degree of probability which is required to satisfy the test of remoteness is that there must have been a serious possibility that the type of loss in question would occur[1]. Thus, it suffices that the plaintiff's loss is such as may reasonably be supposed to have been in the parties' contemplation as a serious possibility, had their attention been drawn to the possibility of the breach which has in fact occurred. It must be emphasised that the particular breach itself need not have been contemplated. Suppose that the loss has been caused by some defect in the subject-matter of the contract which is unknown, or even unknowable, when the contract is made. The court has to assume, even though it is contrary to the facts, that the parties had in mind the breach which has occurred when it considers whether the plaintiff's loss was within their reasonable contemplation.

---

1 *The Heron II* [1969] 1 AC 350, [1967] 3 All ER 686, HL.

12.6 The application of the contractual rule of remoteness can best be illustrated by reference to past decisions. In *Hadley v Baxendale*[1], the plaintiffs' mill at Gloucester was brought to a halt when a crank shaft broke. The shaft had to be sent to its makers in Greenwich as a pattern for a new one. The defendant carriers undertook to deliver it at Greenwich the following day, but in breach of contract delayed its delivery so that the duration of the stoppage at the mill was extended. The plaintiff's claim to recover damages for loss of profits caused by the defendants' delay was unsuccessful since this loss was held to be too remote. The basis of the court's decision was that the defendants only knew that they were transporting a broken shaft owned by the plaintiffs. The court applied the two sub-rules in turn, and held:

a. the plaintiffs might have had a spare shaft or been able to borrow one, and therefore the loss of profits did not arise in the usual course of events from the defendants' breach; and

b. on the facts known to the defendants (they were unaware of the lack of a substitute shaft), the loss of profits could not be supposed to have been within the reasonable contemplation of the parties at the time they made the contract as the probable result of the breach.

In *Victoria Laundry (Windsor) Ltd v Newman Industries Ltd*[2], the defendants agreed to sell to the plaintiffs, who were launderers and dyers, a boiler to be delivered on a certain date. The boiler was damaged in a fall and was not delivered until five months after the agreed delivery date. The plaintiffs claimed damages for loss of profits that would have been earned during the five month period through the extension of their business, and also for loss of several highly lucrative dyeing contracts which they would have obtained with the Ministry of Supply. The Court of Appeal held that the plaintiffs could recover for the loss of 'normal' profits (i.e. those which would have been earned through an extension of the business) but not for the loss of 'exceptional' profits (i.e. loss of the highly lucrative contracts), which it treated as a different type of loss. This decision was based on the following application of the two sub-rules:

a. the defendants knew at the time of the contract that the plaintiffs were laundrymen and dyers and required the boiler for immediate use in their business and, with their technical experience and knowledge of the facts, it could be presumed that loss of 'normal' profits was foreseeable by them, and therefore within both parties' reasonable contemplation, as likely to result from their breach; but

b. in the absence of special knowledge, they could not reasonably foresee the loss of the 'exceptional' profits under the highly lucrative contracts.

The case was, therefore, remitted to an Official Referee for a decision as to the amount of 'normal' profits which had been lost in the circumstances.

In *The Heron II*[3], the plaintiff sugar merchants chartered The Heron II from the defendant to carry a cargo of sugar from Constanza to Basrah. The defendant shipowner deviated in breach of contract and the ship arrived in Basrah nine days later than expected. Because of a fall in the market price of sugar the plaintiffs obtained £3,800 less for it than would have been obtained if the sugar had arrived on time. The defendant did not know of the plaintiffs' intention to sell the sugar in Basrah, but did know that there was a market for sugar at Basrah and that the plaintiffs were sugar merchants. The House of Lords held that the plaintiffs' loss of profit (£3,800) was not too remote under sub-rule a. since knowledge could be imputed to the defendant that the goods might be sold at market price on their arrival in Basrah and that market prices were apt to fluctuate daily, and therefore the defendant ought to have contemplated that a loss of profit might result from the breach.

---

1 (1854) 23 LJ Exch 179.
2 [1949] 2 KB 528, [1949] 1 All ER 997, CA.
3 [1969] AC 350, [1967] 3 All ER 686, HL.

Measure of damages

12.7 Assuming that the loss is not too remote from the breach of contract, the next question which the court has to consider is the measure (i.e. quantification) of damages for that loss. In quantifying the damages payable, the court is seeking to fulfil the object of damages which, as we said earlier, is to put the injured party into the same position, so far as money can do it, as he would have been in had the contract been performed.

Generally, there are no specific rules for the quantification of damages. One exception relates to contracts for the sale of goods, where the Sale of Goods Act 1893 has provided a number of rules, which we discuss in paras. 22.83 to 22.85, such as that where there is an available market for the goods in question a buyer who fails to accept them is liable, prima facie, to pay the difference between the contract price and the market or current price. However, apart from such specific rules, it is up to the court to quantify adequate compensation for the plaintiff's loss as best it can. The fact that the precise assessment of damages is difficult does not prevent an award being made, as is shown by *Chaplin v Hicks*[1]. The defendant advertised that he would employ, as actresses, 12 women to be selected by him out of 50 chosen by the readers of various newspapers, in which the candidates' photographs appeared, as the most beautiful. The plaintiff was one of the 50 chosen by the readers but the defendant made an unreasonable appointment for an interview with her, and selected 12 out of the 49 who were able to keep the appointment. In an action for breach of contract, the defendant contended that only nominal damages were payable, since the plaintiff would only have had a one in four chance of being selected. Nevertheless, the Court of Appeal refused to disturb an award of £100 damages for the loss of her chance of being selected.

---

1   [1911] 2 KB 786, CA.

Effect of tax liability
12.8   One consequence of the fact that damages are designed to compensate the plaintiff for his actual loss is that, whenever a claim for damages includes a claim for loss of income or profit, the income tax which would have been payable on it may have to be taken into account[1]. Tax liability must certainly be taken into account in quantifying the damages in a contractual claim for wrongful dismissal[2], but the extent to which it should be taken into account in other cases of breach of contract is uncertain although it seems that it should be ignored in commercial cases.

Tax liability can only be taken into account if, and to the extent that, the sum awarded as damages is not taxable in the plaintiff's hands. The result is that tax liability is generally excluded in quantifying damages for loss of profits because such damages are normally subject to tax in the plaintiff's hands as part of the profits of his business[3]. In the case of damages for wrongful dismissal from employment, these are subject to tax in the plaintiff's hands, except for the first £5,000[4]. The result is that in assessing damages of under £5,000 for wrongful dismissal the court must take into account the plaintiff's tax liability and reduce the award accordingly; but in the case of damages exceeding £5,000 the court must take the plaintiff's tax liability into account to the extent of the first £5,000, and reduce that part of the award accordingly, but not in relation to the excess over that sum. In *Parsons v B.N.M. Laboratories Ltd*[5], for instance, the plaintiff claimed, as damages for wrongful dismissal, loss of salary and commission amounting to £1,200. The Court of Appeal held that that sum must be reduced by £320, which was the amount of income tax payable on the lost salary and commission.

---

1 *British Transport Commission v Gourley* [1956] AC 185, [1955] 3 All ER 796, HL.
2 *Beach v Reed Corrugated Cases Ltd* [1956] 2 All ER 652, [1956] 1 WLR 807; *Parsons v B.N.M. Laboratories Ltd* [1964] 1 QB 95, [1963] 2 All ER 658, CA.
3 *Diamond v Campbell-Jones* [1961] Ch 22, [1960] 1 All ER 583.
4 Income and Corporation Taxes Act 1970, ss. 187, 188 and Sched. 4, as amended.
5 [1964] 1 QB 95, [1963] 2 All ER 658, CA.

Mitigation

12.9 The plaintiff cannot recover for loss which he could reasonably have avoided. Thus, the seller of goods which have been wrongly rejected by the buyer must not unreasonably refuse another's offer to buy them. Similarly, an employee who has been wrongfully dismissed must not unreasonably refuse an offer of employment from another[1]. If such refusals occur, the plaintiff is said to be in breach of his duty to mitigate his loss and cannot recover his unmitigated loss but only the loss which he would have suffered if the damage had been mitigated. If he would have suffered no loss at all, only nominal damages are recoverable[2].

A leading case on the duty to mitigate is *Payzu Ltd v Saunders*[3]. A contract for the sale of goods by the defendant to the plaintiffs provided that delivery should be as required over a nine month period and that payment should be made within one month of delivery. The plaintiffs failed to make prompt payment for the first instalment and the defendant, in breach of contract, refused to deliver any more instalments under the contract. He did, however, offer to deliver goods at the contract price if the plaintiffs would pay cash with each order. The plaintiffs refused to do so and brought an action for breach of contract, claiming the difference between the contract price and the market price (which had risen). The Court of Appeal held that the plaintiffs should have mitigated their loss by accepting the defendant's offer, and therefore the damages which they could recover were to be measured by the loss which they would have suffered if the offer had been accepted, not by the difference between the contract and market prices.

The following points may be noted about the duty to mitigate:

a. The duty to mitigate may require the plaintiff to do something positive. In the examples given earlier on this page, the seller and the employee would equally have been in breach of their duty to mitigate if they had not made reasonable efforts to seek other offers to buy the goods or alternative equivalent employment: it would not necessarily excuse them that no one had spontaneously made them an offer.

b. The duty to mitigate only requires the plaintiff to take reasonable steps to minimise his loss. He is not required to embark on hazardous litigation or to risk his commercial reputation in order to minimise his loss. In *Pilkington v Wood*[4], for instance, the plaintiff failed to bring an action against a third party, which, if successful, would have reduced the loss suffered by him consequent on the defendant's breach of contract. It was held that since the litigation would have been hazardous the plaintiff's failure to embark on it did not involve a breach of the duty to mitigate: the duty did not extend this far.

c. If the plaintiff has to spend money in an endeavour to mitigate his loss, he can recover it as part of the damages awarded provided the expenditure was reasonable, and he can so recover notwithstanding that those steps subsequently prove to have aggravated the damage[5].

---

1   *Brace v Calder* [1895] 1 QB 253, CA.
2   *Ibid.*
3   [1919] 2 KB 581, CA.
4   [1953] Ch 770, [1953] 2 All ER 810.
5   *Hoffberger v Ascot International Bloodstock Bureau Ltd* [1976] 120 Sol Jo 130, CA.

12.10 In some cases the duty to mitigate does not apply:

a. It does not apply where the buyer of either goods or land has a cause of action in damages for defects in the goods or land or for some other breach of contract and the seller offers to re-purchase the property. A refusal by the buyer, however capricious, will not prevent him recovering substantial damages[1].

b. As we said in para. 10.12, where there is an anticipatory breach of contract, the injured party has an option *either* to rescind the contract and sue immediately for damages *or* to affirm the contract and await the time of performance, in which case he can then bring an action for damages if the other party is still in breach. If the injured party elects to rescind he is under a duty to mitigate his loss[2]. On the other hand, the injured party is under no duty to mitigate his loss if he affirms the contract. This is shown by the decision of the House of Lords in *White and Carter (Councils) Ltd v McGregor*[3]. The plaintiffs were advertising contractors. They carried on a business of supplying free litter bins to local authorities, the bins being paid for by businesses which hired advertising space on them. The plaintiffs agreed with the defendant garage proprietor to display advertisements for his garage on bins for three years. On the same day, the defendant renounced the contract and asked the plaintiffs to cancel it. They refused, thereby affirming the contract, and proceeded to prepare advertisement plates which they then attached to bins and displayed for three years. When the defendant failed to pay at the appropriate time, the plaintiffs sued for the full contract price. The House of Lords held that they could recover the full contract price despite the fact that they had made no effort to mitigate their loss by getting other advertisers in substitution for the defendant and had increased their loss after the renunciation by performing their side of the contract.

---

1   *Strutt v Whitnell* [1975] 2 All ER 510, [1975] 1 WLR 870, CA.
2   *Roth & Co v Taysen, Townsend & Co* (1895) 1 Com Cas 240.
3   [1962] AC 413, [1961] 3 All ER 1178, HL.

Liquidated damages and penalties

12.11 So far we have been concerned with *unliquidated damages*, i.e. damages which are assessed by the court and not by the agreement of the parties. It is, however, possible for the parties to agree in their contract that in the event of a breach the damages shall be a fixed sum or be calculated in a specified way. Such damages are called *liquidated damages*. Liquidated damages have the obvious advantage that the amount recoverable as damages is always certain whereas in the case of unliquidated damages it is uncertain until the court has decided the matter. Provision for liquidated damages is often found in contracts which have to be completed within a certain time. Thus, contracts for building or civil engineering work normally provide for a specified sum to be paid for every day or week of delay.

If a contract containing a liquidated damages provision is broken, the injured party can recover the specified sum, whether this is greater or less than the actual loss suffered. This rule may benefit a plaintiff who has suffered little or no loss but can be to his disadvantage if the loss suffered greatly exceeds the specified sum. In *Cellulose Acetate Silk Co Ltd v Widnes Foundry (1925) Ltd*[1], the defendants agreed to build machinery for the plaintiffs in 18 weeks and, in the event of taking longer, to pay 'by way of penalty £20 per working week'. The machinery was completed 30 weeks late and the plaintiffs lost £5,850 in consequence. The House of Lords held that the provision for payment was one for liquidated damages and that the plaintiffs could only recover 30 x £20, i.e. £600.

---

1   [1933] AC 20, HL.

12.12 Liquidated damages provisions must be distinguished from two other provisions:

a. *Exemption clauses limiting liability* A liquidated damages, clause is not an exemption clause limiting liability because it fixes the sum payable for breach whether the actual loss is greater or less, whereas (assuming it is valid) such an exemption clause merely fixes the maximum sum recoverable and if the actual loss is less than that sum, only that sum can be recovered.

b. *Penalty clauses* Where the sum fixed by the contract is a genuine pre-estimate of the loss which will be caused by its breach, the provision is one for liquidated damages, but if instead the sum is intended to operate as a threat to hold a potential defaulter to his bargain it is a penalty[1]. The distinction between a penalty and liquidated damages is crucial because their effects are different.

---

1   *Law v Redditch Local Board* [1892] 1 QB 127 at 132.

Penalty
12.13 If the actual loss suffered by a plaintiff is less than the sum specified in a penalty clause, he can only recover his actual loss[1]. Suppose that a broken contract contains a penalty clause for £1,000 penalty but the plaintiff's actual loss is only £100, the plaintiff can only recover £100 damages (whereas if the clause had been one for liquidated damages the plaintiff could have recovered £1,000). On the other hand, if the penalty is less than the actual loss suffered by the plaintiff, e.g. because of inflation since the contract was made, he cannot recover more than the penalty if he sues for it, although if he sues instead for (unliquidated) damages he can recover the whole of his loss[2]. This option is not, of course, open in the case of a liquidated damages provision.

---

1   *Wilbeam v Ashton* (1807) 1 Camp 78.
2   *Well v Rederaktiebolaget Luggude* [1915] 3 KB 66.

Parties' intention
12.14 Whether an agreed sum is liquidated damages or a penalty depends on the parties' intention and, as is shown by the *Cellulose Acetate* case[1], the use of the words 'penalty' or 'liquidated damages' in the contract is not conclusive. The crucial question is whether the parties intended the specified sum to be a genuine pre-estimate of the damage likely to be caused by the breach or to operate as a fine or penalty for

breach. This intention is to be gathered from the terms and inherent circumstances of the contract at the time it was made, not at the time of its breach[2]. The determination of the parties' intention is aided by a number of rebuttable presumptions of intention summarised by Lord Dunedin in *Dunlop Pneumatic Tyre Co Ltd v New Garage and Motor Co Ltd*[3]:

a. 'It will be held to be a penalty if the sum stipulated for is extravagant and unconscionable in amount in comparison with the greatest loss that could conceivably be proved to have followed from the breach.'

b. 'It will be held to be a penalty if the breach consists only in not paying a sum of money, and the sum stipulated is a sum greater than the sum which ought to have been paid.' In *Kemble v Farren*[4], for example, the defendant agreed with the plaintiff to appear at Covent Garden for four seasons at £3.6s.8d a night. The contract provided that if either party refused to fulfil the agreement, or any part of it, he should pay the other £1,000 as 'liquidated damages'. The defendant refused to act during the second season. It was held that the stipulation was a penalty. The obligation to pay £1,000 might have arisen simply on the plaintiff's failure to pay £3.6s.8d and was therefore quite obviously a penalty.

c. 'There is a presumption (but no more) that it is a penalty when a single lump sum is made payable by way of compensation, on the occurrence of one or more or all of several events, some of which may occasion serious and others but trifling damage.' This was a second reason for the decision in *Kemble v Farren*. On the other hand —

d. 'It is no obstacle to the sum stipulated being a genuine pre-estimate of damage, that the consequences of the breach are such as to make precise pre-estimation almost an impossibility.' This is illustrated by the *Dunlop* case itself. The plaintiffs supplied tyres to the defendants subject to an agreement that the defendants would not sell below the list price and would pay £5 by way of liquidated damages for every tyre sold in breach of the agreement. The House of Lords held that the stipulated sum was one for liquidated damages. (The agreement would now be void under the Resale Prices Act 1976.)[5] Clearly, the figure of £5 was, at most, only a rough and ready estimate of the possible loss which the plaintiffs might suffer if their price list was undercut.

---

1 Para. 12.11.
2 *Dunlop Pneumatic Tyre Co Ltd v New Garage & Motor Co Ltd* [1915] AC 77 at 86–87.
3 [1915] AC 77 at 86.
4 (1829) 6 Bing 141.
5 Para. 15.43.

Interest

12.15 Section 3 of the Law Reform (Miscellaneous Provisions) Act 1934 provides that the court may allow interest, at such rates as it thinks fit, on all claims for debt or damages for the whole or any part of the period between the date when the cause of action arose and the date of judgment. Interest cannot be given on interest. The Act of 1934 does not apply to a debt on which interest is payable as of right, viz.

a. where there is an express or implied agreement to pay it;

b. where the usage of the trade requires it[1];

c. where the money was obtained, or is retained, by fraud[2];

d. where by Act of Parliament it is provided that interest shall be payable. For example, under the Bills of Exchange Act 1882 interest from time of maturity, or (in the case of a bill payable on demand) from date of presentment for payment, is payable by the party liable on a dishonoured bill[3].

The measure of damages for failure to pay money by a due date is, generally, interest at the market rate.

---

1 *Re Anglesey* [1901] 2 Ch 548.
2 *Johnson v R* [1904] AC 817, HL.
3 S.57.

QUANTUM MERUIT

12.16 In a particular situation, a claim on a *quantum meruit* is available to a plaintiff as an *alternative* to a claim for damages for breach of contract.

If a party to a contract unjustifiably prevents the other party performing his contractual obligations, as where he states that he will not accept performance or renders performance impossible, his conduct will normally constitute a repudiatory breach of contract and the injured party can recover damages for breach of contract, whether he elects to rescind or to affirm the contract. Alternatively, if the injured party has partly performed his obligations under the contract he can claim on a *quantum meruit* the reasonable value of the work done, provided he has elected to rescind the contract[1]. These rules apply even though the obligation which has not been wholly performed by the injured party is entire[2]. *Planché v Colburn*[3] is a leading authority. A had agreed to write for 'The Juvenile Library', a series published by B, a book on costume and ancient armour. After A had written part of the book, B abandoned the series. It was held that A could recover 50 guineas as reasonable remuneration on a *quantum meruit*.

One distinction between these two types of remedy is that, whereas an award of damages depends on the existence of a contract and its breach, the right to claim on a *quantum meruit* does not arise under the law of contract but by virtue of the law of quasi-contract, which we discuss in Chapter 17. Another distinction relates to the quantum recoverable. As we have already stated, damages are compensatory, their object being to put the plaintiff into the same position, so far as money can do it, as if the contract had been performed. Thus, if the injured party in a case like *Planché v Colburn* decides to sue for damages, the damages awarded will be equivalent to the sum payable to him on completion of his work, less any savings (e.g. on labour and materials) made through not completing performance. But, if it is shown that the plaintiff would in any event have been unable to perform his entire obligation, he will at most be entitled to nominal damages[4]. On the other hand, a *quantum meruit* award is restitutory, its object being to restore the plaintiff to the position in which he would have been if the contract had never been made by awarding him an amount equivalent to the value of the work which he has done. Generally, an award of damages will be more generous than a *quantum meruit* award, but the converse may be true if the plaintiff originally made a bad bargain or if only nominal damages would be awarded.

---

1   *Planché v Colburn* (1831) 8 Bing 14 at 16.
2   Paras. 10.14—10.16.
3   (1831) 8 Bing 14.
4   *The Mihalis Angelos* [1971] 1 QB 164, [1970] 3 All ER 125, CA.

SPECIFIC PERFORMANCE

12.17   The court may grant a decree of specific performance to the injured party, instead of, or in addition to, awarding him damages. Such a decree orders the defaulting party to carry out his contractual obligations.

12.18   Specific performance will not be granted in the following cases:

a. *Where damages are an adequate remedy* It is for this reason that specific performance of a contract to sell goods is not normally ordered: the payment of damages enables the plaintiff to go out into the market and buy the equivalent goods[1]. However, in exceptional cases, e.g. where the contract is for the sale of specific goods of a unique character or of special value or interest, the contract will be specifically enforced[2].

By way of contrast, every plot of land is unique, with the result that contracts for the sale or lease of land are always specifically enforceable. This has produced the rule that, since the contract is specifically enforceable in favour of the purchaser or lessee, a vendor or lessor of land can obtain an order of specific performance even though, in his case, damages would be an adequate remedy[3].

It is because damages are normally adequate that a contractual obligation to pay money is not normally specifically enforceable. However, in addition to the exception mentioned at the end of the last paragraph, there are other exceptions, for instance:

i. as the House of Lords held in *Beswick v Beswick*[4], a contract to pay money to a third party is specifically enforceable (because any damages awarded would probably be nominal);

ii. where the contract is for an annuity or other periodical payment it is specifically enforceable (thereby avoiding the need to sue for damages every time a payment is not made)[5].

b. *Where consideration has not been provided* The remedy of specific performance is an equitable one and, since equity does not recognise a seal as an effective substitute for consideration, specific performance cannot be awarded in favour of a person who has not provided consideration ('equity will not assist a volunteer') and he is left to his common law remedy of damages[6].

c. *Where the court's constant supervision would be necessary to secure compliance with the order* An example is provided by *Ryan v Mutual Tontine Westminster Chambers Association*[7]. In the lease of a flat in a block of flats the lessors agreed to keep a resident porter, who should be in constant attendance and perform specified duties. The person appointed got his duties done by deputies and was absent for hours at a time at another job. The court refused to order specific performance against the lessor of the agreement relating to the porter because such an order would have required its constant supervision. As part of the present principle a contract to build or repair is normally not specifically enforceable, the only exception being where:

i. the work is defined by the contract in a sufficiently definite way for the court to be able to see the exact nature of the work it is asked to specifically enforce; and

ii. the plaintiff has a substantial interest in the work which cannot be compensated by damages; and

iii. the defendant has possession of the land on which the work is contracted to be done[8].

d. *Where the contract is for personal services* The obvious example of such a contract is one of employment. Section 16 of the Trade Union and Labour Relations Act 1974 prohibits an order of specific performance against an *employee* to compel him to do any work or to attend at any place for the doing of any work. It is well established by the cases that contracts for personal services not covered by the Act cannot be specifically enforced either, nor can an order of specific performance be made against an employer. Reasons given are that such contracts would require constant supervision and that it is contrary to public policy to force one person to submit to the orders of another. However, in very exceptional circumstances it may be possible to obtain an order for the specific performance of a contract of employment against an employer.

e. *Lack of mutuality* There is a rule that in certain cases a plaintiff cannot obtain specific performance against the defendant if, in the circumstances, it would not be available to the defendant against the plaintiff. In *Flight v Bolland*[9], for instance, it was held that a minor could not be awarded specific performance of a contract because such an order could not be made against him in the circumstances. While there is no doubting the present rule, its extent is uncertain.

---

1 Apart from its inherent jurisdiction to order specific recovery of goods, the court has power under the Sale of Goods Act 1893 to order the specific performance of contracts for the sale of specific or ascertained goods. This power has not been used more liberally than the inherent power. We discuss it further in para.
2 *Thorn v Public Works Comrs* (1863) 32 Beav 490; *Phillips v Lamdin* [1949] 2 KB 33, [1949] 1 All ER 770; *Sky Petroleum Ltd v VIP Petroleum Ltd* [1974] 1 All ER 954, [1974] 1 WLR 576.
3 *Cogent v Gibson* (1864) 33 Beav 557.
4 [1968] AC 58, [1967] 2 All ER 1197, HL; para. 6.26.
5 *Beswick v Beswick* [1968] AC 58, [1967] 2 All ER 1197, HL.
6 *Cannon v Hartley* [1949] Ch 213, [1949] 1 All ER 50.
7 [1893] 1 Ch 116.
8 *Wolverhampton Corpn v Emmons* [1901] 1 KB 515, CA; *Carpenters Estates Ltd v Davies* [1940] Ch 160, [1940] 1 All ER 13.
9 (1828) 4 Russ 298.

12.19 If the case does not fall within one of the above cases, specific performance may be ordered, but it must not be forgotten that since specific performance is an equitable remedy its award does not lie as of right (unlike the common law remedy of damages) but lies in the court's discretion. Factors which make it unlikely that the court will exercise its discretion in favour of specific performance include:

a. mistake on the part of the defendant, such that it would be unjust to specifically enforce the contract against him[1];
b. delay in bringing an action for specific performance which

resulted in the defendant so changing his position that it would be unjust to specifically enforce the contract against him[2];

c. breach by the plaintiff of his contractual obligations[3].

---

1 Paras. 13.1, 13.6.
2 *Stuart v London and North Western Rly Co* (1852) 1 De G M & G 721; *Lazard Bros & Co Ltd v Fairfield Properties Co (Mayfair) Ltd* (1977) *Times*, 12 October.
3 *Walsh v Lonsdale* (1882) 21 Ch D 9.

INJUNCTION

12.20 An injunction is a court order restraining a party to a contract from acting in breach of a negative stipulation contained in it. By way of comparison, specific performance is concerned with the enforcement of positive contractual stipulations.

12.21 While it is correct to say that injunctions are concerned with restraining breaches of negative contractual stipulations, it would be erroneous to assume that only an express negative stipulation can be remedied by an injunction. Generally, a breach of a positive stipulation can be enjoined if the stipulation can properly be construed as impliedly being a negative stipulation. Thus, in *Manchester Ship Canal Co v Manchester Racecourse Co*[1], a stipulation for the grant of a 'first refusal' was construed as a stipulation, enforceable by injunction, *not* to sell to anyone else in breach of the stipulation. Similarly, in *Metropolitan Electric Supply Co Ltd v Ginder*[2], where the defendant had undertaken to take all the electricity required for his premises from the plaintiffs, it was held that this was impliedly an undertaking *not* to take electricity from any other person, which could be enforced by an injunction. However, the courts have refused to enforce by injunction an undertaking by an employee which, although positive in form, is impliedly negative. In *Whitwood Chemical Co v Hardman*[3], for instance, an employee undertook to devote the whole of his time to his employer. It was held that this undertaking could not be enforced by an injunction, despite the fact that it clearly implied the negative undertaking that the employee would not give his time to another employer.

---

1 [1901] 2 Ch 37.
2 [1901] 2 Ch 799.
3 [1891] 2 Ch 416.

12.22 Although the courts are prepared to enforce an expressly negative stipulation in a contract for personal services, consistency with the rule that such a contract cannot normally be the subject of a decree of specific performance means that an injunction will not be issued to restrain an employee or the like from breaking a promise not to work for any other person, if this would indirectly amount to compelling him to perform his contract with his employer[1]. This is given statutory force by s.16 of the Trade Union and Labour Relations Act 1974, which provides that no court may, by an injunction restraining a breach or threatened breach of a contract of employment, compel an employees to do any work or to attend at any place of work.

On the other hand, an expressly negative promise by an employee or the like will be enforced against him by injunction if it does not indirectly force him to work for his employer. For example, in *Lumley v Wagner*[2], the defendant, an opera star, agreed to sing at the plaintiff's theatre for three months and nowhere else during that time. An injunction was granted restraining her from singing for another during the three month period. *Warner Bros Pictures Inc v Nelson*[3] is a similar case. The defendant, whose stage name was Bette Davis, agreed not to work as a film actress for any other film company for a year or to be engaged in any other occupation. During the year she contracted to work for another film company. Branson, J, stated that, while an injunction enforcing all the negative stipulations in the contract could not be granted (because it would force Bette Davis either to be idle or to perform her contract with the plaintiffs), the injunction requested would be granted because it was limited to prohibiting Bette Davis from working in a film or stage production for anyone other than the plaintiffs. Bette Davis would still be free to earn her living in some other less remunerative way.

---

1   *Rely-a-Bell Burglar and Fire Alarm Co Ltd v Eisler* [1926] Ch 609.
2   (1852) 1 De GM & G 604.
3   [1937] 1 KB 209, [1936] 3 All ER 160.

12.23   The law is similar where an employee seeks to enforce a negative stipulation against his employer. Thus, generally, an injunction will not be issued if its effect is to compel the employer to continue employment. But an injunction may be granted in certain exceptional cases where employer and employee retain their mutual confidence. In *Page One Records Ltd v Britton*[1], The Troggs, a pop group, appointed the plaintiff as their manager for five years, agreeing not to let anyone else act as their manager during that time. After a year, The Troggs dismissed the plaintiff, who sought an injunction restraining them from appointing anyone else as their manager. It was held that an injunction would indirectly compel The Troggs to continue to employ the plaintiff because pop groups could not operate successfully without a manager, and it would be bad to pressure The Troggs into continuing to employ a person in whom they had lost confidence. Therefore the injunction sought was not granted. In comparison, one may note the very exceptional case of *Hill v C. A. Parsons & Co Ltd*[2]. The defendant employers were forced by union pressure to dismiss the plaintiff in breach of contract. An injunction was granted to restrain this breach, even though its effect was to compel the reinstatement of the plaintiff. As the Court of Appeal pointed out, the circumstances were special, in particular because the parties retained their mutual confidence.

1 [1967] 3 All ER 822, [1968] 1 WLR 157.
2 [1972] Ch 305, [1971] 3 All ER 1345, CA.

12.24 An injunction is like specific performance in that:

a. it may be granted with or without an order for damages;

b. where it is applicable, the grant of an injunction is discretionary (since it is an equitable remedy) and is likely to be refused where, for example, the plaintiff is guilty of delay or is in breach of his own obligations under the contract. In particular, an injunction will normally be refused if damages would be an adequate remedy.

On the other hand, an injunction is a much wider remedy than specific performance, partly because it can be ordered in many situations other than contractual situations, and partly because it can be ordered in contractual situations where specific performance could not, e.g. where enforcement of the contract would require the court's constant superintendence or where the contract is one for personal services.

LIMITATION OF ACTIONS

12.25 An action will be barred if it is not brought within the relevant limitation period. The rules relating to these periods are statutory, the principal Act being the Limitation Act 1939. If an action is statute-barred this does not extinguish the plaintiff's substantive right but simply bars the procedural remedies available to him. Two consequences of this are that if a debtor pays a statute-barred debt, he cannot recover the money as money not due[1], and if a debtor who owes a creditor two or more debts, one of which is statute-barred, pays money to the creditor without appropriating it to a debt which is not statute-barred, the creditor is entitled to appropriate it to the statute-barred debt[2].

1 *Bize v Dickason* (1786) 1 Term Rep 285 at 287.
2 *Mills v Fowkes* (1839) 5 Bing NC 455.

Limitation periods

12.26   Under the Limitation Act 1939:

a. Actions founded on a simple contract cannot be brought after the expiration of six years from the date on which the cause of action accrued, which is normally when the breach of contract occurs and never when the damage is suffered[1]. However, if the damages claimed consist of or include damages for personal injuries caused by a breach of contract, the time limit is reduced to three years[2], although by the Limitation Act 1975 this period may be extended in certain circumstances.

b. Actions founded on a contract under seal cannot be brought after the expiration of 12 years from the date on which the cause of action accrued[3].

---

1   Limitation Act 1939, s.2(1).
2   Limitation Act 1975, s.1.
3   Limitation Act 1939, s.2(3).

Minors and the mentally ill
12.27   If a plaintiff is a minor or mentally unsound when the cause of action accrues, the action may be brought within six years of the removal of the disability or of his death, whichever event happens first[1]. On the other hand, if the limitation period has begun to run, the fact that the plaintiff subsequently becomes of unsound mind does not suspend the running of time, and, if a person is under a disability when his cause of action accrues but dies and is succeeded by someone who also is under a disability, there is no extension of time by reason of the latter's disability[2].

If the plaintiff is a minor when his cause of action accrues and later becomes of unsound mind, the extension of time continues to apply if the mental unsoundness started during his minority but if there was an interval in between (i.e. he became insane after reaching 18) the extension of time does not apply and the six year period runs from the time he attains 18[3].

---

1   Limitation Act 1939, ss. 22 and 31(2). The period is three years if damages for personal injuries are claimed: Limitation Act 1975, s.2.
2   Limitation Act 1939, s.22(b).
3   *Borrows v Ellison* (1871) LR 6 Exch 128.

Fraud or mistake
12.28   Generally, the fact that the plaintiff is unaware that he has a cause of action does not prevent the limitation period starting to run, even if the plaintiff does not know that he has a cause of action until

after the limitation period has expired. However, the Limitation Act 1939, s.26, provides that if —

    a. the action is based on the fraud of the defendant or his agent; or

    b. the right of action is concealed by the fraud of such a person; or

    c. the action is for relief from the consequences of mistake,

the limitation period does not begin to run until the plaintiff has discovered the fraud or the mistake or could with reasonable diligence have discovered it.

In relation to fraudulent concealment under b., 'fraud' is not limited to common law which would give rise to a separate cause of action but includes 'equitable fraud', i.e. conduct which, having regard to some special relationship between the two parties concerned, is an unconscionable thing for one to do to the other. This is illustrated by *Applegate v Moss*[1]. The defendant, who was a property developer, agreed to build two houses for the plaintiff on a concrete raft. Eight years later the plaintiff discovered that the houses were unsafe and irreparable because the foundations were not as specified. The Court of Appeal held that, despite the lapse of more than six years from the time of the breach of contract, the plaintiff was entitled to sue because his right of action had been concealed by the defendant's fraud in covering up what Lord Denning, MR, described as the 'rubbishy foundations' so that the bad work might not be discovered for a long time.

The proviso to s.26 protects the position of third parties. It provides that nothing in the section shall enable any action to be brought to recover, or set aside a transaction affecting, any property which has been purchased for valuable consideration by a person who neither knew nor had reason to believe that a fraud or mistake had occurred. The proviso also applies to an action for damages for wrongful interference with goods[2].

---

1 [1971] 1 QB 406, [1971] 1 All ER 747, CA.
2 *Eddis v Chichester Constable* [1969] 2 Ch 345, [1969] 2 All ER 912, CA.

Revival of the remedy

12.29   An acknowledgement or part payment of a debt or other liquidated pecuniary claim may start time running again, even though the right of action is already statute-barred. This rule illustrates another aspect of the fact that if an action is statute-barred the plaintiff's substantive rights are not extinguished but his remedies are simply barred. The basic provision is s.23(4) of the Limitation Act 1939, which provides that where any right of action has accrued to recover any debt or other liquidated pecuniary claim and the person liable or accountable therefore acknowledges the claim or makes any payment in respect thereof, the right of action is deemed to have accrued on the date of the acknowledgement or the *last* payment. Such revival is only possible in the case of a debt or other liquidated sum, but it is not essential that an acknowledgement should quantify the amount due since it suffices if that amount can be assessed by extrinsic evidence without further agreement of the parties[1]. A cause of action for unliquidated damages cannot be revived.

---

1 *Dungate v Dungate* [1965] 3 All ER 818, [1965] 1 WLR 1477.

Acknowledgement

12.30 The acknowledgement must be in writing and signed by the person making it or his agent, and must be made to the person or his agent whose claim is acknowledged[1]. An acknowledgement is only sufficient to start time running again if it amounts to an admission of liability, but it is not necessary that a promise to pay should be implied. An acknowledgement by one debtor does not bind a joint debtor[2], unless the acknowledgor can be regarded as an agent for himself and the joint debtor, which will happen, for instance, if they are partners.

---

1 Limitation Act 1939, s.24(1) and (2).
2 *Ibid.*, s.25(5) and (8).

Part payment

12.31 In order to start time running again, part payment must be clearly referable to the debt. A creditor who is owed several debts by a debtor cannot revive his right of action to a statute-barred debt simply by exercising his power of appropriation of payments[1] and appropriating a general payment by the debtor in part payment of that debt[2]. Part payment must be made to the person or to the agent in respect of whose claim the payment is made. If part payment is made by a joint debtor *before* the debt has become statute-barred time starts running again against all the joint debtors, but the right of action against the others is not revived if he makes the part payment *after* the debt has become statute-barred[3].

---

1 Para. 9.9.
2 But see para. 9.10.
3 Limitation Act 1939, s.25(6) and (8).

Equitable relief

12.32 The provisions of the Limitation Acts do not apply to claims for equitable relief[1]. However, in cases where, before the Judicature Act 1873, the claim for relief could have been entertained in either the common law courts or in the Court of Chancery, the limitation periods under the Limitation Act 1939 are applied to equitable claims by analogy[2]. The position is different in the case of purely equitable claims, i.e. claims which could only have been entertained by the Court of Chancery before the Act of 1873, such as claims for specific performance or an injunction. Here, the claim may fail under the equitable doctrine of laches (delay). Traditionally, the rule has been that the plaintiff must show himself to be 'ready, desirous, prompt and eager' to assert his rights[3], otherwise he may be barred from claiming the equitable relief. But there is recent authority that, at least where the claim is for specific performance, even gross delay will not bar the claim for equitable relief if it has done the defendant no harm at all[4]. The avoidance of fixed limitation periods in this area is obviously more appropriate to the discretionary nature of equitable remedies.

---

1 Limitation Act 1939, s.2(7).
2 *Knox v Gye* (1872) LR 5 HL 656 at 674.
3 *Milward v Earl of Thanet* (1801) 5 Ves 720n.
4 *Lazard Bros & Co Ltd v Fairfield Properties Co (Mayfair) Ltd* (1977) *Times*, 12 October.

Chapter 13
Mistake

13.1   In certain cases a contract[1] which is made in circumstances where one or both parties are labouring under a mistake is void. If a contract is void for mistake it has no legal effect: consequently, it is unenforceable by either party, and title to property cannot pass under it. A party who has received goods under a void contract may be liable to the transferor in tort if he wrongfully interferes with them, and so may a third party who has bought them from him.

Because of the serious consequences of finding a contract void for mistake, the law defines the situations in which a mistake will render a contract void very narrowly. It follows from this that many mistakes made by a party in concluding a contract are legally irrelevant. Even mistakes which are induced by the other contracting party may not render the contract void, although there may be a remedy for misrepresentation[2].

A contract *may* be void for mistake:

a. if the parties have reached an agreement, but have done so on the basis of some fundamental mistake which they share; or

b. if, because of a mistake which the parties do not share, they are fundamentally at cross-purposes.

As a preliminary point it should be noted that a mistake of law will generally be held to be legally irrelevant[3].

---

1   It is traditional, although perhaps inaccurate, to describe agreements void for mistake as contracts.
2   Chap. 14.
3   *Solle v Butcher* [1950] 1 KB 671, [1949] 2 All ER 1107, CA.

SHARED MISTAKE
Common law

13.2 If the parties have reached an agreement on the basis of a misapprehension as to the facts which is shared by both of them, the contract may be void for mistake. Whether the rules relating to mistake come into play is a matter of construction of the contract. If the contract provides that the risk as to the particular fact or event falls on one party, the law gives effect to the express intention of the parties. If the contract does so provide, then the contract is not void but enforceable. The terms of the contract may not expressly state on whom the risk falls, but the courts may be able to determine an intention that one or both parties should bear it from the terms of the contract. In either case, the position is as follows: if, to take, as an example, the case of a contract for the sale of specific goods which it turns out have never existed, the buyer assumed the risk of the goods' existence, he must pay the contractual price; but if the seller assumed that risk he will be liable in damages for breach of contract. In the Australian case of *McRae v Commonwealth Disposals Commission*[1], the Commission sold to McRae the right to salvage a tanker which was, they claimed, lying on a specified reef. There was no reef of that name at the map reference given, nor was there any tanker. The court found as a matter of construction that the Commission had impliedly undertaken that the tanker existed and thus McRae could claim damages for breach of this undertaking. This case can be contrasted with *Clark v Lindsay*[2], where A had agreed with B to hire a room along the route of Edward VII's coronation procession. When they made the contract both parties were unaware that the coronation had been postponed because of the King's illness, but the contract expressly provided that, if the procession was postponed, A should have the use of the room on any later day on which it took place. Consequently, it was held that the contract was not void for mistake and both parties were bound to perform their obligations on the re-arranged day.

This approach seems to have been adopted also by the House of Lords in *Couterier v Hastie*[3]. Here, a cargo of grain being shipped to the United Kingdom was sold to the defendant after the cargo had ceased to exist, in that it had already been sold by the ship's captain. The seller demanded payment for the cargo. The House of Lords found that on a true construction of the contract the risk that the cargo did not exist had not been placed on the buyer and therefore he did not have to pay for the goods. It was not necessary for the House to decide whether the risk was placed on the seller, who could thus have been sued for non-delivery, or whether the contract was void.

---

1 (1950) 84 CLR 377.
2 (1903) 88 LT 198.
3 (1856) 5 HL C as 673, HL.

13.3 If, on its true construction, the contract does not allocate the risk in the matter concerning which the parties share a mistake, the rules relating to mistake must be looked at. Under them, not every shared mistake renders a contract void: it must be fundamental. If it is not fundamental the contract is enforceable at common law. What is a fundamental mistake in this context? It is established that a shared mistake as to the existence of the subject-matter of the contract is fundamental. In *Galloway v Galloway*[1], for instance, a separation agreement based on a marriage, which unknown to the parties was invalid, was held void. Clearly, in such a case, the separation agreement would not attempt to throw the risk of the marriage being invalid on either party and so it is not surprising that the court did not first consider the question of construction.

Similarly, a contract is void if it is made under a shared mistaken belief that it is possible to perform it, unless on the true construction of the contract one party or the other has agreed to run the risk of impossibility of performance. Thus, it has been held that a contract, whereby X agrees to lease land to Y, which Y already owns, is void at common law[2], and so is a contract whereby X agrees with Y to cut and process a certain tonnage of a particular crop on land, when there is not that tonnage to be cropped[3]. It would be different, however, if X had warranted (as a seller normally does) that he had title to the land or had guaranteed the yield (in that case, X would be liable for breach of contract) or if Y had agreed to run the risk (i.e. to pay in any event).

Another example is provided by *Griffiths v Brymer*[4]. As in *Clark v Lindsay*, this case concerned an agreement for the hire of a room along the route of Edward VII's coronation procession which had been made by the parties in ignorance of the cancellation of the procession. The court did not specifically deal with the construction of the contract, but presumably the contract had not allocated the risk of the cancellation. It held that the contract was void for mistake and that the plaintiff could recover money he had paid under it.

---

1 (1914) 30 TLR 531, DC.
2 *Cooper v Phibbs* (1867) LR 2 HL 149, HL.
3 *Sheikh Bros v Ochsner* [1957] AC 136, PC.
4 (1903) 19 TLR 434.

13.4 If the facts in *Couturier v Hastie* occurred today, the decision would almost certainly be different because there is now a special statutory provision dealing with the *perishing* of *specific* goods before a contract for their sale is made. Section 6 of the Sale of Goods Act 1893 provides that in such a case the contract is void[1]. Presumably, this provision can be displaced if the contract expressly places the risk as to the goods' continued existence on one of the parties. Section 6 does not apply to unascertained goods or goods which have never existed.

In such cases, the contract is first construed and if the risk is placed on either party, expressly or impliedly, the contract governs; but if the risk is not allocated, the contract is void.

1 For a further discussion see para. 22.24.

13.5 A vexed question is whether a shared mistake as to the quality of the subject-matter of the contract can ever be sufficiently fundamental to render it void. Frequently, of course, the risk that the goods lack that quality is borne by the seller because the supposed quality of the goods is a term of the contract. If this occurs, the law of mistake is irrelevant because the parties have determined that the seller shall be liable for breach of contract if the quality is absent. But if the contract does not allocate the risk that the quality is lacking, is the contract *ever* void for mistake? The case of *Bell v Lever Bros Ltd*[1] suggests that in some cases a contract can be void for a shared mistake as to quality. In that case, Bell was employed by Lever Bros under a contract of employment for five years at £8,000 per annum. Lever Bros agreed to pay Bell £30,000 to relinquish this contract. Subsequently, they discovered that they could have terminated the contract without compensation because of breaches of it by Bell. Bell had forgotten about these breaches and he and Lever Bros were treated as being under a shared mistake as to the quality of the contract of employment, in that they had believed it was valid when in truth it was voidable. Lever Bros' claim to recover back the compensation paid failed before the House of Lords, who held the contract of compensation valid despite the shared mistake, although three of their Lordships stated that a sufficiently fundamental mistake as to quality might render a contract void. The reader may think that, if the mistake as to quality in this case was not sufficiently fundamental, it is hard to imagine when a mistake as to quality will be. No case has actually been decided on the basis that a contract was void because of a fundamental mistake as to quality, although it was held, obiter, in *Nicholson and Venn v Smith-Marriott*[2], that the contract in issue was void for mistake. In that case, a set of linen napkins and table cloths was put for sale, described as dating from the seventeenth century. Unknown to both the buyers and the sellers, it was in fact Georgian, and the buyers were able to recover for breach of contract since the sellers were in breach of the implied condition under the Sale of Goods Act 1893[3] that the goods corresponded with their description. The judge added that, had the buyers claimed for breach of contract he would have held the contract void for mistake as to quality.

1 [1932] AC 161, HL.
2 (1947) 177 LT 189.
3 See para. 22.47.

13.6 The dicta in support of the proposition that a contract can be void for a fundamental mistake as to quality can be contrasted with the actual decisions in a number of cases. In *Solle v Butcher*[1], the fact that both parties to a lease mistakenly believed that the premises were free from rent control did not render the contract void. Similarly, in *Magee v Pennine Insurance Co Ltd*[2], a compromise of a claim under an insurance policy, which both parties mistakenly believed to be valid when in fact it was voidable, was held not to be void for mistake. Again, we are prompted to ask, if these mistakes were not fundamental, what sort of mistake would have been? Another example of a mistake as to quality which was not legally relevant occurred in *Harrison & Jones Ltd v Bunten & Lancaster Ltd*[3]. In this case, the parties bought and sold 'Sree brand' kapok. Both parties believed Sree brand to be pure kapok, when in fact it contained other substances. The judge admitted that the purchasers considered it vital that the kapok was pure, but refused to hold that the contract was void for mistake.

---

1 [1950] 1 KB 671, [1949] 2 All ER 1107, CA. Also see *Grist v Bailey,* para. 13.9.
2 [1969] 2 QB 507, [1969] 2 All ER 891, CA.
3 [1953] 1 QB 646, [1953] 1 All ER 903.

13.7 Our conclusion is that at law a contract can never be void because of a mistake as to quality, however fundamental.

Equity

13.8 If a contract is void at law for mistake, it is of no legal effect and no damages can be awarded for non-performance or faulty performance. Further, equity, following the law, will not grant specific performance. But it is difficult to establish mistake in law, and equity has intervened and granted relief where contracts are based on a mistake shared by the parties which is not sufficient to make the contract void. This relief may take the form of refusing specific performance (which will not affect liability in damages), or of awarding specific performance on terms which do justice, or of rescinding the contract for *mistake*.

13.9 A decision that a contract is void means that it never existed, but rescission sets aside a contract which may previously have existed, and the parties are restored to their former positions. In addition, the court may impose terms on the parties in the interests of justice and equity. Thus, if a contract of sale of goods is rescinded for mistake, this may be done on terms that the buyer is compensated for any improvements which he has made to the goods.

It is not certain which mistakes equity will take into account in determining whether to set aside a contract. Certainly, all mistakes which the law considers relevant will be relevant in equity and so will other types of mistake, although the limits are not clearly established. Some examples of where equity has set aside a contract are *Solle v Butcher*[1], *Grist v Bailey*[2] and *Magee v Pennine Insurance Co Ltd*[3], all of which involve mistakes of quality.

In *Solle v Butcher*, a lease was granted at a specified rent in the common mistaken belief that the nature of the flat demised had been so changed as not to be a rent-controlled property. As we have said, the Court of Appeal refused to find the contract void but set it aside in equity. At the time there was a housing shortage, and rescission was ordered on terms that the tenant should have an option either to surrender the lease or stay in the premises under a new lease at the maximum rent which the landlord could charge under the statutory provisions then in force.

In *Grist v Bailey*, the plaintiff agreed to buy a house from the defendant at approximately one-third of its value because the house was sold subject to an existing tenancy which both parties mistakenly believed was protected by the Rent Acts (which would have given the tenant a right to remain in the property indefinitely). On discovering that the tenancy was not protected, the plaintiff sought specific performance and the defendant sought to have the agreement set aside because of the mistake. The contract was not void at law but the mistake was a sufficiently fundamental mistake as to quality to allow equitable intervention. The action for specific performance was dismissed and the agreement to sell set aside, but only on the term that the defendant should give the defendant a chance to enter into a new contract of sale at the full value of the property.

In *Magee v Pennine Insurance Co Ltd*[4], an insurance company paid Magee £375 in settlement of an insurance claim on his car. The company then discovered the insurance contract was voidable for innocent misrepresentation and sought to recover the £375, alleging that they had agreed to pay it in the mistaken belief, shared by Magee, that the contract of insurance was valid. The majority of the Court of Appeal found the agreement to pay the money was not void at law but were prepared to set it aside in equity.

Strangely, the court did not impose terms on the parties so that, while the company recovered its £375, Magee was awarded nothing to compensate him for the insurance premiums he had paid.

---

1   [1950] 1 KB 671, [1949] 2 All ER 1107, CA.
2   [1967] Ch 532, [1966] 2 All ER 875.
3   [1969] 2 QB 507, [1969] 2 All ER 891, CA.
4   [1969] 2 QB 507, [1969] 2 All ER 891, CA.

MISTAKES NOT SHARED BY THE PARTIES

Common law

13.10 The fact that a party entered into an apparent contract under a mistake does not normally render the contract void, and the same is true if both parties were labouring under *different* mistaken beliefs. However, a contract will be void if such a mistake relates to:

a. the identity of the other party; or

b. a fundamental matter relating to the subject-matter of the contract; or

c. whether a particular matter is a term of the contract,

and the mistake is an operative mistake in the sense discussed below.

Mistake as to identity

13.11 A mistake as to identity can make an apparent contract void; a mistake which merely relates to an attribute, e.g. credit-worthiness, of the other party can never do so.

In *Cundy v Lindsay*[1], the plaintiffs sold goods to Blenkarn, a rogue who carried on business at 37 Wood Street, believing him to be Blenkiron & Co, a respectable firm of 137 Wood Street. Blenkarn had deliberately signed his offer to buy so that the signature appeared to be Blenkiron, and the House of Lords found that the plaintiffs had intended to sell only to Blenkiron. They had purported to accept an offer made by Blenkiron and had never intended to contract with Blenkarn at all. In consequence, the apparent contract with Blenkarn was void and the innocent party to whom Blenkarn had resold the goods was liable for the tort of conversion. The unfortunate defendants could, of course, have sued Blenkarn for the torts of conversion and deceit[2] if they could have traced him. In *Cundy v Lindsay*, the plaintiffs were able to establish that they meant to deal only with Blenkiron and not with the sender of the letter; there was thus a mistake as to identity. On the other hand, in *King's Norton Metal Co Ltd v Edridge, Merrett & Co Ltd*[3], the mistake made by the plaintiffs who sold goods to a rogue who resold them to the defendants was one as to attribute, not identity. In this case, a rogue, one Wallis, offered to buy goods in a letter written on paper headed Hallam & Co and embellished with references to depots and a picture of a factory. The plaintiffs mistakenly believed Hallam & Co to be a respectable firm but they did not think that they were dealing with someone other than the writer of the letter. Their mistake was as to the credit and reliability of Hallam & Co, and not as to the identity of the other party. Thus, they had intended to contract with the writer of the letter and they were bound by the contract.

---

1   (1878) 3 App Cas 459, HL.
2   Para. 14.14, a.
3   (1897) 14 TLR 98.

13.12 When the parties contract face to face, it is much more difficult to establish that a mistake relates to the identity, as opposed to attributes, of the other party, and it can normally be presumed that a party intended to deal with the person in front of him. However, every case turns on its facts and it may be possible to establish a mistake as to identity if the identity of one party was of particular importance to the other.

In *Phillips v Brooks Ltd*[1], a jeweller sold goods to a customer who wrote out a cheque for the price. At some point in the negotiations, possibly prior to the contract of sale being made, the customer announced that he was Sir George Bullough of St. James' Square. The customer departed with some of his purchases, which he pledged to the defendant, and his cheque was later dishonoured. If the contract was void for mistake, the plaintiff had the better title to the goods, but the judge found that the jeweller had intended to contract with the person in the shop. The jeweller's mistaken belief related to an attribute of the customer (his credit-worthiness), not his identity. It would have been different if the jeweller had established that the identity of his customer was of particular importance to him. He had, it is true, consulted a directory to see whether there was a Sir George Bullough of St. James' Square, but this was not sufficient to rebut the presumption that he intended to deal with the customer before him, whoever he was. A similar case is that of *Lewis v Averay*[2], where a rogue, claiming to be Richard Greene, the well-known actor, bought from the plaintiff a car which he then sold to the defendant, who was innocent. The plaintiff sued the defendant for the conversion of his car but failed to establish that he had made a mistake as to the identity of the other party to the agreement. He had to be presumed to intend to deal with the person in front of him, said the Court of Appeal, unless he could establish that the identity of the buyer was of fundamental importance to him. In this case, the only attempt to check whether the rogue was Richard Greene was the perusal of a Pinewood Studio pass in the name of Richard Greene, which was produced by the rogue, and this was insufficient to establish that he intended to deal only with Richard Greene, the actor.

1 [1919] 2 KB 243.
2 [1972] 1 QB 198, [1971] 3 All ER 907, CA.

13.13 Two cases where the plaintiff was able to establish a mistake as to the identity of the other party are *Ingram v Little*[1] and *Sowler v Potter*[2]. In *Ingram v Little*, the plaintiffs, two elderly sisters, were confronted by a rogue who called himself Hutchinson. They agreed to sell him their car, but refused to continue the sale when the rogue proposed to pay by cheque. He then announced himself to be P. G. M. Hutchinson of Stanstead House, Caterham. One sister slipped out to the Post Office, consulted the telephone directory and found that

there was a P. G. M. Hutchinson of Stanstead House, while the other
sister plied the rogue with conversation. They accepted the cheque,
which was dishonoured, and the rogue sold the car to the defendant,
whom the sisters sued in conversion. The Court of Appeal found that
on the facts of the case the plaintiffs had done sufficient to establish
that they intended to deal only with P. G. M. Hutchinson of Stanstead
House, and not with the person in front of them. This case has been
greatly criticised but, since all cases turn on their own facts, it may
have been correctly decided.

In *Sowler v Potter*[2], the lease of a café was granted to Potter, who
had previously been convicted of keeping a disorderly café under
another name, Robinson. Tucker, J, held that the lease was void because
of the lessor's mistaken belief that Potter was not Robinson. The
judge found that the lessor's agent, who had concluded the contract,
only intended to deal with the person in front of him if that person was
not Robinson, a convicted criminal. This case has also been doubted,
and indeed, since the contract could have been rescinded for misrepresentation, its authority on the law of mistake is limited.

---

1   [1961] 1 QB 31, [1960] 3 All ER 332, CA.
2   [1940] 1 KB 271, [1939] 4 All ER 478.

Fundamental mistake as to subject-matter
13.14   A mistake as to the subject-matter of a contract may render it
void. In *Raffles v Wichelhaus*[1], for example, there was a contract to
buy cotton which was arriving from Bombay on a ship called 'Peerless'.
There were two ships called 'Peerless', both sailed from Bombay with
cotton, one leaving in October and one in December. The buyer refused
to take delivery of the cotton despatched in December on the ground
that he had intended to buy cotton despatched in the 'Peerless' which
sailed in October. It was established that the parties genuinely had
different consignments in mind at the time of contracting, and the
contract was held void for mistake. There was no genuine agreement,
for the parties were at cross-purposes. Similarly, if X agrees to buy a
consignment of wheat from Y, thinking that it is a consignment of oats,
his mistake is sufficiently fundamental[2].

On the other hand, a mistake which simply relates to a quality,
but not the essential nature of the thing, is not sufficiently fundamental
to render the contract void. Thus, if X agrees to buy oats from Y,
mistakenly believing that they are old oats, the contract cannot be void
for mistake[3].

---

1   (1864) 2 H & C 906.
2   *Scriven & Co v Hindley & Co* [1913] 3 KB 564.
3   *Smith v Hughes* (1871) LR 6 QB 597.

Mistake as the terms of the contract

13.15 A contract may be void if a party mistakenly believes that a particular matter is a term of the contract, even though the mistake does not relate to the identity of the other party or the essence of the subject-matter. Thus, if X mistakenly believes that Y warrants that the oats which he is selling him are old oats, the contract may be void for mistake[1].

In *Hartog v Colin and Shields*[2], the sellers mistakenly offered to sell goods at a given price per pound when they had intended to offer to sell at that given price per piece. The buyer accepted the offer. The contract was held void because of the sellers' mistake as to the price (a term of the contract). All the preliminary negotiations had been on the basis of price per piece and trade custom also related to price per piece. The effect of this was that the court found that the buyer must have realised that the sellers had made a mistake and could not rush in and accept what would have been a most advantageous offer.

---

1 *Smith v Hughes* (1871) LR 6 QB 597.
2 [1939] 3 All ER 566.

Operative mistake

13.16 It is not enough that a party was mistaken as to the identity of the other party or the essence of the subject-matter or a term of the contract. Such a mistake must be operative to render the contract void and it will only be so if:

a. The other party knew of the mistake, as in *Cundy v Lindsay, Ingram v Little, Sowler v Potter* and *Hartog v Colin & Shields*; or

b. The circumstances are so ambiguous that a reasonable person could not say whether the contract meant what one party thought it meant or what the other party thought it meant. It is only in exceptional cases that the circumstances are so ambiguous. The approach taken by the courts is that if, whatever A's real intention may be, he so conducts himself that a reasonable person would believe that he was assenting to the contract proposed by the other party (B), and B contracts with A in that belief, there is a contract with the meaning and terms understood by B[1]. In *Wood v Scarth*[2], the defendant wrote to the plaintiff, offering to let him a public house at £63 a year. After an interview with the defendant's clerk, the plaintiff accepted the offer by letter. The defendant had intended also to take a premium for the tenancy and thought that the clerk had made this clear to the plaintiff. The plaintiff accepted the offer, thinking that his only financial obligation was to pay the rent. It was held that there was a contract in the sense understood by the plaintiff.

Wood v Scarth can be contrasted with *Raffles v Wichelhaus*, which we referred to in para. 13.14, where the circumstances were such that neither party's understanding of the contract into which they were entering could be said to be the more reasonable and the contract was held to be void. In *Scriven v Hindley*[3], the defendants successfully bid at an auction sale for a lot which consisted of tow, thinking that they were bidding for hemp, an infinitely superior product. Both tow and hemp were sold at the auction and samples of each were on display, although the defendants had not inspected them because he had already seen samples of hemp at the plaintiffs' showroom. However, the lot in question was misleadingly described in the auctioneer's catalogue and the samples were confusingly marked. It was held that the contract was void. Clearly, in the special circumstances a reasonable person could not say whether there was a contract for the sale of hemp or for the sale of tow.

1 *Smith v Hughes* (1871) LR 6 QB 597 at 607.
2 (1858) 1 F & F 293.
3 [1913] 3 KB 564.

Equity

13.17 Where a contract is void at common law because an operative mistake was not shared by the parties, equity follows the law and will not grant specific performance[1] of the contract and may, to put the matter beyond doubt, rescind the contract.

In addition, the equitable remedy of specific performance may be refused if justice so demands, and it is reasonable to do so, even though the contract is not void for mistake at common law. It was refused, for instance, in *Wood v Scarth*[2], although the plaintiff was able to recover the common law remedy of damages. On the other hand, in *Tamplin v James*[3], where the defendant had successfully bid for a property under the mistaken belief as to its extent, specific performance was ordered: the defendant's mistake was his own fault since he had failed to check the plans to which the auctioneer had drawn attention.

1 *Webster v Cecil* (1861) 30 Beav 62.
2 (1855) 2 K & J 33, (1858) 1 F & F 293; para. 13.16.
3 (1880) 15 Ch D 215.

MISTAKE AND DOCUMENTS

Rectification

13.18 We are concerned here with the case where the parties have made a perfectly valid oral agreement but it is later embodied in a document which *records their agreement inaccurately*. In such a case, the equitable remedy of rectification is available. This enables a court to rectify the document so that it embodies the agreement of the parties accurately. Oral evidence is admissible to show that the written document does not represent the agreement of the parties even if the contract at issue is one which must be made or evidenced in writing.

Rectification will normally only be ordered if the document does not represent the intentions of *both* parties. However, it can be ordered if one party mistakenly believed a particular term was included in the document and the other party knew of that mistake but nevertheless allowed the document to be executed[1]. On the other hand, if the document simply fails to mention an obligation which one party, but not the other, had intended to be a term of the contract there is no case for rectification[2].

A document may be rectified to accord with the previously expressed intentions of the parties provided there was a *concluded antecedent agreement*, whether or not it was a binding contract. In *Joscelyne v Nissen*[3], which finally determined the point, the plaintiff proposed that his daughter-in-law, the defendant, who shared the same house, should take over his car-hire business. It was clearly agreed that if the defendant took over the business she would pay many of the household bills relating to the plaintiff's part of the house. The subsequent written contract did not impose an obligation to pay the relevant household bills on the defendant and, though taking the profits of the car-hire business, she failed to pay these household bills after a while. The Court of Appeal permitted the written contract to be rectified so as to accord with the oral agreement, even though the latter was not binding.

There is no right of rectification and it will only be ordered where it is just and equitable to do so. For example, the existence of third party rights dependent on the written contract will bar rectification unless the third party knows of the mistake. Lapse of time may also prevent rectification, and certain written documents cannot be rectified[4].

---

1 *A. Roberts & Co v Leicestershire County Council* [1961] Ch 555, [1961] 2 All ER 545.
2 *Riverlate Properties Ltd v Paul* [1975] Ch 133, [1974] 2 All ER 656, CA.
3 [1970] 2 QB 86, [1970] 1 All ER 1213, CA.
4 For example, the Articles of Association of a company, although the company may alter the Articles under the Companies Act 1948.

Documents mistakenly signed

13.19 It is accepted that where a person signs a document which contains a contract he is bound by that contract. This is so even if it is not the contract which he expected and whether or not he has read or understood the agreement. An exception to this has been established; it is the plea of *non est factum* (it is not my deed), which, if proved, permits the signatory of a written contract to deny liability on that contract.

To escape liability on a signed contract, the signatory must prove:

a. that the signed document was radically different in effect from that which he thought he was signing; and

b. that he was not careless in signing the document.

The leading case is the House of Lords decision in *Saunders v Anglia Building Society*[1]. Mrs. Gallie, an elderly widow, occupied a house under a lease. Her nephew, Parkin, wished to raise money using the house as security. Mrs. Gallie was happy for this to happen, provided she could live in the house rent-free until her death[2]. Because Parkin did not want to pay maintenance to his estranged wife, he adopted a circuitous method of raising money so as to appear not to have any funds. The scheme was for Mrs. Gallie to assign the property to a friend of Parkin, Lee, who would mortgage it and pay the money to Parkin. A document which assigned the property was drawn up and Mrs. Gallie signed it without reading it: she had, in fact, broken her glasses. She thought the document was transferring the house to Parkin so that he could mortgage it. Lee mortgaged the property to the Building Society but paid Parkin nothing. The Building Society claimed they had better title to the house than Mrs. Gallie, but she denied their title, claiming that she was not bound by the signed document which, unknown to her, assigned the lease of the property to Lee.

The House of Lords rejected Mrs. Gallie's plea of *non est factum* and found that Lee had good title which he could pass to the Building Society. They found that the document she had signed was not radically different in effect from what she had intended to sign. Legally, there may be a great difference between an assignment and a deed of gift, but the effect in this case was the same — to enable Parkin to raise money on the security of the house. Even if the signed document had been radically different from what was intended, Mrs. Gallie had failed to establish that she had not been careless. She had not read the document nor asked for it to be read to her; she had consulted no professional advisors and she had not acted sensibly. In deciding if a party has established that he was not careless, the standard of the reasonable man applies to those of full age and understanding. On the other hand, the House of Lords seemed to suggest that if the party was illiterate or lacked mental capacity or was blind, he should be judged by his own standard. So, in considering the 'incapable' signatory, the court might consider whether the signatory used such care as a reasonable man with the incapacity of the signatory should use. If a blind man is proposing to sign a document, he should ask for it to be read to him by a trustworthy person, and, if he fails to do so, he cannot rely on *non est factum.*

1 [1971] AC 1004, [1970] 3 All ER 961, HL.
2 Mrs. Gallie died before the case was heard by the House of Lords. Saunders was her executrix.

13.20 In *United Dominions Trust Ltd v Western*[1], the defendant agreed to buy a car on hire-purchase. He signed a document which was in fact a loan agreement with the plaintiffs and which did not specify the price of the car or the deposit paid. Incorrect figures were subsequently inserted by the sellers of the car, and the defendant later learnt of this. He failed to pay any instalments and was sued. The Court of Appeal refused to allow the defendant to rely on the doctrine of *non est factum* because, firstly, the document signed was not radically different from that which he thought he was signing, and, secondly, while he did not sign a document with the incorrect figures, but one in blank, the same legal principles relating to carelessness must apply. In seeking to rely on *non est factum,* the defendant must prove that, in signing a document of this type in blank, he exercised due care. Clearly, in this case, he had not.

1 [1976] QB 513, [1975] 3 All ER 1017, CA.

13.21 Since *Saunders v Anglia Building Society*[1], it seems unlikely that *non est factum* will be successfully pleaded in more than a few cases.

1 [1971] AC 1004, [1970] 3 All ER 961, HL.

Chapter 14
Misrepresentation, Duress and Undue Influence

MISREPRESENTATION

14.1 Where a person makes a contract under a mistake induced by the misrepresentation of the other party his legal position may be resolved by the application of the law relating to misrepresentation. It should be noted that, unless, as rarely happens, a mistake induced by a misrepresentation is such as to render the contract void under the rules discussed above, it is the rules which follow which govern the situation. These rules are somewhat involved and different rules apply depending on whether there has been an active misrepresentation or a misrepresentation through non-disclosure.

ACTIVE MISREPRESENTATION

14.2 When one is faced with an 'active misrepresentation' situation one must first ask whether the representation has become a term of the contract or not, applying the rules set out in paras. 8.8 to 8.15 above. The division between active misrepresentations which have remained pre-contractual representations (mere representations) and those which have become terms of a resulting contract is fundamental since the remedies are different.

Active misrepresentations which have remained mere representations

14.3 If the misrepresentation has not become a contractual term, the misrepresentee, provided certain requirements are satisfied, can refuse to carry out his contractual obligations, and plead the misrepresentation

as a defence to an action for damages for non-performance of the contract or for specific performance. In addition, two remedies may be available, rescission of the contract (unless this is barred) and (in many cases) damages. The requirements mentioned above are that:
the misrepresentation must be one of fact;
it must have been addressed to the person misled; and
it must have induced the contract.

Misrepresentation of fact
14.4 There must be a misrepresentation by words or conduct of a past or existing fact. It follows that there are many misrepresentations for which no relief is available. The following must be distinguished from misrepresentations of fact:

a. *Mere puffs* A representation which is mere vague sales talk is not regarded as a representation of fact, as is shown by *Dimmock v Hallett*[1]. At a sale of land by auction, it was said to be 'fertile and improvable'; in fact it was partly abandoned and useless. The representation was held to be a 'mere flourishing description by an auctioneer' affording no ground for relief. It is a question of fact whether a particular statement is merely vague sales talk or the assertion of some verifiable fact.

b. *Statements of opinion* A statement which merely expresses an opinion or belief does not give grounds for relief if the opinion or belief turns out to be wrong. In *Bisset v Wilkinson*[2], the vendor of a farm which had never been used as a sheep farm, told a prospective purchaser that in his judgment the land would support 2,000 sheep. It was held that, this being an honest statement of the vendor's opinion of the farm's capacity, no relief was available. It would have been different if there had been a misrepresentation of its actual capacity since this would have been a misrepresentation of fact.

What has been said in the last paragraph must be qualified by pointing out that in two cases statements of opinion can involve an implied misrepresentation of fact and so give rise to relief.
i. If a person represents an opinion which he does not honestly hold he will at the same time make a misrepresentation of fact, the fact that he honestly holds the opinion[3].
ii. If a person represents an opinion for which he does not have reasonable grounds he will at the same time make a misrepresentation of fact if he impliedly represents that he has reasonable grounds for his opinion. A classic example is *Smith v Land and House Property Corpn*[4]. The vendor of a hotel described it as let to 'Mr. Frederick Fleck (a most desirable tenant) . . . for an unexpired term of 27½ years, thus offering a first-class investment'. Fleck had not paid the last quarter's rent and had paid the previous one by instalments and under pressure. The Court of

Appeal held that the above statement was not merely of opinion but also involved a misrepresentation of fact because the vendor impliedly stated that he had reasonable grounds for his opinion. Too much should not be read into this decision because the court will only find such an implied representation where the facts on which the opinion is based are particularly within the knowledge of the person stating the opinion, and not when the facts are equally known to both parties[5].

c. *Statements as to the future* Such statements, the best example of which is a statement of intention, are obviously not statements of fact in themselves and no remedy is available if the future event does not occur. However, a statement as to the future will involve a misrepresentation of fact if its maker does not honestly believe in its truth. In the case of a misrepresentation of intention this rule is well summarised by the statement of Bowen, LJ, in *Edgington v Fitzmaurice*[6], that the state of a man's mind is as much a fact as the state of his digestion. In this case the plaintiff was induced to lend money to a company by representations made in a prospectus by the directors that the money would be used to improve the company's buildings and to expand its business. The directors' true intention was to use the money to pay off the company's debts. They were held liable in deceit (fraudulent misrepresentation) on the basis that their misrepresentation of present intentions was a misrepresentation of fact.

d. *Statements of law* A person who is induced to contract by a misrepresentation of law has no remedy[7]. The sole possible exception is where, as in the case of a statement of opinion, the representor wilfully misrepresents the fact that he does not believe his statement of the law[8].

A difficulty in this area is distinguishing a statement of law from a statement of fact. Clearly, a representation as to the meaning of a statute is one of law. However, in *West London Commercial Bank v Kitson*[9], it was held that a misrepresentation of the contents of a Private Act was one of fact. The directors of a company represented that the company had power to accept bills and that they had authority to accept on its behalf. Under the Private Act which incorporated it the company had no power to accept bills or authorise anyone to do so. It was held that the representation was one of fact since it related to the contents of a Private Act. It is doubtful whether this decision would be extended to the contents of a Public Act because such a misrepresentation seems clearly to be one as to the general law. The distinction between meaning and contents drawn in the case of a Private Act also exists in relation to misrepresentations as to documents. This is shown by *Wauton v Coppard*[10]. The plaintiff contracted to buy a house from the defendant for use as a preparatory school. He made the contract after the defendant's agent had told him that there was nothing in the deed of restrictive covenants to prevent the running of a school. When the plaintiff received the deed he discovered that it prohibited any business or occupation whereby disagreeable noise or nuisance might be caused and he sought to rescind the contract. Romer, J, held that the misrepresentation made by the defendant's agent was one of fact, and that the contract would be set aside, because it concerned the contents of the deed. It would have been different, he held, if the agent had merely been asked the construction, i.e. meaning, of the deed: that would have resulted in a misrepresentation of law.

e. *Silence* Not surprisingly, silence cannot generally constitute an active misrepresentation[11]. However, there are two exceptions:

i. Where silence distorts a positive assertion of fact there will be an active misrepresentation of fact. Thus, in *Dimmock v Hallett*[12], it was said that if a vendor of land states that farms are let, but omits to say that the tenants have given notice to quit, his statement will be a misrepresentation of fact.

ii. Where a representation is falsified by later events, before the conclusion of the contract, there will be an active misrepresentation if the representor fails to notify the other of the change. This is shown by *With v O'Flanagan*[13]. Negotiations for the sale of a medical practice were begun in January 1934. The defendant vendor represented to the plaintiff that the practice was producing £2,000 per annum, which was then true. Between January and May the defendant was seriously ill and the practice was looked after by a number of locum tenentes with the result that the receipts had fallen to £5 per week by 1 May 1934. On 1 May 1934, the plaintiff, who had not been informed of the change of circumstances, signed a contract to purchase the practice. The Court of Appeal rescinded the contract on the ground that the defendant ought to have communicated the change of circumstances to the plaintiff. It said that the representation made to induce the contract must be treated as continuing until the contract was signed and what was initially a true representation had turned into a misrepresentation.

---

1 (1866) 2 Ch App 21.
2 [1927] AC 177, PC.
3 *Brown v Raphael* [1958] Ch 636 at 641, [1958] 2 All ER 79, CA.
4 (1884) 28 Ch D 7, CA.
5 Also see *Brown v Raphael* [1958] Ch 636, [1958] 2 All ER 79, CA.
6 (1884) 29 Ch D 459, CA.
7 *Beattie v Lord Ebury* (1872) 7 Ch App 777.
8 *West London Commercial Bank v Kitson* (1884) 13 QBD 360 at 362–363.
9 (1884) 13 QBD 360, CA.
10 [1899] 1 Ch 92.

11 See further para. 14.22.
12 (1866) LR 2 Ch App 21.
13 [1936] Ch 575, [1936] 1 All ER 727, CA.

The misrepresentation must have been addressed by the misrepresentor to the person misled

14.5   A leading authority for this requirement is *Peek v Gurney*[1]. The appellant purchased shares on the faith of misrepresentations contained in a prospectus issued by the promoters of a company. The appellant was not a person to whom shares had been allotted on the first formation of the company but had merely purchased shares from such allottees. The House of Lords held that the appellant could not succeed in his suit against the promoters because the prospectus was only addressed to the first applicants for shares and could not be supposed to extend to others.

The present requirement is not as stringent as may appear at first sight because:

a. It is possible for a representation to be made to the public in general, as in the case of an advertisement.

b. A representation need not be made directly to the person misled, or his agent, in order to satisfy the present requirement. It suffices that the representor intended that the person to whom he made the misrepresentation would pass it on to the plaintiff. This is shown by *Pilmore v Hood*[2]. The defendant wished to sell a public house to X and fraudulently misrepresented that the annual takings were £180. X was unable to buy and with the defendant's knowledge persuaded the plaintiff to buy by repeating the defendant's misrepresentation. The defendant was held liable in damages to the plaintiff for his fraudulent misrepresentation. An important limit on the rule in *Pilmore v Hood* is that, if the person (A) to whom the misrepresentation is originally made by the defendant (D), contracts with D as a result, the misrepresentation is deemed to be exhausted. Thus, if A then contracts to sell the property to B, repeating D's misrepresentation, as D knew he would, B has no redress against D because D's misrepresentation, being exhausted, is not regarded as addressed to B[3]. Of course, in such a case B is not remediless because he can pursue the normal remedies for misrepresentation against A who passed on the misrepresentation.

---

1   (1873) LR 6 HL 377, HL.
2   (1838) 5 Bing NC 97.
3   *Gross v Lewis Hillman Ltd* [1970] Ch 445, [1969] 3 All ER 1476, CA.

The misrepresentation must have induced the misrepresentee to make the contract

14.6 The question of inducement is one of fact but, if the misrepresentor made a statement of a nature likely to induce a person to contract and with a view to inducing this, it will normally be inferred that it did induce the misrepresentee to contract. However, this inference is rebutted in three cases:

a. If the misrepresentee, or his agent acting for him within the scope of his authority, actually knew the truth[1].

b. If the misrepresentee was ignorant of the misrepresentation when the contract was made. In *Re Northumberland and Durham District Banking Co, ex parte Bigge*[2], the plaintiff, who had bought some shares in a company, sought to have the purchase rescinded on the ground that the company had published false reports of its financial state. He failed and one of the reasons was because he was unable to prove that he had read any of the reports or that anyone had told him of their contents.

c. If the misrepresentee did not allow the representation to affect his judgment. Thus, if the representee investigates the truth of the representation and relies on his investigation rather than the representation in making the contract the inference of inducement is rebutted except in the case of fraud. In *Attwood v Small*[3], the appellant offered to sell a mine, making exaggerated representations as to its earning capacity. The respondents agreed to buy if the appellant could verify his representations and appointed agents to investigate the matter. The agents, who were experienced, visited the mine and were given every facility. They reported that the representations were true and the contract was made. The House of Lords held that the contract could not be rescinded for misrepresentation because the respondents had not relied on the misrepresentations but on their own independent investigations.

---

1 *Begbie v Phosphate Sewage Co* (1875) LR 10 QB 491; *Redgrave v Hurd* (1881) 20 Ch D 1, CA.
2 (1859) 28 LJ Ch 50.
3 (1838) 6 Cl & Fin 232, HL.

14.7 Before leaving the requirement of inducement a general point must be noted. Provided that it was one of the inducements the misrepresentation need not be the sole inducement. This is shown by *Edgington v Fitzmaurice*[1], where the plaintiff was induced to take debentures in a company partly by a misrepresentation in the prospectus and partly by his own mistaken belief that debenture holders would have a charge on the company's property. He was held entitled to rescission.

---

1 (1885) 29 Ch D 459, CA.

Remedies for active misrepresentations which have remained mere misrepresentations

14.8 Provided the above requirements are satisfied one or more of the following remedies are available to the misrepresentee.

Rescission

14.9 The effect of a misrepresentation is to make the contract voidable — not void, so that it remains valid unless and until the misrepresentee elects to rescind it on discovering the misrepresentation. Rescission entails setting the contract aside as if it had never been made, the misrepresentee recovering what he transferred under the contract but having to restore what he obtained under it. The effect of a misrepresentation is important in relation to the rights of third parties. If A sells a car to B under a contract which is voidable for B's misrepresentation, a voidable title passes to B and if C, an innocent purchaser, buys the car from B before A has decided to rescind, A loses the right to rescind and C obtains a valid title[1]. This must be distinguished from the situation where the contract is void for mistake. Here title to the goods never passes and they can always be recovered, or damages obtained in lieu, from the other party or a third person to whom they have been transferred[2].

---

1 *White v Garden* (1851) 10 CB 919.
2 *Cundy v Lindsay* (1878) 3 App Cas 459, HL.

14.10 Rescission can be effected in two ways. First, by bringing legal proceedings for an order for rescission. This may be necessary where a formal document or transaction, such as a lease, has to be set aside by a court order. In other cases a court order is not essential but may be advantageous if the misrepresentor is likely to prove unwilling to return what he has obtained under the contract.

Secondly, rescission can be effected by the misrepresentee making it clear that he refuses to be bound by the contract. Normally, communication of this decision to the misrepresentor is required, but there is an exception. If a fraudulent misrepresentor absconds, it suffices that the misrepresentee records his intention to rescind the contract by some overt act that is reasonable in the circumstances. This was decided by the Court of Appeal in *Car and Universal Finance Co Ltd v Caldwell*[1]. The defendant sold his car to N in return for a cheque which was dishonoured when he presented it the next day. The defendant immediately informed the police and the Automobile Association of the fraudulent transaction. Subsequently, N sold the car to X who sold it to Y who sold it to Z who sold it to the plaintiffs who bought it in good faith.

It was held that in the circumstances the defendant had done enough to rescind the contract before the plaintiffs bought the car, title had therefore re-vested in him and the plaintiffs had not got title.

---

1   [1965] 1 QB 525, [1964] 1 All ER 290, CA.

14.11   There are five bars to the right to rescind:

a. *Affirmation of contract by the misrepresentee* This occurs if, after discovering that the representation is untrue, the misrepresentee declares his intention to waive his right to rescission or acts in a way that such an intention can be inferred. This inference was drawn in *Long v Lloyd*[1]. The plaintiff bought a lorry as the result of the defendant's misrepresentation that it was in excellent condition. On the plaintiff's first business journey the dynamo broke and he noticed several other serious defects. On the next business journey the lorry broke down and the plaintiff, realising it was in a very bad condition, sought to rescind the contract. The Court of Appeal held that the second journey constituted an affirmation because the plaintiff knew by then that the representation was untrue. Similarly, if a person, who has applied for, and been allotted, shares in reliance on a misrepresentation subsequently discovers the falsity but nevertheless attempts to sell them, or retains dividends paid on them, or neglects to have his name removed from the register of shareholders, an intention to affirm will be inferred[2]. Once the election to rescind or affirm has been made it is irrevocable[3].

b. *Lapse of time* This can provide evidence of affirmation where the misrepresentee fails to rescind for a considerable time after discovering the falsity[4]. In addition, lapse of time can operate as a separate bar to rescission in cases where the misrepresentee has not delayed after discovering the falsity. This is shown by *Leaf v International Galleries*[5], where the plaintiff bought from the defendant a picture of Salisbury Cathedral which the latter had innocently represented to be by Constable. Five years later the plaintiff discovered that this was a misrepresentation and immediately sought to rescind the contract. The Court of Appeal held that his right to rescind had been lost through lapse of a reasonable time to discover the falsity. This bar probably does not apply in the case of a fraudulent misrepresentation.

c. *Inability to restore* The main objects of rescission are to restore the parties to their former position and to prevent unjust enrichment[6]. Thus, if either party has so changed or otherwise dealt with what he has obtained under the contract that he cannot restore it, rescission is barred[7]. So, for example, the purchaser of a cake cannot rescind the contract if he has eaten it[7].

There are three qualifications on the present bar:

i. A fraudulent misrepresentor cannot rely on his own dealings with what he has obtained as a bar to rescission by the misrepresentee[8].

ii. The fact that a seller has spent the money which he has received does not make restitution impossible since one bank note is as good as another and the seller can restore what he obtained under the contract by handing over other notes.

iii. Precise restitution is not required for rescission. Provided the property obtained under the contract can substantially be restored, rescission can be enforced even though the property has deteriorated, declined in value or otherwise changed. For example, in *Armstrong v Jackson*[9], a broker fraudulently sold shares to the plaintiff. Later, when the shares had fallen to one-twelfth of their value at the time of sale, the plaintiff claimed rescission. It was held that, since the plaintiff could return the actual shares, rescission would be ordered, subject to the defendant's repayment of the purchase price being credited with the dividends received by the plaintiff. However, where the deterioration or loss of value results from the voluntary dealings with it by the person who obtained it under the contract he must not only account for any profits derived from it but also pay compensation for such deterioration or loss of value[10]. If both parties have benefited from the property obtained by them the court, in ordering rescission, can set off the benefits received by one party against those received by the other[11].

d. *Bona fide purchaser for value* As has been indicated in para. 14.9, if, before the misrepresentee elects to rescind, a third party has innocently purchased the property, or an interest in it, for value from the misrepresentor, his rights are valid against the misrepresentee who loses the chance to rescind. This is illustrated by *White v Garden*[12], where a rogue bought 50 tons of iron from Garden by persuading him to take in payment a fraudulent bill of exchange. The rogue then sold the iron for value to White who acted in good faith (i.e. was unaware of the rogue's fraudulent misrepresentation) and Garden delivered the iron to White. The bill of exchange was subsequently dishonoured and Garden seized and removed some of the iron. Garden was held liable for what is now the tort of conversion; he had purported to rescind the contract with the rogue too late, the rogue's voidable title having been made unavoidable when White innocently bought the iron from him. In *Car and Universal Finance Co Ltd v Caldwell*[13], on the other hand, rescission was not barred because it occurred before the intervention of a bona fide purchaser for value.

e. *The wound up company* Under the rule in *Oakes v Turquand*[14], if a shareholder wishes to rescind his contract to take up shares in a company on the ground of misrepresentation he must do so before a winding up of the company commences.

---

1 [1958] 2 All ER 402, [1958] 1 WLR 753, CA.
2 [1958] 1 WLR 753, CA.
3 *Re Hop and Malt Exchange and Warehouse Co, Ex parte Briggs* (1866) LR 1 Eq 483; *Re Scottish Petroleum* (1883) 23 Ch D 413, CA.
4 *Clough v London and North Western Rly Co* (1871) LR 7 Exch 26 at 35.
5 [1950] 2 KB 86, [1950] 1 All ER 693, CA.
6 *Spence v Crawford* [1939] 3 All ER 271 at 288–289.
7 *Clarke v Dickson* (1858) EB & E 148; *Mackenzie v Royal Bank of Canada* [1934] AC 468, PC.
8 *Spence v Crawford* [1939] 3 All ER 271 at 280–282.
9 *Armstrong v Jackson* [1917] 2 KB 822.
10 *Erlanger v New Sombrero Phosphate Co* (1878) 3 App Cas 1218 at 1278–1279, HL.
11 *Hulton v Hulton* [1917] 1 KB 813, CA.
12 (1851) 10 CB 919.
13 Para. 14.10.
14 (1867) LR 2 HL 325, HL.

14.12 Before leaving the bars to rescission it should be noted that the courts have power, in the case of non-fraudulent misrepresentations, to refuse rescission, or to refuse to recognise a purported rescission, and to award damages in lieu. This power is discussed in para. 14.14, e.

Damages
14.13 It must be emphasised at the outset that we are concerned here with damages for misrepresentation and not with damages for breach of contract, which we have discussed in Chapter 12 and which are a different species. Sometimes damages for misrepresentation can be recovered under the common law of tort: sometimes under the Misrepresentation Act 1967. Rescission and damages are alternative remedies in many cases, but if the victim of a fraudulent or negligent misrepresentation has suffered consequential loss he may rescind *and* sue for damages.

14.14 The discussion of the rules of assessment of damages for misrepresentation requires the division of the relevant law into five classes:

a. *Fraudulent misrepresentation* Fraudulent misrepresentation gives rise to an action for damages for the tort of deceit. The classic definition of fraud in this context was given by Lord Herschell in *Derry v Peek*[1]. Lord Herschell stated that fraud is proved where it is shown that a misrepresentation has been made (i) knowingly, or (ii) without belief in its truth, or (iii) recklessly, careless whether it be true or false. A misrepresentation would not be fraudulent if there was an honest belief in its truth when it was made, even though there were no reasonable grounds for that belief. Motive was irrelevant: an intention to cheat or injure was not required.

Turning to the assessment of damages for the tort of deceit, the measure of damages is assessed according to the 'out of pocket rule', i.e. an amount is awarded which puts the injured party into the position in which he would have been had the fraudulent misrepresentation never been made. In relation to the actual subject-matter of the contract, this is achieved by awarding the misrepresentee the difference between what he paid for the thing in question and its actual value at that time, as is shown by *McConnel v Wright*[2], where a person who had been induced to buy shares by a fraudulent misrepresentation in a prospectus recovered the difference between the purchase price and the actual value of the shares, assessed as at the time of the contract. The 'out of pocket rule' should be contrasted with the measure of damages for breach of contract. Here the 'loss of the bargain rule' applies, as has been explained in para. 12.2, and the injured party recovers an amount (the difference between the 'represented value' at the time of the contract and the actual value) which puts him into the position in which he would have been if the representation had been true. This distinction can be demonstrated by the following example. E, a numismatist, is induced to buy a coin by F who deceives him as to its rarity. E pays £100 for the coin which in fact was worth £50. If F's representation had been true the coin would have been worth £200. F's representation does not become a term of the contract and therefore E's only claim for damages is for damages for fraudulent misrepresentation (deceit). These amount to £50 under the 'out of pocket rule'. If the misrepresentation had become a contractual term E could have chosen to sue instead for damages for breach of contract, which would have amounted to £100 under the 'loss of the bargain rule'. It is, of course, possible to envisage situations where the 'out of pocket' rule, would afford a more generous measure than the 'loss of the bargain rule', as where if F's representation had been true the coin would have been worth £125.

The 'out of pocket rule' also applies to any consequential loss for which the injured party may recover. In the tort of deceit the rule of remoteness of damage (which determines for what consequential loss recovery may be made) appears to be that the defendant is liable for all actual damage or loss directly flowing from the deceit[3], a more liberal rule than that which applies in other torts[4], and also more liberal than the rule of remoteness which applies in the case of damages for breach of contract, where damages are limited to compensation for consequential loss which was within the parties' reasonable contemplation when the contract was made as the probable result of its breach[5].

b. *Negligent misrepresentation under the Misrepresentation Act 1967*
Section 2(1) of the Act of 1967 provides that where a person has
entered into a contract after a misrepresentation has been made to him
by another party thereto and as a result of it has suffered loss, then, if
the misrepresentor would be liable to damages for misrepresentation if
it had been made fraudulently he is to be so liable notwithstanding that
the misrepresentation was not made fraudulently, unless he proves that
he had reasonable grounds to believe and did believe up to the time the
contract was made that the facts represented were true. In other words,
the misrepresentor is deemed negligent, and liable to pay damages,
unless he proves in the stated way that he was not negligent. Whether
the misrepresentor can prove this will depend, for instance, on whether
he was an expert or not, the length of the negotiations and whether he
himself had been misled by another.

Section 2(1) does not state how damages are to be assessed in
cases falling within it. Although the matter is not free from doubt, it
appears that the measure of damages is governed by the 'loss of the
bargain rule'[6], rather than the 'out of pocket rule' which applies in
fraudulent misrepresentation. The misrepresentee can only recover for
consequential loss if it is not too remote and, in this context, the same
rule of remoteness applies as in fraudulent misrepresentation, that of
direct consequences[7].

c. *Negligent misrepresentation at common law* The victim of a negligent
misrepresentation may be able to sue the misrepresentor under the
principles in *Hedley Byrne & Co Ltd v Heller & Partners Ltd*[8], which
we discuss fully in paras. 20.12 to 20.15. If the misrepresentee chooses
to do so, he must prove (i) that the misrepresentor owed him a duty to
take reasonable care in making the representation, which duty only
arises if there is a 'special relationship', which will arise where the
misrepresentor has some special knowledge or skill relevant to the
representation and knows, or it is reasonably foreseeable, that the misrepresentee will rely on the representation; (ii) that the misrepresentor
was in breach of that duty, and (iii) that damage resulted from that
breach.

The *Hedley Byrne* principles were applied to a representation
made in pre-contractual negotiations by the Court of Appeal in *Esso
Petroleum Co Ltd v Mardon*[9]. In negotiations in 1963 for the tenancy of
a filling station Esso negligently told Mr. Mardon that the station had an
estimated annual throughput of 200,000 gallons. Mr. Mardon was
induced to take the tenancy but the actual annual throughput never
exceeded 86,000 gallons and Mr. Mardon was awarded damages against
Esso. One reason for its decision given by the Court of Appeal was that
Esso, having special knowledge and skill in estimating petrol throughput,
were under the duty of care imposed by *Hedley Byrne* — which applied

to pre-contractual statements — and were in breach of that duty. In this case Mr. Mardon could not have relied on the Misrepresentation Act 1967, s.2(1), because the misrepresentation had occurred before the Act came into force. In practice, it is normally better to rely on s.2(1) in the case of a negligent misrepresentation because the onus of disproving negligence is placed on the defendant under that section, whereas if he relies on the *Hedley Byrne* principles the plaintiff must prove that they are satisfied. In addition, no special relationship need be proved under s.2(1). However, the *Hedley Byrne* principles are still important in pre-contractual misrepresentation situations in two cases: where the misrepresentation concerns a matter of opinion or as to the future; and where the misrepresentation is made by a third party to the contract. In both cases, assuming its requirements are satisfied, there can be tortious liability under the principles in *Hedley Byrne,* although there can be no rescission for misrepresentation or damages under the Act of 1967.

The measure of damages under *Hedley Byrne* is governed by the 'out of pocket rule' and questions of remoteness of damage by the test of foreseeability at the time of the breach of duty[10].

d. *Innocent misrepresentation* Subject to what is said in e. below, damages cannot be awarded for a misrepresentation which is not fraudulent or negligent, as defined above, however an indemnity — which is different from damages — may be awarded.

e. *Damages in lieu of rescission* Section 2(2) of the Misrepresentation Act 1967 provides that where a person has entered into a contract after a non-fraudulent misrepresentation has been made to him which would entitle him to rescind the contract then, if it is claimed in proceedings arising out of the contract that the contract ought to be or has been rescinded, the court or arbitrator may declare the contract subsisting and award damages in lieu of rescission, if of the opinion that it would be equitable to do so. The rationale for this power is that the rescission may be too drastic in some cases, e.g. where the misrepresentation was trifling. In exercising his discretion, a judge or arbitrator is required by s.2(2) to have regard to the nature of the misrepresentation and the loss that would be caused by it if the contract was upheld, as well as the loss that rescission would cause to the other party.

It must be emphasised that this power to award damages in lieu of rescission can only be exercised if rescission has not been barred, e.g. by affirmation of the contract, and cannot be exercised in the case of a fraudulent misrepresentation. The assessment of damages under s.2(2) is uncertain. Probably, the misrepresentor is liable to pay the difference between the price he received and the actual value of the property and, in the case of consequential loss, compensation for those items for which an indemnity could have been awarded if rescission had been granted. Where a person has been held liable to pay damages under s.2(1) of the Act of 1967, the judge or arbitrator, in assessing damages thereunder, must take into account any damages in lieu of rescission under s.2(2)[11].

---

1 (1889) 14 App Cas 337, HL.
2 [1903] 1 Ch 546, CA.
3 *Doyle v Olby (Ironmongers) Ltd* [1969] 2 QB 158, [1969] 2 All ER 119, CA.
4 Paras. 20.26, 20.27.
5 Paras. 12.3, 12.4.
6 *Gosling v Anderson* (1972) 223 Estates Gazette 709, CA; *Jarvis v Swan Tours Ltd* [1973] 1 QB 233, [1973] 1 All ER 71, CA; *Davis & Co (Wines) Ltd v Afa-Minerva (E.M.I.) Ltd* [1974] 2 Lloyd's Rep 27; *Watts v Spence* [1975] 2 All ER 528.
7 *Davis etc. v Afa-Minerva.*
8 [1964] AC 465, [1963] 2 All ER 575, HL.
9 [1976] QB 801, [1976] 2 All ER 5, CA.
10 Paras. 20.26, 20.27.
11 Misrepresentation Act 1967, s.2(3).

Indemnity

14.15 It has already been noted that the object of rescission is to restore the contracting parties to their former position as if the contract had never been made. As part of this restoration the misrepresentee can claim an indemnity against any *obligations necessarily created by the contract*[1]. The italicised words must be emphasised since they indicate that an indemnity is far less extensive than damages, as was recognised by the Court of Appeal in *Newbigging v Adam*[2]. A classic example of this distinction is provided by *Whittington v Seale-Hayne*[3]. The plaintiffs, breeders of prize poultry, were induced to take a lease of the defendant's premises by his innocent misrepresentation that the premises were in a thoroughly sanitary condition. Under the lease the plaintiffs covenanted to execute all works required by any local or public authority. Owing to the insanitary condition of the premises the water supply was poisoned, the plaintiffs' manager and his family became very ill, and the poultry became valueless for breeding purposes or died. In addition, the local authority required the drains to be renewed. The plaintiffs sought an indemnity for the following losses: the value of the stock lost; loss of profit on sales; loss of breeding season; rent and removal of stores, and medical expenses on behalf of the manager. Farwell, J, rescinded the lease and held that the plaintiffs could recover an indemnity for what they had spent on rent, rates and repairs under the covenants in the lease, because these expenses arose necessarily out of the occupation of the premises or were incurred under the covenants in the lease and were thus obligations necessarily created by the contract. However, Farwell, J, refused to award an indemnity for the loss of stock, loss of profits, loss of breeding season or the medical expenses, since to do so would be to award damages, not an indemnity, there being no obligation created by the contract to carry on a poultry farm on the premises or to employ a manager, etc.

---

1 *Whittington v Seale-Hayne* (1900) 82 LT 49, adopting the view of Bowen, LJ, in *Newbigging v Adam* (1886) 34 Ch D 582, CA.
2 (1886) 34 Ch D 582, CA.
3 (1900) 82 LT 49.

14.16 Two further points may be made concerning the award of an indemnity:

a. Being ancillary to rescission, an indemnity cannot be awarded if rescission is barred.

b. The remedy of an indemnity is redundant where the court can, and does, award damages for misrepresentation. However, where there has merely been an innocent misrepresentation and the court decides not to award damages in lieu of rescission, the availability of an award of an indemnity is very important.

Active misrepresentations which have become contractual terms

14.17 Whether a misrepresentation made during pre-contractual negotiations has become a term of the resulting contract, or of a contract collateral to it, is determined in accordance with the rules set out in paras. 8.8 to 8.15 above.

If the misrepresentation has become a contractual term the misrepresentee normally has a choice between two courses of action.

Breach of contract
14.18 As in the case of the breach of any other contractual term the misrepresentee can sue for breach of contract. If he does so he can recover damages for breach of contract (as opposed to damages for misrepresentation). The measure of damages will be according to the normal contractual rule, the 'loss of the bargain rule', and recovery can be had for all consequential loss within the parties' reasonable contemplation at the time the contract was made as a probable result of the breach. The relevant law has already been discussed in detail in Chapter 12. In addition, if the misrepresentation has become a condition of the contract, or if there has been a sufficiently serious breach of an 'intermediate term', the misrepresentee can also rescind the contract for *breach,* a matter which we discussed in paras. 10.3 to 10.22.

Misrepresentation Act 1967, s.1(a)

14.19 The misrepresentee's alternative course of action is to make use of the Misrepresentation Act 1967, s.1(a). Under this provision a person who is induced to enter into a contract by a misrepresentation of fact, which has become a term of the contract, can elect to rescind the contract for *misrepresentation* subject to the bars to rescission mentioned in para. 14.11 above. However, if he does so rescind he cannot recover damages for breach of contract since rescission for misrepresentation sets the contract aside for all purposes, including his right to claim damages for its breach, although he may be able to claim damages for misrepresentation, depending on the circumstances, in accordance with the rules set out in paras. 14.13 and 14.14 above.

14.20 The choice of a particular course of action will depend very much on whether greater damages will be obtained for breach of contract or for misrepresentation and on whether the plaintiff wishes, and is able, to rescind for misrepresentation.

Avoidance of provision excluding or limiting liability for misrepresentation

14.21 Section 3 of the Misrepresentation Act 1967[1] provides that if a contract contains a term which would exclude or restrict —

a. any liability to which a party to a contract may be subject by reason of any misrepresentation made by him before the contract was made; or

b. any remedy available to another party to the contract by reason of such a misrepresentation,

that term is of no effect except in so far as it satisfies the requirement of reasonableness; and it is for the person claiming that it satisfies that requirement to show that it does. The requirement of reasonableness is that the term must have been a fair and reasonable one to be included having regard to the circumstances which were, or ought reasonably to have been, known to or in the contemplation of the parties when the contract was made[2].

Section 3 not only applies where the relevant misrepresentation has remained a mere representation but also where it has become a contractual term — at least, as far as rescission for misrepresentation and damages for misrepresentation are concerned, although it is uncertain whether it applies if the misrepresentee elects to treat it as a breach of contract.

---

1 As substituted by the Unfair Contract Terms Act 1977, s.8.
2 Unfair Contract Terms Act 1977, s.11(1).

MISREPRESENTATION THROUGH NON-DISCLOSURE

14.22 Generally, mere silence as to a material fact or tacit acquiescence in another's erroneous belief concerning such a fact does not constitute a misrepresentation. Thus, in *Turner v Green*[1], where two solicitors arranged a compromise of certain legal proceedings, the failure of the plaintiff's solicitor to inform the defendant's of a material fact was held not to be a ground for relief even though the defendant would not have made the compromise if he had known of that fact.

1 [1895] 2 Ch 205.

14.23 However, in certain situations there is a duty to disclose material facts, breach of which gives rise to relief. Two of these situations have been referred to already: where silence distorts a positive assertion and where a positive assertion is falsified by later events (see para. 14.4, e). In these cases silence is deemed to be an active misrepresentation. In addition, in the case of contracts uberrimae fidei — of the utmost good faith — a duty to disclose fully all material facts is imposed, breach of which is regarded as a misrepresentation through non-disclosure for which relief is available.

Contracts uberrimae fidei can be divided into three types:

a. insurance contracts;

b. contracts preliminary to family arrangements; and

c. contracts where one party is in a fiduciary relationship with the other.

Insurance contracts

14.24 An intending assured is under a duty to disclose all material facts known to him[1]. In the case of marine insurance this duty of disclosure is now imposed by the Marine Insurance Act 1906, s.18(1), but otherwise it rests on the common law. A material fact in this context is one which would influence the mind of a prudent insurer in fixing the premium, or determining whether he will take the risk[2]. In marine insurance the assured is deemed by s.18(1) of the Act of 1906 to know every fact which ought to be known to him but otherwise the duty of disclosure only extends to those facts which are actually known to him[3]. However, there is nothing to stop the contract imposing a more stringent duty to disclose all facts whether material or not, and whether known or not, by providing that the accuracy of the information given by the assured is a condition of the validity of the policy. This is a regrettably common practice.

1 An early authority is *Carter v Boehm* (1766) 3 Burr 1905.
2 *London Assurance v Mansel* (1879) 11 Ch D 363; Marine Insurance Act 1906, s.18(2).
3 *Joel v Law Union and Crown Insurance Co* [1908] 2 KB 863, CA.

Contracts preliminary to 'family arrangements'

14.25 Examples of 'family arrangements' are the settlement, or re-settlement, of land between members of a family and an agreement by one member of a family to surrender some proprietary right to another member. Persons making contracts for such purposes are under a duty imposed by equity to make full disclosure of all material facts known to them[1].

---

1 *Gordon v Gordon* (1821) 3 Swan 400.

Contracts where one party is in a fiduciary relationship with the other

14.26 Where one prospective contracting party stands in a fiduciary relationship with the other he is under a duty imposed by equity to disclose any material fact known to him which might be considered likely to affect the contract between them. Examples of such relationships are: solicitor or accountant and client; trustee and beneficiary; principal and agent; partner and partner; parent and child; and doctor and patient. In such cases, the first named party is deemed to have such influence over the other that the contract will be rescinded unless he proves that he has fulfilled his duty of disclosure, and that the contract is advantageous to the other. Thus, in *Armstrong v Jackson*[1], where a stockbroker, who was employed to buy shares for his client, sold the client his own shares without disclosing this fact, it was held that the contract could be rescinded because of his breach of his duty of disclosure.

---

1 [1917] 2 KB 822.

14.27 The effect of a breach of the duty of disclosure in contracts uberrimae fidei is that the person to whom the duty was owed can refuse to carry out the contract, resist any claim for specific performance, and, if necessary, have the contract rescinded, in which case an indemnity can be awarded where appropriate. The Misrepresentation Act 1967 does not apply to misrepresentation through non-disclosure in contracts uberrimae fidei.

14.28 In conclusion, it may be noted that the Companies Act 1948, s.38, sets out certain matters which a company's prospectus inviting subscriptions for shares must contain. Failure to disclose such facts does not of itself give rise to a right to rescind, but a subscriber who has suffered loss as a result of the non-disclosure may have a statutory right of action against the directors for damages.

DURESS AND UNDUE INFLUENCE

Duress

14.29 We are concerned here with the situation where a contract has been procured by intimidation or pressure. Such a contract may be avoided at common law or in equity even though the coercion was not the sole or predominant reason for the contract being made, provided it was a reason[1]. The common law doctrine of duress is narrower than that of equity but, since its consequences may be different, it would be wrong to regard it as redundant.

---

1 *Barton v Armstrong* [1976] AC 104, [1975] 2 All ER 465, PC.

Duress at common law

14.30 It was thought that duress at common law consisted only of actual or threatened personal violence or imprisonment[1], but it has recently been held that this is not so and that any other threat, e.g. a threat to goods or to break a contract, can constitute duress of the present type[2].

To constitute duress at common law, the coercive act must be unlawful (i.e. a tort or a crime)[3] so that, for instance, a threat of lawful imprisonment, e.g. a criminal prosecution, does not suffice[4]. There is recent authority that the will of the other party must have been coerced so as to vitiate his consent: the test being whether his consent has been so overcome as to deprive him of contractual intention[5]. If this statement is correct the difficulties of applying the test are manifest.

It is uncertain whether duress at common law renders the contract voidable, in which case it is valid unless and until the coerced party rescinds it, or void. If the coerced party's consent must have been overcome so as to deprive him of contractual intention the latter consequence would seem to be more appropriate.

---

1 Co Litt 253b; *Cumming v Ince* (1847) 11 QB 112 at 120.
2 *The Siboen and The Sibotre* [1976] 1 Lloyd's Rep 293.
3 *Barton v Armstrong* [1976] AC 118 at 121. It may be noted that a threat to break an existing contract has been held to be an unlawful act for the purpose of the tort of intimidation: *Rookes v Barnard* [1964] AC 1129, [1964] 1 All ER 367, HL.
4 *Smith v Monteith* (1844) 13 M & W 427.
5 *The Siboen and The Sibotre.*

Duress in equity

14.31 A contract is voidable under this doctrine where threats have made it impossible for the coerced party either to consider the relevant matter normally or to feel a free agent. As in the case of other voidable contracts, the coerced party can rescind the contract or rely on the duress as a defence if sued. An important distinction between duress at common law and in equity is that under the equitable doctrine the coercive act need not be unlawful. For instance, in *Williams v Bayley*[1], where a banker had made it clear to a father, whose son had given the banker promissory notes on which he had forged his father's signature, that the son would be prosecuted if some arrangement was not reached, it was held by the House of Lords that an agreement by the father to make a mortgage to the bank in return for the delivery to him of the promissory notes should be rescinded.

---

1 (1866) LR 1 HL 200, HL.

Undue influence

14.32 A contract which falls within the equitable doctrine of undue influence is voidable at the instance of the party influenced. 'Duress in equity' can be regarded as part of this doctrine but, since the relevant rules are rather different, we prefer to limit the subject-matter under this heading to cases where one party's consent to a contract[1] has been procured by the use of improper means, other than threats, by the other.

Although the courts have avoided giving precise limits to the doctrine of undue influence, two situations can be stated as falling within it.

---

1 Or a gift.

Fiduciary relationships

14.33 A fiduciary relationship, i.e. a special relationship between two persons such that, while it continues, one necessarily places confidence in the other, has been held to exist between the following: parent and child[1], doctor and patient[2], solicitor or accountant and client[3], religious adviser and disciple[4], principal and agent, and trustee and beneficiary[5]. In the absence of evidence to the contrary, a contract between persons in such a fiduciary relationship is presumed to have been made under the undue influence of the first-named persons in the above list.

While the list of fiduciary relationships giving rise to the presumption of undue influence is not closed[6], it has been held that not all such relationships give rise to the presumption. For instance, the relationship between husband and wife does not[7].

---

1 *Bainbrigge v Browne* (1881) 18 Ch D 188.
2 *Mitchell v Homfray* (1881) 8 QBD 587, CA.
3 *Wright v Carter* [1903] 1 Ch 27, CA.
4 *Allcard v Skinner* (1887) 36 Ch D 145, CA.
5 *Beningfield v Baxter* (1886) 12 App Cas 167, PC.
6 *Lloyds Bank v Bundy* [1975] QB 326, [1974] 3 All ER 757, CA.
7 *Howes v Bishop* [1909] 2 KB 390, CA.

14.34 Two cases serve to illustrate the range of fiduciary relationships giving rise to a presumption of undue influence. In *Tufton v Sperni*[1], the plaintiff and defendant were both members of a committee formed to establish a Moslem cultural centre in London, it being understood that the plaintiff would provide the money for it. The plaintiff was induced to buy a house from the defendant at an over-value and at the same time to make it available for the defendant on lease at ridiculously favourable terms. The Court of Appeal rescinded the contract on the ground that, since all members of the committee necessarily had confidence in each other in regard to all matters related to the committee's objective, each member possessed the influence over the others which naturally grows out of confidence. There was therefore a fiduciary relationship from which undue influence could be presumed. In *Lloyds Bank v Bundy*[2], the defendant was an elderly farmer. The company which was run by his son got into difficulties and the defendant guaranteed its overdraft with the plaintiff bank, mortgaging his farmhouse, which was his home and only asset, to the bank as security for the guarantee. In relation to this transaction he had placed himself entirely in the hands of the assistant bank manager for financial advice and had thereby placed his confidence in the bank. Normally, there is no fiduciary relationship between a creditor and a guarantor, but it was held by the Court of Appeal that in the exceptional circumstances there was a fiduciary relationship between the plaintiff bank and the defendant and that not only could the mortgage not be enforced but it, and the guarantee, should be set aside.

---

1 [1952] 2 TLR 516, CA.
2 [1975] QB 326, [1974] 3 All ER 757, CA.

Position of personal ascendancy and influence
14.35 Even though a fiduciary relationship did not exist between the parties, the doctrine of undue influence applies if it is positively proved

that one party has gained almost complete domination over the mind of another. Once this is proved a transaction between them will be presumed to result from the undue influence of the dominant party until the contrary is proved[1].

---

1 *Smith v Kay* (1859) 7 HL Cas 750, HL; *Morley v Loughnan* [1893] 1 Ch 736.

Rebutting the presumption

14.36 The presumption that undue influence has been exercised can only be rebutted by proof that the party presumed to have been influenced has been placed in such a position as will enable him to form an entirely free and unfettered judgment, independent altogether of any sort of control[1]. The onus of proving this is on the party presumed to have exercised undue influence. The best, but not the only[2], way of doing so is by proving that the other party received independent and informed advice, particularly legal advice, before making the contract.

---

1 *Archer v Hudson* (1844) 7 Beav 551 at 560.
2 *Inche Noriah v Shaik Allie Bin Omar* [1929] AC 127, PC.

Unconscionable bargains

14.37 There is old authority that the court will rescind a contract on the basis that unfair advantage has been taken of a party who was poor, ignorant or weak-minded, by the other[1]. This principle has not been applied in a modern case, although there are statements in a number of recent decisions to support it[2].

The law on unconscionable bargains has the same basis as the other areas of equitable intervention which have just been mentioned: inequality of bargaining power. It remains to be seen whether this 'common thread' will be adopted by the courts as a basis of intervention in contractual situations other than those involving pressure or influence on a poor, ignorant or weak-minded party.

---

1 *Evans v Llewellin* (1787) 1 Cox Eq Cas 333 is an example.
2 *Lloyds Bank v Bundy* [1975] QB 326 at 339, [1974] 3 All ER 757 at 765, CA; *Clifford Davis Management Ltd v W.E.A. Records Ltd* [1975] 1 All ER 237 at 240, CA; *A. Schroeder Music Publishing Co Ltd v Macaulay* [1974] 3 All ER 616 at 623.

Bars to rescission[1]

14.38 Where a contract is voidable for duress or undue influence, or because it is an unconscionable bargain, it is valid unless and until it is rescinded. Rescission will be barred in two cases.

Affirmation

Rescission is barred if, after the pressure or influence or relationship giving rise to a presumption of undue influence has ceased, the party influenced expressly or impliedly affirms the contract[2]. An unreasonable lapse of time after removal of the influence before seeking rescission of the contract is a particularly important evidential factor suggesting affirmation[3]. A person can be held to have affirmed even though he has not had independent advice after the removal of the influence[4] and did not know that he could have the contract rescinded, provided he was aware that he might have rights and deliberately refrained from finding out[5].

Purchasers without notice

The right to rescission is lost if a third party acquires an interest for value in the property transferred by the party influenced without notice of the pressure or influence, or fiduciary relationship giving rise to a presumption of undue influence, in question[6]. Rescission is, of course, not barred if the third party does not provide consideration or has notice of the facts[7].

---

1 These bars also apply to gifts made in similar circumstances.
2 *Allcard v Skinner* (1887) 36 Ch D 145, CA; *Fry v Lane* (1888) 40 Ch D 312.
3 *Allcard v Skinner.*
4 *Mitchell v Homfray* (1881) 8 QBD 587, CA.
5 *Allcard v Skinner* (1887) 36 Ch D 45 at 92.
6 *Bainbrigge v Browne* (1881) 18 Ch D 188.
7 *Lancashire Loans Ltd v Black* [1934] 1 KB 380, CA.

Statutory protection

14.39 Two modern statutes provide some protection against certain types of oppressive or unfair bargaining in particular transactions.

Consumer Credit Act 1974

This Act empowers the court to re-open 'extortionate credit bargains' and 'do justice between the parties'. This power is considered further in paras. 23.67 to 23.69.

Fair Trading Act 1973

Part II of the Act, which was discussed in para. 10.60, provides a procedure for making Statutory Instruments to control, inter alia, consumer trade practices which have, or are likely to have, the effect of subjecting consumers to undue pressure to enter into consumer transactions or of causing the terms or conditions on which consumers enter into them to be so adverse to them as to be inequitable.

If they are detrimental or unfair to consumers, the two types of consumer trade practice in issue here may also result in a reference to the Restrictive Practices Court under Part III of the Act for an order restraining the objectionable course of conduct. This procedure was discussed in para. 10.60.

Chapter 15

Void and Illegal Contracts

15.1 A contract which would otherwise be valid may be invalid on the ground that it is void or illegal. For convenience, such contracts will be discussed in the following order:
Wagering and gaming contracts.
Other contracts void on grounds of public policy.
Illegal contracts.

WAGERING AND GAMING CONTRACTS

Nature

Wagering contracts
15.2 A wagering contract is one by which two persons, who hold opposite views concerning the outcome of a future uncertain event, or who express different views about a fact of which they are uncertain[1], agree that, dependent on the determination of that event or fact, one shall win from the other a sum of money or other stake; neither of the contracting parties having any other interest in that contract than the sum or stake he will so win or lose. It is essential to a wagering contract that each party may under it either win or lose[2]. It must be emphasised that, while wagers normally concern a stake on the outcome of a future uncertain event, such as a horse race or a general election, they can also concern the ascertainment of some past or present fact of which the parties are uncertain and express opposite views, such as whether Oxford or Cambridge won the Boat Race in a particular year or whether the Eiffel Tower is taller than Blackpool Tower.

---

1 *Hampden v Walsh* (1876) 1 QBD 189.
2 *Carlill v Carbolic Smoke Ball Co* [1892] 2 QB 484 at 490.

15.3 The above definition reveals the following requirements of a wager:

a. *Each party must stand to win or lose* There is no wagering contract unless under the terms of the contract each party can win or lose[1]. Thus, people who 'place' money with the Horseracing Totalisator Board or with a football pools company do not make a wagering contract because the Board or company cannot win or lose on the outcome of events but merely divides the amount received, less expenses etc., among the successful contributors[2].

b. *Two parties or sides* For no apparent reason a contract is not one of wager if there are more than two parties or two sides who can lose[3]. It is for this reason that a sweepstake is not a wager (although it may be illegal as a lottery)[4].

c. *No other interest* A wagering contract can only exist if each party has no other interest in the contract than the sum he will win or the stake he will lose. One result of this rule is that if a person insures against some risk to property or matter in which he has a legally recognised right or interest the contract is not one of wager and is valid[5]. Thus, if A insures his house against fire (or the life of himself or his wife, or his potato crop against failure) with B there will be a valid contract of insurance. But if C insures A's house, life or crop, in none of which he has any right or interest, the contract will be one of wager since C's only interest in the fate of the house, life or crop is that if the specified event occurs he recovers the assured sum.

Another result of the present rule can be shown by reference to Stock Exchange dealings. If C agrees with D to buy shares from him, the shares to be transferred at the next Stock Exchange settlement day in a week's time and the price to be their market price on that day, the element of chance does not make the contract one of wager because C has an interest in the subject-matter of the contract (the shares) which extends beyond winning (if the price has gone down by settlement day) or losing (if the price has gone up)[6]. The situation is otherwise in the case of a 'contract for differences'. Here E buys shares from F on the understanding that they are neither to be transferred nor paid for, but that on settlement day one party shall pay the other the difference between the price then and the price on the contract day; depending on whether it has gone up or down. Here E has no interest in the contract other than winning or losing and it is therefore a wagering contract and void[7].

Whether the parties have an interest in addition to mere winning or losing depends on the substance, and not the form, of the transaction. In *Brogden v Marriott*[8], for instance, the defendant agreed to sell, and the plaintiff to buy, a horse. The price was to be £200 if the horse trotted at 18 m.p.h. within a month, or a shilling if it did not. The horse failed in its attempt and the plaintiff claimed it at a shilling. He was unsuccessful because it was held to be a wager: in substance it was merely a bet on whether the horse would attain 18 m.p.h.. It would have been different if the difference in price had represented a genuine attempt to assess the value of a horse with the capacity to trot at that speed and without it.

---

1 *Ellesmere v Wallace* [1929] 2 Ch 1, CA.
2 *Tote Investors Ltd v Smoker* [1968] 1 QB 509, [1967] 3 All ER 242, CA.
3 This point is discussed further in *Ellesmere v Wallace* [1929] 2 Ch 1, CA.
4 Lotteries and Amusements Act 1976, ss. 1–6.
5 *Wilson v Jones* (1867) LR 2 Exch 139 at 150. Also see Marine Insurance Act 1906, s.4.
6 *Ironmonger & Co v Dyne* (1928) 44 TLR 497 at 499, CA.
7 *Universal Stock Exchange Ltd v Strachan* [1896] AC 166, HL.
8 (1836) 3 Bing NC 88.

Gaming contracts

15.4 'Gaming' means the playing of any game (which includes horse racing)[1] for money or money's worth[2]. A gaming contract is simply a contract in which the parties agree *to take part in playing such a game*[2]. A gaming contract does not necessarily involve a wagering contract since there may be more than two sides involved.

Parenthetically, it may be noted that many types of wagering and gaming are regulated by statute, especially the Betting, Gaming and Lotteries Acts 1963–71 (which, inter alia, govern legalised betting) and the Gaming Act 1968. In the statutes just mentioned 'gaming' bears a special meaning, being limited to the playing of a game of chance for winning in money or money's worth, whether any person playing the game is at risk of losing any money or money's worth or not[3]. No game is per se illegal but becomes so if the Gaming Act 1968 is infringed. The relevant provisions are outside the scope of this book but it may be noted that they differ depending on whether the gaming takes place on premises licensed or registered for gaming, or elsewhere. With the exception of s.16 of the 1968 Act *these statutes do not affect the law relating to wagering and gaming contracts*.

---

1 *Applegarth v Colley* (1842) 10 M & W 723.
2 *Ellesmere v Wallace* [1929] 2 Ch 1 at 55, CA.
3 Betting, Gaming and Lotteries Act 1963, s.55 (as amended); Betting, Gaming and Lotteries Act 1963, s.52.

Effects

Enforcement of gaming and wagering contracts

15.5 The first part of s.18 of the Gaming Act 1845, provides that all contracts by way of gaming or wagering, whether oral or written, are null and void. Thus, if A makes a bet with B on the result of the Grand National, and wins, he cannot sue B for his winnings. But, unlike the situation in most void contracts, it has been held that if A loses and pays B his winnings he confers a good title to the money on B and cannot recover it back[1].

---

1 *Bridger v Savage* (1885) 15 QBD 363 at 367, CA.

15.6 The second part of s.18 provides that 'no suit shall be brought or maintained in any Court . . . for recovering any sum of money or valuable thing alleged to be won on any wager'. These words do not simply repeat the first part of s.18 but extend to fresh promises to honour the lost bet which are supported by a fresh consideration, as was held by the House of Lords in *Hill v William Hill (Park Lane) Ltd*[1]. The committee of Tattersalls, which acts as a court of honour for bets on horse racing, ordered the appellant, a race horse owner, to discharge betting debts due to the respondent bookmakers, but he failed to do so. If the respondents had reported this failure to the Jockey Club the appellant would have been posted as a defaulter and warned off Newmarket Heath, thereby being precluded from entering any horse at, or even attending, race meetings. However, the respondents agreed not to report the appellant in consideration of the appellant giving them a post-dated cheque for part of the debt and promising the balance by instalments. The cheque was not honoured and none of the instalments was paid. The House of Lords held that the respondent could not sue on this subsequent contract because, while it was not one of gaming or wagering and therefore not struck down by the first part of s.18, the action was brought to recover a 'sum of money alleged to be won upon any wager' and was barred by the second part. It is a moot point whether a subsequent promise of the above type would be enforceable if it was not for the amount of the betting debt but for some other thing, as, for instance, where the loser promises to give the winner a car if he does not report his failure to pay a betting debt of £5,000 to Tattersalls, because it cannot be said that the car was 'alleged to be won on the wager'.

---

1 [1949] AC 530, [1949] 2 All ER 452, HL.

Principal and agent

15.7 First, three situations will be discussed which can arise where A (the principal) instructs B (the agent) to effect a bet for him.

a. Where the agent has acted within the scope of his authority in paying out *money* on a bet he cannot recover that amount from his principal. This is provided by s.1 of the Gaming Act 1892, which created an exception to the general rule of law that an agent is entitled to be indemnified by his principal against liability incurred by him in executing his lawful instructions[1]. Section 1 of the Act of 1892 goes on to provide that the agent cannot recover any money by way of commission which he has been promised for acting as a betting agent.

b. Where the agent has failed to carry out his instructions the principal cannot sue him for breach of the contract of agency[2], because a contract which is void cannot be the basis, directly or indirectly, of a legal claim[3].

c. Where the agent has made successful bets on behalf of his principal and received the winnings, he is obliged to hand them over to the principal[4]. This is in accordance with the general rule that a person who has received money on behalf of another cannot resist an action for its recovery by pleading that he received it in respect of a void transaction[5].

---

1 Para. 18.23.
2 *Cohen v Kittell* (1889) 22 QBD 680.
3 *Cheshire & Co v Vaughan Bros and Co* [1920] 3 KB 240 at 254—5.
4 *Bridger v Savage* (1885) 15 QBD 363, CA.
5 *Cheshire & Co v Vaughan Bros & Co* [1920] 3 KB 240 at 255.

15.8 Another situation which must be discussed arises where the parties to a bet deposit their bets with a stakeholder. In such a case the stakeholder is the agent of each party to the bet. Nevertheless, the winner of the bet cannot sue the stakeholder to recover his opponent's stake. This is provided by the third part of s.18 of the Gaming Act 1845: 'no suit or action shall be brought or maintained in any Court . . . for recovering any sum of money or valuable thing which shall have been deposited in the hands of any person to abide the event on which any wager shall have been made'. However, s.18 has been construed so as not to prevent each party recovering his own stake *before* it has been paid over to the winner (a limitation which is of obvious importance to the loser)[1].

---

1 *Diggle v Higgs* (1877) 2 Ex D 422, CA.

Securities

15.9 If a security, such as a cheque or other bill of exchange, is given to the winner by the loser in payment of a gaming or wagering debt the winner can no more sue on the security than he could sue for the amount he has won[1]. Thus, as between the parties the loser can stop the cheque with impunity.

---

1 *Richardson v Moncrieffe* (1926) 43 TLR 32.

15.10 The position is more complex where the security is a negotiable instrument which subsequently comes into the hands of a third party. Here the position is as follows:

a. *Gaming and wagers on games* The Gaming Act 1710, s.1, as amended by the Gaming Act 1835, s.1, provides that securities given in respect of any money or valuable thing won by playing at any game or betting on any game shall be deemed to have been given for an illegal consideration. As a result, a subsequent holder of a bill of exchange given must prove that, subsequent to the illegality, value has been given for the notice that it was so given[1]. However, such a bill can be enforced by a subsequent holder if he is a holder in due course (i.e. one who took it in good faith, for value, and without notice of the illegality)[2]. Normally, a holder of a bill is presumed to be a holder in due course, but once it is admitted that the bill was given for an illegal consideration a holder must prove that, subsequent to the illegality, value has been given for the bill without notice of the illegality (namely, the circumstances in which it was given)[3].

The same sections of the Gaming Acts 1710 and 1835 also apply to securities given for the repayment of money lent for gaming, or betting on gaming. 'Money' in this context has been held to include 'chips' representing money[4].

b. *Non-gaming wagers* Where a security is given in respect of a wager on some event other than a game, e.g. the result of a general election, the Gaming Acts of 1710 and 1835 do not apply and the consideration for the security is not illegal. The security becomes enforceable as soon as it is transferred for value, and a subsequent holder is deemed to be a holder in due course, unless the original drawer proves that value was not given, so that it will be presumed to have been transferred for value. Thus, if A makes an unsuccessful bet with B on the speed of Concorde and gives B a cheque or other negotiable instrument, which B indorses in favour of C, C will be able to sue A on the cheque even though he was aware of the circumstances in which it was made out to B and it would be for A to try to establish that no value had been given for it[5].

The above discussion of securities is subject to special rules under the Gaming Act 1968, s.16(4), which apply where a *cheque is given for a loan for gaming on premises licensed or registered for gaming.* If the licensee of such premises accepts a non-post-dated cheque in exchange for cash or tokens to be used for gaming on those premises the cheque is enforceable, *even between the parties,* provided the cheque is for the value of the cash or tokens (e.g. 'chips') exchanged and it is presented for payment or collection within two 'banking days'.

---

1 *Woolf v Hamilton* [1898] 2 QB 337, CA.
2 Bills of Exchange Act 1882, ss. 29(1), (2) and 38(2).
3 *Ibid.,* s.30(2).
4 *Stuart v Stephen* (1940) 56 TLR 571.
5 *Lilley v Rankin* (1886) 56 LJQB 248.

Loans

15.11 Whether money lent to pay betting losses or for the purpose of betting is recoverable depends on whether it was lent subject to an express or implied stipulation that it was to be used for such a purpose. If it was, the loan is irrecoverable[1]: if it was not, it is recoverable by the lender even though he was aware that the money would be used for such a purpose[2] (except that a loan for gaming is not recoverable if it is given in return for a security)[3]. A loan made for the purpose of enabling the borrower to take part in gaming which is conducted illegally (i.e. in contravention of the Gaming Act 1968) is never recoverable[4].

---

1 Gaming Act 1892, s.1; *MacDonald v Green* [1951] 1 KB 594, [1950] 2 All ER 1240, CA.
2 *Re O'Shea* [1911] 2 KB 981, CA; *C.H.T. v Ward* [1965] 2 QB 63 at 86, [1963] 3 All ER 835 at 842.
3 *Carlton Hall Club v Laurence* [1929] All ER Rep 605, DC. S.16(4) of the Gaming Act 1968 has introduced a qualification on this rule in cases where loans for gaming are made in return for *cheques* on premises licensed or registered for gaming (see para. 15.10).
4 *M'Kinnell v Robinson* (1838) 3 M & W 434.

OTHER CONTRACTS VOID ON GROUNDS OF PUBLIC POLICY

15.12 The following matters must be discussed —
The types of contracts void on grounds of public policy.
The legal effects of such contracts.

15.13 Contracts which are void on grounds of public policy can be divided into three types:
Contracts prejudicial to the married state or to parental obligations.
Contracts ousting the jurisdiction of the courts.
Contracts in restraint of trade.

Contracts prejudicial to the married state or to parental obligations

15.14 The following categories of contract fall within this type:

Marriage brokerage agreements
An obvious example of such an agreement is one to procure a marriage with a particular person, but an agreement to introduce a number of persons with a view to promoting a marriage with one or other of them also falls within this category and is therefore void[1]. This is of obvious importance to marriage bureaux.

Agreements for future marital separation
An agreement for an immediate separation between spouses is perfectly valid but an agreement providing for a possible future separation is not[2], unless it forms part of a reconciliation agreement between spouses who *are* separated[3]. Thus, the law only strikes down those contracts which are likely to lead to a weakening of marital bonds and upholds contracts made between parties whose marriage has already broken down.

Agreements to surrender parental rights or duties
Such an agreement is void[4], except that an agreement in a separation deed between spouses for the surrender by the father of his right to custody of their children is enforceable provided it is not unbeneficial to the children[5].

---

1 *Hermann v Charlesworth* [1905] 2 KB 123, CA.
2 *H v W* (1857) 3 K & J 382.
3 *Harrison v Harrison* [1910] 1 KB 35.
4 *Cartwright v Cartwright* (1853) 3 De G M & G 982.
5 Custody of Infants Act 1873, s.2.

Contracts purporting to oust the jurisdiction of the courts

Arbitration clauses[1]
15.15 These clauses are perfectly valid if they merely require the parties to refer a relevant disagreement to arbitration for settlement as a condition precedent to an action in the courts. This was held

in *Scott v Avery*[2]. An insurance policy provided that if there was a dispute relating to the policy the assured could not bring any action in the courts in relation to it until the dispute had been referred to arbitrators and the arbitrators had reached a decision. The House of Lords held that the clause was valid since it did not purport to oust the jurisdiction of the courts but simply laid down a condition which had to be satisfied before the courts might exercise jurisdiction. On the other hand, an arbitration clause purporting to deprive the parties absolutely of recourse to the courts is unenforceable and void. This is shown by *Czarnikow v Roth, Schmidt & Co*[3]. A contract for the sale of sugar provided that disputes should be submitted to arbitration and that no party should require the arbitrator to state a case on any point of law for the opinion of the court. The clause was held to be unenforceable and void, since it purported to oust the jurisdiction of the courts to determine points of law. However, a clause which simply makes the arbitrator the final arbiter on questions of fact is valid[4].

1 Also see paras. 2.40—2.49.
2 (1855) 5 HL Cas 811, HL.
3 [1922] 2 KB 478, CA.
4 *Lee v Showmen's Guild of Great Britain* [1952] 2 QB 329 at 342, [1952] 1 All ER 1175 at 1181, CA.

Maintenance agreements
15.16 If a maintenance agreement between spouses contains a promise by one of them not to apply to the courts for a financial provision order in return for a promise of maintenance by the other, the former spouse's promise is void and unenforceable[1]. In the case of written agreements, this is now provided by the Matrimonial Causes Act 1973, s.34, which goes on to state, however, that any other financial arrangements in the agreement are valid (unless they are void or unenforceable for any other reason).

1 *Hyman v Hyman* [1929] AC 601, HL.

Contracts in restraint of trade

15.17 These contracts give rise to more complications than other contracts which are void on grounds of public policy. Contracts in restraint of trade may be void at common law or, in some cases (which we deal with in paras. 15.33 to 15.45), by statute.

Contracts in restraint of trade which are void at common law can be divided into five principal categories:

a. agreements restricting the subsequent occupation of an employee;

b. agreements between employers regulating labour;

c. agreements between the vendor and purchaser of the goodwill of a business restricting competition by the vendor;

d. exclusive dealing agreements; and

e. cartel agreements.

It must be emphasised that this list is not exclusive and that other types of agreement in restraint of trade are, or may be, void unless they satisfy the tests mentioned in the next paragraph[1]. On the other hand, some agreements which restrain trade are not covered by the present doctrine. Two examples of these appear in paras. 15.23 and 15.26. Meanwhile, it may be noted that the purposes of a trade union or employers' association do not, by reason of the fact that they are in restraint of trade, make void any agreement[2].

---

1 *Esso Petroleum Co Ltd v Harper's Garage (Stourport) Ltd* [1968] AC 269, [1967] 1 All ER 699, HL.
2 Trade Union and Labour Relations Act 1974, ss. 2(5) and 3(5).

15.18 The general tests of validity applicable to contracts falling within the restraint of trade doctrine are as follows:
  A contract in restraint of trade is prima facie void. But —
  Such a contract will be valid and enforceable if —
    first, the person seeking to enforce it shows that the restraint is reasonable between the parties to the contract; *and*
    secondly, the other party does not show that the restraint is unreasonable in the public interest[1].
The tests of reasonableness must be applied as at the date the contract was made and in the light of the then existing facts and of what might possibly happen in the future. Anything else which has occurred subsequently must be ignored[2]. The application of these tests can be demonstrated by reference to the five categories of agreement mentioned above.

---

1 These tests have their foundation in *Nordenfeldt's* case [1894] AC 535, HL and *Herbert Morris Ltd v Saxelby* [1916] 1 AC 688, HL.
2 *Putsman v Taylor* [1927] 1 KB 637 at 643; *Gledhow Autoparts Ltd v Delaney* [1965] 3 All ER 288 at 295.

Agreements concerning the subsequent occupation of an employee
15.19 A contract between employer and employee, normally the contract of employment, may contain a covenant (promise) by the employee that he will not be employed in, or conduct, a business

competing with his employer's after leaving his employment. This restriction will normally be limited in duration and area. Such a restriction, being in restraint of trade, is prima facie void and will only be valid and enforceable if the tests of reasonableness referred to above are satisfied. The precise nature of these tests in the present context will now be examined.

a. *Reasonable between the parties* Two things must be proved to satisfy this test:

i. The restriction must protect a legally recognised interest of the employer. Only two interests are so recognised:

a. *Protection of trade secrets and secret processes* An example is provided by *Forster & Sons Ltd v Suggett*[1]. The defendant was the plaintiff company's works manager. He was instructed in secret methods relating to the production of glass which the plaintiff company produced. He agreed that during the five years after the end of his employment with the plaintiff company he would not carry on in the United Kingdom, or be interested in, glass bottle manufacturing or any other business connected with glass making carried on by the company. It was held that this restriction was reasonable to protect the plaintiff company's trade secrets and an injunction was ordered to restrain breach of it.

b. *Protection of business connections* An employer is entitled to prevent an employee misusing influence which he has obtained over the employer's customers and thereby enticing them away[2]. Thus, in *Fitch v Dewes*[3], where the contract provided that a Tamworth solicitor's managing clerk (who was himself a solicitor) should never practice within seven miles of Tamworth Town Hall, the House of Lords held that the restriction was valid because it constituted a reasonable protection of the employer's business connections against an employee who could gain influence over his clients.

It is not enough merely to show that the restriction purports to protect trade secrets or connections: it must also be shown that they require protection against the particular employee. Thus, the restriction will be invalid if the employee did not know enough about a trade secret to be able to use it or was insufficiently acquainted with customers to be able to influence them. This is shown, for example, by *S.W.Strange Ltd v Mann*[4], where a restriction imposed on a bookmaker's manager was held to be void because the business was mostly conducted by telephone and the manager had no chance to get to know his employer's customers or to influence them.

No other interests can be protected validly by the present type of restriction[5] with the result that a restriction whose object is simply to protect the employer against competition or to protect, for instance, a special method of organisation of a business is invalid[6].

ii. Reasonableness. To be reasonable between the parties, the restriction must be no wider than is reasonably necessary to protect the employer's trade secrets or business connections. Reasonableness is a matter of degree: the terms of the restriction must be measured against the degree of knowledge or influence which the employee has gained in his employment. A fortiori, a restriction will be void if it relates to a wider range of occupations than is reasonably necessary to protect the relevant interest. Two other factors which are particularly important are the duration and area of the restriction.

a. Duration In *M and S Drapers v Reynolds*[7], a collector-salesman of a credit drapery firm covenanted not to canvass his employers' customers for a period of five years after leaving their employment. The restriction was held to be void: in view of the lowly position of a collector-salesman it was for a longer period than was reasonably necessary to protect the employers' business connections. On the other hand, the restriction in *Fitch v Dewes* was upheld, even though it was to last for life, because of the degree of influence which the solicitor's clerk would gain over his employer's clients.

b. Area In *Mason v Provident Clothing and Supply Co Ltd*[8], a canvasser in the plaintiff company's Islington branch district covenanted not to work in any similar business for three years within 25 miles of London. The restriction was held to be void because it extended further than was reasonably necessary to protect the plaintiff company's business connections. On the other hand, a covenant by a sales representative that, for two years after leaving his employment, he would not canvass (in the same goods) people *who had been customers of his employer during his employment,* was upheld in *G.W.Plowman & Son Ltd v Ash*[9] even though it was unlimited in area.

b. Reasonable in the public interest The operation of this test is demonstrated by *Wyatt v Kreglinger and Fernau*[10]. The employers of a wool broker promised to pay him a pension on his retirement provided he did not re-enter the wool trade and did nothing to their detriment (fair competition excepted). The broker subsequently sued for arrears of pension but the Court of Appeal held that he could not succeed since the contract was void for two reasons: i. the restriction was unreasonable as between the parties; ii. the contract was unreasonable in the public interest because the permanent restriction on the broker working anywhere in the wool trade deprived the community of services from which it might benefit.

Provided the restriction is reasonable between the parties, employer-employee restrictions will rarely be invalidated on the ground that they are unreasonable in the public interest. However, where the employee has a special skill of particular value to the community, the restriction may well be found unreasonable in the public interest even though it affords reasonable protection for the employer's trade secrets or connections[11].

It may be noted in passing that, even in the absence of an express restraint, where an employee or ex-employee uses or discloses an employer's trade secrets, or an employee solicits an employer's customers, the employer can obtain an injunction to restrain this[12].

---

1 (1918) 35 TLR 87.
2 *Herbert Morris Ltd v Saxelby* [1916] 1 AC 688 at 709, HL.
3 [1921] 2 AC 158, HL.
4 [1965] 1 All ER 1069, [1965] 1 WLR 629.
5 *Herbert Morris Ltd v Saxelby* [1916] 1 AC 688 at 710, HL.
6 *Ibid.*
7 [1956] 3 All ER 814, [1957] 1 WLR 9, CA.
8 [1913] AC 724, HL.
9 [1964] 2 All ER 10.
10 [1933] 1 KB 793, CA.
11 *Bull v Pitney-Bowes Ltd* [1966] 3 All ER 384.
12 *Printers and Finishers Ltd v Holloway* [1964] 3 All ER 731, [1965] 1 WLR 1 (trade secrets); *Wessex Dairies Ltd v Smith* [1935] 2 KB 80 (business connections).

Agreements between employers regulating labour

15.20 The same principles apply to agreements between employers attempting to regulate their labour and imposing mutual restrictions on the re-employment of each other's former employees. This is illustrated by *Kores Manufacturing Co Ltd v Kolok Manufacturing Co Ltd*[1]. The plaintiff and defendant companies were manufacturers of carbon paper and typewriter ribbons. They agreed that neither would employ at any time any person who had been employed by the other during the then past five years. The defendant company broke this agreement. The Court of Appeal held that the agreement was void because it covered all employees, whether or not they knew of the parties' trade secrets, and was also excessive in duration. It was therefore unreasonable as between the parties since it imposed on them a restriction grossly in excess of what was necessary to protect their trade secrets.

A question which is not finally resolved is whether agreements of the present type can ever be valid if their purpose is not to protect the employers' trade secrets or connections but to protect the adequacy and stability of labour forces or some other interest. In the *Kores* case, the Court of Appeal took the view that such an agreement could not be valid. However, in *Eastham v Newcastle United Football Club Ltd*[2], Wilberforce, J, was prepared to accept that the proper organisation of football was an interest which could be protected by an agreement between football clubs, although he found that the 'retain and transfer' system (the agreement between these employers) was invalid because it went further than was reasonably necessary to protect that interest. Unless the protectable interests in agreements between employers are legally limited to trade secrets and connections, employers will be able to circumvent the restrictions on employer-employee restraint of trade agreements by making agreements between themselves protecting interests other than their trade secrets or connections.

---

1 [1959] Ch 108, [1958] 2 All ER 65, CA.
2 [1964] Ch 613, [1963] 3 All ER 139.

15.21 As the *Eastham* case shows, an employee affected by the present type of contract can challenge it by seeking a declaration that it is void. If he is successful, the declaration will not set the contract aside but it has strong persuasive force on the parties' future conduct.

Agreements between the vendor and purchaser of the goodwill of a business restricting competition by the vendor

15.22 Such an agreement is prima facie void for restraint of trade but will be valid and enforceable if it is reasonable between the parties and not unreasonable in the public interest. The following can be said concerning the requirement of reasonableness between the parties:

a. *The restriction must protect the business sold* An agreement whereby one business surrenders to another its liberty to trade in a particular field is void since mere competition is not a protectable interest[1]. The restriction must relate to an actual business which has been sold. Thus, even though it is contained in what purports to be a contract for the sale of a business, a restriction will be void if there is no actual business to protect. This is shown by *Vancouver Malt and Sake Brewing Co Ltd v Vancouver Breweries Ltd*[2]. The appellants held a licence to brew beer and other liquors but the only trade actually carried on by them under the licence was brewing sake. They purported to sell the goodwill of their licence, so far as it related to brewing beer, to the respondents and covenanted not to brew beer for 15 years thereafter. The Privy Council held that the covenant was void because, if there was a sale, it was merely a sale of the appellants' liberty to brew beer since there was no goodwill of a beer brewing business to be transferred and the covenant was simply a bare restriction on competition.

Other aspects of the rule that the covenant must protect the business actually sold are demonstrated by *British Reinforced Concrete Engineering Co Ltd v Schelff*[3]. The defendant, who ran a small business for the *sale* of 'Loop' road reinforcements, sold it to the plaintiff company, a large company which manufactured and sold 'B.R.C.' road reinforcements. In the contract of sale the defendant covenanted that, for three years after the end of the First World War, he would not 'either alone or jointly or in partnership with any other person or persons whomsoever and either directly or indirectly carry on or manage or be concerned or interested in or act as servant of any person concerned or interested in the business of the manufacture or sale of road reinforcements in any part of the United Kingdom'. It was held that this covenant was too wide because it extended to the manufacture of road reinforcements as well as their sale, and thus sought to protect more than the actual business sold (the *sale* of road reinforcements).

b. *The restriction must go no further than is reasonably necessary to protect the business sold* As was pointed out in the *Schelff* case, the reasonableness of the restriction must be judged by reference to the extent and circumstances of the business sold, and not by the extent and range of any business already run by the purchaser. Reasonableness is judged from the standpoint of both parties. For example, in the *Schelff* case it was held that the 'servant clause' was unreasonable because it would preclude the defendant from becoming the servant of a trust company which, as part of its investments, held shares in a company manufacturing or selling road reinforcements.

The duration and area of the restriction are particularly important factors to be taken into account in assessing its reasonableness. The approach of the courts is more liberal here than in the case of employer-employee restrictions because buyers and sellers of businesses are more obviously equal bargaining partners. A good example of this liberality is provided by *Nordenfeldt v Maxim Nordenfeldt Guns and Ammunition Co Ltd*[4]. The appellant, who had obtained patents for improving quick-firing guns, carried on, among other things, business as a maker of such guns and of ammunition. He sold the goodwill and assets of the business to a company, entering into a covenant which restricted his future activities. The company later merged with another to become the respondent company and the appellant's earlier covenant was substantially repeated with it. This covenant provided that for 25 years the appellant would not engage, except on behalf of the company, directly or indirectly in the trade or business of a manufacturer of guns, gun mountings or carriages, gunpowder, explosives or ammunition, or in any business competing or liable to compete in any way with that for the time being carried on by the respondent company. The first part of the covenant, relating to engaging in a business manufacturing guns etc., was held by the House of Lords to provide reasonable protection for the business acquired by the company, even though the restriction was world-wide and was to last for 25 years, and was therefore valid. It was recognised, however, that the second part of the covenant, relating to engaging in any business competing with that carried on by the company, was void because it went further than was reasonable to protect the business acquired by the company. Similarly, the restriction in the *Schelff* case, even as it related to the management etc. of a business selling reinforcements, was held void because it applied to the whole of the United Kingdom, which was regarded as a wider area than was necessary to protect the actual business sold.

---

1 *Vancouver Malt and Sake Brewing Co Ltd v Vancouver Breweries Ltd* [1934] AC 181, PC.
2 [1934] AC 181, PC.
3 [1921] 2 Ch 563.
4 [1894] AC 535, HL.

Exclusive dealing agreements
15.23 One type of agreement under this heading is a 'solus agreement' whereby A agrees to buy all his requirements of a particular commodity from C. In *Esso Petroleum Co Ltd v Harper's Garage (Stourport) Ltd*[1], the House of Lords held that such exclusive purchasing agreements were subject to the restraint of trade doctrine and were prima facie void. However, as their Lordships recognised, there are exceptions. The House of Lords held that where a person acquires land by conveyance or lease, and an exclusive dealing agreement relating to the land is inserted into the conveyance or lease, it is not subject to the restraint of trade doctrine. Thus, if an oil company sells or leases a filling station to X, inserting a covenant into the conveyance or lease that X shall only buy petrol supplies from the company, the covenant falls outside the restraint of trade doctrine and is valid. Lord Reid said that the reason for this was that the restraint of trade doctrine only applied where a person gave up a freedom which he would otherwise have enjoyed, and a person buying or leasing land had no previous right to trade there and thus gave up no previously held freedom. The limits of this exception are shown by *Amoco Australia Pty Ltd v Rocca Bros Motor Engineering Co Pty Ltd*[2], where Rocca, who owned a garage, leased it to Amoco who immediately leased it back to them. The underlease contained a provision that Rocca should buy all its petrol supplies from Amoco. The Privy Council applied the restraint of trade doctrine to this restriction: Rocca had given up a previously held freedom to trade on the land as they wished.

---

1 [1968] AC 269, [1967] 1 All ER 699, HL.
2 [1975] AC 561, [1975] 1 All ER 968, PC.

15.24 Where the restraint of trade doctrine applies to an exclusive purchasing agreement the restraint is, of course, valid only if it is reasonable between the parties and is not shown to be unreasonable in the public interest. It appears that, as opposed to the heads of agreements in restraint of trade already mentioned, an exclusive purchasing agreement can be valid even though its object is simply to protect a party against competition (and this is true of the other types of exclusive dealing agreements). The operation of the restraint of trade doctrine to exclusive purchasing agreements is demonstrated by *Esso Petroleum Co Ltd v Harper's Garage (Stourport) Ltd.* Harper's agreed to buy all their petrol requirements from Esso. They also agreed to operate their two garages in accordance with the 'Esso co-operation plan' under which they had to keep the garages open at all reasonable hours and not sell them without getting the purchaser to enter into a similar agreement with Esso. In return Harper's got a 1¼d rebate a gallon off the list price of petrol. In the case of one garage the agreement was to last for four years five months. The agreement relating to the other garage was to last for 21 years, being contained in a mortgage of the garage to Esso for 21 years which was not redeemable before that time had expired. The House of Lords held that both agreements were prima facie void since neither fell within an exception to the restraint of trade doctrine, even though one was contained in a mortgage. The question was therefore whether the restrictions in the two agreements were reasonable:

a. The House held that the agreement for four years five months was reasonable between the parties. It was reasonably required to protect Esso's legitimate interest in securing continuity of their sales outlets, their system of distribution and the stability of their sales. In return Harper's not only got a rebate on the price of the petrol they purchased but could also rely on the financial backing of a big company if they were short of funds. The agreement was also reasonable in the public interest.

b. The House held that the agreement for 21 years was unreasonable between the parties, because it was for longer than necessary to protect Esso's interests, and therefore void.

The public interest in this context refers to the interest of the public that a person should not be subjected to unreasonable restrictions on his freedom to work or trade, and not to any ultimate economic or social or other advantage to the public at large[1].

---

1 *Texaco Ltd v Mulberry Filling Station Ltd* [1972] 1 All ER 513.

15.25 Another type of agreement which may be said to fall under the heading of exclusive dealing agreements is an agreement whereby A agrees to provide his services solely to B for a period. Normally, such a contract does not fall within the restraint of trade doctrine even though it necessarily involves restriction of one of the party's right to exercise any lawful activity he chooses, but if the contractual restriction appears to be unnecessary or to be reasonably capable of enforcement in an oppressive manner it is prima facie void and its validity depends upon the twin tests of reasonableness[1]. An example of an exclusive services contract which fell within the restraint of trade doctrine for the reasons just given is *Schroeder Music Publishing Co Ltd v Macaulay*[2]. M, a young and unknown song writer, entered into a contract with S Ltd, who were music publishers, whereby they engaged his exclusive services for five years. Under the contract M assigned to S Ltd full copyright for the whole world in anything composed by him during the period of the contract or before it. If M's royalties exceeded £5,000 during the five year period the contract was to be automatically extended for another five years. S Ltd reserved the right to terminate the contract with one month's notice, but M had no such rights. S Ltd were not obliged by the contract to publish anything composed by M. The House of Lords held that the contract fell within the restraint of trade doctrine and was void, the main reason for its decision being that the agreement was unreasonable between the parties because, while S Ltd were given the sole right to publish M's songs, they were not bound to do so and could simply leave them lying in a drawer.

---

1 *Schroeder Music Publishing Co Ltd v Macaulay* [1974] 3 All ER 616, [1974] 1 WLR 1308, HL; *Clifford Davis Management Ltd v W.E.A. Records Ltd* [1975] 1 All ER 237, [1975] 1 WLR 61, CA.
2 [1974] 3 All ER 616, [1974] 1 WLR 1308, HL.

15.26 Before leaving exclusive dealing agreements it should be noted that 'sole agency agreements', i.e. agreements giving a person the sole right to supply a manufacturer's goods, are exempt from the restraint of trade doctrine because they have gained general commercial acceptance[1].

---

1 *Esso Petroleum Co Ltd v Harper's Garage (Stourport) Ltd* [1968] AC 269 at 336, [1967] 1 All ER 699 at 731.

Cartel agreements
15.27 These are agreements in which manufacturers or traders undertake to restrict their output, supply or purchase of goods or services, or to restrict competition between them or to maintain prices. At common law a cartel agreement, like any other agreement governed by the restraint of trade doctrine, is prima facie void and to be enforceable must be justified as reasonable between the parties and not be shown to be unreasonable in the public interest.

a. *Reasonable between the parties* Although protection against competition is not in itself an interest which can be validly protected by a cartel agreement, the interests which can be so protected have been liberally defined so as to include, for instance, a manufacturer's interest in the maintenance of his list of customers[1]. Because the parties are equal bargaining partners, the courts have been reluctant to find that a cartel agreement is unreasonable between them, and have only done so in cases where the agreement imposed a perpetual restraint from which a party could not withdraw or could only withdraw with great difficulty[2].

b. *Reasonable in the public interest* A cartel agreement is also unlikely to fall foul of this test because it will only be found contrary to the public interest if it is calculated to produce 'a pernicious monopoly, that is to say, a monopoly calculated to enhance prices to an unreasonable extent'[3].

We show in paras 16.33 to 16.45 how these common law rules concerning cartel agreements have been rendered almost completely obsolete by statute.

---

1 *McEllistrim v Ballymacelligott Co-operative Agriculture and Dairy Society* [1919] AC 548, HL.
2 *Ibid.*
3 *A-G of South Australia v Adelaide SS Co Ltd* [1913] AC 781, PC.

Effects

Enforcement of the contract

15.28 Provided that the part of the contract which is void on grounds of public policy can be severed from the rest of the contract, the latter, as opposed to the void part, is enforceable. However, if the void part cannot be severed the whole contract is void and unenforceable. Severance can operate in two ways.

15.29 *Severance of the whole of an objectionable promise* If this can be done the rest of the contract is valid and enforceable. Severance of a whole promise is not possible if it is the whole or a substantial part of the consideration furnished by a party. Thus, in *Wyatt v Kreglinger and Fernau*, which we discussed in para. 15.19. b, it was held that the ex-employee could not enforce the promise to pay him a pension since he had given no valid consideration for it, his only promise — not to compete — being void under the restraint of trade doctrine. The present rule can be demonstrated by contrasting *Bennett v Bennett*[1] with *Goodinson v Goodinson*[2]. In the former case, Mrs. Bennett petitioned for divorce and sought maintenance for herself and her son in the petition. Before the decree nisi was granted she entered into a deed with her husband in which she promised to withdraw her existing application and not to apply to the courts for maintenance for herself or her children, to maintain the son and to indemnify the husband against any legal expenses arising out of the deed. In return, the husband covenanted to pay the wife and son an annuity and to convey certain property. He failed to make the promised payments and the wife sued him on the deed. The Court of Appeal held that the wife's promise not to apply to the courts was void on the ground that it purported to oust the jurisdiction of the courts and that it could not be severed from the rest of her promises because it formed the main consideration from her for the contract. The whole contract was therefore void and unenforceable.

On the other hand, in *Goodinson v Goodinson*[2], the void promise was held to be severable. A husband and wife who were separated made an agreement whereby the husband promised to pay the wife a weekly sum if she would indemnify him against any debts incurred by her, not pledge his credit for necessaries and not bring maintenance proceedings against him. The husband fell into arrears under the agreement and the wife sued to recover them. The Court of Appeal held that the wife's last promise was void for the same reason as in *Bennett v Bennett* but that it could be severed from the other promises, leaving the rest of the contract valid and enforceable. *Bennett v Bennett* was distinguished because the other promises made by Mrs. Goodinson were substantial and the promise not to take the husband to court did not form the main consideration provided by her.

It must be noted that, while these two cases provide the best available illustrations of severance of a whole promise, *Bennett v Bennett* would be decided differently now because, by a subsequent statute, a written maintenance agreement can be enforced even though a party has provided no consideration other than a void promise not to apply to the courts for financial provision[3].

---

1   [1952] 1 KB 249, [1952] 1 All ER 413, CA.
2   [1954] 2 QB 118, [1954] 2 All ER 255, CA.
3   Para. 15.16.

15.30 *Severance of the objectionable part of a promise* This is particularly relevant in restraint of trade contracts. If severance is possible of part of a promise, the rest of the contract, including the unsevered part of the promise, can be enforced. Severance of this type is only possible if two tests are satisfied:

> a. The 'blue pencil' test. This test is only satisfied if the objectionable words can be struck out of the promise *as it stands*.

This was possible in relation to the offending part of the promise in the *Nordenfeldt* case, which has been discussed in para.15.22,b.. Another example is provided by *Goldsoll v Goldman*[1]. The defendant sold his imitation jewellery business in Old Bond Street to the plaintiff, another jeweller. The defendant covenanted that for two years he would not 'either solely or jointly with or as agent or employee for any person or company . . . carry on or be interested in the business of a vendor of or dealer in real or imitation jewellery in the county of London, England, Scotland, Ireland, Wales, or any part of the United Kingdom and the Isle of Man or in France, the United States of America, Russia or Spain, or within 25 miles of Potsdamerstrasse, Berlin, or St. Stephan's Kirche, Vienna'. The defendant joined a rival jeweller's in New Bond Street within two years and the plaintiff sought an injunction to restrain breach of the covenant. The Court of Appeal held that the covenant was unreasonably wide in respect of subject-matter (for the defendant had not dealt in real jewellery) and also in respect of area (because the defendant had not traded abroad) but that the reference to foreign places and real jewellery could be severed because it was possible to delete them from the covenant *as it stood*. After severance the covenant merely prohibited dealing in imitation jewellery in the United Kingdom and the Isle of Man, and an injunction was granted to prevent such dealing.

If the unreasonable part of the promise cannot be deleted from the promise as it stands severance of it is not possible. The court cannot re-write the promise by adding or altering even one word so as to make it reasonable. Thus, in *Mason v Provident Clothing and Supply Co Ltd*[2], which has already been referred to[3], where the contract in question contained a promise that the employee would not work within 25 miles of London after leaving his employment, the House of Lords held that the promise was too wide in area, and therefore unreasonable, and refused to re-draft the clause so that it would be reasonable and enforceable. The whole promise was therefore held void and unenforceable.

b. Severance of the objectionable part must not alter the nature (as opposed to the extent) of the original contract. This means that severance of part of a promise is impossible unless it can be construed as being divisible into a number of separate and independent parts. This rule is sensible — otherwise the mechanical deletion of the objectionable part of the promise could radically change the whole contract — but difficult to apply.

The application of this test can be illustrated by two cases. In *Attwood v Lamont*[4], the plaintiffs owned a general outfitter's business in Kidderminster. The business was divided into a number of departments. The defendant was the head of the tailoring department but had no concern with any other department. In his contract of employment the defendant had undertaken that, after the termination of his employment, he would not 'be concerned in any of the following trades or businesses: that is to say, the trade or business of a tailor, dressmaker, general draper, milliner, hatter, haberdasher, gentlemen's, ladies' or children's outfitter' within ten miles of Kidderminster. Later the plaintiffs sought to enforce this covenant. They admitted that it was too wide in terms of the trades covered but argued that the references to aspects of the business other than tailoring could be severed, leaving the tailoring restraint enforceable. The Court of Appeal rejected this course because such severance would have altered the whole nature of the covenant: the covenant as it stood was one indivisible covenant for the protection of the whole of the plaintiffs' business, not several covenants for the protection of the plaintiffs' several departments, and to alter it would be to alter its nature.

This case can be contrasted with *Putsman v Taylor*[5]. The plaintiff carried on business as a tailor at three places in Birmingham: Snow Hill, Bristol Road and Aston Cross. He employed the defendant at his Snow Hill branch, although under the defendant's contract of employment he could have been directed to work at any of the three branches. The defendant covenanted that for five years after leaving the plaintiff's employment he would not carry on any business similar to that of the employer ... or be employed in any capacity by any person ... carrying on a business similar to that of the employer in Snow Hill ... or within half-a-mile radius of Aston Cross ... or Bristol Road'. The Divisional Court held that the Aston Cross and Bristol Road restrictions were unreasonable to protect the plaintiff's business connections but could be severed from the Snow Hill part of the covenant which, presumably, was held to be divisible in substance into several covenants.

---

1   [1915] 1 Ch 292, CA.
2   [1913] AC 724, HL.
3   Para. 15.19, a.
4   [1920] 3 KB 571, CA.
5   [1927] 1 KB 637, DC.

Other effects
15.31   In *Hermann v Charlesworth*[1], a woman who had paid a fee to a 'marriage broker' was held to be entitled to recover it despite the fact

that he had introduced her to a number of men. Probably, money or property transferred under other contracts which are wholly void on grounds of public policy, or under a severable part of a contract which is void on such grounds, is recoverable, even though the contract has been performed.

---

1 [1905] 2 KB 123, CA; para. 15.14.

15.32 A collateral or subsequent transaction founded on a contract which is wholly void on grounds of public policy, or on a severable void part of such a contract, is itself void.

Statute and restraint of trade

Restrictive Trade Practices Act 1976
15.33 The narrow common law rules concerning cartel agreements considered in para. 15.27, which reflect a laissez-faire attitude towards economic matters, were rendered almost completely obsolete with the passing of the Restrictive Trade Practices Act 1956 most of which, together with subsequent amendments, has been consolidated in the Restrictive Trade Practices Act 1976 (which has been amended slightly by the Restrictive Trade Practices Act 1977). Under this Act many cartel agreements (whether or not intended to be legally enforceable) are made subject to registration and judicial investigation.

15.34 The agreements which are subject to this procedure are:

a. *Restrictive agreements as to goods* These are defined as any agreement or arrangement, between two or more persons carrying on business in the United Kingdom in the production, supply or processing of goods, by which restrictions are accepted by two or more parties as to:
 i. the prices to be charged, made, quoted or paid for goods; or
 ii. the price to be recommended in respect of the resale of goods supplied; (agreements for the *collective enforcement* of conditions as to resale prices are absolutely prohibited and illegal[1]); or
 iii. the conditions on which goods are to be supplied, acquired or processed; or
 iv. the quantities or descriptions of goods to be produced, supplied or acquired; or
 v. the processes of manufacture to be applied to any goods; or
 vi. the persons to or from whom, or the areas or places in or from which, goods are to be supplied or acquired[2].

b. *Restrictive agreements as to services* These are defined as any agreement or arrangement between two or more persons carrying on business in the United Kingdom in the supply of services of a class designated by

the Secretary of State whereby restrictions are accepted by two or more parties as to:
  i. the charges to be made, quoted or paid for designated services; or
  ii. the conditions on which designated services are to be supplied or obtained; or
  iii. the extent to which, or the form in which, designated services are to be made available, supplied or obtained; or
  iv. the persons or classes of persons for whom or from whom, or the areas or places in or from which, designated services are to be made available or supplied or are to be obtained[3].
All services have now been made designated services except those professional services, which include accounting and auditing services, exempted by the Act[4].

c. *Information agreements as to goods or services* The Secretary of State has power to extend the requirement of registration to any class of 'information agreement' as to goods or services[5]. An information agreement is defined as an agreement, between two or more persons carrying on a business of the types referred to above, which provides for the furnishing by two or more parties to each other or to others of information relating to matters specified in the Secretary of State's order. These matters are the prices or charges to be asked for goods or services, or the conditions on which they are provided, and other matters corresponding to the restrictions mentioned in relation to restrictive agreements as to goods and services[6].

---

1 Resale Prices Act 1976, s.1; paras. 15.42–15.45.
2 Restrictive Trade Practices Act 1976, s.6.
3 *Ibid.*, s.11.
4 Restrictive Trade Practices (Services) Order 1976; Restrictive Trade Practices Act 1976, Sched. 1.
5 Restrictive Trade Practices Act 1976, ss. 7 and 12; so far only information agreements as to the price and conditions of supply of goods have been made registrable: Restrictive Trade Practices (Information Agreements) Order 1969.
6 Restrictive Trade Practices Act 1976, ss. 7 and 12.

15.35 *Exempt agreements* Certain agreements, such as 'solus agreements' and 'know how' agreements are excluded from the provisions of the Act[1], and certain agreements of importance to the national economy or for holding down prices may be exempted by the Secretary of State[2].

---

1 Restrictive Trade Practices Act 1976, s.28 and Sched. 3.
2 *Ibid.*, ss.29–31.

15.36 *Registration* Registrable agreements must be registered with the Director-General of Fair Trading before they take effect or within three months of being made, whichever is the earlier[1]. Failure to do so renders the agreement void in respect of all restriction or information provisions therein and it is unlawful for a party to give effect to them. In addition, a third party injured by such provisions in an unregistered agreement can sue for damages for breach of statutory duty, and the Director can obtain an injunction to stop the parties enforcing or carrying out the restriction or information provisions[2].

1 Restrictive Trade Practices Act 1976, ss. 1 and 24.
2 *Ibid.*, s.35.

15.37 *Judicial investigation* Once an agreement has been registered the Director must generally refer it to the Restrictive Practices Court which has to determine whether or not the restriction or information provisions in the agreement are 'contrary to the public interest'. If the Court finds that they are, the agreement is rendered void in respect of the offending provisions and the parties can be restrained from enforcing or carrying them out and from making a similar agreement[1].

A restriction or information provision is presumed to be contrary to the public interest unless it is shown to be beneficial in one of the eight ways specified in the Act *and* to be not unreasonable having regard to the balance between those circumstances and any detriment to the public or to persons not parties to the agreement (such as purchasers, consumers, users or sellers of goods, and users or suppliers of services) resulting or likely to result from the operation of the restriction[2].

1 Restrictive Trade Practices Act 1976, s.2.
2 *Ibid.*, ss. 10 and 19.

15.38 *Trade and service supply associations* The above provisions concerning registration and investigation also apply to specific recommendations made by such associations to their members if they concern the action to be taken or not to be taken in relation to any particular class of good, process of manufacture or service in respect of a matter which, if contained in an agreement, would make the agreement registrable[1].

1 Restrictive Trade Practices Act 1976, ss. 8 and 16.

15.39 The result of these statutory provisions is that the common law rules concerning cartel agreements are now only of practical relevance in relation to the rare cartel agreement which is not registrable under the Act or which satisfies the criteria in the Act but is unreasonable between the parties. The statutory system outlined above has two important advantages over the common law provisions:

a. At common law the validity of a cartel agreement can only come before the courts if a party breaks it or wishes to challenge it. Now, agreements covered by the Act of 1976 must be registered and investigated by the Restrictive Practices Court.

b. The Act provides tests of validity more in accord with modern economic attitudes.

EEC Treaty, Article 85

15.40 Cartel agreements may also be void on the ground that they conflict with article 85 of the Treaty establishing the European Economic Community. Article 85(1) prohibits:

'all agreements between undertakings, decisions by associations of undertakings and concerted practices which may affect trade between Member States [of the European Economic Community] and which have as their object or effect the prevention, restriction or distortion of competition within the common market, and in particular those which:

a. directly or indirectly fix purchase or selling prices or any other trading conditions;

b. limit or control production, markets, technical development, or investment;

c. share markets or source of supply;

d. apply dissimilar conditions to equivalent transactions with other trading parties, thereby placing them at a competitive disadvantage;

e. make the conclusion of contracts subject to acceptance by the other parties of supplementary obligations which, by their nature or according to commercial usage, have no connection with the subject of such contracts.'

The following comments must be made concerning article 85. First, article 85 only applies to agreements etc. affecting trade between two member states of the European Community. Of course, an agreement between two undertakings in one state may have this effect, as where two companies in this country agree to divide up their European export markets.

Secondly, infringement of article 85(1) makes the prohibited agreement automatically void[1] and unenforceable in English law. The EEC Commission also has power to impose a fine or order the discontinuance of the agreement. However, under Community regulations an agreement can be notified to the EEC Commission for an individual exemption or for a declaration that the agreement does not fall within article 85[2]. Despite the use of the phrase 'automatically void' an agreement is regarded as 'provisionally valid' if it has been notified to the Commission for exemption[3].

Finally, the Restrictive Trade Practices Act 1976 deals with the situation which arises where an agreement is or may be void under both the Act and article 85. In particular, the Director-General of Fair Trading is given a discretion not to refer an agreement to the Restrictive Practices Court, and the Court has power to decline or postpone the exercise of its jurisdiction having regard to article 85 and to the effect of any exemption granted thereunder[4].

---

1 Treaty of Rome, art. 85(2).
2 *Ibid.*, art. 85(3); Reg. 17/62.
3 *Case 13/61: Bosch v De Geus* [1962] CMLR 1, CJEC.
4 Restrictive Trade Practices Act 1976, ss. 5 and 21.

15.41 The wording of article 85(1) is apt to cover not only cartel agreements but also exclusive dealing agreements such as 'solus agreements'. However, its applications to these was severely restricted by Regulation 67/67 which provides that article 85(1) is inapplicable to three groups of agreements between no more than two undertakings:

a. those in which one undertakes to supply the other exclusively with certain products for the purpose of resale in certain geographical areas;

b. those in which one undertakes to buy only from the other for the purpose of resale;

c. those in which both have undertaken the agreements provided under a. and b..

The provisions of article 85(1) and the rules of the common law restraint of trade doctrine are cumulative so that a cartel agreement and an exclusive dealing agreement to which article 85(1) applies will be invalid in English law unless it is valid under both sets of rules.

Resale Prices Act 1976

15.42 This Act, a consolidation Act, replaces the Resale Prices Act 1964 whose object was to abolish resale price maintenance in the United Kingdom, except where it could be shown to be in the public interest. The Act is not concerned with arrangements imposing maximum prices, which remain perfectly valid.

15.43 The Act of 1976 provides that, except in the case of classes of goods exempted by the Restrictive Practices Court, a term or condition of a contract for, or relating to, the sale of goods by a manufacturer or other supplier to a dealer which provides a minimum resale price is void, although this does not affect the enforceability of the rest of the contract[1]. In addition, it is unlawful for any supplier of goods to include, or require the inclusion of, any minimum resale price provision in any such contract, or to notify to dealers or otherwise to publish minimum resale prices (although publication of a recommended price is permitted)[1].

The Act also prohibits the indirect enforcement of such minimum price provisions by providing that it is unlawful to withhold supplies from dealers who have undercut the stipulated price or supplied third parties who have done so, or who are likely to so undercut or to supply third parties who are likely to undercut. For the purpose of this prohibition a person is treated as withholding supplies of goods if he refuses or fails to supply those goods to the order of the dealer; or if he refuses to supply them to the dealer except at prices or on terms as to credit or other matters which are significantly less favourable than those at or on which he normally supplies those goods to other similar dealers; or if, although he contracts to supply the goods to the dealer, he treats him significantly less favourably than he normally treats other such dealers in respect of the times or methods of delivery or other matters arising in the execution of the contract. However, a supplier is not to be treated as withholding supplies of goods if, in addition to the ground of actual or apprehended price-cutting, he has other grounds which, standing alone, would have led him to withhold those supplies[2]. Moreover, the withholding of supplies of any goods from a dealer is not unlawful if the supplier has reasonable cause to believe that within the previous 12 months the dealer, or another dealer supplied by him, has been using as loss-leaders any goods of the same or a similar description[3].

The unlawful practices mentioned above can result in civil actions brought by the Crown for an injunction 'or other appropriate relief', and for breach of statutory duty brought by any person affected by the contravention[4].

1 Resale Prices Act 1976, s.9.
2 *Ibid.*, ss. 11 and 12.
3 *Ibid.*, s.13.
4 *Ibid.*, s.25.

15.44 The Act of 1964 gave suppliers a period of three months from 16 August 1964 to register with the Registrar of Restrictive Trading Agreements (whose functions are now vested in the Director-General of Fair Trading) claims for exemption in respect of goods of a particular class supplied by them. All such claims had to be referred to the Restrictive Practices Court. Pending the outcome of the Court's investigation goods of the class in question were treated as exempted goods. Applications for exemption which have not been registered in the above time period may be made to the Court with its leave[1].

1 Resale Prices Act 1976, s.16.

15.45 The Court may make an exemption order in relation to a particular class of goods if the supplier proves that in default of a minimum resale price system applicable to them:

a. the quantity or variety of the goods available for sale, or the number of retail establishments in which the goods are sold, would be substantially reduced; or

b. the retail prices of the goods would in general and in the long run be increased; or

c. the goods would be sold by retail under conditions likely to cause danger to health in consequence of their misuse by the public as consumers or users of them; or

d. the provision of after-sales service would be substantially reduced,

and in any such case that the resulting detriment to the public as consumers or users of the goods in question would outweigh the detriment to them as consumers or users resulting from the maintenance of minimum prices in respect of the goods[1].

Only two exemption orders have been made: in respect of books and related goods, and of medicaments and related goods. These are, therefore, the only goods in respect of which minimum resale price maintenance is now permissible.

---

1   Resale Prices Act 1976, s.14.

ILLEGAL CONTRACTS

15.46   A contract may be illegal in one of three ways, because,
its formation is prohibited by statute; or
it is performed in a manner which is prohibited by statute; or
it involves an element which is unlawful, immoral or prejudicial to the interests of the state.
These three types of illegality, with their effects on the enforcement of a contract, will be discussed in turn, followed by a discussion on the other effects of illegal contracts generally.

Contracts whose formation is prohibited by statute

15.47   A contract is illegal in itself if a statute expressly or impliedly prohibits its making.

15.48 An example of a contract which was *expressly* so prohibited is provided by *Re Mahmoud and Ispahani*[1]. Under wartime delegated legislation it was forbidden to buy or sell linseed oil without a licence. A agreed to sell and deliver some linseed oil to B but B subsequently refused to accept delivery because, unknown to A, he did not have a licence to buy linseed oil. The Court of Appeal held that, there being a clear statutory prohibition of the making of such a contract without a licence, it was illegal and unenforceable by A.

A modern example of a statute expressly prohibiting the formation of a contract is provided by the Resale Prices Act 1976, s.1. We mentioned in paras. 15.33 to 15.38 that cartel agreements may be *void* under the Restrictive Trade Practices Act 1976 but the Resale Prices Act 1976, s.1, makes *illegal* agreements for the *collective* enforcement of price maintenance conditions. Section 1 strikes at such agreements between suppliers and between dealers. Any agreement or even any arrangement between two or more persons carrying on business in the United Kingdom as suppliers of goods is illegal if it provides:

a. that goods shall be withheld from dealers who have infringed a condition as to the prices at which those goods may be sold (this includes putting a dealer's name on a stop-list); or

b. that goods shall not be supplied to such dealers except on terms which are less favourable than those applicable to similar dealers (e.g. by cancellation of a trade discount); or

c. that goods will only be supplied to persons who undertake to withhold or refuse supplies of goods in the above two ways.

In addition, agreements or arrangements authorising the recovery of penalties from offending dealers are illegal, as is the conduct of any domestic proceedings in connection therewith.

There are similar provisions relating to agreements between dealers in goods which provide for the like sanctions against suppliers who fail to observe or enforce resale price conditions.

The consequences of a contract which is illegal under s.1 are not simply that it is unenforceable. In addition, the Crown may obtain an injunction 'or other appropriate relief', and a person affected by the agreement can bring an action for breach of statutory duty.

---

1   [1921] 2 KB 716, CA.

15.49 The question whether a statute *impliedly* prohibits the making of a particular contract is productive of uncertainty since its answer depends on the judicial interpretation of the statute to ascertain whether Parliament intended to forbid the making of the particular contract.

Because of the harsh consequences of such a finding, a contract will not be held to be prohibited unless there is a clear implication that this was Parliament's intention[1]. One factor which is particularly relevant is whether the object of the statute is to protect the public or a class of persons, e.g. to protect the public against unqualified persons or to protect licensed persons from competition[1]. If so, this suggests that Parliament intended a contract made in breach of the statute to be prohibited. In *Cope v Rowlands*[2], for instance, a statute provided that anyone who acted as a broker in the City of London without a licence should pay a penalty for each offence. The plaintiff, who was unlicensed, acted as a broker for the defendant whom he later sued for the work which he had done for him. Parke, B, dismissed the action because although the statute did not expressly prohibit the contract in question, Parliament had intended to protect the public in stockbroking transactions. The statute therefore had to be taken as impliedly prohibiting the making of stockbroking contracts by unlicensed persons.

On the other hand, the fact that the statute's object is sufficiently served by the imposition of the statutory penalty suggests that Parliament did not intend a contract made in breach of the statute to be prohibited. In *Smith v Mawhood*[3], the plaintiff, a tobacconist, sued the defendant for the price of tobacco which he had delivered to him. The defendant pleaded that the contract was illegal because the plaintiff did not have a licence to sell tobacco, nor was his name painted on his premises, as required by statute. It was held that, although the plaintiff had committed a statutory offence, the contract was not illegal because the object of the statute was the imposition of a penalty for revenue purposes, and not the prohibition of contracts of sale by unlicensed dealers.

Another factor to which regard may be made is the inconvenience and injury which would be caused by holding the contract to be illegal[4].

The approach of the courts is well demonstrated by the decision of the Court of Appeal in *Archbolds (Freightage) Ltd v S. Spanglett Ltd*[5]. The defendants contracted with the plaintiffs to carry whisky from Leeds to London. The whisky was stolen en route through the negligence of the defendants' driver and the plaintiffs claimed damages for its loss. The defendants raised the defence that, under the Road and Rail Traffic Act 1933, it was illegal for a person to use a vehicle to carry goods for another for reward unless the vehicle held an 'A' licence, that the vehicle used did not hold an 'A' licence (in fact none of their vehicles held an 'A' licence), and that therefore the contract was illegal and unenforceable. The trial judge dismissed this defence and awarded the plaintiffs damages. The Court of Appeal dismissed the defendant's appeal. It held that if, as had been found, the contract merely provided for the carriage of whisky from Leeds to London, the *formation* of that contract could not be illegal because, even had both parties contemplated that an unlicensed vehicle would be used, this would not be a contractual term. However, the Court continued, even if the contract was to carry goods in a vehicle which did not in fact have an 'A' licence the contract would still not be illegal in its formation. This was because the Act of 1933 did not expressly prohibit the formation of such a contract; nor did it impliedly prohibit it, since its object was not to interfere with the owner of goods or his facilities for transport but to control competition between transport firms and improve efficiency, and that object was sufficiently served by the penalties prescribed for the transport undertaking using the unlicensed vehicle.

1 *St. John Shipping Corpn v Joseph Rank Ltd* [1957] 1 QB 267, [1956] 3 All ER 683.
2 (1836) 2 M & W 149.
3 (1845) 14 M & W 452.
4 *St. John Shipping Corpn v Joseph Rank Ltd* [1957] 1 QB 267, [1956] 3 All ER 683.
5 [1961] 1 QB 374, [1961] 1 All ER 417, CA.

Enforcement
15.50 Where a contract is statutorily illegal as formed neither party can enforce it, subject to the exception mentioned in the next paragraph, even though he was unaware of the facts constituting the illegality. Thus, in *Re Mahmoud and Ispahani*[1], the seller could not sue the buyer for refusing to take delivery of the linseed oil despite the fact that he was unaware that the buyer did not have the necessary licence, and had been assured between contract and attempted delivery by the buyer that he had a licence.

A contract which is statutorily illegal as formed can be enforced in part if the illegal portions are severable. The rule is that where a party makes a number of promises, one of which is illegal and the rest legal, the illegal promise can be severed and the others enforced provided the illegal promise does not constitute the main or only consideration given by that party for the other's promises.

1 [1921] 2 KB 716, CA; para. 15.48.

15.51 Although a party to an illegally formed contract cannot recover damages for its breach if severance is impossible, he may be able to recover damages for misrepresentation if he has been induced to contract by a misrepresentation of fact (which may be of a fact affecting the legality of the contract)[1].

1 Para. 14.4.

Contracts which become illegal because they are performed in a manner which constitutes a statutory offence

15.52 The fact that an offence is committed in performing an initially lawful contract does not necessarily make the contract illegal[1], and generally it does not have that effect. Thus, for reasons which will become apparent shortly, the fact that an employee of a road haulage company exceeds the speed limit while delivering goods does not render the contract of carriage made by the company illegal.

---

1   *St. John Shipping Corpn v Joseph Rank Ltd* [1957] 1 QB 267, [1956] 3 All ER 683.

15.53 Some statutes expressly state whether breach of their provisions does or does not invalidate a contract. However, generally, it depends on the interpretation of the statute to see whether Parliament intended that the particular type of contract in question should be prohibited if performed in contravention of the statute. The approach here is the same as that to the question whether a contract is impliedly illegal as formed. Breach of a statute in performing a contract will only be held to invalidate it if there is a clear implication that Parliament so intended. A statute whose object is the protection of the public or a class of persons is likely to give rise to such an implication, as will a statute which says that the type of contract in question can only be performed in one way. In *Anderson Ltd v Daniel*[1], for instance, the statute required a seller of artificial fertilisers to give a buyer an invoice stating the percentage of certain chemicals. The plaintiffs sold 10 tons of artificial fertiliser to the defendants but did not provide the necessary invoice. It was held that since the statute had specified the only way in which the contract could be performed, and since this had not been done, the contract was rendered illegal and the plaintiffs could not recover the price of the fertiliser. On the other hand, if the purposes of the statute are sufficiently served by the prescribed penalties the statute is unlikely to be construed as prohibiting the contract. Another factor to be taken into account is the inconvenience or injury to a party which would result from a finding that the contract is prohibited.

These factors were taken into account by Devlin, J, in *St. John Shipping Corpn v Joseph Rank Ltd*[2]. By statute it is an offence to load a ship to such an extent that the load line is below water. The plaintiffs chartered their ship to X to carry grain from the United States to England. The plaintiffs overloaded the ship so that the load line was submerged. The defendants, who were consignees of part of the cargo, withheld part of the freight charge (the equivalent of the amount due on the excess cargo), contending that the plaintiffs could not enforce the contract because they had performed it unlawfully. Devlin, J, held that the plaintiffs could recover the amount due. He held that the illegal performance of the contract of carriage did not render it illegal because the Act merely punished infringements of the load line rules and was not intended to prohibit a contract of carriage performed in breach of them.

---

1 [1924] 1 KB 138, CA.
2 [1957] 1 QB 267, [1956] 3 All ER 683.

Enforcement

15.54 Where a contract has become illegal through performance in breach of a statute the party who has so performed it cannot enforce the contract, as is shown by *Anderson Ltd v Daniel*[1], where the plaintiffs' claim for the price of the fertiliser which they had delivered was dismissed because of their illegal performance. A limited exception was recognised in *Frank W. Clifford Ltd v Garth*[2], namely that, if the performance was initially legal but became illegal and the legal and illegal parts of the performance can be precisely valued, the illegal part can be severed and the party who has illegally performed the contract can recover the amount of the contractual price which is attributable to the legal performance. In this case, the defendant engaged the plaintiffs to convert premises into a coffee bar for her. At the time in question it was illegal to do more than a £1,000 worth of such work on any single property in any year without a licence. The defendant had already had £146 worth of work done that year by another contractor. Her contract with the plaintiffs was not for a fixed figure but on a 'cost-plus' basis, and because of various difficulties the plaintiffs' bill was far in excess of £1,000. The Court of Appeal held that, although the plaintiffs could not recover the full amount claimed, they could recover £854 because until the work in the particular year exceeded £1,000 in value it was perfectly lawful and only became unlawful in relation to the excess. Thus, the plaintiffs could recover the amount which fell within the free limit.

---

1 [1924] 1 KB 138, CA.
2 [1956] 2 All ER 323, [1956] 1 WLR 570, CA.

15.55 The other party to a contract which is illegal as performed can sue on it, unless he knew of the mode of performance adopted (although he need not have known that it was illegal[1]) and allowed the performance to proceed. It is for him to establish his innocence. In *Marles v Philip Trant and Sons Ltd (No.2)*[2], for instance, the Court of Appeal held that although a contract for the sale of wheat was illegal, because the seller had not given the buyer certain written details as required by statute, the buyer could nevertheless sue the seller for breach of contract (the wheat having been mis-described as 'spring wheat') because of his innocence. Similarly, in the *Archbolds (Freightage)* case[3], the Court of Appeal did not find it necessary to pursue the question whether the hauliers' unlawful performance of the contract rendered it illegal, because the plaintiffs had been ignorant that it was to be so performed and could have sued on the contract of carriage anyway. On the other hand, the plaintiffs failed to recover damages for breach of contract in *Ashmore, Benson, Pease and Co Ltd v A. V. Dawson Ltd*[4], where a contract of carriage performed by the defendants in breach of maximum load regulations was held to be illegal, because their transport manager had watched the lorries being overloaded and, by allowing it, had participated in the illegal performance of the contract.

1 *Archbolds (Freightage) Ltd v S. Spanglett Ltd* [1961] 1 QB 374, [1961] 1 All ER 417, CA.
2 [1954] 1 QB 29, [1953] 1 All ER 651, CA.
3 [1961] 1 QB 374, [1961] 1 All ER 417, CA. The facts are set out in para. 15.49.
4 [1973] 2 All ER 856, [1973] 1 WLR 828, CA.

15.56 If, a party, who cannot sue on the illegal contract because he has illegally performed it, can prove that a collateral contract existed whereby the other party assumed responsibility for ensuring that the performance would be lawful, as by obtaining a necessary licence; he can recover damages for breach of that collateral contract[1].

1 *Strongman (1945) Ltd v Sincock* [1955] 2 QB 525, [1955] 3 All ER 90, CA. In addition, he may be able to recover damages for misrepresentation.

Contracts involving an element which is unlawful, immoral or prejudicial to the interests of the state

15.57 Sometimes an agreement will be overtly for an unlawful, immoral or state-prejudicial purpose: at other times an overtly lawful agreement, or its subject-matter, will be intended by one or both of the parties, when the contract is made, to be exploited for such a purpose. Both types of contract are illegal ab initio but their consequences differ.

15.58 Any agreement to commit a crime or tort falls within this head, so that an agreement to assault X is illegal[1], as is an agreement to publish a libel about X[2]. The width of the present head may be demonstrated by reference to *Miller v Karlinski*[3] and *Alexander v Rayson*[4]. In the former, the terms of an employment contract were that the employee should be paid £10 a week plus travelling expenses. The contract also provided that he could recover the amount of income tax payable on the £10 by claiming it as travel expenses. The employee later claimed ten weeks' arrears of salary plus 'expenses', most of which related to what was payable in income tax. It was held that since the contract was overtly for an illegal purpose – to defraud the Revenue – it could not be enforced by the employee and his action was dismissed. In contrast, the contract in *Alexander v Rayson*, which was not overtly for an unlawful purpose, was held to be illegal because it was intended to be exploited for such a purpose. The plaintiff let a flat to the defendant at £1,200 p.a.. The transaction was effected by two documents: a lease of the flat at £450 p.a., which provided for certain services to be rendered by the plaintiff, and an agreement that in consideration of £750 p.a. the plaintiff would render certain services, which were substantially the same as in the lease. Subsequently, the defendant refused to pay an instalment due under the documents. When sued for this, the defendant raised the defence that the object of the two documents was that only the lease was to be disclosed to the local authority to deceive them into reducing the rateable value of the property. The Court of Appeal held that if the documents were intended to be used for an unlawful purpose the plaintiff could not enforce either the lease or the service agreement.

---

1   *Allen v Rescous* (1676) 2 Lev 174.
2   *Apthorp v Neville & Co* (1907) 23 TLR 575.
3   [1945] 62 TLR 85.
4   [1936] 1 KB 169, CA.

15.59   Turning to agreements involving immorality, a contract to pay a woman in return for her agreeing to become a mistress is an obvious example of a contract which is illegal on the ground that its purpose is overtly immoral[1], while a contract to hire to a prostitute a car which is intended for use in her profession will be held illegal because the subject-matter of the contract is intended to be used for an immoral purpose[2].

---

1   *Walker v Perkins* (1764) 1 Wm Bl 517.
2   *Pearce v Brooks* (1866) LR 1 Ex 213.

15.60   Agreements which involve an element prejudicial to the interests of the state include agreements which are hostile to a friendly foreign state[1], agreements which tend to injure the public service (under which heading an agreement to assign a salary earnt in a public office is illegal)[2] and agreements prejudicial to the administration of justice. An example of the last type of agreement is one to suppress, or not to prosecute, a criminal prosecution[3], but this is limited to crimes of a public nature, e.g. riot or rape, so that the compromise of a prosecution for a trade marks offence or a domestic assault is not illegal[4]. An agreement not to appear at the public examination of a bankrupt, nor to oppose his discharge, is another example of an agreement which has another in a case in which he has no legitimate interest. Champerty support shall have a share in anything recovered as a result of the litigation. justice are those tainted by maintenance or champerty. Maintenance occurs if a person without just cause or excuse supports litigation by another in a case in which he has no legitimate interest. Champerty is maintenance plus a further agreement that the person giving such support shall have a share in anything recovered as a result of the litigation.

---

1 *Foster v Driscoll* [1929] 1 KB 470.
2 *Re Mirams* [1891] 1 QB 594.
3 *Keir v Leeman* (1846) 9 QB 371.
4 *Fisher & Co v Appollinaris & Co* (1875) 10 Ch App 297; *McGregor v McGregor* (1888) 21 QBD 424, CA.

Enforcement
15.61 The enforceability of a contract which is illegal because it involves an element which is unlawful, immoral or prejudicial to the interests of the state depends on whether or not is overtly involves such an element. If it does, neither party can enforce it however innocent he may be[1]. On the other hand, where the contract is not overtly for one of the above purposes but is intended to be, or its subject-matter is intended to be, exploited for such a purpose the situation is as follows:

a. the contract cannot be enforced by a party who intended to exploit it unlawfully, immorally or 'prejudicially'[2]; nor

b. can it be enforced by a party who knew the other had such an intention[3]; but

c. it can be enforced by a party who did not know of the other's unlawful, immoral or 'prejudicial' intentions before he performed or tendered performance of his contractual obligations[4].

Thus, in *Cowan v Milbourn*[5], where the defendant, who had agreed to let a room to the plaintiff but later refused to fulfil the agreement on learning that the plaintiff intended to use the room for an unlawful purpose (a blasphemous lecture), was sued for breach of contract, it was held that the plaintiff's action failed because of his unlawful intention in relation to the subject-matter of the contract. Bramwell, B, added that the defendant could have sued the plaintiff for the hire charge if he had let him into possession not knowing of his unlawful intentions, but not if he had previously learnt of them. In the *Archbolds (Freightage)* case[6] the Court of Appeal held that the fact that the hauliers had intended ab initio to carry out the contract of carriage in an unlawful way did not prevent the other party to the contract suing on it because they were ignorant of that intention. A party will have sufficient knowledge in the present context if he has full knowledge of what the other party intends to do, he need not know that it is unlawful[7].

Although the matter is not free from doubt, the better view is that in contracts involving an element of unlawfulness, immorality or prejudice to the interests of the state it is not possible to sever the illegal part and enforce the rest of the contract[8].

---

1 *Miller v Karlinski* (1945) 62 TLR 85; *Keir v Leeman* (1846) 9 QB 371.
2 *Alexander v Rayson* [1936] 1 KB 169, CA.
3 *Pearce v Brooks* (1866) LR 1 Ex 213.
4 *Cowan v Milbourne* (1867) LR 2 Ex 230.
5 (1867) LR 2 Ex 230.
6 [1961] 1 QB 374, [1961] 1 All ER 417, CA; the facts are set out in para. 15.49.
7 *J. M. Allan (Merchandising) Ltd v Cloke* [1963] 2 QB 340, [1963] 2 All ER 258, CA; cf. *Waugh v Morris* (1873) LR 8 QB 202.
8 *Bennett v Bennett* [1952] 1 KB 249 at 252–254, [1952] 1 All ER 413, CA; *Kuenigl v Donnersmark* [1955] 1 QB 515, [1955] 1 All ER 46. Cf. *Fielding and Platt Ltd v Najjar* [1969] 2 All ER 150 at 153.

Other effects of illegal contracts

Recovery of money or property transferred under an illegal contract

15.62   The general rule is that a person cannot recover back money or property which he has transferred under an illegal contract. An authority is *Parkinson v College of Ambulance Ltd*[1]. The secretary of the defendant charity promised the plaintiff that, if he would make a certain donation to the charity, he would procure a knighthood for him. The knighthood did not materialise and the plaintiff sought to recover the £3,000 he had paid. It was held that the contract was illegal (as tending to injure the public service) and that the plaintiff's action, being based on it, must fail. This general rule is normally described by the Latin maxim *in pari delicto potior est conditio defendentis* (where the parties are equally guilty the defendant is in a more favourable position).

---

1 [1925] 2 KB 1.

15.63   In the following exceptional cases a party who cannot enforce the contract can nevertheless recover from the other what he has transferred under it.

a. *Fraudulent misrepresentation by the other party that the contract was lawful* Instead of suing for damages for deceit[1], the party deceived can recover back what he has transferred under the contract. This is shown by *Hughes v Liverpool Victoria Legal Friendly Society*[2], where a woman who had been induced to take out an insurance policy by a fraudulent misrepresentation that it was valid was held able to recover the premium which she had paid. The present exception does not apply where the misrepresentation as to the legality of the contract was not fraudulent[3]. However, where a person has been induced to enter into an illegal contract by a misrepresentation of *fact* he can *rescind the contract for misrepresentation* and recover back what he transferred under it, provided rescission is not barred, even though the misrepresentation was innocent[4].

b. *Contract procured through oppression by the other party* In *Atkinson v Denby*[5], for example, the plaintiff, a debtor, offered his creditors five shillings in the pound. The defendant, who was one of the creditors, told the plaintiff that he would only accept this dividend if the plaintiff first paid him £50 and gave him a certain bill of exchange. The plaintiff agreed and did so. The contract was illegal because of the fraud on the other creditors, but it was held that the plaintiff could recover the £50 because the contract to defraud had been procured by oppression, since the other creditors would not accept the composition if the defendant did not. The basis of this exception, like the previous one, is that the parties are not *in pari delicto*.

c. *No reliance on the illegal contract* A party to an illegal contract can recover back what he has transferred under it if he can establish his right to it without relying on the terms of the illegal contract or its illegality. This exception is of limited application, partly because the ownership of property can pass under an illegal contract (in accordance with the ordinary rules concerning the passing of ownership)[6] if the parties so intend[7]; and where this occurs, as in the case of goods sold under an illegal contract of sale, the transferor cannot recover the property back.

However, where an owner of property has merely transferred some limited interest to another under an illegal contract, as by pledging goods with him or hiring them to him, any rights which he may have independent of his illegal contract will be recognised and enforced. Thus, if A hires goods to B under an illegal contract he can recover them back, or recover damages in lieu, when B's right to possess them has ended. This is because A's right to immediate possession will have revived thereby and consequently he will be entitled to sue B in tort for conversion of the goods without having to base his claim in any way on the terms of the illegal contract or its illegality[8]. On the other hand, if E deposits property with F to secure payment of charges under an illegal contract the property is irrecoverable, unless the charges have been paid, because, once F has pleaded that the property has been pledged with him, E can only base his claim to possession by showing that the pledge was invalid because of the illegality of the contract[9].

d. *Unlawful purpose not yet carried into effect* This exception is relevant to contracts which are illegal because their purpose is unlawful. A party can recover back what he has transferred under an illegal contract if he genuinely repents (which he will not do if his change of mind is brought about by the other's failure to perform the contract or because the illegality has been discovered by the authorities)[10] and withdraws from the contract before the unlawful purpose is partially performed in a substantial way[11].

e. *Class protecting statutes* If a statute which makes a particular type of contract illegal as formed was passed to protect a particular class of persons, rather than simply to impose a penalty and prohibit the contract[12], a member of that class who is a party to such a contract can recover back money or property which he has transferred under it, even though the contract has been completely performed[13]. The basis of this exception is that the parties are not *in pari delicto*[14]. Some class protecting statutes which make particular contracts illegal expressly provide for recovery by a member of the protected class of what he has transferred under them.

---

1 Para. 14.14, a.
2 [1916] 2 KB 482, CA.
3 *Harse v Pearl Life Assurance Co* [1904] 1 KB 558, CA.
4 *Edler v Auerbach* [1950] 1 KB 359, [1949] 2 All ER 692. For these bars see para. 14.11.
5 (1862) 7 H & N 934.
6 See, for example, paras. 22.11–22.22.
7 *Singh v Ali* [1960] AC 167, [1960] 1 All ER 269, PC; *Belvoir Finance Co Ltd v Stapleton* [1971] 1 QB 210, [1970] 3 All ER 664, CA.
8 *Bowmakers Ltd v Barnet Instruments Ltd* [1945] KB 65, [1944] 2 All ER 579, CA.
9 *Taylor v Chester* (1869) LR 4 QB 309.
10 *Bigos v Bousted* [1951] 1 All ER 92; *Alexander v Rayson* [1936] 1 KB 169 at 190.
11 *Kearley v Thomson* (1890) 24 QBD 742, CA; cf. *Taylor v Bowers* (1876) 1 QBD 291, CA.
12 *Green v Portsmouth Stadium Ltd* [1953] 2 QB 190, [1953] 2 All ER 102, CA.
13 *Browning v Morris* (1778) 2 Cowp 290; *Kiriri Cotton Co Ltd v Dewani* [1960] AC 192, [1960] 1 All ER 177, PC.
14 *Ibid.*

Subsequent or collateral transactions founded on the illegal contract
15.64 Such transactions between the parties to the illegal contract are themselves illegal and unenforceable to the same extent as the

contract[1]. Thus, a security, such as a bond or bill of exchange, given to secure performance of an illegal contract is illegal.

Transactions between a party to the illegal contract and a third party which aid the fulfilment of the illegal contract are illegal and unenforceable by the third party if he knows of the prior illegality. One authority is *Spector v Ageda*[2], where it was held that X, who had lent Y money to enable him to pay off a loan from Z under a moneylending agreement which was statutorily illegal, could not recover the amount which she had lent (plus interest) because she had known of the illegal nature of the moneylending agreement.

---

1 *Fisher v Bridges* (1853) 2 E & B 118.
2 [1973] Ch 30, [1971] 3 All ER 417.

Chapter 16

Capacity to Contract

MINORS

16.1 The age of majority was reduced from 21 to 18 by the Family Law Reform Act 1969, s.1. Persons under that age are known as minors or infants. The rules relating to the contractual capacity of minors are based on the common law but they were amended extensively by the Infants' Relief Act 1874. Minors' contracts can be divided into four types:

valid contracts;

voidable contracts;

contracts absolutely void under s.1 of the Infants' Relief Act 1874;

other invalid contracts.

It should be noticed at the outset that a parent or guardian is never liable for a minor's contract unless the minor acts as his agent, nor can a minor's invalid contract be validated by subsequent parental ratification.

Valid contracts

16.2 Three types of contract made by a minor fall within this heading: contracts for necessary goods for the minor; contracts for necessary services for the minor, and contracts of employment, apprenticeship and analogous contracts which are beneficial to the minor. These contracts were not affected by the Infants' Relief Act 1874[1].

---

1 Paras. 16.12–16.14.

Contracts for necessary goods for the minor

16.3 Proof that goods were necessaries requires two conditions to be satisfied:

a. *The goods must be suitable to the minor's position in life* Necessaries are not limited to the necessities of life but they do not extend to mere luxuries[1]. They can include anything fit to maintain the minor in his station in life. Dicta in two nineteenth century cases provide useful illustrations. In *Bryant v Richardson*[2], Martin, B, said: 'A coat of superfine broadcloth may be a necessary for the son of a nobleman, although it is impossible not to say that the coarser material of a ploughman's coat would be sufficient to keep a nobleman's body warm'. In *Ryder v Wombwell*[3], Bramwell, B, said that 'ear rings for a male, spectacles for a blind man, a wild animal, . . . a daily dinner of turtle and venison for a month for a clerk with a salary of £1 a week' could not be necessaries. In this case the defendant, a minor with an annual income of £500, was the son of a deceased baronet and moved in the highest society. He bought from the plaintiff an antique goblet in silver gilt and a pair of crystal, ruby and diamond solitaires (cuff links). On appeal[4], it was held that neither of these things could be necessaries since they were mere luxuries and the plaintiff's claim for the price failed.

b. *The goods must be necessaries according to the minor's actual requirements at the time of delivery* In *Nash v Inman*[5], the defendant was an undergraduate at Cambridge. The plaintiff, a tailor, supplied him with clothes, including 11 fancy waistcoats. The plaintiff's action for the price of the clothes failed because, the evidence showing that the defendant was amply provided already with clothes suitable to his position, there was no proof of the present condition.

---

1 *Peters v Fleming* (1840) 6 M & W 42.
2 (1866) 14 LT 24 at 26.
3 (1868) LR 3 Exch 90 at 96.
4 (1869) LR 4 Exch 32 (affg. (1868) LR 3 Exch 90).
5 [1908] 2 KB 1, CA.

Contracts for necessary services for the minor

16.4 These must satisfy the same tests as contracts for necessary goods. In *Chapple v Cooper*[1], the following examples of necessary services were given: education, training for a trade, and medical advice. Of course, as was emphasised in that case, whether services are necessaries in a particular case·depends on the state and condition of the minor. In *Chapple v Cooper*, funeral expenses for the minor's husband, who had died leaving no estate to defray them, were held to be necessaries; it was stated that necessaries for a minor included necessaries for the minor's spouse or child so that a contract for such necessaries is also valid.

---

1   (1844) 13 M & W 252.

General points concerning contracts for necessaries

16.5   a. A contract which would otherwise be enforceable against the minor as a contract for necessaries cannot be so enforced if it contains terms which are harsh or onerous on him[1].

b. A question of some importance is whether a contract for necessaries can be enforced against a minor if it is still executory. In other words, can a minor be sued if he repudiates the contract before the necessary goods have been delivered or the necessary services performed? The answer depends on whether the minor's liability arises *consensu* (because he has made the contract) or *re* (because the necessaries have been supplied or performed). If liability arises *consensu* the minor is liable under the contract and can be sued for breach if he repudiates the contract while it is still executory. If liability arises *re* the minor is liable only under the law of quasi-contract; he is liable not because he agreed but because the necessary was supplied or performed.

Although the matter is not entirely free from doubt, it seems that in the case of contracts for necessary goods a minor is only liable if the goods have actually been delivered and cannot be sued if he repudiates the contract before delivery[2]. In this context it may also be noted that the Sale of Goods Act 1893, s.2, provides that where necessary goods are sold and delivered to a minor he must pay a reasonable price for them, which is not necessarily the contract price.

Unlike a contract for necessary goods, a contract for necessary services is enforceable against a minor even though it is executory when the minor repudiates it. The authority is *Roberts v Gray*[3]. Roberts was a famous billiards player. He agreed to take Gray, a minor, on a world billiards tour and to pay his expenses. This was a contract for necessary services, a contract for education and instruction, because its object was to instruct Gray in the profession of a billiards player. Roberts spent time and trouble and incurred liabilities in making preparations for the tour, but before the tour began Gray repudiated the contract. The Court of Appeal held that Roberts could recover damages even though Gray had not received any instruction from him.

---

1   *Fawcett v Smethurst* (1914) 84 LJKB 473.
2   *Nash v Inman* [1908] 2 KB 1 at 8, (contrast p.12), CA; *Pontypridd Union v Drew* [1927] 1 KB 214 at 220, CA.
3   [1913] 1 KB 520, CA.

Contracts of employment or apprenticeship and analogous contracts
16.6 Such a contract is valid and enforceable against the minor even though executory. In *Clements v London and North Western Rly Co*[1], a minor entered into a contract of employment as a porter with the railway company, promising to accept the terms of an insurance scheme to which the company contributed, and to forego any claims he might have against the company under the Employers' Liability Act 1880. The terms of the scheme were in some ways more beneficial to him and in other ways less beneficial than those of the Act. It was held that the contract, taken as a whole, was for his benefit and that he was bound by it. This case can be contrasted with *De Francesco v Barnum*[2]. An apprenticeship deed was made between a minor, aged 14, and the plaintiff. The minor bound herself apprentice to the plaintiff for seven years to learn dancing. In the deed she agreed not to take any professional engagement without the plaintiff's consent, nor to marry. She was to be paid for any performances she might give, but there was no provision for other pay, nor did the plaintiff undertake to find her other work. The minor accepted a professional engagement with the defendant without the consent of the plaintiff, who then sued the defendant for inducing a breach of the apprenticeship deed. The plaintiff's success depended on whether the deed was enforceable against the minor. Fry, J, held that the deed was unenforceable because on the whole it was not beneficial to the minor, being unreasonably harsh and oppressive.

---

1   [1894] 2 QB 482, CA.
2   (1889) 43 Ch D 165, CA.

16.7 'Analogous contracts' in this context include contracts whereby a minor earns a fee in his profession or occupation, or obtains a licence to follow his profession or occupation or becomes a member of a professional body. In *Doyle v White City Stadium Ltd*[1], a minor made a contract with the second defendants, the British Board of Boxing Control, whereby he agreed to be bound by the Board's rules in all his professional fights in consideration of receiving a professional boxer's licence. One of the Board's rules was that prize money or fees could be withheld from a boxer who had been disqualified. These rules were incorporated in a contract which the minor made to fight for the heavyweight championship of Great Britain for £3,000. The minor was disqualified for hitting below the belt in breach of the rules and the promoter paid the £3,000 to the Board pending an inquiry. The Board withheld the £3,000. It was held that the minor could not recover that sum: the rules were binding on him since the contract with the Board was, on the whole, for his benefit because the rules encouraged clean fighting. Another case involving an 'analogous contract' is *Chaplin v*

Leslie Frewin (Publishers) Ltd[2]. The plaintiff, a minor and a son of Charlie Chaplin, contracted in return for an advance on royalties to give the defendant publishers the exclusive rights to publish his autobiography, entitled 'I couldn't smoke the grass on my father's lawn'. Later he alleged that the completed work, written by ghost writers with his assistance, showed him to be a depraved creature and he sought to repudiate the contract. By a majority, the Court of Appeal held that he could not do so. The contract was binding on him since it was, on the whole, beneficial to him: it would enable him to start as an author and to earn money to keep himself and his wife and child.

---

1   [1935] 1 KB 110, CA.
2   [1966] Ch 71, [1965] 3 All ER 764, CA.

16.8   For no apparent reason, a minor's trading contract does not fall within the present heading and is not enforceable against him however beneficial to him it may be. For instance, in *Cowern v Nield*[1], it was held that a contract to deliver hay could not be enforced against a hay and straw dealer who was a minor, and therefore he was not obliged to return the purchase price despite his non-delivery. Similarly, in *Mercantile Union Guarantee Corpn Ltd v Ball*[2], it was held that a minor who was a haulage contractor was not liable to pay the hire-purchase instalments on a lorry which he had purchased for use in his business.

---

1   [1912] 2 KB 419, DC.
2   [1937] 2 KB 498, [1937] 3 All ER 1, CA.

Voidable contracts

16.9   A person who makes one of these voidable contracts while he is a minor is bound by it, unless and until he expressly repudiates it during minority or within a reasonable time of attaining his majority. An adult party to such a contract cannot repudiate it[1] but, of course, he will no longer be bound by the contract if the person who contracted as a minor makes a valid repudiation. There are four types of voidable contract:

a. A contract by a minor to take a lease or to buy land or to let or sell land[2].

b. A contract by a minor to buy shares[3].

c. A contract to bring property into a marriage settlement[4].

d. A partnership agreement. A minor who makes a partnership agreement is in a special position compared with the other types of voidable contract. Although he is entitled to share in the profits resulting from the partnership he is not liable for partnership debts while he is still a minor; but once he attains majority he can be sued for subsequent partnership debts, unless he has repudiated the partnership agreement before the debt in question was incurred and given adequate notice of repudiation to people dealing with the partnership[5].

Apart from the present types of contract and the valid contracts mentioned above, a contract made by a minor is invalid. The present types of contract are said to be voidable because under them the minor acquires an interest in property of a fairly permanent nature to which continuous rights and duties attach. It would be unjust, the argument continues, to let the minor retain the benefits without fulfilling the obligations and this is prevented by making the contract voidable. This explanation is open to the objection that it could equally apply to other contracts made by a minor which are void in law. Moreover, it is possible to envisage a voidable contract of the present type which does not involve continuous rights and duties thereunder, as in the case of the purchase of freehold land for a lump sum.

1 *Clayton v Ashdown* (1714) 2 Eq Cas Abr 516.
2 *Whittington v Murdy* (1889) 60 LT 956; *Davies v Beynon-Harris* (1931) 47 TLR 424.
3 *North Western Rly Co v M'Michael* (1850) 5 Exch 114.
4 *Edwards v Carter* [1893] AC 360, HL.
5 *Goode v Harrison* (1821) 5 B & Ald 147.

The time of repudiation

16.10 A voidable contract can be repudiated during minority or within a reasonable time of reaching majority. A repudiation during minority is not conclusive and can be withdrawn within a reasonable time of majority[1]. It depends on the facts of each case whether a repudiation after majority was within a reasonable time of reaching that age. In *Edwards v Carter*[2], a minor became a party to a marriage settlement under which he benefited. He covenanted to bring into the settlement any property he might receive under his father's will. One month later he reached majority. Nearly four years later his father died leaving him property. More than a year after his father's death he purported to repudiate the settlement. The House of Lords held that he had not repudiated within a reasonable time of majority. It held that in determining reasonableness of time it was irrelevant that for most of the time the ex-minor had been ignorant of his right to repudiate and, moreover, could not decide whether or not it was beneficial for him to repudiate until he knew what his father had left him.

1 *North Western Rly Co v M'Michael* (1850) 5 Exch 114 at 127.
2 [1893] AC 360, HL.

Effect of repudiation

16.11 Repudiation relieves the minor or former minor from contractual liabilities accruing after his repudiation[1], but it is uncertain in the light of conflicting dicta whether repudiation relieves him from liabilities which have accrued before repudiation[2].

A person who exercises the right to repudiate the voidable contract cannot recover money paid under it unless there has been a total failure of consideration, which will not occur unless he has received nothing of what he has bargained for[3]. This is demonstrated by *Steinberg v Scala*[4]. The plaintiff, a minor, applied for, and was allotted, shares in a company. She paid the amounts due on application and allotment, and also on the first call. She received no dividends and after 18 months claimed to repudiate the allotment and recover the money she had paid. The Court of Appeal held that, while she could repudiate the contract and thereby avoid liability for future calls, she could not recover what she had already paid because she had got the shares she bargained for and it was immaterial that she had not received any real benefit by way of dividends: there had been no total failure of consideration.

---

1 *Steinberg v Scala (Leeds) Ltd* [1923] 2 Ch 452, CA.
2 Contrast *North Western Rly Co v M'Michael* (1850) 5 Exch 114 at 125 (retrospective) with *Blake v Concannon* (1870) Ir 4 CL 323 (not retrospective). There is dicta in support of both views in the Court of Appeal decision in *Steinberg v Scala (Leeds) Ltd.*
3 *Corpe v Overton* (1833) 10 Bing 252.
4 [1923] 2 Ch 452, CA.

Contracts governed by the Infants Relief Act 1874, s.1

16.12 At common law all contracts made by a minor, other than those previously described, were *negatively* voidable in that they did not bind the minor unless he ratified them within a reasonable time of reaching the age of majority. Negative voidability must be sharply distinguished from the positive voidability of the contracts just mentioned, which bind the minor ab initio and continue to do so unless and until he repudiates before, or within a reasonable time after, attaining majority. The negatively voidable type of minor's contract was abolished by the Infants Relief Act 1874.

16.13 Section 1 of the Infants Relief Act 1874 provides that the following contracts are 'absolutely void', whether made under seal or not:

a. *Contracts for the repayment of money lent or to be lent to a minor*
Thus, any loan of money to a minor is irrecoverable, even if the money

was lent to buy necessaries. However, if money is lent for this purpose and is actually spent on it by the minor, the lender is subrogated to the rights of the seller and has the same right of recovery of the purchase price that the seller would have had if not paid[1].

b. *Contracts for goods (other than necessary goods) supplied or to be supplied to a minor* This head covers contracts of exchange[2], of hire and of hire-purchase[3], as well as contracts of sale.

c. *Accounts stated* An account stated is merely the acknowledgement by a debtor that he owes a sum certain to his creditor. Nowadays it is merely prima facie evidence of this debt, and this evidence may be rebutted by proof that there is no debt, or no valid debt, owing at all[4]. Thus, the inclusion of account stated in the list of 'absolutely void' contracts appears unnecessary.

---

1 *Re National Permanent Benefit Building Society* (1869) LR 5 Ch App 309 at 313.
2 *Pearce v Brain* [1929] 2 KB 310, DC.
3 *Yeoman Credit Ltd v Latter* [1961] 2 All ER 294 at 296, CA.
4 *Siqueira v Noronha* [1934] AC 332 at 337, PC.

The effects of s.1 on the three types of contract
16.14 The use of the words 'absolutely void' suggests that these contracts are complete nullities and of no legal effect, but this suggestion is not totally correct. The effects of one of these absolutely void contracts are as follows:

a. The contract cannot be enforced against the minor. Moreover, a ratification of a debt under such a contract, or a fresh promise to pay, made after attaining majority does not, by virtue of s.2 of the Act of 1874, make the debt enforceable[1].

b. In the absence of authority, it would seen that the words 'absolutely void' render the contract unenforceable by the minor.

c. With one exception, the contract is of no legal effect for other purposes. In *R v Wilson*[2], it was held that a minor could not be made bankrupt in respect of debts which were void under s.1. Similarly, it was held in *Coutts & Co v Brown-Lecky*[3], that a guarantee by an adult of a minor's overdraft with a bank was itself void and unenforceable since, the loan by way of overdraft being void, there was no 'debt' to be guaranteed. It should be noted, however, that lenders of money to minors are not completely unprotected: if they get an indemnity against loss from an adult this can be enforced against him. This is shown by *Yeoman Credit Ltd v Latter*[4]. The plaintiff company lent a minor money and got the second defendant, an adult, to indemnify them. The indemnity was held enforceable by the Court of Appeal on the ground that its object was to protect the plaintiff company against loss rather than to make good the minor's legally non-existent debt. As Harman, LJ, pointed out, the distinction between a guarantee and an indemnity raises 'hair-splitting distinctions of exactly that kind which brings the law into hatred, ridicule and contempt by the public'. In cases of doubt the court will lean in favour of construing a contract between the creditor and adult as being intended to be one of indemnity, rather than of guarantee of the minor's debt[5].

The exceptional case where the present type of contract does have legal effect is that the property passes in goods delivered to the minor under a void contract[6]. This rule has the merit of protecting those who purchase the goods from the minor but it may be contrasted with the rule that property does not pass on delivery under a contract void for mistake[7].

d. Money paid, or property transferred, under the void contract by the minor is only recoverable by him if there has been a total failure of consideration, which will only occur if the minor received nothing of what he bargained for. In *Pearce v Brain*[8], a minor exchanged his motor cycle for the defendant's car. The car broke down after 70 miles. The contract, being for the supply of non-necessary goods, was void under s.1 but it was held that the minor could not recover the motor cycle because he had got what he had bargained for (the car) and there was therefore no total failure of consideration.

---

1 The Betting and Loans (Infants) Act 1892, s.5, extends the minor's protection. It provides that an agreement by a person of full age to repay money lent to him during his minority, together with any negotiable instrument given to give effect to the agreement, shall be absolutely void.
2 (1879) 5 QBD 28.
3 [1947] KB 104, [1946] 2 All ER 207, DC.
4 [1961] 2 All ER 294, CA.
5 *Yeoman Credit Ltd v Latter.*
6 *Stocks v Wilson* [1913] 2 KB 235 at 246.
7 Para. 13.1.
8 [1929] 2 KB 310; relying on *Valentini v Canali* (1889) 24 QBD 166, DC.

Other invalid contracts

16.15 This head covers all contracts made by a minor which are not for necessaries or of beneficial employment, etc., not positively voidable by him, nor absolutely void under the Infants Relief Act 1874, s.1. Contracts covered by this heading therefore include contracts for the supply of goods, or the loan of money, *by* a minor, contracts to render non-necessary services to a minor and contracts of employment made by a minor which are not beneficial to him. These contracts are governed by common law rules, as amended by the Act of 1874, s.2, and their effect is:

a. They do not bind the minor.

b. They bind the adult party[1] but, while the minor may recover damages, the minor cannot obtain specific performance of the contract[2].

c. It appears that a minor can only recover money paid, or property transferred, under the contract if there has been a total failure of consideration.

d. In certain cases such a contract made by a minor becomes binding on him if he makes a fresh promise to perform after reaching majority.

At common law these contracts were of the *negatively* voidable type referred to in para. 16.12, so that they became binding on the minor if he *ratified* them within a reasonable time of reaching majority. This rule was amended by the Infants Relief Act 1874, s.2, which provides that a debt contracted during minority cannot be rendered enforceable against the minor by a promise to pay (or by ratification of the debt) made after majority, nor is the promise to pay in itself enforceable[3]. In the case of contracts other than those giving rise to a debt on the part of the minor, such as a contract by a minor to supply goods, s.2 provides that they can no longer be made enforceable against him by virtue of his ratification after majority. However, if the former minor makes a fresh promise to perform after reaching majority the promise is enforceable. Whether there has been mere ratification or a fresh promise is a difficult question of fact, depending on the former minor's intentions. It is unlikely that a court will infer a fresh promise unless new terms supplementing or varying the original contract are introduced after majority[4].

---

1 *Bruce v Warwick* (1815) 6 Taunt 118.
2 *Flight v Bolland* (1828) 4 Russ 298.
3 *Smith v King* [1892] 2 QB 543.
4 *Ditcham v Worrall* (1880) 5 CPD 410; *Brown v Harper* (1893) 68 LT 488.

Liability for torts connected with contracts

16.16 Generally, a minor is liable for his torts, but he is not so liable if he commits a tort in performing or procuring a contract which is not binding on him, otherwise such a contract could be indirectly enforced by means of a tortious action. Thus, in *Jennings v Rundall*[1], a minor who had hired a mare and injured her by excessive and improper riding was held not liable in tort, and in *R. Leslie Ltd v Sheill*[2], it was held that a minor who obtained a loan of money by a fraudulent misrepresentation as to his age was not liable in the tort of deceit.

The only exception to the rule, that a tortious action cannot be brought for a tort connected with a contract which is not binding on the minor, is where the minor does something, which is not simply a wrongful performance of something authorised or contemplated by the contract, but is the performance of something prohibited by the contract or not contemplated by it. An example is *Burnard v Haggis*[3]. A minor hired a mare for riding and was given strict instructions 'not to jump or lark with her'. He lent her to a friend who jumped her, causing fatal injuries. The minor was held liable in tort because the jumping was a prohibited act, *Jennings v Rundall* being distinguished on the ground that the minor there had not done a prohibited act but merely an authorised act (riding) improperly. A more modern case is *Ballett v Mingay*[4], where the plaintiff lent the defendant, a minor, a microphone and amplifier at a weekly rent. The defendant delivered these improperly to X. The Court of Appeal held that the defendant was liable in tort because parting with possession of the goods fell outside the purview of the contract.

1 (1799) 8 Term Rep 335.
2 [1914] 3 KB 607, CA.
3 (1863) 14 CB NS 45.
4 [1943] KB 281, [1943] 1 All ER 143, CA.

Restitution for fraud by the minor

16.17 The most common fraudulent misrepresentation in this context is that the minor is over the age of majority. A minor who induces a contract which is *not otherwise binding on him* by fraud is not only not liable in tort[1], but is also not liable on the contract or in quasi-contract[2]. However, as a matter of equitable intervention, it may be possible to order the restitution of what the minor obtained under such a contract, since equity required a minor who obtained an advantage by fraud to restore his ill-gotten gains, although it scrupulously stopped short of enforcing the contractual obligation against him[3]. Restitution for fraud is best discussed by distinguishing these three types of case:

a. Where the minor obtains goods by fraud and remains in possession of them an order for restitution can clearly be made, as in *Clarke v Cobley*[4], where a minor was ordered to restore two promissory notes which he had obtained by fraud in return for his execution of a (void) bond.

b. Where the minor obtains a loan of money by fraud restitution cannot be ordered, unless, as is unlikely, he still possesses the actual notes or coins and they can be identified. The leading authority is *R. Leslie Ltd v Sheill*[5], where registered moneylenders lent a minor £400 after he had represented he was of full age. The minor spent the £400 and the moneylenders' claim for the restitution of the money was dismissed by the Court of Appeal on the ground that to compel the minor to refund the money would be an indirect enforcement of the void contract of loan, not a restoration of ill-gotten gains.

c. Where the minor obtains goods by fraud but ceases to possess them because he has sold or exchanged them it would seem in principle that it should not be possible to order him to restore their proceeds because this would be equivalent to enforcing the contract. However, restoration was ordered in such circumstances in *Stocks v Wilson*[6], where the minor was ordered to account for the proceeds of sale. Lush, J's, decision in this case is hard to reconcile with that of the Court of Appeal in *R. Leslie Ltd v Sheill*, since an order for account is in effect enforcing the contract rather than restoring ill-gotten gains. The decision in *Stocks v Wilson* was criticised, but not overruled, in *Sheill's* case.

---

1 Para. 16.16.
2 *Levene v Brougham* (1909) 25 TLR 265, CA; *R. Leslie Ltd v Sheill* [1914] 3 KB 607, CA.
3 *R. Leslie Ltd v Sheill* [1914] 3 KB 607 at 618.
4 (1789) 2 Cox Eq Cas 173.
5 [1914] 3 KB 607, CA.
6 [1913] 2 KB 235.

16.18 The law concerning the contractual capacity of minors is less important now that the age of majority has been reduced to 18. The rules discussed above are not only unduly complex but they are also unsatisfactory in that the balance between the protection of the adult and minor parties to a contract is unduly weighted in favour of the minor. There is good reason for making certain contracts unenforceable against the minor but it seems wrong that, subject to restitution for fraud, he should be able to retain what he has received under such a contract while refusing to perform his side of the bargain.

MENTALLY DISORDERED AND INTOXICATED PERSONS

16.19 If the Court of Protection[1] has assumed jurisdiction to manage the property and affairs of a person suffering from mental disorder, its powers include making contracts for the benefit of that person and carrying out contracts already made by him[2]. It is possible that such a person is absolutely incapable of entering into a contract which binds him; certainly, he cannot make one purporting to dispose of property since this would interfere with the Court's jurisdiction[3].

Apart from this, mentally disordered persons generally have full contractual capacity, although their contracts may be voidable in the circumstances outlined next.

If a mentally disordered or intoxicated person proves that he was incapable, at the time of making the contract, of understanding its nature *and* that the other party knew of this, the contract is voidable at his option[4]. This option can only be exercised when the person is of sane and sober understanding, and if he decides to affirm the contract rather than avoid it he is bound by it[5].

---

1 Para. 2.37.
2 Mental Health Act 1959, s.103.
3 *Re Walker* [1905] 1 Ch 160, CA; *Re Marshall* [1920] 1 Ch 284.
4 *Imperial Loan Co v Stone* [1892] 1 QB 599, CA.
5 *Matthews v Baxter* (1873) LR 8 Exch 132.

16.20 A person who is not contractually liable under the above rules is nevertheless liable to pay a reasonable price for necessary goods sold *and delivered* to him since the Sale of Goods Act 1893, s.2, which has already been mentioned in relation to minors' contracts[1], also applies to persons who are incompetent to contract 'by reason of mental incapacity or drunkenness'.

---

1 Para. 16.5. b.

CORPORATIONS AND UNINCORPORATED ASSOCIATIONS

16.21 We dealt with the contractual capacity of corporations and unincorporated associations in paras. 4.8 to 4.16.

Chapter 17
Quasi - Contract

17.1 In certain cases a person is required by law to pay money to another on the ground that he would be unjustly enriched if he was entitled to retain it. For historical reasons, such cases are known as quasi-contracts, which is somewhat misleading because the liability to pay does not arise from any agreement between the parties concerned but is imposed by law. Quasi-contractual obligations only relate to the payment of money: they do not extend to the transfer of other property.

Quasi-contracts can be divided into the following types:

money paid by the plaintiff to the use of the defendant;

money had and received by the defendant to the use of the plaintiff;

quantum meruit;

money had and received by the defendant from a third party to the use of the plaintiff.

Money paid by the plaintiff to the use of the defendant

Payment which relieves the other of a legal liability to pay
17.2 This covers two types of case. The first is where P pays money to T and, although P is liable to pay the money to T, the principal liability to pay, as between P and D, was on D. In such a case P can recover the money paid from D, as is shown by *Brook's Wharf and Bull Wharf Ltd v Goodman Bros*[1]. The defendants imported skins from Russia and stored them in the plaintiffs' bonded warehouse. The skins were stolen, without any negligence on the plaintiffs' part, but they were required to pay the customs duty on them. By statute, the plaintiffs were liable to pay the duty, although the primary liability was on the defendants. It was held that the plaintiffs could recover the amount of duty paid because they had been compelled by law to pay money for which the defendants were primary liable. Under the present

331

principle a guarantor who pays the debt of the principal debtor is entitled to be indemnified by him for that amount, and a co-guarantor who has paid more than his due share is entitled to a contribution from the other co-guarantor[2].

The second type of case is where P discharges D's legal liability to T under compulsion. Thus, if P, a tenant, pays the rent owed by D, his landlord, to T, a superior landlord, to prevent distress by T, D must pay P the amount paid by him.

---

1   [1937] 1 KB 534, [1936] 3 All ER 696.
2   Paras. 26.34 and 26.35.

Money paid at the request of the other
17.3   This is a very different sort of case. If P pays money to T at the express or implied request of D, P can recover that sum from D[1].

---

1   *Brewer Street Investments Ltd v Barclays Woollen Co Ltd* [1954] 1 QB 428, [1953] 2 All ER 1330, CA.

Money had and received by the defendant to the use of the plaintiff

Money paid under a mistake of fact
17.4   Money paid under a mistake of fact which, if true, would have entitled the payee to payment is recoverable by the payer. In *Kelly v Solari*[1], for example, the plaintiff was the director of a life insurance company which had paid out insurance money to the defendant under her husband's life insurance policy. The policy had, in fact, lapsed because the last premium had not been paid. The company had noted this, but the lapse had been overlooked when the defendant claimed the money. It was held that the plaintiff could recover the money because it had been paid under a mistaken belief in facts which, if true, would have entitled the defendant to payment.

A vexed question is whether, as in *Kelly v Solari*, the mistake must have led the plaintiff to believe facts which, if true, would have meant that he was *legally* obliged to pay. Although this requirement has been re-iterated in a number of cases[2], the Court of Appeal in *Larner v LCC*[3] held that money paid under a mistake of fact which, if true, would have morally (but not legally) obliged its payment was recoverable. The LCC passed a resolution to make up the pay of their employees who were on war service to the amount of their civil salaries. L was one of their employees and he joined the RAF. Although he had agreed to inform the LCC of any increase in his service wages, he failed to do so and, consequently, was overpaid by the LCC. If the facts had been as supposed, the LCC would only have been morally, not legally[4], obliged to make the payments, but the mistake was held to be sufficient to entitle the Council to recover the amount of the over-payment. *Larner v LCC* can be contrasted with *Morgan v Ashcroft*[5], where the Court of Appeal held that a bookmaker who had mistakenly overpaid a client could not recover the excess because, inter alia, even if the facts had been as they had been believed to be, the bookmaker would not have been legally liable to pay gaming winnings[6]. However, dicta in this case suggest that a *voluntary* payment might be recoverable if the mistake was sufficiently fundamental, e.g. as to the identity of the payee or the substantial nature of the transaction.

Subject to what we have just said, if the mistake of fact was induced by a third person, the payment can nevertheless be recovered from the payee[7].

---

1 (1841) 9 M & W 54.
2 E.g. *Aiken v Short* (1856) 1 H & N 210 at 215; *Maskell v Horner* [1915] 3 KB 106.
3 [1949] 2 KB 683, [1949] 1 All ER 964, CA.
4 Para. 6.3.
5 [1938] 1 KB 49, [1937] 3 All ER 92, CA.
6 Para. 15.6.
7 *R. E. Jones Ltd v Waring & Gillow Ltd* [1926] AC 670, HL.

17.5 The mistake must be one of fact: money paid under a mistake of law is not recoverable, generally. A mistake as to the construction of a statute[1], or of regulations[2], or of a contract[3], is one of law, but a mistake as to the existence of a private right, such as a person's title to property, is, oddly enough, regarded as a mistake of fact[4]. An exception to the general rule is that if money is paid to an officer of the court, such as a trustee in bankruptcy or a solicitor, under a mistake of law it is recoverable[5].

---

1 *National Pari-Mutuel Association Ltd v R* (1930) 37 TLR 110.
2 *Holt v Markham* [1923] 1 KB 504, CA.
3 *Ord v Ord* [1923] 2 KB 432.
4 *Cooper v Phibbs* (1867) LR 2 HL 149, HL.
5 *Re Condon, ex parte James* (1874) 9 Ch App 609, CA.

Money paid under improper pressure
17.6 Money paid under improper pressure on the part of the payee is recoverable if, quite apart from the pressure, the payer was not legally obliged to pay it[1].

---

1 *Maskell v Horner* [1915] 3 KB 106.

Money paid in pursuance of an ineffective contract

17.7 a. *Money paid in pursuance of a void or illegal contract* Money paid in pursuance of a void contract is generally recoverable, except in the case of a gaming contract and in certain other cases.

Money paid under an illegal contract is generally not recoverable but we would remind the reader of the exceptional cases where it is, which we enumerated in para. 15.63.

b. *Total failure of consideration* Here we are concerned with the case where the plaintiff has deposited or paid money in pursuance of a contract which is perfectly valid but is rendered ineffective by a total failure of consideration on the part of the defendant (i.e. a total failure to perform his part of the contract). In such a case the plaintiff has an option[2], either

   i. to rescind the contract for breach, in which case he can recover the money which he has paid under quasi-contract[3], or

   ii. to seek damages for its breach.

Thus, if P pays D £500 as a deposit on a car but D fails to supply the car, P can rescind the contract and recover the £500 which he paid.

If the failure of consideration is not total but only partial, the quasi-contractual action for the recovery of money paid is not available, so that, whether the contract is rescinded or not, the appropriate remedy is an action for damages for breach of contract. There will only be a total failure of consideration if the plaintiff has not got any part of what he bargained for. Thus, if P employs D to build a house for him and pays in advance, and D abandons the work before it is finished, P cannot recover any part of his payment and must claim damages for breach of contract[4]. However, if —

   i. the partial performance is such as to entitle the plaintiff to rescind the contract, and he elects to do so, and

   ii. he is able to restore what he has received under the contract, and does so before he has derived any benefit from it[5],

he will bring about a total failure of consideration and be entitled to recover any money which he has paid[6]. A common example of this is where the buyer of defective goods rejects them immediately and claims back his payment.

For the sake of completeness, we must add that in a contract for the sale of goods or of hire-purchase, there will be a total failure of consideration if the seller or bailor fails to pass a good title to the goods to the buyer or bailee, even though the buyer or bailee has derived benefit from them before being deprived of them by the true owner. It follows that the buyer or bailee can recover what he has paid for the goods. In *Rowland v Divall*[7], the plaintiff bought a car from the defendants for £334 and used it for four months. It then transpired that the car had been stolen, although the defendant had dealt with it in good faith, and the plaintiff had to surrender it to the true owner. The Court of Appeal held that the defendant was in breach of the implied condition in the Sale of Goods Act 1893, s.12(1)[8], and the plaintiff was entitled to recover the £334 which he had paid. Its reasoning was that the plaintiff had not received what he had contracted to receive, viz. the property and right to possession of the car, and therefore there was a total failure of consideration entitling him to recover the whole purchase price without any set-off for his use of the car. The decision that there had been a total failure of consideration seems somewhat strained when the buyer had had four months' use of the car before he had to return it to the true owner.

So far we have assumed that the total failure of consideration constitutes a breach of contract. If it does not, e.g. because there is a lawful excuse for the failure, money paid may nevertheless be recovered under the present principle, but the reader is reminded that where the total failure of consideration is due to the frustration of the contract the situation will normally be governed by the Law Reform (Frustrated Contracts) Act 1943[9].

c. *Money paid by party in breach of contract* If a party who has made an advance payment under the contract then refuses, in breach of contract, to perform it, e.g. to take delivery of goods which he has agreed to buy, he can recover his payment if it was intended to be a part-payment of the purchase price, unless the contract otherwise provides[10]. On the other hand, if his advance payment was intended as a deposit (i.e. a guarantee that he would perform his side of the contract) it is not recoverable[11], unless the contract otherwise provides[12].

---

1 Para. 15.5. Also see para. 16.14, d.
2 Paras. 10.3—10.8.
3 *Wilkinson v Lloyd* (1845) 7 QB 27.
4 *Whincup v Hughes* (1871) LR 6 CP 78.
5 *Hunt v Silk* (1804) 5 East 449.
6 *Baldry v Marshall* [1925] 1 QB 260.
7 [1923] 2 KB 500, CA. See also *Warman v Southern Counties Car Finance Corpn Ltd* [1949] 2 KB 576, [1949] 1 All ER 711 (a hire-purchase case).
8 Para. 22.43.
9 Paras. 11.15—11.18.
10 *Mayson v Clouet* [1924] AC 980.
11 *Harrison v Holland* [1921] 3 KB 297 (affd. [1922] 1 KB 211).
12 *Palmer v Temple* (1839) 9 Ad & El 508.

Quantum meruit

17.8 A *quantum meruit* is a claim for reasonable remuneration for services performed or things supplied. Sometimes, the remedy is contractual in that it enables a reasonable remuneration to be recovered under a contract which has not fixed a precise sum. We have mentioned examples of this in the relevant parts of this book[1] and confine ourselves here to quasi-contractual *quantum meruit* claims. These can be made in the following cases:

a. Where the other party to a contract unjustifiably prevents the plaintiff (who has partly performed his contractual obligations) completing them, as where he states that he will not accept performance or renders performance impossible, and the plaintiff has elected to rescind the contract. Here, the remedy of a *quantum meruit* is an alternative to an action for damages, and may be less generous[2].

b. Where the plaintiff has performed services in pursuance of a contract which is void. For example, in *Craven-Ellis v Canons Ltd*[3], the plaintiff was employed as the managing director of a company under a contract which was void because the directors who made it were not qualified to act. It was held by the Court of Appeal that the plaintiff could recover reasonable remuneration on a *quantum meruit* for services rendered under the contract.

c. Where necessary goods are supplied to minors, or to mentally disordered or drunken persons, they are liable to pay a reasonable price for them, and the basis of this liability is quasi-contractual[4].

---

1 Paras. 5.19, 5.25, 18.21 for example.
2 Para. 12.17.
3 [1936] 2 KB 403, [1936] 3 All ER 1066, CA.
4 Paras. 16.5, b, 16.20.

Money had and received by the defendant from a third party to the use of the plaintiff

17.9 The following two situations are among those comprehended by this heading:

a. Where a deposit or other sum of money is paid to a stakeholder pending the determination of the entitlement of two persons to it, the person who becomes entitled to it can recover it[1].

b. Where D receives money from T, or is otherwise under a monetary obligation (e.g. a debt) to T, and he is instructed by T to pay the money to P, and he promises P that he will pay him, P may recover the money from T[2].

---

1 *Sadler v Smith* (1869) LR 5 QB 40.
2 *Shamia v Joory* [1958] 1 QB 448, [1958] 1 All ER 111.

Chapter 18
Agency

18.1 The words 'agent' and 'agency' are familiar ones. The expressions 'estate agent' and 'travel agent' are equally well known. Company directors may act as agents of their companies, accountants as agents of their clients and auctioneers as agents of the vendors (and sometimes the purchasers as well) of property. These agents, indeed all agents, share several basic characteristics and are subject to the same legal rules. Agency is the relationship between two legal persons, whereby one person, the principal, appoints another, the agent, to act on his behalf in effecting a transaction. Agents are usually appointed by contract and they may be authorised to make contracts or undertake other tasks on behalf of their principal. For example, an agent may, sign documents on behalf of his principal[1] unless a statute requires personal signature[2], execute deeds if duly authorised[3], or execute a bill of sale[4]. In addition, he may render his principal liable for his torts[5].

---

1 *LCC v Agricultural Food Products Ltd* [1955] 2 QB 218, [1955] 2 All ER 229, CA.
2 For example, under certain provisions of the Bankruptcy Act 1914.
3 *Steiglitz v Egginton* (1815) Holt NP 141; para. 18.45.
4 *Furnivall v Hudson* [1893] 1 Ch 335.
5 For example, *Lloyd v Grace, Smith & Co* [1912] AC 716, HL; and see also paras. 18.32, 18.37 and 21.30.

Other relationships contrasted
18.2 *Agents and independent contractors* Whether a person is acting on his own behalf or as the agent of another is not always immediately obvious. Each case turns on its own particular facts. For example, a retailer of vacuum cleaners may be described as 'the agent of X Ltd', manufacturers of vacuum cleaners, but he is not necessarily an agent in the legal sense. If the retailer is contracting on his own behalf and not

on behalf of X Ltd, and if he intends to make a profit on the sale of vacuum cleaners rather than earn commission for conveying orders to X Ltd, he is trading on his own behalf and not as an agent. If he is acting as the agent of X Ltd, then purchasers of vacuum cleaners enter into a contract which binds X Ltd but probably does not bind the agent[1].

Agents and commission merchants If one person appoints another his commission merchant, he appoints that other to effect some transaction on his behalf but he intends the commission merchant to deal in his own name and not to bind his appointer. The relationship of principal and agent exists between appointer and appointee but it is a limited agency, because the 'agent' has no power to affect the legal relationship of the 'principal' and third parties.

---

1 For a discussion of this basic principle of agency, which is an exception to the doctrine of privity, see paras. 18.39 and 18.40.

Three issues
18.3 The three issues with which we are concerned in this chapter are:

a. the relationship of principal and agent; the appointment of agents, their rights and duties and the termination of agency; and

b. the changes in the legal relationship of the principal and third parties which may be effected by an agent; and

c. the legal relationship, if any, between the agent and third parties.

PRINCIPAL AND AGENT

Appointment

18.4 Agency may be created by agreement, express or implied, by ratification or by virtue of necessity. In determining whether a principal (P) has appointed another person to act as his agent (A), it is necessary to decide if P had the capacity to appoint an agent and whether A had the capacity to act as an agent, before considering how an agent is appointed.

Capacity to act as principal or agent
18.5 An agent can be appointed to effect any transaction for which the principal has capacity. However, a principal cannot evade a contractual incapacity by appointing an agent to act on his behalf. A minor can appoint an agent to buy necessaries but cannot enter into

trading contracts merely by the interpositioning of an adult agent[1]. Companies can only made intra vires contracts (contracts within the powers bestowed on them in the memorandum of association[2]) and cannot extend their contractual capacity by the use of an agent[3]. A mentally disordered person can appoint an agent to purchase or obtain necessaries[4]. However, an agent who acts on behalf of a mentally disordered principal has to bear the risk that he may be personally liable for breach of warranty of authority[5]. If such an agent is liable for breach of warranty of authority he is entitled to be indemnified by his mentally disordered principal, unless he knew at the time of acting of his principal's incapacity[6]. An agent who incurs expenses in carrying out the instructions of his mentally disordered principal is entitled to be reimbursed for those expenses.

Anyone not suffering from a mental disorder can act as an agent. A minor can act as agent in a transaction which he would not have capacity to effect on his own behalf. For example, a father could appoint his infant son to purchase non-necessary goods on his behalf even though the infant son could not make a binding contract for non-necessary goods on his own behalf. However, an agent who lacks full contractual capacity can only be made personally liable on those contracts which he would have had capacity to make on his own behalf[7].

---

1 *G(A) v G(T)* [1970] 2 QB 643, [1970] 3 All ER 546, CA.
2 Para. 4.9.
3 But see the effect of the European Communities Act 1972, s.9 on the position of a third party who enters into a contract with a company which the company lacks capacity to make; para. 4.11.
4 For the contractual capacity of a mentally disordered person see paras. 17.19 and 17.20.
5 For breach of warranty of authority, see para. 18.50.
6 *Yonge v Toynbee* [1910] 1 KB 215, CA; *Thacker v Hardy* (1878) 4 QBD 685, CA.
7 *Smally v Smally* (1700) 1 Eq Ca Abr 6; for when an agent is personally liable on contracts see paras. 18.39, 18.45–18.48.

Appointment by express agreement

18.6 An agent may be appointed by express agreement between principal and agent. This agreement is frequently, but not necessarily, a contract. If the appointment is by contract the usual rules for the formation of contracts must be complied with. Normally, the appointment can be made informally even if the agent is to transact contracts which must be evidenced in writing. All that is necessary is a desire to appoint A your agent and consent to act as such. However, in some cases certain formalities are necessary to create agency. For instance, if an agent has to execute a deed his appointment must be by deed[1].

The agreement which appoints the agent will specify the authority which the principal bestows upon the agent, though this may be extended between the parties by implication[2]. The authority of the agent to bind the principal to a contract with a third party may also be extended by ostensible authority[3].

1 *Steiglitz v Egginton* (1815) Holt NP 141, and see also the Powers of Attorney Act 1971, ss. 1 and 7, and para. 18.45 for the consequences of an appointment not under seal.
2 Para. 18.32.
3 Paras. 18.34–18.38.

Appointment by implied agreement

18.7 If the parties have not expressly agreed to become principal and agent it may be possible to find an implied agreement based on their conduct or relationship. If the parties have so conducted themselves towards one another that it would be reasonable for them to assume that they have consented to act as principal and agent, then they are principal and agent[1]. For example, the agent of a finance company or an insurance company may also be held to be the agent of the party seeking finance or insurance if the circumstances warrant an implication of agreement to such an agency relationship[2]. Factors which have been found relevant in determining whether agency has been created by implied agreement are whether one party acts for the other at the other's request and whether commission is payable.

An implied agreement to agency by virtue of the relationship of the parties arises in the case of husband and wife. A wife has authority to pledge her husband's credit for household necessaries even if he has not expressly appointed her his agent[3].

Since there is no express appointment in this case, the authority which the principal bestows upon the agent is implied authority[4]; but, as with agents expressly appointed, agents impliedly appointed may have the power to bind the principal to contracts with third parties by virtue of ostensible authority[5].

1 *Ashford Shire Council v Dependable Motors Pty Ltd* [1961] AC 336, [1961] 1 All ER 96, PC.
2 *Newsholme Bros v Road Transport and General Insurance Co Ltd* [1929] 2 KB 356, CA.
3 *Debenham v Mellon* (1880) 6 App Cas 24, HL.
4 Para. 18.32.
5 Paras. 18.34–18.38.

Ratification

18.8 If a party acts or purports to act for another in a particular transaction, but either has no authority to effect the transaction or exceeds his authority in so doing, he has no power to bind the party for whom he was allegedly acting. A person cannot create himself an agent by purporting to act for someone else, nor bind his principal, if he is an agent, if he exceeds the authority bestowed upon him by his principal. However, the relationship of principal and agent can arise, and unauthorised acts can be validated, by ratification[1]. If the alleged principal ratifies the transaction of the 'agent' this ratification is retrospective — the agent is deemed to have been acting as an authorised agent when he effected the transaction[2]. Thus, the relationship of principal and agent can be created (or authority bestowed or extended) if ratification can and has occurred. However, ratification only creates agency for the past and does not operate for the future, although frequent acts of ratification may create agency by implied agreement or bestow ostensible authority on the 'agent' in future dealings with third parties[3].

---

1 *Wilson v Tunman* (1843) 6 Man & G 236.
2 *Bolton Partners v Lambert* (1889) 41 Ch D 295, CA.
3 *Midland Bank v Reckitt* [1933] AC 1, HL.

18.9 *Effects of ratification* If the principal ratifies a transaction entered into on his behalf he must be taken to have ratified all that transaction and not merely those parts which are to his advantage[1]. The effect of ratification is to make the transaction (which is usually a contract) binding on the principal from the moment it was made by the agent[2]. Since the acts of the agent are retrospectively validated, the agent cannot be liable to a third party for breach of warranty of authority[3] and can claim commission and an indemnity[4]. Once a contract is ratified the agent generally ceases to be liable on the contract. However, ratification cannot deprive a third party of his right to sue the agent for breach of warranty of authority if he has suffered loss despite ratification. Nor can ratification vary rights in property which had vested before ratification[5]. Perhaps the most controversial effect of ratification is that it allows the principal to decide whether to accept a contract or reject it. The third party may repudiate an agreement with the agent because of the agent's lack of authority yet find himself bound by the contract if the principal subsequently ratifies[6]. However, if a contract is made 'subject to ratification' the third party can withdraw prior to ratification and, if he does so, ratification cannot bind him[7]. Because the effects of ratification are at least potentially unfair to third parties, ratification is only possible in some circumstances.

---

1 *Cornwal v Wilson* (1750) 1 Ves Sen 509.
2 *Bolton Partners v Lambert* (1889) 41 Ch D 295, CA.
3 *Smith v Cologan* (1788) 2 TR 188n. For breach of warranty of authority see para. 18.50.

4 *Hartas v Ribbons* (1889) 22 QBD 254, CA. For indemnities see para. 18.23.
5 *Bird v Brown* (1850) 4 Exch 786.
6 *Bolton Partners v Lambert* (1888) 41 Ch D 295, CA.
7 *Warehousing and Forwarding Co of East Africa Ltd v Jafferali & Sons Ltd* [1964] AC 1, [1963] 3 All ER 571, PC.

18.10 *Who can ratify* Only the alleged principal can ratify the actions of his alleged agent and then only if the latter purported to act on his behalf[1]. Therefore, if an agent has not revealed he was acting as an agent, i.e. he has an undisclosed principal, the undisclosed principal cannot ratify. A leading illustration of this is the case of *Keighley, Maxsted & Co v Durant*[2]. In this case an agent purchased wheat at a price which was higher than he had been authorised to pay. The agent had not revealed that he was acting as an agent when he bought the grain, and because of this the House of Lords found the defendant principal was not liable for breach of contract when he refused to accept delivery of the grain, even though he had purported to ratify the contract of sale. Provided that an agent reveals that he is acting as agent, his principal, even though unnamed, can ratify his unauthorised actions[3]. However, an unnamed principal should be identifiable[4], unless, perhaps, the third party has shown that he is uninterested in the identity of the principal. Further, there is a strange provision which provides that unnamed, and possibly unidentifiable, principals can ratify contracts of marine insurance[5].

A company which is a disclosed principal can only ratify if it is in existence at the time the agent enters into any contract[6]. If a company takes the benefit of a pre-incorporation contract it is not liable on it. But the company will be liable if it makes a new contract post-incorporation on the same subject-matter[7]. Any new contract will not be implied merely because the company takes the benefit of the pre-incorporation contract[8] and any new contract is of course only prospective in effect. The agent who makes the pre-incorporation contract on behalf of the non-existent company is personally liable on the contract unless personal liability has been excluded 'by contract or otherwise'[9].

To be able to ratify, the disclosed principal must have had the capacity to make the contract himself at the date when the 'agent' contracted[10].

1 *Wilson v Tumman* (1843) 6 Man & G 236.
2 [1901] AC 240, HL.
3 *Watson v Swann* (1862) 11 CB NS 756.
4 *Ibid.*
5 *Boston Fruit Co v British and Foreign Marine Insurance Co* [1906] AC 336, HL.
6 *Kelner v Baxter* (1866) LR 2 CP 174.
7 *Howard v Patent Ivory Manufacturing Co* (1888) 38 Ch D 156.

8 *Touche v Metropolitan Railway Warehousing Co* (1871) LR 6 Ch App 671.
9 European Communities Act 1972, s.9.
10 *Boston Deep Sea Fishing and Ice Co Ltd v Farnham (Inspector of Taxes)*
   [1957] 3 All ER 204, [1957] 1 WLR 1051.

18.11 *What can be ratified* Apparently any action of an agent can be ratified (even where the agent was seeking to benefit himself) except void acts[1]. An illustration of a void and thus unratifiable action is an unauthorised act on behalf of, but ultra vires, a company[2].

Considerable difficulty has arisen over forged signatures. Such a forgery could be regarded as a void act and in early cases was so regarded. However, subsequent interpretation of the leading case, *Brook v Hook*[3], has suggested that, while forgeries are generally regarded as unratifiable, it is for a different reason. Current opinion is that a forged signature by an agent is unratifiable because in forging a signature the 'agent was not purporting to be an agent' but to be the person whose signature he forged.

---

1 *Re Tiedemann and Ledermann Frères* [1899] 2 QB 66.
2 *Ashbury Railway Carriage and Iron Co v Riche* (1875) LR 7 HL 653; for a discussion of ultra vires see paras. 4.9–4.12.
3 (1871) LR 6 Exch 89.

18.12 *How to ratify* Ratification may be made by express affirmation of the unauthorised actions of the agent by the principal. There is no special form for ratification but it must be done within a reasonable time[1]. How long can elapse before ratification becomes impossible is a question of fact in every case, but certainly if the time for performance of a contract has passed ratification is impossible[2].

Ratification may also be effected by conduct[3], although mere passive acceptance of the benefit of a contract may be insufficient[4], and if the conduct of the purported principal amounts to ratification he cannot repudiate the actions of his agent[5]. Examples of ratification are provided by the following cases. In *Lyell v Kennedy*[6], A received rent from property for many years and the owner sued him for an account of the rents; it was held that the owner's action constituted ratification of such receipts. Similarly, in *Cornwal v Wilson*[7], A bought some goods in excess of the price authorised by P. P objected to the purchase but sold some of the goods; it was held that he had ratified by selling the goods. An action by the alleged principal will only be implied ratification if the principal had a choice of whether to act or not. If the alleged principal had no real choice other than to accept the benefit of the unauthorised actions of his agent, accepting such benefit is not ratification. For example, if an agent has had unauthorised repairs done on a ship, merely retaking the ship with these repairs is not ratification by the principal because if he wished to recover his property he had to have it with the unauthorised repairs[8].

Ratification will, generally, only be implied if the alleged principal has acted with full knowledge of the facts[9]. But, if the alleged principal is prepared to take the risk of what his agent has done, he can choose to ratify without full knowledge. For instance, in *Fitzmaurice v Bayley*[10], an agent entered into an unauthorised contract for the purchase of property. The principal wrote a letter saying he did not know what his agent had done but would stand by all that he had done. This was an express ratification by the principal; he had agreed to bear the risk of being bound by the unauthorised acts of his agent, whatever they were.

---

1 *Re Portuguese Consolidated Copper Mines Ltd* (1890) 45 Ch D 16, CA.
2 *Metropolitan Asylums Board of Managers v Kingham & Sons* (1890) 6 TLR 217.
3 *Lyell v Kennedy* (1889) 14 App Cas 437, HL.
4 *Hughes v Hughes* (1971) 221 Estates Gazette 145, CA.
5 *Cornwal v Wilson* (1750) 1 Ves Sen 509.
6 (1889) 14 App Cas 437, HL.
7 (1750) 1 Ves Sen 509.
8 *Foreman & Co Pty Ltd v The Liddesdale* [1900] AC 190, PC.
9 *The Bonita, The Charlotte* (1861) Lush 252.
10 (1856) 6 E & B 868.

Agency of necessity

18.13 Agency of necessity is a limited exception to the concept that agency is based on a consensual relationship between the parties. When certain emergencies occur, immediate action may be necessary and the courts may be prepared to find that the person taking such action was thereby acting as an agent of necessity. A common example of agency of necessity is that masters of ships faced with an emergency are agents of the shipowner, and have authority to enter into contracts with third parties on behalf of him[1]. Frequently, agency of necessity will merely extend the authority of existing agents but in other cases it may create agency where none existed previously — for example, between masters of ships and cargo owners. In other cases, if a person claims to be an agent of necessity, such agency will only affect the relationship of the alleged principal and agent, and will confer no power on the 'agent' to deal with third parties on behalf of the 'principal'. This type of agency of necessity is more likely than the former if the parties were not already principal and agent; for example, someone who salvages a ship.

Agency of necessity will only arise if the 'agent' has no practical way of communicating with the 'principal'[2], if the action of the 'agent' is reasonably necessary to benefit the 'principal'[3] and if the 'agent' has acted bona fide.

1 *The Gratitudine* (1801) 3 Ch Rob 240.
2 *Springer v Great Western Rly Co* [1921] 1 KB 257, CA.
3 *Burns, Philp & Co Ltd v Gillespie Bros Pty Ltd* (1947) 74 CLR 148.

A postscript
18.14 In some cases a person will be held to have authority to affect the legal relationship of the principal and third parties even if the person whose actions bind the principal is not technically an agent. This is not a method of creating agency between principal and agent but it may result in an alleged principal being unable to deny that his apparent agent was authorised to act on his behalf[1].

1 Paras. 18.34–18.38.

Duties of an agent

18.15 An agent appointed by agreement, express or implied, or an agent of necessity is under certain obligations towards his principal. An agent whose agency is *created* by ratification cannot be under any obligations to his principal since the agency arises retrospectively.

Duty to act
18.16 A paid agent is under a duty to act and any loss suffered by the principal because of failure to act is recoverable by the principal[1]. If the agent does not intend to act he should inform his principal of this fact, but the agent cannot be made liable for failure to perform acts which are illegal or void[2].

1 *Turpin v Bilton* (1843) 5 Man & G 455.
2 *Cohen v Kittell* (1889) 22 QBD 680, DC.

Obeying instructions
18.17 The primary obligation imposed on an agent is to act strictly in accordance with the instructions of his principal insofar as they are lawful and reasonable. If an agent who is appointed to sell goods for cash exchanges them for other goods he is in breach of his duty, however valuable the goods acquired. If an agent carries out his instructions he cannot be liable for loss suffered by the principal because the instructions were at fault[1]. If the instructions which the agent receives are not

complied with he will be responsible to his principal for any loss thereby suffered, even if the loss is not occasioned by any fault of the agent[2]. However, if the instructions received by an agent are ambiguous the agent is not in breach of his duty. if he makes a reasonable but incorrect interpretation of those instructions[3]. If instructions confer a discretion on the agent, the agent will not be liable for failure to obey instructions if he exercises the discretion reasonably[4].

The instructions which an agent should obey may be clarified or extended by virtue of custom or trade usage applying in the trade or profession which the agent follows.

1 *Overend and Gurney Co v Gibb* (1872) LR 5 HL 480.
2 *Lilley v Doubleday* (1881) 7 QBD 510.
3 *Weigall & Co v Runciman & Co* (1916) 85 LJKB 1187, CA.
4 *Boden v French* (1851) 10 CB 886.

Care and skill
18.18   In carrying out his instructions an agent is required to display such care and skill as is reasonably necessary to carry out his duties, and also such care and skill as might reasonably be expected from a person in his profession[1]. For example, an accountant acting as an agent should acquaint himself with such relevant legislation as a competent accountant would, as well as exercising proper care in pursuing his principal's instructions. A gratuitous agent is not under any contractual duty to display care, but he is under a duty of care imposed by the law of tort, subject to the operation of any disclaimer. The duty of care may be overridden by express instructions from the principal.

1 *Beal v South Devon Rly Co* (1864) 3 H & C 337.

Fiduciary duties
18.19   An agent owes a fiduciary duty to his principal because of the confidential relationship between them. There are two fiduciary duties — a duty of disclosure and a duty not to take bribes or make secret profits.

a. *Disclosure*   No fiduciary should put himself in a position where his duty to his principal and his own interests conflict. For instance, an agent cannot sell his property to his principal[1] nor purchase the property of the principal[2] which he is commissioned to sell, unless he has made full disclosure of all relevant facts. However innocent the behaviour of the agent, if duty and interest conflict and there is no full disclosure, any transaction entered into by the agent will be voidable, i.e. subject to rescission, or will not be specifically enforceable, depending on the context. In *Boardman v Phipps*[3], a solicitor, who was the agent of trustees, purchased shares in a company in which the trust was considering investing. The House of Lords said there was a potential conflict between the solicitor's duty to give independent advice to the trustees and his interest in the affairs of the company.

b. *Bribes and secret profits* If an agent is offered a bribe while acting as an agent he is liable to account for such bribe to his principal, even if the bribe was not attended by an evil motive and even if the principal has suffered no loss thereby[4]. The taking of a bribe entitles the principal to dismiss the agent[5], recover any loss suffered thereby from the agent or a third party (as well as the bribe)[6], and entitles him to repudiate any transaction connected with the bribe[7]. The agent also loses his right to commission[8]. A secret profit (or benefit) obtained by the agent in the course of his agency is likewise recoverable by the principal, even if the principal has suffered no loss, or indeed benefited, and even if the agent acted honestly throughout[9]. Any use of the principal's property, including confidential information acquired during the course of the agency, which brings benefits to the agent, is a secret profit and, unless the agent has revealed the position to the principal before the profit is made, he must account for such profit to the principal[10], even if it is made after the agency has terminated.

---

1 *Gillett v Peppercorne* (1840) 3 Beav 78; see para. 15.26.
2 *McPherson v Watt* (1877) 3 App Cas 254, HL.
3 [1967] 2 AC 46, [1966] 3 All ER 721, HL.
4 *Industries and General Mortgage Co Ltd v Lewis* [1949] 2 All ER 573.
5 *Boston Deep Sea Fishing and Ice Co v Ansell* (1888) 39 Ch D 339.
6 *Salford Corpn v Lever* [1891] 1 QB 168, CA.
7 *Taylor v Walker* [1958] 1 Lloyd's Rep 490.
8 *Meadow Schama & Co v C. Mitchell & Co Ltd* (1973) 228 Estates Gazette 1511, CA.
9 *Regal (Hastings) Ltd v Gulliver* [1967] 2 AC 134n, [1942] 1 All ER 378, HL; *Boardman v Phipps* [1967] 2 AC 46, [1966] 3 All ER 721, HL.
10 *Industrial Development Consultants Ltd v Cooley* [1972] 2 All ER 162, [1972] 1 WLR 443. In *Boardman v Phipps* [1967] 2 AC 46, [1966] 3 All ER 721, HL, the solicitor was liable to account for the profits made on the shares. The House of Lords held that he had acquired them by using confidential information even though he acted honestly throughout and his share dealings conferred benefits on the trust.

Other duties
18.20 An agent also has a duty not to delegate his responsibilities to a sub-agent without the authority of the principal[1]. An agent must also pay over to the principal any money received for the use of the principal

in the course of the agency, even if it is claimed by third parties[2], and an agent must keep proper accounts.

---

1 *De Bussche v Alt* (1878) 8 Ch D 286, CA.
2 *Blaustein v Maltz, Mitchell & Co* [1937] 2 KB 142, [1937] 1 All ER 497, CA.

Rights of agents

Remuneration

18.21 An agent may be entitled to be paid for his services. The right to be paid may be an express term of the contract of agency or, in the absence of such a term, may be implied if it was clearly the intention of the parties that the agent was to be paid[1]. The agent will only be entitled to remuneration where he has performed, precisely and completely, the obligations in the agency agreement — it is an entire contract[2]. If an agent does less than he is contractually required to do he can recover for what he has done only if the contract so provides.

If the contract of agency expressly provides the amount of remuneration for a given task, this is the amount payable. If the contract merely provides that the agent is to be paid without specifying an amount, he is entitled to recover a reasonable amount[3]. If the contract mentions remuneration, but on its true construction does not entitle the agent to payment, he can recover nothing. For instance, in *Kofi Sunkersette Obu v Strauss & Co Ltd*[4], the Privy Council refused to allow an agent to recover any commission in a case where the contract of agency provided that the amount of commission, *if any*, was to be fixed by the principal. If there is an implied term providing for payment, the amount of such payment must be determined by the courts. Usually it will be on the basis of what is reasonable, but it may be possible to imply the fixed scale costs of professional men[5].

In the absence of a contract of agency the agent is entitled to be paid on a *quantum meruit* basis[6].

---

1 *Reeve v Reeve* (1858) 1 F & F 280.
2 Para. 10.14.
3 *Way v Latilla* [1937] 3 All ER 759, HL.
4 [1951] AC 243, PC.
5 For when the courts will imply terms into contracts see paras. 8.19—8.28.
6 For *quantum meruit* generally see para. 17.8.

18.22 The occurrence of the transaction which the agent is commissioned to effect does not entitle the agent to remuneration: the occurrence must be brought about by the agent unless the contract provides that he is to be paid however the desired result occurs[1].

If the principal hinders the earning of commission by the agent, the agent cannot recover any commission thereby lost or sue the principal. In *Rhodes v Forwood*[2], the plaintiff was appointed the defendant's sole agent for the sale of his coal in Liverpool for seven years. The House of Lords refused to find the defendant liable for breach of contract when he sold his colliery. The contract of agency may contain a term that the principal will not hinder the agent in his efforts to earn his commission, but if it is not an express term the courts are reluctant to imply such a term into the contract of agency[3].

Even if an agent complies with the instructions in the contract of agency, he cannot recover any commission if the transaction he was engaged to effect was unlawful or rendered void by the Gaming Acts[4], nor, of course, if he is in breach of his obligations under the contract. Neither can an agent claim commission if he earned it acting in a capacity in which he was not legally qualified to act.

---

1 *Millar, Son & Co v Radford* (1903) 19 TLR 575, CA.
2 (1876) 1 App Cas 256, HL.
3 *Luxor (Eastbourne) Ltd v Cooper* [1941] AC 108, [1941] 1 All ER 33, HL.
4 For illegality and the Gaming Acts see Chap. 15, especially para. 15.7.

Indemnity
18.23 An agent who has suffered loss or incurred liabilities in the course of carrying out authorised actions for his principal is entitled to be reimbursed or indemnified by the principal[1]. However, he has no right to reimbursement or an indemnity for losses or liabilities arising because of breaches of duty or in carrying out an illegal transaction or a transaction rendered void by the Gaming Acts[2]. In *Ex parte Mather*[3], a principal employed an agent to purchase smuggled goods. The agent was not entitled to recover the cost of these goods from the principal even though the principal had obtained possession of them.

---

1 *Hooper v Treffry* (1847) 1 Exch 17.
2 *Capp v Topham* (1805) 6 East 392; *Gasson v Cole* (1910) 26 TLR 468.
3 (1797) 3 Ves 373.

Termination

18.24 A contract of agency may be terminated in any way that any other contract can be terminated: that is by agreement[1], by performance[2], by breach[3] or by frustration[4]. However, there are also special methods of termination available for contracts of agency. It is necessary to remember that termination of agency between principal and agent may not affect the ostensible authority of the agent, who can, therefore, bind the principal in dealings with third parties who do not know of the termination of the agent's authority.

---

1 Paras. 6.31–6.36.
2 Chap. 9.
3 Chap. 10.
4 Chap. 11.

Special methods for termination of agency

By notice

18.25 If the agency agreement so provides, either party can terminate it by serving notice. If the agency was established by contract any notice must be in accordance with that specified by the contract and, in the absence of any period of notice being specified, there must be reasonable notice[1]. If the contract of agency is for a definite period it may be a breach of contract to attempt to terminate the contract by notice. If notice is given the authority of the agent determines[2] but if there is a breach of contract the party in breach can be liable in damages[3]. The courts will not order specific performance of the contract because it is a contract for personal services.

We have already seen[4] that if an agent accepts a bribe his contract of agency can be terminated without notice. There are other contracts which on their true construction allow either principal or agent to terminate the agreement without any notice[5]. If an agent is employed on a commission basis, so that he is only entitled to remuneration when he does the act required by the agency agreement, for example, sells a house, then it would seem that such contract can be terminated without notice[6]. Agency contracts which resemble contracts of employment, in that the agent is paid merely for being an agent, require notice[7].

There are some cases where the authority of an agent is irrevocable. Under the Powers of Attorney Act 1971, s.4, a power of attorney expressed to be irrevocable, and given to secure a proprietary interest of the donee of the power, cannot be revoked by the donor of that power without the consent of the donee nor by the death, insanity or bankruptcy of the donor. Also, if the agent is given authority by deed, or for valuable consideration, to effect a security or to protect an interest of the agent, that authority is irrevocable while the security or interest subsists[8]. Again, an authority coupled with an interest is not revoked by the death, insanity or bankruptcy of the donor.

---

1 *Martin-Baker Aircraft Co Ltd v Murison* [1955] 2 QB 556, [1955] 2 All ER 722.
2 Actual authority determines but see para. 18.36 for ostensible authority.

3 There is no breach if the contract is one which can be terminated without notice.
4 Para. 18.19. b.
5 *Atkinson v Cotesworth* (1825) 3 B & C 647.
6 *Motion v Michaud* (1892) 8 TLR 253, affd. by the Court of Appeal (1892) 8 TLR 447, CA.
7 *Parker v Ibbetson* (1858) 4 CB NS 346.
8 *Gaussen v Morton* (1830) 10 B & C 731.

By conduct

18.26 If the principal (or agent) acts in such a way that he must be taken to have terminated the agency agreement, this can be an effective termination. If the termination is a breach of a contract of agency, the party in breach will be liable to pay damages. As has been mentioned above[1], certain contracts can be terminated without giving notice and if such a contract is terminated by conduct there is no breach[2]. Termination by conduct can arise where the principal does what the agent was engaged to do or where the principal effectively prevents the agent from doing what he was engaged to do, albeit through no fault of his own[3]. For example, if A is engaged as agent to sell cookers manufactured by P, and P ceases to manufacture cookers, the contract of agency must terminate. If the contract of agency could be terminated without notice the principal incurs no liability. An agency contract which is for a specified period can be terminated by conduct but this may constitute breach depending on the construction of the contract[4]. If the contract was on a commission basis it is more likely that the courts will find there is no requirement for the principal to allow his agent to earn commission for the specified period and the contract can be terminated by conduct without involving breach. In *French & Co Ltd v Leeston Shipping Co Ltd*[5], agents, who chartered a ship for 18 months, were to be paid commission on the hire paid. The owners sold the ship to the charterers after four months and it was found that the agents were not entitled to commission on hire which would have been paid if the charter had lasted another 14 months. The conduct of the principals (the charterers) had terminated the agency and they were not in breach of contract. However, in *Turner v Goldsmith*[6], an agent, who was to be employed for five years as a traveller selling shirts, was not released from his obligation when the principal's shirt factory burnt down.

1 Para. 18.25.
2 *Atkinson v Cotesworth* (1825) 3 B & C 647.
3 *Rhodes v Forwood* (1876) 1 App Cas 256, HL.
4 *Ibid.*
5 [1922] 1 AC 451, HL.
6 [1891] 1 QB 544, CA.

By death

18.27 The death of principal or agent determines the agency[1]. The agent's right to remuneration ceases with the death of the principal, as does his right of indemnity[2]. Most importantly, the actual authority of the agent ceases on the death of the principal and any transactions entered into after the death of the principal bind the agent, but not the principal's estate, even if the agent does not know of the death[3].

1 *Blades v Free* (1829) 9 B & C 167; *Friend v Young* [1897] 2 Ch 421.
2 *Farrow v Wilson* (1869) LR 4 CP 744; *Pool v Pool* (1889) 58 LJP 67.
3 *Blades v Free* (1829) 9 B & C 167.

By virtue of insanity

18.28 If the principal becomes insane the agency is terminated, and the agent can presumably claim no commission in relation to transactions entered into after his actual authority is determined by the insanity. Any contract entered into by the agent after the determination of actual authority by reason of insanity binds the principal[1], unless the third party knew of the insanity. Provided that the third party did not know of the insanity, the agent can be liable for breach of warranty of authority even if he did not know of the insanity[2].

1 *Drew v Nunn* (1879) 4 QBD 661, CA.
2 *Yonge v Toynbee* [1910] 1 KB 215, CA.

By virtue of bankruptcy

18.29 The bankruptcy of a principal terminates a contract of agency[1]. On the other hand, the bankruptcy of an agent does not automatically determine the agency, unless it prevents the agent acting as agents[2].

1 *Elliott v Turquand* (1881) 7 App Cas 79, HL.
2 *McCall v Australian Meat Co Ltd* (1870) 19 WR 188.

Effects of termination

18.30 Obviously, accrued rights are unaffected by the termination of agency. It should be remembered that, while actual authority is terminated if agency is terminated, the agent may still be invested with ostensible authority[1] and, thus, may still bind his principal unless a third party with whom the agent deals has notice of the termination of the agency.

1 Paras. 18.34–18.38.

PRINCIPAL AND THIRD PARTIES

18.31 If an agent makes an *authorised* contract on behalf of his principal then the principal is deemed to have made the contract. Indeed, if the principal is a disclosed principal, he alone is deemed to have made the contract and not the agent — except in certain limited circumstances. The principal may, contrary to the doctrine of privity, sue and be sued on authorised contracts made by his agent. If the principal is undisclosed then both principal and agent can sue or be sued on the authorised contract. If a contract or transaction is not authorised then it does not bind the principal but it does bind the agent. An agent may be authorised in any of several ways.

The authority of agents

Actual authority
18.32 An agent who has been expressly appointed may have both express and implied actual authority. An agent appointed by implied agreement has implied actual authority.

Express authority is the authority conferred by the agreement (which is usually a contract) creating agency. Implied authority consists of those terms which will be implied into the contract of agency by applying the usual rules for the implication of terms into contracts[1]. Certain types of implied actual authority are well recognised, for instance, incidental and customary authority. Incidental authority has been described as conferring authority to do 'all subordinate acts incident to and necessary for the execution of [actual] authority'[2]. Thus, incidental authority supplements the actual authority of the agent and gives the agent authority to undertake tasks which are incidental to his authorised task. It is a question of fact in every case whether a particular action is incidental to the authorised purpose of the agent. For example, an agent authorised to sell property has incidental authority to sign a memorandum so as to satisfy the Law of Property Act 1925, s.40[3]. Customary authority means that an agent operating in a particular market or business has the authority which an agent operating in that market or business usually has[4]. If an agent has a particular position, for example, company secretary, foreman or bailiff, then he has a type of customary authority commonly called usual authority, which confers on him the authority to undertake any tasks which an agent in that position usually has authority to make[5]. In *Panorama Developments Ltd v Fidelis Furnishing Fabrics Ltd*[6], the company appointed X their company secretary. As such he was an agent of the company, and the company was liable to pay for cars hired by X, even though he used them for his own and not the company's purposes, because hiring cars was within the customary usual authority of an agent holding the position of company secretary.

---

1 Paras. 8.19—8.28.
2 *Collen v Gardner* (1856) 21 Beav 540.
3 *Rosenbaum v Belson* [1900] 2 Ch 267.
4 *Bayliffe v Butterworth* (1847) 1 Exch 425.
5 *Hely-Hutchinson v Brayhead Ltd* [1968] 1 QB 549, [1967] 3 All ER 98; affd. on other grounds by the Court of Appeal.
6 [1971] 2 QB 711, [1971] 3 All ER 16, CA.

18.33 Actual authority can only arise where the parties have been created principal and agent. Actual authority operates in two ways. It delimits what the agent is authorised to do and renders him liable to his principal if he oversteps those limits, and it defines those transactions which will bind the principal and a third party. The agent can only bind principals to third parties on transactions which he was authorised to make (subject to ostensible authority).

Ostensible authority
18.34 Ostensible authority may result in:

a. a person who is not an agent being regarded as an agent of a person for whom he acts or appears to act in a particular transaction; or

b. the extension of the authority of an agent[1].

It does not extend the actual authority of the agent in relation to his principal.

---

1 The important case of *Freeman and Lockyer v Buckhurst Park Properties (Mangal) Ltd* [1964] 2 QB 480, [1964] 1 All ER 630, CA, re-affirmed that ostensible authority operates in these two ways.

18.35 Ostensible authority can arise when the alleged principal makes to a third party a representation of fact, usually by conduct, which the third party relies on, that a person is authorised to act as his agent[1]. If the third party can show that such was the case, the alleged principal cannot deny the authority of the person he has held out as being his agent. Thus, a person who permits someone to act on his behalf may find himself unable to deny that he is his agent. Ostensible authority can operate in a single transaction. For instance, if a person stands by and watches someone acting for him, he conveys the impression to a third party that the person is authorised to act for him. But ostensible authority can operate in a series of transactions; if a person frequently allows an unauthorised person to act for him, he may be unable to deny that the person had ostensible authority to act for him in other similar future transactions. For example, if a company allows X to act as managing director, even though he has not been appointed as such, third parties are entitled to assume that he is managing director.

If there is a single transaction, the ostensible authority of the agent is to effect that transaction and no more. That is all the 'principal' has represented to the world that the agent has authority to undertake. If the 'principal' has allowed a person to act on his behalf more than once, that person has ostensible authority to effect such transactions and similar transactions in the future, and may also have ostensible usual authority. Ostensible usual authority means that where a person is held out as occupying a particular position, for example, managing director, then he will have all the usual authority that a person would have if properly appointed to that position[2]. This can be compared with customary usual authority which operates where the agent has been properly appointed[3]. If a person has invested an agent with ostensible authority, it is not necessarily limited to exactly the same transactions as those from which the ostensible authority arose. In *Swiss Air Transport Co Ltd v Palmer*[4], an agent who was held out as having authority to ship wigs was held to have ostensible authority to arrange the shipment of wigs and other items over the same route but not to buy himself an air-ticket.

---

1 *Freeman and Lockyer v Buckhurst Park Properties (Mangal) Ltd* [1964] 2 QB 480, [1964] 1 All ER 630, CA.
2 *Ibid.*
3 Para. 18.32.
4 [1976] 2 Lloyd's Rep 604.

18.36 Ostensible authority can also operate if the principal of a validly appointed agent has restricted or terminated the actual authority of the agent. Such action is binding between principal and agent but cannot bind a third party who does not know of the restriction or termination[1].

Ostensible authority in relation to mercantile agents (who are defined in para. 18.52) has been codified by statute[2]. Statute allows mercantile agents to deal with goods, or documents of title to goods (which they hold with the consent of the owner), by sale, pledge or disposition, in their ordinary course of business, and any transaction so entered into binds the owner of the goods or documents of title (the principal) even if not authorised by him, providing that the person taking under the disposition by the mercantile agent acted in good faith and without notice of any lack of authority.

---

1 *Trickett v Tomlinson* (1863) 13 CB NS 663.
2 Factors Act 1889, s.2.

18.37 Ostensible authority is based on the belief raised in the mind of the third party by the representation of the 'principal' that a particular person is his agent. It follows that a third party, who knows, or ought to know, that the alleged principal has not invested with authority the person whom he appears to hold out as his agent, cannot rely on the doctrine of ostensible authority — because he cannot say that he was led to believe that that person was the alleged principal's agent. This may cause particular difficulties with companies. The public documents of the company[1] may reveal that a person whom the company appears to be holding out as an agent lacks authority. Because these documents are open to public inspection, they are deemed to give notice to the whole world of this lack of authority even if, as is usual, a particular third party has not read them. This has been amended in relation to directors, but not other agents of the company, by the European Communities Act 1972, s.9. Since 1973, a company cannot deny the ostensible authority of a director or person whom it has held out as director, by claiming that the public documents gave notice of any lack of authority. On the other hand, if the public documents extend the authority of an agent or a person held out as an agent of the company, the third party cannot rely on such extension unless he has read the public documents.

Acts within the ostensible authority of an agent bind the principal even if they are entered into for the agent's own purposes or are fraudulent, provided the fraud occurs while he is purporting to carry out what he is ostensibly authorised to do[2].

---

1 Para. 4.9.
2 *Lloyd v Grace, Smith & Co* [1912] AC 716, HL.

18.38 It must be emphasised that ostensible authority operates to make someone an agent with authority for the purposes of his dealings with third parties. It does not create an agency relationship, though it may prevent the 'principal' denying that a person was acting on his behalf.

The disclosed principal

18.39 A disclosed principal is one whose existence was known to the third party at the time of contracting. It is sufficient for the third party to know of the existence of the principal: he need not know the name of the principal.

If the agent of a disclosed principal makes an authorised contract, the principal is bound by that contract and is considered to be a party to it, whereas, generally, the agent is not. The principal can sue and be sued on the contract[1].

However, the agent may be jointly or solely liable on the contract, entered on behalf of his disclosed principal, if the contract expressly or impliedly reveals this to be the intention of the parties. Under the Partnership Act 1890, s.5, a partner who contracts on behalf of the partnership is jointly liable with the rest of the partners on that contract. In other cases, whether there is an implied intention that the agent shall be jointly or solely liable on the contract is a question of construction[2]. Particular note is taken of the description of the agent in a written contract and how the agent signed a written contract. If the document describes the agent as an agent and he signs 'as agent' he is not liable on the contract[3]. If neither document nor signature describes him as an agent he is liable on the contract[4] even if he is known to be acting as an agent. If either the signature or document reveals him to be an agent, the question of his personal liability is one of fact[5]. If the contract is oral and the agent is known to be an agent, the above rules for written contracts do not apply and every case is determined by reference to its particular facts[6]. If an agent is liable on a contract he will probably also have the benefit of that contract unless, as a matter of construction, the contract reveals the agent is to be liable without having the benefit of the contract. There are other circumstances in which agents are personally liable on authorised contracts[7].

---

1   *Montgomerie v United Kingdom Mutual SS Association* [1891] 1 QB 370.
2   But see the doctrine of election, para. 18.43.
3   *Lucas v Beale* (1851) 10 CB 739.
4   *Basma v Weekes* [1950] AC 441, [1950] 2 All ER 146, PC.
5   *Burrell v Jones* (1819) 3 B & Ald 47.
6   *N. and J. Vlassopulos Ltd v Ney Shipping Ltd* [1977] 1 Lloyd's Rep 478, CA.
7   Paras. 18.45—18.48.

18.40   If money due under a contract is paid to an agent authorised to receive money this is a sufficient discharge of any obligation owed to the principal. If an agent not authorised to receive money in fact does so, this is not a good discharge unless the action of the agent is ratified; acceptance of the money by the principal can, of course, constitute ratification[1].

---

1   *Brown v Staton* (1816) 2 Chit 353.

The undisclosed principal

18.41   If the third party is unaware that he is dealing with an agent, the principal is called an undisclosed principal. An undisclosed principal can sue and be sued on authorised contracts entered into on his behalf[1].

The agent can also sue and be sued on such contracts[2]. It may seem odd that the third party can be sued by someone with whom he did not know he was contracting and with whom he may not have wished to contract. To protect the third party certain limitations have been placed on the right of the undisclosed principal to sue.

---

1   *Scrimshire v Alderton* (1743) 2 Stra 1182; *Thomson v Davenport* (1829) 9 B & C 78.
2   *Saxon v Blake* (1861) 29 Beav 438.

Limitations on the right of the undisclosed principal to sue
18.42   An undisclosed principal cannot sue:

a. If the principal did not exist or lacked capacity at the time the agent contracted[1].

b. If the contract expressly prohibits the intervention of an undisclosed principal[2].

c. If the contract impliedly excludes the intervention of an undisclosed principal. For example, if the contract 'shows' the agent to be contracting as principal. In *Humble v Hunter*[3], the agent of an undisclosed principal signed a charter party as 'owner' of the ship. This contract was found to impliedly regard the agent as owner, and the true owner (the principal) could not sue on the contract.

d. If the third party can establish that he had some reason for wishing to deal with the agent personally. For example, if the agent was a man of fine reputation and acknowledged skill, and the contract involved reliance on such integrity and skill[4].

e. If the third party can establish that he had a reason for not wishing to deal with the principal.

f. If the third party could not have been sued by the agent[5].

g. If the third party has paid the agent what is due under the contract (even if the third party exercises a set-off). However, if the belief that the agent was not an agent was not induced by the principal, the third party is not discharged from liability by paying the agent unless he pays the agent in full[6].

---

1   Para. 18.5.
2   *United Kingdom Mutual SS Assurance Association Ltd v Nevill* (1887) 19 QBD 110, CA.
3   (1848) 12 QB 310.
4   *Collins v Associated Greyhound Racecourses Ltd* [1930] 1 Ch 1, CA; *Nash v Dix* (1898) 78 LT 445.
5   *Ludgater v Love* (1881) 44 LT 694, CA.
6   *Cooke v Eshelby* (1887) 12 App Cas 271, HL.

Election

18.43 If the agent has acted as agent of an undisclosed principal, or in any other case where the agent is jointly liable on a contract with his principal, the third party must elect whether to sue the principal or the agent[1]. This election may be express or implied. An implied election will only occur if a third party with full knowledge of all the relevant facts indicates clearly which party he intends to hold liable on the contract[2]. What constitutes implied election is a question of fact — beginning legal proceedings[3], demanding payment, and debiting an account[4] are all relevant but not conclusive factors. If a third party obtains judgment against either principal or agent he cannot sue the other one, even if he did not have full knowledge of all relevant facts at the date of judgment[5].

1   *Paterson v Candasequi* (1812) 15 East 62.
2   *Thomson v Davenport* (1829) 9 B & C 78.
3   *Clarkson, Booker Ltd v Andjel* [1964] 2 QB 775, [1964] 3 All 260, CA.
4   *Young & Co Ltd v White* (1911) 28 TLR 87.
5   *Kendall v Hamilton* (1879) 4 App Cas 504, HL.

AGENTS AND THIRD PARTIES

18.44 We have seen that agents can be jointly liable on authorised contracts made on behalf of a disclosed principal if, on its true construction, the contract imposed such liability on the agent[1]. However, the agent of a disclosed principal is the only party capable of suing or being sued in certain cases.

1   Para. 18.39; for the doctrine of election see para. 18.43. The agent of a disclosed principal can be solely liable on a contract if the contract on its true construction imposes such liability.

Contracts under seal

18.45 At common law, an agent who enters into a contract under seal is liable on it, even if he is known to be contracting as an agent[1], and the principal is not liable unless he was named as a party to the deed and it was executed in his name[2]. In equity, the principal can sue on a deed if the agent contracted as trustee for the principal and the agent is made co-plaintiff[3].

If an agent who was the donee of a power of attorney executed a contract under seal on behalf of the principal, the principal can sue on it[4], although there is authority to suggest that he must still be named in the deed[5].

1   *Schack v Anthony* (1813) 1 M & S 573.
2   *Ibid.*
3   *Harmer v Armstrong* [1934] Ch 65, CA.
4   Powers of Attorney Act 1971, s.7.
5   *Harmer v Armstrong* [1934] Ch 65, CA.

Trade usage

18.46 If a trade custom, not inconsistent with the contract, makes an agent liable on a contract the courts will give effect to that custom[1].

---

1   *Barrow & Bros v Dyster, Nalder & Co* (1884) 13 QBD 635, DC.

Negotiable instruments

18.47 An agent will be personally liable on a negotiable instrument if he signs his name as a party to the instrument unless he indicates that he is signing on behalf of a principal[1]. Merely signing 'as agent' will not suffice to exempt the agent from personal liability if he signs as acceptor, and the bill is drawn on him[2]. If the agent indorses or draws a bill of exchange he is personally liable unless he clearly indicates he is acting as an agent[3].

---

1   Bills of Exchange Act 1882, s.26.
2   *Mare v Charles* (1856) 5 E & B 978.
3   *Elliott v Bax-Ironside* [1925] 2 KB 301, CA.

Where the principal is in fact agent

18.48 If an agent contracts on behalf of a non-existent principal then the agent must be contracting on his own behalf[1]. If the agent purports to contract as agent but is in fact the principal, he can sue and be sued on the contract[2]. But, if X, a purported agent who is in fact a principal, appears to contract on behalf of a named principal, he cannot sue or be sued on the contract[3]. The agent can sue if he contracts on his own behalf and the contract indicates, but does not name, a principal and shows that the identity of the principal is not relevant[4]. The cases in this area are generally considered to be unsatisfactory.

---

1   European Communities Act 1972, s.9.
2   *Gardiner v Heading* [1928] 2 KB 284, CA.
3   *Fairlie v Fenton* (1870) LR 5 Exch 169.
4   *Schmaltz v Avery* (1851) 16 QB 655.

Rights of third parties against agents

On the contract

18.49 If the agent is jointly or solely liable on the contract, the third party can, subject to the doctrine of election[1], sue the agent.

---

1   Para. 18.43.

For breach of warranty of authority

18.50 If a person acts as agent, knowing that he has no authority, he is liable to the third party for breach of warranty of authority if he has represented to the third party that he had authority[1]. Purporting to act as agent constitutes a representation of authority, unless the third party knew or ought to have known of the lack of authority[2].

Even if the agent genuinely and reasonably believes he has authority, when he has not, he may be liable to the third party[3]. In *Yonge v Toynbee*[4], an agent acting on behalf of his principal was held liable for breach of warranty of authority when, entirely unknown to him, his authority had been terminated by the insanity of his principal. The third party can sue even if he has not entered into a contract, provided he has altered his position in reliance on the representation.

If the representation made by the agent is one of law, not fact, he is not liable if it is untrue[5]. An action for breach of warranty cannot lie if the principal ratifies the unauthorised act.

The amount of damages which may be awarded under this head is the amount which would put the third party in the same position as if the representation (of authority) had been true[6]. Therefore, if the third party could recover nothing from the principal, even if the agent had had authority, he can recover nothing for breach of warranty of authority.

---

1 *Collen v Wright* (1857) 8 E & B 647.
2 Para. 18.37.
3 *Yonge v Toynbee*, [1910] 1 KB 215, CA.
4 [1910] 1 KB 215, CA.
5 *Beattie v Ebury* (1872) 7 Ch App 777, HL.
6 *Richardson v Williamson and Lawson* (1871) LR 6 QB 276.

In Tort

18.51 An agent may be liable even if his principal is also vicariously liable. Therefore, an agent may be liable in deceit, or under the rules in *Hedley Byrne & Co Ltd v Heller & Partners, Ltd*[1], or, of course, for such actions as knocking down a third party by negligent driving.

---

1 [1964] AC 465, [1963] 2 All ER 575, HL.

TYPES OF AGENT

Del credere agents

18.52 A *del credere* agent is an agent who guarantees that third parties with whom he contracts will pay any sums due under their contracts. He is paid an extra commission for this guarantee to the principal.

General agents

A general agent has authority to act for his principal in all aspects of a particular trade or business.

Special agents

A special agent has authority to effect a particular transaction.

Mercantile agents or factors

A mercantile agent or factor is an agent 'having in the customary course of his business as such agent authority either to sell goods, or to consign goods for the purpose of sale, or to buy goods, or to raise money on the security of goods'[1].

---

1   Factors Act 1889, s.1.

Chapter 19
Assignment

19.1 In this chapter we are concerned with the circumstances in which a right or obligation can be transferred from one person to another.

VOLUNTARY TRANSFER

Assignment of choses in action

19.2 A chose in action comprises all personal rights of property which can only be claimed or enforced by action, and not by taking physical possession[1]. This definition includes not only contractual rights such as a debt, but also rights which are not contractual such as patent rights, copyright, rights of action in tort and rights under a trust.

Contractual rights, as well as the other choses in action, may be transferred to another by a process called assignment. Thus, while a contract cannot generally confer rights upon a third party[2], it is possible for a right created by a contract to be assigned by its owner to a third party. The effect of the assignment of any chose in action is that the assignor (the person making the assignment) transfers to the assignee the right in question, which the assignee can enforce by action on his own initiative and in his own name.

---

1 *Torkington v Magee* [1902] 2 KB 427 at 430.
2 Para. 6.19.

19.3 The following choses in action can only be assigned in accordance with special statutory provisions:
bills of lading according to the Bills of Lading Act 1855[1];
negotiable instruments according to the Bills of Exchange Act 1882[2].

These special provisions fall outside the scope of this Chapter, and we confine ourselves for the present to the general rules which relate to all other choses in action, concentrating in particular on the assignment of ordinary contractual rights, the most common example of which is the assignment of a debt. Rights under a contract and other choses in action can be assigned by their owner to a third party *either* by statutory assignment under the Law of Property Act 1925, s.136(1), *or* by an equitable assignment where s.136(1) is not complied with.

1   Para. 27.30.
2   Para. 24.20.

Statutory assignment
19.4   General statutory provisions for the assignment of choses in action were first made by the Judicature Act 1873. They are now contained in the Law of Property Act 1925, s.136(1)[1], under which there are four requirements for a valid statutory assignment:

a. the assignment must be in writing;

b. it must be signed by the assignor;

c. it must be absolute; and

d. the debtor, trustee or other person from whom the assignor would have been entitled to claim the debt or other chose in action must be given written notice.

It must be emphasised that a statutory assignment may be voluntary, in other words the assignee can enforce it even though he has not provided any consideration[2]. If the requirements for a statutory assignment are satisfied the assignee obtains the exclusive legal right to the debt or other chose in action and can bring an action in his own name to enforce it without joining the assignor as a party to the proceedings.

Three of the four requirements require further examination.

1   Although the wording of s.136 refers only to 'legal' choses, it was held in *Torkington v Magee* [1902] 2 KB 427, CA, that equitable choses as well as legal choses can be assigned under s.136. The distinction between legal and equitable choses is outlined in para. 19.10.
2   *Re Westerton* [1919] 2 Ch 104.

19.5   *Assignment in writing* The written document must purport to be an assignment but it need not be made in a particular form nor under seal.

19.6 *Assignment absolute* For an assignment to be absolute the *whole interest* of the assignor in the chose in action must be transferred *unconditionally* to the assignee and *placed completely under his control*. Provided these criteria are satisfied it is not necessary that there should be an out and out transfer depriving the assignor of all further interest in the chose: the unconditional transfer for the time being of the whole of the assignor's interest in the chose is an absolute assignment. This is shown by *Tancred v Delagoa Bay Rly Co*[1], where a debt was assigned as security for a loan, with the proviso that, if the assignor repaid the loan, the debt should be re-assigned to him. This was held to be an absolute assignment.

Absolute assignments must be distinguished from three other types of assignment which, not being absolute, cannot be made under s.136(1):

a. *Conditional assignments* These are assignments which automatically take effect or cease on the happening of a future uncertain event. *Durham Bros v Robertson*[2] provides an example. A firm of building contractors, to whom £1,080 was due under a building contract, borrowed money from the plaintiffs and assigned the £1,080 to them as security for the loan *'until the money lent . . . be repaid to you'*. It was held that this was a mere conditional assignment and therefore it could not take effect under s.136. The distinction between this case and *Tancred v Delagoa Bay Rly Co* is that in *Durham Bros v Robertson* the assignment did not transfer the debt unconditionally to the plaintiffs, but only until the loan was repaid, on which event the plaintiffs' interest in the debt would automatically cease, with the result that the debtor would not be certain that he was paying his debt to the right person without knowing the state of accounts between assignor and assignee. On the other hand, in *Tancred v Delagoa Bay Rly Co*, the debt was transferred completely to the assignee and did not automatically revert to the assignor on repayment of the loan but required a re-assignment, of which the debtor would have notice so that he would be in no doubt as to who was entitled to payment at any particular time without looking at the state of accounts between assignor and assignee.

b. *Assignments by way of charge* Assignments purporting to be by way of charge are expressly excluded from s.136. An assignment by way of charge merely gives the assignee a right to payment out of a particular fund or property without transferring that fund or property to him[3]. It must be distinguished from the transaction known as a mortgage of a chose in action which, in its ordinary form as in *Tancred v Delagoa Bay Rly Co*, involves the transfer of the fund or property with a proviso for re-assignment[3]. An example of an assignment by way of charge is provided by *Jones v Humphreys*[4]. A schoolmaster, who had borrowed £15 from a moneylender, assigned to him so much of his salary as should be necessary to repay the amount which he had already borrowed or any further sums which he might borrow. It was held that this was not an absolute assignment of a definite debt, but a mere security purporting to be by way of charge.

c. *Assignments of part of a chose* In *Williams v Atlantic Assurance Co Ltd*[5], for instance, it was held that the assignment of part of a debt was not an absolute assignment.

---

1 (1889) 23 QBD 239.
2 [1898] 1 QB 765, CA.
3 *Tancred v Delagoa Bay Rly Co* (1889) 23 QBD 239 at 242.
4 [1902] 1 KB 11, DC.
5 [1933] 1 KB 81, CA.

19.7 *Written notice* Express written notice of the assignment must be given by the assignor or the assignee to the debtor, trustee or other person from whom the assignor would have been able to claim the debt or other chose in action. The written notice need not be in any particular form but it must clearly indicate the fact of the assignment[1]. It is effective from the date on which it is received and the statutory assignment is not perfected until then[2].

---

1 *Denney, Gasquet and Metcalfe v Conklin* [1913] 3 KB 177.
2 *Holt v Heatherfield Trust Ltd* [1942] 2 KB 1, [1942] 1 All ER 404.

19.8 Section 136(1) does not apply to certain choses in action, whose assignment is subject to special provisions. Examples are shares in companies registered under the Companies Act 1948 (which provides that the assignment must be in the manner provided by the articles of the particular company and be registered in the books of the company) and copyrights (which must be transferred in accordance with the provisions of the Copyright Act 1956).

Equitable assignment
19.9 At common law, choses in action were not generally assignable, but from the early seventeenth century equity enforced assignments of choses in action. The provisions relating to statutory assignment do not supersede equitable assignment but limit its operation to cases where the requirements for statutory assignment have not been satisfied[1]. Since 1 November 1875, when the Judicature Act 1873 came into force, any equitable assignment is recognised by all Divisions of the High

Court, but the rules governing such assignments are based on those existing before the Act was passed and came into force.

---

1 *Brandt's Sons & Co v Dunlop Rubber Co Ltd* [1905] AC 454 at 461, HL.

19.10 At the outset, we must mention the effect of an equitable assignment on the enforcement of the chose in action assigned. This differs depending upon whether a legal chose in action or an equitable chose in action is involved. A legal chose in action is a right which before 1875 could only be enforced by an action in a common law court, for example, a debt under a contract: an equitable chose in action is a right which before 1875 could only be enforced by an action in the Court of Chancery, such as a right under a trust.

The effect of an equitable assignment of an equitable chose is that, as in the case of a statutory assignment, the assignee can enforce the chose by bringing an action in his own name without joining the assignor as a party[1]. The sole exception is where the assignment is not absolute, i.e. the assignor still has some interest in the chose in action, in which case the assignor must be joined as a party to the proceedings so that the court can make a final adjudication binding on all those concerned with the chose in action[2]. On the other hand, the effect of an equitable assignment of a contractual right or other legal chose in action is that that right etc. can only be enforced by the assignee joining the assignor as co-plaintiff, if he is willing to co-operate, or as co-defendant, if he is not[3]. The reasons for this rule are historical and their explanation is not appropriate to a book such as this. This procedural complication makes it highly desirable to ensure that the absolute assignment of a legal chose in action complies with the requirements for a statutory assignment.

---

1 *Donaldson v Donaldson* (1854) Kay 711.
2 *Re Steel Wing Co Ltd* [1921] 1 Ch 349.
3 *Performing Right Society Ltd v London Theatre of Varieties Ltd* [1924] AC 1, HL.

19.11 Unlike statutory assignment, an equitable assignment need not be absolute (so that it may be conditional, or by way of charge, or of part of a debt)[1], writing is not always required and notice to the debtor is not essential, but consideration is sometimes necessary.

---

1 *Durham Bros v Robertson* [1898] 1 QB 765, CA; *Re Steel Wing Co Ltd* [1921] 1 Ch 349.

19.12 *Writing* The equitable assignment of an equitable chose in action must be in writing signed by the assignor or his agent authorised to do so[1], but the equitable assignment of a legal chose may be oral. In general, no particular form of words is required so long as the assignor's intention that the chose should become the assignee's property can fairly be collected from the words written or said or even from a course of conduct[2]. In *Thomas v Harris*[3], for instance, a father, shortly before his death, handed certain insurance policies on his life to his son with the request that the son should erect a tombstone for him and pay for it out of the insurance monies. It was held that this was a valid oral equitable assignment of the policies by way of charge for the amount spent by the son on the tombstone.

---

1   Law of Property Act 1925, s.53(1)(c).
2   *Brandt's Sons & Co v Dunlop Rubber Co Ltd* [1905] AC 454, HL.
3   [1947] 1 All ER 444, CA.

19.13 *Notice* Notice to the debtor or other person from whom the assignor would have been entitled to claim the chose in action is not essential to perfect the assignee's title under an equitable assignment[1]. However, it is advisable to give such notice because:

a. An assignment does not bind the debtor etc. until he has received notice, written or otherwise, of the assignment. Thus, if before notice, the debtor pays the assignor he gets a good discharge of his debt[2] and the assignee will have the trouble and expense of seeking to recover the payment from the assignor.

b. Notice to the debtor etc. prevents him from setting up new equities which may mature between himself and the assignor thereafter[3].

c. Notice to the debtor etc. is necessary to establish priority under the rule in *Dearle v Hall*[4]. Where an assignor makes two or more assignments of the same chose in action, the priority of the respective claims of the assignees depends on the order in which they gave notice of their assignment. The notice must be clear and unequivocal and, in the case of an equitable chose in action only, must be in writing[5]. However, an assignee who at the time of the assignment actually knows, or would have known if he had made proper inquiries, of a previous assignment cannot gain priority over it by being first to give notice. There is authority that the rule in *Dearle v Hall* also applies to determine priorities in statutory assignment[6].

---

1   *Gorringe v Irwell India Rubber Works* (1886) 34 Ch D 128, CA.
2   *Stocks v Dobson* (1853) 4 De G M & G 11.
3   Para. 19.16.

4 (1828) 3 Russ 1.
5 Law of Property Act 1925, s.137(3).
6 *Marchant v Morton Down & Co* [1901] 2 KB 829.

19.14 *Communication to assignee* Unless it is made in pursuance of a previous agreement between assignor and assignee, an equitable assignment is not binding until it is communicated to the assignee[1]. Until then it may be revoked by the assignor.

---

1 *Re Hamilton* (1921) 124 LT 737, CA.

19.15 *Consideration* An equitable assignment will be enforced, even though the assignee has not furnished consideration, provided the assignor has done everything required to be done by him in order to transfer the chose in action, whether the chose is legal[1] or equitable[2]. Thus, in *IIolt v Heatherfield Trust Ltd*[3], an absolute written assignment of a debt, which failed to be a statutory assignment because written notice had not been given to the debtor, was held to be effective as an equitable assignment even though it was not supported by consideration.

However, consideration is a requirement for enforcement in the following cases, even though the assignment is made by deed:

a. *Future choses in action* A future chose is a pure expectancy, such as a legacy hoped for under the will of a living person. It must be contrasted with an existing right to be paid in the future, which is an existing, not a future chose. Other examples of future choses are future royalties, future income and future book debts. Future choses are not statutorily assignable, but in equity an assignment of them made for consideration has always been treated as a contract to assign[4]. Thus, if an assignor who has received consideration becomes possessed of the chose he is compelled by equity to perform his contract, and the beneficial interest in the property passes to the assignee immediately the property is acquired[5].

b. *Contracts to assign* Similarly, consideration is required for a contract to assign even an existing chose in action in the future[6].

c. *Assignments by way of charge* The rights of an assignee under such an assignment are founded in contract and therefore the assignee must have provided consideration[7].

---

1 *Kekewich v Manning* (1851) 1 De G M & G 176.
2 *Harding v Harding* (1886) 17 QBD 442, DC; *Holt v Heatherfield Trust Ltd* [1942] 2 KB 1, [1942] 1 All ER 404.
3 [1942] 2 KB 1, [1942] 1 All ER 404.
4 *Warmstrey v Tanfield* (1628) 1 Rep Ch 29.

5 *Holroyd v Marshall* (1862) 10 HL Cas 191, HL.
6 *Re McArdle* [1951] Ch 669, [1951] 1 All ER 905, CA.
7 *Re Earl of Lucan* (1890) 45 Ch D 470.

Rules common to both statutory and equitable assignments

19.16   a. *Assignee takes subject to the equities* An assignee only steps into the shoes of his assignor, so that he takes the right to the chose in action 'subject to the equities', i.e. subject to any defence or counter-claim which the debtor etc. had against the assignor. This is so even though the assignee provided value for the assignment and was ignorant of the assignor's claims when he took the assignment.

Where the debtor's claim arises directly out of the *same* contract or transaction as the subject-matter of the assignment, the debtor may set it up against the assignee *whether it accrued to him before or after he had received notice of the assignment*[1]. Thus, where contractual rights have been assigned, the debtor can rescind the contract on the ground that he was induced to enter it by the assignor's fraud[2] or set-off against the assignee any claim for damages for breach of the contract by the assignor[3].

Where the debtor's claim arises out of a contract or transaction *other* than that which forms the subject-matter of the assignment the debtor may *only set it up if it accrued to him before the time when he received notice of the assignment*[4]. Thus, if X owes Y £100 and Y assigns this debt to Z, X can only set-off against Z a debt of £50 owed to him by Y if that debt has arisen before he (X) received notice of the assignment.

A limitation which applies in both cases is that nothing in the nature of a personal claim against the assignor, such as a claim to damages for fraud, can be set up against an assignee[5].

b. *Choses in action incapable of assignment*
   i. The right to the salary or pension of a public officer is not assignable[6]. A public officer is a person employed in the public service whose pay comes out of national, and not local, funds. Thus, a civil servant cannot, but a local government officer can, assign the right to his pay.
   ii. A contractual right is not assignable if this is expressly forbidden by the contract.
   iii. A bare right of litigation is not assignable on the ground that it savours of maintenance or champerty[7]. What this means is that if all that is purported to be assigned is the right to recover *unliquidated damages*[8] for a tort or a breach of contract[9] or to rescind for fraud[10] the assignment is void. The only exceptions are an assignment of a bare right to litigation by a trustee in bankruptcy or a liquidator of a company[11] and an assignment by an insured person

to his insurer, who has compensated him, of his rights against the person who has caused him the loss[12].

The assignment of a *bare* right of action must be distinguished from the assignment of a right of litigation which is *incidental* to an interest in property which the assignee acquires from the assignor at the same time. Thus, an agreement by the seller of land that the purchaser shall be entitled to sue X for damage already done to the land is a valid assignment of a right of litigation[13].

iv. Where a contractual right is conferred on a party for reasons personal to him, e.g. because of his qualifications or because of confidence reposed in him, he cannot assign it. The basis of this rule is that an assignment of a contractual right must not prejudice the party who owns the corresponding obligation[14]. Thus, an employer cannot assign his contractual right to an employee's service[15]: the identity of his employer is of obvious importance to an employee. Similarly, the holder of a motor insurance policy cannot assign his rights under it[16]: the skill and driving record of the policy holder is a matter on which the insurer relies. On the other hand, it may be a matter of indifference to the seller or buyer in a contract for the sale of goods or other property as to whom he performs his obligations, in which case the right to them is assignable. But even a contract for the sale of goods may be of a personal nature, as is shown by *Cooper v Micklefield Coal and Lime Co Ltd*[17]. In this case it was held that a retail coal merchant's contractual right to have coal supplied on credit could not be assigned to his successor because, in making the contract, the sellers had relied on the coal merchant's business experience, and to force them to give credit to another would subject them to a different business risk.

1 *Newfoundland Government v Newfoundland Rly* (1888) 13 App Cas 199, PC.
2 *Graham v Johnson* (1869) LR 8 Eq 36.
3 *Young v Kitchin* (1878) 3 Ex D 127.
4 *Roxburghe v Cox* (1881) 17 Ch D 520, CA.
5 *Stoddart v Union Trust Ltd* [1912] 1 KB 181, CA.
6 *Grenfell v Dean and Canons of Windsor* (1840) 2 Beav 544.
7 *Dawson v Great Northern and City Rly Co* [1905] 1 KB 260 at 270; *May v Lane* (1894) 64 LJQB 236, CA.
8 Para. 12.12.
9 *Defries v Milne* [1913] 1 Ch 98, CA.
10 *Prosser v Edmonds* (1835) 1 Y & C Ex 481.
11 Bankruptcy Act 1914, s.48; Companies Act 1948, s.245.
12 *Compania Colombiana de Seguros v Pacific Steam Navigation Co* [1965] 1 QB 101, [1964] 1 All ER 216.
13 *Dawson v Great Northern and City Rly Co* [1905] 1 KB 260, CA.
14 *Tolhurst v Associated Portland Cement Manufacturers (1900) Ltd* [1903] AC 414, HL.

15 *Nokes v Doncaster Amalgamated Collieries Ltd* [1940] AC 1014, [1940] 3 All ER 549, HL.
16 *Peters v General Accident and Life Assurance Corpn Ltd* [1937] 4 All ER 628. Also see para. 25.9.
17 (1912) 107 LT 457.

Novation of contractual rights

19.17   Novation is another process whereby a third party to a contract can acquire a right provided by it. By a novation contractual rights are transferred indirectly to a third party by means of a new contract between the debtor, creditor and the third party, in substitution for the original one, which provides that the debt owed by the debtor to the creditor shall henceforth be owed to the third party. A novation is not enforceable by the third party unless he has provided consideration for the debtor's promise to pay him[1]. Novation is most common in the case where A owes B £x, and B owes T £x. If the three agree that A shall pay T instead of B, in discharge of his indebtedness to B and of B's to T, there will be a novation; and T can sue A for the money because he has provided consideration for A's promise to pay him by the promise to discharge B's debt.

---

1   *Tatlock v Harris* (1789) 3 Term Rep 174 at 180; *Wharton v Walker* (1825) 4 B & C 163.

19.18   There are three essential distinctions between assignment and novation:

a. the process of assignment is not limited to contractual rights;

b. in an assignment the debtor is not a party to the transaction;

c. the debtor's consent is not necessary to the validity of an assignment.

These distinctions illustrate why assignment is far more common than novation.

Assignment of contractual liabilities

19.19   Contractual obligations cannot be assigned (i.e. transferred without the creditor's consent) by a party to a third party[1]. But if the creditor consents, a party can transfer a contractual obligation to a third party. The transaction will be one of novation and releases the party and imposes the obligation on the third party[1]. What is required for the novation of a contractual obligation is a new contract between the creditor, debtor and third party that the obligation owed by the debtor under the original contract to the creditor shall henceforth be owed by the third party in substitution. Such a novation is only binding if supported by consideration. Usually, the creditor provides consideration for the third party's promise to perform by promising to release the debtor (and so can enforce the obligation against the third party) and the debtor provides consideration for the creditor's promise to release him by providing the third party (and so is effectively released). An example of a novation of liability is *Miller's* case[2]. M insured his life with the N Co. The N Co became amalgamated with the O Co and ceased to carry on business. The O Co agreed to become liable on the policy if M paid future premiums to it. Subsequent premiums were paid to the O Co by M and it was held that, there being a complete novation, he could enforce the policy against the O Co.

Novation is frequently used where there is a change in the membership of a partnership, the old and new partners and the firm's creditors agreeing, expressly or by implication, that the creditors will look to the new partner (and the remaining ones), in place of the retiring partner, for payment of their debts.

---

1 *Tolhurst v Associated Portland Cement Manufacturers (1900) Ltd* [1902] 2 KB 660 at 668, CA.
2 (1876) 3 Ch D 391, CA.

19.20 There is no other way in which a party can extinguish his contractual liability by transferring it to a third party. It is, of course, possible in some cases for him to arrange for a third party to perform his obligations so as to discharge him, as we stated in para. 9.18, but in such a case there is no assignment of contractual liability so that the party remains liable if the third party fails to perform or performs defectively.

INVOLUNTARY ASSIGNMENT

19.21 A person's rights and liabilities are automatically assigned by operation of law in the event of his death or bankruptcy.

Death

19.22 On the death of a person, his property (including any choses in action which survive him) goes to his personal representatives, i.e. his executors (if he leaves a will) or administrators (if he dies intestate). It is the personal representatives' duty, after paying the deceased's debts and testamentary and funeral expenses, to distribute his estate in accordance with his will or, in the case of intestacy, in accordance with the Administration of Estates Act 1925.

The law of succession is a large subject but the scope of this book merely requires us to consider in more detail the devolution by death of the deceased's contractual rights and liabilities. Under the Law Reform (Miscellaneous Provisions) Act 1934, s.1, all causes of action subsisting against or vested in a party to a contract survive against or, as the case may be, for the benefit of his estate on his death[1]. The result is that his personal representatives may sue for debts due to the deceased and recover damages for any breach committed in his lifetime, and conversely they can be sued by the other party to the contract for a breach of contract committed during the deceased's lifetime (though they are not personally liable, but only to the extent of the assets in their hands, so that there is not strictly an assignment of liability).

---

1 The same rule applies to causes of action in tort, with the exception of defamation.

19.23 Where a contract has not been fully performed at the time of death, the general rule is that the benefit and the burden pass to the personal representatives so that they are entitled to any outstanding performance on the part of the party and must perform any outstanding obligation on the part of the deceased, failure to do so rendering them liable to the extent of their assets. There are two exceptions:

a. Where the parties intended the contract to be for life only.

b. Where the contract depends on the personal skill or service of a party, as in the case of an employment contract or a contract of agency, the death of either party frustrates the contract[1] and the deceased's obligation to continue serving, or right to be served (as the case may be), does not devolve to his personal representatives, although of course they can sue for money earned by the deceased or sue or be sued for breaches committed before his death[2].

---

1 Paras. 11.5 and 11.6.
2 *Stubbs v Holywell Rly Co* (1867) LR 2 Exch 311.

Bankruptcy

19.24 If a person is adjudicated a bankrupt, property (including choses in action) belonging to him at the time of his bankruptcy passes to his trustees in bankruptcy, with the exception of the tools of his trade, clothing and bedding to a total value of £250[1]. Choses in action pass to the trustee without an assignment by the bankrupt and are 'deemed to have been duly assigned' by him[2].

The scope of this book only necessitates a further discussion of the effects of bankruptcy on the bankrupt's contractual rights and liabilities.

---

1 Bankruptcy Act 1914, s.38 (as amended by the Insolvency Act 1976).
2 *Ibid.*, s.48.

19.25 The trustee in bankruptcy is generally in the position of an assignee of all the contractual rights of the bankrupt, and he alone can recover debts due to the bankrupt and claim damages for breach of any contract with the bankrupt (even if it was committed before the bankruptcy) — the bankrupt having no further interest[1]. However, the following contractual rights do not pass to the trustee in bankruptcy:

a. A right of action for wages earned *after* the bankruptcy, or for damages for breach of a contract of employment (e.g. wrongful dismissal) committed *after* the bankruptcy, does not pass to the trustee but remains vested in the bankrupt, subject to the power of the trustee to intervene and retain out of the sum recovered what is not required to maintain the bankrupt and his family[2].

b. A right of action for damages for breach of contract resulting immediately in injury to the character, feelings or reputation of a bankrupt does not pass to the trustee but remains vested in the bankrupt, whether the breach was committed before or after the bankruptcy. This is shown by *Wilson v United Counties Bank Ltd*[3]. The plaintiff, a trader, entrusted the financial side of his business to the defendant bank during his absence on military service in the First World War. The bank conducted the business so negligently that the plaintiff was adjudicated bankrupt. In an action which he and the trustee brought against the bank, damages of £45,000 were awarded for the loss to his estate and of £7,500 for the injury to his credit and reputation. It was held that the £7,500 belonged personally to the bankrupt as compensation for damage to his reputation, while the £45,000 went to the trustee for the benefit of the creditors.

---

1 *Farrow v Wilson* (1869) LR 4 CP 744.
2 *Bailey v Thurston & Co Ltd* [1903] 1 KB 137, CA.
3 [1920] AC 102, HL.

19.26 Where the contract is executory, the trustee may (subject to the provisions of the Bankruptcy Act 1914) perform it and claim payment from the other party[1]. However, he is not entitled to do so if the contract is one which is personal in nature, such as one whose execution requires the skill and judgment of the bankrupt. For example, in *Knight v Burgess*[2], it was held that the trustee in bankruptcy was not entitled to complete the building of a chapel because the contract involved the personal skill of the bankrupt builder.

1 Bankruptcy Act 1914, s.56.
2 (1864) 33 LJ Ch 727.

19.27 The bankrupt's contractual liabilities pass to the trustee in bankruptcy, in the sense that the trustee must distribute the bankrupt's assets (including those which he has acquired by enforcing the bankrupt's contractual rights) among the bankrupt's creditors. This, of course, does not strictly involve an assignment because the trustee is not personally liable but only to the extent of the bankrupt's property which he has collected.

19.28 The trustee also has power to disclaim an executory contract on the ground that it is onerous or unprofitable. The effect of his doing so is to discharge the contract but a person injured by the disclaimer can prove in the bankruptcy for any damage which he suffers by such disclaimer[1].

1 Bankruptcy Act 1914, s.54.

Part III
Elements of the Law of Tort

Chapter 20
Negligence

20.1 A tort is a civil wrong, the commission of which renders a person (the tortfeasor) liable to the victim, the normal remedy being damages. The mere fact that a person has been caused damage or loss by another does not mean that there is necessarily tortious liability[1]. The damage or loss must be of a type which the law recognises, and it must have been caused in a way which the law regards as giving rise to civil liability. This means that the plaintiff in a tortious action can only succeed if the requirements of a particular tort are satisfied. The tort of negligence is the most commonly committed.

---

1 *Bell v Travco Hotels Ltd* [1953] 1 QB 473, [1953] 1 All ER 638, CA.

20.2 The tort of negligence occurs when a person, who is under a legal duty to take care, fails to take adequate care and thereby causes damage to the plaintiff. This cannot be called a definition in that it leaves many questions open, but it provides some guidance as to the scope of negligence. It is somewhat artificial to divide negligence into the components of duty, breach and damage because there is really only one question before the court — whether the injured party will receive compensation — and many cases do not discuss each component separately, but this breakdown is traditional and helps clarify the requirements of the tort.

Duty of care

20.3 In any action for negligence the party injured must establish that the injury was caused by a person who owed him a duty of care. Duty of care has two elements:

a. *The notional duty* Were the facts of the case such that the law recognises that there could be a duty of care?

b. *The actual duty* If a duty of care was legally capable of existing, was there, in fact, a duty of care in this case?

20.4 Whether there is a notional duty of care is a question of law. In determining whether or not there could be a duty of care, reference must be made to the leading case. In *Donoghue v Stevenson*[1], Lord Atkin propounded the classic definition of duty of care, 'you must take reasonable care to avoid acts or omissions which you can reasonably foresee would be likely to injure your neighbour. Who, then, in law is my neighbour? The answer seems to be — persons who are so closely and directly affected by my act that I ought reasonably to have them in contemplation as being so affected when I am directing my mind to the acts or omissions which are called in question.' This famous 'neighbour principle' established that whether or not there was a duty of care depended upon reasonable foresight. Reasonable foresight means 'would a reasonable man in the position of the defendant have foreseen that his actions might adversely affect people within the range of those actions?' In *Donoghue v Stevenson*, the plaintiff alleged that she had suffered injury by consuming part of a bottle of ginger beer manufactured by the defendant, which contained a partially decomposed snail.

The principle that the duty of care in negligence is based on reasonable foreseeability could mean that whenever damage was reasonably foreseeable a party causing such damage could be under a notional duty of care. However, while the courts are prepared to extend the scope of negligence, certain types of cases have been held to disclose no notional duty of care, even if the damage occurring was reasonably foreseeable. The result is that there are certain established areas where the non-existence of a duty of care is clear, although the House of Lords may change its mind on the non-existence of a duty[2]. The House of Lords has recently stated that the courts should presume that, where the application of the 'neighbour test' would disclose a duty of care, a notional duty of care should be found to exist unless there is some good reason why it should not apply[3]. One good reason for finding no notional duty of care despite the fact that damage was reasonably foreseeable is where past cases have established the absence of such a duty.

---

1   [1932] AC 562, HL.
2   See, for example, the decision in *Hedley Byrne & Co Ltd v Heller & Partners Ltd* [1964] AC 465, [1963] 2 All ER 575, HL.
3   *Home Office v Dorset Yacht Co* [1970] AC 1004, [1970] 2 All ER 294, HL.

Cases where the absence of a duty of care has been established

20.5 *Third parties* Generally, a defendant owes no duty of care in relation to the actions of third parties[1]. For instance, in *Smith v Scott*[2], the local authority was held not responsible for the depredations of a known problem family whom it had rehoused next door to the plaintiff. However, a defendant may owe a duty of care to a plaintiff, where a third party causes reasonably foreseeable damage, if he has control over the property of the plaintiff or over the third party. In *Stansbie v Troman*[3], a painter, who, contrary to the instructions of the plaintiff, left a house he was working on unlocked during a two hour absence, was held liable in negligence when property was stolen from the house. In the important case of *Home Office v Dorset Yacht Co Ltd*[4], the Home Office was held responsible for the damage caused by Borstal boys in an escape from a camp on Brownsea Island. The duty of care to people whose property might be damaged in any escape was based on the control which the Home Office has over Borstal boys.

1 *Deyong v Shenburn* [1946] KB 227, [1946] 1 All ER 226, CA.
2 [1973] Ch 314, [1972] 3 All ER 645.
3 [1948] 2 KB 48, [1948] 1 All ER 599, CA.
4 [1970] AC 1004, [1970] 2 All ER 294, HL.

20.6 *Land law* There seems no good reason why cases involving property should not be subject to the principles enunciated in *Donoghue v Stevenson*[1], and stated to be of general application in *Home Office v Dorset Yacht Co Ltd*[2]. It is settled, however, that no duty of care is owed to a neighbouring landowner whose land, it is reasonably foreseeable, will be adversely affected by the abstraction of percolating water[3]. Also, the vendor or lessor of a dwelling owes no duty of care at common law to a purchaser or tenant, and cannot be liable in negligence if such a person suffers injury due to the defective state of the premises[4]. There may, of course, be contractual liability to the purchaser or tenant but not to others, for example, visitors. However, if the vendor or lessor was also the person who constructed or converted the dwelling, he owes a duty of care towards people who might be affected by defects in the property. This duty, imposed by the Defective Premises Act 1972, is not abrogated by the sale or demise of the dwelling house. This Act also imposes a duty of care on those who assist or advise on the building or conversion of dwelling houses.

1 [1932] AC 562, HL.
2 [1970] AC 1004, [1970] 2 All ER 294, HL.
3 *Langbrook Properties Ltd v Surrey County Council* [1969] 3 All ER 1424, [1970] 1 WLR 161.
4 *Cavalier v Pope* [1906] AC 428, HL; *Bottomley v Bannister* [1932] 1 KB 458, CA.

20.7 *Judicial process* 'It is well settled that judges, barristers, solicitors, jurors and witnesses enjoy an absolute immunity from any form of civil action being brought against them in respect of anything they say or do in court during the course of a trial'[1]. Therefore, no duty of care is owed by those specified in respect of proceedings in court. Barristers are also immune from actions in negligence in respect of work connected with litigation[2]. This immunity is probably also available to solicitors. There is no such immunity for work unconnected with litigation. Arbitrators are immune from actions in negligence when acting as arbitrators and deciding disputes, but valuers have no such immunity[3].

---

1 *Sutcliffe v Thackrah* [1974] AC 727, [1974] 1 All ER 859, HL.
2 *Rondel v Worsley* [1969] 1 AC 191, [1967] 1 All ER 993, HL.
3 *Arenson v Casson, Beckman, Rutley & Co* [1975] 3 All ER 901, [1975] 3 WLR 815, HL.

Cases where a duty of care may exist
20.8 *Economic loss* Economic loss may be pure economic loss, which is financial loss unassociated with physical injury or injury to property, or consequential economic loss, which is financial loss consequential on such injury (e.g. loss of earnings). Consequential economic loss is recoverable, but pure economic loss is not[1] except where it is caused by a negligent mis-statement made to the plaintiff[2], or if the loss is recoverable by statute.

A case which illustrates the difference between pure economic loss and consequential economic loss is *Spartan Steel and Alloys Ltd v Martin & Co (Contractors) Ltd*[3]. In this case the defendant's employees severed an electricity cable leading to the plaintiff's factory. When the electricity failed the plaintiff was melting material in a furnace, and the melt was ruined. The plaintiff was able to recover for damage to the materials in the furnace (direct physical loss) and for the loss of profit on that melt (consequential economic loss) but not for the loss of profit on melts which could not take place because of the power failure (pure economic loss).

It has proved difficult in some cases to decide if loss is physical or pure economic, particularly where the loss consists of a diminution in the value of the property of the plaintiff. This issue has been discussed most thoroughly in relation to real property but it is thought that the same principles apply to personal property. In two cases, houses were constructed on defective foundations after a negligent approval or lack of inspection of the foundations by the local authorities. The local authorities were sued by the owners of the houses for the diminution in their value. In *Dutton v Bognor Regis UDC*[4], one judge thought such loss was physical loss and recoverable, while another considered it to be economic loss, but economic loss which was recoverable. In *Anns v London Borough of Merton*[5], the House of Lords said, obiter, that damages were recoverable and the amount of damages should be assessed by reference to the cost of making the premises safe, but without explaining if the loss was physical or pure economic.

---

1   *Cattle v Stockton Waterworks Co* (1875) LR 10 QB 453.
2   Paras. 20.13—20.15.
3   [1973] QB 27, [1972] 3 All ER 557, CA. See also *SCM (United Kingdom) Ltd v Whittall & Son Ltd* [1971] 1 QB 337, [1970] 3 All ER 245, CA.
4   [1972] 1 QB 373, [1972] 1 All ER 462, CA.
5   [1977] 2 All ER 492, HL.

20.9   Nervous shock The principles of *Donoghue v Stevenson*[1], which established the existence of a general duty of care based on reasonable foreseeability did not distinguish between physical and mental injury. However, it is clear that there is in general, no duty of care not to cause reasonably foreseeable nervous shock[2]. The cases draw highly artificial distinctions between 'recoverable' and 'irrecoverable' shock and can only be explained on the basis of policy. It is considered that to allow recovery in negligence for all cases of nervous shock would 'open the floodgates of litigation'. Recovery can never be had for more mere mental upset. The defendant is only liable if his negligence caused physical injury as well as nervous shock, or if the nervous shock resulting from the defendant's negligence produces a physical or mental injury or illness[3] and the plaintiff:

a. was in fear of immediate physical injury because of the defendant's negligence[4]; or

b. saw, heard or apprehended through his own unaided senses, i.e. was not told by someone else, that a relative or, probably, a friend had suffered, or apparently suffered, injury because of the defendant's negligence[5]; or

c. apprehended, because of the defendant's negligence, some particularly unpleasant event was likely to affect a relative, although in the event it did not[6].

---

1   [1932] AC 562, HL.
2   *Bourhill v Young* [1943] AC 92, [1942] 2 All ER 396, HL.
3   *Hinz v Berry* [1970] 2 QB 40, [1970] 1 All ER 1074, CA.
4   *Dulieu v White & Sons* [1901] 2 KB 669, DC.
5   *Hinz v Berry* — wife recovered for shock of seeing her husband and children injured (£4000); *Dooley v Cammell Laird & Co Ltd* [1951] 1 Lloyd's Rep 271 — crane driver who reasonably believed a workmate had been crushed recovered for nervous shock (£377); *Boardman v Sanderson* [1964] 1 WLR 1317, CA — father who heard screams of his son as the son was run over, recovered for nervous shock (£75).

6 This is based on the doubtful case of *Owens v Liverpool Corpn* [1939] 1 KB 394, [1938] 4 All ER 727, CA — in which relatives of a deceased person recovered small sums for the shock of believing the coffin would be overturned when the hearse was hit by a tram.

20.10 If nervous shock is caused by a deliberate, rather than negligent, action or statement, the plaintiff can always recover damages[1].

1 *Wilkinson v Downton* [1897] 2 QB 57.

20.11 *Statutory powers* A statute may confer on a person or body a power, but not a duty, to do something, e.g. to inspect the foundations of a building in the course of erection, and the question may arise as to the liability of that person or body if the power is not exercised and injury is caused to another person or his property in consequence. Depending on the interpretation of the statute, that person or body may owe a duty of care in relation to the exercise of the statutory power but such a duty is only broken if there is a total failure to exercise discretion as to whether or not the power should be exercised[1]. Thus, if the person or body with the statutory power has thought about exercising it, but decided not to do so, there can be no liability for damage resulting from its non-exercise.

1 *Anns v London Borough of Merton* [1977] 2 All ER 492, HL.

Liability for negligent mis-statements
20.12 There is no reason in principle why liability for negligent words should differ from liability for negligent conduct, and where negligent words cause physical injury no difficulty has been experienced in finding that the person uttering those words owes a duty of care to those persons who suffer reasonably foreseeable injury by relying on them[1]. If negligent words cause pure economic loss the position is less straightforward.

1 *Sharp v Avery* [1938] 4 All ER 85, CA.

20.13 *Economic loss* As we have said in para. 20.8, there is no duty not to cause pure economic loss. However, in some circumstances there may be a duty of care not to cause such loss by a negligent mis-statement. This duty of care was established in 1963 in *Hedley Byrne & Co Ltd v Heller & Partners Ltd*[1]. In this case, inquiries were made of the defendants by the plaintiffs' bankers on their behalf, as to the financial standing of a company called Easipower Ltd. The plaintiffs initiated these inquiries because they had entered into contracts on behalf of Easipower and, in the event of Easipower failing to meet their contractual obligations, the plaintiffs would be liable on these contracts. The defendants' replies, though somewhat non-committal, were sufficient to encourage the plaintiffs to continue their dealings with Easipower. Easipower went into liquidation and the plaintiffs became liable on the contracts, involving them in liabilities of £17,661 18s 6d. The replies made by the defendants to the inquiries as to the financial standing of Easipower were found to be negligent and the House of Lords had to decide:

a. if the defendants could owe the plaintiffs a duty of care; and

b. if such a duty of care could exist, whether such a duty actually existed in this case.

The House of Lords held, by a majority, that a duty of care could exist in relation to negligent mis-statements in certain circumstances. The duty of care arises if there is a fiduciary relationship between the party making the negligent mis-statement and the party relying on such statements[2], or if a contract imposes such a duty on an adviser, or if there is a special relationship between the parties.

A special relationship will arise, said the House of Lords in *Hedley Byrne*, if advice or information is given by the defendant and it is reasonable for the plaintiff to rely on that advice, providing that the defendant realises or should realise that his words will be relied on either by the person whom he is addressing or a third party. If a party occupies a particular position, for example, a professional man, it is reasonable for a person to rely on his advice in relation to professional matters. Advice given on a social occasion will almost certainly not give rise to a duty of care; but a duty could arise if the party giving advice realised or should have realised it would be relied on and it is reasonable for the party relying on such advice to do so. The House of Lords found that the defendants in *Hedley Byrne could* owe a duty of care to the plaintiffs. It was irrelevant that the request for information was not made by the plaintiffs because the defendants realised that someone intended to rely on their replies.

However, on the facts of *Hedley Byrne & Co Ltd v Heller & Partners Ltd*[3], no duty of care *actually* arose because the advice given by the defendants was prefaced by a disclaimer of responsibility for the accuracy of their replies. Since February 1978, such a disclaimer of responsibility for negligent advice made in the course of business is only effective to exclude liability in so far as such exclusion is reasonable[4].

---

1 [1964] AC 465, [1963] 2 All ER 575, HL.
2 *Nocton v Lord Ashburton* [1914] AC 932, HL.

3 [1964] AC 465, [1963] 2 All ER 575, HL.
4 Unfair Contract Terms Act 1977, s.2. The requirement of reasonableness is the same as that discussed in para. 10.45.

20.14 Subsequent cases have accepted that, if there is a special relationship between the parties, a duty not to make negligent misstatements arises, but their interpretation of what constitutes a special relationship displays less unanimity. In *Mutual Life and Citizens' Assurance Co Ltd v Evatt*[1], the Privy Council took a restrictive view of when a special relationship would arise. They considered that a duty of care could only arise if the adviser was either in the business of giving advice or had held himself out as possessing the skill to give the requested advice. However, there are dicta by the Court of Appeal in *Esso Petroleum Co Ltd v Mardon*[2] which criticise the decision in *Mutual Life v Evatt* and suggest that it is too narrowly formulated. In this case there was approval for the view of the House of Lords in *Hedley Byrne v Heller*. Indeed, it seems reasonable to suppose that a special relationship, and thus a duty of care, exists where one party relies on the advice of another, providing such reliance is reasonable and that the party giving the advice realises or should realise that his advice will be relied on. In *Esso Petroleum Co Ltd v Mardon*[3], advice as to the expected annual throughput of a new filling station made by an expert in the petrol trade gave rise to a duty of care, even though the parties subsequently entered into a contract. In *W. B. Anderson & Sons Ltd v Rhodes (Liverpool) Ltd*[4], information as to the financial standing of X given by the commission agent of X, who was buying goods from the plaintiff for X, gave rise to a duty of care.

1 [1971] AC 793, [1971] 1 All ER 150, PC.
2 [1976] 2 QB 801, [1976] 2 All ER 5, CA. See also para. 15.14, c.
3 [1976] 2 QB 801, [1976] 2 All ER 5, CA.
4 [1967] 2 All ER 850.

20.15 The standard of care which the person owing a duty of care under *Hedley Byrne* is expected to satisfy is a duty to act honestly and exercise reasonable care. It is not a duty to give correct advice.

The decision in *Hedley Byrne & Co Ltd v Heller & Partners Ltd*[1], is of great importance to professional advisers who may incur liability for losses suffered by those relying on their advice, particularly since attempts to exclude liability have been curtailed by statute.

1 [1964] AC 465, [1963] 2 All ER 575, HL.

Actual duty of care

20.16   Whether there is an actual duty of care is a question of fact. If it is theoretically possible for a duty of care to exist, the court must then decide whether a duty of care actually arose in the particular case before it. For instance, motorists owe a notional duty of care to all road users but in a particular case no actual duty may arise because the plaintiff was not reasonably foreseeable. For an actual duty of care to arise it is not necessary to reasonably foresee the particular plaintiff, it is sufficient that the plaintiff belongs to a reasonably foreseeable class, for example, pedestrians or the blind[1].

---

1   *Haley v London Electricity Board* [1965] AC 778, [1964] 3 All ER 185, HL.

Breach of duty

The reasonable man

20.17   If there is a duty of care, liability can only arise when there is a breach of that duty. The duty is a duty to take care not to injure, not a duty not to injure, so that in every case it is necessary to determine if the defendant took care which was reasonable in the circumstances. This is not assessed subjectively but objectively; the defendant is not entitled to escape liability by alleging he did *his* incompetent best. The court determines what standard of care would have been reached by a reasonable man in the position of the defendant and in the situation faced by the defendant. If the defendant fails to reach that standard he is in breach of his duty of care[1]. The standard of care for a car driver is the standard of the reasonably competent driver, which is treated by the court as a very high standard. There is no escape for a learner driver: he too must reach the same standard[2]. The standard of care of an accountant is the standard of the reasonably competent accountant[3]. If a doctor is employed by the plaintiff to pierce her ears he is expected to reach the standard of a reasonably competent doctor, but if a jeweller is employed to carry out the same task he is only expected to reach the standard of a reasonably competent jeweller engaged in ear piercing[4]. The standard which the reasonable man is expected to reach is judged by the circumstances and state of knowledge at the time of the injury. It is not a failure to reach the required standard simply to fail to implement a safety precaution not recognised as necessary until after the injury[5].

---

1   *Vaughan v Menlove* (1837) 3 Bing NC 468.
2   *Nettleship v Weston* [1971] 2 QB 691, [1971] 3 All ER 581, CA.

3 *Greaves & Co (Contractors) Ltd v Baynham, Meikle & Partners* [1975] 3 All
   ER 99, [1975] 1 WLR 1095, CA.
4 *Philips v William Whiteley Ltd* [1938] 1 All ER 566.
5 *Roe v Minister of Health* [1954] 2 QB 66, [1954] 2 All ER 131, CA.

The concept of risk

20.18 In determining whether the defendant has reached the standard
of care which could be expected of a reasonable man in his position,
the courts, while applying the overall concept of reasonable foreseeability, tend to pay particular regard to the risk of harm to which the
plaintiff is exposed by the defendant. The concept of risk can be
subdivided into particular areas, namely:

a. whether the conduct of the defendant was likely to cause harm;

b. whether the harm to which the plaintiff was exposed by the defendant
was serious;

c. whether the defendant was engaged on some useful task when he
placed the plaintiff at risk.

20.19 *Likelihood of injury* A defendant who owes a duty of care is
only required to take reasonable care to guard against breach of that
duty. He is not required to guard against remote possibilities of injury[1].
Two cases concerning cricket grounds may be contrasted. In *Bolton v
Stone*[2], the plaintiff was struck by a cricket ball, while standing in the
street outside her house. 'Sixes' of such mammoth proportions had
occurred about six times in the previous 30 years. The House of Lords
found that a duty of care existed but that no breach of that duty had
occurred. The chances of such accidents were too fantastic a possibility
to require the club to guard against them. In *Miller v Jackson*[3], the
plaintiffs occupied a house adjacent to a cricket ground. Balls flew into
their garden and neighbouring gardens more regularly than in *Bolton v
Stone*, and in the preceding season five balls had landed in their garden.
The Court of Appeal found that the risk of harm to the plaintiffs or
their property was a far from remote possibility and the club was
liable in negligence.

   If the likelihood of injury is small there will probably be no
liability for failing to prevent that injury, but in every case the courts
must balance the likelihood of injury against the ease or difficulty of
preventing that injury. A risk which may easily be guarded against
should be guarded against even if the injury is comparatively unlikely
to happen, whereas failure to guard against an equally unlikely injury
which could only be prevented with comparative difficulty may give
rise to no liability[4].

---

1 *Fardon v Harcourt-Rivington* (1932) 146 LT 391, HL.
2 [1951] AC 850, [1951] 1 All ER 1078, HL.

3 [1977] QB 966, [1977] 3 All ER 338, CA.
4 *The Wagon Mound (No.2)* [1967] 1 AC 617 at 642, [1966] 2 All ER 709, PC; *Latimer v AEC Ltd* [1953] AC 643, [1953] 2 All ER 449, HL.

20.20 *Seriousness of harm* Where the harm which is reasonably likely to occur if there is a breach of the duty of care is serious harm, it will be considered reasonable for the defendant to exercise greater care than where the foreseeable harm is slight. In *Paris v Stepney Borough Council*[1], the local authority were liable for the loss of sight sustained by the plaintiff while in their employment. The defendant had failed to provide the plaintiff with goggles and, while such failure might be reasonable for the usual employee, it was not reasonable in the case of the plaintiff, who had only one good eye. The seriousness of the harm likely to affect the plaintiff (blindness) required a reasonable employer to provide goggles.

1 [1951] AC 367, [1951] 1 All ER 42, HL.

20.21 *Usefulness of the defendant's conduct* If the defendant causes injury in the course of some socially useful activity, he may not be in breach of his duty of care. Once again, the courts have to balance two issues — social utility and the harm caused. The more worthy the object which the defendant sought to attain, the less likely is he to be held liable in negligence[1]. In *Watt v Hertfordshire County Council*[2], a fireman who was injured by heavy equipment which was being carried in a lorry not designed for such equipment could not recover damages. The fire authorities had used this lorry because they were rushing to the scene of an accident to try to save someone trapped under a heavy vehicle: the risk which they took in an attempt to save life was not a breach of the duty of care which they owed to the plaintiff.

1 *Daborn v Bath Tramways Motor Co Ltd* [1946] 2 All ER 333, CA.
2 [1954] 2 All ER 368, CA.

Res ipsa loquitur
20.22 In an action for negligence the burden of proving all the elements of the tort is on the plaintiff. However, in seeking to prove breach of duty he may be assisted by the maxim *res ipsa loquitur* ('the thing speaks for itself', i.e. the circumstances are such that a breach of duty can be inferred). If a plaintiff shows that this maxim applies, the effect is to establish a breach of duty unless the defendant can prove otherwise[1].

The classic definition of *res ipsa loquitur* was given by Erle, CJ, in *Scott v London and St. Katherine Docks Co*[2]: 'There must be reasonable evidence of negligence. But where the thing is shown to be under the management of the defendant or his servants, and the accident is such as in the ordinary course of things does not happen if those who have the management use proper care, it affords reasonable evidence, in the absence of explanation by the defendants, that the accident arose from want of care.' Therefore, if the maxim is to apply the plaintiff must show first that the thing which caused the accident was under the control of the defendant or his servants. In *Easson v London and North Eastern Rly Co*[3], the defendants were found not to have control over the doors of their railway carriages, at least not where it was equally likely that a passenger had failed to latch adequately the door through which the plaintiff fell. The accident in question occurred seven miles from the last station. Had it occurred as the train was pulling out of a station the defendants might have been found still to have control over the doors of their train. The second thing which the plaintiff must establish to raise an inference of negligence, is that the accident is such that it would not normally happen unless there had been negligence. For example, in *Ward v Tesco Stores Ltd*[4], the plaintiff slipped and fell on a patch of yoghourt while patronising the defendant's store. The Court of Appeal found that such an accident would not have occurred in the ordinary course of things if spillages had been promptly dealt with.

---

1 *Henderson v Henry E. Jenkins & Sons* [1970] AC 282, [1969] 3 All ER 756, HL.
2 (1865) 3 H & C 596.
3 [1944] 2 KB 421, [1944] 2 All ER 425, CA.
4 [1976] 1 All ER 219, [1976] 1 WLR 810, CA.

Liability for damage

20.23 The plaintiff can recover damages if he can prove that his injuries were a consequence of a breach of duty. In deciding whether the plaintiff's injuries were such a consequence the court must consider two things:

a. whether the breach of duty in fact caused the injuries; and

b. whether the injuries are too remote.

Causation in fact
20.24 The plaintiff in an action for negligence must prove that the actual cause of his injuries was the breach of duty by the defendant. If the immediate cause of the injury was the fault of the plaintiff, the plaintiff cannot recover. For example, in *McWilliams v Sir William Arrol & Co Ltd*[1], the defendants failed to provide safety equipment for steel erectors, one of whom fell to his death. His widow was unable to

recover damages because, it was conclusively established that the deceased would not have used the safety equipment even if it had been provided. Thus, the House of Lords held that the cause of the accident was the default of the deceased, and not the employer's failure to provide safety equipment. Furthermore, if the cause of the injury is the default of a third party, the defendant will not be liable. In *Barnett v Chelsea and Kensington Hospital Management Committee*[2], hospital treatment, or lack of treatment, in breach of a duty of care was found not to have caused the death of the plaintiff's husband, who had been poisoned by an unknown person, since it was established that, even if correct medical treatment had been forthcoming, death would have ensued.

---

1 [1962] 1 All ER 623, [1962] 1 WLR 295, HL.
2 [1969] 1 QB 428, [1968] 1 All ER 1068.

20.25 Sometimes, the plaintiff's injuries may be suffered in two or more unrelated accidents. If such is the case, a defendant who caused the first injuries is not responsible for subsequent injuries, unless he causes them. But the defendant is still liable for the initial injuries even if the subsequent injuries overwhelm them. For example, in *Baker v Willoughby*[1], the defendant negligently injured the plaintiff's left leg. Before the trial concerning this the plaintiff was the victim of an armed robbery at work and his left leg suffered gunshot wounds and had to be amputated. The defendant was liable to compensate the plaintiff for the damage he had caused to the leg, and the fact that the leg had been amputated was ignored in the assessment of damages. If the robbers had been sued they would only have been responsible for injury to an already damaged leg[2].

---

1 [1970] AC 467, [1969] 3 All ER 1528, HL.
2 Also *Performance Cars Ltd v Abraham* [1962] 1 QB 33, [1962] 3 All ER 413, CA, no liability for damage to paintwork of a car which already needed a respray.

Remoteness of damage
20.26 If the defendant's breach of duty caused the plaintiff's injuries, the plaintiff can recover damages if his injuries were not too remote. The test of remoteness, that of foreseeability of damage, is to be found in a decision of the Privy Council, *The Wagon Mound*[1]. In *The Wagon Mound*, a ship, the Wagon Mound, was taking on fuel oil at a wharf in Sydney harbour. Because of the carelessness of the servants of the defendant charterers of the ship, large amounts of fuel oil were spilt, some of which spread to another wharf owned by the plaintiff, where

welding was taking place. Two days later the oil was ignited by splashes from the welding falling onto the oily water. This caused extensive damage to the plaintiff's wharf. It was found as a fact that it was unforeseeable that fuel oil on water would burn, but it was foreseeable that the oil might foul parts of the plaintiff's wharf. The fire was a direct consequence of the breach of duty by the defendants, but it was unforeseeable. The Privy Council, therefore, rejected the plaintiff's claim for damages.

---

1 [1961] AC 388, [1961] 1 All ER 404, PC.

20.27 This test of remoteness has been discussed in subsequent cases and it has been established that an injury is not too remote if a reasonable man would have foreseen at the time of the breach of duty, the type of injury which has occurred. It is not necessary to foresee the exact way in which the injury occurs, nor the extent of the injury[1]. In *Hughes v Lord Advocate*[2], some workmen left a manhole unattended but surrounded by paraffin lamps. A child playing with one of the lamps fell through the manhole and was severely burned when the lamp exploded. It was foreseeable that a child might break a lamp and be burnt but it was totally unforeseeable that a lamp should explode. The child was able to recover damages because the type of injury, burning, was foreseeable. In contrast, in *Doughty v Turner Manufacturing Co Ltd*[3], workmen were not able to recover for injuries caused by the eruption of a cauldron of molten metal, which occurred when a cover fell into the cauldron and suffered chemical change. Injury by splashing molten metal was foreseeable, but not injury by eruption of the molten metal.

---

1 *Bradford v Robinson Rentals Ltd* [1967] 1 All ER 267, [1967] 1 WLR 337.
2 [1963] AC 837, [1963] 1 All ER 705, HL.
3 [1964] 1 QB 518, [1964] 1 All ER 98, CA.

Some cases where damage will not be too remote
20.28 There are two situations where the plaintiff can recover even though it might seem difficult to reconcile such recovery with the rule that only reasonably foreseeable damage is recoverable. First, intended consequences are not too remote[1]. Secondly, the defendant must take his victim as he finds him. Provided the type of damage (e.g. personal injury) was reasonably foreseeable, it is no defence that the injuries suffered by the plaintiff far exceed the injuries that would be suffered by an average person, because of some inherent weakness of the plaintiff.

This rule is known as the 'thin skull rule'. In *Robinson v Post Office*[2], the Post Office was held responsible for brain damage suffered by an employee, who had suffered a cut at work and had been sent to a doctor to have an anti-tetanus injection. Unfortunately, he was allergic to the serum and this caused the brain damage.

---

1   *Scott v Shepherd* (1773) 2 Wm Bl 892.
2   [1974] 2 All ER 737, [1974] 1 WLR 1176, CA.

Some cases where damage will be too remote
20.29   The defendant will not be responsible for injuries suffered by the plaintiff, even if he is in breach of his duty to the plaintiff, if the injuries were caused by a third party[1] or the plaintiff himself[2]. However, not every act of a third party or the plaintiff absolves the defendant from responsibility for his breach of duty. In *Haynes v Harwood*[3], a horse drawn van belonging to the defendants was left unattended in a street in which children were playing. A child threw a stone at the horse, which bolted and injured the plaintiff. The court found the defendants liable despite the act of the child, because their breach of duty consisted of leaving the horse where a child might well cause it to bolt. An action by the plaintiff, which, combined with the defendant's breach of duty, occasions the plaintiff injury, will normally be an act of contributory negligence[4]. However, sometimes the action of the plaintiff is regarded as the cause of his injuries, as in *McKew v Holland and Hannen and Cubitts (Scotland) Ltd*[5]. In this case, the plaintiff had been injured in an accident by the negligence of the defendant and as a consequence was afflicted with a leg which sometimes gave way beneath him. After the accident he visited a flat which was approached by a steep staircase without a handrail. When descending the stairs the plaintiff felt his leg giving way and jumped to try and land upright, sustaining a fractured ankle. The House of Lords found the defendant was not responsible for the broken ankle, the cause of the plaintiff's accident was his foolhardiness in using the stairs without any assistance, knowing his leg was liable to give way.

---

1   *The Oropesa* [1943] P 32, [1943] 1 All ER 211, CA.
2   *McKew v Holland and Hannen and Cubitts (Scotland) Ltd* [1969] 3 All ER 1621, HL.
3   [1935] 1 KB 146, CA.
4   Paras. 21.39–21.43.
5   *McKew v Holland and Hannen and Cubitts (Scotland) Ltd* [1969] 3 All ER 1621, HL.

RELATED TOPICS

Employers' liability[1]

20.30   An employer owes a duty of care to his employees because they are his employees. An employer fulfils this duty, which is to exercise reasonable care, by providing a competent staff, adequate materials, a proper system of work and effective supervision[2]. As well as this common law duty in negligence, an employer may also be liable for breach of statutory duty[3] or be vicariously responsible[4] for accidents occurring at work. The standard of care expected from an employer is high and he cannot discharge his duty of care merely by entrusting a task to an independent contractor. Furthermore, an employer is liable in negligence for defects in equipment which he provides, even if the defects are caused by the fault of a third party[5].

---

1 See also paras. 28.64–28.82.
2 *Wilsons and Clyde Coal Co Ltd v English* [1938] AC 57, [1937] 3 All ER 628, HL.
3 Paras. 21.1–21.5.
4 Paras. 21.14–21.20.
5 Employer's Liability (Defective Equipment) Act 1969.

Manufacturers' liability

20.31   The leading case is *Donoghue v Stevenson*[1], where it was held that a manufacturer of a product owes a duty of care to the ultimate consumer of his product, at least if the goods are not intended to be subject to inspection between manufacture and sale, and such inspection is not reasonably probable. The manufacturer in that case owed a duty to the retailer of the ginger beer in contract, but this was held not to prevent a concomitant duty of care to the consumer in the tort of negligence.

---

1 [1932] AC 562, HL; para. 20.4.

20.32   A duty of care will not arise if examination was reasonably foreseeable[1]. But, otherwise the fact that there is an actual inspection of goods between manufacture and the loss or damage caused by the goods does not abrogate the duty of care. Whether an intermediate examination was probable is determined objectively, but it is a decision influenced by policy factors. Essentially, it is a decision whether a manufacturer should have to bear the risk of loss or damage caused by the product he has manufactured. Absence of control by the manufacturer once the goods have left his hands does not abrogate the duty of care. However, where there is a considerable time-lag between manufacture and the causing of injury the manufacturer is less likely to be liable, especially if the ultimate consumer or an intermediate owner is in a better position to know if the product is satisfactory. In *Paine v Colne Valley Electricity Supply Co Ltd*[2], the housing for electrical equipment caused the death of an employee because it was improperly insulated. The employers had purchased the housing over two years previously and had themselves installed it. The employers, and not the manufacturer of the defective housing, were held responsible for the death. The rules can apply to those who construct or manufacture buildings as well as chattels[3]. If a manufacturer is liable because he manufactured a defective article he is liable for any damage to persons or property using the product and apparently also for damage to the product itself[4].

1 *Driver v William Willett (Contractors) Ltd* [1969] 1 All ER 665.
2 [1938] 4 All ER 803.
3 *Dutton v Bognor Regis UDC* [1972] 1 QB 373, [1972] 1 All ER 462, CA; *Anns v London Borough of Merton* [1977] 2 All ER 492, [1977] 2 WLR 1024, HL.
4 *Ibid.*

20.33 If a manufacturer was not in breach of his duty of care in manufacturing the defective item, he cannot, of course, be liable in negligence. Establishing that his production methods are practically foolproof will absolve him from liability for the odd defective product[1].

1 *Daniels and Daniels v White & Sons Ltd* [1938] 4 All ER 258.

20.34 The manufacturer of defective products cannot exclude liability for negligence by means of an exemption clause if the goods are not to be used for business purposes and the purported exemption clause was contained in a guarantee. Anything in writing containing a promise to repair or replace defective goods is a guarantee in this context[1].

1 Unfair Contract Terms Act 1977, s.5. See also para. 22.62.

The liability of occupiers of property to lawful visitors

20.35 The occupier of premises owes a common duty of care to all lawful visitors. The duty, which is a duty to make sure that lawful visitors are reasonably safe while visiting premises, is imposed by the Occupiers' Liability Act 1957, s.2. The common duty of care closely resembles the duty of care in negligence.

Premises
20.36   Premises for the purposes of the Act include ships in dry dock[1], lifts[2] (at least in relation to their defective state rather than their defective operation), a large mechanical digger engaged in extending the London Underground[3], and scaffolding[4], as well as buildings and land.

---

1   *London Graving Dock Co Ltd v Horton* [1951] AC 737, [1951] 2 All ER 1, HL.
2   *Haseldine v Daw & Son Ltd* [1941] 2 KB 343, [1941] 3 All ER 156, CA.
3   *Bunker v Charles Brand & Son Ltd* [1969] 2 QB 480, [1969] 2 All ER 59.
4   *Kearney v Eric Waller Ltd* [1967] 1 QB 29, [1965] 3 All ER 352.

Lawful visitors
20.37   The common duty of care is owed to all lawful visitors[1]. A person may be a lawful visitor because he has been invited onto the occupier's premises, or has a contractual right to be on them, or is on them as of right (e.g. under a statutory power of entry such as that possessed by officials of gas or electricity boards in certain cases), or because he has been permitted, expressly or impliedly, to be on them. The occupier of premises does not owe the common duty of care under the Occupiers' Liability Act to trespassers, and a lawful visitor may become a trespasser if he visits parts of the premises of the occupier to which he has not been invited or allowed to enter. It was said in one case, that you do not invite visitors into your home for them to slide down the bannisters; in other words, a visitor remains a lawful visitor only while within the ambit of his lawful visit. Lawful visitors have an implied permission in many cases to seek out a lavatory, and such searchings will not render the visitor a trespasser.

---

1   Occupiers' Liability Act 1957, ss. 1(2) and 2(6).

20.38   Difficulty can be experienced in distinguishing between persons entering premises under an implied permission to do so (implied licensees) and trespassers. There is an implied licence, for instance, for visitors of tenants to use parts of premises still occupied by the landlord[1], who therefore owes such visitors a common duty of care. There is an implied licence to visit public parks to take recreation there or to visit public libraries to consult or borrow books. If the occupier of private premises has not expressly permitted the entry of people he may be found to have impliedly authorised such entry. An implied licence can arise if the occupier of premises knows of the incursion of trespassers and acts in such a way that assent to those incursions can be assumed. There may be an implied licence if, despite a notice saying 'No Trespassers', the occupier of land makes no attempt to seek a remedy against persistent and regular trespassing[2]. However, the absence of such a notice does not give an implied licence to enter premises[3]. In *Lowery v Walker*[4], an implied licence was found to exist in favour of people using a field as a short cut to a railway station. This short cut had been used for 35 years and, although the owner of the field had often sought to prevent its use, he had never taken proceedings against anyone. It was held that people using the short cut had an implied licence to do so, and therefore the plaintiff, who was savaged by a horse which the defendant had put in the field, could recover. Children will also have an implied licence if they have been 'allured' onto the occupier's premises. Among the things which have been held to be 'allurements' are poisonous shrubs[5] and a horse and cart[6].

---

1 *Jacobs v LCC* [1950] AC 361, [1950] 1 All ER 737, HL.
2 *Addie & Sons (Collieries) Ltd v Dumbreck* [1929] AC 358, HL.
3 *Edwards v Railway Executive* [1952] AC 737, [1952] 2 All ER 430, HL.
4 [1911] AC 10, HL.
5 *Glasgow Corpn v Taylor* [1922] 1 AC 44, HL.
6 *Lynch v Nurdin* (1841) 1 QB 29.

Occupiers
20.39 The common duty of care is owed to lawful visitors by the occupier of the premises[1].

The crucial determinant of whether a person is an occupier of premises is whether he has control of them. Ownership in itself is not enough. Different parts of the same premises may be occupied by different people for the purposes of the Occupiers Liability Act. In *Wheat v Lacon & Co Ltd*[2], the owners of a public house which was managed for them by X, were found to be occupiers of the public house because they retained a degree of control over the premises. The House of Lords found the defendants and X were in occupation of X's flat, though X's responsibility extended only to his belongings not to the structure of the premises.

---

1 Occupiers' Liability Act 1957, s.1(1).
2 [1966] AC 552, [1966] 1 All ER 582, HL; *Harris v Birkenhead Corpn* [1976] 1 All ER 341, [1975] 1 WLR 379, CA.

The common duty of care
20.40 The duty which the occupier of property owes towards the person and property of his lawful visitors is the common duty of care.

This duty is defined in the Occupiers' Liability Act 1957, s.2, as a duty to take such care as, in all the circumstances of the case, is reasonable to see that the visitor will be reasonably safe in using the premises for the purposes for which he is invited or permitted by the occupier to be there. The common duty of care imposed by the statute closely resembles the standard and duty of care which are the basis of the common law tort of negligence. The common duty of care is further explained in the Occupiers' Liability Act which says that:

a. an occupier is entitled to assume that lawful visitors will display ordinary prudence while on his premises[1]; and

b. an occupier must expect children to be less careful than adults[2]. However, in *Phipps v Rochester Corpn*[3], the Court of Appeal held that an occupier is entitled to assume that very young children (in this case aged five and seven) will be accompanied by a responsible adult; and

c. an occupier can assume that lawful visitors carrying out their job on his premises will recognise and guard against any special risks attaching to that job. However, this only applies where the occupier leaves his visitors a discretion as to how to carry out their job[4].

---

1 S.2(3).
2 *Ibid.*
3 [1955] 1 QB 450, [1955] 1 All ER 129.
4 S.2(3); *Roles v Nathan* [1963] 2 All ER 908, CA.

20.41 If an occupier warns his lawful visitors of a danger he discharges his duty of care, providing that the notice in itself is enough to render a visitor reasonably safe[1]. Further, an occupier will not be liable for a danger caused by the faulty work of an independent contractor whom he has employed, if it was reasonable for him to entrust the work to an independent contractor, and he made a reasonable attempt to check that the independent contractor was competent and that the work was properly done[2].

An occupier is entitled to exclude, by contract or by means of a notice or warning, the common duty of care in relation to premises not used for business purposes. There are exceptions: an occupier cannot exclude, by contract, the common duty of care owed to those lawful visitors who enter by virtue of a contract but who are not parties to that contract[3], nor can an occupier or business premises exclude liability by contract or otherwise for causing death or personal injury to visitors and he can only exclude liability for causing other types of injury if such exclusion is reasonable[4].

---

1 Occupiers' Liability Act 1957, s.2(4).
2 *Ibid.;* liability for the torts of independent contractors is discussed in paras. 21.21–21.29.

3   *Ibid.* s.2(1) and 3(1).
4   Unfair Contract Terms Act 1977, s.2; para. 21.35.

20.42   Landlords are in a special position under the Occupiers Liability Act. They only owe a duty to those likely to be affected by a want of repair in the demised premises if they have a duty to repair the premises or if they have a right to enter and repair those premises[1].

1   Occupiers' Liability Act 1957, s.4.

Defences
20.43   The occupier can rely on the defences of volenti and contributory negligence[1].

1   Paras. 21.35–21.43.

Activities carried on by an occupier of premises
20.44   Of course, the occupier of premises owes a duty of care to all lawful visitors in respect of activities which he carries on on his premises, but this duty is owed under the common law tort of negligence and not under the Occupiers' Liability Act.

Liability of occupiers to trespassers
20.45   People who are not lawful visitors are trespassers.
        The occupier owes them a lesser duty than he owes to lawful visitors. It is long established that, in respect of activities carried out or the state of the premises, an occupier cannot deliberately seek to injure trespassers nor recklessly disregard their presence[1]. Otherwise the duty owed to trespassers is the duty of common humanity. This duty was formulated by the House of Lords in *British Railways Board v Herrington*[2]. This case provides that if a reasonable man would have realised that there was a strong probability that trespassers were on the occupier's premises at a point where they were subject to danger, then the occupier must make some attempt to protect such trespassers. The standard of conduct demanded of the occupier is to act with common humanity, this is assessed *subjectively*, i.e. what is required of an individual occupier is determined by reference to such factors as their age, strength and financial resources. From the aged or the infirm or the poor a warning notice might suffice, from a wealthy company more will be demanded. In addition, attempts to exclude liability by means of notices are subject to statutory restrictions[3]. In *Herrington*, trespassers used to play by the side of the railway line and used the line as a short cut. The fences at this point were dilapidated and the defendant's employees, who knew of the defects in the fences and the presence of

trespassers, did no more than report the trespass to the police. The plaintiff, a child of six, was severely injured when he came into contact with a live rail. The House of Lords found that the defendant owed the plaintiff a duty, viz. the duty of common humanity, and that they had failed to satisfy that duty[4].

---

1 *Bird v Holbrook* (1828) 4 Bing 628; *Mourton v Poulter* [1930] 2 KB 183, DC.
2 [1972] AC 877, [1972] 1 All ER 749, HL.
3 Unfair Contract Terms Act 1977, s.2. See para. 20.41.
4 See also *Penny v Northampton Borough Council* (1974) 118 SJ 628, CA.

Chapter 21
Other Torts and Procedural Matters

BREACH OF STATUTORY DUTY

21.1 Not every breach of a duty imposed by statute gives rise to an action in tort. However, if it was the intention of Parliament, express or implied, to permit a civil action for statutory breach, an action is possible. In determining the implied intention of Parliament, various factors are considered:

a. If a statute is intended to prevent the type of injury which the plaintiff has suffered then it is probable that a civil action can be founded on breach of statutory duty[1].

b. The fact that a statute provides that any fine levied for breach of a statutory duty can be used to compensate a victim of that breach does not necessarily mean there can be no civil remedy[2].

c. If a statutory duty is owed to the general public rather than individuals then probably no civil action will lie for breach of statutory duty.

d. The fact that a victim of a breach of a statutory duty has a common law remedy, e.g. in negligence, will not prevent a civil action for breach of statute. Employees, in particular, will frequently have an action for breach of statutory duty and for negligence against their employer[3].

The Factories Acts are examples of statutes for breach of which a civil action will nearly always lie.

---

1 *Monk v Warbey* [1935] 1 KB 75, CA.
2 *Groves v Lord Wimborne* [1898] 2 QB 402, CA.
3 See also para. 20.30.

21.2 An action for breach of statutory duty can only be maintained by a plaintiff:

a. If the statutory duty was owed to *him*[1]. For example, if a statute imposes an obligation on employers to provide adequate lighting in factories for employees, a visitor to a factory who falls and because of defective lighting is injured cannot recover damages for breach of statutory duty; and

b. If the injury was of a kind which the statute sought to prevent[1]. In *Gorris v Scott*[2], a shipowner failed to provide pens for livestock on board his ship in breach of statutory duty. The plaintiff, whose sheep were washed overboard because of the lack of pens, failed to recover for breach of statutory duty because the statute sought to prevent the spread of disease, not to prevent animals being lost overboard.

---

1 *Hartley v Mayoh & Co Ltd* [1954] 1 QB 383, [1954] 1 All ER 375, CA.
2 *Gorris v Scott* (1874) LR 9 Exch 125.

The standard of liability
21.3 The standard which a party who is under a statutory duty must reach to avoid liability is determined by reference to the statute in issue. If a statute provides that X must be done, failure to do X in even the slightest degree is a breach of statutory duty[1]. For example, the Factories Acts require a grinding wheel to be securely fenced, and it is no defence, to an action by an employee injured by an unfenced grinding wheel, that fencing the wheel would render the wheel unusable[1].

---

1 *John Summers & Sons Ltd v Frost* [1955] AC 740, [1955] 1 All ER 870, HL.

Causation
21.4 Injury to the plaintiff must be caused by the breach of statutory duty if he is to recover[1]. In *Ginty v Belmont Building Supplies Ltd*[2], the plaintiff was required by statute to use crawling boards while engaged on roofwork and the defendant was required to see the plaintiff used such boards. Boards were provided by the defendant, but the plaintiff failed to use them and fell through a roof and was injured. His claim for damages for breach of statutory duty failed, the immediate cause of the plaintiff's injury being his own default.

---

1 See *McWilliams v Sir William Arrol & Co Ltd* [1962] 1 All ER 623, [1962] 1 WLR 295, HL; para. 20.24.
2 [1959] 1 All ER 414.

Defences

21.5 Contributory negligence and *volenti* which are discussed in paras. 21.35 to 21.43 are defences to an action for breach of statutory duty.

SOME OTHER TORTS

Defamation

21.6 Defamation consists of publishing a statement which tends to lower a person in the estimation of right-thinking members of society or which would tend to make them shun or avoid that person. It is not necessary for anyone to actually think the worse of the plaintiff or shun or avoid him.

Defamation is subdivided into libel and slander. A defamation which is published in a relatively permanent form, e.g. in a film or newspaper, is libel and words or pictures broadcast over the radio or television are by statute considered to be libel. Libel is actionable without proof of any damage, whereas slander is only actionable if there has been some damage caused to the plaintiff *or* the slander imputes:

a. that the plaintiff has committed a criminal offence; or

b. that he is unfit for his trade, profession or office; or

c. where the plaintiff is a woman, that she is unchaste.

21.7 If the plaintiff is to sue successfully for defamation, he must prove:

a. that the words, picture, film or other material were defamatory (either in their natural and ordinary meaning or because of facts known to people to whom the words were published); and

b. that they referred to the plaintiff, (the reference need not be by name if the plaintiff is clearly indicated); and

c. that the words were published. Publication to a single person, other than the publisher's spouse, will suffice, but there is no publication if the alleged defamation is only revealed to the plaintiff.

Every repetition of a defamatory statement is a publication so that not only is the writer or speaker of the defamation liable but so is a printer or publisher etc.. Even a distributor of papers and books can be liable if he knew or ought to have known that the paper or book contained defamatory material.

21.8 The defences that are available to an action for defamation are:

a. That the defamation was published innocently and an offer to apologise has been made.

b. Justification, i.e. that the defamation was true; this defence is not destroyed by the fact that the defamation was prompted by spite or malice. An exception is the case where the defamation relates to the criminal conviction of a person who has been 'rehabilitated' under the Rehabilitation of Offenders Act 1974, in which case justification is destroyed by proof of malice.

c. Fair comment. The comment must be on a matter of public interest, it must be an expression of opinion and it must be fair.

d. Absolute privilege. Certain communications are absolutely privileged and cannot form the basis of an action for defamation, e.g. statements in Parliament and in judicial proceedings.

e. Qualified privilege. A number of communications are privileged but the privilege disappears if there is malice. An example is a fair and accurate report of Parliamentary proceedings.

Interference with chattels

21.9 The Torts (Interference with Goods) Act 1977 provides that a person who 'wrongfully interferes' with goods (all chattels except a chose in action or money) is liable in tort either to return the goods and pay consequential damages; or to return the goods, or pay damages for their value and consequential damages; or to pay damages.

21.10 Wrongful interference consists of the following torts:

a. conversion;

b. trespass to goods;

c. negligence resulting in damage to goods or an interest in goods;

d. any other tort resulting in damage to goods or to an interest in goods.

Conversion can consist of loss or destruction of goods by a bailee in breach of duty; taking possession of another's goods, even if innocently; or abusing possession of another's goods, e.g. by selling them. Contributory negligence is not a defence to an action for wrongful interference. If the tortfeasor has improved the goods or honestly acquired them after improvement, paying more for them because of the improvement, the plaintiff may be required to pay an allowance for the improvement.

Private nuisance

21.11 Every occupier of property must expect his property and his enjoyment of that property to be affected to some extent by the actions carried on on adjoining land. However, if this interference exceeds what one can be expected to endure, it is an actionable private nuisance. In deciding whether the interference with the property or its enjoyment exceeds what the plaintiff can be expected to endure, the court has regard to the character of the neighbourhood, unless the property has actually been damaged, in which case this factor is irrelevant. If the alleged interference would not affect a normal person but affects the plaintiff because of some abnormal sensitivity then the nuisance is not actionable. The mere fact that the defendant's conduct is useful is no defence, and a nuisance not apparently actionable can become so if prolonged or activated by malice.

If an actionable nuisance is established, the plaintiff can sue for damages or apply for an injunction to restrain the nuisance. Only the owner or occupier of property can sue successfully in nuisance but he can recover for damage to himself, his property and his enjoyment of his property.

21.12 If the defendant is the occupier of property from which the nuisance emanated and he created that nuisance, it is no defence for him to say that he exercised reasonable care not to create a nuisance. However, if the defendant is the occupier of property from which the nuisance emanated and the nuisance was created by a third party, e.g. a trespasser, or occurred naturally, e.g. a tree struck by lightning, then the defendant will not be liable in nuisance if he can prove that he was not negligent in failing to prevent the nuisance interfering with the plaintiff's property.

The person who created a nuisance can always be sued. Among the defences which are available are nuisance prescription, i.e. that an actionable nuisance has continued for 20 years and the plaintiff has not sued during that period, *volenti non fit injuria*, contributory negligence and statutory authorisation.

The rule in *Rylands v Fletcher*

21.13 This tort is one of strict liability, i.e. liability can arise without fault, although some defences are available. It resembles nuisance in that it is an action brought by one land owner or occupier against another land owner or occupier. Liability under this rule arises where the defendant, for his own purposes, brings onto his land, and collects there, something which constitutes a non-natural user of the land, and which is likely to cause mischief if it escapes, and which does escape.

The vital elements are the collection of the mischievous items, e.g. water, yew trees or cars, and the escape from land within the control of one person to land within the control of another, always providing that what is collected constitutes non-natural user of the land. This does not mean unnatural user but use of land which is unusual having regard to modern conditions. Therefore, a factory is probably not a non-natural user. The owner or occupier of the land adversely affected by the escape can sue for damage to person or property, and it is thought that a non-occupier can sue for physical injury.

The defences available are *volenti non fit injuria*, that the collecting and keeping, etc., was partly for the defendant's benefit, that the escape was caused by the unforeseeable act of a stranger, contributory negligence, statutory authority and, in very extreme cases, that the escape was an act of God.

VICARIOUS LIABILITY

21.14 Vicarious liability enables the victim of a tort to sue a person standing in a particular relationship to the tortfeasor, if the commission of that tort is referable to that relationship. An example of a relationship giving rise to vicarious liability is that of employer and employee; an employer is vicariously liable for torts committed by an employee in the course of his employment. To a lesser extent a principal may be vicariously liable for the torts of his agent, and an employer for the torts of his independent contractor. If a person is vicariously liable for the torts of the tortfeasor this does not exempt the tortfeasor from liability, it merely enables the victim to choose the person whom he wishes to sue. Since an employer or principal will generally be better able to satisfy a judgement made against him than would the tortfeasor, the victim of the tort will usually choose to sue the employer or principal. Where there is no vicarious liability at common law, responsibility for the torts of another may be imposed by statute. Police officers are not the employees of their chief constable but, by virtue of the Police Act 1964[1], he is liable for torts committed by them in the performance of their duties. Any damages awarded against a chief constable are payable out of public funds.

---

1 S.48.

Employers and employees

21.15 Because employers are vicariously liable for the torts of their employees in situations when they would not be so liable for the torts

of their independent contractors, it is necessary to determine whether
a particular tortfeasor is an employee.

Who is an employee?
21.16 In many cases there is no difficulty in deciding whether a person
is an employee. Where the decision is less straight-forward these are
various tests which the courts have devised as aids to their deliberations.
These are discussed more fully in paras. 28.3 to 28.5, but every case
entails the consideration and balancing of various factors. For example,
what the parties call their relationship, whether the employer controls
the method of working used by the tortfeasor, whether the work done by
the tortfeasor is an integral part of the business, who provides the
equipment for the job, whether payment is in the form of wages, who
engages helpers to assist the tortfeasor in his work and whether the
tortfeasor has any financial stake in the business.

Particularly difficulty has arisen in determining whether skilled
professional staff, for example, doctors, nurses and surgeons working
in a hospital, are employees. Hospitals have been held vicariously liable
for the torts of their full-time personnel[1] and, in some cases, even part-
time staff. A hospital may be in breach of its own duty of care, which
it owes to patients, if it negligently injures them, so that it is not always
necessary to decide the difficult question of whether a member of the
hospital staff is an employee[2].

---

1 *Cassidy v Ministry of Health* [1951] 2 KB 343, [1951] 1 All ER 574, CA.
2 *Ibid.*

Who is an employer?
21.17 An employee who works for employer A, his usual or general
employer, may be lent or hired to employer B, his temporary employer,
for a period of time or for a particular purpose. If the employer commits
a tort while working for employer B, the courts have to decide which
employer is to be vicariously liable. In *Mersey Docks and Harbour
Board v Coggins and Griffith (Liverpool) Ltd*[1], the House of Lords
attempted to formulate some guidelines for the courts. In this case,
a crane driver and his crane were hired to Coggins under a contract
which provided that the crane driver was to be the employee of Coggins.
Coggins told the crane driver what they required to be done but did not
attempt to instruct him how to operate his crane. In carrying out
Coggins' instructions, the driver injured X when he operated his crane
negligently. The general employer, the Harbour Board, were held
vicariously liable for their driver's tort. The House of Lords held that,
unless the general employer established otherwise, he should be the
employer held vicariously liable. The general employer does not necessarily avoid vicarious liability by providing in his contract with the

temporary employer that the employee is the employee of the temporary employer. The House stated that the most important factor in determining who is to be vicariously liable is who controlled the way the employee was to work, but other relevant factors are who paid his wages and who was entitled to dismiss him. In the *Mersey Docks* case, the temporary employer controlled what the crane driver was to do, but not how he was to do it. Obviously, the less skilled the employee, the more likely it is that the temporary employer controls the way the employee works and therefore the more likely it is that the temporary employer is vicariously liable.

---

1 [1947] AC 1, [1946] 2 All ER 345, HL.

When is the employer liable?
21.18 An employer is only vicariously liable for torts committed by his employees in the course of their employment. An employee is acting in the course of his employment if the act which constitutes the tort is:

a. expressly authorised by his employer; or

b. impliedly authorised by his employer; or

c. incidental to an authorised act; or

d. a method, even if an improper method, of carrying out an authorised act.

21.19 If an employee departs so radically from what he is authorised to do, or adopts a method of performance which is totally different from that authorised, that he can no longer be regarded as acting in the course of his employment, his employer ceases to be vicariously liable for his torts; the employee is 'on a frolic of his own'.

In *Staton v National Coal Board*[1], a first-aid attendant, who was employed by the defendant, was found to be acting in the course of his employment when cycling across the defendant's premises to collect his wages. However, in *Hilton v Thomas Burton (Rhodes) Ltd*[2], some employees, who had permission to use their employer's van for reasonable purposes, were found not to be acting in the course of their employment when they had an accident in the van while returning from a totally unauthorised tea-break taken seven miles from their workplace. If an employee has an express or implied authority to act, the employer will be vicariously liable for torts committed in exercising that authority, even if the employee carelessly or in an excess of misguided zeal exceeded his authority. For example, an employee usually has implied authority to protect his employer's property and, if the employee injures someone in the belief that he is protecting that property, the employer is vicariously liable, unless the actions of the employee are so unreasonable that he must be regarded as on a frolic of his own[3]. In *Kay v ITW Ltd*[4], the defendant's storekeeper was authorised to drive fork-lift trucks and small vans. In attempting to return a fork-lift truck to a warehouse, he moved a lorry belonging to a third party, which was blocking his path, without asking permission from the lorry driver. In moving the lorry, he injured the plaintiff, and his employer was held liable for the plaintiff's injuries, even though the storekeeper was not authorised to drive lorries and there was no pressing need to return the fork-lift truck to the warehouse. The Court of Appeal held that he had not acted so unreasonably in moving the lorry that he was no longer acting in the course of his employment.

Even disregarding the express instructions of the employer does not necessarily take an employee out of the course of his employment, if the employee is still doing what he is authorised to do, albeit in an improper manner. In *Limpus v London General Omnibus Co*[5], the employer was vicariously liable for damage to the plaintiff's bus which had been caused by their employee racing his bus contrary to his express instructions. The employee was employed to drive buses and, therefore, the employer was liable for torts committed while he was driving buses, even if his method of driving was not an authorised method. Similarly, in *Rose v Plenty*[6], the employers of a milkman were vicariously liable for the injuries caused to the plaintiff by the negligent driving of the milk-float by their employee. This was so even though the plaintiff was a child whom the milkman, contrary to express instructions, was using as an assistant. The Court of Appeal said that the milkman, by disregarding his instructions, had not ceased to be acting on behalf of his employer.

---

1 [1957] 2 All ER 667, [1957] 1 WLR 893.
2 [1961] 1 All ER 74, [1961] 1 WLR 705.
3 *Poland v John Parr & Sons* [1927] 1 KB 236.
4 [1968] 1 QB 140, [1967] 3 All ER 22, CA.
5 (1862) 1 H & C 526.
6 [1976] 1 All ER 97, [1976] 1 WLR 141, CA.

21.20 If the employee is acting in the course of his employment, the employer is vicariously liable for his torts, even when the employee committed the tort for his own benefit. For example, an employer has been held to be vicariously liable for thefts and frauds perpetrated by his employees[1].

---

1 *Morris v C. W. Martin & Sons Ltd* [1966] 1 QB 716, [1965] 2 All ER 725, CA.

Employers and independent contractors

21.21 While an employer is not generally vicariously liable for torts committed by independent contractors whom he has engaged, liability is imposed in a number of cases. Such liability is not comparable with the liability of an employer for the torts of his employees because it only arises if:

a. *the employer* owes a particular type of duty of care to the plaintiff, and, although he does not personally break it, a tortious act *in the particular circumstances by the independent contractor is regarded as the employer's act and therefore his breach;* or

b. *the employer* owes a duty of care to the plaintiff, and *the breach of duty is the employer's failure to engage an independent contractor who is competent* to carry out the task entrusted to him.

Non-delegable duties

21.22 Cases which fall into category a. above are described as non-delegable duties. These duties are ones of strict liability, i.e. absence of fault is no defence. Nor is it a defence that a competent independent contractor was employed.

21.23 *Operations on or adjoining a highway* If an independent contractor is engaged to work on or adjoining the highway, the employer is liable for the tortious activities or omissions of the contractor which cause damage[1].

---

1 *Tarry v Ashton* (1876) 1 QBD 314.

21.24 *Employers liability* We have seen in para. 20.30 that an employer owes a duty of care in negligence to his employees. This duty of care, to see that the employees are reasonably safe, cannot be discharged by entrusting the organisation of safety at work to an independent contractor, however competent. The employer is, of course, only liable if there is a breach of his duty either by himself or his employees or his independent contractors.

21.25 *Rylands v Fletcher*[1] Apart from the particular application of the rule in *Rylands v Fletcher*, mentioned above, an employer is liable under the rule in *Rylands v Fletcher* for the torts of his independent contractor.

---

1 (1866) LR 1 Exch 265; para. 21.13.

21.26 *Extra-hazardous activities* By analogy with the rule in *Rylands v Fletcher*, an employer owes a duty of care to those likely to be affected by his pursuance of acts which clearly involve danger to others because of the dangerous equipment used. This duty, which involves a duty to see that care *is* taken, cannot be discharged merely by employing a competent independent contractor. In *Honeywill and Stein Ltd v Larkin Bros Ltd*[1], the plaintiffs engaged the defendant to take photographs of the interior of X's cinema by flashlight and were responsible when the defendant's negligent use of magnesium flash powder resulted in damage by fire to the cinema.

1 [1934] 1 KB 191, CA.

21.27 *Strict statutory duties* Certain statutes impose liability for the defaults of an independent contractor on his employer. An example is the Factories Act 1961[1].

1 Paras. 28.79 and 28.80.

Negligent selection of contractor
21.28 Cases which fall within category b. above are those in which, while it is reasonable to employ an independent contractor, in that an ordinary person can delegate tasks involving skill and competence, the employer has failed to exercise reasonable care to choose an apparently competent contractor. The employer will be in breach of his duty in such cases if he does not use due care to see that his contractor is properly qualified for the task entrusted to him, or if he fails to give the contractor adequate instructions in relation to matters not within the contractor's professional knowledge but incidental to the task for which the contractor is engaged[1].

1 *Robinson v Beaconsfield RDC* [1911] 2 Ch 188, CA.

21.29 In relation to either case, the employer can only be liable where the tort of the independent contractor is committed in carrying out the work which he was engaged to do.

Principal and agent[1]

21.30 A principal is vicariously liable for torts committed by his agent when the agent was acting within his actual, usual or ostensible authority[2]. For example, in *Lloyd v Grace, Smith & Co*[3], a firm of solicitors was vicariously liable for a fraud practised by their agent, a clerk, which was within his ostensible authority.

Such liability can arise even when there is no contractual relationship between principal and agent. A vexed question is that of the relationship of a vehicle owner and a person who drives the vehicle with his permission. If the driver is an agent, the principal (the car owner) is vicariously liable for accidents caused negligently involving the vehicle (so that his insurers will have to pay any damages). It appears that the car driver is the agent of the car owner if he drives the car with the owner's permission *and* the owner had some interest or concern in the journey of the driver[4].

---

1 Chap. 18.
2 Paras. 18.32—18.38; *Heatons Transport (St Helens) Ltd v Transport and General Workers' Union* [1973] AC 15, [1972] 3 All ER 101, HL.
3 [1912] AC 716, HL.
4 *Morgans v Launchbury* [1973] AC 127, [1972] 2 All ER 606, HL; *Ormrod v Crosville Motor Services Ltd* [1953] 2 All ER 753, [1953] 1 WLR 1120, CA.

DEATH

21.31 Causing death does not itself give rise to any cause of action in tort. However by virtue of the Law Reform (Miscellaneous Provisions) Act 1934, the estate of a tort victim can recover damages where the deceased could have recovered damages. In addition to claims under the 1934 Act, the tortfeasor may be liable under the Fatal Accidents Act 1976 to the dependent relatives for depriving them of their means of support.

21.32 *The Law Reform (Miscellaneous Provisions) Act 1934* Section 1 of this Act provides that any action except defamation subsisting *against or vested in* a person prior to death is not terminated by the death of either party. If a person is injured by the negligent driving of another he has a cause of action for any injury suffered, and his death will not terminate that cause of action which can be pursued by his estate. Any damages which are awarded are paid to the estate and therefore benefit those entitled under the will or the intestacy of the deceased. In assessing damages when the victim of the tort has died, the court can award a sum for loss of expectation of life (conventionally £1,000) and for loss suffered by the deceased between the date of the tort and his demise, which if death is instantaneous will be nothing[1]. Damages awarded to the deceased's estate may be reduced if the deceased contributed to his death[2] but there is no reduction because the deceased's estate has benefited by his death, e.g. if life insurance becomes payable.

In one case, a deceased's estate can be sued even if the cause of action did not arise until after the decease. This is when a tort is committed prior to death but does not cause damage until after the death. For example, if a manufacturer negligently produces a defective product, and then dies, a person injured in using that product can sue the manufacturer's estate.

---

1 *Rose v Ford* [1937] AC 826, [1937] 1 All ER 359, HL.
2 Paras. 21.39—21.43.

21.33 *Fatal Accidents Act 1976* This Act provides that dependent relatives whose breadwinner has been killed by the tortious acts of another can sue that other. Their action is not because a person has been killed but because they have been deprived of the person on whom they were dependent. Damages payable under this Act are paid directly to the relatives and do not form part of the deceased's estate, but damages are only payable if the deceased could have sued if he were alive. In assessing damages the court can award a sum for earnings which the deceased could have earned (unlike claims under the Law Reform (Miscellaneous Provisions) Act) and which he would have expended on his dependents. Because damages can be awarded for the deceased's loss of future earnings, and because damages are paid directly to them, it is generally beneficial for relatives to seek damages under this Act rather than the 1934 Act, though a joint action embracing both Acts is common. The damages awarded by the court under the 1976 Act will be reduced by the amount of any benefits accruing to dependent relatives because of the death of their breadwinner, including benefits actually accruing to them from the damages payable to the deceased's estate under the Law Reform (Miscellaneous Provisions) Act[1]. However, the Fatal Accidents Act provides that, in awarding damages, no reduction is to be made in respect of insurance money, pensions or gratuities payable because of the death. Damages awarded under this Act can be reduced if the deceased breadwinner, or a dependent relative, contributed to his decease[2].

---

1 *Davies v Powell Dyffryn Collieries Ltd* [1942] AC 601, [1942] 1 All ER 657, HL.
2 Paras. 21.39—21.43.

JOINT TORTFEASORS

21.34 If two or more people acting in pursuance of a common design thereby commit a tort, they are joint tortfeasors. Each joint tortfeasor is jointly and severally liable for damages recoverable by the victim of their tort[1]. Thus, the victim of a joint tort can sue:

a. All or some of the tortfeasors in a joint action, and one sum by way of damages will be awarded[2].

b. Any one tortfeasor, and it is possible for all the tortfeasors to be sued in turn, although damages can only be recovered once[3].

If the victim of a joint tort obtains damages from one tortfeasor that tortfeasor can obtain contributions from his fellow tortfeasors. The amount of contribution payable by any tortfeasor can be fixed by the court at a just and equitable amount up to 100 per cent, having regard to the relative responsibility of that tortfeasor for the damage. The court can provide that a joint tortfeasor shall not have to make any contribution, or that a particular tortfeasor shall have to indemnify his fellow tortfeasors for all the damages awarded against them[4].

---

1 *Clark v Newsam* (1847) 1 Exch 131.
2 *Wah Tat Bank Ltd v Chan* [1975] AC 507, [1075] 2 All ER 257, PC.
3 Law Reform (Married Women and Tortfeasors) Act 1935, s.6.
4 *Ibid.*

DEFENCES

Volenti non fit injuria

21.35 If a defendant establishes expressly or impliedly that the plaintiff consented to the action which caused him injury, it is a complete defence to any action in tort for that injury[1]. For example, a sportsman who is injured in the course of a game is *volens*, at least in relation to injuries which were not the result of a gross violation of the rules of the game. 'Consent' means not merely consent to the risk of harm but also a waiver of any legal remedy for such harm. Consent can be express in that the plaintiff either enters into a contract which excludes the defendant's liability in tort or otherwise agrees to assume the risk that the defendant may cause him harm. However, statute imposes severe constraints on a defendant, who seeks to establish express consent. First, a defendant cannot exclude liability to passengers who travel in his car[2]. Secondly, the Unfair Contract Terms Act 1977 states that a defendant cannot exclude liability for negligently[3] causing death or physical injury if the duty of care arises from things done in the course of business or from the occupation of business premises. Furthermore, liability for other types of injury can only be excluded by an exemption clause or notice if the clause or notice is fair and reasonable[4]. In the absence of express consent, consent may be implied from the circumstances of the case.

---

1   *Imperial Chemical Industries Ltd v Shatwell* [1965] AC 656, [1964] 2 All ER 999, HL.
2   Road Traffic Act 1972, s.148(3).
3   'Negligence' in this context includes breach of the common duty of care owed under the Occupiers' Liability Act 1957.
4   Ss. 1 and 2. For 'reasonable' see para. 10.41.

21.36   The essence of the defence is consent to the absence of a legal remedy for injuries, and merely because a plaintiff knew of a risk does not mean that he consented to that risk. In *Nettleship v Weston*[1], the Court of Appeal found that an instructor who had agreed to give the defendant driving lessons was not *volens*. The defence was rejected by two judges because they seemed to regard only express consent as capable of founding *volenti*, and by the third judge because the plaintiff had inquired if the defendant was insured before getting into the car, thereby rebutting any implied consent to the risk. Even if the plaintiff has continued to act over a lengthy period with full knowledge of a risk, this will not necessarily raise an implication of consent, particularly in cases involving employers and employees[2].

There can be no consent to risk where there is no choice whether or not to accept the risk. Therefore, *volenti* cannot be a defence where the plaintiff did not have 'full knowledge of the circumstances on which the exercise of choice is conditional . . .' or where he was under 'a feeling of restraint' which interfered with the 'freedom of his will'[3]. Once again, because of this requirement, it is very difficult for an employer to be able to establish *volenti*.

---

1   [1971] 2 QB 691, [1971] 3 All ER 581, CA.
2   See for example, *Smith v Charles Baker & Sons* [1891] AC 325, HL.
3   *Bowater v Rowley Regis Corpn* [1944] KB 476, [1944] 1 All ER 465, CA.

21.37   The courts have displayed a generous attitude towards rescuers who are injured in an attempt to save a third party or the defendant or his property from the consequences of the defendant's tort. A rescuer will not be denied a remedy merely because he chose to attempt a rescue. In *Haynes v Harwood*[1], a policeman, who was injured in attempting to save a woman and children, who were at risk because the defendant's horses had bolted due to the defendant's negligence, was able to recover for the severe personal injuries he thereby suffered.

---

1   [1935] 1 KB 146, CA.

21.38 Sometimes, *volenti* cannot be a defence, for example, where a statute imposes an absolute duty on the defendant.

Contributory negligence

21.39 Section 1(1) of the Law Reform (Contributory Negligence) Act 1945 provides that 'where any person suffers damage as the result partly of his own fault and partly of the fault of any other person or persons, a claim in respect of that damage shall not be defeated by reason of the fault of the person suffering the damage, but the damages recoverable in respect thereof shall be reduced to such extent as the court thinks just and equitable having regard to the claimant's share in the responsibility for the damages'. Thus, contributory negligence by the plaintiff is not a complete defence to the plaintiff's claim but it does enable the court to reduce the damages payable by the defendant.

Contributory negligence, i.e. negligence contributing to the accident, can arise without the plaintiff having owed the defendant a duty of care. The defendant need only prove that the plaintiff failed to take reasonable precautions to guard against the danger which occurred and that this contributed to his injury[1]. It is contributory negligence if a passenger fails to wear a seat-belt and is thereby injured in a road accident[2].

---

1 *Jones v Livox Quarries Ltd* [1952] 2 QB 608, CA.
2 *Froom v Butcher* [1976] QB 286, [1975] 3 All ER 520, CA.

21.40 The plaintiff will not be contributorily negligent merely because his action or inaction contributed to the accident: he must reasonably foresee that if he failed to act as a reasonable and prudent man he might be hurt. Therefore, if the reasonable man would not have foreseen any injury, or if the plaintiff did all that a reasonable man could be expected to do, he will not be contributorily negligent[1]. The reasonable man is expected to foresee and therefore guard against the carelessness of other people. In cases involving employees the standard of care must, of course, be assessed having regard to the conditions prevailing in the factory.

---

1 *Caswell v Powell Dyffryn Quarries Ltd* [1940] AC 152, [1939] 2 All ER 722, HL.

21.41 Contributory negligence is not limited to actions in negligence; it can apply to cases under the Occupiers' Liability Act 1957 and actions for breach of statutory duty. However, in relation to actions for breach of statutory duty, regard must be had to the wording of the statute. This may impose an absolute obligation on the defendant who will then find it difficult to establish contributory negligence[1].

1 It is not an impossible task; see, for example, *Uddin v Associated Portland Cement Manufacturers Ltd* [1965] 2 QB 15, [1965] 1 All ER 347.

21.42 If the defendant can establish that the plaintiff alone caused the accident, he is not liable at all. Whether a plaintiff caused or merely contributed to the accident is, of course, a question of fact[1].

1 *Stapley v Gypsum Mines Ltd* [1953] AC 663, [1953] 2 All ER 478, HL.

21.43 The apportionment of damages is on the basis of what is just and equitable, having regard to the responsibility which the plaintiff must bear for the accident. The degree of responsibility borne by the plaintiff is a question of fact depending on his blameworthiness and the degree of causation attributable to him.

Exemption clauses

21.44 Liability in tort may be excluded by an exemption clause or notice[1].

1 Paras. 10.23–10.60 and particularly paras. 20.33, 20.41 and 21.35.

Statutory exclusion

21.45 Certain statutes provide that the only compensation available to the victim of a breach of that statute is derived from the statute and that there is no liability in tort. Every case depends upon the interpretation of the particular statute and if a statute is ambiguous the court may decide that it only provides a defence where the powers conferred by the statute were exercised with due care[1].

1 *Metropolitan Asylum District Managers v Hill* (1881) 6 App Cas 193, HL.

Limitation of actions

21.46 The right to sue in tort must be exercised within a given period of the time when the right of action accrued. The Limitation Act 1939 provides generally that claims for personal injuires must be exercised within three years, whereas for most other claims six years is allowed. The Limitation Act 1975 allows a plaintiff with a personal injury claim to apply for leave to bring his claim after three years in some circumstances.

REMEDIES

Damages

21.47 Damages, which are the principal remedy in tort, are recoverable if they are not too remote a consequence of the defendant's tort. In most torts, remoteness is based on foreseeability of damage; this is certainly the rule in negligence[1]. However, the rule of remoteness in some torts, such as deceit, is that of direct consequences[2].

Damages are designed to compensate the plaintiff for the loss he has suffered: to place him in the same position as if the tort had not been committed, in so far as it is possible to do so[3]. Money cannot replace a severed limb or restore sight but it can help to ease the life of such tort victims. While damages are awarded as a once-and-for-all lump sum, that sum, especially in personal injury claims, can include compensation for several heads of damage or loss suffered. Examples are: pain and suffering[4]; loss of expectation of life, which is a conventional £1000 in all cases[5]; loss of amenity, even if the victim is in a coma, including the liability to pursue hobbies etc; and loss of earnings (subject to a deduction for tax which those earnings would have borne)[6].

---

1 Para. 20.26.
2 Para. 15.14. a.
3 Though exemplary damages may be awarded in some cases to 'punish' the defendant.
4 *H. West & Son Ltd v Shephard* [1964] AC 326, [1963] 2 All ER 625, HL.
5 *Rose v Ford* [1937] AC 826.
6 *British Transport Commission v Gourley* [1956] AC 185, [1955] 3 All ER 786, HL; para. 12.8.

Other remedies

21.48 Where damages would not form an adequate remedy, the courts may be prepared to award an injunction restraining the defendant from committing further torts. It is an equitable and therefore discretionary remedy, and it is thought that an injunction is only available to restrain certain torts — principally, nuisance. The Court of Appeal has stated recently that an injunction will not be awarded in the case of negligence[1].

---

1 *Miller v Jackson* [1977] QB 966, [1977] 3 All ER 338, CA.

21.49 An order for the restitution of land or chattels may in some circumstances be made for the torts of trespass to land and wrongful interference with goods.

21.50 In limited circumstances, the victim of a tort may use self-help. For example, he can abate a nuisance but only where it is reasonable to do so and probably only after notice to the tortfeasor. The victim of a tort, who in seeking to abate a nuisance, goes further than is necessary to protect his rights may himself be liable in tort.

Part IV
Commercial Law

Chapter 22
The Sale of Goods

22.1 One of the most common types of contract is a contract of sale of goods. The law relating to such a contract was codified by the Sale of Goods Act 1893 which, as amended, is still in force. It must be emphasised that the general principles of the law of contract, which we dealt with in Part II, continue to apply to contracts for the sale of goods, save in so far as they are inconsistent with the express provisions of the Act of 1893[1].

Unless otherwise stated, references in this chapter to sections are to sections of the Act of 1893.

---

1 S.61(2).

CONTRACT OF SALE OF GOODS

22.2 Section 1 defines a contract of sale of goods as a contract, whether absolute or conditional, 'whereby the seller transfers or agrees to transfer the property in goods to the buyer for a money consideration, called the price'. A number of the terms used in this definition require further discussion.

'Transfers or agrees to transfer'
22.3 Where the property in the goods is transferred from the seller to the buyer under the contract of sale (i.e. at once) the contract is called a sale; but where the transfer of the property in the goods is to take place at a future time or subject to some condition thereafter to be fulfilled, such as the payment of the price, the contract is called an agreement to sell[1]. An agreement to sell becomes a sale when the time

elapses or the conditions are fulfilled subject to which the property in the goods is to be transferred[2].

---

1 S.1(3).
2 S.1(4).

'Goods'
22.4 By s.62(1), 'goods' include all chattels personal other than choses in action[1] and money. Section 62(1) goes on to provide that 'goods' also include:

a. emblements and industrial growing crops, which are cultivated crops such as corn and potatoes; and

b. things attached to and forming part of the land (such as things growing spontaneously on the land (*fructus naturales*), e.g. grass and trees, and fixtures) *provided* they are to be severed before sale or under the contract.

---

1 Para. 19.2.

22.5 In the light of the above it can be seen that a contract of sale of a motor car, or of a dog, or of a crop of potatoes growing in a field, or of timber which is to be cut down before sale or under the contract, is a contract of sale of goods, whereas a contract of sale of an estate or some other interest in land is not. The dividing line can be illustrated by the following example. A contract which gives a person a right to enter upon land to dig from the earth in situ gravel or coal, or to remove slag from slag heaps, at so much a ton is not a contract of sale of goods but instead a contract to grant an interest in land; on the other hand, if the coal or gravel or slag has already been detached from the land a contract for its sale is a contract of sale of goods[1].

In addition, a contract of sale of goods does not include a contract for work and materials. This is a contract which involves the delivery of a chattel but whose substance (or main object) is the exercise of skill and experience in the production of the chattel, it being only subsidiary (or incidental) to that that there will pass to the customer some materials in addition to the skill involved in the production of the chattel. This test was applied by the Court of Appeal in *Robinson v Graves*[2], where it was held that a contract to paint a portrait was a contract for work and materials, and not a contract of sale of goods, because the substance of the contract was the artist's skill, and it was only ancillary to that that there would pass to the customer some materials, namely the paint and canvas. Similarly, a contract involving the repair of a car and the supply of parts for that purpose has been held to be a contract for work and materials, not one for the sale of goods[3]. In contrast, in *Marcel (Furriers) Ltd v Tapper*[4], a contract for a mink jacket of a special colour and style to be made to a customer's requirements was held to be a contract of sale of goods, despite the degree of skill and experience involved in its production, because the actual acquisition by the customer of the materials involved was not subsidiary to that.

Of course, the various terms implied by the Sale of Goods Act, such as that the goods supplied are of merchantable quality or reasonably fit for their purpose, cannot be implied into a contract for work and materials. However, the courts will imply analogous terms into such a contract. Thus, a term will be implied into a contract for work and materials that the materials used will be reasonably fit for the purpose for which they are required[3], provided that the customer has made known, expressly or impliedly, the particular purpose for which the materials are required, so as to show that he relies on the contractor's skill and judgement[5]. Similarly, a term will be implied that the materials used will be of good quality[6].

Until the Unfair Contract Terms Act 1977, liability for breach of such terms implied by law into a contract for work and materials could be excluded or restricted by an exemption clause but, as we have seen[7], such exclusion or restriction has been limited by that Act, especially in the case of consumer transactions.

---

1 *Morgan v Russell & Sons* [1909] 1 KB 357.
2 [1935] 1 KB 579, CA.
3 *Myers & Co v Brent Cross Service Co* [1934] 1 KB 46.
4 [1953] 1 All ER 15, [1953] 1 WLR 49.
5 *Ingham v Emes* [1955] 2 QB 366, [1955] 2 All ER 740, CA.
6 *Young and Marten Ltd v McManus Childs Ltd* [1969] 1 AC 454, [1968] 2 All ER 1169, HL.
7 Para. 10.48.

'Property in goods'
22.6 In order to be a contract of sale of goods, the seller must transfer, or agree to transfer, under the contract the property in goods to the buyer. 'Property' means the right of ownership, i.e. a right which is good against the whole world. It is for this reason that a contract of hire, including one of hire-purchase (where the hirer has an option to purchase the goods at the end of the period of hire), is not a contract of sale of goods and is not governed by the Sale of Goods Act. However, terms analogous to those implied by the Sale of Goods Act are implied into hire-purchase contracts by other legislation and the courts are prepared normally to imply a term into any other contract of hire that the goods are as fit for the purpose for which they are hired as reasonable skill and care can make them, as well as additional types of implied terms in different categories of contracts of hire.

'Money consideration'

22.7 In order to be a contract of sale of goods, the consideration for the transfer of the property in goods must be *money* (the price). If the consideration for the goods is other goods the contract is one of exchange, not of sale. In *Esso Petroleum Ltd v Customs and Excise Commrs*[1], the House of Lords held that World Cup coins which were advertised as 'free' with every four gallons of Esso petrol purchased were not sold, since the contract under which they would be transferred would be one collateral to a contract of sale of petrol and the consideration provided under the collateral contract would be the purchase of petrol, no price being paid for the coins. However, if the consideration is partly in money and partly in goods or something else of value, as in the case of a part-exchange transaction, the contract is one of sale of goods. In *Aldridge v Johnson*[2], it was accepted that a contract for the exchange of 52 bullocks for 100 quarters of barley, the difference in value to be made up in cash, was one of sale.

By s.8(1), the price in a contract of sale may:

a. be fixed by the contract, as is normally the case; or

b. be left to be fixed in a manner thereby agreed, e.g. by a third party valuer; or

c. be determined by the course of dealing between the parties. This enables a court, where the parties have not expressly agreed a price or the manner of its determination, to imply the price which the parties intended by reference to the price paid in earlier similar transactions between the parties.

Section 8(2) provides that where the price is not determined in one of the above ways the buyer must pay a reasonable price.

Where the contract provides that the price is to be fixed by a third party, and such third party cannot or does not do so, the agreement is avoided[3]; except that:

a. if the goods or part thereof have been delivered to and appropriated by the buyer he must pay a reasonable price for them[4]; and

b. if the third party is prevented from fixing the price by the fault of the buyer or seller, as where the seller refuses to allow him to examine them, the party not in fault may maintain an action for damages against the party in default[5].

---

1   [1976] 1 All ER 117, [1976] 1 WLR 1, HL.
2   (1857) 7 E & B 885.
3   S.9(1).
4   *Ibid.*
5   S.9(2).

Other introductory matters

Form

22.8   There are generally no formal requirements for the making of a contract of sale, so that it may be made in writing, or orally, or partly in writing and partly orally, or be implied from the conduct of the parties[1]. An exception is that certain contracts of conditional sale or credit sale have to be in a specified written form, otherwise they are enforceable only on an order of the court[2].

---

1   S.3.
2   Para. 23.26.

Existing goods and future goods

22.9   The goods which form the subject-matter of a contract of sale may be either existing goods, owned or possessed by the seller, or goods to be manufactured or acquired by the seller after the making of the contract of sale, which are called 'future goods'[1]. Where, by a contract of sale, the seller purports to effect a present sale of future goods, the contract operates as an agreement to sell goods[2].

---

1   S.5(1).
2   S.5(3).

Specific goods and unascertained goods

22.10   The goods, whether existing or future, which form the subject-matter of a contract of sale can also be classified as specific goods or as unascertained goods. This distinction is important because in several respects, such as in relation to the passing of the property in the goods, different rules apply depending on whether the goods are specific or unascertained. Specific goods are defined by s.62(1) as goods identified and agreed on at the time a contract of sale is made. Thus, a sale by X of his M.G. car or a sale by Y of all the wheat in his granary is a sale of specific goods. Unascertained goods are goods not specifically identified but described by reference:

a. to goods of a particular kind, as where a wine merchant agrees to sell a dozen bottles of Chateau Le Carney 1973; or

b. to an unidentified part of a specified whole, as where there is an agreement to sell 500 tons of wheat out of 1,000 tons on board a ship[1].

Of course, future goods are generally unascertained goods, but if future goods are identified and agreed on at the time the contract of sale is made they will be specific goods, as where an art dealer agrees to sell a particular painting by Stanley Spencer, which he has not yet acquired, to a customer.

---

1   *Re Wait* [1927] 1 Ch 606, CA.

TRANSFER OF PROPERTY

22.11   The precise time when the property (i.e. ownership) in the goods is transferred from the seller to the buyer is of great importance. Two reasons are that:

a. generally, it is only when ownership has passed to the buyer that the seller is entitled to sue him for the price, as opposed to damages for breach of contract[1];

b. generally, only a person with ownership can pass a good title by resale or otherwise dealing with the goods[2].

In addition, the question of ownership of goods is crucial if the buyer or the seller becomes bankrupt. For instance, on the bankruptcy of the buyer his goods become the property of his trustee in bankruptcy so that, if the ownership of the goods has already passed to him and the seller has not been paid in full, the seller can only claim a dividend on the price due along with all the other unsecured creditors, whereas if the ownership has not yet passed to the buyer the seller can recover them.

---

1   Para. 22.87.
2   Para. 22.28.

22.12   Another reason why the time when ownership is transferred is important is that by s.20 the goods generally remain at the seller's risk until the ownership of them is transferred to the buyer, after which they are at the buyer's risk whether delivery has been made or not. Thus, if the goods which are the subject-matter of a contract of sale are accidentally destroyed the loss will be borne by the seller if the ownership of the goods has not been transferred to the buyer, but if it has been transferred to the buyer he must bear the loss, whether or not the goods have been delivered, and he cannot recover the price from the seller, if he has paid it, nor refuse to pay the price, if he has not yet paid it in full.

22.13   Before turning to the rules governing the transfer of ownership, we wish to emphasise that, unless otherwise agreed, the buyer is entitled to delivery of the goods only if he has tendered the price for them, even if the ownership of them has already passed to him.

Transfer of property in specific goods

22.14 Section 17 provides that in a contract of sale of specific or ascertained goods the property (i.e. ownership) in them passes to the buyer at such time as the parties intend it to pass, and for the purpose of ascertaining the parties' intention regard must be had to the terms of the contract, the conduct of the parties, and the circumstances of the case. In addition, s.18 lays down a number of rules for ascertaining the parties' intention as to the time when the property in the goods is to pass to the buyer. These rules, which apply unless a contrary intention appears from the contractual terms, the parties' conduct or the circumstances of the case, are as follows.

22.15 *Rule 1* 'Where there is an unconditional contract for the sale of specific goods, in a deliverable state, the property in the goods passes to the buyer when the contract is made, and it is immaterial whether the time of payment or the time of delivery, or both, be postponed.'

In order to be 'in a deliverable state' the goods must be in such a state that the buyer would be bound under the contract to take delivery of them[1]. In *Underwood Ltd v Burgh Castle Brick and Cement Syndicate*[2], S agreed to sell to B 'free on rail' a horizontal condensing engine weighing 30 tons and embedded in a floor of concrete. Before it could be delivered on rail the engine had to be detached from its base and dismantled. S detached the engine but accidentally damaged part of it in loading it on a truck, and B refused to accept it. S's action for the price failed. The Court of Appeal held that the property in the engine had not passed under r.1 when the contract was made because it then had to be detached and dismantled by S before it was in such a condition that B would be bound to take delivery of it; therefore it was not 'in a deliverable state' when the contract was made.

---

1 S.62(4).
2 [1922] 1 KB 343, CA.

22.16 *Rule 2* 'Where there is a contract for the sale of specific goods and the seller is bound to do something to the goods [e.g. repair or alter them], for the purpose of putting them into a deliverable state, the property does not pass until such thing be done, and the buyer has notice thereof.' This rule was held to apply in *Underwood Ltd v Burgh Castle Brick and Cement Syndicate*. Consequently, the risk was still on S so that B were entitled to reject the machine and refuse to pay the price.

22.17 *Rule 3* 'Where there is a contract for the sale of specific goods in a deliverable state, but the seller is bound to weigh, measure, test, or do some other act or thing with reference to the goods for the purpose of ascertaining the price, the property does not pass until such act or thing be done, and the buyer has notice thereof'.

This rule does not apply if the weighing, measuring, or testing etc. is to be done by the buyer[1]. In such a case the property passes at the time of the contract under r.1.

---

1   *Nanka-Bruce v Commonwealth Trust Ltd* [1926] AC 77, PC.

22.18 *Rule 4* 'When goods are delivered to the buyer on approval or 'on sale or return' or other similar terms the property therein passes to the buyer:—

(a) When he signifies his approval or acceptance to the seller or does any other act adopting the transaction:

(b) If he does not signify his approval or acceptance to the seller but retains the goods without giving notice of rejection, then, if a time has been fixed for the return of the goods, on the expiration of such time, and, if no time has been fixed, on the expiration of a reasonable time. What is a reasonable time is a question of fact.'

It has been held, for the purposes of r.4(a), that if the person taking the goods does any act in relation to them consistent only with his having become the purchaser, such as selling the goods or pledging them, then that is an 'act adopting the transaction' and the property in the goods passes to him[1]. However, since all the rules are subject to a contrary intention appearing, the property will not pass in such a case if the buyer received the goods from the seller on the terms that they were to remain the seller's property until they were paid for[2].

Rule 4(b) only applies if it is the buyer who retains the goods. Thus, if goods on sale or return are seized from the buyer and detained to pay his creditors, the property will not pass under r.4(b)[3].

For the purposes of r.4 a contract for the sale or return of goods includes a contract where goods are delivered to a person who intends not to buy them himself but to sell them to third parties[4].

---

1   *Kirkham v Attenborough* [1897] 1 QB 201, CA.
2   *Weiner v Gill* [1906] 2 KB 574, CA.
3   *Re Ferrier, ex parte Trustee v Donald* [1944] Ch 295.
4   *Poole v Smith's Car Sales (Balham) Ltd* [1962] 2 All ER 482, [1962] 1 WLR 744, CA.

Transfer of property in unascertained goods

22.19 Whatever the parties' intentions, the property in unascertained goods which are the subject-matter of a contract of sale cannot pass unless and until there exist goods which are identifiable as *the* goods under the contract. Thus, s.16 provides that, in a contract for the sale of unascertained goods, no property in the goods is transferred to the buyer until the goods are *ascertained*, i.e. identified *after* the contract as being in accordance with the agreement[1]. The result is that if A agrees to sell B 200 quarters of maize out of 600 quarters lying in a warehouse the property in the 200 quarters cannot pass until 200 quarters of maize are identified by severance from the rest as the maize to which the contract relates[2].

Rule 5 of s.18 shows that, subject to a contrary intention on the part of the parties, goods are 'ascertained' when goods of the description agreed and in a deliverable state are unconditionally appropriated to the contract by one party with the other's assent.

Rule 5(1) provides: 'Where there is a contract for the sale of unascertained or future goods by description, and goods of that description and in a deliverable state are unconditionally appropriated to the contract, either by the seller with the assent of the buyer, or by the buyer with the assent of the seller, the property in the goods thereupon passes to the buyer. Such assent may be express or implied, and may be given either before or after the appropriation is made.'

---

1 *Re Wait* [1927] 1 Ch 606 at 630.
2 *Laurie and Morewood v Dudin & Sons* [1928] 1 KB 223, CA.

22.20 An appropriation of goods by the seller or the buyer occurs when he irrevocably sets aside or selects goods for the particular contract. It is irrelevant whether delivery takes place then or later[1]. It is only if the unconditional appropriation is made with the assent, express or implied, of the other party, which may be given before or after the appropriation, that the property in the appropriated goods passes. If A goes into an off-licence and asks for a bottle of a type of gin not on display, and the shopkeeper takes one out and hands it to him, and he accepts it, there is an appropriation by the shopkeeper from his stock with A's express assent, and the property in the bottle of gin passes. If A writes to a bookshop asking to be sent a copy of *Wuthering Heights*, the shopkeeper appropriates it unconditionally by putting a copy in the post and, since A has, by his conduct, impliedly assented to the appropriation, the property in the book selected passes to A[2].

Another example of implied assent to an appropriation occurs where the seller sends notice of an appropriation to the buyer and the buyer does not object within a reasonable time. In *Pignataro v Gilroy*[3], S sold to B 140 bags of rice, the particular bags being unascertained. On 27 February, B sent a cheque for the price and asked for a delivery order. The next day S sent a delivery order for 125 bags from a wharf and also sent an accompanying letter saying that the remaining 15 bags were ready for delivery at his place of business. B did not send for the 15 bags until 25 March, when it was found that they had been stolen shortly beforehand, without any negligence on S's part. It was held that B could not recover the price which he had paid for the 15 bags, because his subsequent assent to S's appropriation of those bags to the contract could be inferred from his conduct in not objecting to the appropriation. Therefore, the property in the 15 bags had passed to B, and the goods were at his risk, by the time they were stolen.

---

1 *Furby v Hooey* [1947] 1 All ER 236.
2 *Ibid.*
3 [1919] 1 KB 459.

22.21 A particular example of an unconditional appropriation within r.5(1) is provided by r.5(2) which states that: 'Where, in pursuance of the contract, the seller delivers the goods to the buyer or to a carrier or other bailee . . . (whether named by the buyer or not) for the purpose of transmission to the buyer, and does not reserve the right of disposal, he is deemed to have unconditionally appropriated the goods to the contract.' Rule 5(2) does not apply if the goods form part of a larger quantity of identical goods destined for different owners and delivered to the carrier. In *Healy v Howlett & Sons*[1], S was a fish exporter carrying on business in Valentia, Ireland. He agreed to sell 20 boxes of mackerel to B, whose business was in London. S sent 190 boxes of mackerel by rail from Valentia to England, instructing the railway officials at Holyhead to deliver 20 boxes to B and specified numbers of the remaining boxes to two other customers. The boxes were delayed en route to Holyhead and the fish had deteriorated before any of the 190 boxes were earmarked there for B in accordance with S's instructions. When the mackerel was delivered to B they rejected them. It was held that there had been no appropriation of the 20 boxes to the contract with B when the 190 boxes had been delivered to the railway company in Valentia. Such an appropriation had only occurred when the 20 boxes had been earmarked for B at Holyhead. Since the property in the 20 boxes of mackerel did not pass until then and the mackerel had deteriorated before that time, the mackerel was at S's risk when it deteriorated. B were therefore entitled to reject the mackerel and were not liable to pay the price.

In addition, r.5(2) expressly does not apply where the seller reserves the right of disposal, which is discussed below.

Rule 5 is not limited to contracts for the sale of unascertained existing goods. It also applies to an agreement for the sale of future goods, whether specific or unascertained. In the case of specific future goods they will normally be appropriated by the seller with the buyer's implied consent when the seller acquires ownership of them, so that the property in them will pass to the buyer at that time.

Where there is a contract for the sale of unascertained or future goods and the goods, when ascertained, are delivered to the buyer on approval or on sale or return, or other similar terms, r.4 determines when the property in them has passed, subject to the parties' contrary intention appearing.

---

1   [1917] 1 KB 337.

Reservation of the right of disposal

22.22   Under r.1 the effect of an unconditional contract for the sale of specific goods, in a deliverable state, is that the property passes to the buyer when the contract is made. Under r.5, as we have just mentioned, the property in unascertained or future goods in a deliverable state passes when they are unconditionally appropriated by one party with the other's consent. We now turn to consider the case where there is a contract for the sale of specific goods or where goods are subsequently appropriated to the contract, and the seller, by the terms of the contract or the appropriation, reserves the right of disposal of the goods until a condition is fulfilled, the most common example being the payment of the price. Section 19(1) provides that in such a case, notwithstanding the delivery of the goods to the buyer, or to a carrier or other bailee for transmission to the buyer, the property in the goods does not pass to the buyer until the condition is fulfilled.

Apart from an express reservation of the right of disposal, the seller is presumed by s.19(2) to reserve the right of disposal where goods are shipped, and by the bill of lading (the document signed by the ship's master which acknowledges receipt of the goods on board) the goods are deliverable to the order of the seller or his agent. The result is that the property in the goods shipped remains in the seller until he indorses the bill of lading in favour of the buyer and the price is paid or tendered. However, the presumption that a right of disposal is reserved in such a case is rebuttable by evidence that the parties intended that the property should pass to the buyer on shipment.

PERISHING OF THE GOODS

22.23 The situation where goods have perished prior to the contract of sale, or after the contract but before the risk has passed to the buyer, is governed by the Sale of Goods Act in some cases and by the general principles of the law of contract in others.

In this context the 'perishing' of goods includes cases not only where they have been physically destroyed or stolen, but also where they are so damaged as to have ceased to exist commercially as goods of the description under which they were sold, as, for instance, where dates carried on a ship which sinks but is later recovered, are irretrievably contaminated with sewage[1]. On the other hand, goods have not perished if, despite deterioration, they still answer to the contractual description[2].

---

1 *Asfar & Co v Blundell* [1896] 1 QB 123, CA.
2 *Horn v Minister of Food* [1948] 2 All ER 1036.

Perishing prior to the contract

Specific goods
22.24 Section 6 provides that where there is a sale of specific goods, and the goods without the knowledge of the seller have perished at the time when the contract is made, the contract is void. The result is that the seller cannot sue the buyer for the price, and the buyer cannot sue the seller for breach of contract in failing to make delivery.

If only part of the specific goods have perished the whole contract is nevertheless void under s.6, provided that the goods were sold as an indivisible whole. In *Barrow, Lane and Ballard Ltd v Philip Phillips & Co Ltd*[1], the plaintiffs sold to the defendants 700 bags of Chinese groundnuts 'marked E.C.P., and known as lot 7 of Chinese groundnuts in shell, then lying at the National Wharves in London' for £727. Unknown to the parties, 109 of the bags had been stolen at the time of the sale. It was held that, as the contract was for an indivisible parcel of goods, the contract was void under s.6 even though only part of the goods had been stolen and therefore the plaintiffs could not recover the price.

Section 6 does not apply to goods which have never existed but a contract for the sale of goods which have never existed will be void under the general principles of the law of contract relating to mistake, unless one of the parties agrees to bear the risk that they do not exist[2]. It may be that s.6 would similarly be ousted, so that a contract for the sale of specific goods which had previously perished would not be void, if one of the parties had undertaken to bear the risk that the goods no longer existed. If s.6 is ousted in such a case, and the seller has undertaken the risk of the goods' non-existence by guaranteeing their existence, the seller will be liable to the buyer if they have perished, and likewise the buyer will be liable to the seller if he has undertaken to bear the risk by promising to pay even if the goods have perished.

---

1 [1929] 1 KB 574.
2 Paras. 13.2–13.4.

Unascertained goods
22.25 Section 6 does not apply to sales of unascertained goods. Thus, if B agrees to sell S 100 tons of wheat but, unknown to B, the wheat he had in mind had already been destroyed by fire, s.6 would be inapplicable, because the wheat would not be specific goods, and reference to the general principles relating to mistake in contract would show that the contract would not be void for mistake, so that B would still be liable to supply 100 tons of wheat or pay damages. These general principles would supply the same answer if the wheat had never existed.

Goods perishing after contract but before the risk has passed

Specific goods
22.26 Section 7 provides that where there is an agreement to sell specific goods, and subsequent to the agreement the goods, without any fault on the part of the seller or buyer, perish before the risk passes to the buyer, the agreement is thereby avoided. The result is that the seller cannot sue the buyer for the price, and the buyer cannot sue the seller for breach of contract in failing to make the delivery. If only part of the specific goods have perished the *whole* contract is nevertheless avoided under s.7, provided that the goods were sold as an indivisible whole.

Section 7 is a statutory application of the doctrine of frustration[1] to cases where the risk in the specific goods which have perished after an agreement for their sale has not yet passed[2] to the buyer. However, the provisions of the Law Reform (Frustrated Contracts) Act 1943 do not apply[3], with the result that the effect of the avoidance of a contract by s.7 is governed by the common law principles preceding that Act. These principles were laid down by the House of Lords in the *Fibrosa* case[4]. Under them the buyer can recover money which he has paid before the goods perished if, but only if, there has been a total failure of consideration, in the sense that he has got nothing of what he had bargained for. On the other hand, the seller who is ordered to repay such sums has no right of set-off for any expenses he may have incurred, e.g. in putting the goods into a deliverable state, in seeking to perform the contract before the goods perished.

Whether a contract for the sale of specific goods is avoided by some event other than their perishing, such as their being requisitioned by the Government, before the risk has passed depends on the application of the doctrine of frustration, since s.7 does not apply. If the contract is frustrated thereby its effects are governed by the Law Reform (Frustrated Contracts) Act 1943[5].

---

1 Para. 11.3.
2 Para. 22.12.
3 Law Reform (Frustrated Contracts) Act 1943, s.2(5)(c); paras. 11.15–11.18. Nor does the Act apply to contracts where the risk has passed to the buyer before the specific goods have perished.
4 [1943] AC 32, [1942] 2 All ER 122, HL; para. 11.14.
5 Paras. 11.15–11.18.

Unascertained goods

22.27 Section 7 does not apply to agreements to sell unascertained goods but the doctrine of frustration is, of course, applicable. Thus, if the contract required that the goods should come from a particular source, such as the seller's stock, or be grown by the seller, the contract is frustrated if the seller's stock or crops perish. On the other hand, if the sale is of generic goods, i.e. goods of a general description, such as 20 tons of coal, the contract is not frustrated by the subsequent perishing of the goods which the seller had it in mind to supply, and he remains liable to obtain similar goods of a like description for delivery to the buyer or to pay damages if he does not. If a contract for the sale of unascertained goods is frustrated the effects are governed by the Law Reform (Frustrated Contracts) Act 1943.

TRANSFER OF TITLE

General rule

22.28 As a general rule, the sale of goods by a person who is not the owner does not give good title to them to the buyer, even if the buyer bought in good faith and without notice of the seller's lack of title. This common law rule, which is confirmed by s.21(1), is often referred to by the maxim *nemo dat quod non habet* (a person cannot give what he has not got). If X steals a car owned by O from O's garage and sells it to Y, an innocent purchaser, Y does not get good title to the car and can be sued by O for the tort of conversion and so can an innocent purchaser of the car from Y.

The general rule clearly protects the owners of goods, but there are a number of exceptions to it which protect innocent buyers from those without title in certain cases, at the expense of the true owner.

Exceptions

Agency

22.29 Section 21(1) recognises that a person who sells goods under the authority[1], or with the consent, of the owner can give good title to the buyer. It also provides that a buyer obtains good title if the owner of the goods is precluded from denying the seller's authority to sell. Thus, if the owner of the goods represents to the buyer that the seller is the owner of the goods or deliberately enables the seller to hold himself out as their owner, the owner is estopped (i.e. precluded) from denying the title of the buyer and the buyer gets good title to the goods. In *Eastern Distributors Ltd v Goldring*[2], M, the owner of a van, wanted to buy a car from C, a car dealer, but lacked the deposit. To overcome this, C suggested that M should raise the deposit on the security of the van and that he, C, should pretend to the plaintiffs, a finance company, that M wished to purchase both the van and the car and had paid the necessary deposit on both. C would keep the balance of the purchase price received from the finance company and M would pay the hire-purchase instalments. M agreed and signed blank hire-purchase documents. C completed the documents and forwarded them to the finance company, who accepted the proposal on the van but rejected that on the car. *C had no authority from M to proceed in respect of the van, unless the transaction with the car proceeded*, but he nevertheless purported to sell the van to the plaintiff finance company. The Court of Appeal held that M was estopped from denying C's authority to sell the van to the plaintiff finance company because he had enabled C to represent to the company that he was the owner of the van and had the right to sell it.

On the other hand, the mere fact that the owner of goods has permitted someone to have possession of them does not estop the owner from denying that person's authority to sell. In *Central Newbury Car Auctions Ltd v Unity Finance Ltd*[3], the plaintiffs agreed with C that they would sell a car to a finance company which would let it on hire-purchase to C. Before the arrangements were completed the plaintiffs handed the car and its log book to C. The finance company refused to complete but meanwhile C sold the car to X. The Court of Appeal held that by entrusting the car to C together with the log book, which clearly showed that it did not prove legal ownership, the plaintiffs had not represented that C was entitled to deal with the car on his own nor deliberately allowed him to hold himself out as so entitled. Thus, they were not estopped from disputing C's title and X had not got title to the car.

---

1 S.61 provides that the rules relating to the law of principal and agent continue to apply to contracts of sale of goods. Thus, a sale by an agent without actual authority will give the buyer a good title if the sale is within the agent's ostensible authority or usual authority. See paras. 18.34–18.38.
2 [1957] 2 QB 600, [1957] 2 All ER 525, CA.
3 [1957] 1 QB 371, [1957] 3 All ER 905, CA.

Sale by a mercantile agent

22.30 Under the Factors Act 1889, a mercantile agent[1] who is not the owner of goods can in certain circumstances sell them and give a good title to the buyer. Section 2(1) of the Factors Act 1889 provides that where a mercantile agent who is, with the consent of the owner, in possession of goods or of documents of title to goods, sells, pledges, or makes any other disposition of the goods, when acting in the ordinary course of his business as a mercantile agent, that sale, pledge or other disposition is as valid as if the mercantile agent had been expressly authorised to make it by the owner of the goods; provided that the person taking under the disposition acts in good faith and does not have notice at the time of the disposition that the mercantile agent lacked authority to make it. Documents of title include bills of lading, warrants for delivery of goods and any other document used in the ordinary course of business as proof of the possession or control of goods[2], but not the log book of a car.

---

1 Para. 18.52.
2 Factors Act 1889, s.1(4).

Second sale by seller in possession

22.31 Section 25(1) provides that if a person, having sold goods, continues or is in possession of the goods, or of the documents of title[1] to them, with or without the buyer's consent, any delivery of the goods or transfer of the documents by him or his mercantile agent under any sale, pledge, or other disposition of them, to a person who takes them in good faith and without notice of the previous sale, has the same effect as if the person making the delivery or transfer was expressly authorised by the owner of the goods to make it[2].

The effect of s.25(1) is that if S, a shopkeeper, sells a television to B1 and promises to deliver it, and before doing so sells *and delivers* it to B2, who takes it in good faith and without notice of the previous sale to B1, B2 will get a good title to the television, notwithstanding that the property in it had passed to B1 beforehand. Of course, if the property in the goods had not passed to B1 by the time of the sale to B2, e.g. because S had to do something to the television to put it into a deliverable state and B1 had not had notice that this was done, S would give B2 good title by virtue of his ownership and B2 would not need to rely on s.25(1).

Section 25(1) applies even though the seller, who'continues in possession', does so not as a seller but as a bailee or trespasser[3]. Thus, where A, the owner of a car, sells it to a finance company and immediately hires it back under a hire-purchase agreement without ever transferring possession of the car, and then fraudulently sells it to a third party, title will pass to the third party under s.25(1) even though A is merely in possession as a bailee at the time of the fraudulent sale, and not as a seller of the car.

Section 25(1) does not affect the rights of the original buyer against the seller, so that he can sue the seller in conversion, or for breach of contract when he fails to deliver the goods.

---

1 S.62(1) provides that 'document of title' bears the same meaning as under the Factors Act 1889 (see para. 22.30).
2 A similar provision is contained in the Factors Act 1889, s.8.
3 *Worcester Works Finance Ltd v Cooden Engineering Co Ltd* [1972] 1 QB 210, [1971] 3 All ER 708, CA, applying the Privy Council's view in *Pacific Motor Auctions Pty Ltd v Motor Credits (Hire Finance) Ltd* [1965] AC 867, [1965] 2 All ER 105, PC.

Sale by buyer in possession

22.32 Section 25(2) provides that if a person, having bought or agreed to buy goods, obtains, *with the seller's consent*, possession of the goods or of the documents of title[1] to them, the delivery of the goods or transfer of the documents by him or by his mercantile agent under any sale, pledge, or other disposition of them, to a person who takes them in good faith and without notice of any lien or other right of the original seller in respect of the goods, will have the same effect as if the person making the delivery or transfer were a mercantile agent in possession of the goods or documents with the owner's consent[2]. It must be emphasised that this provision only applies where the person who has bought or agreed to buy goods has obtained possession of them with the seller's consent. However, provided this consent has been given, the fact that it was obtained by deception does not exclude the provision[3].

The effect of s.25(2) is that if S agrees to sell a radio to B1 and gives him possession of it, but the contract provides that the property in the radio is not to pass to B1 until B1 has paid for it, and before that time B1 sells and *delivers* the radio to B2, who takes it in good faith and without notice that the property in the radio is still in S, B2 will acquire a good title to it. Of course, if the property in the radio had already passed to B1 at the time of the sale to B2, B1 would give B2 a good title to it by virtue of his ownership and B2 would not need to rely on s.25(2).

---

1 For definition, see para. 22.30.
2 A similar provision is contained in the Factors Act 1889, s.9.
3 *Du Jardin v Beadman Bros Ltd* [1952] 2 QB 712, [1952] 2 All ER 160.

22.33 Section 25(2) refers to a person who has 'bought or agreed to buy' goods. Consequently, it cannot apply where the sale, pledge or other disposition is by a person with a mere option to purchase, for instance under a hire-purchase agreement[1], nor where the sale etc. is by a person who has only received the goods on sale or return or on approval[2]. In addition, the buyer under a 'conditional sale agreement' is deemed by s.25(2)(i)[3] not to be a person who has bought or agreed to buy goods. A 'conditional sale agreement' is an agreement for the sale of goods which is 'a consumer credit agreement within the meaning of the Consumer Credit Act 1974 under which the purchase price or part of it is payable by instalments, and the property in the goods is to remain in the seller ... until such conditions as to payment of instalments or otherwise as may be specified in the agreement are fulfilled[4].'

On the other hand, a person who has made a conditional agreement to buy goods, other than a 'conditional sale agreement', is a person who 'has agreed to buy' within s.25(2). Another example of a person who has 'agreed to buy' is provided by *Cahn v Pockett's Bristol Channel Steam Packet Co Ltd*[5]. S sold copper to B1, a foreign buyer, and sent him a bill of lading indorsed in blank, together with a bill of exchange for the price for acceptance by B1. B1 was insolvent and did not accept the draft but he transferred the bill of lading to B2, an innocent third party, in fulfilment of a contract for the sale of the copper to B2. S stopped the copper *in transitu*. The Court of Appeal held that although the property in the copper had not been transferred to B1 by virtue of s.19(3)[6], because he had not satisfied the condition about acceptance, nevertheless he was a person who had 'agreed to buy' the copper and had passed a good title to the copper to B2 because he was in possession of the bill of lading with S's consent.

---

1 *Helby v Matthews* [1895] AC 471, HL; *Belsize Motor Supply Co v Cox* [1914] 1 KB 244.
2 *Edwards Ltd v Vaughan* (1910) 26 TLR 545.
3 Para. (i) was inserted into s.25(2) by the Consumer Credit Act 1974, Sched. 4.
4 S.25(2)(ii) (inserted by the Consumer Credit Act 1974, Sched. 4).
5 [1899] 1 QB 643, CA.

6   S.19(3) provides: 'Where the seller of goods draws on the buyer for the price, and transmits the bill of exchange and bill of lading to the buyer together to secure acceptance or payment of the bill of exchange, the buyer is bound to return the bill of lading if he does not honour the bill of exchange, and if he wrongfully retains the bill of lading the property in the goods does not pass to him.'

Sale of motor vehicles

22.34   A person in possession of goods under a hire-purchase agreement or conditional sale agreement cannot pass a good title to them under the Sale of Goods Act 1893, s.25(2). However, Part III of the Hire-Purchase Act 1964[1] provides that where a person (whom we will call X) in possession of a *motor vehicle* under a hire-purchase or conditional sale agreement disposes of it by sale or hire-purchase to a *private purchaser* who takes it in good faith and without notice of the agreement the disposition takes effect as if the title of the owner of the vehicle had been vested in X immediately before the disposition[2], so that the purchaser obtains a good title to the vehicle in the same way and at the same time as he would if X had been entitled to make the disposition. In addition, if X disposes of the vehicle to a dealer in motor vehicles or a finance company, then, if the *first* private purchaser of the vehicle after that disposition takes it in good faith and without notice of the hire-purchase or conditional sale agreement, the disposition of the vehicle to him has effect as if the title of the owner of the vehicle had vested in X immediately before he disposed of it to the dealer or finance company[3].

A 'private purchaser' is a purchaser who at the time of the disposition does not carry on a business as a motor vehicle dealer or of providing finance for motor vehicle deals[4]. While a private purchaser is not protected by the Act of 1964 if he has actual knowledge that the vehicle is subject to a hire-purchase or conditional sale agreement, he is protected if he honestly believed that, although the vehicle was once subject to such an agreement, all the instalments have been paid off[5].

---

1   Part III of the Act of 1964 was reproduced with minor changes of terminology in Sched. 4 of the Consumer Credit Act 1974.
2   Hire Purchase Act 1964, s.27(1) and (2).
3   *Ibid.*, s.27(3).
4   *Ibid.*, s.29(2).
5   *Barker v Bell* [1971] 2 All ER 867, [1971] 1 WLR 983, CA.

Sale in market overt

22.35   Section 22(1) provides that where goods are sold in market overt, according to the usage of the market, the buyer obtains a good title to the goods, provided he buys the goods in good faith and without notice of any defect or want of title on the part of the seller.

'Market overt' means any market in England which is open, public and legally constituted by royal charter, custom or statute but only on the market days prescribed thereby[1]. In addition, by local custom, that part of every shop within the City of London to which the public are admitted without special invitation is market overt[2]. However, a sale in a shop in the City of London will only be in market overt if the following requirements are satisfied:

a. The goods in question must be of the kind usually sold in that shop. Thus, the sale of a watch in a tobacconist's shop will not be a sale in market overt.

b. The sale must be by, and not to, the shopkeeper[3] (unlike sales in markets overt other than shops in the City of London which need not be by a tradesman)[4].

c. The sale must be on a business day, i.e. not on a Sunday or Bank Holiday.

The following rules must also be satisfied for a sale to be in market overt, whether the sale takes place in a shop in the City of London or in some other market:

a. The sale must take place between sunrise and sunset[4].

b. The bulk, not merely a sample, of the goods must have been exposed for sale[5].

In order for a buyer in market overt to obtain a good title to the goods, he must buy them in good faith and without notice of the seller's defect or want of title and the goods must have been sold in accordance with the usage of the market. In *Bishopsgate Motor Finance Corpn Ltd v Transport Brakes Ltd*[6], S had a car on hire-purchase from the plaintiffs. In breach of the hire-purchase agreement, S took the car to Maidstone market, which was constituted by royal charter, and handed it to auctioneers to sell. The car was not sold by the auctioneers but, later that day, S sold the car to an innocent purchaser, B. The Court of Appeal held that, as the usage of the market allowed sales by private treaty in the market after an auctioneer had failed to sell, B had acquired good title to the car.

The rules concerning sales in market overt are of great importance where the goods sold are stolen goods. The conviction of the offender does not deprive a person of good title to stolen goods which he has obtained through purchase in market overt or otherwise[7].

---

1   *Lee v Bayes* (1856) 18 CB 599 at 601.
2   *Hargreave v Spink* [1892] 1 QB 25.
3   *Ibid.*

4 *Reid v Police Comr of the Metropolis* [1973] QB 551, [1973] 2 All ER 97, CA.
5 *Crane v London Dock Co* (1864) 33 LJQB 224.
6 [1949] 1 KB 322, [1949] 1 All ER 37, CA.
7 Theft Act 1968, s.31(2). The Sale of Goods Act 1893, s.24(1), which provided that the goods revested in the original owner on conviction of the offender, was repealed by the Theft Act 1968, Sched. 3.

Sale by person with a voidable title

22.36   Section 23 provides that where the seller has a *voidable* title (e.g. because he has obtained the goods by misrepresentation) but his title has not been avoided at the time of the sale, the buyer acquires a good title, provided he buys in good faith and without notice of the seller's defect of title.

The circumstances in which a contract is voidable, and the way in which it is avoided, were considered in Chapter 14.

Special powers of sale

22.37   Section 21(2) provides that the general rule does not affect the validity of any contract of sale under any special common law or statutory power of sale or under the order of a court of competent jurisdiction.

There are many common law or statutory powers whereby a non-owner is enabled to pass a good title. At common law, for instance, a pledgee can sell an unredeemed pledge[1] and pass good title to the goods to the buyer as against the pledgor[2], and a mortgagee has the same power if the mortgagor makes default[3]. Innkeepers and hotel proprietors have a statutory power to sell goods, left on their premises or deposited with them by guests, in satisfaction of unpaid debts, but it can only be exercised after a certain period and after notice of the intended sale has been advertised[4]. Such a sale passes a good title to the buyer as against the guest[5]. Persons, such as repairers, with whom goods are deposited have a statutory power to sell goods which have not been collected. To be entitled to sell, such a person must notify the depositor (who is in law the bailor of the goods) of his intention to sell, or at least take reasonable steps to communicate with him, and he must be reasonably satisfied that the depositor is the owner of the goods. If he wishes, a court order may be obtained authorising the sale, and if it is obtained it is conclusive, as against the depositor, of the bailee's entitlement to sell the goods. This is a useful course to adopt if the situation is at all doubtful. Provided the various requirements are satisfied, or the sale is authorised by the court, a buyer gets a good title as against the depositor.

Under the Rules of the Supreme Court the High Court has jurisdiction to order the sale of goods which it may be desirable, for good reason, to have sold at once[6], e.g. where the goods are perishable. This power can be used, for instance, where a bailee wishes to enforce a lien which he has over goods in his possession. The buyer gets a title which is good against the whole world.

---

1   *Re Morritt* (1886) 18 QBD 222 at 232.
2   *Burrows v Barnes* (1900) 82 LT 721, DC.
3   *Re Morritt* (1886) 18 QBD 222 at 232.
4   Innkeepers Act 1878, s.1.
5   Torts (Interference with Goods) Act 1977, ss. 12 and 13.
6   Rules of the Supreme Court, Order 29, r.4.

Effect on title of writs of execution

22.38   Section 26(1) provides that a writ of execution against goods binds the property in the goods of the execution debtor as from the time when the writ is delivered to the sheriff to be executed. This simply means that on delivery of the writ the sheriff acquires a legal right to seize sufficient of the debtor's goods to sell and thus satisfy the judgment debt. However, the proviso to s.26(1) states that, until the goods are seized, the writ does not prejudice the title to such goods of a person who has bought them in good faith, unless at the time he acquired title he had notice that a writ of execution against the debtor's goods had been delivered to the sheriff. The proviso does not apply once the debtor's goods have been seized by the sheriff. Where a person buys goods from the debtor which have been seized, but not yet sold, by the sheriff, he gets a good title to them, but it is subject to the sheriff's right to sell the goods even though he did not have notice of the seizure[1].

---

1   *Lloyds and Scottish Finance Ltd v Modern Cars and Caravans (Kingston) Ltd* [1966] 1 QB 764, [1964] 2 All ER 732.

TERMS OF THE CONTRACT

22.39   Some of the terms in a contract of sale of goods can be classified as conditions, others as warranties. As we said in para. 10.17, a condition is a statement of fact, or a promise, which forms an essential term of the contract, any breach of which entitles the injured party to rescind the contract for breach (or, as it is described in the Sale of Goods Act 1893, treat the contract as repudiated), which he will do if he rejects the goods or refuses to accept further deliveries under an instalment contract. A warranty is a term concerning a fact or promise which is a less important or subsidiary element of the contract (or, in the words of the Sale of Goods Act 1893[1], 'collateral to the main purpose' of the contract), the breach of which does not entitle the injured party to rescind the contract but only to sue for damages[2].

---

1 S.62(1).
2 *Ibid.*

22.40 The distinction between conditions and warranties is subject to the following important qualifications:

a. Section 11(1)(a) provides that on breach of a condition to be fulfilled by the seller, the buyer may waive the breach of condition altogether, or may elect to treat its breach as a breach of warranty, and not as a ground for rescinding the contract.

b. Section 11(1)(c)[1] provides that where a contract of sale is not severable, and the buyer has accepted the goods, or part of them, he can only treat a breach of condition as a breach of warranty, 'and not as a ground for rejecting the goods and treating the contract as repudiated', unless there is a term of the contract, express or implied, to that effect.

Section 11(1)(c) only applies where the contract of sale is not severable, so that it is inapplicable to a contract under which goods are to be delivered by instalments, each of which is to be separately paid for, because this is a severable contract[2]. On the other hand, a contract for a lump sum price payable after the completion of delivery is not severable even though it provides for delivery by instalment or the seller has an option to fulfil his obligations by one delivery or two or more[3], with the result that if the buyer accepts an instalment he is precluded by s.11(1)(c) from rejecting later instalments.

By s.35 (as amended by the Misrepresentation Act 1967, s.4(2)), a buyer is deemed to have accepted goods:

i. *When he intimates to the seller that he has accepted them;* or

ii. *When the goods have been delivered to him and he does any act in relation to them which is inconsistent with the ownership of the seller,* such as re-selling and despatching the whole or part of them to a sub-buyer[4]. However, this is subject to the provisions of s.34 to the effect that where goods are delivered to a buyer, which he has not previously examined, he is not deemed to have accepted the goods unless and until he has had a reasonable opportunity of examining them for the purpose of ascertaining whether they conform to the contract. The result is that if a buyer, who has not had a reasonable opportunity to examine the goods, re-sells and despatches them to a sub-buyer, he is deemed

445

not to have accepted them by s.34, whereas if he had had a reasonable opportunity to examine them he would have been deemed by s.35 to have accepted them; or

iii. *When, after the lapse of a reasonable time, he retains the goods without intimating to the seller that he has rejected them.* Again, this is subject to s.34 so that a buyer is not deemed to have accepted the goods unless he has had a reasonable chance of examining them.

c. We said in para. 10.21 that under the general law of contract there is a third type of contractual term, the 'intermediate term', whose breach may or may not entitle the injured party to rescind the contract, depending on whether the effect of the breach is such as to deprive him of substantially the whole benefit which it was intended he should obtain under the contract. It is clear from the decision of the Court of Appeal in *The Hansa Nord*[5] that intermediate terms can exist in contracts of sale of goods because, although the Sale of Goods Act only refers expressly to conditions and warranties, the general law of contract is expressly preserved by s.61(2). Consequently, a term in a contract of sale may be a condition *or* an intermediate term *or* a warranty. If the term broken by the seller is classified as an intermediate term the buyer is entitled to rescind the contract by rejecting the goods if, but only if, the effect of the breach substantially deprives him of his intended benefit under the contract.

---

1 As amended by the Misrepresentation Act 1967, s.4(1).
2 Para. 10.17.
3 *J. Rosenthal & Sons Ltd v Esmail* [1965] 2 All ER 860, [1965] 1 WLR 1117, HL.
4 *Hardy & Co v Hillerns and Fowler* [1923] 2 KB 490, CA.
5 [1976] QB 44, [1975] 3 All ER 739, CA.

Express terms

22.41 We dealt in Chapters 8 and 10 with how one determines whether a pre-contractual representation has become a contractual term and, if so, how one ascertains its classification in order to determine the legal consequences of its breach. All we need do here is to mention again the special rule that a term as to the time of payment is deemed by s.10(1) not to be of the essence of a contract of sale, and therefore not a condition, unless a contrary intention appears from the terms of the contract. Section 10(1) also provides that whether any other terms as to time are of the essence of such a contract depends on the terms of the contract, but they are usually construed as making time of the essence, and therefore conditions[1]. For example, a term as to the time of delivery is normally construed as a condition, so that if the seller fails to deliver on time the buyer may reject the goods[2].

---

1 *Bowes v Shand* (1877) 2 App Cas 455 at 463.
2 *Hartley v Hymans* [1920] 3 KB 475.

Implied terms

22.42 In addition to the express terms of a contract of sale which have been agreed by the parties, a number of terms are implied into it by the Sale of Goods Act 1893, ss. 12 to 15 (as amended by the Supply of Goods (Implied Terms) Act 1973). Unlike express terms, there is no problem of classifying these implied terms because each of them is classified as a condition or warranty by the statute, and there is no possibility of one of them being an 'intermediate term'. Until the Supply of Goods (Implied Terms) Act 1973, the terms implied by ss. 12 to 15 could be excluded or modified by the parties but, as we have seen[1], such exclusion or modification is restricted by statute, now the Unfair Contract Terms Act 1977, especially in the case of a consumer sale. The terms implied by ss. 12 to 15 are as follows.

---

1 Para. 10.47.

Implied undertakings as to title
22.43 Section 12(1) provides that the following undertakings as to title are implied in every contract of sale, other than one in which there appears from the contract or is to be inferred from its circumstances an intention that the seller should transfer only such title as he or a third person may have in the goods:
'(a) an *implied condition* on the part of the seller that in the case of a sale, he *has a right to sell* the goods, and in the case of an agreement to sell, he will have a right to sell the goods at the time when the property is to pass; and
(b) an *implied warranty* that the *goods are free, and will remain free until the time when the property is to pass, from any charge or encumbrance not disclosed or known to the buyer* before the contract is made *and* that the *buyer will enjoy quiet possession* of the goods except so far as it may be disturbed by the owner or other person entitled to the benefit of any charge or encumbrance so disclosed or known.'

22.44 If there has been a breach of the *implied condition* that the seller has the right to sell the goods, the buyer who is forced to hand them over to the true owner is entitled to recover the full price he has paid, on the ground that there has been a total failure of consideration, *notwithstanding that he has used the goods for some time.* It appears that s.11(1)(c)[1] has no application to a breach of s.12(1)(a) because there is not really a contract of sale at all if the seller has no right to sell the goods[2].

A seller is in breach of the implied condition not only where he lacks the right to pass the property in the goods to the buyer but also where he can be stopped by process of law from selling the goods. Thus, in *Niblett v Confectioners' Materials Co Ltd*[3], where cans of condensed milk which were labelled in such a way as to infringe the trade mark of a third party, who could have obtained an injunction to restrain their sale, were sold by the defendants to the plaintiffs, it was held that the defendants were in breach of the implied condition that they had the right to sell the cans.

---

1 Para. 22.40. b.
2 *Rowland v Divall* [1923] 2 KB 500, CA.
3 [1921] 3 KB 387, CA.

22.45 The *implied warranty* under s.12(1)(b) of quiet possession and freedom from encumbrances adds little to the implied condition but will be useful in the following situations:

a. Where the seller has the right to sell, but only subject to the rights of a third party which have not been disclosed to the buyer before the contract is made. Thus, if D, an execution debtor, sells goods which have been seized by the sheriff under a writ of execution, without disclosing this, D will be in breach of the implied warranty because, although he had the right to sell the goods, and is therefore not in breach of the implied condition, the title passed is not free from the rights of the sheriff[1].

b. Where the seller had the right to sell but a third a party has subsequently acquired the benefit of any charge or encumbrance not disclosed or known to the buyer before the contract was made. Thus, if S sells goods to B and after the sale T acquires a patent involving interference with B's use, S will be in breach of the implied warranty but not in breach of the implied condition because he had the right to sell when the contract was made[2].

---

1 *Lloyds and Scottish Finance Ltd v Modern Cars and Caravans (Kingston) Ltd* [1966] 1 QB 764, [1964] 2 All ER 732.
2 *Microbeads AG v Vinhurst Road Markings Ltd* [1975] 1 All ER 529, [1975] 1 WLR 218, CA.

22.46 Section 12(2) deals with those contracts of sale excluded from s.12(1), viz. those 'in which there appears from the contract or is to be inferred from the circumstances an intention that the seller should transfer only such title as he or a third person may have in the goods'. As these words indicate, s.12(2) is concerned with cases where the seller intends to sell a limited title because, for instance, the title to the goods is encumbered or doubtful. Section 12(2) can only apply, however, if the contract expressly provides, or it can be inferred from the circumstances, that the seller intends to transfer only such title as he or a third person may have in the goods. Such an intention will probably be inferred where, for example, a pawnbroker sells an unredeemed pledge or where a sheriff sells goods which have been seized in execution.

Where the contract is one to which s.12(2) applies there is no implied condition that the seller has a right to sell. In addition, the implied warranty under s.12(1)(b) is modified so that there is an implied warranty that all encumbrances known to the seller have been disclosed to the buyer before the contract is made, and also an implied warranty that neither the seller, nor (in the case where it is intended to pass only such title as a third person may have) the third person, nor anyone claiming under them, will disturb the buyer's quiet possession.

Sale by description
22.47 Section 13(1) provides:

'Where there is a contract for the sale of goods *by description*, there is an *implied condition* that the goods shall correspond with the description; and if the sale be by sample[1], as well as by description, it is not sufficient that the bulk of the goods corresponds with the sample if the goods do not also correspond with the description.'

There will be a sale by description where the buyer contracts in reliance on a description, express or implied, of the goods in the contract[2]. Thus, if the buyer has not seen the goods there is necessarily a contract of sale by description. In *Varley v Whipp*[3], for instance, S offered to sell to B a second-hand reaping machine, which he described as new the previous year and to have been used only to cut 50–60 acres. B agreed to buy on the faith of this description without having seen the machine. When the machine was delivered, B discovered that it was of extreme antiquity and returned it to S, who then sued for the price. It was held that this was a sale by description, that the machine did not correspond with the description, that B was therefore entitled to reject it for breach of the condition implied by s.13 and that consequently the plaintiff could not recover the price. Even if the buyer has seen the goods before buying them there will be a sale by description, provided he can prove that he still relied essentially on the description and that any discrepancy between the goods and the description was not apparent. In *Nicholson and Venn v Smith-Marriott*[4], a set of linen napkins and table cloths put up for auction by the defendants was described in the sale catalogue as dating from the seventeenth century. The plaintiffs, who were antique dealers, read the description, saw the linen and bought it. It later transpired that the set dated from the eighteenth century. It was held that, notwithstanding their inspection of the set, the plaintiffs had relied, not on its appearance, but on the catalogue description, with the result that there was a sale by description and the defendants were liable for breach of the term implied by s.13.

A sale can be by description even though the goods may have been selected by the buyer[5], as in a self-service shop, in which case the description will be implied from the words on the packaging or labelling of the goods.

The term 'description' refers to any words used in relation to the goods which identify them. It covers not only words which go to the nature of the goods, such as their size or age, but also other attributes expressed or implied in the contract, such as the origin or mode of packing of the goods, which are a substantial ingredient in identifying the goods sold[6].

---

1   Para. 22.60.
2   *Wallis, Son and Wells v Pratt and Haynes* [1911] AC 394, HL.
3   [1900] 1 QB 513.
4   (1947) 177 LT 189.
5   S.13(2).
6   E.g. *Re Moore & Co and Landauer & Co* [1921] 2 KB 519, CA.

22.48   The reader is reminded that apart from civil liability under the Sale of Goods Act 1893, a seller who applies a false description to goods may be criminally liable under the Trade Descriptions Act 1968.

Implied condition as to merchantable quality
22.49   Normally, there is no implied term in a contract of sale as to the quality of the goods sold or their fitness for a particular purpose[1]. However, in addition to conditions and warranties implied by usage[2], other important exceptions to this general principle of *caveat emptor* (let the buyer beware) are provided by ss. 14(2), 14(3) and 15, which we propose to consider in turn after we have dealt with an element common to s.14(2) and s.14(3).

22.50   Unlike ss. 12 and 13, sub-s. (2) and (3) of s.14 only apply where goods are sold *in the course of a business*. 'Business' is not limited to commercial activities in the ordinary sense because it is defined to include 'a profession and the activities of any government department, or local or public authority'[3]. Consequently, if an accountant sells one of his office typewriters which is surplus to requirements, the two subsections are applicable, but not if he sells the family washing machine. However, if a private individual sells goods through an agent acting in the course of a business, such as an auctioneer, the two subsections apply to the sale by him unless the buyer knows that the seller is a private individual or reasonable steps have been taken to bring that fact to the buyer's notice before the contract is made[4].

---

1 S.14(1).
2 S.14(4).
3 This definition was inserted into s.62(1) by the Supply of Goods (Implied Terms) Act 1973, s.7, as amended by the Unfair Contract Terms Act 1977, Sched. 3.
4 S.14(5).

22.51 The implied condition as to merchantable quality is provided by s.14(2):

'Where the seller sells goods *in the course of a business,* there is an *implied condition* that the *goods supplied* under the contract are of *merchantable quality,* except that there is no such condition —

(a) as regards defects specifically drawn to the buyer's attention before the contract is made; or

(b) if the buyer examines the goods before the contract is made, as regards defects which that examination ought to reveal.'

22.52 By s.62(1A)[1], goods of any kind are of merchantable quality if they are *as fit for the purpose or purposes for which goods of that kind are commonly bought as it is reasonable to expect* having regard to any description applied to them, the price (if relevant) and all the other relevant circumstances. The reference to the *'purpose or purposes for which goods of that kind are commonly bought'* means that, if the goods have only one purpose, they are unmerchantable if they are not as fit for that purpose as it is reasonable to expect. Thus, a pair of underpants containing an excess of sulphite which gave the wearer dermatitis have been held to be not of merchantable quality[2]. On the other hand, where the goods are commonly bought for several purposes, and they are unfit for one of them, it may be that this does not make them unmerchantable, provided a buyer would accept them without a substantial abatement in price[3].

As s.62(1A) confirms, the term 'merchantable quality' is a relative one. In deciding whether the goods are *as fit* for the purposes for which goods of that kind are commonly bought *as it is reasonable to expect,* regard must be had:

a. *To any description applied to them.* If motor horns are sold as 'new' but it transpires that they are dented and scratched, they will not be of merchantable quality[4], but if they are sold as 'second-hand' or 'shop soiled', they will be[5], unless there is something radically wrong with them.

b. *To the price*. If the goods are sold at market price a higher standard of quality can properly be expected than if they are sold at a 'cut' price[6].

c. *To other relevant circumstances*. For instance, if there is a clause in the contract giving the buyer an allowance of the price for particular shortcomings, regard must be had to that in deciding whether they are of merchantable quality[7].

---

1 S.62(1A) was added to the Sale of Goods Act by the Supply of Goods (Implied Terms) Act 1973, s.7.
2 *Grant v Australian Knitting Mills Ltd* [1936] AC 85, PC.
3 This was the position before 'merchantable quality' was given a statutory definition: *B. S. Brown & Son Ltd v Craiks Ltd* [1970] 1 All ER 823, [1970] 1 WLR 752, HL.
4 *Jackson v Rotax Motor and Cycle Co* [1910] 2 KB 937, CA.
5 *Bartlett v Sidney Marcus Ltd* [1965] 2 All ER 753, [1965] 1 WLR 1013, CA.
6 *B. S. Brown & Son Ltd v Craiks Ltd* [1970] 1 All ER 823, [1970] 1 WLR 752, HL.
7 *The Hansa Nord* [1975] 3 All ER 739 at 749.

22.53 The implied condition as to merchantable quality is not confined to the goods actually 'sold' but extends to all goods 'supplied under the contract'. Thus, if a detonator is included in a consignment of coal, or lemonade is supplied in a defective returnable bottle, there can be a breach of the implied condition as to the merchantable quality of the goods supplied even though neither the detonator nor the bottle was part of the respective contracts of sale and the coal and lemonade were in themselves of merchantable quality[1].

---

1 *Wilson v Rickett, Cockerell & Co Ltd* [1954] 1 QB 598, [1954] 1 All ER 868, CA (detonator in 'Coalite'); *Geddling v Marsh* [1920] 1 KB 668, DC (lemonade in defective returnable bottle).

22.54 The implied condition as to merchantable quality is excluded:

a. as regards defects specifically drawn to the buyer's attention before the contract is made; or

b. if the buyer examines the goods before the contract is made, as regards defects which *that* examination ought to reveal.

Implied condition of fitness for purpose
22.55 Section 14(3)[1] provides:
'Where the seller sells goods *in the course of a business and the buyer, expressly or by implication, makes known* —

(a) to the seller, or

(b) where the purchase price or part of it is payable by instalments and the goods were previously sold by a credit-broker to the seller, to that credit-broker,

any particular purpose for which the goods are being bought, there is an *implied condition* that the *goods supplied* under the contract are *reasonably fit for that purpose*, whether or not that is a purpose for which such goods are commonly supplied, except where the circumstances show that the buyer does not rely, or that it is unreasonable for him to rely, on the skill or judgment of the seller or credit-broker . . .'

The reference to a credit-broker[2] is significant only in a credit sale agreement, which is an agreement for the sale of goods under which the price or part of it is payable by instalments but, unlike a conditional sale agreement, the property passes at once.

---

1 As amended by the Consumer Credit Act 1974, as well as by the Supply of Goods (Implied Terms) Act 1973.

2 A 'credit-broker' is defined by the rest of s.14(3) as a person carrying on a business of introducing *individuals* desiring to obtain credit to persons carrying on any business so far as it relates to the provision of credit, or to other credit-brokers.

22.56 The implied condition under s.14(3) is that the goods supplied are reasonably fit for the *particular purpose for which they are being bought* and it can only apply where the buyer makes that purpose known to the seller or (where relevant) the credit-broker expressly or by implication. Where the purpose for which the goods are bought is obvious, because they only have that one ordinary purpose, it need not be made known expressly because it is clearly implied. If a person buys a bath bun, his particular purpose, to eat it, is impliedly made known to the seller, so that if it contains a stone which breaks the buyer's tooth the seller will be in breach of the condition implied into the contract of sale by s.14(3)[1]. Similarly, a buyer of underpants need not specify his particular purpose, viz. to wear them next to the skin, because this is the only purpose for which anyone would ordinarily want underpants; thus, if they contain an excess of sulphite which gives him dermatitis the seller will be in breach of the implied condition as to fitness for purpose[2]. On the other hand, if the goods can be used for a variety of ordinary purposes, or if they are bought for a special or extraordinary purpose, the implied condition under s.14(3) can only apply if the particular purpose for which they are bought is made known expressly to the seller[3].

---

1 *Chaproniere v Mason* (1905) 21 TLR 633, CA.

2 *Grant v Australian Knitting Mills Ltd* [1936] AC 85, PC.

3 *Griffiths v Peter Conway Ltd* [1939] 1 All ER 685, CA. The approach taken in this paragraph was confirmed by the House of Lords in *Henry Kendall & Sons v William Lillico & Sons Ltd* [1969] AC 31, [1968] 2 All ER 444, HL.

22.57 The implied condition of fitness for purpose is, like the condition of merchantable quality, not limited to the goods actually 'sold' but extends to all goods 'supplied under the contract'. It is not broken simply because those goods are not absolutely fit but only if they are *not reasonably fit for the particular purpose* for which they are bought. In *Heil v Hedges*[1], pork chops, which were infested with a parasite worm and would have been harmless if cooked properly, were held to be reasonably fit for their purpose, so that the seller was not liable to the buyer who had only had them partly cooked and become ill. Nor was the seller liable for breach of the implied condition of merchantable quality, because the chops were merchantable if properly cooked.

1 [1951] 1 TLR 512.

22.58 Where the particular purpose is broadly made known, there will be no breach of the implied condition as to the fitness for purpose if the goods are suitable for most types of use within that purpose even though they are unsuitable for an improbable use within it[1]. Thus, if S sells meal to B, after B has made known to him that he wishes to include it in animal feeding stuff, the meal is only required to be reasonably fit for inclusion in feeding stuffs for any animals to which S ought to have contemplated it might be fed.

The implied condition as to fitness for purpose does not apply where the circumstances show that the buyer does not rely, or that it is unreasonable for him to rely, on the skill or judgment of the seller or credit-broker.

1 *Ashington Piggeries Ltd v Christopher Hill Ltd* [1972] AC 441, [1971] 1 All ER 847, HL.

22.59 There is obviously some overlap between the conditions implied by s.14(2) and s.14(3). However, if the buyer buys the goods for some *special or extraordinary* purpose, and the goods turn out to be unfit for it, only s.14(3) is relevant, and only then if that purpose has expressly been made known. Only if the goods are unfit for the purpose for which goods of that kind are *commonly* bought can there be a breach of the implied condition of merchantable quality under s.14(2).

Sale by sample

22.60 By s. 15(1), a contract of sale is a contract of sale by sample where there is a term in the contract, express or implied, to that effect. The mere display of a sample during negotiations does not make the contract one of sample: there must, at least, be evidence that the parties intended the sale to be by sample.

Three conditions are implied into contracts of sale by sample by s.15(2):

'In the case of a contract by sample —

(a) There is an *implied condition* that *the bulk shall correspond with the sample in quality*:

(b) There is an *implied condition* that the buyer shall have a *reasonable opportunity of comparing the bulk with the sample*:

(c) There is an *implied condition* that the goods shall be *free from any defect, rendering them unmerchantable, which would not be apparent on reasonable examination of the sample.*'

Implied condition (a) is broken if the bulk does not correspond completely with the sample in quality, even though only a small amount of work or expense is required to achieve complete correspondence[1].

The seller is in breach of implied condition (c) if the goods have a latent defect, but not if the defect could have been discovered by a reasonable examination of the sample, whether or not the buyer made any examination.

---

1   *E. and S. Ruben Ltd v Faire Bros & Co Ltd* [1949] 1 KB 254, [1949] 1 All ER 215.

Trading Stamps Act 1964

22.61 The Trading Stamps Act 1964, s.4[1], provides that where trading stamps are redeemed for goods *warranties* as to title, freedom from encumbrances, quiet possession and merchantable quality are implied, notwithstanding any terms to the contrary on which the redemption is made.

---

1   As amended by the Supply of Goods (Implied Terms) Act 1973, s.16.

Non-contractual liability for defective goods

22.62 Because of the doctrine of privity of contract[1], only the seller of defective goods can be liable for breach of the express or implied terms of the contract of sale, and then only to the buyer. However, if a buyer by retail, who has been injured by defective goods wishes to sue the manufacturer, he may be able to recover damages in tort for negligence[2]. Similarly, if, for instance, the buyer's wife is injured by the defective goods she may be able to recover damages for negligence from the seller or manufacturer.

There is no reason why a buyer who has been injured by defective goods should not sue the seller for negligence rather than for breach of contract, but normally he will not do so because the seller's contractual liability for breach of the implied terms discussed above is strict, so that it is no defence for the seller to prove that the defect was latent and could not have been discovered by the exercise of reasonable care[3]; whereas if he sues in negligence the buyer will have to prove that the seller failed to take reasonable care.

Sometimes manufacturers and distributors issue 'guarantees' which contain or purport to contain a promise that defects will be made good, but which also attempt to exclude or restrict their liability for loss or damage. Section 5 of the Unfair Contract Terms Act 1977 provides that such 'guarantees' are void in the case of goods of a type ordinarily supplied for private use or consumption, where loss or damage arises from the goods proving defective in consumer use, and results from the negligence of a person concerned in their manufacture or distribution[4].

---

1 Para. 6.19.
2 Paras. 20.31–20.34.
3 *Frost v Aylesbury Dairy Co Ltd* [1905] 1 KB 608, CA.
4 This provision only applies to 'business liability' as defined by the Act; para. 10.40.

DELIVERY AND ACCEPTANCE OF THE GOODS

22.63 By s.27, it is the duty of the seller to deliver the goods, and of the buyer to accept and pay for them, in accordance with the contract of sale.

Unless otherwise agreed, delivery and payment are concurrent conditions, that is to say, the seller must be ready and willing to give possession of the goods to the buyer in exchange for the price and the buyer must be ready and willing to pay the price in exchange for possession of the goods[1]. An example of an agreement to the contrary is where the seller agrees to give the buyer credit and, therefore, must deliver the goods before payment.

---

1 S.28.

Delivery

22.64 'Delivery' is defined by s.62 as the 'voluntary transfer of possession from one person to another'. This can be achieved either by actually placing the buyer in possession or constructively, by handing to the buyer the means of obtaining possession such as the key of the warehouse where the goods are stored or a document of title to them (e.g. a bill of lading, which will entitle the holder to receive the goods on the arrival of the ship).

22.65 Section 29 lays down the following rules as to delivery:

a. Although s.27 places the seller under the duty to deliver, he is not obliged by the Act to carry or send the goods to the buyer. Whether it is for the buyer to take possession of the goods or for the seller to send them to him depends on the terms of the contract, express or implied.

b. In the absence of any such terms, the place of delivery is the seller's place of business, if he has one, and if not, his residence; except that, if the goods are specific goods known to both parties to be in some other place, then that place is the place of delivery.

c. Where the seller is bound by the terms of the contract to send the goods to the buyer, and no time for sending them is fixed, he must send them within a reasonable time.

d. Demand or tender of delivery may be treated as ineffectual unless made at a reasonable hour.

e. Where the goods are in the possession of a third person, there is no delivery by the seller to the buyer unless and until the third person acknowledges to the buyer that he holds the goods on his behalf. However, this rule does not affect the operation of the issue or transfer of any document of title to goods, such as a bill of lading. Consequently, if the seller of goods which are in the possession of a third party, e.g. a carrier, transfers a document of title to the buyer this operates as a delivery of the goods.

f. Unless otherwise agreed, the expenses of putting the goods into a deliverable state[1] must be borne by the seller.

---

1 Para. 22.15.

22.66 *Delivery to carrier* This is governed by s.32. Where, in pursuance of a contract of sale, the seller is authorised or required to send the goods to the buyer, delivery of the goods to a carrier, whether named by the buyer or not, is prima facie deemed to be a delivery of the goods to the buyer, so that, unless otherwise agreed, the buyer's concurrent obligation to pay the price then becomes operative.

However, unless otherwise authorised by the buyer, the seller must make a reasonable contract with the carrier on behalf of the buyer, and if he does not do so, and the goods are lost or damaged in transit, the buyer may decline to treat the delivery to the carrier as a delivery to himself, or may hold the seller responsible in damages.

Unless otherwise agreed, when the goods are sent by sea, the seller must give sufficient notice to the buyer to enable him to effect any usual insurance, otherwise the goods will be at the seller's risk during their sea transit.

22.67 *Risk of deterioration in transit* Section 33 provides that where the seller agrees to deliver goods at his own risk at a place other than that where they were sold, the buyer must, nevertheless, take any risk of deterioration necessarily incident to the course of transit, unless otherwise agreed.

22.68 It may also be noted at this juncture that, if the seller agrees to deliver the goods at the buyer's premises and delivers them there without negligence to a person having apparent authority to receive them, he discharges his obligations, so that if that person misappropriates them the loss falls on the buyer and not on the seller[1].

---

1 *Galbraith and Grant Ltd v Block* [1922] 2 KB 155.

Acceptance

22.69 We stated in para. 22.63 that, by s.27, a buyer must accept and pay for goods in accordance with the terms of the contract. Consequently, a failure by a buyer to accept the goods delivered, in the sense described above, renders him liable for breach of contract unless he has a right to reject them (i.e. refuse to accept them) for breach of a condition (as opposed to a warranty) of the contract, or for the breach of an intermediate term entitling him to rescind, or for one of the reasons described in the following paragraphs (paras. 22.70 to 22.71). The reader is reminded that once a buyer has accepted all or part of the goods under an entire or indivisible contract he is bound by s.11(1)(c)[1] to treat any breach of condition as a breach of warranty and therefore cannot reject the goods.

Unless otherwise agreed, a buyer is not obliged to accept delivery of the goods by instalments[2].

---

1 Para. 22.40, b.
2 S.31(1).

22.70 Section 30 shows that the seller's obligation to deliver is an obligation to deliver the correct quantity of goods precisely, subject to 'microscopic' divergence[1], and is a condition precedent to the buyer's obligation to accept the goods and pay the price. Section 30 (1) and (2) provides that where the seller delivers to the buyer a larger or smaller quantity of goods than he contracted to sell, the buyer may:

a. reject the whole; or

b. accept the whole (in which case he must pay for them at the contract rate); or

c. in the case of a larger quantity only, accept the goods included in the contract and reject the rest.

Section 30(3) provides that if the seller delivers the goods he contracted to sell mixed with goods of a different description, the buyer may:

a. accept the goods which are in accordance with the contract and reject the rest; or

b. reject the whole.

It should be noted that the fact that the buyer can accept the goods which are in accordance with the contract and reject the rest means that this provision prevails over s.11(1)(c).

Because of the difficulty of delivering the precise amount where a contract concerns a large quantity of goods, sellers often try to protect themselves by inserting an expression such as 'say about' or 'more or less' into the contractual provision relating to quantity. In addition, such terms may be imported into a contract by trade usage or a course of dealing between the parties[2]. Where a contract contains such a term the effect is to provide, in favour of the seller, a reasonable latitude between the contract quantity and the quantity delivered, so that the buyer is not entitled to reject the goods unless the reasonable margin is exceeded.

---

1 *Shipton, Anderson & Co v Weil Bros & Co* [1912] 1 KB 574; para. 9.2.
2 S.30(4).

Delivery by instalments

22.71 So far we have concentrated our discussion of delivery and acceptance on the position in relation to entire or indivisible contracts. We now consider contracts for delivery by instalments which are severable contracts because each instalment is to be separately paid for[1].

Section 31(2) provides that where there is a contract for the sale of goods to be delivered by stated instalments, which are to be separately paid for, and the seller makes defective deliveries in respect of one or more instalments, or the buyer neglects or refuses to take delivery of, or pay for, one or more instalments, it is a question in each case depending on the terms of the contract and the circumstances of the case, whether the breach of contract is a repudiation of the whole contract entitling the buyer to rescind it, or whether it is a severable breach giving rise to a claim for damages but not to a right to treat the whole contract as repudiated.

As s.31(2) indicates, where the terms of the contract do not indicate what is to be the position if one or other party is in default in relation to an instalment, the answer depends on the circumstances of the case. In *Mersey Steel and Iron Co Ltd v Naylor, Benzon & Co²*, S sold to B 5,000 tons of steel, to be delivered at the rate of 1,000 tons monthly, payments to be made within three days after receipt of shipping documents. After the delivery of two instalments, but before payment for them became due, a petition for winding-up S was presented. Thereupon, B refused to make any payment unless the leave of the court was obtained, being under the erroneous impression that this was necessary. The House of Lords held that it was impossible to ascribe to the conduct of B the character of a repudiation of the contract. It was just the reverse: they were desirous of fulfilling the contract and had expressed anxiety that the supposed difficulty should be removed as soon as possible by obtaining the leave of the court. There was therefore no repudiatory breach of the contract by B, and S were not entitled to rescind the contract. Consequently, they remained liable to make further deliveries.

It is not always easy to decide whether a particular breach of a severable contract for delivery by instalments amounts to a repudiation of the whole contract by the party in default. However, in *Maple Flock Co Ltd v Universal Furniture Products (Wembley) Ltd³*, it was indicated that the principal considerations are not the subjective mental state of the party in breach, but first, the ratio quantitatively which the breach bears to the contract as a whole, and secondly, the degree of probability that such a breach will be repeated. In addition, the further the parties have proceeded with the contract the less likely it is to be inferred that a breach constitutes a repudiation of the whole contract⁴. In the *Maple Flock* case, there was a contract for the sale of 100 tons of flock, to be delivered in instalments of 1½ tons at the rate of three instalments a week, the weekly deliveries to be separately paid for. The first fifteen loads were satisfactory but the sixteenth contained an excessive amount of chlorine and the buyers claimed to rescind the whole contract for repudiatory breach, consequently refusing to accept any further deliveries. The Court of Appeal held that the buyers were not entitled to do this because there was no probability that the breach would be repeated and the breach which had occurred related to a single instalment which bore only a small quantitative ratio to the contract as a whole.

---

1   Para. 10.17.
2   (1884) 9 App Cas 434, HL.
3   [1934] 1 KB 148, CA.
4   *Cornwall v Henson* [1900] 2 Ch 298 at 304.

REMEDIES FOR BREACH OF CONTRACT OF SALE

Breach by the seller

22.72   We have shown that the seller of goods is under a duty to deliver the goods in accordance with the contract of sale and to observe the terms, express or implied, of the contract. In the event of a breach by the seller of his contractual duties the remedies available to the buyer are as follows.

Remedies for non-delivery
22.73   *Damages*   By s.51, where the seller wrongfully neglects or refuses to deliver the goods to the buyer, the buyer has a right of action for damages[1]. The measure of damages is the estimated loss directly and naturally resulting, in the ordinary course of events, from the seller's breach of contract[2], which, where there is an available market for the goods in question (i.e. they can be freely and readily bought) is prima facie the amount, if any, by which the market or current price exceeds the contract price at the time when they ought to have been delivered, or, if no time was fixed, at the time of the refusal to deliver[3]. Any sub-sale made by the buyer in the expectation of receiving the goods is generally ignored, so that if the resale price is below the market price the damages are not reduced[4], and if the resale price is above the market price they are not increased[5]. Where there is no available market for the goods in question, the measure of damages is still the loss directly and naturally resulting from the breach, but the court has to assess this loss as best it can on the evidence before it, including the resale price if they have been resold.

The rules just stated are concerned with valuing one element of the buyer's loss, his expectation of getting the goods. In addition, where the buyer has resold the goods at a profit he can recover special damages for loss of the profit *provided* the seller can reasonably be supposed to have contemplated when the contract was made that the goods were required for resale, otherwise the loss will be too remote under the rules of remoteness of damage discussed in paras. 12.3 to 12.6[6].

---

1 S.51(1).
2 S.51(2). This puts into statutory effect the first sub-rule in *Hadley v Baxendale*, para. 12.3, a.
3 S.51(3).
4 *Williams Bros v Ed. T. Agius Ltd* [1914] AC 510, HL.
5 *Williams v Reynolds* (1865) 6 B & S 495.
6 S.54.

22.74 *Specific performance* An action for damages is the buyer's main remedy for non-delivery, but in a limited number of cases a decree of specific performance may be awarded. By s.52, where the contract is for the delivery of specific or ascertained goods the court may, on the application of the buyer, direct that the contract shall be specifically enforced, i.e. the goods be delivered. The decree may be unconditional or upon such terms and conditions as to damages, payment of the price, and otherwise, as to the court may seem just. This remedy is, of course, a discretionary one and will normally only be granted when the goods are unique in character or of special value or interest so that damages would be an inadequate remedy. In *Cohen v Roche*[1], an order of specific performance of a contract for the sale of eight Hepplewhite chairs was refused because the chairs were 'ordinary articles of commerce and of no special value or interest' and the plaintiff was merely awarded damages for non-delivery. On the other hand, in *Behnke v Bede Shipping Co Ltd*[2], an order for specific performance for a contract of sale of a ship was made because the ship was of 'peculiar and practically unique value to the plaintiff'.

In *Sky Petroleum Ltd v V.I.P. Petroleum Ltd*[3], it was held that a court has an inherent jurisdiction to order specific performance of a contract for unascertained goods where the remedy of damages would be inadequate, such as where there is no alternative source of supplies available to the buyer.

---

1 [1927] 1 KB 169.
2 [1927] 1 KB 649.
3 [1974] 1 All ER 954, [1974] 1 WLR 576.

22.75 *Recovery of price* If the seller fails to deliver or tender delivery, the buyer is, of course, not liable to pay the price. If the buyer has paid the price but the seller fails to deliver the goods, the buyer may recover the price in a quasi-contractual action on the basis of a total failure of consideration[1].

---

1 S.54. Also see para. 17.7, b.

Remedies for breach of condition
22.76 What is said here is also applicable, with certain exceptions, to the breach of an intermediate term where the effect of the particular breach entitles the buyer to treat the contract as repudiated (i.e. to rescind it).

22.77 *Rejection of the goods* As we have seen, where the seller is in breach of a condition, the buyer may treat the contract as repudiated and reject the goods. Unless otherwise agreed, a buyer who rejects goods is not bound to return them to the seller: it is sufficient if he intimates to the seller that he refuses to accept them[1].

The right to reject is lost if the buyer:

a. has waived the condition[2]; or

b. has elected to treat the breach of condition as a breach of warranty[3]; or

c. where the contract is not severable, has 'accepted'[4] the goods (unless there is a term of the contract, express or implied, which still permits rejection)[5]; or

d. cannot let the seller have the goods back, even though he has not 'accepted them', because, for instance, he has sold and delivered them to X, who will not return them.

---

1 S.36.
2 This is expressly provided in relation to breach of condition by s.11(1)(a).
3 S.11(1)(a).
4 For the definition of 'acceptance' in relation to a breach of condition, see para. 24.40, b.
5 S.11(1)(c).

22.78 *Recovery of the price* Of course, if the buyer validly rejects the goods, the price is no longer payable, if he has not yet paid it, since the contract has been rescinded. Where the buyer validly rejects the goods after he has paid the price, he can recover it in a quasi-contractual action on the basis of a total failure of consideration[1], but he is not entitled to retain the goods until the money is returned[2].

---

1 S.54. Also see para. 17.7, b.
2 *J. L. Lyons & Co Ltd v May and Baker Ltd* [1923] 1 KB 685.

22.79 *Damages* If the buyer has rejected the goods, he may sue for damages and the case will be treated in the same way as if the goods had not been delivered at all.

Remedies for breach of warranty

22.80   Section 53(1) provides that where there is a breach of warranty by the seller, or where the buyer elects, or is compelled (by 'acceptance' or inability to let the seller have the goods), to treat a breach of condition[1] by the seller as a breach of warranty, the buyer is not entitled to reject the goods; but he may:

a. set up the breach of warranty in diminution or extinction of the price; or

b. maintain an action against the seller for damages for breach of warranty.

The measure of damages for breach of warranty is the estimated loss directly and naturally resulting, in the ordinary course of events, from the breach of warranty[2].

In the case of a breach of a warranty of quality, this loss is prima facie the difference between the value of the goods at the time of delivery to the buyer and the value they would have had if they had answered to the warranty[3]. This prima facie rule is concerned with valuing the buyer's loss of expected benefit. In addition, the buyer will be able to recover damages for consequential loss caused by the defect in quality, e.g. personal injury or damage to other property, provided it is not too remote[4].

If the seller commits a breach by late delivery, the buyer's loss directly and naturally resulting from the breach is prima facie the difference between the market price at the time when the goods ought to have been delivered and the market price of the goods when they are delivered[5]. Thus, if S should have delivered the goods to B on 1 May when the market price was £10 a ton but does not deliver until 1 July when the market price was £9 a ton, the measure of damages is prima facie £1 a ton. However, where the buyer has re-sold the goods at a price higher than the market price at the time of actual delivery the damages are reduced to the difference between the market price when the goods ought to have been delivered and their resale price[6]. Consequently, if B, in the above example, has resold the goods to X at £9.50 a ton, the measure of damages will be the difference between £10 and £9.50, i.e. 50p a ton. Of course, in cases of late delivery, the buyer may also recover for any other damage which has resulted from the breach, provided it is not too remote.

What has been said about the buyer's remedies for breach of warranty is, presumably, applicable in cases where the seller breaks an intermediate term and the effect of the breach does not entitle the buyer to reject the goods or it does so entitle him but he elects or is compelled not to do so.

---

1   Or, presumably, the breach of an intermediate term justifying rejection.

2 S.53(2).
3 S.53(3).
4 Para. 12.3, b.
5 *Elbinger AG v Armstrong* (1874) LR 9 QB 473.
6 *Wertheim v Chicoutimi Pulp Co* [1911] AC 301, PC.

Breach by the buyer

22.81 As we said in para. 22.63, the buyer is under a duty to accept and pay for the goods in accordance with the contract. In the event of a breach by the buyer of his contractual duties the remedies available to the seller are as follows.

Remedy for failure to take delivery
22.82 Section 37 provides that when the seller is ready and willing to deliver the goods, and requests the buyer to take delivery, and the buyer (wrongfully) fails to comply with this request within a reasonable time, the seller can recover —

a. any loss occasioned by the buyer's neglect or refusal to take delivery; and

b. a reasonable charge for the care and custody of the goods.

This provision is without prejudice to the seller's right to rescind the contract if the buyer's neglect or refusal to take delivery amounts to a repudiation of the contract, as where the refusal is absolute[1], in which case the seller, apart from being able to rescind and thereby terminate his obligation to deliver, has a right of action for damages under provisions mentioned in the following paragraphs. On the other hand, if the buyer's neglect or refusal does not amount to a repudiation, e.g. because the buyer merely requests a short postponement, the seller cannot rescind and therefore remains liable to deliver.

---

1 Paras. 10.10—10.13.

Remedy for failure to accept
22.83 Section 50(1) provides that where the buyer wrongfully neglects or refuses to accept and pay for the goods, the seller may maintain an action against him for damages for non-acceptance. By s.50(2), the measure of damages is the estimated loss directly and naturally resulting, in the ordinary course of events, from the buyer's breach of contract.

Where there is an available market for the goods in question (i.e. they can be freely and readily sold), the measure of damages is prima facie the difference between the contract price and the market or current price at the time or times when the goods ought to have been accepted or, if no time was fixed for acceptance, then at the time of refusal (s.50(3)). Consequently, if there is an available market for the goods and –

a. their market price is *lower* than their contract price, the seller is entitled to substantial damages representing the difference; but if

b. their market price is the *same as or even higher* than the contract price, the seller is only entitled to nominal damages.

Section 50(3) only lays down a prima facie rule which can be displaced if it would work injustice or otherwise be inappropriate[1].

---

1 *W. L. Thompson Ltd v Robinson (Gunmakers) Ltd* [1955] Ch 177, [1955] 1 All ER 154.

22.84 Where there is no available market, the court has to rely on the basic provision, s.50(2), and determine the loss directly and naturally resulting from the buyer's breach. The following situations can be considered further.

There is no available market if the goods are made or procured to the buyer's specification and cannot be sold to another because of their specialised nature. In such a case, the seller can recover damages amounting to the cost incurred in making or procuring them and his loss of profit, i.e. the contract price.

There is no available market if at the time the supply of the goods in question exceeds the demand. In such a case the seller *may* be able to recover his loss of profit. In *W. L. Thompson Ltd v Robinson (Gunmakers) Ltd*[1], B contracted to buy a new Vanguard car from S, who were car dealers, at the recommended retail price. B then refused to accept the car and were sued by S for loss of their profit of £61 on the sale. B argued that S could not recover loss of profit, but only damages measured under s.50(3) which, since there was no difference between the contract price and the market or current price, would have to be nominal. This argument was rejected because, first, s.50(3) only laid down a prima facie rule which could be displaced if it worked injustice, and, secondly, s.50(3) was inapplicable anyway because there was no available market for Vanguard cars since at the time supply exceeded demand. The measure of damages was therefore that specified by s.50(2), the loss directly and naturally resulting from the breach. As a result of the breach, the plaintiffs had sold one Vanguard less than they might and so were entitled to claim loss of profit.

The situation in *Thompson v Robinson* must be contrasted with two others. First, if demand for the goods exceeds supply, so that, for instance, a car dealer can sell all the cars of a particular make which he can obtain from the manufacturers, he cannot recover loss of profit in an action for non-acceptance since he cannot be said to have made only one sale instead of two and can only recover nominal damages[2]. Secondly, although there is no available market for second-hand cars and other unique goods, the seller cannot recover his loss of profit under s.50(2) in an action for non-acceptance because it is not the direct and natural result of the buyer's breach that the seller will sell one car, for instance, instead of two[3]. Instead, the seller's damages will be the particular loss which he has suffered as a direct and natural result of the breach, i.e. the difference between the contract price and the price at which he ultimately sells the car to another, if that price is higher, or, if it is lower, nominal damages only.

---

1 [1955] Ch 177, [1955] 1 All ER 154.
2 *Charter v Sullivan* [1957] 2 QB 117, [1957] 1 All ER 809, CA.
3 *Lazenby Garages Ltd v Wright* [1976] 2 All ER 770, [1976] 1 WLR 459, CA.

22.85 Quite apart from the loss directly and naturally resulting from the breach, the seller may also recover for any other damage which he has suffered provided it ought to have been in the contemplation of the parties, when they made the contract, as the probable result of the breach, otherwise it will be too remote under the rules of remoteness of damage discussed in paras. 12.3 to 12.6[1].

---

1 S.54.

Remedies for non-payment of the price

22.86 The Sale of Goods Act gives an unpaid seller two types of remedy –

a personal remedy against the buyer for the price; and
real remedies against the goods themselves.

The remedy against the buyer for the price

22.87 Section 49 provides that where the buyer wrongfully neglects or refuses to pay for the goods, the seller has a right of action against him for the *price* of the goods (as opposed to damages) in two cases:

a. where the property (i.e. ownership) in the goods has passed to the buyer; of course, since the obligations to deliver and pay are concurrent conditions, unless otherwise agreed[1], the seller cannot normally bring an action for the price unless he has delivered or is ready and willing to deliver the goods;

b. where, under the contract, the price is payable on a specified date irrespective of delivery. Under this provision the seller can sue for the price although the property in the goods has not passed to the buyer, and the goods have not been appropriated to the contract.

The relationship between the remedies of the seller against the buyer which we have just mentioned can be illustrated as follows. If the property has passed to the buyer and he has accepted the goods but wrongfully defaults in paying the price, the seller can sue him for the price under s.49. If the property in the goods has not passed and the buyer wrongfully fails to accept them, the seller can sue him for damages for non-acceptance under s.50. If the property in the goods has passed to the buyer and the seller wrongfully fails to accept and pay for them, the seller can sue for the price under s.49 or for damages for non-acceptance under s.50. If the seller sues for the price he may also claim under s.37 for any loss occasioned by the failure to take delivery and for storage charges etc. If the seller sues for damages for non-acceptance, such losses and expenses will be taken into account in quantifying the damages.

Remedies against the goods themselves

22.88   Section 39 provides that an 'unpaid seller' has the following real rights against the goods themselves, even though the property in the goods may have passed to the buyer:

a. a lien on the goods while he is in possession of them;

b. in the case of the insolvency of the buyer, a right of stopping the goods in transitu after he has parted with the possession of them;

c. a right of resale as limited by the Act.

If the property in the goods has *not* passed to the buyer, an 'unpaid seller' has, in addition to his other remedies, a right of withholding delivery similar to and co-extensive with his rights of lien and stoppage in transitu where the property has passed to the buyer[1].

These rights against the goods are only available to an 'unpaid seller'. In this context 'seller' includes any person in the position of a seller, such as a consignor or agent who has himself paid, or is directly responsible for paying, the price to the seller[2].

---

1   S.39(2).
2   S.38(2).

22.89   *Lien*   The fact that the buyer has obtained the property (i.e. ownership) in the goods (which, in the case of specific goods, will normally happen when the contract of sale is made)[1] does not mean that the seller has to deliver them before the buyer has paid the price, because so long as the unpaid seller is in possession of the goods he has a lien over them. A lien is the right to retain possession of the goods owned by the buyer until the payment or tender of payment of their *price*. If the property in the goods has not passed to the buyer, e.g. because the right of disposal has been reserved[2], the unpaid seller has an equivalent right of withholding possession.

These rights only exist in the three cases laid down by s.41(1):

a. where the goods have been sold without any stipulation as to credit; or

b. where the goods have been sold on credit, but the term of credit has expired; or

c. where the buyer becomes insolvent, which he will be deemed to be if he has ceased to pay his debts in the ordinary course of business or cannot pay his debts as they become due, whether or not he has committed an act of bankruptcy[3].

Where part delivery has been made under an indivisible contract, the unpaid seller may exercise his right of lien on the remainder of the goods, unless the part delivery has been made under such circumstances as to show an agreement to waive the lien[4].

---

1   Para. 22.15.
2   Para. 22.22.
3   S.62(3).
4   S.42.

22.90   Since the lien depends on possession, s.43 provides that the unpaid seller loses his right of lien if:

a. he delivers the goods to a carrier or other bailee for the purpose of transmission to the buyer without reserving the right of disposal of the goods; or

b. the buyer or his agent lawfully obtains possession of the goods; or

c. he (the unpaid seller) waives his lien.

But the right of lien is not lost simply because the unpaid seller has obtained judgment for the price.

By s.47, the unpaid seller's lien is not affected by any sale or other disposition of the goods which the buyer may make, unless the seller assents to it; it is not enough that the unpaid seller acknowledges the sale etc. There will only be such an assent if the circumstances show that the unpaid seller intended to renounce his rights against the goods and to take the risk of the buyer's dishonesty[1].

However, if a document of title, e.g. a bill of lading or a delivery warrant, is lawfully transferred by the unpaid seller to any person as buyer or owner, and that person transfers the document to a third person who takes it in good faith and for value, the proviso to s.47 applies, whereby —

a. if the transfer to the third party is by way of *sale*, the unpaid seller's *lien is totally defeated*;

b. if such transfer is by way of a *pledge* or other disposition for value, the unpaid seller can only exercise his *lien subject to the right of the pledgee* or other transferee for value.

---

1   *D. F. Mount Ltd v Jay and Jay (Provisions) Co Ltd* [1960] 1 QB 159, [1959] 3 All ER 307.

22.91   *Stoppage in transitu*   Section 44 provides that the unpaid seller who has parted with possession of the goods to a carrier or other bailee for transmission to the buyer is entitled to stop the goods, resume possession of them and *retain them until payment or tender of the price*. This right is *only* available *if the buyer becomes insolvent* (as defined in para. 22.89, c) *and if the goods are still in transit*. The right of stoppage *in transitu* provided by s.44 is not available if the property in the goods has not passed to the buyer but in such a case the equivalent and co-extensive right of withholding delivery is available to an unpaid seller.

By s.46, stoppage in transitu is effected by the unpaid seller by:

a. taking actual possession of the goods; or

b. giving notice of his claim to the carrier or other bailee in whose possession the goods are. Such notice may be given to the person in actual possession of the goods or to his principal. If it is given to the principal, the notice is ineffectual unless it is given under such circumstances that he can, with reasonable diligence, communicate it to his servant or agent in time to prevent delivery to the buyer.

On notice being given, the carrier or other bailee must re-deliver the goods to, or according to the directions of, the unpaid seller, otherwise he is liable in tort for conversion. The seller must bear the expenses of re-delivery.

22.92   Since the right of stoppage can only be exercised while the goods are still in transit, it is important to define when this begins and ends. By s.45(1), goods are deemed to be in the course of transit from the time when they are delivered to a carrier or other bailee (such as a warehouseman)[1] for the purpose of transmission to the buyer, until the buyer or his agent takes delivery of them from such carrier or other bailee.

The point at which transit ceases must be determined on the facts of each case. Obviously, transit is at an end when the goods are delivered, actually or constructively[2], by the carrier or other bailee to the buyer or his agent, e.g. the buyer's warehouseman or the master of the buyer's *own* ship[3]. In addition, s.45 provides that, inter alia, transit is at an end:

a. if the buyer or his agent obtains possession of the goods before they reach their appointed destination, whether or not this is against the carrier's will;

b. when, after the goods have arrived at their appointed destination, e.g. the carrier's depot, the carrier or other bailee acknowledges to the buyer or his agent that he holds the goods on his behalf and *continues in possession of them as bailee for the buyer or his agent,* and it is immaterial that a further destination may have been indicated by the buyer; but if the buyer rejects the goods and the carrier or other bailee continues in possession of them, the transit is not ended, even if the seller has refused to have them back;

c. where the carrier or other bailee wrongfully refuses to deliver the goods to the buyer or his agent.

It may be added that if part delivery of the goods has been made to the buyer or his agent, the right of stoppage in transitu can still be exercised on the remainder of the goods, unless the part delivery has been made under such circumstances as to show an agreement by the seller to give up possession of the whole of the goods[4].

---

1 Of course, as this paragraph shows, if the carrier or other bailee is the agent of the buyer the transit never begins for the purposes of stoppage in transitu.
2 Para. 22.64.
3 If the goods are delivered to a ship chartered by the buyer it is a question depending on the circumstances of the case, whether they are in the possession of the master as agent for the buyer (transit ends) or as a carrier (transit does not end), s.45(5).
4 S.45(7).

22.93 Section 47, and the proviso thereto, protects the unpaid seller's right of stoppage in transitu in the event of a sale, pledge or other disposition to the same extent as it protects the right of lien. Thus, for instance, if the buyer sells the goods, the unpaid seller's right of stoppage is not defeated unless he has assented to the sale. But his right of stoppage is defeated if he has transferred a document of title to the buyer and the buyer transfers it for value by way of sale to X who takes it in good faith[1].

---

1 In *Cahn v Pockett's Bristol Channel Steam Packet Co Ltd* [1899] 1 QB 643, CA; para. 22.33, it was held X's right of stoppage in transitu was defeated by virtue of the proviso to s.47.

22.94 *Resale* Section 48 provides an unpaid seller who has exercised his right of lien or stoppage in transitu with the right to resell the goods in three cases:

a. where the goods are of a perishable nature;

b. where the unpaid seller gives notice to the buyer of his intention to resell, and the buyer does not pay or tender the price within a reasonable time;

c. where the seller expressly reserves the right of resale in case the buyer should make default.

The exercise of one of these rights of resale rescinds the contract with the result that, if the property in the goods has passed to the original buyer, it reverts to the unpaid seller, and, consequently, the seller loses the right to sue the original buyer under s.49 for the price. In addition, whether or not the property has passed to the original buyer, the seller may keep any proceeds made on the resale and sue the original buyer for damages under s.50 for non-acceptance if the resale, after deducting its extra expenses, realises less than the contract price[1].

The exercise by the unpaid seller of his right of lien or of stoppage in transitu does not rescind the contract of sale[2]. It is for this reason that, subject to the exceptions mentioned above, the unpaid seller who has exercised such a right is not entitled to resell the goods, and if he does he will be liable for breach of contract to the original buyer. However, if, notwithstanding, the unpaid seller who has exercised his right of lien or of stoppage does resell the goods, the new buyer gets a good title to them as against the original buyer[3].

---

1 S.48(4); *R. V. Ward Ltd v Bignall* [1967] 1 QB 534, [1967] 2 All ER 499, CA (in relation to the rights to resell under s.48(3)).
2 S.48(1).
3 S.48(2).

PARTICULAR TYPES OF CONTRACT OF SALE

Contracts of sale involving shipment of goods

22.95 These contracts can take a variety of forms, but we shall limit ourselves to three types.

FOB contracts
22.96 FOB stands for free on board. Under such a contract the seller is obliged to place the goods on board a ship, which is usually named by the buyer, and to pay the charges for doing so. Delivery on board is

prima facie deemed to be a delivery to the buyer. The buyer pays freight and insurance but, unless otherwise agreed, the seller must give such notice to the buyer as may enable him to insure goods during their sea transit, otherwise they are deemed to be at his risk[1]. Under an FOB contract the risk passes to the buyer when the goods cross the ship's rail and so, prima facie, does the property (unless the goods are unascertained and part of a larger consignment, in which case the property does not pass until they are ascertained[2]).

---

1 Para. 22.66.
2 Para. 22.19.

CIF contracts
22.97 CIF stands for cost, insurance and freight. A CIF contract is one for the sale of goods to be performed by the delivery of documents representing the goods. Under such a contract the seller is obliged: to arrange shipment of the goods; to pay the freight; to arrange and pay for marine insurance on the goods on terms current in the trade and which will be for the benefit of the buyer; to procure a contract of carriage by sea, which will be indorsed by a bill of lading; to make out an invoice for the goods; and to tender the bill of lading, the insurance policy and the invoice (which are the documents representing the goods). If, as often happens, the contract so provides, the seller can deliver a delivery order and insurance certificate instead of the bill of lading and insurance policy.

The tender of the shipping documents represents the seller's duty to deliver the goods, with the result that the buyer is obliged to pay the price on tender of the documents if the documents are in order, even though the goods are already lost[1]. In a CIF contract the risk passes to the buyer when the goods cross the ship's rail[2] but normally the property only passes when the shipping documents are tendered to him.

---

1 *C. Groom Ltd v Barber* [1915] 1 KB 316.
2 *Biddell Bros v Horst Co* [1911] 1 KB 214; affd. [1912] AC 18, HL.

'Ex ship' contracts
22.98 Under such a contract the seller is obliged not only to ship the goods but to deliver them to the buyer from a ship which has arrived at the port of delivery and at a place customarily used for the unloading of the particular type of goods. Until this is done, the price is not payable, nor does the property or risk pass to the buyer until then. The seller is not obliged to insure, but if he does so it will be for his own benefit[1].

---

1 *Yangtsze Insurance Association Ltd v Lukmanjee* [1918] AC 585, PC.

International sales

22.99 The rules of English law relating to the sale of goods do not necessarily apply to a contract of international sale of goods. Different rules are contained in two international conventions, the Uniform Law on the International Sale of Goods (ULIS) and the Uniform Law on the Formation of Contracts for the International Sale of Goods (ULFIS), and these may be applicable by virtue of the Uniform Laws of International Sales Act 1967, which gives them effect in this country. ULIS and ULFIS apply to international contracts between parties carrying on business or habitually resident in different 'contracting states', unless the parties exclude them in whole or part.

In addition, even if the parties both carry on business or are habitually resident in the United Kingdom, they may adopt ULIS and ULFIS as the law of contract in preference to the Sale of Goods Act. However, in this case the parties cannot evade the mandatory provisions of ss. 12 to 15 of the Sale of Goods Act by making such an adoption[1].

So far, businessmen in this country have shown little inclination to adopt ULIS and ULFIS in preference to English law, but no doubt the Uniform Laws will be adopted increasingly in international trade.

---

1 Supply of Goods (Implied Terms) Act 1973, s.5(2) (as amended by the Unfair Contract Terms Act 1977, Sched. 4).

Chapter 23

Consumer Credit

23.1 There has been a gradual increase in statutory control over hire-purchase and other forms of consumer credit in order to protect consumers against unfair practices by traders. The Consumer Credit Act 1974, which is a comprehensive piece of legislation and far wider ranging than the statutes replaced by it, is the culmination of the legislative process in this area. Although the whole of the Act had not been brought into force when this book went to press, we propose to discuss the law as it will be when the Act is fully in force. Unless otherwise indicated, references in this chapter to 'the Act', or to sections, relate to the Consumer Credit Act 1974.

Even when the Act is fully in force, it will not be the only source of the legal rules relevant to credit transactions because, quite apart from the fact that essentially it is only concerned with regulated consumer credit and consumer hire agreements, it assumes the continued application of the law of contract and of certain specific rules relating to particular types of transactions, such as hire-purchase or conditional sale agreements.

We propose to discuss the provisions of the Act first and then turn to some of these other matters at the end of the Chapter.

Supervision of the system of protection

23.2 The system of protection established by the Act is supervised by the Director-General of Fair Trading. By s.1, the Director's duty is:

a. to administer the licensing system set up by the Act;

b. generally to superintend the working and enforcement of the Act and regulations made under it;

c. where necessary or expedient, to enforce the Act and regulations;

d. to keep under review, and advise, the Secretary of State for Prices and Consumer Protection, about —
    i. social and commercial developments relating to the provision of credit or bailment of goods to individuals; and
    ii. the working and enforcement of the Act and regulations made under it.

DEFINITIONS AND SPECIAL CHARACTERISTICS

23.3   The provisions of the Consumer Credit Act 1974 can only be understood if the meaning of a number of basic terms used by it, especially the definitions of various types of transactions, are firmly understood. Section 189 of the Act contains a very long list of definitions, many of which are amplified elsewhere in the Act. In addition, Schedule 2 puts flesh on the statutory definitions by providing examples of factual situations designed to illustrate the application of the various terms. Unless the contrary is indicated, all definitions which we mention in this part are derived from s.189.

23.4   With the notable exception of the provisions relating to extortionate credit bargains[1], the protective provisions of the Act are limited to regulated agreements. *A regulated agreement is a consumer credit agreement, or a consumer hire agreement, other than an exempt agreement.*

---

1   Paras. 23.67—23.69.

Regulated consumer credit agreement

23.5   By s.8, a consumer credit agreement is a credit agreement by which the creditor (who may be an individual or a corporation) provides the debtor (who must be an individual) with credit not exceeding £5,000. An 'individual' in this context includes a partnership or other unincorporated body of persons not consisting entirely of bodies corporate. It should be noted that a consumer credit agreement can be made by a sole trader or by a partnership (unless all the partners are bodies corporate) as debtor, despite the fact that he or it is not a 'consumer' in the popular sense of that term.

23.6   'Credit' is widely defined by s.9. It includes a cash loan, and any other form of financial accommodation, but an item entering into the total charge for credit, such as a broker's fee or legal fees, is not treated as credit even if time is allowed for its payment. It must be emphasised that the question of whether an agreement, e.g. for hire-purchase, is regulated does not depend on whether the value of the goods does not exceed £5,000 but on whether the credit provided does not exceed that sum. In a hire-purchase agreement the credit provided is deemed to be the difference between the total price of the goods *and* the aggregate of the deposit (if any) and the total charge for credit. Suppose that an individual enters into a hire-purchase agreement as debtor, that the agreement provides for the property in the goods to pass to him on payment of a total of £7,500 and the exercise by him of an option to purchase, and that the sum of £7,500 includes a down-payment of £1,000 and a total charge for credit of £1,500. The agreement will be a regulated consumer credit agreement because the credit under the above formula is deemed to be £7,500 − (£1,000 + £1,500) = £5,000[1].

---

1   Sched. 2, Example 10.

23.7   Section 10 provides that credit can be divided into two types: running-account credit and fixed-sum credit.

Running-account credit   Running-account credit is a facility under a credit agreement between an individual (the debtor) and another (the creditor) whereby the debtor is entitled to receive from time to time from the creditor or a third party cash, goods or services (or any of them) to an amount or value such that, taking into account payments made by or to the credit of the debtor, the credit limit (if any) is not exceeded. Examples are bank overdrafts, credit cards and shop budget accounts.

A running-account credit facility constitutes a regulated consumer credit agreement if the 'credit limit' does not exceed £5,000. 'Credit limit' means the maximum debit balance which, under the credit agreement, is allowed to stand on the account, disregarding any term of the agreement allowing that maximum to be exceeded merely temporarily. A running-account credit is deemed by s.10(3) not to exceed £5,000 if the credit limit does not exceed £5,000 *or* if, although there is no credit limit or there is a credit limit in excess of £5,000:

a. the debtor is not enabled to draw more than £5,000 credit at any time; or

b. the agreement provides that, if the debit balance rises above a given amount (not exceeding £5,000), the credit charge is to increase or any other conditions favouring the creditor or his associate are to come into operation; or

c. at the time the agreement is made, it is probable that the debit balance will not at any time rise above £5,000 (but if the agreement contains a term signifying that in the parties' opinion this provision does not apply, it shall be taken not to apply unless the contrary is proved)[1].

These are anti-avoidance provisions designed to ensure that a fictitiously high credit limit is not set when in fact the credit to be taken is within the £5,000 limit. An example of an unlimited running-account credit agreement which is nevertheless a regulated consumer credit agreement is where a bank grants an individual an unlimited overdraft with an increased rate of interest on so much of any debit balance as exceeds £2,000. Although the overdraft purports to be unlimited, the stipulation for increased interest above £2,000 brings the agreement within b. above[2]. Another example is where an 'individual' shopkeeper, whose business normally carries a stock worth about £1,000, makes an agreement with X whereby X undertakes to provide on short-term credit the stock needed from time to time by the shopkeeper without any specified limit. Although the agreement seems to provide unlimited credit, it is a regulated consumer credit agreement because it is probable, having regard to the stock usually carried by the shopkeeper, that his indebtedness to X will not at any time exceed £5,000 and therefore the agreement falls within c. above[3].

Fixed-sum credit Fixed-sum credit is any other facility under a credit agreement whereby a debtor who is an 'individual' is enabled to receive credit of a definite amount (whether it is taken in one amount or by instalments). Examples are bank loans, personal loans, pawnbrokers' loans, hire-purchase, and conditional sale and credit sale agreements.

---

1 S.171(1).
2 Sched. 2, Example 6.
3 Sched. 2, Example 7.

Restricted-use and unrestricted-use credit
23.8 Regulated consumer credit agreements are, by s.11, classifiable on the basis of the form of the loan into restricted-use credit agreements and unrestricted-use credit agreements. Section 11 lays down a rather complex definition of a restricted-use credit agreement, from which it distinguishes an unrestricted-use credit agreement. For the purposes of this book it suffices to state that the following are examples of restricted-use credit agreements: hire-purchase, conditional sale and credit sale agreements, check and voucher trading, shop budget accounts, loans made for the purchase of goods or services where the loan is paid direct to the supplier, and agreements to pay off the debtor's existing debts in return for the debtor's promise to repay the loan with interest[1]. Examples of unrestricted-use credit facilities are overdraft facilities, cheque cards, and loans of money which are at the free disposition of

the debtor (whether or not the purpose of the loan is known to the creditor) such as bank loans, personal loans and pawnbrokers' loans[2]. If a credit card is used to purchase goods or services this gives rise to restricted-use credit, but if it is used to obtain cash it gives rise to unrestricted-use credit[3].

---

1   Sched. 2, Examples 10, 12, 13, 14, 16.
2   Sched. 2, Examples 8, 12, 16, 17, 18, 21.
3   S.18 and Sched. 2, Example 16.

Debtor-creditor-supplier and debtor-creditor agreements

23.9   Sections 12 and 13 provide a further classification of regulated consumer credit agreements based on the relationship between the creditor and the supplier: debtor-creditor-supplier agreements and debtor-creditor agreements.

By s.12, there are three types of debtor-creditor-supplier agreements:

a. A restricted-use credit agreement financing a transaction between the debtor and the creditor, whether forming part of that agreement or not. (The description of such an agreement as a debtor-creditor-supplier agreement may seem surprising. This type of agreement embraces a hire-purchase, conditional sale or credit sale agreement between a customer and a dealer who finances his own instalment credit, and also the very common tripartite arrangement between a customer, dealer and finance company whereby the finance company buys the goods from the dealer and then lets them to the customer on hire-purchase, or sells them to him under a credit sale or conditional sale arrangement.)

b. A restricted-use credit agreement financing a transaction between the debtor and a person (the 'supplier') other than the creditor, and which is made by the creditor under pre-existing arrangements, or in anticipation of future arrangements, between himself and the supplier. (This covers the sort of case where a loan for the purchase of furniture is made by the creditor under pre-existing arrangements, or in contemplation of future arrangements, between him and the dealer (supplier).)

c. An unrestricted-use credit agreement which is made under pre-existing arrangements between the creditor and a person (the 'supplier') other than the debtor in the knowledge that the credit is to be used to finance a transaction between the debtor and the supplier, even though the loan theoretically remains at the debtor's free disposition.

Section 13 defines debtor-creditor agreements. Essentially, they comprise any agreement which is not a debtor-creditor-supplier agreement.

Credit-token agreements

23.10 Credit-token agreements are a particular type of regulated consumer credit agreement, to which a number of special provisions apply, either in addition to, or in substitution for, the general rules relating to regulated agreements. Section 14 provides that a credit-token agreement is a regulated agreement for the provision of credit in connection with the use of a credit-token. Section 14(1) defines a 'credit-token' and in the light of that definition, the following are obvious examples of a credit-token: credit cards issued by a retailer or other supplier for the purchase on credit of goods or services provided by him; credit cards issued by banks; checks and vouchers issued by check and voucher trading companies, and cash cards issued by banks so that money can be obtained from cash-dispensing machines (unless the user's account is immediately debited so that no credit is given).

Exempt agreements

23.11 As we have already stated, a consumer credit agreement is not a regulated agreement if it is an 'exempt agreement'. One type of exempt agreement is a debtor-creditor-supplier agreement financing the purchase of land, or the provision of dwellings on any land, and secured by land mortgage on that land, *provided* the creditor is a local authority or building society, or a body, such as an insurance company or friendly society, specified in an order made by the Secretary of State for Prices and Consumer Protection[1]. A large number of such bodies have been specified in the Consumer Credit (Exempt Agreements) Order 1977.

The Secretary of State has power by order to specify other types of exempt agreements[2] and he has specified a number of agreements in the Order just mentioned.

---

1 S.16(1)—(4). A debtor-creditor agreement secured by land mortgage is also exempt if the creditor is such a body.
2 S.16(5).

Regulated consumer hire agreement

23.12 By s.15, a consumer hire agreement is an agreement made by the owner of goods with an individual (as defined above), who is called 'the hirer', for the bailment of goods to the hirer, being an agreement which —

a. is not a hire-purchase agreement, and

b. is capable of subsisting for more than three months, and

c. does not require the hirer to make payments exceeding £5,000.

Thus, if O agrees with H, an individual, to bail goods to H for a period of three years certain at £2,000 a year, payable quarterly, the agreement is not a consumer hire agreement. The reason is that, while the agreement is not one of hire-purchase (because it contains no provision for the passing of property to H) and is capable of subsisting for more than three months, condition c. is not fulfilled because the payments which H is required to make exceed £5,000. However, the agreement would have been a consumer hire agreement if the hire charge was £1,500 a year, or if it provided that H could terminate the agreement at some stage before the hire charge exceeded £5,000[1].

Most types of consumer hire agreements will be regulated agreements because the range of exempt agreements is limited to consumer hire agreements:

a. where the owner is a body corporate authorised by or under any enactment to supply electricity, gas or water *and* the subject of the agreement is a meter or metering equipment; or

b. where the owner is the Post Office or Hull Borough Council and the subject-matter of the agreement is telecommunication apparatus, other than apparatus which is part of an internal telephone system[2].

---

1 Sched. 2, Example 20.
2 S.16(6).

Definitions common to all regulated agreements

Small agreements[1]
23.13 A small agreement is:

a. a regulated consumer credit agreement for credit not exceeding £30, other than a hire-purchase or conditional sale agreement; or

b. a regulated consumer hire agreement which does not require the hirer to make payments exceeding £30,

being an agreement which is either unsecured or secured by a guarantee or indemnity only.

Generally, small agreements are not excluded from the application of the Act, but there are exceptions. For example, most of the provisions relating to entry into a regulated agreement do not apply to small debtor-creditor-supplier agreements for restricted-use credit. As an anti-avoidance measure, it is provided that where it appears probable that two or more small agreements were made instead of a single agreement in an endeavour to avoid the operation of any provision of the Act which is not applicable to small agreements, the Act applies to the agreements as if they were regulated agreements other than small agreements.

---

1 S.17.

Multiple agreements[1]
23.14 A multiple agreement is an agreement whose terms are such as —

a. to place a part of it within one category of regulated agreement (e.g. a fixed-sum credit), and another part of it within a different category of regulated agreement (e.g. a running-account credit) or within a category of agreement which is not a regulated agreement (e.g. the provision under that part of credit in excess of £5,000);

b. to place it, or a part of it, within two or more categories of regulated agreement, as in the case of a credit card which may be used to obtain cash from the creditor (a debtor-creditor-supplier agreement for un-restricted-use credit) or to obtain goods or services from suppliers (a debtor-creditor-supplier agreement for restricted-use credit).

If any part of the agreement falls within a category of regulated agreement, that part is treated as a separate agreement. In addition, if the terms of the agreement place it, or a part of it, within two or more categories of regulated agreement at once, it is treated as an agreement in each of those categories.

---

1 S.18.

Linked transactions
23.15 'Linked transactions', which are referred to in various parts of the Act, are defined by s.19. A transaction entered into by the debtor or hirer, or a relative of his, with any other person ('the other party'), except one for the provision of security, is a linked transaction in relation to an actual or prospective regulated agreement (the 'principal agreement') of which it is not part if one of the three following criteria are satisfied:

a. the transaction is entered into in compliance with a term of the principal agreement, e.g. a contract for the maintenance or insurance of goods which are subject to a hire-purchase contract (the principal agreement); or

b. the principal agreement is a debtor-creditor-supplier agreement and the transaction (e.g. a contract for the purchase of goods or services) is financed by the principal agreement; or

c. the other party is the creditor or owner, or someone such as an associate of his, *and* he initiated the transaction by suggesting it to the debtor or hirer, or his relative, who enters into it —

   i. to induce the creditor or owner to enter into the principal agreement, or

   ii. for another purpose related to the principal agreement, or

   iii. where the principal agreement is a restricted-use credit agreement, for a purpose related to a transaction financed, or to be financed, by the principal agreement.

A life insurance policy, for example, will be a linked transaction under c. if the debtor takes it out at the creditor's suggestion and does so to induce the creditor to contract with him (or to cover his repayments in the event of his death).

A linked transaction entered into before the making of the principal agreement has no effect until such time (if any) as that agreement is made.

Other terms

23.16 The meaning of certain other terms which are frequently used in the Act may conveniently be given here. When the Act refers to *notice* being given, notice in writing is required. Some provisions do not apply to a *non-commercial agreement*, which is a consumer credit or consumer hire agreement not made by the creditor or owner in the course of *any* business carried on by him. Often the Act refers to a *prescribed* manner or *prescribed* period etc. and this means prescribed by regulations made by the Secretary of State for Prices and Consumer Protection.

CONTROLS OVER CONSUMER CREDIT OR CONSUMER HIRE BUSINESSES

Licensing

23.17 Part III of the Act (ss.21—42) introduces a licensing system administered by the Director-General of Fair Trading. Generally, a licence is required to carry on any business as far as it comprises or relates to —

a. the provision of credit under regulated consumer credit agreements ('consumer credit business'), or

b. the bailment of goods under regulated consumer hire agreements ('consumer hire business').

The only bodies exempt from the licensing requirement are local authorities and any body corporate which is empowered by a Public General Act *naming it* to carry on a business. In addition, of course, a business will not be required to be licensed if it:

a. provides credit or bails goods only to companies; or

b. provides credit or bails goods to individuals but only in circumstances where the credit or hire exceeds £5,000; or

c. provides credit or bails goods only under 'exempt agreements',

because in such cases the business would not comprise or relate to regulated consumer credit or consumer hire agreements.

23.18   Normally, the licence issued will be a 'standard licence', but it is possible for a 'group licence' to be issued. A *standard licence* is a licence issued to the person, partnership or unincorporated body of persons named in it. This licenses such activities by the licensee as are specified in the licence for a period of three years from the date specified in the licence[1].

The Director must grant a standard licence if an applicant satisfies him that the name under which he applies to be licensed is not misleading or otherwise undesirable *and* that he is a fit person to engage in activities covered by the licence. A standard licence held by one individual terminates on his death or bankruptcy or if he becomes a mental patient, although the termination is deferred for 12 months during which time the licensee's business can be carried on by certain authorised people[2]. A *group licence* licences such persons and activities as are specified in it. It may only be issued if the Director considers that the public interest is better served by doing so than obliging the persons concerned to apply separately for standard licences. The persons covered by a group licence need not be named but can be described by general words, whether or not coupled with the exclusion of named persons. Neither type of licence is assignable.

The Director has powers to vary, suspend or revoke licences. The interests of the licence-holder are safeguarded in such a case by the requirement that he must be given an opportunity to make representations. Such a safeguard also exists where the Director decides not to issue a licence in accordance with an application. An appeal against the Director's decision in one of these matters lies to the Secretary of State, with a further appeal to the High Court on a point of law.

The consequences of unlicensed activities are twofold:

a. *Criminal consequences* A person who engages in any activities for which a licence is required when he is not a licensee under a licence covering those activities commits an offence.

b. *Civil consequences* If a regulated agreement, other than a non-commercial agreement, was made when the creditor or owner was unlicensed, it is unenforceable against the debtor or hirer unless the Director has made an order that such agreements made by that unlicensed person during that period are to be treated as if he had been licensed. If the Director decides not to make an order in accordance with the application, the applicant must be given an opportunity to make representations. There is the same right of appeal against the Director's decision as that outlined above.

---

1 Consumer Credit (Period of Standard Licence) Regulations 1975.
2 Consumer Credit (Termination of Licenses) Regulations 1976.

23.19 The provisions of the Act relating to licences, including their issue, variation, suspension or revocation, also apply to an ancillary credit business[1]. An ancillary credit business is any business so far as it comprises or relates to a number of activities, such as debt-collecting or credit-brokerage. The Act gives an involved definition of 'credit-brokerage', the term covers not only 'brokers' in the ordinary sense but also dealers in goods, such as retailers, providers of services financed by consumer credit agreements, accountants, estate agents, and others who *habitually* put their clients in touch with finance companies and so effect introductions to them. Group licences have been issued to a number of bodies, e.g. the Law Society in relation to solicitors holding a current practising certificate and the National Association of Citizens Advice Bureaux in respect of bureaux registered with the Association. If a regulated agreement results from an introduction effected by an unlicensed *credit-broker*, it is unenforceable against the debtor or hirer unless the Director makes an order that regulated agreements made as the result of introductions effected by the unlicensed broker are to be treated as licensed at the time of the introduction. A person carrying on an unlicensed ancillary credit business cannot claim commission or other fees from a client without an order from the Director. In relation to these types of order, the same provisions concerning representations and appeals apply as in the case of unlicensed consumer credit businesses.

---

1 Ss. 145—149.

Seeking business

23.20 Part IV of the Act (ss.43—54) endeavours to protect consumers by controlling advertisements and other methods of seeking business. The controls over advertisements are not limited to consumer credit or hire businesses.

Advertisements

23.21 The provisions (ss.43—47) mentioned below apply to *any* advertisement, published for the purposes of a business carried on by the advertiser, indicating that he is willing to provide credit or to enter into an agreement for the bailment of goods by him (unless he indicates that he is unwilling to enter into a consumer hire agreement), provided he carries on a consumer credit or hire business or a business in the course of which he provides credit to individuals secured on land. The only cases where the Act does not apply are where the advertisement indicates that:

a. the credit must exceed £5,000 and that no security is required or the security is to consist of property other than land; or

b. the credit is available only to a body corporate.

23.22 The Act provides three offences relating to advertising:

a. *Breach of regulations* The Secretary of State for Prices and Consumer Protection has power to make regulations concerning the form and content of advertisements so as to ensure that an advertisement conveys a fair and reasonably comprehensive indication of the nature of the credit or hire facilities offered by the advertiser and of their true cost to persons using them. Breach of such regulations is an offence[1].

b. *False or misleading advertisements* If an advertisement conveys information which is false or misleading in a material respect, the advertiser commits an offence.

c. *Lack of preparedness to sell goods etc. for cash* It is an offence to advertise a restricted-use credit agreement relating to goods or services to be supplied by any person if that person does not hold himself out as prepared to sell the goods or provide the services for cash.

Liability for these offences extends to persons, other than the advertiser, who published, devised or procured the publication of the advertisement, e.g. newspaper proprietors and advertising agencies. A publisher, however, has a special defence if he proves that he received the advertisement in the course of business, and did not know and had no reason to suspect its publication would be an offence.

---

1 S.167.

Canvassing

23.23 The Act provides the following offences:

a. soliciting the entry by an individual into a regulated debtor-creditor agreement off trade premises, unless in response to a signed written request[1];

b. canvassing off trade premises the services of a credit-brokerage, debt-adjusting or debt-counselling business, unless in response to a prior request[2];

c. sending an unsolicited credit-token[3];

d. sending a circular to a minor inviting him to obtain credit or hire goods. It is a defence to a charge of this offence that the sender did not know and had no reasonable cause to suspect that the addressee was a minor[4].

---

1 Ss. 48 and 49.
2 Ss. 153 and 154.
3 S.51.
4 S.50.

ENTRY INTO REGULATED AGREEMENTS

23.24 Part V of the Act (ss.55–74) contains provisions, whose principal purpose is to ensure that the debtor or hirer knows what obligations he is taking on and has the chance to weigh up all the considerations. The provisions which follow apply to all regulated agreements, with the following principal exceptions:

a. a non-commercial agreement;

b. unless otherwise stated, a debtor-creditor agreement enabling the debtor to overdraw on a current account (e.g. an ordinary bank overdraft), provided that the Director determines that this exception shall apply;

c. unless otherwise stated, a small debtor-creditor-supplier agreement for restricted-use credit.

Disclosure

23.25 Certain information must be disclosed to the debtor or hirer in the prescribed manner before a regulated agreement is made, otherwise it is not properly executed and cannot be enforced against the debtor or hirer except on a court order[1]. This requirement extends to the small agreements mentioned in para. 23.24, c.

---

1 Ss. 55, 65.

Form and contents of the agreements

23.26 A regulated agreement is not properly executed and cannot be enforced against the debtor or hirer except on a court order, unless:

a. a document in the prescribed form itself containing all the prescribed terms (such as the debtor's or hirer's rights and duties, the protection and remedies available to him under the Act, and the amount and rate of the total charges for credit) is signed in the prescribed manner both by the debtor or hirer and by or on behalf of the creditor or owner; and

b. the document sets out all the express terms of the agreement or refers to another document containing them; and

c. the document is, when presented or sent to the debtor or hirer for signature, in such a state that all its terms are readily legible[1].

---

1 Ss. 60, 61, 65.

Duty to supply copies[1]

23.27 When a regulated agreement is presented or sent to the debtor or hirer for his signature a copy of the agreement, and of any other document referred to in it, must accompany it. In addition, if but only if, the agreement does not become an executed agreement on the debtor's or hirer's signature, because the creditor or owner has not yet signed it, a copy of the executed agreement, and of any other document referred to in it, must be given to him within seven days following the 'making' of the agreement (normally, the debtor's or creditor's signing of the agreement).

In the case of a cancellable agreement, the second copy (where necessary) must be sent by post and each copy must give details of the cancellation rights in the prescribed form. If only one copy of a cancellable agreement has to be supplied, the creditor or owner must also send by post a notice giving details of the cancellation rights within seven days of the 'making' of the agreement.

Unless the above provisions are complied with, a regulated agreement is improperly executed and cannot be enforced against the debtor or hirer except on a court order. Moreover, in the case of a cancellable agreement, a court cannot make an enforcement order unless a copy of the agreement and other documents was given to the debtor or hirer before the commencement of the enforcement order proceedings. If the creditor or owner is in breach of the requirements for the giving of notice of cancellation rights, the agreement can never be enforced[2].

---

1 Ss. 62–65.
2 S.127(4).

Cancellation

23.28 A regulated agreement is a 'cancellable agreement' if *its antecedent negotiations included oral representations* made in the presence of the debtor or hirer by, or on behalf of, the person conducting the negotiations, *provided the debtor or hirer signs the agreement at a place other than a place of business of* —

a. the creditor or owner; or

b. a party to a linked transaction (other than the debtor or hirer or a relative of his); or

c. the negotiator in any antecedent negotiations[1].

'Antecedent negotiations' include negotiations conducted by the creditor or owner or his employee in relation to the making of any regulated agreement, or by a dealer in relation to goods sold or proposed to be sold by him to a finance company before forming the subject-matter of a regulated agreement[2].

It follows that, unless all the antecedent negotiations were in writing or by telephone, an agreement is cancellable if the debtor or hirer signs it in his own home or at his own place of business, and this is so even though the antecedent negotiations took place at, for instance, the creditor's or owner's place of business.

A regulated agreement secured on land, a restricted-use credit agreement to finance the purchase of land and an agreement for a bridging loan in connection with the purchase of land are not cancellable agreements[3].

---

1 S.67.
2 S.56.
3 S.67(a). Special provision for reflection in these cases is provided by s.61(2).

23.29 Where an agreement is cancellable, the debtor or hirer has a 'cooling-off' period, which starts at the time he signs the agreement and terminates at the end of the fifth day following the day on which he receives the second copy of the agreement (where necessary) or notice of cancellation rights (if there is no second copy)[1]. Thus, if a debtor signs an unexecuted agreement on 1 August and receives the second copy (the copy of the executed agreement) on 7 August, the cooling-off period will expire at midnight on 12 August.

If the debtor or hirer wishes to cancel a cancellable agreement, he must serve a written notice of cancellation on the creditor or hirer, or on the person specified in the notice of cancellation rights, or on a person who is, or is deemed to be (e.g. a credit-broker, who was the negotiator in antecedent negotiations), the creditor's or owner's agent, indicating his intention to withdraw. A notice of cancellation sent by post is deemed to be served on the addressee at the time of posting, whether or not received by him[2].

---

1 S.68.
2 S.69.

23.30 *The effect of cancellation* Sections 69 to 73 provide as follows:

a. The service of a notice of cancellation operates to cancel the agreement, and any linked transaction, and to withdraw any offer by the debtor or hirer, or his relative, to enter into a linked transaction.

b. An agreement or transaction which has been cancelled is thereafter treated as if it had never been entered into.

c. Any sum paid by the debtor or hirer or his relative under, or in contemplation of, the agreement is repayable by the person to whom it was originally paid. However, in the case of a debtor-creditor-supplier agreement the creditor and supplier are under a joint and several liability to repay so that the creditor can be made liable even though the money was paid to the supplier. Obviously, this is of particular importance where the supplier becomes insolvent. The creditor is entitled to be indemnified by the supplier for loss suffered by the creditor in satisfying his liability. The debtor etc. has a lien on any goods in his possession for any sum repayable to him.

d. No further sums are payable by the debtor or hirer or his relative.

e. In the case of a debtor-creditor-supplier agreement, any sum paid on the debtor's behalf to the supplier becomes repayable to the creditor.

f. Where the total charge for credit includes an item in respect of a fee, commission or other sum payable to a credit-broker that sum is repayable, except for the first £1 thereof.

g. If a debtor under a consumer credit agreement has received the credit and repays the whole or part of it before the expiry of one month following the service of his notice of cancellation, or, in the case of credit repayable by instalments, before the first instalment is due, he does not have to pay interest on the amount repaid. Moreover, where, in the case of credit repayable by instalments, the whole of the credit is not repaid before the first instalment, the debtor is not liable to repay any of the credit until he has received a written requirement in the prescribed form, signed by or on behalf of the creditor, stating the amounts of the remaining instalments but excluding any sum other than the principal and interest.

h. Where the possession of goods has been transferred under a cancellable restricted-use debtor-creditor-supplier agreement or consumer hire agreement, or a linked transaction to which the debtor or hirer or his relative is a party, and the agreement or transaction is thereafter cancelled, then the possessor of the goods is under a duty, subject to his right of lien mentioned in c. above, to restore the goods to the person from whom he obtained them. However, this duty only extends to delivering the goods up for collection at his own premises after service of a written request by the other party.

The possessor is, from the time he receives possession, under a duty to retain possession of the goods and to take reasonable care of them. These duties continue after cancellation but subject to two qualifications:

i. if no request for delivery up of the goods is received within 21 days of cancellation, the possessor's duty to take reasonable care of the goods ceases, although his duty to retain them does not;

ii. if the possessor receives a request for delivery up within 21 days, but refuses or fails to comply with it, his duty to take reasonable care continues until he does so comply.

Once the goods have been delivered up (or delivered or sent) the possessor's duties to restore the goods, to retain them and to take reasonable care of them cease, except that if he elects to send them he is obliged to take reasonable care to see that they are received by the person from whom he obtained them and not damaged in transit.

Any breach by a possessor of the above duties is actionable as a breach of statutory duty.

j. Where the negotiator has received goods in part-exchange, the debtor or hirer can recover the part-exchange allowance from the negotiator unless the part-exchanged goods are re-delivered to him in substantially the same condition within 10 days of cancellation. The debtor has a lien on the goods to which the cancelled agreement relates for the return of the part-exchanged goods or allowance. An obvious case where the part-exchange allowance will have to be paid to the debtor is where the part-exchanged goods have already been disposed of to another.

There are special provisions concerning debtor-creditor-supplier agreements for restricted-use credit financing the doing of work or supply of goods in an emergency, or the supply of goods which, before service of the notice of cancellation, had by the act of the debtor or his relative become incorporated in any land or thing not comprised in the agreement or any linked transaction. In these cases the notice of cancellation operates only to extinguish the credit arrangements and does not affect the debtor's obligation to pay for the work or goods. Nor do the duties to retain, restore and take reasonable care of the goods apply in these cases, or in the case of perishable goods or goods which by their nature are consumed by use and which, before cancellation, were so consumed.

23.31 If a party to a *prospective* regulated agreement, whether of the cancellable variety or not, unequivocally indicates to the other party or to his agent his intention to withdraw from it, this has the same effect as the cancellation of a concluded agreement[1].

---

1 S.57.

MATTERS ARISING DURING THE CURRENCY OF AN AGREEMENT

Liability of creditor for breaches by supplier

23.32 Section 75 of the Act provides that if the debtor under a debtor-creditor-supplier agreement has, in relation to a transaction financed by that agreement, a claim against the supplier in respect of a misrepresentation or breach of contract, he has a similar claim against the creditor, who, with the supplier, is jointly and severally liable to the debtor. However, subject to any agreement between them, the creditor is entitled to be indemnified by the supplier for his loss in satisfying such liability. This provision is of obvious significance where the debtor buys defective goods with a personal loan or with a credit card voucher, especially if the supplier is insolvent. It does not apply to a claim —

a. under a non-commercial agreement; or

b. so far as it relates to any single item to which the supplier has attached a cash price not exceeding £30 (thereby exempting many transactions, for instance, entered into by the use of a credit card or voucher) or more than £10,000.

Where the creditor is himself the supplier or hirer of goods under a credit sale, conditional sale or hire-purchase agreement, the position is different because he is directly liable e.g. under the Sale of Goods Act 1893 or the Supply of Goods (Implied Terms) Act 1973, and not under s.75.

Duty to give additional information

23.33 Sections 77 to 79 provide that the creditor under a regulated agreement for fixed-sum credit or running-account credit and the owner under a regulated consumer hire agreement must, after receiving a written notice to that effect from the debtor or hirer and payment of 15p, give him a copy of the executed agreement and of any other document referred to in it, together with a statement signed by or on behalf of the creditor or owner showing the state of the account between them and certain other details. These provisions do not apply —

a. to an agreement under which no sum is, or will or may become, payable by the debtor or hirer; or

b. to a request made less than one month after a previous request relating to the same agreement was complied with; or

c. to a non-commercial agreement.

If the creditor or owner fails to comply with the request within the prescribed period he is not entitled, while the default continues, to enforce the agreement *and* if the default continues for one month he commits an offence.

23.34 Two other provisions concerning the giving of information may be noted. First, s.78(4) provides that the creditor under a regulated running-account credit agreement for credit in excess of £30 must *automatically* give the debtor statements in the prescribed form showing the state of the account at regular intervals not exceeding 12 months and, where the agreement provides for the periodic making of payments by the debtor or periodic charging of interest against him, statements showing the state of account at the end of each of those periods in which there is any movement in the account. Secondly, where a regulated agreement requires the *debtor or hirer* to keep goods to which the agreement relates in his possession or control, he must tell the creditor or owner where they are within seven working days after receiving a written request to that effect; if he fails to do so and his default continues for 14 days he commits an offence[1]. Neither of these provisions applies to a non-commercial agreement.

---

1 S.80.

Appropriation of payments

23.35 We have seen in paras. 9.7 to 9.9 that the normal contractual rule, where several debts are owed by a debtor to a creditor, is that the debtor may, when making a payment which is insufficient to discharge the total debts, appropriate the money in or towards the satisfaction of a particular debt or debts; but that if he does not do so, the creditor may appropriate the payment to such debts as he wishes. Section 81 provides that, while a debtor who is liable to a creditor under two or more regulated agreements is entitled to appropriate a payment towards a particular debt or debts, a failure by him to make any such appropriation results in a special rule applying where one or more of the agreements is a hire-purchase or conditional sale agreement or a consumer hire agreement or an agreement in relation to which any security has been provided. This special rule is that the payment shall automatically be appropriated towards the sums due under the several agreements respectively in the proportions which those sums bear to one another.

Variation of agreements[1]

23.36 Where, *under a power contained in a regulated agreement*, the creditor or owner varies the agreement, the variation does not take place before notice is given to the debtor or hirer in the prescribed manner.

23.37 Where an agreement (a 'modifying agreement') varies or supplements an earlier agreement, the modifying agreement is treated as:

a. revoking the earlier agreement, and

b. containing provisions reproducing the combined effect of the two agreements, and obligations outstanding in relation to the earlier agreement remain outstanding in relation to the modifying agreement. A modifying agreement is treated as a regulated agreement even though it results in the credit exceeding £5,000. The debtor or hirer is further protected by the provision that if the earlier agreement is a cancellable agreement, and the modifying agreement is made in the cooling-off period applicable to the earlier agreement, then, whether or not the modifying agreement would otherwise be a cancellable agreement, it can be cancelled during that period. Otherwise the modifying agreement is never cancellable.

These provisions do not apply to a non-commercial agreement.

---

1   S.82.

Death of the debtor or hirer

23.38 We are concerned here with whether the death of the debtor or hirer entitles the creditor or owner under a regulated agreement to do one of the following specified acts:

a. to terminate the agreement (assuming it has not expired); or

b. to demand payment of any sum; or

c. to recover possession of any goods or land; or

d. to treat any right conferred on the debtor or hirer by the agreement as terminated, restricted or deferred; or

e. to enforce any security.

The law is as follows. If the agreement is fully secured, the creditor or owner is not entitled by reason of the debtor's or hirer's death to do any of the specified acts. On the other hand, if the agreement is unsecured or only partly secured he is entitled to do such acts, *but only on a court order*[1]. The court will make such an order only if the creditor or owner proves that he has been unable to satisfy himself that the present and future obligations of the deceased debtor or hirer are likely to be discharged[2]. These provisions do not prevent the creditor from treating the right to draw on any credit as restricted or deferred by reason of the debtor's death, nor do they affect the operation of any agreement providing for payments of debts under a regulated agreement (or becoming due on the debtor or hirer's death) out of the proceeds of an insurance policy on his life.

---

1 S.86.
2 S.128.

ENFORCEMENT AND TERMINATION

Restrictions on the rights of the creditor or owner

Default cases

23.39 A creditor or owner's entitlement to claim damages for breach of a regulated agreement by the debtor or hirer is not restricted by the Act, but he cannot, by reason of such a breach, do any of the following acts unless he first serves a 'default notice':

a. terminate the agreement; or

b. demand earlier payment of any sum; or

c. recover possession of any goods or land; or

d. treat any right conferred on the debtor or hirer by the agreement as terminated, restricted or deferred (apart from the restriction or deferment of the right to draw further on any credit); or

e. enforce any security[1].

---

1 S.87.

23.40 The default notice must be in the prescribed form and specify:

a. the nature of the alleged breach;

b. if the breach is capable of remedy, what action is required to remedy it and the date before which that action is to be taken; and

c. if the breach is not capable of remedy, the sum (if any) required to be paid as compensation for the breach, and the date before which it is to be paid[1].

The notice must also contain information in the prescribed form about the consequences of failure to comply with it. A date specified in accordance with the above must be not less than seven days after service of the default notice, and the creditor or owner must not take any of the five listed actions before the date specified in the notice or (if no requirement of remedying or compensation is made) before those seven days have elapsed.

Where a default notice requires action or payment by the debtor or hirer, it may include a provision for the taking of any of the five listed actions at any time after the above period has elapsed, together with a statement that the provision will be ineffective if the breach is duly remedied or the compensation duly paid[2]. If the debtor or hirer duly remedies the breach, or pays compensation for it, before the date specified for that purpose in the default notice, the breach is treated as not having occurred[3].

Service of a default notice enables the debtor or hirer to apply to the court for a time order, which we discuss in paras. 23.61 and 23.62.

---

1 S.88(1), (2) and (4).
2 S.88(5).
3 S.89.

23.41 In the case of *regulated hire-purchase and conditional sale agreements* there are additional restrictions on the creditor's right to re-take possession of goods or land in the event of default by the debtor.

Where a debtor, who has paid or tendered to the creditor one-third or more of the total price of the goods, is in breach of such an agreement relating to goods and the property in the goods remains in the creditor, the creditor is not entitled to recover possession of the goods from the debtor without an order of the court. Such goods are known as 'protected goods'. Where the creditor is required under the agreement to install the goods, the reference to one-third of the total price refers to the aggregate of the installation charge and one-third of the remainder of the total price[1]. In such a case the one-third rule can be expressed as follows where T = the amount payable under the one-third rule, I = the installation charge and P = the total price:

$$T = \frac{I + (P - I)}{3}$$

These provisions do not apply if the debtor terminates the agreement, as by exercising an option to terminate. In such a case the creditor can recover possession without a court order whether or not one-third of the total price has been paid, and the same is true if the debtor consents to the recovery when it occurs. The restriction on recovery only applies to recovery from the debtor and not to the recovery of goods which are in the wrongful possession of a third party or have been abandoned by the debtor. On the other hand, where goods are protected goods at the time of a debtor's death, the restriction continues to apply (in relation to the possessor of the goods) until the grant of probate or letters of administration[2].

If the creditor recovers possession of protected goods without a court order in contravention of the above restriction:

a. the regulated agreement, if not previously terminated, terminates; and

b. the debtor is released from all liability under the agreement and can even recover all sums which he has paid under the agreement[3].

---

1 S.90(1), (2) and (7).
2 Ss. 90(5), (6) and 173(3).
3 S.91.

23.42 Another restriction on the recovery of goods is that, except under a court order, the creditor is not entitled to enter premises to recover goods subject to the regulated agreement. This is of obvious importance where the goods are not protected goods[1].

If the debtor is in breach of a regulated conditional sale agreement relating to land, the creditor is only entitled to recover possession of the land from the debtor, or any person claiming under him, on an order of the court[2].

Entry or recovery of possession with the debtor's consent is not a contravention of either of these provisions. Contravention of either provision is a breach of statutory duty[3].

---

1 S.92(1).
2 S.92(2).
3 Ss. 92(3) and 173(3).

Non-default cases

23.43 Sections 76 and 98 of the Act deal with regulated agreements which are so drafted as to allow a creditor or owner to call in a loan, or to terminate the agreement or any particular right conferred on the debtor or hirer by it, even in the absence of any breach.

The two sections provide that where a regulated agreement specifies a period for its duration, and that period has not expired, then, notwithstanding that the agreement is terminable before the end of the period, the creditor or owner is not entitled:

a. to terminate the agreement (s.98); or

b. to demand earlier payment of any sum; or

c. to recover possession of any goods or land; or

d. to treat any right conferred on the debtor or hirer by the agreement as terminated, restricted or deferred (s.76),

except by or after giving the debtor or hirer not less than seven days' notice in the prescribed form of his intention to do so. This provision does not prevent a creditor from treating the right to draw on any credit as restricted or deferred.

Service of a notice under s.76 or s.98 enables the debtor or hirer to apply to the court for a time order.

The restrictions on the creditor or owner's rights on the debtor or hirer's death have already been discussed (para. 23.38).

Termination by the debtor or hirer

23.44 The debtor or hirer can terminate the agreement either by completing his payments, and he may do this ahead of time, or by exercising his statutory right to terminate.

Debtor's right to complete payments ahead of time
23.45 A debtor under a regulated consumer credit agreement is entitled at any time to discharge his indebtedness by notice to the creditor and the payment to him of all amounts payable by the debtor to him under the agreement (less any rebate allowable under regulations). The notice given by the debtor may embody the exercise by him of any option under the agreement to purchase the goods[1]. Any term limiting the right is void[2].

---

1 S.94.
2 S.173(1).

23.46 Two other provisions are relevant to the debtor's right of early payment. First, s.96 provides that early payment discharges the debtor, or his relative, from any future liability under a linked transaction. Secondly, by s.97 the creditor must, within the prescribed period of receiving a written request from the debtor, give the debtor a statement of the amount needed to discharge the debtor's indebtedness.

Debtor's statutory right of termination
23.47 This right is governed by ss. 99 and 100. At any time before the final payment under a *regulated hire-purchase or conditional sale agreement* falls due, the debtor is entitled to terminate the agreement by giving written notice to any person authorised or entitled to receive payments under the agreement. However, the debtor is not so entitled in the case of a conditional sale agreement relating to land after the title to the land has passed to him. In addition, if, in the case of a conditional sale agreement relating to goods, the property in the goods, having become vested in the debtor, is transferred to a third person (e.g. a buyer) who does not become the debtor under the agreement, the debtor's statutory right of termination ceases.

23.48 The effect of a valid termination by the debtor is that:

a. He remains liable to pay any sums which have accrued due under the agreement before the termination.

b. Subject to exceptions, he is liable to bring his payments up to one-half of the total price. Where an installation charge is payable by the debtor under the agreement, the reference to one-half of the total price means the aggregate of the installation charge and one-half of the remainder of the total price. This formula can be expressed thus:

$$H = I + \frac{(P - I)}{2}$$

where H = the statutory one-half, I = the installation charge and P = the total price. The 'one-half rule' does not apply where the agreement provides for a smaller payment, or does not provide for any payment, nor where the court is satisfied that a lesser sum would be equal to the loss sustained by the creditor in consequence of the termination, in which case the court can order the payment of that lesser sum instead.

c. He is *also* liable to compensate the creditor for any damage to the goods if he has failed to take reasonable care of them.

d. He must permit the creditor to recover possession of the goods, and if he wrongfully retains them the court will order the delivery of them to the creditor without giving the debtor the option to pay their value, unless satisfied that it would not be just to do so.

e. Where a debtor under a conditional sale agreement relating to goods terminates it after the property in the goods has become vested in him, the property in the goods thereupon vests in the person in whom it was vested immediately before it became vested in the debtor.

Hirer's statutory right of termination

23.49 The hirer under a *regulated consumer hire agreement* is entitled under s.101 to terminate the agreement by giving written notice to any person entitled or authorised to receive payments under the agreement. Such termination does not affect any liability under the agreement, e.g. to pay money, which has already accrued.

A notice cannot expire, i.e. an agreement can never be terminated, within 18 months of the agreement being made, but apart from that the minimum period of notice is one instalment period or three months, whichever is the less, unless the agreement specifies a shorter period.

23.50 There is no statutory right of termination in the case of an agreement:

a. where the total hire payments exceed £300 a year; or

b. where goods are bailed to the hirer for the purpose of his business, and the goods were selected by the hirer and acquired by the owner (at the hirer's request) from any person other than the hirer's associate; or

c. where the hirer requires the goods for the purpose of bailing them to other persons in the course of his business; or

d. where the agreement is made by a person carrying on a consumer hire business specially exempted from the termination rules by the Director-General of Fair Trading.

Termination statements

23.51 The debtor or hirer under a regulated agreement has the right to request from the creditor or owner a signed notice that he has discharged his indebtedness and that the agreement has ceased to be operative. The creditor or owner must either comply with the request within a prescribed period or serve a counter-notice, stating that he disputes the matter of discharge. If the creditor or owner fails to comply with these provisions, and his default continues for one month, he commits an offence.

These provisions do not apply to a non-commercial agreement or if the creditor or owner has already given a termination statement relating to the agreement[1].

---

1   S.103.

SECURITY

23.52 Part VIII of the Act (ss. 105—126) deals with securities given in relation to an actual or prospective regulated agreement. In this context, 'securities' include not only real securities, such as a mortgage, charge or pledge, but also personal securities, such as an indemnity or guarantee[1].

---

1 S.189(1).

Form and content of securities
23.53 Any security, other than one given by the debtor or hirer, provided in relation to a regulated agreement, must be expressed in writing. This document, which is known as a security instrument, will not be properly executed unless it is in the prescribed form, contains the prescribed information, embodies all the express terms of the security, is signed by or on behalf of the surety, and a copy of it has been given to the surety. If a security is not expressed in writing or is improperly executed it is enforceable against the surety on an order of the court only[1].

---

1 S.105.

Duty to give information to surety
23.54 If the surety is a different person from the debtor or hirer, then, on receipt of a written request from the surety, and the payment of a fee of 15p, the creditor or owner must give him specified information, such as, in the case of a hire-purchase agreement, the total sum paid, the total sum payable but unpaid, and the total sum to become payable, under the agreement, as well as copies of the regulated agreement and of the security instrument (if any). If the creditor or owner fails to comply in this way he is not entitled, while the default continues, to enforce the security; and if the default continues for one month he commits an offence[1].

---

1 Ss. 107—109.

Duty to give surety copy of default etc. notice
23.55 If a default notice or a notice of the type mentioned in para. 23.43 is served on a debtor or hirer, a copy of it must be served by the creditor or owner on any surety. Failure to do so renders the security enforceable against the surety (in respect of the breach or other matters to which the notice relates) only on an order of the court[1].

---

1 S.111.

Act not to be evaded by use of security

23.56 Where a security is provided in relation to a regulated agreement, the security may not be enforced so as to benefit the creditor or owner, directly or indirectly, to a greater extent as respects payment than would be the case if the security were not provided and any obligations of the debtor or hirer, or his relative, were carried out to the extent that they would be enforced under the Act[1]. Thus, if T indemnifies C or guarantees payment by D of his debts under a regulated hire-purchase or conditional sale agreement with C, and D terminates the agreement, C cannot enforce the security against T to a greater extent than is necessary to bring the payment up to one-half of the total price because D's liabilities cannot exceed that amount under s.100 and C cannot evade this limit by suing T for a greater amount.

In addition, where a regulated agreement is enforceable on an order of the court (e.g. an improperly executed agreement) or of the Director-General of Fair Trading only, any security provided in relation to that agreement is only enforceable where such an order has been made in relation to that agreement[2].

---

1 S.113(1). If an indemnity is given where the debtor or hirer is a minor, or otherwise not of full capacity, the reference to the extent to which his obligations would be enforced is to be read as a reference to the extent to which they would be enforced if he was of full capacity: s.113(7). Thus, for instance, if the debtor or hirer is a minor, a contract of indemnity does not become unenforceable merely by reason of his minority.
2 S.113(2).

Restrictions on taking and negotiating instruments[1]

23.57 A creditor or owner is not entitled to take a negotiable instrument, other than a bank note or cheque, in payment of, or as security for, any sum payable by the debtor or hirer under a regulated agreement, or by a surety in relation to such an agreement. Likewise, if he takes a cheque in payment he must not negotiate it except to a banker. These restrictions do not apply in the case of a non-commercial agreement.

---

1 S.123.

Enforcement of land mortgages

23.58 A land mortgage securing a regulated agreement is enforceable on an order of the court only[1]. This is of great importance because it means that, in the case of such a mortgage, the mortgagee (i.e. the creditor) is not permitted to exercise a mortgagee's rights of taking possession and of sale without a court order in the event of default by the mortgagor (debtor).

---

1 S.126.

JUDICIAL CONTROL

23.59 Any action by the creditor or owner to enforce a regulated agreement, or any related security, must be brought in a county court[1], as must an action to enforce any linked transaction[2]. A county court has wide powers in connection with these matters, and also has the power to reopen extortionate credit bargains, whether regulated or not.

---

1 S.141(1).
2 S.137(1).

Enforcement orders[1]

23.60 We have already stated that an improperly executed regulated agreement or security instrument, or a security not expressed in writing, cannot be enforced without an order of the court. Generally, the court has a discretion as to whether to make such an enforcement order, but it must not make such an order in the following cases:

a. An enforcement order must not be made if a document in the prescribed form, itself containing all the prescribed terms and conforming to regulations as to form and content, has not been duly signed, unless a document (whether or not in the prescribed form and complying with the regulations) itself containing all the prescribed terms of the agreement was signed by the debtor or hirer. If such a document was signed and an enforcement order is made, it may direct that the agreement is to have effect as if it did not include a term omitted from that document.

b. Where, in the case of a *cancellable* agreement, there has been non-compliance with the duty to supply a copy or copies of the agreement, and the creditor or owner has not rectified the situation by giving a copy of the agreement, and of any other document referred to in it, to the debtor or hirer before the commencement of the proceedings for an enforcement order, an enforcement order must be refused.

c. An enforcement order can never be made if the creditor or owner is in breach of the requirement for the giving of notice of cancellation rights.

d. Apart from these cases, the court is obliged to dismiss an application for an enforcement order only if it considers it just to do so having regard to:
    i. prejudice caused to any person by the contravention in question, and the degree of culpability for it; and
    ii. its powers, in an order, to reduce or discharge any sum payable by the debtor or hirer, or any surety, so as to compensate him for prejudice suffered as a result of the contravention, or to

impose conditions or suspend the operation of the order, or to vary agreements and securities.

---

1 S.127.

Time orders[1]
23.61 A 'time order' is an order for one or both of the following:

a. the payment, by the debtor or hirer or any surety of any sum owed under a regulated agreement or a security, by such instalments and at such times as the court considers reasonable, having regard to the means of the debtor or hirer and any surety; and/or

b. the remedying by the debtor or hirer of any breach of a regulated agreement (other than the non-payment of money) within a period specified by the court.

---

1 Ss. 129 and 130.

23.62 A time order may be made by the court, provided it considers it just to do so, in the following cases:

a. on an application by the debtor or hirer after service on him of a default notice or, in a non-default case, of a notice of the type mentioned in para. 23.43; or

b. where the creditor or owner applies for an enforcement order or brings an action to enforce a regulated agreement or any security, or recover possession of any goods or land to which the agreement relates.

The court has power to vary or revoke a time order[1].

Where, after a time order has been made in relation to a regulated hire-purchase, conditional sale or consumer hire agreement, the debtor or hirer is in possession of the goods, he is treated (except in the case of a debtor to whom the creditor's title has passed) as a bailee of the goods under the terms of the agreement, notwithstanding that it has been terminated.

---

1 S.131.

Protection orders
23.63 The court may make orders to protect the property of a creditor or owner under a regulated agreement, or property subject to

any security, from damage or depreciation pending the determination of proceedings under the Act, including orders restricting or prohibiting the use of property or giving directions as to its custody[1].

---

1 S.131.

Financial relief for hirer

23.64 Although a creditor cannot, in the case of regulated hire-purchase or conditional sale agreements, recover possession of protected goods except on an order of the court[1], there is no corresponding provision in the case of a regulated consumer hire agreement. However, a hirer is afforded some protection by s.132 which provides that where the owner of goods subject to a consumer hire agreement recovers possession of them, otherwise than by a court action, the hirer may apply to the court for an order that the whole or part of any sum paid by the hirer to the owner shall be repaid, and that the obligation to pay the whole or part of any sum owed by the hirer to the owner shall cease. The court may make the order applied for if it considers it just to do so, having regard to the extent of the hirer's enjoyment of the goods.

If the owner brings an action for repossession of goods subject to a regulated consumer hire agreement, the court may include such provisions in the delivery order.

---

1 Para. 23.41.

Transfer orders and return orders

23.65 In relation to a regulated *hire-purchase or conditional sale agreement*, the court has power, if it appears to be just to do so, to make a transfer order or a return order under s.133 —

a. on an application for an enforcement order or a time order, or

b. in an action brought by the creditor to recover possession of goods to which the agreement relates.

A 'return order' is an order for the return to the creditor of goods to which the agreement relates. A 'transfer order' is an order for the transfer to the debtor of the creditor's title to certain goods to which the agreement relates (the 'transferred goods') and the return to the creditor of the remainder of the goods. A transfer order cannot be made unless the paid-up sum exceeds the part of the total price referable to the transferred goods by an amount equal to at least one-third of the unpaid balance of the total price. This formula can be expressed thus:

$$G = P - \frac{U}{3}$$

where G = the total price referable to the transferred goods (and thus the maximum value of goods transferable), P = the paid-up sum, and U = the unpaid balance of the total price. The operation of this formula can be demonstrated as follows. Assuming that the total price is £600, that the goods can be separated, and that £300 (the paid-up sum) has been paid by the debtor under the agreement, the maximum value of the goods transferable is £200. The reason is that £100 is one-third of the unpaid balance of the total price and the paid-up sum (£300) exceeds the part of the total price referable to the transferred goods (£200) by £100.

Notwithstanding the making of a return order or a transfer order, the debtor may, before the goods enter the creditor's possession, claim those goods on payment of the balance of the total price and the fulfilment of any necessary conditions. Similarly, if the total price is paid under a time, return or transfer order, and any other necessary conditions are fulfilled, the creditor's title vests in the debtor.

Supplemental provisions as to orders

23.66 Where the court makes one of the orders outlined above in relation to a regulated agreement, it may, if it considers it just to do so, make the operation of any term of the order conditional on the doing of specified acts by any party to the proceedings or suspend the operation of any term[1]. In addition, if the court makes one of the orders outlined above, it may include in it such provisions as it considers just for amending any agreement or security in consequence of a term of the order[2].

---

1 S.135.
2 S.136.

Extortionate credit bargains

23.67 If the court finds a credit bargain extortionate it has power to reopen the credit agreement so as to do justice between the parties[1]. It may exercise this power —

a. on an application for this purpose by the debtor or any surety; or

b. at the instance of the debtor or a surety in any proceedings to which the debtor and creditor are parties, being proceedings to enforce the credit agreement, any related security, or any linked transaction; or

c. at the instance of the debtor or a surety in other court proceedings where the amount paid or payable under the credit agreement is relevant[2].

The power to reopen a credit agreement is not confined to regulated agreements but extends to all credit agreements other than those where the debtor is a body corporate or a partnership of bodies corporate. Whether such an agreement can be reopened depends on whether the credit *bargain* is extortionate, and a credit bargain is not necessarily just the credit agreement because, if one or more other transactions (such as a maintenance contract) are to be taken into account in computing the total charge for credit, the credit bargain is the credit agreement and the other transaction(s) taken together[3].

---

1 S.137(1).
2 S.139(1).
3 S.137(2).

23.68 A credit bargain is extortionate if the payments to be made under it are 'grossly exorbitant' or if it 'otherwise grossly contravenes the ordinary principles of fair dealing'. Factors to be taken into account in determining this matter include:

a. the prevailing level of interest rates when the credit bargain was made;

b. matters affecting the debtor, such as his age, experience, business capacity and state of health, and the degree to which he was under financial pressure when he made the bargain;

c. matters affecting the creditor, such as the degree of risk accepted by him (having regard to the value of any security provided), his relationship to the debtor, and whether or not a colourable cash price was quoted for any goods or services included in the credit bargain[1].

If the debtor or any surety alleges that a credit bargain is extortionate, the creditor must prove that this is not so[2].

---

1 S.138(2)–(4).
2 S.171(7).

23.69 In reopening the credit agreement, the court may, to relieve the debtor or a surety from payment of any sum in excess of that fairly due and reasonable, order:

a. the taking of accounts;

b. the setting aside of the whole or part of any obligation imposed on the debtor or a surety by the credit bargain or any related agreement;

c. the creditor to repay the whole or part of any sum paid under the credit bargain or a related agreement by the debtor or a surety;

d. securities to be returned to a surety; or

e. the alteration of the terms of the agreement or any security instrument[1].

However, an order cannot be made which affects a judgment[2].

---

1   S.139(2).
2   S.139(4).

SPECIFIC RULES OUTSIDE THE ACT

23.70   At the start of this chapter we mentioned that the Consumer Credit Act 1974 assumes the continued application of certain specific rules relating to particular types of transaction, whether or not they are regulated agreements, and we now propose to consider these.

Hire-purchase agreements

23.71   A hire-purchase agreement is an agreement, other than a conditional sale agreement, under which –

a. goods are bailed (i.e. possession of them is delivered) to a person (the debtor) in return for periodical payments by him, and

b. the property (i.e. ownership) in the goods will pass to the debtor if the terms of the agreement are complied with and one or more of the following occurs –
   i.   the exercise of an option to purchase by the debtor;
   ii. the doing of any other specified act by any party to the agreement;
   iii. the happening of any other specified act[1].

---

1   This definition is provided by the Consumer Credit Act 1974, s.189, for the purposes of that Act, but it is also apt to describe hire-purchase agreements generally.

23.72   In its usual form, the debtor under a hire-purchase agreement pays an initial payment which is normally a percentage of the cash price and then pays periodical (i.e. weekly or monthly) instalments representing the balance of the cash price plus the hire-purchase charges. As an anti-inflation measure, Government orders often require a minimum deposit for certain types of goods and specify a maximum period in which instalment payments must be made. Breach of such an order renders the agreement illegal and unenforceable by either party. Once the debtor has paid the requisite instalments, he can exercise an option to purchase the goods, provided he has complied with the terms of the agreement and (in the ordinary sort of case) paid a nominal sum, such as £1. If the debtor exercises this option, there is a contract of sale which makes him the owner of the goods already in his possession.

23.73 When the system of hire-purchase transactions originated in the late nineteenth century, a hire-purchase transaction simply involved a hire-purchase contract between the dealer and the customer. Since then there has evolved a more complex arrangement between the dealer, the customer and a finance company, whereby, if the customer wishes to take goods on hire-purchase, the dealer does not make a hire-purchase contract with the customer but instead sells the goods to a finance company for cash. The finance company, having now become the owner, then lets the goods to the customer under a hire-purchase agreement, under which rights and obligations exist between the customer (debtor) and finance company (creditor) and to which the dealer is not a party. In such a case the dealer is a credit-broker for the purposes of the Consumer Credit Act 1974. At the same time, the finance company frequently enters into a 'recourse agreement' with the dealer, whereby the dealer agrees to purchase the goods back from the company if the debtor defaults, or agrees to guarantee the debtor's liability to the company, or agrees to indemnify the company for any loss which it may incur if the hire-purchase agreement is terminated.

Another way in which a finance company may become involved in a hire-purchase transaction is by 'block discounting'. Here, the dealer enters into hire-purchase agreements directly with customers and then assigns his rights under them to a finance company for cash, although he may continue to collect instalments from the debtor as agent for the finance company. Block discounting normally also involves the transfer of ownership of the goods by the dealer to the finance company.

23.74 As we have indicated in Chapter 22, a person in possession of goods under a hire-purchase agreement cannot pass a good title to them to a third party. Two exceptions, which we have already noted, concern certain sales of motor vehicles and sales in market overt[1]. In addition, if the debtor, having wrongfully sold goods subject to a hire-purchase agreement, subsequently acquires title to them by completing the instalment payments and exercising his option to purchase, the good title acquired by him is said to 'feed the title' of the buyer from him (or a subsequent transferee) and vests a good title forthwith in that person[2].

The obligations of persons involved in a hire-purchase transaction are as follows.

---

1   Paras. 22.34 and 22.35.
2   *Butterworth v Kingsway Motors Ltd* [1954] 2 All ER 694, [1954] 1 WLR 1286.

23.75 *Obligations of the creditor* By the Supply of Goods (Implied Terms) Act 1973, ss. 8 to 11 (as amended by the Consumer Credit Act 1974, Sched. 4), terms as to title, description, quality, fitness for purpose and as to sample are implied into *all* hire-purchase agreements, whether regulated or not. These terms are virtually identical to those implied into sale of goods contracts by the Sale of Goods Act 1893, ss. 12 to 15 (as amended)[1], and as we have shown in para. 10.47 the right to exclude them has been severely restricted in the same ways.

If the creditor is in breach of an express or implied term of the hire-purchase contract, the debtor's remedies depend upon the nature of the term broken in the same way as in a contract for the sale of goods[2]. There is one exception: there is no equivalent of the Sale of Goods Act 1893, s.11(1)(c), so that a debtor under a hire-purchase agreement does not lose the right to rescind it simply because he has 'accepted' the goods by keeping them after he has had a reasonable opportunity to examine the goods. On the other hand, of course, if he continues with the contract once he has discovered the breach of condition, as where he continues to pay instalments, he affirms the contract and loses his right to rescind.

The reader is reminded that breach of the implied condition as to title constitutes a total failure of consideration, even though the debtor has derived benefit from the goods, and the debtor can recover back what he has paid under the agreement if he has to return the goods to their true owner[3].

---

1   Paras. 22.42–22.60.
2   Paras. 22.39 and 22.40.
3   *Warman v Southern Counties Car Finance Corpn Ltd* [1949] 2 KB 576, [1949] 1 All ER 711; para. 17.7, b.

Duties of the dealer
23.76 If the dealer is also the creditor he will of course owe the debtor the duties outlined above. But if the hire-purchase contract is between the debtor and a finance company, to whom the dealer has sold the goods, the dealer cannot be sued for breach of any express or implied term of that contract since he is not a party to it. However,

if the dealer has induced the debtor to contract with the finance company by making a statement which turns out to be false, this statement may form a term of a collateral contract between the debtor and the dealer, in which case the debtor will be able to sue the dealer for damages[1]. Alternatively, if a dealer makes a significant mis-statement he may be liable in tort[2].

Normally, the debtor will prefer to sue the finance company, but these remedies are useful where the finance company is not worth suing for some reason, or if the dealer gave undertakings going beyond those contained in the hire-purchase contract.

---

1 Para. 6.21.
2 Para. 20.13.

Duties of the debtor
23.77 The following duties are either expressed or implied in a hire-purchase contract:

a. To take delivery of the goods.

b. To take reasonable care of the goods. Like any other bailee, the debtor has the onus of disproving negligence if the goods are lost or damaged. For the sake of completeness, it should be noted that if the debtor purports to bring about a change of ownership, e.g. by sale, or otherwise deals with the goods in a manner which unjustifiably denies the creditor's title, he is liable in conversion irrespective of negligence.

c. To pay instalment charges. The agreement may give the debtor an option to terminate it and return the goods. More important, in the case of regulated agreements the debtor is given such an option by the Consumer Credit Act 1974, subject to certain conditions, as we have shown in paras. 23.47 and 23.48. Unless the debtor exercises an option to terminate, he remains liable to pay all the instalment charges; if he fails to do so he is liable for all arrears and for damages for any consequential loss, and the creditor may exercise any power in the contract to terminate it and resume possession. However, if the contract is a regulated agreement, the creditor's rights are restricted by the Consumer Credit Act 1974 in the way which we have outlined in paras. 23.39 to 23.42.

Conditional sale agreements

23.78 A conditional sale agreement is an agreement for the sale of goods or land under which the purchase price or part of it is payable by instalments, and the property in the goods or land is to remain in the seller (notwithstanding that the buyer is to be in possession of the goods or land) until such conditions as to the payment of instalments or otherwise as may be specified in the agreement are fulfilled[1].

The situation with regard to the passing of title to goods subject to such an agreement is the same as in the case of a hire-purchase agreement[2]. However, since the agreement is one of sale, the provisions of the Sale of Goods Act 1893, including the implied terms under ss. 12 to 15, generally apply to a conditional sale agreement. An exception is that s.11(1)(c) of that Act does not apply to conditional sale agreements which are agreements for consumer sales[3]. But a breach of condition, express or implied, to be fulfilled by the seller under any such agreement is treated as a breach of warranty, and not as grounds for rejecting the goods and treating the agreement as repudiated, if (but only if) it would have fallen to be so treated had the condition been contained in a corresponding hire-purchase agreement as a condition to be fulfilled by the creditor[4]. Thus, if the buyer, knowing of the breach, affirms the contract he loses the right to rescind and can only claim damages.

---

1 This definition is provided by the Consumer Credit Act 1974, s.189, for the purposes of that Act, but it is also apt to describe conditional sale agreements generally.
2 Paras. 22.33 and 23.74.
3 Supply of Goods (Implied Terms) Act 1973, s.14(1).
4 *Ibid.*, s.14(2) (as amended by the Consumer Credit Act 1974, Sched. 4).

Credit sale agreements

23.79 A credit sale agreement is an agreement for the sale of goods, under which the purchase price or part of it is payable by instalments, but which is not a conditional sale agreement[1]. Consequently, the property passes immediately to a buyer under a credit sale agreement and he can pass title to a third party in the same ways as any other buyer of goods. It also follows that the agreement is subject to those terms implied by the Sale of Goods Act 1893 (as amended) and to all the other provisions of that Act.

---

1 This definition is provided by the Consumer Credit Act 1974, s.189, for the purposes of that Act, but it is also apt to describe credit sale agreements generally.

Chapter 24
Negotiable Instruments

24.1 In this chapter we are concerned with the nature of negotiability, the rules relating to bills of exchange, with particular reference to the law of cheques, and the relationship of the parties to a bill of exchange or cheque.

The nature of negotiability

24.2 A negotiable instrument has been defined as a chose in action[1] which is freely transferable and in respect of which a transferee can acquire a better title than that possessed by the transferor. The fact that a transferee can acquire this good title, even from a thief who has stolen the negotiable instrument, in appropriate circumstances, is most important. A negotiable instrument differs from a contractual right in several ways. For example, only parties to a contract can enforce it, subject to certain limited exceptions[2], whereas any holder (i.e. the bearer or, a person in possession of the instrument to whom the money due under the instrument is payable) can bring an action to enforce it. Rights dependent on a contract arise out of that contract and not from possession of the documents in which the terms of the contract are written. However, rights can arise merely from the possession of a negotiable instrument, and it is possible to describe a person as the owner of a negotiable instrument but there is no one who can be described as the owner of a contract.

Contractual rights, and other choses in action, can be transferred by assignment[3] but assignment and assignability differ radically from negotiation and negotiability. For example, a statutory assignment of a chose in action must be in a particular form whereas a negotiable instrument can be transferred by indorsement and delivery, or by mere delivery in appropriate cases. Furthermore, no notice of transfer is necessary and a transferee of a negotiable instrument can always enforce it without joining the transferor as a party to the action. Also, the transferee of certain negotiable instruments, if he is a holder in due course, can acquire a better title than the transferor since he takes free of any equities between the debtor and the transferor[4]. A transferee of a negotiable instrument need not provide consideration for the transfer and yet can still be regarded as a holder for value providing that consideration has been given for the negotiable instrument at some time[5].

Cheques, bills of exchange and promissory notes are all recognised as negotiable instruments by the Bills of Exchange Act 1882, which is the principal source of the law relating to negotiable instruments. All statutory references are to the Bills of Exchange Act 1882, unless otherwise stated. Other negotiable instruments derive their validity from mercantile custom.

---

1 A chose in action is defined in para. 19.2.
2 For the doctrine of privity and its exceptions, see paras. 6.19 and 6.20.
3 Chap. 19.
4 Para. 24.27; *Miller v Race* (1758) 1 Burr 452.
5 Para. 24.12; Bills of Exchange Act 1882, s.27.

RULES COMMON TO BILLS OF EXCHANGE AND CHEQUES

24.3 We are all familiar with at least some of the uses of a cheque; the same may not be true of bills of exchange. A bill of exchange is a negotiable instrument by which its maker agrees to pay money at some future date; it is a form of credit. However, the person to whom a bill is payable can raise money on it immediately by selling it or using it as security for a loan. It can also be used as a means of discharging an existing debt; a cheque, which is merely a particular form of bill, is generally used for just this purpose.

24.4 A bill of exchange is defined in s.3(1):
'An unconditional order in writing, addressed by one person to another, signed by the person giving it, requiring the person to whom it is addressed to pay on demand, or at a fixed or determinable future time, a sum certain in money to or to the order of a specified person, or to bearer.'
A cheque is defined in s.73 thus:
'A cheque is a bill of exchange drawn on a banker payable on demand. Except as otherwise provided in this Part [of this Act] the provisions of this Act applicable to a bill of exchange payable on demand apply to a cheque.'

Before we consider the meaning of these sections we must define some of the parties to a bill or cheque. They are the 'drawer' (the person who authorises payment), the 'drawee' (the person who is authorised to make payment), and the 'payee' (the person to whom payment, initially, is to be made). For example, in relation to a cheque, the drawer is the person who signs the cheque, the bank is the drawee and the person to whom the cheque is payable is the payee.

The combination of ss.3 and 73 discloses the following requirements for the formation of a valid cheque. Most of these requirements are, of course, equally necessary for the formation of a bill.

An unconditional order in writing
24.5   The order is considered to be in writing even when it is printed[1] or typewritten, and if the order is written it need not be in ink or in any particular form[2]. Cheques, of course, are usually in the form of a printed order issued by a bank. The order to pay must be an *order* and it must be *unconditional*. While politeness will not prevent a request for payment constituting an order, e.g. 'please pay', the request must require payment, not merely permit it, in order to be a valid bill or cheque. An order is not unconditional if it is subject to a qualification or limitation, so that an order by X to pay Y £200 'when my account exceeds £1,000' would not be a valid order. However, if a qualification or limitation is addressed to the payee and not to the drawee the order is not conditional. Determining to whom the limitation is addressed is not always easy. Every case turns on its own facts but the courts have had regard to the position of the limitation. A limitation which appears after the amount payable and above the drawer's signature is treated as addressed to the drawee. A banker who is in doubt about whether a limitation is addressed to payee or drawee would be wise to obtain an indemnity from his customer before paying a cheque. Section 11 provides that an instrument expressed to be payable on a contingency is not to be regarded as a bill or cheque even if the contingency occurs. Furthermore, s.3(3) states that an order to pay out of a particular fund is conditional, unless the order to pay is unqualified and either the order indicates the fund out of which the drawee is to reimburse himself, e.g. 'debit my current account', or the order is coupled with a statement naming the transaction occasioning the bill or cheque, e.g. 'to pay for the car I have bought'.

---

1   S.2.
2   People have drawn cheques in many curious forms. On one occasion the order to pay was written on the side of a cow; it was honoured by the bank.

Addressed by one person to another
24.6   A person cannot be both drawer and drawee so that, for example, one branch of a bank cannot draw a cheque on another branch of the

same bank[1]. The drawee, who must be named or indicated reasonably clearly, can be an individual or a company, and a bill or cheque can be drawn on two drawees providing that they are not named in the alternative or in succession[2].

---

1   *Capital and Counties Bank Ltd v Gordon* [1903] AC 240, HL.
2   S.6.

Signed by the person giving it

24.7   A document which is unsigned cannot be a valid bill or cheque but a duly authorised agent can sign on behalf of his principal[1]. The signature can be in the form of a mark if the person purporting to sign habitually so signs[2], or reproduced, at least in the case of an individual, by means of a rubber stamp. A bank will usually require an indemnity before paying on a cheque signed by means of a rubber stamp.

---

1   Paras. 18.32—18.38.
2   *George v Surrey* (1830) Mood & M 516.

To pay . . . a sum certain in money

24.8   Section 3(2) qualifies s.3(1) by providing that an order addressed to the drawee to pay a sum of money is not a bill or cheque if the order is to pay a sum of money *and* do something else.

However, s.9 says that a sum payable by a bill or cheque does not cease to be a sum certain because it is to be paid:

a. with interest; or

b. by instalments, even if the whole sum becomes due in default of payment of any instalment; or

c. in accordance with a specified rate of exchange.

If a bill is payable with interest, interest runs from the date of the bill, or its date of issue if it is undated, unless the bill specifies some other date[1]. Section 9(2) provides that, if the sum payable is expressed in words and figures and they do not coincide, the amount specified in writing is the sum payable. In practice, a banker would return a cheque on which the words and figures did not agree, drawing the discrepancy to the attention of the drawer.

---

1   S.9(3).

On demand or at a fixed or determinable future time
24.9 If an order to pay is to constitute a cheque it *must* be payable on demand. A bill is valid if payable on demand or at a fixed or determinable future time. Section 14, as amended[1], states that where a bill is not payable on demand it is due and payable on the last day of the time allowed for payment in the bill, or, if that is a non-business day (essentially weekends, bank holidays and other public holidays), the following day. Section 10 defines a bill payable on demand as a bill which is expressed to be payable on demand, or at sight, or on presentation, or a bill in which no time for payment is specified[2]. While a cheque may not bear the words 'on demand' or 'at sight', it is an instrument payable on demand because it does not specify a time for payment. A bill not payable on demand is a 'time bill', i.e. one payable at a fixed future date, or one payable on the happening of a specified event provided that the event is certain to occur[3]. An order to pay on the happening of some future event which is not certain to occur is not a bill, neither is an order to pay on or before a specified date[4]. If an order to pay is payable at a specified period after the giving of notice this may be a valid bill[5].

---

1 By the Banking and Financial Dealings Act 1971, s.3.
2 An overdue bill, if accepted or indorsed, is a bill payable on demand as regards the acceptor or indorser.
3 S.11.
4 *Williamson v Rider* [1963] 1 QB 89, [1962] 2 All ER 268, CA.
5 *Ibid.*

To or to the order of a specified person or to the bearer
24.10 If the payee of a bill or cheque is not sufficiently delineated the purported bill or cheque is not a valid bill or cheque[1].

A bill or cheque which is payable 'to X' or 'to X or order' is a valid bill or cheque even if X is the drawer or drawee. Such a bill or cheque is called an order bill or an order cheque[2]. The name of the payee need not be used, but the payee must be indicated with reasonable certainty and the safest plan is, of course, to actually name the payee[3]. Parol evidence is admissible to establish who is the payee, where the name of the payee has been mis-spelt[4], and if the payee whose name has been mis-spelt wishes to indorse the bill or cheque he can do so, using the incorrect name[5].

A bill or cheque which is payable 'to bearer' or 'to X or bearer', or which is indorsed 'to bearer' or indorsed in blank[6], is a valid bill or cheque. Such a bill or cheque is called a bearer bill or a bearer cheque[7]. Section 7(3) also provides that, where a bill or cheque is payable to a payee who is in fact fictitious or non-existent, the bill or cheque is to be regarded as payable to bearer. If the payee is not fictitious but has been named as payee as a result of fraud, it is a vexed question whether the bill or cheque can be regarded as payable to bearer. In *Bank of England v*

Vagliano Bros[8], V's clerk forged certain instruments purporting to be bills drawn on V in favour of X, who were a perfectly respectable firm. The clerk then forged an indorsement by X in favour of M, under which name he obtained payment of the bills. The question at issue was whether the bank could debit V's account with the amount of these bills. If the payee could be regarded as fictitious then the bills became payable to bearer and the bank could debit V's account. The House of Lords held that a bill could be regarded as payable to bearer if the payee, while not fictitious, had not, and had never been intended to have, any rights in the bill or cheque or, in other words, if the insertion of the payee's name was a mere pretence. On the other hand, if there was an intention to benefit the payee named in a bill or cheque it cannot be regarded as payable to bearer, even if the payee's name has been inserted because of fraud[9].

Cheques frequently specify that they are payable to 'cash' or 'wages'. This is not a sufficient specification of the payee and bank to whom such a cheque is presented can require it to be indorsed, but in practice indorsement is rarely required. It is thought that a cheque payable to 'cash' etc. can be cashed by a bearer, but a bank should be careful before cashing such a cheque. It has been suggested that, unless the bank can prove that the customer intended the cheque to be cashed by a bearer, it is not entitled to debit the customer's account.

A bill or cheque which bears no name is not a valid instrument even if it bears the words 'or order', and such an instrument is not payable to bearer[10]. However, a bill of cheque payable 'to . . . Order' has been held to be valid and is payable to the drawer[11].

---

1 S.7.
2 S.8(4), provided there is no limitation on transfer.
3 S.7.
4 *Willis v Barrett* (1816) 2 Stark 29.
5 S.32.
6 For indorsement, see para. 24.13.
7 S.8(3).
8 [1891] AC 107, HL.
9 *North and South Wales Bank v Macbeth* [1908] AC 137, HL.
10 *R v Randall* (1811) Russ & Ry 195.
11 *Chamberlain v Young and Tower* [1893] 2 QB 206, CA.

Other requirements for the formation of a valid bill or cheque
24.11 Section 3(4) provides that a bill, and therefore a cheque, is not invalid merely because it is not dated or because it does not specify the place where it was drawn or is to be paid. Cheques, of course, usually have the branch on which they are drawn printed on them. The fact that a bill or cheque is ante-dated, post-dated or dated on a Sunday will not invalidate it[1]. A bank can refuse to pay an undated cheque. A post-

dated cheque is regarded as a valid cheque, even though it cannot be described as payable on demand. However, a bank should exercise care in cashing such a cheque because the drawer can stop the cheque at any time before the specified date.

Section 12 states that if a bill is payable at a fixed time after its date and the bill is undated, any holder can insert the true date. If a bill or indorsement is dated, there is a presumption that the date is correct[2].

---

1 S.13.
2 S.13.

Consideration

24.12 A bill or cheque, if it is to be valid, must be supported by consideration[1]. There are, however, some variations from the usual rules relating to consideration. First, there is a presumption that consideration has been provided by any signatory of the bill or cheque[2]. Secondly, consideration need not move from the promisee, and past consideration may be good consideration[3]. Section 27(2) provides that, where value has been given *at any time* for a bill or cheque, a holder of that bill or cheque is deemed to be a holder for value as regards the acceptor of the bill[4] and all parties to the bill or cheque who were parties prior to the time when the consideration was provided.

---

1 Chap. 6.
2 S. 30.
3 S.27(1); para. 6.4.
4 Para 24.54.

Who can be liable on a bill or cheque

24.13 Before discussing who is liable on a bill or cheque it is necessary to define an 'indorser' and an 'indorsee' of a bill or cheque and mention a 'holder in due course'. An 'indorser' is a person who writes his name on the back of a cheque or bill. This is usually done to negotiate an order cheque or bill to another person. If this other person is specified in the indorsement he is the 'indorsee'. For example, if D draws a cheque on X payable to Y or order, Y can indorse that cheque by signing his name on the back of it. Y can indorse the cheque in favour of Z, in which case Z becomes entitled, after delivery of the cheque, to cash it or indorse it again, and if X fails to pay on the cheque Z can sue Y. A bill or cheque may also be indorsed in blank, i.e. the indorser signs his name on the back of the instrument but does not specify an indorsee. If a bill or cheque is indorsed in blank it becomes a bearer bill or cheque. Apart from the case where a payee or indorsee effects an indorsement, s.56 provides that anyone signing a bill or cheque, other than as drawer or acceptor[1], incurs the liability of an indorser to a holder in due course. A 'holder in due course' is a payee or indorsee of a bill or cheque with possession of that bill or cheque, or a person in possession of a bearer bill or cheque, who has provided consideration for that bill or cheque[2] and who satisfies the requirements of s.29 which we discuss in paras. 24.27 to 24.33.

If a person is to be liable on a bill or cheque three conditions must be complied with.

---

1 Para. 24.54.
2 Actual or deemed consideration within s.27; para. 24.12.

Capacity

24.14 Section 22 provides that capacity to incur liability on a bill or cheque is co-extensive with capacity to contract[1]. Therefore, a minor who purports to draw or indorse a bill or cheque cannot be held liable on that instrument, and a company can only be liable if the drawing, indorsing or accepting of bills or cheques is within its power[2]. However, s.22(2) provides that, while a person who lacks capacity cannot be liable on a bill or cheque, this does not prevent a holder suing other parties to the bill or cheque. Companies usually have express or implied power to draw, indorse and accept bills and cheques, and even if they lack such power they may be liable to a third party under the European Communities Act 1972, s.9[3].

---

1 Chap. 16 and paras. 4.8–4.10.
2 Para. 4.9.
3 Para. 4.11.

Signature

24.15 By s.23, no one can be liable as drawer, indorser or acceptor of a bill or cheque if he did not sign the bill or cheque. This provision is, however, modified in that a person who signs an instrument using a trade name or an assumed name is liable on that instrument[1]. Furthermore, the signature of one partner is treated as a signature by all the partners. The signature of an authorised agent is, of course, regarded as the signature of the principal[2]. However, a signature by an agent which is expressed to be by procuration, usually indicated by such terms as 'per pro' or 'pp' alongside the agent's name, gives notice that the agent has only limited authority to sign and the principal is only bound if the agent was acting within the scope of his actual authority[3]. An agent who signs a bill or cheque, in any capacity, without indicating clearly that he signs as an agent will incur personal liability on that bill or cheque[4]. Section 26 says that merely adding such words as 'agent' or 'director' is not in itself sufficient to exempt an agent from liability.

Personal liability is also incurred by any officer of a company who signs on behalf of the company a bill or cheque in which the full name of the company fails to appear[5].

---

1 S.23(2).
2 S.91.
3 S.25.
4 S.26(1); para. 18.47.
5 Companies Act 1948, s.108.

24.16 A forged or unauthorised signature is inoperative, and s.24 says that there is 'no right to retain the bill or cheque or to give a discharge therefor or to enforce payment thereof against any party thereto' by virtue of such a forged or unauthorised signature. Therefore, if X draws a cheque in favour of Y and either forges Z's signature on the cheque or, being Z's agent, signs on behalf of Z without any authority to do so, Y cannot demand payment of that cheque. Indeed, Y has no right to retain the cheque and Z's bank is not entitled to debit Z's account, even if it paid Y. Section 24 stresses that if an unauthorised signature is ratified[1], a bill or cheque can be regarded as if it had been duly signed from the beginning. A party may sometimes be unable to plead the forged or unauthorised signature because he is estopped from so doing; for example, if he fails to denounce a forged signature with reasonable speed.

Three final points relating to signature:

a. since banks do not sign cheques they cannot be liable to holders in the event of non-payment of those cheques;

b. if the drawer's signature is forged on a 'cheque', the 'cheque' is void ab initio; and

c. in very limited circumstances a person may be able to escape liability on a bill or cheque by pleading *non est factum* successfully[2].

---

1 Paras. 18.8—18.12.
2 Paras. 13.9—13.21.

Delivery
24.17 'Issue', that is the first delivery of a complete bill or cheque to a holder, or 'delivery', that is the transfer of possession (actual or constructive) from one person to another[1], is necessary to complete a contract on a bill or cheque. Therefore, any contract on a bill or cheque

is revocable until delivery[2]. To be effective, delivery must be authorised, so that a person who acquires a bill or cheque by virtue of an unauthorised transfer does not take free of prior claims on that bill or cheque. Therefore, a thief has no title to a bill or cheque because there has been no delivery. However, s.21 provides that a holder in due course is conclusively presumed to have taken under a good delivery and can thus sue all prior parties to the bill or cheque, even if he acquired the bill or cheque from a thief.

Posting a bill or cheque is not delivery unless the creditor requested the use of the post[3].

---

1 S.2.
2 Subject to the exception that when an acceptance has been written on a bill and notice of this fact has been given the acceptance is irrevocable.
3 *Thairlwall v Great Northern Rly Co* [1910] 2 KB 509; para. 9.5.

Negotiation and indorsement

24.18 Negotiation means 'the transfer of a bill [or cheque] to another so as to constitute the transferee the holder of the bill [or cheque]'. A bill or cheque may be transferred from one person to another, but, unless that other is also constituted the holder of the bill or cheque, the instrument is not negotiated to that other. The advantage which flows from a transfer which is a negotiation of the instrument is that the transferee takes free of claims against prior holders of that instrument and he can acquire a better title than his transferor.

24.19 A bearer bill or cheque is negotiated by delivery and an order bill or cheque may be transferred from one person to another, but, allows a drawer to prohibit, expressly or impliedly, the transfer of a bill. This does not affect the validity of the bill between the drawer, drawee and payee but such a bill cannot be transferred or negotiated. The same is true of cheques, except that a cheque which is crossed and expressed to be 'not negotiable' can be transferred whereas a bill can not.

Indorsement
24.20 Section 32 sets out the requirements for a valid indorsement:

a. The indorsement must be written on the bill or cheque, usually, but not necessarily, on the back.

b. It must be signed by the indorser. The indorser's signature by itself constitutes an indorsement, and would be an indorsement in blank.

An indorsement written on an 'allonge', i.e. an attached slip, or a 'copy' of a bill or cheque issued or negotiated in a country where 'copies' are recognised, is deemed to be a indorsement written on the bill[1]. An indorsement which purports to transfer only part of the amount payable under the bill or cheque or which purports to transfer the bill or cheque to two unconnected indorsees does not operate as a negotiation[2]. However, such an indorsement may give the indorsee a lien on the bill.

Section 31 says that where the holder of an order bill or order cheque transfers that bill or cheque for value without indorsing it, i.e. by delivery, the transferee has no better title than the transferor (there is no negotiation because there is no indorsement), but the transferee is entitled to have the bill or cheque indorsed in his favour[3].

In practice very few cheques are indorsed or negotiated.

1 S.32(1).
2 S.32(2).
3 *Walters v Neary* (1904) 21 TLR 146.

Types of indorsement

24.21 *Conditional indorsement* Under s.33, if a bill purports to be indorsed conditionally, for example, 'pay X if he marries Y', the payer can disregard the condition, if he wishes, and payment to the indorsee will be valid whether or not the indorsee has complied with the condition.

Indorsement in blank Such an indorsement does not name or indicate the indorsee; after such an indorsement a bill or cheque becomes a bearer bill or cheque[1].

Special indorsement This type of indorsement specifies to whom, or to whose order, the bill or cheque is to be payable[2]. An indorsement in blank can be converted into a special indorsement if the holder inserts a direction to pay himself, or to his order, or to another, above the indorser's signature[3].

Restrictive indorsement If an indorsement prohibits further transfer or expressly states that it is a mere authority to deal with the bill or cheque as thereby directed, it is a restrictive indorsement. A restrictive indorsement gives the indorsee the right to receive payment of the bill or cheque and to sue anyone whom the indorser could have sued, but, unless expressly authorised, he cannot transfer his rights[4].

Forged indorsements The provisions relating to forged indorsements differ for bills and cheques and are discussed separately in paras. 24.56 and 24.73.

Subsequent indorsements If there are two or more indorsements, the order in which they appear on the bill or cheque is deemed to be the order in which they were made unless the contrary is proved[5].

1 S.3(1).
2 S.34(2).

3 S.34(4).
4 S.35.
5 S.32(5).

Discharge of a bill or cheque

24.22 A bill or cheque is discharged when all rights of action on it are extinguished. Such discharge can be:

a. by payment in due course; or

b. by cancellation; or

c. in some cases, by material alteration.

In addition, a bill of exchange, *but not a cheque*, is discharged when the acceptor becomes the holder of the bill at or after maturity[1] or the holder renounces his rights against the acceptor absolutely and unconditionally *at or after maturity*[2].

---

1 S.61.
2 S.62.

Payment in due course
24.23 Section 59 provides that a bill is discharged by payment in due course, which means payment made at or after the maturity (i.e. the date from which payment becomes due) of the bill or cheque to the holder of it and without notice that the holder's title to the bill or cheque is defective. The holder is a payee or indorsee in possession of an order bill or cheque or the person in possession of a bearer bill or cheque. This is by far the most common method of discharge.

To effect a good discharge, the bill or cheque must be paid by the drawee, or on his behalf. Payment by the drawer or indorser will not discharge the bill or cheque, though in some cases payment to the wrong person will be an effective discharge. For example, payment to the holder of a bearer bill or cheque discharges the bill or cheque even if the holder is a thief who has stolen the instrument, providing that payment is not made in suspicious circumstances, e.g. before the instrument is due[1]. If a bill bears a forged indorsement, payment to a person whose title is derived from that forged indorsement is not a good discharge. The position is different if payment is made on a cheque bearing a forged indorsement, such payment can in some circumstances discharge the cheque. We discuss this important topic in para. 24.73.

---

1 *Smith v Sheppard* (1776) Chitty on Bills of Exchange (11th Edn) 278.

Cancellation

24.24 Under s.63, a bill or cheque is discharged by intentional cancellation by its holder or his authorised agent if the cancellation is apparent on the bill or cheque. For example, writing 'cancelled' across a bill or cheque will discharge it; but merely tearing it in half so that it is capable of re-assembly will not[1]. The holder or his authorised agent can also cancel the liability of any party to a bill or cheque by striking out his signature. Indorsers who would have had a right of recourse against a party whose liability is cancelled also have their liability cancelled.

If the holder can prove that a cancellation was made unintentionally, or mistakenly, or by an unauthorised agent, the cancellation will be inoperative.

---

1 *Ingham v Primrose* (1859) 7 CB NS 82.

Material alteration

24.25 Section 64 provides that, if a bill or cheque is materially altered without the assent of all parties liable on the bill, the bill or cheque is avoided, except as against a party who made, or authorised, or agreed to, the alteration and any subsequent indorsers. But if the alteration is not apparent, then a holder in due course who has possession of the bill or cheque can enforce it as if it had not been altered.

Section 64 only relates to deliberate alterations, so that in a case where a bank note was washed while in the pocket of a garment and parts of it were illegible the section was inapplicable and the holder was able to recover[1].

The section says that the following alterations are material:

a. of the date;

b. of the amount payable;

c. of the time of payment; and

d. of the place of payment[2].

This list is not exhaustive and it has been suggested that any alteration which alters the business effect of the bill or cheque might be material. Alteration of the name of the payee by the addition of an initial has been held to be material[3], as has the insertion of the rate of interest in the corner of a bill which provided for the payment of 'lawful interest'[4].

An alteration will be regarded as apparent if the bill or cheque would normally be examined by a potential holder and a reasonably careful scrutiny would reveal the alteration[5].

---

1 *Hong Kong and Shanghai Banking Corpn v Le Lee Shi* [1928] AC 181, HL.
2 In the case where the bill has been accepted and the addition of the place of payment is without the consent of the acceptor.

3 *Goldman v Cox* (1924) 40 TLR 744, CA.
4 *Warrington v Early* (1853) 23 LJKB 47.
5 *Woollatt v Stanley* (1923) 138 LT 620.

The holder of a bill or cheque

24.26 Before we discuss the rights of a holder, we must determine who is a holder. A holder of a bill [or cheque] is defined by s.2 as 'the payee or indorsee of a bill or note [or cheque] who is in possession of it, or the person in possession of a bill or note or cheque which is payable to bearer'.

   If such a holder has given valuable consideration, or is deemed to have given valuable consideration by virtue of s.27, for a bill or cheque, he is a holder for value. A holder for value who complies with the requirements of s.29 (which are discussed in the next paragraph) is a holder in due course.

24.27 The rights of a holder are set out in s.38:
   '(1) He may sue on the bill [or cheque] in his own name;
   (2) Where he is a holder in due course, he holds the bill [or cheque] free from any defect of title of prior parties, as well as from mere personal defences available to prior parties among themselves, and may enforce payment against all parties liable on the bill.'
As we can see from the above, any holder can sue in his own name, but only a holder in due course takes free from any defect of title of prior parties and from any defences available to prior parties amongst themselves. It is extremely important, therefore, to know whether a holder is a holder in due course. This is determined by reference to s.29, which provides that to be a holder in due course a person must:

a. take a bill or cheque which is complete and regular on its face; and

b. become the holder of that bill or cheque before it becomes overdue, and, if it has been dishonoured, without notice of that fact; and

c. take the bill or cheque in good faith, for value and without notice of any defects in the title of his transferor at the time of negotiation.

Complete and regular on its face
24.28 This is a question of fact, and a bill or cheque will not be complete and regular on its face (which includes the back of the instrument) if any material detail is missing. In *Arab Bank Ltd v Ross*[1], the Court of Appeal found that a negotiable instrument which had been incorrectly indorsed (in that 'company' had been omitted from the name of the indorsing company) was sufficient to pass title to the plaintiff bank but that the bank was not a holder in due course.

---

1 [1952] 2 QB 216, [1952] 1 All ER 709, CA.

Before the bill or cheque becomes overdue
24.29 If a bearer bill or cheque has not been paid within a reasonable time of its issue or when it was drawn, it may be overdue. An order bill or cheque is overdue when the due date for payment has passed.

Take the bill or cheque in good faith
24.30 A holder acts in good faith if he acts honestly; merely being negligent will not constitute a lack of good faith[1]. If a holder wilfully or fraudulently abstains from inquiry or deliberately ignores the truth, this will constitute bad faith, and gross negligence in failing to discover the truth may be evidence of fraud or wilful neglect[2].

---

1 S.90.
2 *Goodman v Harvey* (1836) 4 Ad & El 870.

For value
24.31 This means that a holder must have provided valuable consideration, or be deemed to have given such consideration within s.27[1].

---

1 Para. 24.12; *Barclays Bank Ltd v Astley Industrial Trust Ltd* [1970] 2 QB 527, [1970] 1 All ER 719.

Without notice of any defect
24.32 Section 29(2) provides that the title of the transferor of a bill or cheque is defective when he 'obtained the bill [or cheque], or the acceptance thereof [if a bill], by fraud, duress, or force and fear, or other unlawful means, or for an illegal consideration, or when he negotiates it in breach of faith, or under such circumstances as amount to a fraud'.

The transferee will have notice of such a defect if he has actual notice of the particular facts avoiding the bill or cheque, or if he has notice, or should have known, of something vitiating the bill or cheque without knowing the precise details.

Burden of proof
24.33 Section 30(2) says that a holder is presumed to be a holder in due course. There is an exception: if a bill or cheque is shown to be tainted by fraud or illegality, the holder is presumed *not* to be a holder in due course. However, the presumption that a holder is a holder in due course revives if the holder establishes that subsequent to the fraud or illegality value has been given in good faith for the bill or cheque.

Other matters
24.34 It should be noted that the original payee cannot be a holder in due course because he does not acquire the bill or cheque by negotiation[1].

Therefore, if a payee acquires a bill or cheque which is tainted by fraud or illegality, he cannot enforce the instrument and must refund any money which he received prior to the discovery of the fraud or illegality, even when he has given value and acted in good faith throughout.

A holder who derives his title through a holder in due course, if not a party to the fraud or illegality which taints a bill or cheque, has the rights of a holder in due course as regards the acceptor of a bill and all parties to a bill or cheque prior to the holder in due course, even if he has notice of the fraud or illegality[2].

1 R. E. *Jones Ltd v Waring and Gillow Ltd* [1926] AC 670, HL.
2 S.29(3).

Rights of holders

Rights of a mere holder
24.35 We have seen in para. 24.27 that a mere holder can sue on the instrument in his own name. Since he takes subject to all equities available against previous parties, including immediate parties (i.e. parties with whom he has entered into a contract in relation to the instrument), his position is less secure than that of the holder in due course. The absence of consideration[1] and total failure of consideration have both been successfully pleaded to defeat an action on a bill or cheque by a mere holder. A right against a prior party which is un-connected with the bill or cheque cannot be used to defeat a mere holder's action.

1 *Forman v Wright* (1851) 11 CB 481.

A holder for value
24.36 His position is similar to that of a mere holder.

A holder in due course
24.37 Apart from the protection afforded by s.38, the position of the holder in due course is also protected by the following sections[1]. Section 12 permits such a holder to rely on the date shown in a fixed period bill even when the wrong date has been inserted in an originally undated bill. Section 21(2) provides that a bill or cheque in the hands of a holder in due course is conclusively presumed to have been validly delivered by all parties prior to him, so that they are all liable to him. Section 54(2) says that the acceptor of a bill cannot deny certain matters to such a holder. Section 55(2) provides that an indorser of a

bill or cheque by indorsing that instrument cannot deny to a holder in due course the genuineness and regularity of the drawer's signature and all previous indorsements.

---

1   See also s.64, para. 24.25.

A holder-payee for value
24.38   Since the original payee cannot be a holder in due course he cannot claim the benefit of s.38. However, it is thought that a holder-payee for value who complies with s.29 in all respects, apart from acquisition by negotiation, takes free of defects of title and of any personal defences against a 'remote party'. The acceptor of a bill is a remote party, as is a person who is not a party to a contract with the payee relating to the bill or cheque.

A transferee by delivery
24.39   A bearer bill or cheque is transferred by delivery, and a bona fide possessor of such an instrument is the true owner of the bill or cheque. A bona fide transferee for value of such a bill or cheque is not affected by defects in the title of the transferor, or the drawer, or indorser (if any), or acceptor (if it is a bill). To be bona fide, a transferee must act honestly, he need not act carefully. Therefore, a banker presented with a cheque payable to bearer or indorsed in blank is a bona fide transferee for value if he pays the money due on the cheque, even if he was careless in failing to determine if the bearer had acquired the cheque honestly[1].

---

1   For the duties of a banker to a drawer see paras. 24.67–24.79.

An indorsee
24.40   An indorsee may well be a holder in due course but, even if he is not, an indorsee can sue all the parties whose names are on the bill or cheque. If a party acquires a bearer bill or cheque by delivery without the proper indorsement, he cannot obtain a good title to the instrument if a subsequent indorsement occurs after he has received notice of fraud, if any[1]. We have discussed restrictive indorsements in para. 24.21.

---

1   *Whistler v Forster* (1863) 32 LJCP 161.

Duties of a holder

24.41   A holder who wishes to claim payment of a bill must comply with several requirements. In the event of non-compliance the drawer and any indorsers are discharged from liability on the bill or cheque, and they may also be discharged from liability on the contract to which the instrument relates[1]. The duties imposed on a holder who wishes to enforce payment of a bill or cheque are:

a. a duty to present for payment; the rules for bills and cheques are similar but not identical;

b. a duty to give notice of dishonour; and

c. a duty to note and protest.

In relation to bills there is also a duty to present for acceptance, which we discuss when dealing with acceptance of bills in para. 24.55.

---

1 Chap. 9.

Duty to present for payment
24.42   All bills and cheques must be presented for payment[1] unless presentment is excused[2]. Failure to present the instrument for payment discharges the drawer and the indorsers (if any) of that bill or cheque, but not the acceptor of a bill[3]. Presentment for payment means presentment to obtain the money due on the instrument and therefore the instrument must be presented in the 'proper place'. Section 45 says that the 'proper place' is either the place of payment specified in the bill or cheque, or, if there is no specified place of payment, the address of the drawee or acceptor if given in the bill or cheque. If no address is given, the 'proper place' is the business premises or ordinary residence of the drawee or the acceptor, if the address of such establishments is known. If none of these places is appropriate for a particular bill or cheque, presentment for payment may be made to the drawee or acceptor wherever he can be found, or at his last known business premises or ordinary residence[4]. If the bill or cheque is presented at the proper place but, after the exercise of due diligence, no one authorised to make or refuse payment can be found, no further presentment is necessary[5]. Presentment for payment should be made during normal business hours if the proper place for presentation is business premises, e.g. during banking hours at a bank[6], or at a reasonable time in other cases. Presentment by post may be valid if authorised by agreement or custom. However, there is no banking custom permitting the presentment for payment of bills and cheques by post.

---

1 S.45.
2 For example, ss. 45(5) and 46.

3 S.52; para. 24.54.
4 S.45(4).
5 S.45(5).
6 *Parker v Gordon* (1806) 7 East 385.

24.43 Presentment must also be made at an appropriate time. A *bill* payable on demand must be presented within a reasonable time of issue in order to render the drawer liable, and within a reasonable time of any indorsement to render an indorser liable[1]. A bill not payable on demand, i.e. a time bill, must be presented on the day on which it falls due, or if that is a non-business day[2] on the following day. If the due date for payment of a time bill has passed, the bill is overdue and, once overdue, the drawer and indorsers are discharged, unless the holder can establish that he falls within s.46. This section excuses delay in presentment when such delay is beyond the control of the holder and is not imputable to his default, misconduct or negligence. However, once the delay has ceased, the bill must be presented with reasonable promptitude if it is not to become overdue. Section 46 dispenses with presentment if:

a. after the exercises of reasonable diligence, presentment cannot be effected; or

b. the drawee is fictitious; or

c. presentment is waived.

In addition, if the drawee is not bound to pay the bill, presentment *as regards the drawer* is unnecessary.

---

1 S.45(2).
2 Para. 24.9.

24.44 The time for presentment of *cheques* is the same as for bills in respect or indorsers, but in respect of drawers the rule is different. The drawer of a cheque is not discharged by unreasonable delay in presentment unless s.74 applies. This section says that, subject to s.46 (those cases where no presentment is necessary or delay is excused), only a drawer who has suffered actual loss because of the unreasonable delay in presentment is discharged, and then only to the amount of loss suffered. In determining what is a reasonable time, s.74 provides that 'regard shall be had to the nature of the instrument, the usage of trade and of bankers, and the facts of the particular case'.

If a bill or cheque is presented for payment but dishonoured, in that payment is denied, or if presentment is excused and the bill is overdue or unpaid[1], the holder has an immediate right of recourse against the drawer or indorsers, but before he can proceed any further the holder must serve a notice of dishonour. If a bill is dishonoured by

non-acceptance[2] a notice of dishonour is again necessary if the holder
wishes to enforce his rights.

---

1 S.47.
2 Para. 24.54.

Duty to give notice of dishonour

24.45 If a bill or cheque has been dishonoured the holder, or a person
acting on his behalf, must serve a notice of dishonour on the drawer
and any indorser, and failure to serve such a notice on any party discharges that party from liability on the instrument[1]. However, a holder
in due course subsequent to an omission to serve a notice of dishonour
for non-acceptance is not prejudiced by that omission[2]. A notice of dishonour may also be served by or on behalf of an indorser who is liable
on a bill or cheque. Such notice, if given by the holder, enures for the
benefit of all subsequent holders and all prior indorsers who have a
right of recourse against the party to whom the notice is given. If
notice is given by an indorser it enures for the benefit of the holder
and of all indorsers subsequent to the party to whom it is given[3].

A notice of dishonour must comply with s.49, which says that
the notice may be oral or in writing, or a combination of the two, and
that the mere return of the dishonoured bill or cheque will suffice. The
notice of dishonour need not be signed but it must indicate the dishonoured instrument with sufficient clarity. Notice of dishonour should
be given within a reasonable time of the dishonour. Reasonable time
is the day after dishonour of a bill or cheque, if it would be reasonable
to deliver the notice by hand[4], and in other cases the day after the
dishonour or the following day[5]. A posted notice of dishonour is
served when it is delivered[6], but a correctly posted notice is deemed to
be good notice by the sender even if it fails to arrive[7].

The rules for when a notice of dishonour must be served should
be strictly complied with since delay can deprive the holder or indorser
of his right of action. Section 50 excuses delay if it is caused by circumstances beyond the control of the party desiring to serve notice and is
not imputable to his default, misconduct or negligence. Thus, ignorance
of the residence of the party on whom notice is to be served will excuse
delay, providing that the party seeking to serve the notice did not ignore
the ordinary and obvious methods available for discovering addresses[8].
The section dispenses with notice of dishonour if, after reasonable
diligence, notice cannot be given to the relevant party, or if notice is
waived. Notice to the drawer is dispensed with if the drawee and the
drawer are the same person, or if the drawer lacks capacity (and thus
cannot be liable on the instrument) or is fictitious. Nor is notice to the
drawer necessary when he is the person to whom the cheque was
presented for payment, or when he has countermanded payment, or

when the drawee or acceptor is not obliged to accept or pay on the instrument[9]. Notice to the indorser is dispensed with if the drawee is fictitious or lacks capacity (and this was known to the indorser at the time of the indorsement), or if the indorser was the person to whom the bill or cheque was presented for payment[10].

---

1 S.48.
2 *Ibid.*
3 S.49.
4 S.49(12) and *Hamilton Finance Co Ltd v Coverley Westray Walbaum and Tosetti Ltd* [1969] 1 Lloyd's Rep 53.
5 S.49(12).
6 *Eaglehill Ltd v J. Needham Builders Ltd* [1973] AC 992, [1972] 1 All ER 895, HL.
7 S.49(15).
8 *Beveridge v Burgis* (1812) 3 Camp 262.
9 S.50(2).
10 S.50(2).

Duty to note and protest
24.46 There is a duty imposed on the holder of a bill or cheque to note and protest only when the instrument has been dishonoured *and* the instrument is and appears on its face to be a foreign bill or cheque, i.e. a bill or cheque not drawn and payable in the British Islands or drawn within the British Islands on a person not resident therein[1]. In the case of a dishonoured inland bill or cheque, i.e. not a foreign bill or cheque, noting and protesting is optional.

Failure to note and protest a dishonoured foreign bill or cheque discharges the drawer and any indorsers but not the acceptor[2]. Noting consists of presenting the bill or cheque to a notary public who re-presents the bill or cheque. If it is again dishonoured, he 'notes' on the instrument the date of the presentment, the answer given, his initials and the amount of his fee. After such 'noting', a copy of the 'protest', which is a formal document signed by the notary giving details of the re-presentment and the result, is sent to the drawer and any indorsers of the instrument[3]. 'Noting' must take place on the day of dishonour or the following business day, but 'protest' can be made later. Protesting can be dispensed with in those circumstances in which a notice of dishonour would not be required. Delay in noting or protesting is excused by circumstances beyond the control of the holder and not imputable to his default, misconduct or negligence, provided that, when the cause of delay ceases, noting and protesting occurs with reasonable promptitude[4].

---

1 S.4. Notice that the duty to note and protest is also obligatory if the holder wishes to call upon a referee in case of need (s.15), and before a bill can be accepted or paid for honour (s.65).

2 S.51.
3 S.51.
4 S.51(9).

Liability of parties

The drawee
24.47 Section 53 provides that the drawee of a bill who does not accept it as required by the Act is not liable on the bill. Because cheques are not accepted, it follows that the payee of a cheque cannot enforce payment of it against a banker. However, as we shall see, a banker is required to pay cheques drawn by his customers (if the customer has assets) and failure to pay gives the customer a cause of action.

A drawee who is not liable on the bill, because he has not accepted it, may still be liable on a contract or pre-existing debt in relation to which the bill was drawn.

The drawer or indorser
24.48 An indorser can be regarded as a new drawer of the instrument, and as such he is liable to every succeeding holder of the bill or cheque if the drawee fails to accept or, having accepted, fails to pay on the instrument. Section 55 delineates the liability of a drawer or indorser:
'The drawer of a bill or cheque by drawing it —
(a) engages that on due presentment it shall be accepted and paid according to its tenour, and that if it be dishonoured he will compensate the holder or any indorser who is compelled to pay it, provided that the requisite proceedings on dishonour be duly taken.'
The section also provides that the drawer cannot deny, against a holder by indorsing a bill or cheque, engages that it shall be accepted and paid according to its tenour, on due presentment. If a bill or cheque is dishonoured, an indorser becomes liable to compensate the holder, or any subsequent indorser, who has been made liable on the instrument, provided the requisite proceedings in dishonour have been taken. An indorser cannot, against a holder in due course, deny the genuineness and regularity of the drawer's signature or any indorsements prior to his own. Nor can he deny, to his immediate or any subsequent indorsee, that the bill or cheque was, at the time of indorsement, a valid and subsisting bill or cheque and that he had a good title thereto.

The effect of s.55 is to allow the holder to sue the drawer or any indorser of a bill or cheque if it is not paid by the drawee. Any indorser who is sued can sue a previous indorser and so on until liability passes back to the drawer; this would be a very cumbersome process if a bill or cheque had been indorsed several times. It is, however, possible to shorten the process in certain cases. If a bill or cheque is dishonoured by non-payment and it has been protested for non-payment[1], any person can intervene and pay it for the honour of any party who is liable on the bill or cheque or for the honour of the drawer of it. This is called 'payment for honour', and the effect of such intervention is to discharge parties subsequent to the party for whose honour the bill or cheque was paid and to confer upon the payer the right to sue any party who would have been liable to the party for whose honour the payment was made. This 'payment for honour *supra protest*', as it is described in s.68, must be attested by a notarial act of honour which can be appended to the protest[2].

1 Para. 24.46.
2 A similar process called acceptance for honour is possible when a bill has been protested for dishonour by non-acceptance, ss.65–67.

24.49 Finally, it should be noted that a drawer or indorser can limit his liability on a bill or cheque by words expressly limiting or excluding liability[1]. Also, an indorser, who is obliged to indorse a bill or cheque while acting in a representative capacity, is entitled to indorse the instrument in such a way as to exclude personal liability[2].

1 S.16.
2 S.26.

The acceptor
24.50 The liability of an acceptor of a bill is discussed in relation to acceptance in para. 24.54.

A stranger
24.51 A person who signs a bill or cheque, but is not a party thereto, is regarded as an indorser and can be held liable as such by a holder in due course[1].

1 S.56; para. 24.48.

A transferor by delivery
24.52 If the holder of a bearer bill or cheque negotiates it by delivery without indorsement he is a 'transferor by delivery'[1]. Such a transferor is not liable on the instrument, but, if he negotiates the bill or cheque by delivery, he thereby warrants to the immediate transferee, if that transferee is a holder for value, that:

a. he has a right to transfer it;

b. the bill or cheque is what it purports to be; and

c. at the time of transfer he is not aware of any fact which makes that bill or cheque valueless[2].

Not only is such a transferee not liable on the bill or cheque, he is not liable to refund the consideration he received if the bill or cheque proves to be worthless because of the insolvency of the parties liable on the bill or cheque.

---

1 S.58.
2 S.58 and see *Gompertz v Bartlett* (1853) 23 LJQB 65.

Measure of damages

24.53 The damages awarded for the dishonour of a bill or cheque payable in the United Kingdom consist of:

a. the amount of the bill or cheque;

b. interest thereon from the date of presentment (if the bill or cheque is payable on demand) or the date of maturity (if the bill is payable after a fixed period); and

c. the expenses of noting and protesting where protest is required[1].

If a bill or cheque is payable outside the United Kingdom, the holder is entitled to recover from those liable on the instrument the amount of the re-exchange with interest until the time of payment[2].

---

1 S.57(1).
2 S.57(2). 'Re-exchange' means the cost of purchasing currency to meet the sterling equivalent of the amount due.

AN OUTLINE OF RULES RELATING TO BILLS OF EXCHANGE BUT NOT CHEQUES

Acceptance

24.54 Section 17 provides that acceptance is the 'signification by the drawee of his assent to the order of the drawer'. On acceptance of a bill a drawee becomes an acceptor and liable on the bill and, by virtue of s.54, cannot deny to a holder in due course:

a. the existence of the drawer, the genuineness of his signature and his capacity to draw the bill; or

b. the capacity of the drawer to indorse the bill if it is a bill payable to the drawer's order, but the acceptor can deny the genuineness or validity of the drawer's indorsement; or

c. the existence of the payee and his capacity to indorse a bill payable to a third party's order, but the acceptor can deny the genuineness or validity of the payee's indorsement.

For example, if a bill is drawn by X on Y in favour of Z or his order and Y accepts the bill, Y cannot deny to a holder in due course the existence or capacity of X or the existence or the capacity of Z to indorse, even if in fact Z stole the bill and inserted his own name as payee.

Acceptance must be written on the bill and signed by the drawee; the drawee's signature in itself is considered to be a valid acceptance. Acceptance can be general (i.e. an assent without qualification to the order of the drawer) or qualified (i.e. an assent which varies the effect of the bill as drawn). An acceptance will be qualified if it, for example, is conditional or is only an acceptance of part of the sum payable under the bill[1]. A holder who takes a qualified acceptance loses the right to sue the drawer or an indorser of the bill, because such an acceptance discharges the drawer or indorser from liability, unless the holder has authorised or assented to the qualified acceptance[2]. A qualified acceptance also permits a holder to treat the bill as dishonoured for non-acceptance if he wishes to do so.

---

1 S.19.
2 S.44.

Duty to present for acceptance

24.55 We have seen in para. 24.41 that the holder of a bill is required to comply with certain duties if he wishes to enforce that bill. Another duty which is imposed on him is to present the bill for acceptance if it has not already been accepted. Presentment for acceptance is not required if the bill is payable on demand. The procedure for acceptance is laid down in ss. 39 to 43.

Forged indorsements on bills

24.56 Title to an order bill passes by indorsement and delivery. A forged indorsement is, however, totally inoperative and cannot pass title, even to a holder in due course. The true owner of the bill in question is always entitled to recover it. However, an indorser who indorses the bill after the forgery cannot deny the validity of the forged indorsement to a holder in due course, or to a person who would be a holder in due course but for the forgery.

CHEQUES

24.57 A cheque is a particular form of bill of exchange and the majority of rules relating to bills also apply to cheques. There are, however, some special provisions which are only applicable to cheques and it is one of these which we consider in paras. 24.58 to 24.64. The parties to a cheque are the drawer (the customer) who draws a cheque on a drawee (the banker) in favour of a payee. A cheque can be indorsed but in practice this is rare. In discussing cheques it is necessary to distinguish between the banker to whom the cheque is presented by the payee (the collecting banker) and the banker whose customer is the drawer (the paying banker).

Crossed cheques

24.58 A cheque may be crossed either 'generally' or 'specially', and a crossed cheque must be paid into a bank account; it cannot be paid to the bearer, even if he is the payee, directly. This provides some safeguard if a cheque is stolen in that the thief cannot cash the cheque over the counter but must pay it into his bank account, and this delay gives the drawer a greater opportunity of stopping payment on the cheque.

   Section 76 provides that a cheque is 'crossed generally' if it bears two transverse parallel lines, to which may be added the words 'and company' or an abbreviation thereof, or 'not negotiable', or both. The section further provides that a cheque is 'crossed specially' if it bears the name of a banker, the banker's name will usually be placed between two transverse parallel lines and the cheque may also bear the words 'not negotiable'.

Who may cross a cheque
24.59 Section 77 provides that a cheque may be crossed generally or specially by the drawer or the holder. The holder of a cheque crossed generally may convert it into a cheque crossed specially or add the words 'not negotiable'. If a cheque is crossed specially the banker to whom it is crossed may cross it to another banker for collection. Furthermore, a collecting banker who receives a cheque crossed generally can cross it specially to another banker for collection.

The effect of crossing
24.60 The crossing on a cheque is a material part of the cheque and it is not lawful to obliterate, or add to, or alter that crossing[1]. If a cheque is uncrossed the holder can choose between sending the cheque to his bank and requesting them to seek payment of it from the drawee, or

present the cheque himself and request payment of it to him. However, if a cheque is crossed it must be paid through a banker. Section 79(2) says that if a paying banker pays a cheque crossed generally other than to a banker, or a cheque crossed specially other than to the banker to whom it is crossed (or his agent for collection who is himself a banker), he is liable to the true owner of the cheque for any loss sustained because of the incorrect payment of the cheque. If a crossed cheque is paid to the true owner over the counter the holder cannot have a claim against the banker, but it has been suggested that the drawer might be able to refuse to allow his account to be debited because payment was made in an unauthorised manner[2]. If a crossed cheque is paid over the counter to someone other than the true owner, the banker is liable to the true owner. The Act does not define a 'true owner' but the term includes a holder for value in due course[2]. However, if a crossed cheque has been negotiated after a forged indorsement the true owner is the payee or indorsee immediately prior to the forged indorsement.

---

1   S.78.
2   *Smith v Union Bank of London* (1875) 1 QBD 31, CA.

24.61   Section 79(2) provides a defence for a banker who pays on a crossed cheque, in good faith and without negligence, other than to a banker or other than to the specified banker. The defence is available if the cheque presented for payment appears to be an uncrossed cheque but subsequently transpires to have been crossed at some point in time. If the section is applicable the banker is not liable nor can the payment be questioned. Another statutory protection for bankers is contained in s.80. This section says that if a banker pays a cheque in accordance with its crossing, in good faith and without negligence, he cannot be liable if the payment was in fact made to someone other than the true owner, e.g. where a crossed cheque is paid by a thief into a bank account. If a banker is absolved from liability to the true owner by virtue of s.80, the drawer also ceases to be liable to the true owner provided that the cheque had, at some point, come into the hands of the payee.

'Not negotiable'
24.62   Section 76 allows a person crossing a cheque to add the words 'not negotiable', the effect of so doing is set out in s.81. This section provides that where a person takes a crossed cheque bearing these words 'he shall not have and shall not be capable of giving a better title to the cheque than that which the person from whom he took had'. 'Not negotiable' on a cheque does not prevent that cheque being transferred but it nullifies the basic rule of negotiable instruments, that a transferee can acquire a better title than the transferor. It has been

said that 'everyone who takes a cheque marked "not negotiable" takes it at his own risk'[1].

---

1 *Great Western Rly Co v London and County Banking Co Ltd* [1901] AC 414, HL.

'Account payee only'
24.63   A general crossing will frequently bear the words 'account payee only'. These words require the collecting banker to credit the payee's account with money payable under the cheque[1]. A collecting banker is put on inquiry if such a cheque is presented for payment by someone other than the payee, and if such a cheque is paid into an account other than the payee's, the banker is probably liable to the true owner for conversion of the cheque. It is thought that such words do not prohibit transfer of the cheque.

---

1 *National Bank v Silke* [1891] 1 QB 435, CA.

24.64   The crossing rules also apply to certain documents other than cheques, including banker's drafts and dividend warrants.

BANKER AND CUSTOMER

24.65   A banker is defined by the Act as a body of persons, whether incorporated or not, who carry on the business of banking[1]. A customer has been held to be a person who has an account in his own name with a banker[2], and he becomes a customer when the banker accepts instructions to open an account for him or receives a deposit to be credited to the account. Merely because a banker performs a casual service for a person does not make that person a customer. The relationship of banker and customer can only arise if both parties intend that it should do so. Essentially, the relationship of banker and customer is that of debtor and creditor (though with special obligations), and it is a contractual relationship and not a fiduciary one. However, a fiduciary relationship may arise in a particular transaction, as in the case of *Lloyds Bank Ltd v Bundy*[3], which we discussed in para. 14.34. A customer can usually terminate the relationship when he chooses, but the bank is not entitled to close a customer's account without giving reasonable notice. What is reasonable depends on the facts of the case[4]. The Consumer Credit Act 1974[5] can apply to credit transactions between banker and customer but the provisions of the Act relating to the entry into credit agreements may not apply to overdrafts. The Consumer Credit Act 1974 also imposes restrictions on the use of negotiable instruments in respect of regulated agreements[6].

---

1 S.2.
2 *Lacave & Co v Credit Lyonnais* [1897], 1 QB 148.
3 [1975] QB 326, [1974] 3 All ER 757, CA.
4 *Prosperity Ltd v Lloyds Bank Ltd* (1923) 39 TLR 372.
5 Chap. 23.
6 S.123; para. 23.57.

Duties of the customer

24.66 It is the duty of a customer, in drawing a cheque, to take 'usual reasonable precautions to prevent forgery'[1]. If the customer neglects this duty and forgery occurs, the customer is liable for the loss not the banker[1]. In the leading case of *London Joint Stock Bank Ltd v Macmillan and Arthur*[2], the confidential clerk of M, was entrusted with the task of filling in M's cheques for signature. The clerk prepared a bearer cheque, on which the sum payable was not mentioned in words and which bore the figures '2 0 0', and M signed it. The clerk then added the words one hundred and twenty pounds and added a 1 and a 0 either side of the 2 in the spaces which had been conveniently left. The clerk obtained payment of the cheque from M's banker. The House of Lords allowed the bank to debit their client's account for the full amount of the cheque, finding that the loss was caused by M's breach of the duty of care which he owed to his banker. Whether a customer is in breach of his duty is a question of fact, having regard to what is considered usual practice in drawing cheques.

A customer is under no duty to check that his bank statement represents the true state of his account but, if the bank has in fact credited him with more money than it should, the customer is not necessarily entitled to retain that money. The bank may be estopped from reclaiming the amount over-credited but only if the customer relies on the representation by the bank as to the amount of money in his account and alters his position in reliance on that representation. In *United Overseas Bank v Jiwani*[3], the bank was able to reclaim the money it had over-credited to the defendant's account even though he had used it as part of the purchase price of an hotel, because it was established that he would have bought the hotel anyway and thus did not rely on the representation by the bank.

---

1 *London Joint Stock Bank Ltd v Macmillan and Arthur* [1918] AC 777, HL.
2 [1918] AC 777, HL, which approved *Young v Grote* (1827) 4 Bing 253.
3 [1977] 1 All ER 733, [1976] 1 WLR 964.

Duties of the banker

24.67 A banker owes a contractual duty to take reasonable care in the conduct of business on behalf of a customer. When a customer draws a cheque he authorises the banker to make payment, and also creates the relationship of principal and agent.

Duty to honour cheques
24.68 A banker is under a duty to the customer to honour cheques up to the amount of his credit balance or agreed overdraft. A banker is not in breach of this duty if he dishonours a cheque which exceeds the customer's credit balance when the customer has made a deposit but the banker has not had a reasonable time in which to credit it to the customer's account[1]. Nor can a customer draw against cheques payable to his account before those cheques are cleared or credited. A banker need not honour a cheque presented at a branch at which the drawer does not have an account but, in practice, he will frequently do so. In practice, banks will not honour 'stale' cheques, i.e. cheques outstanding for some period, usually six months or more, or undated cheques. If a banker wrongly dishonours a cheque, a customer can successfully claim substantial damages, without proof of actual loss, if he is a trader or professional man. In other cases a customer is only entitled to nominal damages in the absence of actual loss. A banker should exercise care in writing 'refer to drawer' on a cheque because these words may be libellous[2].

---

1 *Marzetti v Williams* (1830) 1 B & Ad 415.
2 Paras. 21.6–21.8.

Termination of the duty to pay
24.69 The duty and authority of a banker to pay a cheque drawn on him by a customer ceases if a customer countermands or 'stops' payment[1]. Notice to the banker to stop payment should be unambiguous and identify the cheque clearly, because a banker will not be at fault if he disregards an unclear countermand. However, a banker is not entitled to ignore a clear countermand. This point is well illustrated by *Burnett v Westminster Bank Ltd*[2]. In this case, the plaintiff had an account at two separate branches of the defendant bank and had a cheque book for each account. The cheque books requested customers to use the correct cheque book for each branch and the cheques themselves bore a computer code. The plaintiff used a cheque issued by one branch (A) to draw on his other account at the other branch (B) after substituting the address of the B branch. The following day the plaintiff countermanded the cheque at the B branch but the cheque, was of course,

forwarded by the computer to the A branch who honoured it. The court found that the plaintiff had effectively countermanded payment by notice at the B branch. The countermand was unaffected by the business usages of the defendants.

A countermand becomes effective when it reaches the ledger clerk or equivalent; mere delivery of a countermand to the banker's address is insufficient. However, if a letter of countermand is so delivered, but remains unopened for an unreasonably long time, the banker who pays on a cheque countermanded by that letter may be liable in negligence. In *Curtice v London City and Midland Bank Ltd*[3], it was suggested that a countermand by telegram would not be effective, but such a telegram would entitle the bank to postpone payment until it had checked the authority of the countermand. Notice of countermand must be made at the branch on which the cheque is drawn.

---

1 S.75(1).
2 [1966] 1 QB 742, [1965] 3 All ER 81.
3 [1900] 1 KB 293, CA.

24.70 Apart from countermand, the duty to pay ceases in a number of cases such as:

a. on the death of a customer[1]; or

b. on notice of the insanity of the customer; or

c. on notice of an act of bankruptcy on which a petition can be filed; or

d. on notice of a receiving order in bankruptcy; or

e. on notice of the commencement of winding-up, if the customer is a company; and

f. on closure of the bank.

---

1 S.75.

Unauthorised payments
24.71 If a banker pays on a cheque and such payment is authorised he can debit the customer's account. Furthermore, s.59 provides that if a banker pays a bearer cheque, in good faith and without notice of any defect in title of the holder, this is a payment in due course which discharges the cheque and entitles the banker to debit the customer's account. However, if a banker pays on a cheque which is unauthorised, e.g. in that it bears a forged indorsement, he cannot debit the customer's account and is liable in conversion for the face value of the cheque, subject to the exceptions which we now discuss.

24.72 *Negligence* As we have seen in para. 24.66, if the unauthorised payment was a result of the careless manner in which the customer drew the cheque the customer is liable. This only applies to negligence in the method of drawing the cheque; carelessness unconnected with the drawing of the cheque, which gives rise to the unauthorised payment, will not render the customer liable on the cheque.

24.73 *Forged indorsement* If an indorsement is forged on a cheque payable to bearer, or treated as payable to bearer, because of the fact that the payee is fictitious, and the banker pays it to a holder or his agent, this is considered payment in due course and the banker can debit the customer's account. The holder of a bearer cheque takes his title from the delivery, not from the indorsement. However, if an indorsement is forged on an order cheque, a transferee of that cheque cannot be a holder in due course since his title derives from delivery and indorsement, and payment to him is not payment in due course. The banker is protected by s.60, which provides that where an order cheque is paid in the ordinary course of business and in good faith, the banker is deemed to have paid in due course even if the cheque bore a forged indorsement of the payee or a subsequent holder so long as the cheque is regular on its face. The ordinary course of business seems to mean that a method of conducting business adopted by the business community at large — paying a crossed cheque over the counter[1] or honouring a cheque with an irregular indorsement[2] is not acting in the ordinary course of business. It seems that negligent practice by a banker does not mean that he is not acting in the 'ordinary course of business'[3] nor is negligence incompatible with good faith[4].

---

1 *Smith v Union Bank of London* (1875) LR 10 QB 291; affd., (1875) 1 QBD 31.
2 *Charles v Blackwell* (1877) 2 CPD 151, CA.
3 *Carpenters Co v British Mutual Banking Co* [1938] 1 KB 511, [1937] 3 All ER 811, CA.
4 Also see para. 24.39.

24.74 *Irregular or no indorsement* By s.1 of the Cheques Act 1957, a banker, who pays a cheque in the ordinary course of business and in good faith, is deemed to have paid in due course if the cheque is irregularly indorsed or not indorsed. Payment in due course discharges the banker from liability. This provision is subject to a circular of the Committee of London Clearing Bankers which lays down what is ordinary business practice in relation to indorsements so that disregard of the circular is disregard of the ordinary course of business and the Cheques Act 1957, s.1 will not apply. The circular says that if a cheque is cashed over the counter it should be indorsed.

24.75 *Estoppel* The customer may, by his conduct, be estopped from alleging that the banker exceeded his authority by paying a cheque. For example, if a customer assured his banker that the signature on a cheque was genuine, he cannot subsequently deny that the signature was his[1]. A leading case is *Greenwood v Martins Bank Ltd*[2]. In this case the plaintiff's wife forged and cashed many of his cheques over a period of time. The plaintiff discovered this but did not inform his bank. Subsequently he discovered that his wife's explanation of the forgeries was untrue and threatened to reveal what she had done to the bank, whereupon the wife committed suicide. The plaintiff brought an action against the bank reclaiming the money which it had paid on the forged cheques. The House of Lords found that he was estopped by his own conduct from claiming that the bank had exceeded its authority in honouring the forged cheques. In failing to report the forgeries as soon as he had discovered them he had led the bank to believe that its payments were authorised and the bank had been adversely affected by his inaction, in that had it sued the wife during her lifetime it might have been able to recover some of the money.

---

1   *Brook v Hook* (1871) LR 6 Exch 89.
2   [1933] AC 51, HL.

Subrogation
24.76   If a banker pays money on an unauthorised or countermanded cheque and debits the customer's account he is liable to replace the sum debited. However, if the money paid without authority was used to pay an existing debt the banker may be subrogated to the existing debtor's rights, in which case the bank can enforce the debt 'discharged' by the unauthorised payment as if it was an assignee of that debt.

Rights against the payee
24.77   Unless he is estopped, a banker can recover money paid on an unauthorised cheque from the payee[1].

---

1   *National Westminster Bank Ltd v Barclays Bank International Ltd* [1975] QB 654, [1974] 3 All ER 834.

Duty of secrecy
24.78   This duty imposed on bankers by virtue of their confidential relationships with their customers was comprehensively discussed in *Tournier v National Provincial and Union Bank of England*[1]. In this case the Court of Appeal stressed that the duty arose from the nature of the contract between banker and customer. Breach of the duty will entitle

the customer to nominal damages or, if he has suffered actual loss, substantial damages. The duty is qualified and subject to certain reasonable exceptions. The duty itself requires the banker not to reveal any information gained about the customer while acting in his capacity as banker. The exceptions are:

a. Where disclosure is under compulsion of law; for example, an order made under the Bankers' Books Evidence Act 1879 which allows a party to litigation to inspect and take copies of entries in a banker's book if such book is used in the ordinary business of the bank. The Taxes Management Act 1970, s.20, provides that the Inspector of Taxes can require the production of information relating to a taxpayer's financial position in certain cases.

b. Where there is a public duty to disclose, which outweighs the private duty; for example, where there is danger to the state.

c. Where the interests of the bank require disclosure; for example, if the banker is seeking payment of an overdraft he may state the amount of overdraft on the writ.

d. Where the disclosure is made with the express or implied consent of the customer; for example, where the customer gives the name of his banker as a referee.

---

1 [1924] 1 KB 461, CA.

Other duties
24.79 Among the other duties imposed upon a banker are:

a. To give information regarding the credit and standing of a customer, if authorised. In giving such information a bank can be liable for negligent mis-statements causing financial loss[1].

b. To advise on investments. In so doing a banker must use reasonable care[1].

c. To take custody of valuables; the duty of care imposed on a banker is to take reasonable care for the safety of the goods[2]. If the banker deals with the goods in a manner inconsistent with the rights of the true owner, e.g. by delivering them to the wrong person, he is liable in conversion even if he was not negligent.

---

1 *Hedley Byrne & Co Ltd v Heller & Partners Ltd* [1964] AC 465, [1963] 2 All ER 575, HL; para. 20.13.
2 *Giblin v McMullen* (1868) LR 2 PC 317.

The position of the collecting banker

24.80 A banker who collects payment of a valid cheque for a person who is not the true owner can be sued in conversion[1] or for money had and received by the true owner[2]. However, the Cheques Act 1957, s.4 affords some protection to a collecting banker in relation to cheques, bankers' drafts and some other instruments. To claim the protection of s.4, the banker must act in good faith without negligence and either (a) receive payment for the customer of a cheque or banker's draft etc.; or (b) having credited the customer's account with the amount of such an instrument, receive payment of the sum due under the instrument himself. If this is the case and the customer has no title or a defective title to the instrument, the banker does not become liable to the true owner of the instrument, merely because he received payment of the sum due under the instrument.

---

1 *A. L. Underwood Ltd v Barclays Bank* [1924] 1 KB 775, CA.
2 *Bavins Junr and Sims v London and South Western Bank* [1900] 1 QB 270, CA.

Conditions for the application of s.4
24.81 *There must be a customer* This is discussed in para. 24.65.

24.82 *The banker must be a collecting agent* The Cheques Act 1957, s.4, does not protect a banker who takes the cheque as holder for value rather than as a collecting banker, because if he takes the cheque as holder for value he receives it for himself. A banker becomes a holder for value:

a. if he exchanges an uncleared cheque for cash[1]; or

b. if the customer pays in the cheque to reduce his overdraft; or

c. if the customer draws against the cheque before clearance with the express or implied consent of the banker[2].

If the banker takes as a holder for value and is also a holder in due course he obtains a good title to the cheque.

---

1 *Great Western Rly Co v London and County Banking Co Ltd* [1901] AC 414, HL.
2 *A. L. Underwood Ltd v Bank of Liverpool and Martins* [1924] 1 KB 775, CA.

24.83 *Without negligence* A collecting banker must prove he was not negligent if he wishes to rely on the Cheques Act 1957, s.4. What constitutes negligence for this purpose is unclear; it has been equated with carelessness[1], and failure to take reasonable care[1]. In *Marfani & Co Ltd v Midland Bank Ltd*[2], the following was said: 'what enquiries he (the collecting banker) should make, and what facts are sufficient to cause him reasonably to suspect that the customer is not the true owner must depend upon current banking practice, and change as that practice changes'. Certainly, if the cheque or the circumstances are sufficient to put the banker on inquiry he may lose the protection of the section if he proceeds. A banker put on inquiry should ask questions and seek the truth: it is no defence to a claim of negligence that had he inquired he would not have been told the truth. The alleged negligence must relate to, or be in connection with, the *collection* of the cheque. Negligence in any other dealing with the customer is irrelevant. Such a connection can arise where the banker collects on a cheque which opens an account, which cheque is payable to 'account payee only'[3], or where a prospective customer seeks to open his account with a cheque not drawn in his favour[4]. A banker should make more inquiries when collecting a cheque indorsed to a customer with a dubious banking record[5] than when the customer has an unblemished record. A banker is, of course, put on inquiry if the cheque presented for collection on its face gives rise to the suspicion that it has been misappropriated[6]. Such suspicion would arise if a customer presented a cheque for a large sum payable to a third person, or if a customer presented a cheque payable to a public official and apparently indorsed by that official, or if a director presents a cheque payable to the company which he controls. If the banker knows that the customer presenting the cheque is in a fiduciary position and the cheque indicates that the money it represents may be the property of the principal, there is a clear duty to inquire. Again, if an employee presents a cheque drawn in favour of his employer, there is a clear duty to inquire, especially if the employee has indorsed the cheque supposedly on behalf of the employer[6]. Perhaps proof of the absence of negligence can be summed up as requiring honest trading carried on with vigilance and proper conduct. It has been said that, if an inquiry has been made, the banker need not view the answers with abnormal suspicion.

Section 4(3) provides that a banker is not to be regarded as negligent merely because he failed to concern himself with the absence of, or any irregularity of, indorsement, but this may be affected by the circular of the Committee of London Clearing Bankers discussed in para. 24.74.

---

1 *Orbit Mining and Trading Co Ltd v Westminster Bank Ltd* [1963] 1 QB 794, [1962] 3 All ER 565.
2 [1968] 2 All ER 573, [1968] 1 WLR 956, CA.
3 *Ladbroke & Co v Todd* (1914) 111 LT 43.
4 *Harding v London Joint Stock Bank Ltd* (1914) 3 Legal Decisions affecting Bankers 81.

5 *Motor Traders Guarantee Corpn Ltd v Midland Bank Ltd* [1937] 4 All ER 90.
6 *Lloyds Bank Ltd v E.B. Savory & Co* [1933] AC 201, HL.

Measure of damages

24.84 If a collecting banker cannot rely on s.4, the measure of damages
payable to the true owner is the face value of the instrument if the
banker is sued in conversion. Alternatively, the proceeds of the cheque
may be claimed from the banker as money had and received[1].

---

1 *Morison v London County and Westminster Bank Ltd* [1914] 3 KB 356, CA.

Holder in due course

24.85 We have mentioned in para. 24.82, that a collecting banker may
be a holder in due course. By the Cheques Act 1957, s.2, a collecting
banker may also become a holder in due course of an order cheque
which is not indorsed, provided that he gives value for the cheque. If a
collecting banker becomes a holder in due course, he has the usual rights
of such a holder, including the right to sue the drawer if the cheque is
dishonoured. Section 2 is an exception to s.31 of the principal Act,
which requires an order cheque to be indorsed before it can be negotiated.
The section only applies to unindorsed cheques and not to irregularly
indorsed ones. In the important case of *Westminster Bank Ltd v Zang*[1],
an unindorsed cheque drawn on Z was presented for collection by T at
his bank for the benefit of T Ltd's account, which was overdrawn. The
cheque was dishonoured and was returned to T so that he could sue Z,
but he discontinued the action and returned the cheque to his bank.
The bank claimed to be holders in due course and thus able to sue Z.
The House of Lords held that the bank had not given value because
interest was charged on the overdraft unreduced by the cheque.

---

1 [1966] AC 182, [1966] 1 All ER 114, HL.

Cheques and receipts

24.86 The Cheques Act 1957[1] provides that an *unindorsed* cheque
apparently paid by the bank on whom it is drawn is evidence, but not
conclusive evidence, that the payee has received the sum payable by the
cheque. An *indorsed* cheque was evidence of receipt by the payee even
before 1957.

---

1 S.3.

CHEQUES AND OTHER BILLS

Cheques and bills

24.87 A cheque differs from a bill in that it need not be accepted, it is rarely indorsed, delay in presentment does not necessarily discharge the drawer, the rules on crossings do not apply to bills and the provisions relating to payment on forged and unauthorised indorsements vary.

Cheques and promissory notes

24.88 A promissory note, which is defined in s.83, is an unconditional promise by the maker of the note to pay a specified sum at a particular time. A cheque is an order to pay, which must be presented for payment. A note is a promise to pay, and its presentment is not always necessary for payment. Both notes and cheques need not be presented for acceptance, or be accepted, but the rules on overdue instruments vary.

Chapter 25

Elements of Insurance Law

GENERAL

25.1 An insurance contract is one whereby a person or company, known as 'the insurer' (or, in the case of a member of Lloyd's, 'the underwriter'), agrees, in return for the payment of a premium or premiums, to pay to another person or company ('the insured' or 'the assured') a specified sum of money on the occurrence of a specified event, *or* to idemnify the insured up to a specified amount against loss caused by a specified risk.

25.2 As we saw in para. 15.3, c, a contract of insurance is distinguishable from a wagering contract by the fact that, whereas in a wagering contract neither party has any interest other than the sum he will win or the stake he will lose, in insurance the insured has some legally recognised right or interest in the subject-matter insured. Hence, if a contract purports to be one of insurance but the 'insured' has no insurable interest in its subject-matter, the contract is one of wagering and void as such. Moreover, it has been repeatedly held that contracts of insurance, other than those relating to ships, merchandise and goods (which include money in this context), are illegal unless the insured has an insurable interest in their subject-matter. Where the contract is illegal for this reason, the insured cannot recover back premiums paid under it[1], unless he falls within one of the exceptional cases where money paid under an illegal contract is recoverable, e.g. where he was induced by fraud to believe the policy was legal[2].

In the case of insurance on ships, merchandise and goods (including money), an insurable interest need only exist at the time of the loss. On the other hand, in life assurance and all other contracts of insurance an insurable interest must be proved at the time of the contract as well (*in the case of indemnity policies only*) as at the time of loss[3].

---

1   *Harse v Pearl Life Assurance Co* [1904] 1 KB 558, CA; para. 16.63, a.
2   *Hughes v Liverpool Victoria Legal Friendly Society* [1916] 2 KB 482, CA; para. 16.63, a.
3   Life Assurance Act 1774, ss. 1 and 4; Marine Insurance Act 1906, s.6.

25.3   Four types of insurance are especially significant: fire insurance, liability insurance, life assurance and marine insurance. Marine insurance law is a specialised subject outside the scope of this book and we shall not say anything specific about it. Other common types of insurance include property insurance (e.g. house and contents insurance) and personal accident or sickness insurance, but insurance can be obtained for virtually every type of risk.

25.4   Generally, a person wishing to insure makes his offer by filling in a proposal form. If this is accepted by the insurer, the contract of insurance is normally evidenced by a document known as a policy of insurance.

  We saw in para. 15.24 that an intending assured is under a duty to disclose all material facts known to him and that if he fails to do so the insurer can rescind the contract of insurance. This duty of disclosure even applies to any material alteration of risk between submission of the proposal and its acceptance[1].

INDEMNITY POLICIES

Indemnity principle

25.5   With the exception of life insurance and personal accident or sickness insurance, insurance contracts are contracts of indemnity for loss caused by a specified risk. This means that if, for example, an accountant insures himself against professional negligence liability up to a maximum of £100,000, and subsequently claims under the policy, he can only recover the amount of his liability and legal costs, so far as it does not exceed the sum insured, and not £100,000[2]. This principle even applies to the insurance of property, although here the parties may agree beforehand the value of the property so that if it is destroyed, damaged or lost the indemnity will be assessed on the basis of that figure regardless of the real value of the property[3], unless the insured has been fraudulent.

---

1   *Looker v Law Union and Rock Insurance Co Ltd* [1928] 1 KB 554.
2   *Castellain v Preston* (1883) 11 QBD 380, CA.
3   *Elcock v Thomson,* [1949] 2 KB 755 [1949] 2 All ER 381.

25.6   Other aspects of the principle of indemnity are:

a. *Contribution* If a person is insured with more than one insurer *for the same risk and interest* he cannot recover more in total than his actual loss. If a loss occurs, the insured can choose which insurer or insurers to recover from, but an insurer against whom a claim is made has a right to rateable contributions from the others[1]. The right to contribution is not very important in practice because policies normally include a rateable proportion clause, whose effect is to restrict the insurer's liability under the policy to a rateable proportion of the damage, so that the insured will himself have to claim contributions from all the insurers.

b. *Subrogation* When there is a contract of indemnity, and a loss occurs, anything which reduces that loss reduces the amount which the indemnifier has to pay. Consequently, if an insurer under an insurance contract of the indemnifying type has already paid the insured, he is entitled to anything reducing the loss which is in the hands of the insured, or comes into his hands[2]. This is known as the rule of subrogation. It entitles the insurer who has paid the insured to any compensation for loss received by the insured and to any rights and remedies which he may have against third parties in respect of it. Liability policies often give the insurer an express right of subrogation which can be enforced even before payment.

c. *Salvage* If insured property is a total wreck, e.g. a burnt out car, and the insurer pays the insured on the basis of a total loss, he is entitled to the property as salvage: this prevents the insured retaining more than his actual loss.

We emphasise that none of these rules apply to life assurance and other types of non-indemnity insurance.

---

1   *American Surety Co of New York v Wrightson* (1910) 27 TLR 91; *North British and Mercantile Insurance Co v London, Liverpool and Globe Insurance Co* (1877) 5 Ch D 569, CA.
2   *Burnand v Rodocanachi* (1882) 7 App Cas 333 at 339, HL.

Assignment

25.7   It is essential to distinguish between an assignment of the right to recover money payable under an indemnity policy and a transfer of the insurance policy itself.

25.8   *Assignment of the right to recover under the policy* There is no difficulty here. Like any other chose in action, the right can be assigned effectively provided the requirements of the Law of Property Act 1925, s.136, are satisfied, otherwise the transfer operates as an equitable assignment[1].

---

1 Chapter 19.

25.9 *Transfer of the contract of insurance* Insurance being a contract of a personal nature, the policy can only be effectively transferred so as to attach to a different insured if:

a. the insurer consents[1]; and

b. the assignment is accompanied by a contemporaneous transfer of interest in the property insured[2], otherwise there will cease to be a person with an insurable interest.

The requirement of the insurer's consent means that there is in effect a novation[3]. The above rules mean that if X sells property to Y, a contemporaneous attempt to transfer his fire policy on it to Y can only be effective if the insurer consents.

---

1 *Sadler's Co v Badcock* (1743) 2 Atk 554.
2 *Lloyd v Fleming* (1872) LR 7 QB 299.
3 Paras. 19.17 and 19.18.

Fire insurance

25.10 A contract of fire insurance is a contract whereby the insurer agrees to indemnify the insured up to a specified amount against the consequences of a fire to specified property, in return for the payment of a single or periodical premiums. The insured cannot recover if he, or someone acting with his consent, deliberately caused the loss by fire, but the fact that the loss was caused by his negligence does not debar him. In *Harris v Poland*[1], for example, the insured hid her jewellery in the grate of her fireplace. Later, forgetting this, she lit the fire and the jewellery was damaged. It was held that she could recover under a fire policy. Fire policies usually refer to excepted perils, such as riot, war and explosion.

---

1 [1942] 1 KB 462, [1941] 1 All ER 204.

Insurable interest
25.11 The insured will generally have an insurable interest to the extent of any interest in the property insured. Obviously, a person can

always insure his own property. In addition, a trustee can insure trust property, and a mortgagee (the creditor under a mortgage) can insure the mortgaged property[1]. Similarly, a bailee, such as a carrier, can insure the goods bailed, and may do so either to the extent of his own limited interest or for the full value of the goods. If he takes the latter course and is paid insurance money, he may retain so much of it as is necessary to cover his own interest and is a trustee for the owner in respect of the rest[2]. On the other hand, a shareholder in a company does not have an insurable interest in the property of the company, even if he holds virtually all the shares, and nor does an unsecured creditor of the company[3].

The insurable interest must exist at the time of loss for a claim to succeed (which is another corollary of the indemnity principle), and, as we have already indicated[4], in the case of buildings the interest must also have existed when the contract of insurance was made.

---

1 *Westminster Fire Office v Glasgow Provident Investment Society* (1883) 13 App Cas 699, HL.
2 *Waters v Monarch Fire and Life Assurance Co* (1856) 5 E & B 870.
3 *Macaura v Northern Assurance Co Ltd* [1925] AC 619, HL.
4 Para. 25.2.

Reinstatement
25.12 Section 83 of the Fires Prevention (Metropolis) Act 1774, which somewhat surprisingly applies to the whole of England and Wales, provides that *any person* (e.g. a mortgagee or a tenant) interested in a building destroyed by fire can *require the insurer* to spend insurance money on the reinstatement of the building.

'Subject to average' clause
25.13 The general rule is that an insured is entitled to be indemnified to the full extent of his loss, up to the amount specified in the policy, even though the fire only causes partial loss to the insured property. This can produce hardship for insurers where the property is *under-insured* since, in accepting a proposal for insurance against total loss at a particular figure, they will not have calculated that partial loss, which is intrinsically more likely to occur, could reach that figure, and consequently may have fixed a relatively small premium. To protect themselves against under-insurance, insurers frequently insert a 'subject to average' clause in fire and other policies where the risk of partial loss is high. The effect of such a clause is that the insured can only recover such proportion of the actual loss suffered as the sum insured bears to the total value of the insured property. An example is provided by *Acme Wood Flooring Co Ltd v Marten*[1], where timber worth £36,500 was

insured for £11,450. Damage totalling £12,050 was caused. The policy contained a 'subject to average' clause and consequently it was held that the insured could only recover $\frac{11450}{36500}$ £12,850, i.e. the same proportion of the loss suffered as the sum insured bore to the total value of the insured property. But for the clause, the insured could have recovered the full amount of their partial loss.

---

1   (1904) 90 LT 313.

Liability insurance

25.14   Liability insurance means insurance cover indemnifying the insured against his legal liability to third parties. Thus, a householder can insure against his liability to visitors and neighbours, and an accountant or other professional man can insure against liability for professional negligence. Cover against legal liability can be obtained by a special policy against a particular type of liability. Alternatively, such cover may form part of a wider policy, and this is frequently so in the case of house and motor vehicle insurance.

25.15   It is contrary to public policy for a claim under liability insurance to be allowed in respect of a *deliberate* criminal act by the insured[1]. The same is probably true in the case of deliberate tortious acts such as may occur, for instance, in cases of defamation.

---

1   *Gray v Barr* [1971] 2 QB 554, [1971] 2 All ER 949, CA.

Insolvency of insured

25.16   Section 1(1) of the Third Parties (Rights against Insurers) Act 1930 provides that where any person is insured against liabilities to third parties which he may incur, then, if such liability is incurred by him either before or after the events mentioned below, his rights against the insurer are transferred to the third party to whom the liability is incurred. The events on which the transfer of rights operates are:

a. if the insured is an individual, when he becomes bankrupt or makes a composition or arrangement with his creditors;

b. if the insured is a company, when it goes into liquidation (other than voluntary liquidation merely for the purpose of reconstruction or amalgamation with another company), or a receiver or manager is appointed by holders of debenture shares secured by a floating charge.

If a claim is made by a third party under this provision, the insurer can set up any defence available against the insured, including failure to notify a claim within a prescribed time[1], but may not claim a set-off for unpaid premiums[2]. The rights of third parties under the Act cannot be barred or altered by an insurance contract[3].

---

1 *Farrell v Federated Employers' Insurance Association Ltd* [1970] 3 All ER 632, CA.
2 *Murray v Legal and General Assurance Society Ltd* [1970] 2 QB 495, [1969] 3 All ER 794.
3 Third Parties (Rights against Insurers) Act 1930, s.1(3).

Compulsory insurance

25.17 *Employers' Liability (Compulsory Insurance) Act 1969* This Act makes it compulsory for every employer (besides nationalised industries, local authorities and the like) to insure himself against liability for bodily injury or disease sustained by his employees, and arising out of and in the course of their employment in Great Britain or on oil rigs in designated areas[1]. An employer is not required to insure an employee who is a close relative. It is an offence for an employer not to be insured in breach of these requirements.

---

1 Employers' Liability (Compulsory Insurance) Act 1969, s.1.

25.18 *Road Traffic Act 1972*[1] Under this Act it is an offence for a person to use, or cause to permit any person to use, a motor vehicle on a road unless there is in force such an insurance policy[2] in relation to that person or that other person in respect of third party risks as complies with the Act. There are limited exceptions to this requirement of compulsory insurance, for example, invalid carriages and local authority and police vehicles. In order to comply with the statutory requirement, an insurance policy must insure the person or persons specified in it against any liability (other than contractual liability) which may be incurred in respect of death or bodily injury to any person caused by, or arising out of, the use of a vehicle on a road[3]. Persons, other than the insured, named in the policy can enforce their right to an indemnity by personally suing the insurer notwithstanding their lack of privity to the contract of insurance.

A policy is of no effect for the purpose of the statutory requirement until a certificate of insurance is delivered to the insured.

A judgment against the insured in respect of liability covered by compulsory insurance can be enforced against the insurer by the third party, provided that notice of the action in which judgment was obtained was given before or within seven days of its commencement and, of course, an applicable policy was in force. Recovery can be had from the insurer notwithstanding a clause in the policy purporting to restrict the insurance by reference to certain specified matters, such as the age or physical or mental condition of the driver, or the condition of the vehicle, or the number of passengers. Nor is recovery barred by a provision that there shall be no liability under the policy if some specified thing is done (e.g. an admission of liability), or not done, *after* the event giving rise to the third party's claim. On the other hand, the rights of recovery of a third party victim are affected by a provision in the policy limiting it to the use of a vehicle in a particular way, such as use for private purposes only. If a third party is injured while the vehicle is being used in some unauthorised way he cannot recover damages from the insurer.

---

1 Ss.143—149 contain the relevant provisions.
2 As an alternative to an insurance policy, a security for £15,000 (or more in some cases) may be deposited with the Accountant-General of the Supreme Court. This is only done by large undertakings such as bus companies.
3 The policy must also insure the specified person or persons in respect of medical expenses for emergency treatment incurred by him or them.

25.19 In relation to a compulsory risk, third parties are protected against uninsured and untraced drivers by an agreement between the Motor Insurers' Bureau and the Ministry of Transport. In relation to uninsured drivers, the Board will satisfy any judgment which is not satisfied in full within seven days provided certain requirements are satisfied. In the case of untraced drivers the bureau will compensate the third party if on the balance of probabilities the untraced driver would be liable to pay damages to him, provided, again, certain requirements are satisfied.

LIFE ASSURANCE

25.20 In a contract for life assurance the insurer undertakes, in return for the payment of a single premium or periodical premiums, to pay a lump sum or annuity (an annual sum) to the person for whose benefit the insurance is made on the death of the person whose life is insured. Life assurance can involve endowment assurance, in which case the insurer's liability accrues on the death of the assured or his attainment of a specified age, whichever is the earlier.

Insurable interest

25.21 Like any other insurance contract, a life insurance contract is only valid if the insured has an insurable interest in its subject-matter.

The Life Assurance Act 1774, s.1, prohibits an insurance to be made by any person on the life of any person, unless the person for whose benefit the policy was made has an interest in it. The interest, however, need only exist when the policy is effected, with the result that the policy is not invalidated by the termination of that interest before the death of the life assured[1]. Section 3 provides that where the insured has an insurable interest, no greater sum can be recovered from the insurer than the value of that interest at the date of the policy.

Who has an insurable interest in a life? Obviously a person has an insurable interest in his own life[2] and in that of his spouse[3] and can insure it for his own benefit, but where a person insures any other life for his own benefit, he must have a pecuniary interest in that life. The following are examples of people who have an insurable interest in the lives of those mentioned:

a. a creditor has an insurable interest in his debtor's life to the extent of the debt[4];

b. a surety has an insurable interest in the debtor's life for the whole debt[5];

c. an employee has an insurable interest in the life of his employer up to the amount of pay outstanding at the time the policy was effected[6];

d. an employer has an insurable interest in the life of an employee.

On the other hand, a parent does not generally have an insurable interest in the life of his child[7], nor a child in the life of a parent[8], since such persons will not normally have a legally recognised pecuniary interest in the insured life.

1 *Dalby v India and London Life-Assurance Co* (1854) 15 CB 365.
2 *McFarlane v Royal London Friendly Society* (1886) 2 TLR 755; Married Women's Property Act 1882, s.11.
3 *Reed v Royal Exchange Assurance Co* (1795) Peake Add Cas 70; *Griffiths v Fleming* [1909] 1 KB 805, CA.
4 *Godsall v Boldero* (1807) 9 East 72.
5 *Branford v Saunders* (1877) 25 WR 650.
6 *Hebdon v West* (1863) 3 B & S 579.
7 *Halford v Kymer* (1830) 10 B & C 724.
8 *Harse v Pearl Life Assurance Co* [1904] 1 KB 558, CA.

Suicide

25.22 There is no doubt that if the assured kills himself during a period of temporary insanity, the insurance money is recoverable by his personal representatives, unless the policy otherwise provides[1]. The situation is more complex in the case of sane suicide, which was a crime until the Suicide Act 1961. In *Beresford v Royal Insurance Co Ltd*[2], a case decided before the Act of 1961, R insured his life for £50,000. The policy contained a term avoiding it in the event of suicide within one year of its commencement. More than a year after its commencement, and minutes before it lapsed, R committed suicide. He was not insane. The House of Lords held that the insurers had agreed to pay in the events which had occurred, but that the claim by R's personal representatives for the insurance money was contrary to public policy, because they were seeking to recover the fruits of the assured's crime, and must fail. There is a general principle of insurance law that money is not payable under a policy when the assured deliberately brings about the event insured against. Thus, it would seem that despite the abolition of the the crime of suicide, insurance money is still not recoverable if the assured has killed himself, unless the policy expressly provides the contrary.

---

1 *Horn v Anglo-Australian etc Assurance Co* (1861) 30 LJ Ch 511.
2 [1938] AC 586, [1938] 2 All ER 602, HL.

Married Women's Property Act 1882

25.23 The Married Women's Property Act 1882, s.11, provides that where a man effects assurance on his *own* life, and the policy is expressed to be for the benefit of his wife or children[1], or where a woman effects an assurance on her *own* life, and the policy is expressed to be for the benefit of her husband or children, the policy creates 'a trust in favour of the objects therein named'. In such a case, the money payable under the policy does not, so long as the trust remains unperformed, form part of the assured's estate. However, if it is proved that the policy was effected to defraud the assured's creditors, they are entitled to receive, out of the sums payable under the policy, a sum equal to the premiums paid. Section 11, which constitutes an exception to the doctrine of privity of contract, does not apply where the life assured is not that of the person effecting the assurance, nor where the person for whose benefit the policy is expressed to be is someone other than a spouse or child of the assured (but in this case he can be benefited if a trust of the policy is created in his favour by the assured, which, unless express, is very hard to prove)[2].

---

1 Including illegitimate children, Family Law Reform Act 1969, s.19(1).
2 *Re Sinclair's Life Policy* [1938] Ch 799, [1938] 3 All ER 124; para. 6.25.

Assignment

25.24 A policy of life assurance can never be transferred, but the right to recover money payable under it can be assigned in three ways:

a. Under the Policies of Assurance Act 1867 it can be assigned either by indorsement of the policy or by a separate instrument in the form or to the effect set out in the Schedule to the Act, such indorsement or separate instrument being duly stamped[1]. Written notice of the assignment must be given to the insurer in order to perfect it, and it is the date on which notice is received which determines the competing claims of different assignees. In addition, any bona fide payments made in respect of the policy by the insurer before notice is received are valid against the assignee giving notice[2]. If he receives a written request to do so and payment of a fee not exceeding 25p, the insurer must give a written receipt of notice[3].

b. An assignment is also effective if it complies with the Law of Property Act 1925, s.136[4].

c. An assignment which does not satisfy either of the above provisions may nevertheless take effect as an equitable assignment, although there are some disadvantages attached to this[5].

---

1 Policies of Assurance Act 1867, ss. 1 and 5.
2 *Ibid.*, s.3.
3 *Ibid.*, s.6.
4 Para. 19.5.
5 Paras. 19.9—19.15.

25.25 An assignee need not have an insurable interest in the life[1].

---

1 *Ashley v Ashley* (1829) 3 Sim 149.

Chapter 26

Bailments and Securities

BAILMENT

26.1 A bailment is a transaction involving the transfer of *possession* of goods by one person (the 'bailor') to another (the 'bailee') on the condition, express or implied, that the bailee will either keep and deliver back the actual goods to the bailor or otherwise deal with the actual goods according to the bailor's instructions. Bailments can either be gratuitous or for reward.

26.2 *Gratuitous bailments* There will be a gratuitous bailment if a person leaves his valuables with a friend for safe-keeping while he is on holiday. Gratuitous bailments do not involve a contract and any liability for breach of duty is in tort with the result that the tortious limitation periods apply[1].

---

1 *Chesworth v Farrar* [1967] 1 QB 407, [1966] 2 All ER 107.

26.3 *Bailments for reward* Such a bailment involves a contract because consideration is provided for the bailment. The same duties may be owed under a bailment for reward as under a gratuitous bailment, but normally these duties will be increased or restricted by the terms of the contract. If the contract imposes additional obligations on a party, and they are broken, the other party can sue for breach of contract. On the other hand, if a party's obligations are validly restricted[1] the other party loses to that extent the right which he would otherwise have had to sue in tort for their breach. If a purported contract of bailment is void, e.g. the bailment of non-necessary goods by a minor, tortious liability can still be incurred[2]. Examples of bailments for reward are the hire or hire-purchase of goods, the deposit of goods at a warehouse, and the delivery of goods to a carrier or for repair.

---

1 Paras. 10.23—10.60.
2 *Ballett v Mingay* [1943] KB 281, [1943] 1 All ER 143, CA; para. 16.16.

Other transactions distinguished

26.4 A licence simply to leave goods on another's land or premises is not a bailment because no transfer of possession is involved. If X leaves his car in Y's car park, Y does not become a bailee of it, even though X pays a fee, because possession of the car is not transferred to Y[1].

---

1 *Ashby v Tolhurst* [1937] 2 KB 242, [1937] 2 All ER 837, CA.

26.5 A loan of money is not ordinarily a bailment because the borrower is not under an obligation to repay the loan with the actual notes or coins lent and can do what he likes with them[1]. However, there will be a bailment if A lends B a rare coin because there will be an obligation to return the actual coin.

---

1 *R v Hassall* (1861) Le & Ca 56.

26.6 There is no bailment where a person receives goods without his consent, as where they are sent to him by mistake or as part of a sales campaign, because the necessary obligation to deal with the goods in a particular way cannot be imposed on a person without his consent. Such a person is, somewhat surprisingly, called an 'involuntary bailee' and his duty in relation to the goods is simply to refrain from intentional damage. Thus, a theatrical producer who lost the manuscript of a play, which he had not asked to be sent to him, was held not to be liable to the sender in *Howard v Harris*[1]. Moreover, if the provisions of the Unsolicited Goods and Services Act 1971 are satisfied, a person who receives unsolicited goods is under no duty in relation to them and can do what he likes with them without incurring any liability to the sender. Section 1 of the 1971 Act provides that a recipient of unsolicited goods may treat them as if they were an unconditional gift on the part of the sender provided:

a. the goods were sent to him with a view to his acquiring them;

b. he has no reasonable cause to believe that they were sent with a view to their being acquired for the purpose of a trade or business;

c. he has not agreed to acquire nor agreed to return them; and

d. during the six months from his (the recipient's) receipt of the goods, the sender did not take possession of them and the recipient did not unreasonably refuse to permit him to do so; *or* not less than 30 days before the end of the six month period the recipient gave written notice in the specified form to the sender, and the sender did not take possession within the next 30 days and the recipient did not unreasonably refuse to permit him to do so.

---

1   (1884) Cab & El 253.

Duties of a bailee

26.7   *To take reasonable care of the goods bailed*[1]   Traditionally, it was considered that the standard of care required of a bailee varied according to the type of bailment, and, in particular, that greater care was required from a bailee for reward than from a gratuitous bailee. However, in *Houghland v R. R. Low (Luxury Coaches) Ltd*[2], Ormerod, LJ, said that the standard of care required must be determined according to the circumstances of the particular case, and not according to the type of bailment. Although this means that the standard of care is assessed in the same way as in the tort of negligence generally, there is one major distinction: once it has been proved that the goods were lost or damaged during the bailment the bailee has the onus of disproving negligence[3], whereas normally the plaintiff has to prove breach of the duty of care owed to him. A bailee will only disprove negligence if he shows that reasonable care was taken in the circumstances by himself or his employees or, in the case of a bailment for reward, by any independent contractor to whom he entrusted the goods[4]. Factors which can be taken into account in determining this include the fact that the bailee is paid for his services, whether he holds himself out as having some special skill, and the subject-matter of the bailment. Where goods have been lost, the bailee will be liable if in addition he has not taken reasonable steps to recover them, unless he can prove that they could not have been recovered even if those steps had been taken[5].

---

1   *Coggs v Bernard* (1704) 1 Smith's Leading Cases (13th ed.) 175.
2   [1962] 1 QB 694, [1962] 2 All ER 159, CA.
3   *Joseph Travers & Sons Ltd v Cooper* [1915] 1 KB 73, CA.
4   *British Road Services Ltd v Arthur V. Crutchley & Co Ltd* [1968] 1 All ER 811, CA.
5   *Coldman v Hill* [1919] 1 KB 443, CA.

26.8   If the bailee does something to the goods which is fundamentally inconsistent with the bailment, as where a carrier deviates from the agreed route or a warehouseman stores goods in a different warehouse from that agreed on, he is liable for any loss or damage occurring thereafter irrespective of negligence[1].

1   *Lilley v Doubleday* (1881) 7 QBD 510.

26.9   *Not to convert the goods bailed*   If the bailee refuses to let the bailor re-possess the goods at the end of the agreed period he is liable to the bailor for the tort of conversion, unless he can prove some lawful justification such as a lien[1].

1   Para. 26.25.

26.10   If a bailee purports to sell or otherwise dispose of the goods bailed, he is liable to the bailor for conversion irrespective of negligence[1]. The only exceptions are where the bailee is entitled to dispose of the goods by the contract or where he can avail himself of the statutory power of sale conferred by the Torts (Interference with Goods) Act 1977, s.12. The statutory power of sale arises where:

a. the bailor is in breach of an obligation to take delivery of the goods or, if the contract of bailment so provides, to give directions as to their delivery; or

b. the bailee —
   i. could impose such an obligation by giving notice to the bailor, or
   ii. can reasonably expect to be relieved of any duty to safeguard the goods on giving notice to the bailor,
but is unable to trace or communicate with the bailor.

   In order to exercise the statutory power of sale, the bailee must notify the bailor of his intention to sell, or at least take reasonable steps to communicate with him, and he must be reasonably satisfied that the bailor is the owner. Where the bailee does notify the bailor, the notice must contain certain prescribed details. After the sale, the bailee must account to the bailor for the proceeds but may deduct the costs of the sale and, where notice was given to the bailor, any sum then payable by the bailor in respect of the goods. The bailment contract can restrict or extend these provisions.

   Section 13 of the Act provides that a court order may be obtained authorising a sale by a bailee of goods to which s.12 applies. If the bailee cannot notify the bailor of his intention to sell, it is advisable for him to seek such authorisation lest his attempts at communication are subsequently impugned as unreasonable.

1   *Sachs v Miklos* [1948] 2 KB 23, [1948] 1 All ER 67, CA.

Duties of a bailor

26.11 *As to quality and fitness of the goods bailed* In the case of a gratuitous bailment, a bailor is under a duty to disclose to the bailee any defect in the goods of which he is aware[1]. It may be that he must also disclose such defects of which he ought reasonably to have been aware[2]. Where the bailment is for reward, e.g. the goods are hired out, there is an implied term of the contract that the goods are as fit for the purpose for which they are hired as reasonable care and skill can make them[3], unless the defect is apparent to the bailee and he relies on his own skill and judgment and not that of the bailor[4].

---

1 *Coughlin v Gillison* [1899] 1 QB 145, CA.
2 This depends on whether the position has been changed by the principle enunciated in *Donoghue v Stevenson*, para. 20.4.
3 *Reed v Dean* [1949] 1 KB 188; para. 8.21.
4 *Yeoman Credit Ltd v Apps* [1962] 2 QB 508, [1961] 2 All ER 281, CA.

26.12 *As to title* In a bailment for reward there is an implied term in the contract that the bailor's title is such that the bailee's possession will be undisturbed.

26.13 The reader is reminded that we discussed the obligations of a party to a hire-purchase agreement in paras. 23.75 and 23.77.

SECURITIES GENERALLY

26.14 A person's chances of having a liability owing to him satisfied are greatly enhanced if he takes or has a security, whether real or personal. A real security exists if security is provided by the pledge or mortgage of property or if a lien exists over property, whereas a personal security arises where one or more third parties guarantee the debt or other liability.

PLEDGES

26.15 A pledge is a bailment of goods as security for a loan. Land and choses in action cannot be pledged but may be the subject of a mortgage. Normally, a pledge involves the borrower of the money (the 'pledgor' or 'pawnor') transferring actual possession of the goods to the lender (the 'pledgee' or 'pawnee'). However, it may be impossible to transfer actual possession, in which case the transfer of constructive possession, e.g. the delivery of a key to the warehouse where the goods are stored, suffices, provided the pledgee obtains full control over the goods.

The pledgee may sell the goods if the pledgor fails to pay at the stated date, or, if no date is fixed, after the pledgee has made a proper demand for payment, and a reasonable time for payment has elapsed[1]. Any surplus above the amount of the debt and the costs of the sale must be handed over to the pledgor. Like any other bailee, the pledgee is liable for any negligence in relation to the goods, proof of lack of negligence being on him. The pledgee must not use the goods. If the pledgor repays the loan at the stipulated date, or, if no date is fixed, whenever he pays or validly tenders payment, the pledgee must deliver back the goods.

---

1   *Re Morritt* (1886) 18 QBD 222 at 232.

26.16   Where an 'individual' receives a loan not exceeding £5,000 by pledging goods, the agreement constitutes a regulated consumer credit agreement[1] and, apart from being subject to the general provisions of the Consumer Credit Act 1974, it is subject to the special provisions in ss.114 to 122 of that Act. These replace somewhat similar provisions in the Pawnbrokers Acts 1872 to 1960 but cover a wider range of transactions than 'pawnbroking' in its traditional sense. The provisions of the Act do not apply to pledges under a non-commercial agreement[2] or the pledge of title documents. For the purposes of the Act, an article taken subject to a pledge is said to be pawned. The relevant provisions of the Act are as follows.

---

1   Para. 23.5.
2   Para. 23.16.

26.17   *Pawn receipt*   A person who takes an article in pawn under a regulated agreement must, at that time, give to the person from whom he receives it a 'pawn receipt' in the prescribed form. If a creditor under a regulated agreement to take any article in pawn fails in his obligations under the Act to supply copies of the agreement, or to give notice of cancellation rights[1], or to give a pawn receipt, he commits an offence.

---

1   Paras. 23.27—23.29.

26.18   *Redemption*   A pawn is redeemable at any time within six months after it has been taken. Subject to this, the period within which a pawn is redeemable is the same as the period fixed by the parties for the duration of the credit secured by the pledge, or such longer period as they may agree. If the pawn is not redeemed by the end of such periods, it is nevertheless redeemable until the pawnee sells it upon notice (unless, in the case of a small agreement, the property has passed to the pawnee in the circumstances outlined in para. 26.19). A special charge may not be made for redemption after the end of the redemption period nor may charges for safe-keeping of the pawn be at a higher rate thereafter. As long as the pawn is redeemable, the pawnee must deliver the pawn to the person who surrenders the pawn receipt and pays the amount owing: he cannot be liable in tort for so doing.

A person, who is not in possession of a pawn receipt but claims to be the owner of the property pledged or to be otherwise entitled or authorised to redeem it, may do so at any time when it is redeemable, by tendering to the pawnee in place of the pawn receipt a statutory declaration in the prescribed form or, in certain cases where the amount concerned is small, a signed statement in the prescribed form. Once this is done, the redemption procedure mentioned in the last paragraph applies as if the declaration or statement was the pawn receipt and the receipt itself becomes inoperative for redemption purposes.

If the pawnee refuses without reasonable cause to allow the pawn to be redeemed he commits a criminal offence.

26.19 *Consequence of failure to redeem* If the redemption period is six months *and* the pawn is security for fixed-sum credit[1] not exceeding £15 or running-account credit[2] on which the credit limit does not exceed £15, the property passes to the pawnee on failure to redeem at the end of that period.

In any other case the pawn becomes realisable at the end of the redemption period. In such a case, the pawnee may sell it after giving the pawnor not less than the prescribed period of notice of the intention to sell. Within the prescribed period after the sale, the pawnee must give the pawnor the prescribed information in writing as to the sale, its proceeds and expenses. Where the net proceeds of sale are not less than the sum which would have been payable if the pawn had been redeemed on the date of sale, the debt secured by the pawn is discharged and any surplus must be paid to the pawnor. If the net proceeds are less than this sum, the pawnor's debt is reduced by the amount of the net proceeds of sale. 'Net proceeds of sale' is the amount realised less the expenses (if any) of the sale.

---

1 Para. 23.7.
2 Para. 23.7.

MORTGAGES

26.20 A mortgage is a transaction whereby a borrower of money (the 'mortgagor') uses property as security for the repayment of the loan to the lender (the 'mortgagee'). Mortgages of land fall outside the scope of this book, and we confine ourselves to mortgages of personal property. A mortgage of personal property can be contrasted with a pledge in this way: a pledgor transfers immediate possession to the pledgee but retains ownership of it; a mortgagor transfers, contingently, legal or equitable ownership of the property but retains possession of it.

Mortgages of choses in action

26.21　Choses in action[1], e.g. debts, life insurance policies and shares, can be the subject of a legal or equitable mortgage. A legal mortgage of a chose in action is effected by an assignment[2] of the chose to the mortgagee, with a proviso for re-assignment on due repayment of the loan. An equitable mortgage is normally effected by a deposit of the title documents to the chose. In an equitable mortgage the mortgagor retains legal ownership and the mortgage merely operates as an agreement to create a legal mortgage. A mortgage of shares is normally an equitable mortgage and is effected by the deposit of the share certificates with the mortgagee, normally with a blank instrument of transfer executed by the mortgagor, and with a proviso for the return of the documents of title on due repayment. The mortgagee can convert the mortgage into a legal one by completing the blank transfer in his own name and registering the transfer.

　　The mortgagee of a chose in action has power to sell it if the mortgagor fails to pay the amount due at the stipulated date or after reasonable notice if no date is fixed[3]. The mortgagee also has a right to foreclosure. In addition, if the mortgage is by deed executed by the mortgagor, the mortgagee has power to sell if the mortgagor fails to pay an instalment of interest for two months after it falls due, or breaks any other covenant on his part[4].

1　Para. 19.2.
2　Chap. 19.
3　*Deverges v Sandeman, Clark & Co* [1902] 1 Ch 579, CA.
4　Law of Property Act 1925, ss.101 and 103.

Mortgage of goods

26.22　A mortgage of goods may be effected orally, but it is more common to effect it by a document. Such a document must be in the form prescribed by the Bills of Sale Act (1878) Amendment Act 1882 and comply with the rules laid down by the Act. Such a document is known as a conditional bill of sale. The grantor of a conditional bill of sale is entitled to redeem the goods subject to it on due repayment of the loan. A bill of sale cannot be made in respect of shares or other choses in action.

A conditional bill of sale must be in the form set out in the Schedule to the Act of 1882: in particular, it must show the consideration, which must be not less than £30. The conditional bill must be attested by a creditable person not a party to it and must be registered at the Central Office of the Supreme Court within seven days of execution and re-registered every five years. The idea behind registration is to prevent the re-mortgage of goods already mortgaged. If the bill is not in the prescribed form, or if it is given in consideration of any sum less than £30, it is absolutely void, although the mortgagee may recover the loan with reasonable interest as money had and received[1]. Noncompliance with the requirement of attestation or that of registration means that the bill is void as against all persons, including the parties, *in respect of the goods* comprised in it, but it does not become void in other respects. This means that terms as to payment, interest and insurance remain enforceable.

By s.7 of the Act of 1882, the grantee of the bill (the mortgagee) cannot take possession of the goods comprised in it unless the grantor (the mortgagor) fails to perform a convenant in it; or becomes bankrupt; or allows the goods to be distrained for rent, rates or taxes; or fraudulently removes goods from the premises, or in certain other cases. In these cases, the mortgagor has a right to apply to the High Court within five days of the seizure for permission to redeem the goods. If it is satisfied that by payment or otherwise the cause of seizure no longer exists, the Court may make such order as it thinks just. It is implicit in the Act that after seizure the mortgagee has a power of sale[2].

---

1 *Davies v Rees* (1886) 17 QBD 408, CA.
2 *Watkins v Evans* (1887) 18 QBD 386, CA.

26.23   Difficult questions can arise in relation to 're-financing agreements' under which the owner of goods sells them to a finance company which then hires them back to the original owner under a hire-purchase agreement. Whether the agreement is void as an unregistered bill of sale or valid as a genuine hire-purchase agreement depends on the reality of the transaction, not its appearance. However, it seems that the courts will only regard the transaction as a mortgage dressed up to look like a sale followed by hire-purchase if *both* parties intended that the transaction should simply be one of loan and mortgage and did not intend that full ownership should pass to the finance company[1].

---

1 *Snook v London and West Riding Investments Ltd* [1967] 2 QB 786, [1967] 1 All ER 518, CA.

26.24 The Act of 1882 does not apply to mortgages by registered companies. These are governed by special provisions in the Companies Act 1948.

LIENS

26.25 There are three types of lien: maritime liens (rights which attach to, and are enforceable against, a ship or its cargo in respect of the payment of seamen's wages, salvage, payment of compensation for negligent collision and the like); equitable liens (such as the right of a partner on dissolution of the partnership by death, retirement or bankruptcy to have the firm's assets applied in satisfaction of the firm's liabilities); and possessory liens. Only possessory liens require further discussion in this book.

Possessory lien

26.26 A possessory lien is the right of a person in possession of goods belonging to another to retain them until his monetary claims against that other are satisfied. This definition serves to distinguish the other two types of lien since they do not depend on the possession of the thing subject to the lien. A possessory lien can also be distinguished from a mortgage in that it does not involve the transfer of ownership to the person with the lien (the 'lienor'). Possessory liens can be of two types: particular or general.

Particular liens
26.27 A particular lien is the right to retain particular goods in the lienor's possession until payment of a debt in respect of those goods has been made. At common law, people who are legally obliged to provide a service, e.g. common carriers[1], have a particular lien on the goods of those for whom the services are performed, and so do bailees who have done work, which has improved the goods, at the request of the owner[2]. It follows that the repairer of goods has a lien on them at common law, but a person who merely stores them or maintains or services them does not, because this does not amount to improving them[3]. In addition, in *Woodworth v Conroy*[4], the Court of Appeal held that accountants have a particular lien for unpaid fees over any books, files and papers delivered to them in the course of their professional work by clients, and also over any other document which comes into their possession while acting as their clients' agents in the course of their ordinary professional work. Architects and arbitrators have a similar lien. These common law rights of lien cannot arise until

the carriage, work, etc. contracted to be done has been completed, except that, if the bailor revokes his order once work has commenced, the bailee has a lien for the work actually done[5].

By statute, an unpaid seller of goods has a lien on them until payment[6]. It is, of course, possible for a contract to confer a particular lien on the parties in particular circumstances.

---

1 Para. 27.2.
2 *Scarfe v Morgan* (1838) 4 M & W 270.
3 *Hatton v Car Maintenance Co* (1914) 30 TLR 275.
4 [1976] QB 884, [1976] 1 All ER 107, CA.
5 *Lilley v Barnsley* (1884) 2 Mood & R 548.
6 Paras. 22.89 and 22.90.

General lien

26.28 A general lien is the right to retain goods in the lienor's possession until *all* his monetary claims against the person to whom the goods belong have been satisfied, irrespective of whether they relate to those goods. A general lien only arises by contract or by trade usage, as in the case of bankers, solicitors, mercantile agents and stockbrokers[1]. A general lien under trade usage can, of course, be restricted or excluded by an agreement to the contrary.

---

1 *Brandao v Barnett* (1846) 12 Cl & Fin 787, HL (bankers); *ex parte Sterling* (1809) 16 Ves 258 (solicitors); *Cowell v Simpson* (1809) 16 Ves 275 at 280 (mercantile agents); *Re London and Globe Finance Corpn* [1902] 2 Ch 416 (stockbrokers).

Enforcement of lien

26.29 A lien is simply a right to retain goods until satisfaction of the relevant monetary claims. Consequently, no claim can be made for storage or any other expense incurred in exercising the lien[1]. Nor is there a right to sell the goods[2], except where this is provided by trade usage, contract or statute. We have already referred to the unpaid seller's rights to sell goods and to the right of sale over uncollected goods[3]. Apart from these exceptional cases, the lienor must apply to the courts for an order to sell[4]. In comparison, a pledgee always has a right of sale if the goods pledged are not redeemed in a certain period.

---

1 *Spears v Hartley* (1800) 3 Esp 81.
2 *White v Spettigue* (1845) 13 M & W 603.
3 Paras. 22.94 and 26.10.
4 *Larner v Fawcett* [1950] 2 All ER 727 CA.

Termination of lien

26.30 Obviously, a possessory lien is lost if the lienor loses possession of the goods. It is also lost if the debt to which the lien relates is paid, or the valid tender of it is refused, or if the lienor takes a security in substitution for the lien.

GUARANTEES

26.31 We showed in para. 7.8 that a contract of guarantee, otherwise known as a contract of surety, has the following characteristics:

a. Three parties must be involved: a creditor (C); a principal debtor (PD), whose liability may be actual or prospective, contractual or tortious; and the guarantor or surety (G), who undertakes to discharge PD's liability if PD fails to do so himself. If there never has been a person who can be described as the principal debtor, or if the purported principal debtor cannot be legally liable (as in the case of a void loan to a minor)[1], there cannot be a contract of guarantee.

b. The principal debtor must continue to have the primary liability towards the creditor, the guarantor being liable only in the event of his default. Subject to the exceptions mentioned in para. 7.9, a contract of guarantee is unenforceable unless evidenced in writing in the prescribed manner[2].

---

1 *Coutts & Co v Browne-Lecky* [1947] KB 104, [1946] 2 All ER 207, DC; para. 10.16, c.
2 Statute of Frauds 1677, s.4; para. 7.7.

26.32 A guarantee may be intended to cover one transaction, e.g. a particular debt, in which case it normally terminates when the principal liability is discharged. On the other hand, a guarantee may be a continuing guarantee, i.e. one which is intended to cover a series of transactions, as where G guarantees PD's bank overdraft up to £1,000.

Guarantor's liability

26.33 G's liability does not arise until PD has defaulted. Unless there is a term to the contrary, C can sue G immediately the default occurs, without first suing PD. G's liability can never exceed PD's liability but, apart from that, the extent of G's liability depends on the terms of the guarantee: it may be the full amount of PD's liability or some lesser amount, and it may be sole liability or joint and several liability with co-guarantors.

Rights of co-guarantors between themselves

26.34 A guarantor who pays or is required to pay more than his due share under a guarantee is always entitled to a contribution from any co-guarantors of the *same* debt or liability, but not if each guarantor has undertaken liability for a specified part of the debt. It is irrelevant that the guarantors are bound by different instruments, unless they are bound for equal portions of PD's debt and each guarantee is a distinct and separate transaction, in which case there is no right of contribution. Where a right to contribution exists, each co-guarantor must normally contribute an equal amount, but if the co-guarantors have guaranteed different amounts they are only liable to contribute proportionately to their respective liabilities[1]. Thus, if G1 guarantees PD's debts to C up to £200 and G2 guarantees them up to £100, and PD then defaults, owing C £150 which C recovers from G1, G1 can claim a contribution of £50 from G2. If a co-guarantor is insolvent, the contributions of the other co-guarantors are reckoned on the basis of the number of solvent co-guarantors[2].

---

1 *Ellesmere Brewery Co v Cooper* [1896] 1 QB 75.
2 *Ex parte Snowdon* (1881) 17 Ch D 44, CA.

Guarantor's rights

26.35 Once the debt has become payable by PD, G has the following rights.

Rights against the principal debtor G is entitled to call upon PD to relieve him from liability by paying off the debt and can obtain a court order compelling PD to do so. However, if G does pay under the guarantee, he is entitled to be indemnified by PD to the extent of any payment properly made under the guarantee. In addition, G can recover from PD the costs of defending any action brought on the guarantee by C *provided* that these were incurred in reasonable defence of PD's interests or PD authorised the defence.

26.36 *Rights against the creditor* G can require C to call on PD to discharge his liability, but C is not obliged to sue PD before having recourse to G. However, if C sues G on the guarantee G can raise any set-off or counter-claim possessed by PD against C[1]. Once he has paid C, G may sue PD in C's name (although he must give C an indemnity for costs) or in his own name (if he obtains an assignment of the guaranteed debt). In this respect it is important to remember that G is entitled to be subrogated to all C's existing rights against PD in respect of the debt[2]. In addition, G is entitled to have assigned to him any security held by C in respect of the debt[3].

---

1 *Bechervaise v Lewis* (1872) LR 7 CP 372.
2 *Re Lamplugh Iron Ore Co Ltd* [1927] 1 Ch 308.
3 Mercantile Law Amendment Act 1856, s.5.

Discharge of the guarantor

26.37 A contract of guarantee may be discharged in the same way as any other contract. In addition, G may be discharged in a number of other cases, the most important being:

a. Discharge of PD by C[1], unless C reserves his rights against G.

b. Discharge by C of a co-guarantor against whom there is a right of contribution[2].

c. Variation of the contract guaranteed by G without G's consent, unless the alteration is manifestly insubstantial or necessarily beneficial to G[3].

d. Legally enforceable agreement between C and PD whereby PD is given further time to pay, unless G consents. Where there is a continuing guarantee and the agreement simply gives PD time to pay a particular instalment, the extent of G's discharge depends on whether the instalment is payable under one indivisible contract, in which case G is discharged from all further liability under the guarantee[4], or whether each instalment relates to a separate contract in a series, in which case G's discharge only relates to that contract[5]. There is one exception to these rules: G is not discharged if C, when giving time to pay to PD, reserves his rights against G[6].

e. Valid revocation of the guarantee by G. A contract for a non-continuing guarantee can only be revoked if the contract expressly provides for this. In the case of a continuing guarantee of a type whose true nature is that of a standing offer, as where an overdraft is guaranteed, the guarantee can be revoked at any time as to future debts incurred by PD but G will remain liable in relation to existing debts to which the guarantee applies. On the other hand, if the guarantee is given in return for a once and for all consideration by C, as where G guarantees PD's engagements as a Lloyd's underwriter in consideration of him being admitted as such by Lloyd's, it is irrevocable unless there is a term to the contrary[7].

f. Death of G. G's death does not affect liability for past transactions; but if G could have revoked the guarantee in his lifetime, the guarantee

will be revoked in relation to transactions subsequent to the time when
C has notice of G's death and G's estate will not be liable for them[8], but
otherwise the guarantee is irrevocable[9].

---

1   *Hewison v Ricketts* (1894) 63 LJQB 711.
2   *Smith v Wood* [1929] 1 Ch 14, CA.
3   *Holme v Brunskill* (1877) 3 QBD 495, CA.
4   *Midland Motor Showrooms Ltd v Newman* [1929] 2 KB 256, CA.
5   *Croydon Gas Co v Dickinson* (1876) 2 CPD 46.
6   *Kearsley v Cole* (1847) 16 M & W 128 at 135.
7   *Lloyd's v Harper* (1880) 16 Ch D 290, CA.
8   *Coulthart v Clementson* (1879) 5 QBD 42.
9   *Lloyd's v Harper* (1880) 16 Ch D 290, CA.

Chapter 27
Contracts of Carriage

CARRIAGE ON LAND

27.1 The basis of the law relating to contracts of carriage on land is the common law, especially that relating to common carriers, but it has been modified considerably by statute.

Common carriers

27.2 At common law there are two types of carrier: a common carrier and a private carrier. A *common carrier* is a person who, by way of business, holds himself out as being ready for hire to transport goods or persons or both for anyone who chooses to employ him. A person can be a common carrier even though he only holds himself out as a carrier of certain goods or of goods or persons between particular places, provided that he professes that he will carry for *anyone* who requests carriage for hire. A *private carrier* is someone who reserves the right to accept or reject requests for carriage whether or not his vehicle is full[1], or who undertakes carriage only as a casual operation.

The division between the two types of carrier is of great importance because:

a. A private carrier is never bound to carry; but a common carrier is under a duty to carry those goods or passengers which he professes he will carry for anyone offering to pay the hire, unless:

   i. his vehicle is already full; or

   ii. the destination is not one to which he usually carries; or

   iii. the goods are of such a nature as to subject him to extraordinary risk[2]; or

   iv. the goods are not properly packed[3].

b. In relation to goods, a private carrier is like any other bailee and therefore, subject to the express terms of the contract of carriage, is only liable for loss or damage if he, or his employee, has caused it negligently, although he has the burden of disproving negligence. On the other hand, a common carrier's liability in relation to goods is that of an 'insurer'. This means that he is liable for any loss or damage, whether occasioned by fault or not, unless there are express contractual terms validly excluding such liability. However, this general rule of strict liability is subject to four excepted perils, in which cases the common carrier is not liable:

i. *Act of God* To escape liability under this heading the common carrier must prove that the loss or damage was attributable to natural causes directly and exclusively without human intervention, which could not be foreseen and whose consequences could not have been prevented by taking reasonable precautions[4].

ii. *Act of the Queen's enemies* The common carrier is not liable if the loss or damage is caused by acts by a hostile foreign government.

iii. *Negligence of the consignor* The carrier is not liable for loss or damage caused by the consignor's negligence, e.g. defective packing of the goods, even if he was aware of the defect when he received the goods[5].

iv. *Inherent vice of the goods* The carrier is not liable for loss or damage to the goods carried which is caused by something inherent in, or natural deterioration of, them, over which he has no control[6]. In addition, if, for any reason, special care is required, the common carrier must be informed of this otherwise he cannot be liable for damage which *would not have occurred but for it*[7].

c. In relation to passengers, common and private carriers are in the same position, in that they can only be liable if they are negligent.

---

1   *Belfast Ropework Co Ltd v Bushell* [1918] 1 KB 210.
2   *Edwards v Sherratt* (1801) 1 East 604.
3   *Sutcliffe v Great Western Rly Co* [1910] 1 KB 478 at 503.
4   *Nugent v Smith* (1876) 1 CPD 243.
5   *Gould v South Eastern and Chatham Rly Co* [1920] 2 KB 186, DC.
6   *Blower v Great Western Rly Co* (1872) LR 7 CP 655, DC.
7   *Baldwin v London, Chatham and Dover Rly Co* (1882) 9 QBD 582, DC.

Rights and duties of a common carrier
27.3 *Duties* In addition to his obligation to carry goods and his strict obligation as to the safety and security of the goods, a common carrier has a number of rights and other duties provided by the common law in relation to goods. He must carry them without unnecessary delay and by his ordinary route, or such other route as the consignor agrees to,

and must not deviate from it unnecessarily[1]. Another duty is that he must deliver the goods at the place specified by the consignor, unless he is instructed by the consignee to deliver them elsewhere or is so instructed by the consignor (provided that person retained the right to do so)[2]. Delivery must be made within a reasonable time[3]. Where it is customary for the consignee to collect the goods from the carrier, the carrier must keep them for a reasonable time at his own risk and his liability as a common carrier will continue until such time has elapsed (or the consignee has collected the goods)[4].

---

1 *Briddon v Great Northern Rly Co* (1858) 28 LJ Ex 51; *Myers v London and South Western Rly Co* (1869) LR 5 CP 1.
2 *London and North Western Rly Co v Bartlett* (1861) 7 H & N 400; *Scothorn v South Staffordshire Rly Co* (1853) 8 Exch 341.
3 *Sims and Co v Midland Rly Co* [1913] 1 KB 103, DC.
4 *Bourne v Gatliffe* (1844) 11 Cl & Fin 45, HL.

27.4 *Rights* A common carrier is entitled to payment in advance, and if he is not paid he can refuse to carry, but his charge must be a reasonable one for his services. A common carrier has a lien on the goods carried for his charges, which he can enforce against both the consignor and the consignee, but as a rule it is only a particular lien[1]. If goods of a dangerous character are given to a common carrier for carriage, the consignor is deemed to warrant that the goods are fit to be carried safely, unless the carrier knows of the danger. If the goods are not so fit, the consignor is liable in damages for breach of this implied warranty even though he was ignorant of the danger. An example is provided by *Bamfield v Goole and Sheffield Transport Co Ltd*[2], where consignors of casks of ferro-silicon described them to the common carrier as 'general cargo'. Neither the consignors nor the carrier knew that ferro-silicon is dangerous. The carrier was killed by poisonous gases given off by the ferro-silicon. Even though the consignors were not negligent in being ignorant of the danger, they were held liable to the carrier's widow in damages for breach of the implied warranty that the goods were safe to be carried.

---

1 *Rushforth v Hadfield* (1805) 6 East 519, (1806) 7 East 224; para. 26.27.
2 [1910] 2 KB 94, CA.

Carriers Act 1830
27.5 This Act modifies the common law liability of a common carrier *by land* and also, in one respect, restricts his power to limit liability. The principal provisions of the Act are as follows:

a. No common carrier is liable, even if he or his employees are negligent[1], for loss or injury to certain specified articles delivered to him for carriage when their value exceeds £10, unless at the time of delivery their value was declared *and* any increased charge demanded has been paid or agreed to be paid[2]. The specified articles include: gold and silver articles, including coins, jewellery, paintings, watches and clocks, and silks and furs. A common carrier can only demand an increased charge for such parcels if he displays a legible notice of the increased charge scale in a conspicuous place in his office or receiving house. Whether or not an increased charge is demanded, it is only if a declaration of value has not been made that the carrier can claim the exemption from his common law liability.

b. This exemption does not extend to wilful wrongdoing or to criminal acts by employees which cause loss or injury[3], nor to damage caused by delay.

c. A common carrier cannot limit his liability by a public notice[4], but the Act itself does not prevent him limiting or excluding his liability by a clause in the contract of carriage[5].

---

1 *Hinton v Dibbin* (1842) 2 QB 646.
2 Carriers Act 1830, s.1.
3 *Ibid.*, s.8.
4 *Ibid.*, s.4.
5 *Ibid.*, s.6. For limitations on exemption clauses, see paras. 10.23–10.59.

The normal position today

27.6   Although a carrier by road may act as a common carrier, most road hauliers reserve the right to accept or reject goods, and are therefore not common carriers, or use the standard Conditions of Carriage of the Road Haulage Association (or similar conditions) which expressly state that they are not common carriers. By statute, the National Freight Corporation, which is a publicly owned undertaking required, in conjunction with the British Railways Board, to provide, secure or promote the provision of properly integrated services for the carriage of goods in Great Britain by road and rail, is not a common carrier[1], nor is the London Transport Executive[2].

We dealt above with the liability of private, as opposed to common, carriers. Because the Carriers Act 1830 does not apply to them, their liability is theoretically unlimited, although in practice private carriers insert exemption clauses, excluding or limiting their liability, into contracts of carriage.

---

1   Transport Act 1968, s.2(2).
2   Transport (London) Act 1969, s.6(2), applying the Transport Act 1962, s.43(6).

27.7 Three pieces of statutory intervention relating to carriers by road must be mentioned. First, the Road Traffic Act 1960, s.151, enacts that any provision in a contract for the carriage of passengers by road in a public service vehicle (i.e. a bus or coach operating as part of a regular service, the operator normally being a common carrier of the passengers and their luggage) is void if it purports to negate or limit the liability of the carrier in respect of the death of or personal injury to a passenger. Secondly, the Carriage of Goods by Road Act 1965 puts into domestic effect the Convention on Contracts for the International Carriage of Goods by Road, the text of which is set out in the Schedule and which lays down rules (known as the CMR conditions) governing contracts for the carriage of goods by road between the territories of signatory states. The Convention imposes liability on the carrier, except in specified limited cases, for loss of, or damage or delay to, the goods, but limits his liability to 25 gold francs per kilo, unless the consignor declares a higher value, or a special interest in delivery, and pays an agreed surcharge, or the loss or damage is caused by the carrier's wilful misconduct. The provisions of the Convention cannot be contracted out of by carriers. Thirdly, the Carriage of Passengers by Road Act 1974, which is not in force at the time of writing, gives domestic effect to the Convention on the Contract for the International Carriage of Passengers and Luggage by Road. The Convention has similar provisions to those of the Carriage of Goods by Road Convention. The limit on the carrier's liability is 250,000 gold francs in respect of each victim.

27.8 The old railway companies were common carriers, but, since the Transport Act 1962, the British Railways Board is not a common carrier by rail and it has power to demand such charges for its services, and subject to such conditions, as it thinks fit[1].

Goods which are accepted for carriage are usually carried subject to the Railway Board's General Conditions for the Carriage of Goods. There are special conditions for the carriage of livestock and of fuel, and sometimes special contracts are made with trade customers which modify the normal conditions of carriage. The General Conditions are divisible into two main parts:

a. *Carriage at Board's risk* If goods are carried in this way, the Board undertakes a strict liability for loss or damage analogous to that of a common carrier of goods, except that the list of excepted perils is considerably wider. In the case of delay or unreasonable deviation, the Board is liable unless it proves that the consequent loss was not caused by its negligence. There is a maximum limit on the Board's liability of £800 per ton of gross weight of the consignment if the whole of it is lost or a proportionate sum if part of it is lost. The board is not liable where the consignor or consignee has been fraudulent.

b. *Carriage at owner's risk* In this case the goods are carried at a cheaper rate, but the Board's liability is more restricted. Generally, the Board is not liable for loss or damage unless it is proved that this was caused by the wilful neglect of the Board or its employees. There is one exception: in the event of non-delivery of the whole consignment or of any separate package forming part of it, but not mis-delivery, delay, damage etc., the Board is in the same position as it would have been if carriage had been at Board's risk.

---

1 Transport Act 1962, s.43(6).

CARRIAGE OF GOODS BY SEA

Contract of affreightment

27.9 A contract for the carriage of goods by sea is known as a contract of affreightment. Such a contract can take one of two forms:

a. it may be a charterparty contract (i.e. the hire of the ship herself) between the charterer and the shipowner and signed by both of them; or

b. it may be a contract between the shipper and the carrier (e.g. the shipowner) for the carriage of goods in a 'general ship', the terms being evidenced by a bill of lading signed by the master of the ship.

The clauses in a bill of lading are very good evidence of the terms of the preceding contract of affreightment; but the bill of lading does not constitute the contract itself and, in the event of conflict between the oral contract and the bill of lading, the former prevails[1]. However, if the bill of lading is indorsed to a third party it becomes *conclusive* evidence of the terms of the contract of affreightment so that evidence to contradict it can no longer be introduced[2].

---

1 *The Ardennes* [1951] 1 KB 55, [1950] 2 All ER 517.
2 Bills of Lading Act 1855, s.1.

27.10 Where a shipper contracts with a shipowner by way of charterparty, a bill of lading is obviously not required as evidence of the contract of affreightment, but a bill of lading will usually be issued to him because he will require one as a document of title if he wishes to transfer the goods while they are in transit. The terms of the bill of lading sometimes conflict with those in the charterparty, and in such a case the position is as follows. As between the charterer and the shipowner, the charterparty regulates the carriage and the bill of lading merely acts as a receipt and a document of title. On the other hand, if the charterer assigns the bill of lading to a third party for value the contractual relations between the shipowner and the indorsee are governed by the bill of lading[1], and the indorsee is not affected by the charterparty except to the extent that the bill of lading refers to and incorporates any or all of the terms of the charterparty. A term in the charterparty cannot be incorporated if it is inconsistent with an express term of the bill of lading, but apart from this the extent of the incorporation depends on the construction of the incorporating clause. General words of incorporation, such as 'freight and all other conditions as per charter', will only be effective to incorporate charterparty provisions as to freight, discharge, demurrage[2] and the like into the bill[3], depending on the words used. Only if specific words, like 'all the terms, conditions, clauses and exceptions contained in the said charterparty apply to this bill of lading and are deemed to be incorporated herein', are used will there be a complete incorporation of the charterparty provisions in the bill of lading[4].

---

1   *Leduc & Co v Ward* (1888) 20 QBD 475 at 479.
2   Para. 27.13.
3   E.g. *Porteus v Watney* (1878) 3 QBD 227, affd. at 534, CA.
4   *The Annefield* [1971] P 168, [1971] 1 All ER 394, CA.

Charterparties

27.11 A charterparty is a contract providing for the hiring of a whole ship. The charterer may hire the ship to carry his own cargo, or to use her as a 'general ship' carrying others' goods under bills of lading. Normally, the charterer only obtains the use of a ship, the possession and control over her remaining in the owner who continues to be liable to pay the master and crew. Charterparties of this type are:

a. *a voyage charterparty*, which is the charter of a ship for a particular voyage, the consideration for the carriage of the cargo being the agreed charter freight;

b. *a time charterparty*, which is the charter of a ship for a particular period, the consideration for the use of the vessel being the payment of charter hire, usually paid monthly in advance.

Sometimes, however, the possession and control over the ship, as well as the use of her, are transferred to the charterer for the specified duration of the charter, the master and crew becoming the charterer's employees for that period. Such charterparties are described as *charterparties by demise* (or bare-boat charters) and are not very common. We do not consider them any further. In what follows we concentrate on voyage charterparties, although much of what we say is equally applicable to time charterparties.

Express terms

27.12 For example, in a voyage charterparty there are usually express undertakings by *the shipowner* that the ship is in a particular position at the date of the charterparty and expected ready to load on a particular date, that she will proceed to the agreed place of loading with all convenient speed (or so near thereto as she may safely get and lie, always afloat), and that the ship shall proceed with all convenient speed to her destination (or so near thereto as she may safely get and lie, always afloat) and there deliver the cargo on payment of the freight (the consideration for the charter). The words 'as near thereunto as she can safely get' enable the shipowner to demand that the ship be loaded, or to deliver the cargo, at some place other than the specified port or berth if the ship cannot actually get there because of some physical obstacle, such as ice or blockade, which cannot be overcome within a reasonable time. 'Always afloat' means that if the ship cannot load or deliver without touching the ground at the specified port, this may be done at the nearest safe port.

27.13 For his part, *the charterer* usually undertake, upon notification that the ship is ready to load, to bring the cargo to the ship and deliver it to the master of the ship alongside her, the charterer paying stevedores and lightermen. If he fails to do so, he is liable despite the absence of personal fault, in the absence of an express stipulation to the contrary[1]. Other express obligations normally undertaken by the charterer are that he will pay the freight on the arrival of the ship at her destination, as well as all dues and duties on the cargo, and that the ship will be unloaded within the specified number of *lay days*. Lay days are usually either:

a. 'working days', i.e. days on which work is usually done at the port of destination;

b. 'running days', i.e. every day; or

c. 'weather working days', i.e. those 'working days' on which the weather permits the relevant work to be done.

The lay days commence when the ship is an 'arrived ship', i.e. when she has arrived at her destination ready to load or unload. If the charterparty specifies a particular dock or wharf, the ship will only be an 'arrived ship' when she gets there. But when no dock or wharf is named, but simply a port, she will be an 'arrived ship' when she comes to rest in the named port and is at the immediate and effective disposition of the charterer[2]. Another condition which must be fulfilled before laytime can begin to run is that the ship must in every way be ready to load or unload[3]. However, in the case of loading (but not generally unloading) lay days cannot ·commence to run until the charterer has notice that the ship is ready to load[4].

As soon as the lay days have commenced to run the charterer is under an absolute obligation to complete the loading or unloading within the specified lay days[5]. The only exceptions are where delay is caused by the fault of the shipowner[6] or where the loading or unloading are unlawful by the local law. The charterer is entitled to extend the loading or unloading over the whole of the specified lay days, but if he completes it before those days have expired the shipowner is obliged to pay him 'despatch money'.

If no lay time is specified the charterer is obliged to load and unload within a reasonable time. This is important because whereas, for example, a strike of stevedores, does not excuse the charterer if he fails to complete within the specified lay days, it will be taken into account in assessing a reasonable time[7].

A related provision found in a voyage charterparty is one for 'demurrage', i.e. liquidated damages[8], which the charterers undertake to pay for each day's detention if they fail to load or unload within the specified lay days or a reasonable time. In the absence of a demurrage provision (or if a period of demurrage is exceeded) the charterer who detains the ship is liable to pay unliquidated damages to the shipowner.

---

1 *Grant & Co v Coverdale, Todd & Co* (1884) 9 App Cas 470, HL.
2 *E. L. Oldendorff & Co GmbH v Tradax Export SA* [1974] AC 479, [1973] 3 All ER 148, HL.
3 *Government of Ceylon v Société Franco-Tunisienne D'Armement-Tunis* [1962] 2 QB 416, [1960] 3 All ER 797.
4 *Stanton v Austin* (1872) LR 7 CP 651; *Harman v Clarke* (1815) 4 Camp 159.
5 *Porteus v Watney* (1878) 3 QBD 227, affd. at 534, CA.
6 *Budgett & Co v Binnington & Co* [1891] 1 QB 35, CA.
7 *Hick v Raymond and Reid* [1893] AC 22, HL.
8 Para. 12.12.

27.14　Other common express terms relate to the effect on the charterparty of occurrences such as strikes, wars and ice, and to the procedure to be adopted in the event of any dispute arising under it.

27.15 *Exemption clauses* In the absence of express stipulations in the charterparty and subject to certain statutory limitations which we mentioned in para. 27.5, a shipowner who is a common carrier is strictly liable for any loss of or damage to goods in transit (unless, of course, this is caused by act of God, or by the Queen's enemies, or by the negligence of the shipper, or by the inherent vice of the goods)[1]. It is uncertain whether a shipowner who is not a common carrier has the same liability or is only liable, as a bailee, if he cannot prove lack of negligence.

What we have just said is rather academic because charterparties invariably contain a clause exempting the shipowner from liability for lost or damaged cargo or for delay. Such a clause may list a large number of excepted perils in addition to the four mentioned in the last paragraph, e.g. 'arrests or restraints of princes, rulers and peoples' (such as interferences by a government taking forcible possession of the goods, or state prohibitions on unloading), 'fire', 'barratry of the master and crew' (wilful wrongdoing by them against the ship and goods), 'gales', 'stranding' (going aground), and other perils of navigation. However, usually, the exemption is provided more briefly and more completely by a clause limiting the shipowner's liability, for loss of or damage to the cargo or for delay, to cases where this is caused by improper or negligent stowage by or on behalf of the shipowner, or by personal lack of due diligence on the part of the shipowner or his manager to see that the ship is seaworthy and properly manned and equipped. Such a clause also provides that the shipowner is not to be liable for any loss, damage or delay arising from any other cause.

---

1 Para. 27.2. b.

27.16 *Cesser clause* Such a clause provides that the charterer's liability shall cease on the cargo being loaded, and is inserted where the shipowner is to look to the cargo owner, not the charterer, for payment of freight. A cesser clause is usually inserted in consideration of the granting to the shipowner of a lien on the cargo to ensure payment of freight and demurrage, the lien being conferred in the bill of lading. If the cesser clause and the lien are not co-extensive, the cesser clause only relieves the charterer to the extent that the shipowner has an effective lien against the claim in question[1]. A fortiori, if no lien is granted to the shipowner the charterer is not relieved from liabilities[2].

---

1 *Hansen v Harrold Bros* [1894] 1 QB 612, CA.
2 *Clink v Radford & Co* [1891] 1 QB 625, CA.

Implied terms
27.17. The court can imply a term into a charterparty, where this is necessary to give it business efficacy and make it a workable agreement, in such manner as the parties would clearly have done if they had applied their minds to the contingency which has arisen[1].

In addition, there are implied in every charterparty, in the absence of an express provision to the contrary, undertakings by the shipowner as to the seaworthiness of his ship, as to reasonable despatch and as to non-deviation. In addition, there is an implied undertaking by the charterer not to ship dangerous goods.

---

1   Para. 8.22.

27.18   *Undertaking as to seaworthiness*   In a voyage charterparty, the shipowner impliedly undertakes that the ship is actually seaworthy when she sails from the port of loading and that she is fit to receive and carry the particular[1] cargo, but not that she will continue to be so throughout the whole of the voyage[2]. Seaworthiness is a relative concept: the question is whether the ship is fit to undertake the particular voyage[3]. Bad stowage amounts to breach of the undertaking as to seaworthiness if it endangers the ship's safety, but not if it merely affects the cargo[4]. Inefficiency or insufficiency of the crew can also constitute unseaworthiness[5], and so can the fact that the ship is not fitted with the necessary loading and unloading tackle[6]. In a time charterparty there is an implied undertaking as to seaworthiness at the beginning of the time[7], but not at the beginning of each voyage.

---

1   *Ciampa v British India Steam Navigation Co Ltd* [1915] 2 KB 774.
2   *Steel v State Line SS Co* (1877) 3 App Cas 72, HL.
3   *Thin v Richards & Co* [1892] 2 QB 141, CA.
4   *Elder, Dempster & Co Ltd v Paterson, Zochonis & Co Ltd* [1924] AC 522, HL.
5   *Hong Kong Fir Shipping Co Ltd v Kawasaki Kisen Kaisha Ltd* [1962] 2 QB 26, [1962] 1 All ER 474, CA.
6   *Hang Fung Shipping and Trading Co Ltd v Mullion & Co Ltd* [1966] 1 Lloyd's Rep 511.
7   *Giertsen v Turnbull & Co* 1908 SC 1101.

27.19   *Undertaking as to reasonable despatch*   The shipowner impliedly undertakes that the ship shall be ready to commence the voyage and to load the cargo, and shall proceed upon and complete the voyage with reasonable despatch[1]. If delay occurs without the fault of either party and is such as to frustrate the charterparty, both parties are discharged from further liability. The Law Reform (Frustrated Contracts) Act 1943 does not apply to a voyage charterparty[2].

---

1   *MacAndrew v Chapple* (1866) LR ! CP 643.
2   Para. 11.18, a.

27.20   *Undertaking not to deviate*   The shipowner undertakes that the ship shall not deviate unnecessarily from her proper course, which is the stipulated, shortest or usual route. Deviations to protect property are often expressly permitted by a 'liberty to deviate' clause in the charterparty, but in the absence of such a clause a deviation to save property is a breach of this undertaking, although a deviation to save life is not[1].

---

1   *Scaramanga v Stamp* (1880) 5 CPD 295, CA.

27.21 *Undertaking not to ship dangerous goods* The charterer impliedly undertakes not to ship goods which are of such a dangerous character or so dangerously packed that the shipowner could not discover the danger by reasonable diligence, unless notice of the danger is given to the shipowner[1]. Goods may be dangerous in this context if they may involve the detention of the ship, e.g. because they cannot be unloaded at their destination without infringing the local law[2].

---

1   *Brass v Maitland* (1856) 6 E & B 470.
2   *Mitchell, Cotts & Co v Steel Bros & Co Ltd* [1916] 2 KB 610.

Nature of the terms of a charterparty
27.22   Some terms have been classified by the courts as conditions and therefore have this status in every charterparty. An example is the express term that the ship is 'now in the port of . . .'[1]. Other terms may be so classified by the courts when they come up for decision, the test being that which we outlined in para. 10.20. If a condition is broken, the injured party has an option to rescind or affirm the charterparty and, in either event, to bring an action for damages. Other terms, such as the three implied undertakings by the shipowner mentioned above[2] are intermediate terms. The consequences of their breach depend on whether the effect of the breach is such as to deprive the injured party of substantially the whole benefit which it was intended that he should obtain under the charterparty[3]. If it does, his remedies are the same as for breach of a condition; otherwise he can only claim damages[3].

Some undertakings, e.g. the implied undertaking by the shipper that the goods are not dangerous, have been held to be warranties, so that the only remedy for their breach is an action for damages.

---

1   *Behn v Burness* (1863) 3 B & S 751.
2   *Hong Kong Fir Shipping* case [1962] 2 QB 26, [1962] 1 All ER 474, CA.
3   Para. 10.21.

Limitation of liability

Merchant Shipping Act 1894
27.23   This Act, as amended, excludes or restricts the liability of an 'owner' of a ship in certain circumstances. An 'owner' in this context

includes a charterer, and any person interested in or in possession of the ship, and any manager or operator of the ship[1].

---

1 Merchant Shipping (Liability of Shipowners and Others) Act 1958, s.3.

27.24 Section 502 provides that an 'owner' *of a British Ship* shall *not be liable* for the following types of damage *if they occur without his fault or privity*:

a. where any goods on board are lost or damaged by reason of fire on board the ship;

b. where any gold, silver, watches, jewels or precious stones on board are lost by robbery or theft, unless their true nature and value has been declared at the time of shipment, either in the bill of lading or otherwise in writing.

27.25 Section 503 provides that if certain other types of damage occur *without the fault or privity* of the 'owner' his *liability is restricted* to specified amounts, *irrespective of whether the ship is British or foreign*. The types of damage are:

a. loss of life or personal injury to any person being carried in the ship;

b. damage or loss to goods on board the ship;

c. loss of life or personal injury to any person not carried in the ship, or loss or damage to any property not on board, or the infringement of any rights, caused by the act or omission of any person (whether on board or not) in the navigation or management of the ship, or any other act or omission of any person on board.

Where liability is restricted, the 'owner's' liability is restricted:

a. for loss of life or personal injury (alone or together with loss of or damage to vessels or goods), to an aggregate amount not exceeding 3,100 gold francs (£114.89)[1] per ton of the ship's tonnage, a ship of less than 300 tons being treated as though she was of 300 tons for this purpose alone;

b. for damage or loss to vessels or goods (whether or not there is in addition loss of life or personal injury), to an amount equivalent to 1,000 gold francs (£37.06) per ton of the ship's tonnage.

Where two or more liabilities are incurred through the same occurrence, the claimants must share the statutory funds rateably if they are inadequate for all claims[2]. If there are claims in respect of life and of goods and the statutory fund for loss of life (i.e. 3,100 gold francs x ship's tonnage) is insufficient to satisfy the claims, the balance of these claims and the claims for vessels or goods will rank equally against the other statutory fund (i.e. 1,000 gold francs x ship's tonnage)[3].

---

1 Merchant Shipping (Limitation of Liability) (Sterling Equivalent) Order 1975.
2 *Mersey Docks and Harbour Board v Hay* [1923] AC 345, HL.
3 *The Victoria* (1888) 13 PD 125.

27.26 It must be emphasised that these exclusions or restrictions of liability only apply where the loss or damage occurred without the fault or privity of the 'owner'. The onus is on the 'owner' to prove this. Where the 'owner' is a corporation, the fault or privity, within the scope of his authority, of a person who is the directing mind and will of the corporation, will be the fault or privity of the corporation[1], but no owner loses the protection of ss.502 and 503 simply because of the fault or privity of a mere employee.

---

1 *Lennard's Carrying Co Ltd v Asiatic Petroleum Co Ltd* [1915] AC 705, HL; *The Norman* [1960] 1 Lloyd's Rep 1.

Bills of lading

27.27 Apart from being evidence of the contract of affreightment, a bill of lading has two other functions:

a. it is a receipt, signed by the master or the shipowner's loading broker, for the goods loaded by the shipper; and

b. it is a document of title to those goods.

Receipt

27.28 As soon as the goods have been loaded a temporary receipt, signed by the Chief Officer, is always issued. This is known as a 'mate's receipt'. On it will be noted any apparent discrepancies in the condition of the goods. Subsequently, the mate's receipt is handed back in exchange for a bill of lading. However, there is nothing to stop the bill being handed over by the master without the production of the mate's receipt, if the goods have been loaded, so long as he is not aware of any interests in the goods other than those of the shipper[1].

The shipowner is entitled to hand over the bill of lading to the person in possession of the mate's receipt if he is not aware of other claims[2]; but if the mate's receipt and the bill come into the hands of different people, the goods must be delivered to the person in possession of the bill[3].

The master has no authority to sign a bill of lading for goods not actually shipped[4] and, if he does, the shipowner is not bound to deliver the amount specified, nor is he estopped from showing that the goods were not shipped. However, since the master's signature is prima facie evidence against the shipowner that the goods have been shipped, it is for the shipowner to disprove this[5].

The master's liability is dealt with by the Bills of Lading Act 1855, s.3. This provides that the bill of lading is *conclusive* evidence as against the master or other person signing it that the goods have been shipped, unless:

a. the holder of the bill had actual notice at the time of receiving it that the goods had not been shipped; or

b. the master or other person signing the bill shows that the misrepresentation that the goods had been shipped was caused without any fault on his part, and wholly by the fraud of the shipper, or of the holder, or of some person under whom the holder claims.

1 *Hathesing v Laing* (1873) LR 17 Eq 92.
2 *Craven v Ryder* (1816) 6 Taunt. 433.
3 *Baumwoll Manufactur etc. v Furness* [1893] AC 8, HL.
4 *Grant v Norway* (1851) 10 CB 665.
5 *Smith & Co v Bedouin Steam Navigation Co* [1896] AC 70, HL.

27.29 Any remarks noted on the mate's receipt must be transferred to the bill of lading, thereby rendering it a 'dirty' bill. On the other hand, where the goods are shipped 'in good order and condition', in which case there will usually be a declaration to this effect in the bill of lading, the bill is 'clean'. The distinction between clean and dirty bills is important. A dirty bill may prevent the shipper transferring it or using it for the purpose of a banker's commercial credit. Avoidance of these disadvantages can be achieved if the shipowner agrees to issue a clean bill in return for an indemnity against any liability which may ensue. The drawback from the shipowner's point of view is that if he does this he will not be able to enforce the contract of indemnity if its effect is to defraud the consignee, since it will be an illegal contract[1]. Whenever a clean bill is given, the shipowner is estopped from claiming that the condition of the goods is other than as acknowledged by the bill, but this estoppel only relates to those defects which could have been discovered on a reasonable external inspection.

1 *Brown Jenkinson & Co Ltd v Percy Dalton (London) Ltd* [1957] 2 QB 621, [1957] 2 All ER 844, CA.

Document of title

27.30 Unlike a mate's receipt, a bill of lading is a document of title which represents the goods shipped, and it remains the 'key' to the goods until they have come into the hands of a person entitled to them under the bill of lading. Its transference enables the owner of the goods to deal with them while they are still on the high seas.

A bill of lading can be transferred by delivery or by indorsement followed by delivery. The law can be summarised as follows:

a. a bill directing delivery of the goods simply 'unto bearer' is transferable by delivery;

b. a bill directing delivery 'unto A or order' or 'unto B or assigns' is transferable by indorsement followed by delivery;

c. a bill directing delivery to a named person without the addition of 'or order' or 'or assigns' (or with their deletion from a printed form) is not transferable by that person.

The effect of a transfer of a bill is to transfer the property in the goods, if the parties so intended[1] and the transferor is able to pass the property in the goods. If the property has passed, the Bills of Lading Act 1855, s.1, transfers the right to sue on the contract of affreightment, and the obligations under it, to the consignee or indorsee. However, s.2 preserves any right of stoppage in transitu[2] or the shipowner's right to claim freight against the original shipper.

---

1 Para. 27.14.
2 Paras. 22.91–22.92.

27.31 It is customary for bills of lading to be issued in sets, which means that three signed copies are made out: one being kept by the shipper, one by the master, and one being forwarded to the consignee. In such a case the first transferee for value is entitled to the goods[1], but, if the master delivers the goods to the first person presenting one of the signed bills forming the set, he will not be liable if that person is not the first transferee, unless he had notice of any other claims to the goods, or knowledge of any other circumstances raising a reasonable suspicion that the claimant is not entitled to them[2].

---

1 *Barber v Meyerstein* (1870) LR 4 HL 317, HL.
2 *Glyn, Mills & Co v East and West India Dock Co* (1882) 7 App Cas 591, HL.

Terms

27.32 Terms commonly found in a bill of lading are that the goods are 'shipped in good order and condition' and that the goods shall be delivered, 'in the like good order and condition' at a specified port subject to 'excepted perils'[1], to the consignee or his assigns on payment of freight. In addition, there are implied into the contract evidenced by the bill of lading the same three undertakings by the shipowner (seaworthiness, reasonable despatch and not to deviate unnecessarily) as are implied into a voyage charterparty, and so is an undertaking by the shipper that the goods shipped are not dangerous. However, where the Hague Rules, as amended, apply, the rights and obligations attaching to carriers under bills of lading are also governed by them. The Hague Rules are set out in the Schedule to the Carriage of Goods by Sea Act 1971, which came into force in 1977 and replaces an Act of the same name of 1924.

---

1 Para. 27.15.

Carriage of Goods by Sea Act 1971

27.33 The Hague Rules, as amended, apply to the carriage of goods by sea where the port of shipment is a port in the United Kingdom *whether or not the carriage is between ports in two different states*[1], and to a voyage from:

a. a port in one state party to the Rules to a port in another state; or

b. a port in one state to another state where the bill of lading is issued in a state party; or

c. a port in one state to a port in another state where the bill of lading provides that the Rules are to govern the contract of affreightment[2]. In the Rules, 'the carrier' includes the shipowner or the charterer who enters into a contract of carriage with a shipper.

---

1 Carriage of Goods by Sea Act 1971, s.1.
2 Hague Rules, art. X.

27.34 The principal Rules are as follows:

a. The carrier is bound, before and at the beginning of the voyage, to exercise due diligence to: make the ship seaworthy; properly man, equip, and supply the ship; and make the holds, refrigerating chambers etc. fit and safe for the reception, carriage and preservation of the goods.

Unlike the undertaking of seaworthiness implied into charterparties or (where the Rules do not apply) bills of lading, this undertaking is not absolute. The carrier is only liable if he was negligent, although once unseaworthiness is proved, he has the burden of proving due diligence.

b. The carrier must properly and carefully load, handle, stow, keep, care for and discharge the goods carried.

c. After receiving the goods, the carrier, or the master, or the agent of the carrier, must, at his demand, issue the shipper a bill of lading showing among other things —

    i. the leading marks necessary for identification of the goods as the same are furnished in writing by the shipper before the loading of such goods starts;

    ii. either the number of packages or pieces, or the quantity, or the weight, as the case may be, as furnished in writing by the shipper;

    iii. the apparent order and condition of the goods.

But no carrier (or his agent) or master is bound to state in the bill any marks, number, quantity, or weight which he has reasonable ground for suspecting do not accurately represent the goods actually received, or which he has had no reasonable means of checking. Such a bill is prima facie evidence of the receipt by the carrier of the goods as therein described. However, proof to the contrary is not admissible when the bill has been transferred to a third party acting with good faith.

d. Written notice of loss or damage must be given to the carrier or his agent at the port of discharge before or at the time of the removal of the goods into the custody of the consignee or other person entitled to delivery, unless the loss or damage is not apparent, in which case it must be given within three days; *otherwise such removal is prima facie evidence of delivery of the goods as described in the bill of lading*. Any action for loss or damage must be brought *within one year* after delivery, or the date delivery should have occurred, unless the parties agree to an extension.

e. Any term purporting to exempt the carrier or ship from liability for negligence, fault or failure in the duties provided in a. to d., or to lessen it, is void.

f. Neither the carrier nor the ship is responsible for loss or damage resulting from a long list of excepted perils, e.g. act of God, or of war, or of public enemies; restraint of princes, rulers or people; strikes; riots; saving or attempting to save life or property at sea; insufficiency of packing; faulty navigation or management of the ship by the master or a pilot or a member of the crew. The excepted perils cannot be relied on if the carrier is in breach of his obligation to exercise due diligence to make the ship seaworthy and this breach causes the damage.

g. Any deviation to save life or property at sea, or any reasonable deviation, is not a breach of the Rules or of the contract of carriage.

h. Unless the nature and value of the goods has been declared before the shipment and inserted in the bill of lading, the limit of the liability of the carrier or on the ship is 10,000 gold francs (£447.81)[1] per package or 30 gold francs (£1.34)[1] per kilo of gross weight of the goods lost or damaged, whichever is higher. Where a container is used to consolidate goods, the number of packages or units enumerated in the bill as packed in the container are deemed to be the number of packages or units. These limitations of liability do not apply if it is proved that the damage resulted from an act or omission of the carrier done with intent to cause damage, or recklessly and with knowledge that damage would probably result. (Limitation of liability is also dealt with by the Merchant Shipping Act 1894, which we discussed in paras. 27.23 to 27.26.)

i. A servant or agent of the carrier, but not an independent contractor, is entitled to avail himself of the same defences and limits of liability as the carrier himself can.

If, but only if, they are expressly incorporated in a charterparty, the Hague Rules can apply to a charterparty.

---

1 Carriage of Goods by Sea (Sterling Equivalents) Order 1977.

Freight

27.35 'Freight' is the remuneration, usually fixed at a rate of £x per ton of cargo shipped, payable to a shipowner for the carriage of goods under a charterparty or bill of lading.

Normally, freight is not payable until the goods have been delivered at the agreed port of destination, so that the obligation to *deliver* there is entire and no freight is payable until the goods have been so delivered. The shipowner can recover nothing even if he is compelled by perils of the sea to abandon the voyage and discharge the cargo at an intermediate port, even if the peril is an 'expected peril'[1]. However, there are two exceptions:

a. A shipowner who has not delivered to the agreed port in breach of his entire obligation to do so may claim not the agreed freight but a reasonable sum or pro rata renumeration *if the cargo owner voluntarily accepts delivery at another port*. Such acceptance gives rise to an inference that there is a fresh agreement by the parties to pay such a sum for the partial (or substituted) performance[2].

b. *If the cargo owner unjustifiably prevents delivery*, the shipowner may claim damages, or remuneration on a *quantum meruit*[3].

The entire obligation mentioned above only relates to arrival and delivery at the agreed port. If the goods are delivered but are deficient in quantity, the shipowner is entitled to a proportionate part of the freight[4]. If the goods are delivered but are damaged, the shipowner is entitled to the freight, unless the damage is severe[5]. In both cases, of course, the shipowner will be liable to a counter-claim for damages for breach of contract.

---

1 *St Enoch Shipping Co Ltd v Phosphate Mining Co* [1916] 2 KB 624.
2 *Christy v Row* (1808) 1 Taunt 300, para. 10.15.
3 Para. 10.15.
4 *Ritchie v Atkinson* (1808) 10 East 295.
5 *Dakin v Oxley* (1864) 15 CB NS 646.

Who pays?

27.36 Where a contract of affreightment is contained in a charterparty, it is generally the charterer who is responsible for paying freight. However, if the charterparty contains a 'cesser clause' his liability ceases when the goods are loaded and the shipowner then looks to the cargo owner and, as we saw in para. 27.16, has a lien on the goods for payment.

Where a contact of affreightment is evidenced by a bill of lading, the shipper is generally liable for paying freight. In addition, by the Bills of Lading Act 1855, s.1, the consignee named in the bill is liable to pay the freight specified in the bill, as is an indorsee of the bill, if the property in the goods has passed to him. This does not remove the primary liability of the shipper. The shipowner has a lien on the goods for payment.

Other types of 'freight'

27.37 a. *'Lump sum freight'* This is a gross sum stipulated to be paid for the use of the whole ship or a part of her (as opposed to the more normal stipulation of £x per ton of cargo shipped). It is payable even though the shipper does not ship any goods, or though part of the goods shipped are not delivered[1].

b. *'Advance freight'* This is freight which is payable under the contract when the voyage starts or at some other time before it ends. 'Advance freight' is not commonly stipulated. If advance freight has not been paid, the shipowner can recover it even though the ship is lost, if this is due to 'excepted perils'[2]. However, if any part of the goods are destroyed before the ship sails freight is not payable on *those* goods, since no freight could have been earned by the ship in respect of them[3].

c. *'Dead freight'* This is the name given to damages for breach of contract by a charterer in failing to load a full and complete cargo. It is not available where 'lump sum freight' is payable because the shipowner in such a case will not suffer loss from not having a fully laden ship.

d. *'Back freight'* If the cargo owner does not take delivery within a reasonable time after the ship has arrived at her destination, the master must deal with the goods in the cargo owner's interest and at his expense. He may place the goods in a warehouse, or, if this is impracticable, carry the goods to some place convenient for the cargo owner (in which case he can charge 'back freight' — remuneration for such carriage)[4].

---

1 *Merchant Shipping Co v Armitage* (1873) LR 9 QB 99.
2 *Byrne v Schiller* (1871) LR 6 Exch 319.
3 *Weir & Co v Girvin & Co* [1900] 1 QB 45, CA.
4 *Cargo ex The Argos* (1873) LR 5 PC 134, PC.

General average

27.38 Loss which arises in consequence of extraordinary sacrifices or expenditure made for the safety of the ship and cargo comes within the 'general average', and must be borne by proportionate contributions by all those who are interested. The idea behind general average is that those sacrifices made in times of danger for the common safety should be made good by all who shared in the venture and whose goods were thereby saved.

A sacrifice or expenditure will only be classified as a general average loss if the following requirements are satisfied:

a. it must be made to avoid a real danger which is common to all interests[1];

b. it must be reasonably necessary to make the sacrifice[2];

c. the sacrifice must be voluntary[3];

d. part of the imperilled property must be saved through the sacrifice[4];

e. the common danger must not arise through any default rendering the interest claiming a general average contribution legally liable[5].

Examples of sacrifices or expenditure which may give rise to a claim for general average contribution are jettison of the cargo (other than worthless cargo), beaching of the ship to avoid sinking, the sale of part of the cargo to pay for repairs to enable the ship to continue her voyage, and the expenses of being towed into a port of refuge for the preservation of the ship and cargo.

---

1 *Walthew v Mavrojani* (1870) LR 5 Exch 116; *Joseph Watson & Sons Ltd v Firemen's Fund Insurance Co of San Francisco* [1922] 2 KB 355.
2 *Pirie & Co v Middle Dock Co* (1881) 44 LT 426.
3 *Shepherd v Kottgen* (1877) 2 CPD 585, CA.

4 *Pirie & Co v Middle Dock Co* (1881) 44 LT 426.
5 *Strang, Steel & Co v A. Scott & Co* (1889) 14 App Cas 601, PC.

27.39 The following persons can sue for a general average contribution if they have suffered a general average loss:

a. the shipowner (who has a lien on the cargo for the general average contribution due from it until all contributions are paid)[1];

b. the owner of sacrificed cargo (who can sue the shipowner, anyone else entitled to the freight and the other cargo owners for a general average contribution); and

c. the person entitled to the freight, if someone other than the shipowner, as where a charterer is entitled to freight under bills of lading.

Anyone, other than the seamen, who was in a position to be benefited by the general average sacrifice or expenditure is liable to contribute. Thus, the shipowner is liable for the contribution due from the ship and the freight, cargo owners are liable for the contribution due on their cargo, and so is a person entitled to freight for the contribution due on the freight.

---

1 *Strang, Steel & Co v A. Scott & Co* (1889) 14 App Cas 601, PC.

27.40 In the absence of agreement to the contrary, the amount of the contributions to be made is 'adjusted' (determined) at, and according to the law of, the port of discharge when the ship reaches it.

The parties normally make provision for general average liability in the bill of lading, and if they do so the position just outlined may be affected. One set of rules, the York-Antwerp Rules of 1950, are invariably stipulated as applicable.

CARRIAGE BY AIR

International flights

27.41 Some sort of international regulation of carriage by air is obviously essential to avoid disputes between states over the relevant rules. This was provided in 1929 by the Warsaw Convention, which remains the basic provision, and to which a large number of states, including the United Kingdom, are parties. The Convention, which provides uniform rules for the international carriage of passengers, baggage and goods by air, was given effect in English Law by the Carriage by Air Act 1932. The Warsaw Convention was amended by the Hague Protocol in 1955 and the amended and unamended texts of the Convention are both set out in the Schedule to the Carriage by Air Act 1961, which repealed the Act of 1932 when it came into force. Since the basis of the uniform rules is international treaties, the rules only apply to journeys between states which are parties thereto. This poses a special problem because, unlike the United Kingdom, not all the parties to the Warsaw Convention have acceded to the Hague Protocol. The result is that a flight from the United Kingdom to a state which is only a party to the Warsaw Convention is governed by the unamended Warsaw Convention, whereas if the destination was a state party to the Convention and the Protocol it would be governed by the amended Convention. We propose to discuss the law primarily as it is under the amended Convention, but will indicate any differences between the amended and unamended texts of the Convention.

The Convention applies to 'international carriage' as therein defined, viz. any carriage in which the place of departure and of destinationtion are within the territories of different states party to the Convention *or* are within the territory of one state party but there is an agreed stopping place in another state party.

Liability

27.42 The carrier is liable, subject to certain exceptions:

a. For the death of or injury to a passenger caused by an accident which occurs on board the aircraft or during embarcation or disembarcation. This liability is limited to 250,000 gold francs (£11,750)[1] for each passenger (or 125,000 gold francs under the unamended convention), unless a higher figure has been agreed by special contract.

b. For the loss of or damage to any registered baggage or any cargo occurring while it is in charge of the carrier at an airport or on board an aircraft. Here there is a limit of liability of 250 gold francs (£11,70)[2] per kilo, unless a declaration of value was made by the passenger or consignor and any supplementary charge paid.

c. For the loss of or damage to goods of which the passenger himself takes charge. In this case liability is limited to 5,000 gold francs (£234) per passenger.

d. For delay in the carriage by air of passengers, baggage or cargo.

---

1 Carriage by Air (Sterling Equivalents) Order 1977.
2 *Ibid.*

Defences

27.43 The carrier is not liable if he proves that he, his agents or employees took all necessary measures to avoid damage, or that it was impossible to take such measures. In addition, if the carrier proves contributory negligence on the part of the injured person, his liability may be avoided in whole or in part.

Where baggage or cargo are damaged[1], a written complaint must be made to the carrier within seven days (baggage) or 14 days (cargo) of their receipt. In the case of delay, written notice must be made within 21 days. Unless there is fraud on the carrier's part, no action will lie against him on a complaint made out of time.

Actions to recover damages must be brought within two years from the date on which the aircraft arrived, or ought to have arrived, or on which the carriage stopped, otherwise the right to recover is extinguished.

---

1 'Damage' in this context does not include loss of contents: *Fothergill v Monarch Airlines Ltd* [1977] 3 All ER 616.

Other provisions
27.44 The limitations on liability mentioned above do not apply:

a. if it is proved that the damage resulted from an act or omission of the carrier, his agent or employee, done with intent to cause damage or recklessly and with knowledge that damage would result; or

b. if the carrier has accepted a passenger without delivering a ticket containing prescribed particulars to him; nor, in the case of registered baggage or cargo, if he has not delivered a baggage check (although this may be combined with a ticket) in the prescribed form, or (in the case of cargo) required and received an air waybill in the prescribed form.

Any provision purporting to exempt the carrier from liability or to fix a lower limit of liability than that specified is void.

Under the amended Convention, but not the unamended Convention, the limitations on liability in relation to death or injury or loss or damage to goods extend to the agents and employees of the carrier.

27.45 The Carriage by Air (Supplementary Provisions) Act 1962, which gave effect to the Guadalajara Convention of 1961, provides that, where the contract of carriage is entered into with one carrier but performed by another, both carriers' liability is subject to the limitations specified above, and a plaintiff may only recover in total the amounts prescribed.

Non-international carriage
27.46 Pursuant to powers in the Act of 1961, the above provisions have been extended to non-international carriage, with certain modifications[1]. Non-international carriage means:

a. carriage between the United Kingdom and a state not party to the Warsaw Convention; and

b. carriage between two points in the United Kingdom.

The modifications are that the maximum limit for death or personal injury is raised to 875,000 gold francs (£40,950) for each passenger, and that the absence of a ticket, baggage check or air waybill does not prevent the limitations on liability applying.

---

1 Carriage by Air Act (Application of Provisions) Order 1967.

Chapter 28
The Law of Employment

28.1 A contract of employment has effect by virtue of the common law, but its incidents are largely governed by statute.

THE EMPLOYMENT RELATIONSHIP

28.2 In this chapter, we are concerned with the incidents of the relationship of employer and employee. A person who contracts to do work for another may be employed either as an employee under a contract of employment or as an independent contractor under a contract for services. The distinction between these two contracts is of considerable importance in the law. For example, at common law, an employer is liable for all the wrongdoings of his employee in the course of his employment, but an employer is not liable for all the wrong-doings of an independent contractor[1]. Under statute, the distinction is important, for example, in relation to liability to pay taxes and national insurance contributions. There is nothing in law to prevent parties choosing, where appropriate, to enter into the relationship of employer and independent contractor rather than of employer and employee. Such a situation is common, for example, in the building industry where the practice of labour-only sub-contracting ('the lump') obtains. Financial advantages accrue to both parties to a contract for services, but the worker must remember that having made his bed as being 'self-employed' he must lie on it[2] as such and cannot claim the benefit of the majority of the statutory and common law rights outlined in this chapter. That is not to say that the parties can, by the label they give to their relationship, affect its true nature[3]. The courts have for-mulated a number of tests for distinguishing between a contract of employment and a contract for services; nonetheless, if the nature of the relationship remains ambiguous the best evidence is what the parties call their relationship[4].

---

1 Paras. 21.21—21.29.
2 *Massey v Crown Life Insurance Co* [1978] IRLR 31, CA.
3 *Ferguson v John Dawson & Partners (Contractors) Ltd* [1976] 3 All ER 817, CA.
4 *Massey v Crown Life Insurance Co* [1978] IRLR 31, CA.

Control test

28.3 In early cases, the courts sought to identify the contract of employment by reference to the 'control test': if the employer controls not only where and when the work is done, but also *how* it is done, the contract is one of employment. Today, control is not regarded as a decisive test of general application, although it is an important factor to consider, because it is inappropriate when one is dealing with man of some particular skill[1]. While the employer of a labourer may be in a position to control the manner in which he carries out his tasks, the employer of, for example, a ship's captain or an engineer, will rarely have the expertise to do so.

---

1 *Morren v Swinton and Pendlebury BC* [1965] 2 All ER 349, [1965] 1 WLR 576.

Organisation test

28.4 The organisation test, which was resorted to in some cases where the inadequacy of the control test was recognised, laid emphasis on the employer's ability to control when and where the work was done. The court's inquiry was directed to whether the work came within the employer's power of organisation. In *Stevenson, Jordan and Harrison Ltd v Macdonald and Evans*[1], the test was formulated thus: 'under a contract of employment a man is employed as part of the business, and his work is done as an integral part of the business; whereas under a contract for services, his work, although done for the business, is not integrated into it but only accessory to it'. This test has been applied in holding that a hospital authority was vicariously liable for the negligence of doctors on its permanent staff[2] and in holding that a circus trapeze artiste who also acted as an usherette was entitled to industrial injuries benefit[3]. Although the courts still refer to the control and organisation tests, it is now recognised that the variety of situations in which the question 'Is this a contract of employment?' arises cannot adequately be dealt with by a single test.

---

1 [1952] 1 TLR 101, CA.
2 *Cassidy v Ministry of Health* [1951] 2 KB 343, [1951] 1 All ER 574, CA.
3 *Whittaker v Ministry of Pensions and National Insurance* [1967] 1 QB 156, [1966] 3 All ER 531.

Multiple test

28.5 In a number of recent cases the courts have applied an 'entre-preneurial test', asking whether the person who has engaged himself to perform the services is performing them as a person in business *on his own account*[1]. There is no exhaustive list of factors to which regard must be had in answering this question, but relevant factors include control, whether the person provides his own equipment, whether he hires his own helpers, what degree of financial risk he takes, what degree of responsibility for investment and management he has, and whether and how far he has an opportunity of profiting from sound management in the performance of his task[2]. In *Ready Mixed Concrete (South East) Ltd v Ministry of Pensions and National Insurance*[3], the court applied a multiple test in holding that a driver employed by the company was not an employee and therefore the company was not liable to pay national insurance contributions in respect of him. Factors taken into account by the court were that, by arrangement with the company, the driver hire-purchased the vehicle he operated; that, although he was to wear the company's uniform and the vehicle was to be painted in the company's colours and used exclusively on the company's business, the driver was responsible for repairs to the vehicle; that he was empowered to delegate his task, and that he was paid by reference to deliveries made and distance travelled. In *Ferguson v John Dawson & Partners (Contractors) Ltd*[4], a builder's labourer, whom both parties considered to be employed as a 'self-employed labour only sub-contractor', was nonetheless held to be an employee and within the purview of safety legislation relating to construction sites. Considerations which the court took into account in coming to this view were that the company could move its workers from site to site; if tools were required, the company provided them; the company told the workers what to do, and the men were paid, at an hourly rate, what could properly be called a 'wage'.

---

1 *Market Investigations Ltd v Ministry of Social Security* [1969] 2 QB 173, [1968] 3 All ER 732.
2 *Ibid.*
3 [1968] 2 QB 497, [1968] 1 All ER 433.
4 [1976] 3 All ER 817, CA.

TERMS OF EMPLOYMENT

28.6 The terms of a contract of employment may be derived from a number of sources: the express agreement of the parties, whether in writing or oral; the incorporation, express or implied, of collectively agreed or other terms; usage and practice; common law and statute.

28.7 An important source of contractual terms is the collective agreement. Employers, or employers' associations, and trade unions engage in collective bargaining, at plant, local and national level, both to regulate the relations between themselves and to regulate the terms and conditions of employment of workers in the particular trade or industry. Such collective agreements are not normally enforceable between the parties to them[1]. Collectively negotiated terms and conditions of employment may become part of an individual's contract of employment either by express reference to such terms in the individual contract[2] or by implication arising from conduct and acquiescence. It is, by and large, a fiction to regard the individual contract of employment as being negotiated and agreed between the employer and employee. For the majority of workers, the terms of their contracts relating to wages, hours and so forth, will have been negotiated collectively at plant, local or national level.

1 Para. 6.2; Trade Union and Labour Relations Act 1974, s.18.
2 *Morris v C. H. Bailey Ltd* [1969] 2 Lloyd's Rep 215, CA.

28.8 Usage and practice may give rise to the implication of terms. In *Sagar v H Ridehalgh & Son Ltd*[1], an employer was held to be entitled to make a deduction from an employee's wage for faulty work. A term permitting the deduction was incorporated by virtue of a general usage in the Lancashire weaving industry. Alternatively, the term was incorporated through the employer's practice of making deductions over a period of 30 years. Unless the contrary is expressed, the employee enters his employment on the same terms as apply to the other employees and must be deemed to have subjected himself to those terms. On the same principle, the provisions of a collective agreement may become incorporated into an employee's contract.

1 [1931] 1 Ch 310, CA.

28.9 Works rules may be incorporated into individual contracts either by express reference or by implication. Alternatively, they may not be contractual terms at all, but instructions from the employer as to the

proper performance of the job[1]. In either case the employee must abide
by the rules[2]. If, however, the rules are contractual terms they may be
varied only by agreement.

---

1 *Secretary of State for Employment v Associated Society of Locomotive Engineers and Firemen* (No. 2) [1972] 2 QB 455, [1972] 2 All ER 949, CA.
2 Para. 28.14.

Common law implied terms

28.10 We have already considered the basis for the implication of
particular terms into contracts[1]. The courts regard certain terms as
being implied in all contracts of employment by virtue of the nature of
the employment relationship.

---

1 Paras. 8.16—8.23.

Duties of the employee
28.11 The courts regard the employee's fundamental duty as being
one of fidelity to his employer. Rarely is a decision of the courts
founded specifically on the duty of faithful service; however, the cases
cited in the following paragraphs may be regarded as illustrating particular aspects of that general duty. In *Secretary of State for Employment v Associated Society of Locomotive Engineers and Firemen (No.2)*[1],
Buckley, LJ, based his decision that a threatened work-to-rule by railway
workers would be a breach of their contracts of employment on the
view that the implied term to serve the employer faithfully would be
broken by the action. Roskill, LJ, found this a tenable view, but pre-
ferred, with Lord Denning, MR, to base his decision on the existence of
an implied term not to wilfully disrupt the employer's business. In
Hivac Ltd v Park Royal Scientific Instruments Ltd[2], the Court of
Appeal held that employees who in their spare time worked for a
company in competition with their employer were in breach of their
implied duty of fidelity to their employer, even though as yet no
confidential information had been disclosed.

It is, of course, contrary to the employee's duty to the employer
to disclose confidential information relating to his employment. In
Bents Brewery Co Ltd v Hogan[3], a trade union official was held to be
guilty of inducing public house managers employed by the brewery to
break their contracts of employment when he sent round a questionnaire
asking them to disclose the takings, trade, wage bill, etc., of their public
houses. This aspect of the employee's duty applies also to disclosure of
confidential information and trade secrets after the employee has left

his employment. Thus, an employee instructed by his employer in a secret manufacturing process was prevented by injunction from disclosing that process to a rival company with whom he subsequently took up employment[4]. Similarly, it is a breach of implied duty, for an employee intending to set up business on his own, to actively solicit his employer's customers with a view to their transferring their custom to him[5].

---

1 [1972] 2 QB 455, [1972] 2 All ER 949, CA.
2 [1946] Ch 169, [1946] 1 All ER 350, CA.
3 [1945] 2 All ER 570.
4 *Amber Size and Chemical Co Ltd v Menzel* [1913] 2 Ch 239.
5 *Wessex Dairies Ltd v Smith* [1935] 2 KB 80.

28.12 An employee is not entitled to accept bribes or to put into his own pocket commission received in respect of contracts negotiated on behalf of his employer[1]. He must not put himself in a position where he is tempted not to perform his duty to his employer faithfully, nor where he may have personal reasons for not giving his employer the best advice which it is his duty to give. Following this reasoning, in *British Syphon Co Ltd v Homewood*[2], a person employed as a technical adviser who, in his spare time, had invented an improved dispenser for soda syphons was required to assign the benefit of his invention to his employer, a manufacturer of soda syphons.

---

1 *Boston Deep Sea Fishing and Ice Co v Ansell* (1888) 39 Ch D 339, CA.
2 [1956] 2 All ER 897, [1956] 1 WLR 1190.

28.13 It is the duty of every employee to carry out his job with proper care. Thus an employee who injured a fellow employee by his negligent reversing of the vehicle which he was employed to drive was held to be in breach of his contract[1]. This case also decides that an employee has a duty to indemnify his employer in respect of liability incurred as a result of the employee's negligence; however, it is not the practice of insurance companies to insist upon the enforcement of this duty.

---

1 *Lister v Romford Ice and Cold Storage Co Ltd* [1957] AC 555, [1957] 1 All ER 125, HL.

28.14 Finally, it is the employee's duty to obey the orders of his employer which are lawful[1] and reasonable[2].

---

1 *Gregory v Ford* [1951] 1 All ER 121.
2 *Ottoman Bank v Chakarian* [1930] AC 277, PC.

Duties of the employer

28.15 The fundamental obligation of the employer is to continue to pay the employee during the subsistence of the relationship. The contract may, however, expressly or impliedly provide otherwise, for example, in cases of lay-off or absence due to illness. Whether or not there is also an obligation on the employer to provide the employee with work to do depends, we suggest, on the construction of the particular contract of employment. No doubt in general it will be found that the contract does not oblige the employer to provide the employee with work[1]. However, such an obligation has been found to exist in the following cases:

a. Where the contractual obligation to pay imports an obligation to provide work, as where remuneration is by commission[2] or in the case of piece-work[3].

b. Where the contract contemplates an opportunity of publicity as well as a salary. In *Herbert Clayton and Jack Waller Ltd v Oliver*[4], the House of Lords held that the contract between a performer and his employer bound the employer to give him the opportunity of appearing in public in the production for which he had been employed.

c. Where the employee is appointed to a particular office. In *Collier v Sunday Referee Publishing Co Ltd*[5], it was held that the employer, although willing to continue to pay the employee, was in breach of contract by destroying the office of chief sub-editor to which the employee had been appointed.

d. Where the provision of work is required to maintain an employee's skill, or contacts in his profession[6].

We consider the employer's duty in respect of his employee's safety in paras. 28.65. to 28.70.

---

1 *Collier v Sunday Referee Publishing Co Ltd* [1940] 2 KB 647, [1940] 4 All ER 234.
2 *Re Rubel Bronze and Metal Co Ltd and Vos* [1918] 1 KB 315.
3 *Devonald v Rosser & Sons* [1906] 2 KB 728, CA.
4 [1930] AC 209, HL.
5 [1940] 2 KB 647, [1940] 4 All ER 234.
6 *Breach v Epsylon Industries Ltd* [1976] ICR 316, EAT; *Langston v Amalgamated Union of Engineering Workers* [1974] ICR 180, [1974] 1 All ER 980, CA.

Written particulars of terms of employment

28.16 The Contracts of Employment Act 1972, s.4 requires that not later than thirteen weeks after commencing his employment, an employee should be given a written statement of certain of the terms and conditions of his employment. This statement must, inter alia, contain particulars of the terms of the contract relating to pay, hours, holiday and holiday pay entitlement, absence due to sickness or injury, sick pay, pensions and pension schemes, the length of notice require to be given by each party to determine the relationship, and the title of the job. The statement must be accompanied by a note detailing any disciplinary rules and outlining grievance procedures. The statement may, for all or any of the particulars, refer the employee to some other document which is reasonably accessible to him[1]. Such a document may well be a collective agreement and in such a case the courts will normally hold that the provisions of the agreement have been incorporated in the contract[2]. Changes in the relevant terms must also be notified to the employee in writing, within one month of the change[3]. If an employee has a written contract containing the relevant particulars, he need not be given a written statement but must be given a note relating to disciplinary and grievance procedure[4].

The statement under s.4 is *not* the contract, nor does it constitute conclusive evidence of the contract[5]. To sign a receipt in respect of the statement is not to conclude a contract. However, if the employee signs as agreeing to the statement or fails to challenge any inaccuracy, he may be estopped from denying that the statement accurately reflects those contractual terms to which it refers.

If an employer fails to provide a statement or provides a statement which is inaccurate or incomplete, the employee may refer the matter to an industrial tribunal to determine what particulars ought to have been included[6].

---

1 Contracts of Employment Act 1972, s.4.
2 Para. 28.7.
3 Contracts of Employment Act 1972, s.5.
4 *Ibid.,* s.6.
5 *Turriff Construction Ltd v Bryant* [1969] ITR 292.
6 Contracts of Employment Act 1972, s.8.

CONTINUITY OF EMPLOYMENT

28.17 In order to qualify for a large number of statutory rights[1] it is necessary for an employee to have a specified period of 'continuous employment'. Save in the case of proceedings in respect of the statutory minimum notice period (see para. 28.38), employment is presumed to be continuous unless the contrary is proved[2]. The principle of promissory estoppel may prevent an employer from rebutting this presumption. For example, where an employer represented to an employee that service with a previous employer would be regarded as part of the employee's period of continuous employment, it was held that the principle of promissory estoppel prevented the employer from showing that the employment was not, in fact, continuous, since the employer had intended his representation to be acted on and it was acted on in that the employee refrained from claiming a redundancy payment from his previous employer[3].

1 E.g. the right not to be unfairly dismissed and the right to redundancy payment.
2 E.g. Trade Union and Labour Relations Act 1974, Sched. 1.
3 *Evenden v Guildford City Association Football Club Ltd* [1975] QB 917, [1975] 3 All ER 269, CA.

28.18 The period of continuous employment is calculated in accordance with the Contracts of Employment Act 1972, Sched. 1. Except as provided by the Schedule, any week which does not count towards an employee's period of continuous employment breaks the continuity and the reckoning must begin anew. Weeks in which the employee is employed for 16 hours or more, or during the whole or part of which the employment is governed by a contract which normally involves employment for 16 hours or more weekly (here referred to as a full-time contract), count towards a period of continuous employment. It follows that the whole of the week in which the employee commenced employment and the whole of the week in which he was dismissed will, if governed by a full-time contract, count towards the period of continuous employment[1]. If the employment ceases to be governed by a full-time contract and becomes governed by a contract which normally involves employment of eight hours or more, but less than 16 hours weekly (here referred to as a part-time contract), then, for up to 26 weeks until another period governed by a full-time contract, the employment under the part-time contract will be regarded as it would have been had the employee been under a full-time contract. A person who has, for five years or more worked under a part-time contract, is treated as if he had worked under a full-time contract. Once a person has qualified for a particular statutory right by virtue of sufficient continuous employment he is regarded as continuing to qualify until such a time as:

a. his employment is governed by a contract normally involving employment for less than eight hours weekly; and

b. he is employed for less than 16 hours in a week.

Even though no contract of employment exists, up to 26 weeks of absence due to sickness or injury count towards the period of continuous employment; as do periods of absence on account of a temporary cessation of work. Periods when, though absent, the employee is regarded, by arrangement or custom, as continuing in employment for all or any purposes (e.g. for the purposes of a pension scheme[2]) also count towards the period of continuous employment, and so do periods of absence due to pregnancy.

Weeks during any part of which an employee is on strike do not count towards his period of continuous employment but do not break the continuity. Where a business is transferred[3], employment with the transferor counts as employment with the transferee and continuity is not broken. This applies also where an employee is taken on by an associated employer. However, payment of a redundancy payment by the outgoing employer breaks the continuity.

---

1   *Coulson v City of London Polytechnic* [1976] IRLR 212.
2   *Wishart v National Coal Board* [1974] ICR 460.
3   Para. 28.56.

WAGES

Itemised pay statement

28.19   The Employment Protection Act 1975 provides[1] that every employee has the right to a written itemised pay statement to be given at or before the time of payment detailing gross pay, deductions, and net pay. Only the aggregate amount of any fixed deductions need be referred to, if the employee has been given an annual standing statement of fixed deductions, stating the amount, intervals and purpose of each deduction[2]. If an employer fails to comply with these sections, an employee may refer the matter to an industrial tribunal. If the employer has made unnotified deductions from the employee's wages during the 13 weeks prior to his application to the tribunal, the tribunal may order the employer to pay the employee a sum not exceeding the aggregate of those deductions[3].

---

1   Employment Protection Act 1975, s.81.
2   *Ibid.*, s.82.
3   *Ibid.*, s.84.

The Truck Acts

28.20   The Truck Act 1831 was designed to counter certain abuses current at the time of its enactment — e.g. payment in goods, or payment in credits to be exchanged at a 'tommy shop'. The Act remains in force and is of considerable importance in relation to the wages of manual labourers[1] — i.e. those for whom work with the hands is the predominant activity[2]. The Act requires that the entire amount of the wages of a manual worker be paid to him in the current coin of the realm (i.e. coins and banknotes)[3]. Every payment in kind or otherwise than in the current coin is declared illegal, null and void[4]. Any contract which provides for the whole or part of the wages of a manual labourer to be paid other than in the current coin, or which specifies the place where or the manner in which, any wages are to be spent, is illegal, null and void[5]. A contravention of the Act is a criminal offence[6]. An employee may recover from his employer in current coin any amount of his wages which has not been so paid[7]. An employer may not make deductions from the wages of a manual labourer which are, in effect, payments to himself — e.g. deductions in respect of rent[8]; if he does so, the employee may recover the amount deducted, and if, as in *Daley v Radnor*[8], the tenancy agreement cannot be severed from the contract of employment, the employer cannot claim for rent owed as the contract is 'illegal, null and void'. The prohibition against deductions in favour of the employer does not prevent deductions in favour of a third party — 'a payment made by an employer at the instance of a person employed . . . to place the money in the hands of some person in whose hands the person employed desires it to be placed, is . . . a payment to the person employed as much as if the current coin had been placed in his or her hands'[9]. Thus it is permissible for the employer to deduct a manual labourer's union subscription from his wages, if the employee wishes. Statute does, of course, permit deductions in respect of income tax, national insurance contributions and attachment of earnings.

An exception to the strict rule under the 1831 Act is provided by the Payment of Wages Act 1960. If a manual labourer requests his employer to pay his wages into his bank account, or by postal order, money order or cheque, and the employer agrees, the arrangement is not invalidated by the Truck Act. Furthermore, an employer may pay an absentee manual labourer by postal or money order if the employer has reasonable grounds for believing the absence is due to sickness or injury or is for the purpose of carrying out duties in connection with the employment.

---

1 The Act refers to 'artificers'.
2 *J. and F. Stone Lighting and Radio Ltd v Haygarth* [1968] AC 157, [1966] 3 All ER 539, HL.
3 Truck Act 1831, ss. 1 and 3.
4 *Ibid.*, s.3.
5 *Ibid.*, ss. 1 and 2.
6 *Ibid.*, s.9.
7 *Ibid.*, s.4.
8 *Penman v Fife Coal Co Ltd* [1936] AC 45, HL; *Daley v Radnor* (1973) 117 Sol Jo 321.
9 *Hewlett v Allan* [1894] AC 383, HL.

Permitted deductions

28.21 An employee may, by a signed agreement, permit deductions to be made from his wages in respect of a number of matters, including, in particular, food prepared and consumed on the premises[1]. Deductions may be made made in respect of bad or negligent work if the amounts are reasonable and the relevant details are contained in a written contract or easily accessible notice[2].

---

1 Truck Act 1831, s.23.
2 Truck Act 1896.

Fines

28.22 An employer may make a deduction in respect of a fine if:

a. the relevant details are contained in a written contract or easily accessible notice;

b. the acts for which the employee may be fined and the amount are specified;

c. such acts are likely to cause loss or damage to the employer or his business; and

d. the amount is fair and reasonable[1].

---

1 Truck Act 1896, s.1.

Level of Wages

Wages Councils

28.23 In certain traditionally poorly paid industries where no adequate collective bargaining machinery exists, wages councils exist to fix (by wages council order) not only the remuneration but also the holidays and other terms of the employees. Wages councils consist of up to three independent persons together with persons nominated to represent both sides of industry[1]. If the contracts of employment of workers to whom a wages council order applies provide for less remuneration, or less favourable terms and conditions, than are laid down by a wages council order they are to take effect as if the remuneration or terms specified in the order were substituted[2]. An employer who fails to comply with an order is liable to a fine and the court may award any back pay to his employees. An employee will, of course, have a remedy under the contract.

It is intended that the establishment of a wages council should mark the first step in the establishment of the machinery of collective bargaining. The second step is the establishment by the Secretary of State, on an application by the relevant trade union and/or employers' association, or after consultation with them, of a statutory joint industrial council[3]. Such a council performs the functions formerly performed by the wages council[4] but is composed only of equal numbers of representatives of the relevant employers' association and trade union[5]. A statutory joint industrial council may be abolished by the Secretary of State when he is satisfied that adequate collective bargaining machinery will be established and maintained[6].

---

1 Wages Councils Act 1959, Sched. 2, para. 1.
2 *Ibid.*, s.12.
3 Employment Protection Act 1975, s.90.
4 *Ibid.*, s.91.
5 *Ibid.*, Sched. 8.
6 *Ibid.*, s.93.

Government contractors
28.24 Government contractors, i.e. those who have contracts with Government departments, are required by the Fair Wages Resolution of the House of Commons 1946 to pay rates of wages, and observe hours and conditions of labour, not less favourable than those established by collective bargaining machinery for the trade or industry in the district where the work is carried out. In the absence of such rates, hours and conditions, the contractor must pay rates and observe hours and conditions not less favourable than the general level of wages, hours and conditions observed by other employers whose general circumstances in the trade or industry in which the contractor is engaged are similar. The Resolution forms part of the contract between the department and contractor but gives no contractual right to an employee[1].

---

1 *Simpson v Kodak Ltd* [1948] 2 KB 184.

Extension of terms and conditions
28.25 The Employment Protection Act 1975, Sched. 11, contains provisions similar to those in the Fair Wages Resolution discussed above but which are of general application. The Schedule provides for a claim to be made to the Advisory Conciliation and Arbitration Service that an employer is observing terms and conditions which are less favourable than:

a. the recognised terms and conditions — e.g. terms settled for workers in comparable employment in the industry by collective bargaining machinery; or

b. where there are no recognised terms and conditions, the general level of terms and conditions — i.e. the general level observed for comparable workers by employers in the industry in the district whose circumstances are similar.

Schedule 11 makes clear that recognised terms and conditions include minimum terms and conditions. A claim may be presented on ground a. above by an employers' association or trade union which is party to the collective agreement; on ground b. by an employers' association having members in the district or by a trade union of which any worker concerned is a member. The ACAS is to take steps to settle the claim, failing which the claim is to be referred to the Central Arbitration Committee. It is for the party making the claim to satisfy the CAC of the recognised terms and conditions or general level, as the case may be; it is for the employer to show that he is observing those terms. If the CAC upholds the claim it is to make an award that the employer observe the relevant terms. Such terms then take effect as terms of the contracts of employment of relevant employees.

EMPLOYMENT PROTECTION

28.26 The Employment Protection Act 1975 creates a number of statutory rights where previously the law has not interfered. These include the right to a statutory guarantee payment in respect of working days on which an employee is given no work to do; the right to six weeks' maternity pay during absence because of pregnancy and the right to return to work after such absence (up to 29 weeks beginning with the week of confinement); the right to paid time off for trade union officials to carry out duties or to undergo training in connection with industrial relations, and the right to unpaid time off for trade union members to take part in trade union activities (other than industrial action), and for employees who are, for example, justices of the peace or local councillors, to carry out their public duties; the right not to have action (short of dismissal) taken by the employer for the purpose of preventing the employee from being a trade union member or taking part in trade union activities, or penalising him for doing so, and the right to apply to the Secretary of State for a payment out of the Redundancy Fund in respect of, in particular, up to eight weeks' arrears of pay, in a case where the employer is insolvent.

DISCRIMINATION IN EMPLOYMENT

Sex discrimination

28.27 It is unlawful for an employer to discriminate on the ground of sex —

a. against a job applicant, in the arrangements he makes for the purpose of determining who should be offered a job, or in the terms on which he offers her employment, or by refusing or deliberately omitting to offer her a job;

b. against an employee, in the way he affords her access to opportunities for promotion, transfer or training, or to any other benefits, facilities or services, or by refusing or deliberately omitting to afford her access to them, or by dismissing her or subjecting her to any other detriment[1]. Although the Sex Discrimination Act speaks of discrimination against women it is to be read as applying equally to discrimination against men[2].

Discrimination may be either direct or indirect. An employer directly discriminates against a woman if on the ground of her sex he treats her less favourably than he treats or would treat a man. He indirectly discriminates against a woman if he applies to her a requirement or condition which he applies or would apply equally to a man, but –

a. which is such that the proportion of women who can comply with it is considerably smaller than the proportion of men who can comply with it, and

b. which he cannot show to be justifiable irrespective of the sex of the person to whom it is applied, and

c. which is to her detriment because she cannot comply with it[3].

Clearly, an employer indirectly discriminates if he requires that candidates for a job should have a beard, unless he can show this is a justifiable requirement. Equally, if he requires, for example, that candidates possess a professional qualification held by very few women as compared to men, he discriminates against a female job applicant not possessing that qualification unless he can show that the requirement is justifiable, and it cannot be justifiable unless its discriminatory effect is justified by the need – not the convenience – of the business or enterprise[4].

In any comparison of the case of a man and the case of a woman, their relevant circumstances must be the same or not materially different[5].

---

1 Sex Discrimination Act 1975, s.6.
2 *Ibid.*, s.2.
3 *Ibid.*, s.1.
4 *Steel v Post Office* [1977] IRLR 288, EAT.
5 Sex Discrimination Act 1975, s.5.

28.28 It is permissible to discriminate in appointing or promoting a person where being of a particular sex is a genuine qualification for the job, for example, where there is a need for authenticity in a dramatic performance, where there is a need to preserve decency and privacy, or where the law imposes restrictions on the employment of women[1].

---

1 Sex Discrimination Act 1975, s.7.

28.29 It is also discriminatory within the Act to victimise a person, treating her less favourably than others, because she has brought or involved herself in proceedings under the Sex Discrimination Act 1975 or the Equal Pay Act 1970 or has alleged contravention of those Acts[1]. The Act further prohibits direct and indirect discrimination against married persons as compared to single persons[2].

---

1 Sex Discrimination Act 1975, s.4.
2 *Ibid.*, s.3.

28.30 A person who feels he or she has been discriminated against in the employment field may complain to an industrial tribunal which, if it upholds the complaint, may

a. declare the rights of the parties;

b. award damages, including damages for injured feelings; and/or

c. recommend that the employer take action to remedy the discrimination.

28.31 The Equal Opportunities Commission is established by the Act to work towards the elimination of discrimination, to promote equality, and to keep under review the operation of the Act. It is empowered, inter alia, to issue codes of practice relating to discrimination in employment, to investigate discriminatory practices and to take steps to bring them to an end, and to give assistance to individuals in cases of complexity or principle.

Equal pay

28.32 The Equal Pay Act 1970 forms, together with the Sex Discrimination Act 1975, a code for the regulation of discrimination in employment. The Act provides that, where a woman works on like work with a man or on a job which has been rated as equivalent on a job evaluation study, an equality clause in her contract of employment operates to modify terms in her contract which are less favourable than terms of a similar kind in the man's contract so as not to be less favourable, and to include in her contract beneficial terms in the man's contract which were not included in her contract. Again, although the Act is framed with reference to women, it is to be read as applying equally to men[1].

---

1 Equal Pay Act 1970, s.1.

28.33 The two Acts operate together in this way: the Equal Pay Act applies

a. if the employee is treated less favourably than a man who is doing like work or work rated as equivalent and the treatment relates to a matter regulated by the contract of employment of either of them;

b. if the less favourable treatment relates to the payment of money which is regulated by the contract.

The Sex Discrimination Act applies

a. if the less favourable treatment relates to a matter not included in a contract;

b. if the less favourable treatment relates to a matter in a contract (other than the payment of money) and the comparison is with employees not doing like work or work rated as equivalent[1].

---

1 Sex Discrimination Act 1975, ss. 6 and 8.

28.34 If a woman feels there has been a contravention of a term modified or included in her contract by the equality clause, she may present a complaint to an industrial tribunal[1]. It is then for her to show that she is engaged on like work with a man or on work given equal value under job evaluation. A woman is to be regarded as being employed on like work with a man if the work is the same or of a *broadly* similar nature. If the work is broadly similar, it is to be regarded as like work unless the differences between the jobs are of practical importance, i.e. are of a kind which the industrial tribunal in its experience would expect to find reflected in the terms and conditions of employment[2]. In considering whether work is 'like work', the tribunal must concentrate on what work is done in practice rather than on the contractual obligations of the man and woman[3]. Furthermore, the time at which the work is done is to be disregarded in determining whether the work is the same or similar[4].

Once it is determined that a man and woman are engaged on like work, a prima facie case for the operation of the equality clause is established. However, the clause does not operate if the employer can show that the variation between the woman's contract and the man's contract is genuinely due to a material difference (other than sex) between her case and his[5]. Such a difference might be that the woman worked in Nottingham while the man worked in London[6] or that the woman worked on a day shift and the man worked on a night shift[7].

However, the *whole* of the variation between the two contracts must be due to a material difference other than sex, or else the equality clause will apply[8].

---

1 Equal Pay Act 1970, s.2.
2 *Capper Pass Ltd v Lawton* [1977] QB 852; [1977] ICR 83, EAT.
3 *Redland Roof Tiles Ltd v Harper* [1977] ICR 349, EAT.
4 *Dugdale v Kraft Foods Ltd* [1977] ICR 48; [1977] 1 All ER 454, EAT.
5 Equal Pay Act 1970, s.1(3).
6 *Navy, Army and Air Force Institutes v Varley* [1977] 1 All ER 840, [1977] ICR 11, EAT.
7 *Kerr v Lister & Co Ltd* [1977] IRLR 259, EAT.
8 *Spruce v National Coal Board* [1977] IRLR 251; affd. [1978] IRLR 122.

Racial discrimination

28.35 The Race Relations Act 1976 makes unlawful discrimination on racial grounds, i.e. on grounds of colour, race, nationality, or ethnic or national origins[1]. The Act is drafted in very similar terms to the Sex Discrimination Act 1975. It is unlawful for an employer to discriminate directly or indirectly against job applicants and employees. It is specifically provided that segregating a person from others on racial grounds constitutes direct discrimination. As in the case of sex discrimination, it is permissible to discriminate where being of a particular racial group is a genuine qualification for a job, for example, for employment in a play, or in an Indian restaurant. A person who feels an employer has discriminated against him may complain to an industrial tribunal. The Commission for Racial Equality exists to carry out equivalent functions in the field of race relations as are carried out by the Equal Opportunities Commission in relation to sex discrimination.

---

1 Race Relations Act 1976, s.3.

DISMISSAL

28.36 The employment relationship may come to an end by the operation of the doctrine of frustration, a matter which we discussed in para. 11.6; by the employee resigning; or by the employer dismissing him.

Written reasons for dismissal

28.37 An employee who has been continuously employed for 26 weeks prior to his dismissal may request his employer to provide him, within 14 days of the request, with a written statement of the reasons for his dismissal[1]. This statement is admissible in evidence in any proceedings. If the employer unreasonably refuses to provide a statement, or gives inadequate or untrue particulars of his reasons, the employee may present a complaint to an industrial tribunal. If the tribunal upholds the complaint, it may declare what it finds to be the reasons for the dismissal and must order the employer to pay the employee a sum equal to two weeks' pay.

---

1 Employment Protection Act 1975, s.70.

Notice

28.38   At common law, the rule is that every contract of employment is terminable by either party by reasonable notice[1]. What is reasonable depends upon the circumstances of each case, but relevant factors include the nature of the job, length of service, seniority and the payment interval. The Contracts of Employment Act 1972, s.1, lays down the *minimum* period of notice to which an employee is entitled: one week's notice if his period of continuous employment is less than two years; one week's notice for each year if his period of continuous employment is two years or more, but less than 12 years; 12 week's notice if his period of continuous employment is 12 years or more. The minimum notice required to be given by an employee to terminate his contract is one week. The section permits either party to waive his right to notice or to accept payment in lieu of notice. The notice given by either party must contain a certain amount of particularity: if it is to operate on a future day it must specify that date, or at least contain facts from which that date is ascertainable[2]. Once notice has been given by either side it can only be withdrawn by agreement[3].

---

1   *Richardson v Koefod* [1969] 3 All ER 1264, [1969] 1 WLR 1812, CA.
2   *Morton Sundour Fabrics Ltd v Shaw* (1966) 2 KIR 1 at 4.
3   *Harris & Russell Ltd v Slingsby* [1973] 3 All ER 31, [1973] ICR 454.

Summary dismissal

28.39   Where an employee has committed a breach of his contract of employment, such as to show that he no longer regards himself as bound by it or one of its essential terms, his employer is entitled to dismiss him summarily, i.e. without notice[1]. In *Sinclair v Neighbour*[2], the manager of a shop took money from the till and put in an IOU in its stead. The next day he put back the amount he had taken. On learning what had taken place, his employer summarily dismissed him. The Court of Appeal held that the manager's conduct, although not dishonest, was incompatible with his employment as a manager and thus his summary dismissal was justified. A case where dismissal was not justified is *Laws v London Chronicle (Indicator Newspapers) Ltd*[3], where the employee joined her superior in walking out of the room after a dispute between her immediate superior and the company's managing director. The latter had ordered the employee to remain; she left, however, out of loyalty to her 'boss'. Her subsequent summary dismissal was held to be unwarranted.

---

1 This right is preserved by Contracts of Employment Act 1972, s.1.
2 [1967] 2 QB 279, [1966] 3 All ER 988, CA.
3 [1959] 2 All ER 285, [1959] 1 WLR 698, CA.

Wrongful dismissal

28.40 Where an employer dismisses an employee with shorter notice than he is contractually obliged to give, or without notice in circumstances in which summary dismissal is not warranted, he wrongfully dismisses the employee, who has an action for breach of contract. If, before his dismissal, the employee has been guilty of such conduct as would entitle the employer to summarily dismiss him, the employer has a defence to an action for wrongful dismissal, even though at the time he dismissed the employee he was unaware of that conduct[1]. It has generally been accepted that the employer's repudiation of the contract by wrongfully dismissing the employee terminates the contract automatically and forthwith[2]. In the normal case, the employee is left to his remedy in damages against the employer. He gets damages for the time he would have served if he had been given proper notice less, because of his duty to mitigate damages[3], anything he has, or ought to have earned in alternative employment. The general rule is that the courts will not grant the remedies of specific performance or injunction to a wrongfully dismissed employee where the effect of the order would be to continue the employment relationship, a matter which we have discussed in paras. 12.18 and 12.22. However, if the person dismissed has not a mere contract of employment, but has a status or can only be dismissed by a specified procedure which alone confers the power to dismiss him, the employment is not effectively terminated by wrongful dismissal[4], and a declaration to that effect may be obtained.

---

1 *Cyril Leonard & Co v Simo Securities Trust Ltd* [1971] 3 All ER 1313, [1972] 1 WLR 80, CA.

2 *Sanders v Ernest A Neale Ltd* [1974] 3 All ER 327, [1974] ICR 565.
3 Para. 12.9.
4 *Taylor v National Union of Seamen* [1967] 1 All ER 767, [1967] 1 WLR 532.

Unfair dismissal

28.41 As a general rule, every employee has the right not to be unfairly dismissed[1]. Certain employees are, however, excluded from the benefit of the unfair dismissal legislation. Amongst these are:

a. Those who have been continuously employed for less than 26 weeks. This exclusion does not apply where the dismissal is for an inadmissible reason (see para. 28.45)[2].

b. Those employed under a contract for a fixed term of two years or more who have agreed in writing to exclude any claim in respect of unfair dismissal. In this context, 'fixed term' means a term 'which cannot be unfixed by notice'[3].

c. Those who under their contract of employment ordinarily work outside Great Britain. Where a person ordinarily works is to be determined by reference to his contract of employment, and in the general case will be the place indicated in his contract as his 'base'[4].

1 Trade Union and Labour Relations Act 1974, Sched. 1, para. 4.
2 *Ibid.*, Sched. 1, paras. 10 and 11.
3 *British Broadcasting Corpn v Ioannou* [1975] QB 781 at 786, [1975] 2 All ER 999, CA.
4 *Wilson v Maynard Shipbuilding Consultants AB* [1976] IRLR 384, EAT.

28.42 An employee who considers that he has been unfairly dismissed may present a complaint to an industrial tribunal within a prescribed period. It is for the employee to show to the tribunal that he was dismissed, and an employee is regarded as dismissed if[1]:

a. his contract of employment is terminated by the employer with or without notice, or

b. his fixed term contract expires without being renewed under the same contract. ('Fixed term' in this context refers to contracts for a specified term whether or not they can be determined by earlier notice[2]), or

c. the employee terminates the contract, with or without notice, in circumstances such that he is entitled to terminate it without notice because of the employer's conduct. This is known as 'constructive dismissal' and whether there has been such a dismissal depends on whether the employer has committed a repudiatory breach of the employment contract. 'Was the employer guilty of conduct which was a significant breach going to the root of the contract of employment, or which showed that he no longer intended to be bound by its essential terms?'[3]

---

1   Trade Union and Labour Relations Act 1974, Sched. 1, para. 5.
2   *Dixon v British Broadcasting Corpn* [1977] IRLR 337, EAT.
3   *Western Excavating (ECC) Ltd v Sharp* [1978] IRLR 27, CA.

28.43   Once the employee has shown that he was dismissed, the employer is liable unless he shows that the employee was dismissed for one of the following reasons:

a. one related to the capability or qualifications of the employee;

b. one related to the conduct of the employee;

c. redundancy;

d. that the employee could not continue to work in the position which he held without contravention (either by him or his employer) of a statute;

e. some other substantial reason of a kind such as to justify the dismissal of an employee holding the position which that employee held[1].

---

1   Trade Union and Labour Relations Act 1974, Sched. 1, para. 6.

28.44   Proof of one of the above reasons does not alone afford the employer a defence. He must also show that he acted reasonably in the circumstances (having regard to equity and the substantial merits of the case) in treating his reason as a sufficient reason for dismissing the employee[1]. The cases show that the procedure followed by the employer in dismissing the employee is a relevant factor in determining whether the employer acted reasonably in the circumstances. Giving a prior warning and an opportunity for a hearing before dismissal are aspects of procedure stressed in the cases. However, there is no general rule requiring an employee to be given a warning or opportunity for a hearing[2]. Where the dismissal is related to conduct, the provisions of the Arbitration Conciliation and Advisory Service (ACAS) Code of Practice on Disciplinary Practice and Procedures in Employment may be taken into account by the tribunal in determining the reasonableness of the employer's action.

In deciding what was the reason for the dismissal and whether the employer acted reasonably in the circumstances in treating it as sufficient, no account is to be taken of pressure via industrial action or threats thereof exercised on the employer to dismiss the employee: the questions are to be answered as if no such pressure had been exercised[3].

---

1 Trade Union and Labour Relations Act 1974, Sched. 1, para. 6(8).
2 *Lowndes v Specialist Heavy Engineering Ltd* [1976] IRLR 246, EAT.
3 Trade Union and Labour Relations Act 1974, Sched. 1, para. 15.

Inadmissible reasons[1]

28.45 The above provisions as to the reasons for, and reasonableness of, a dismissal do not apply if an employee proves not only that he was dismissed, but that his dismissal was for an inadmissible reason.

A dismissal is automatically unfair if the reason for it was that the employee was, or proposed to become, a member of a trade union; or had taken, or proposed to take part in trade union activities at an appropriate time; or refused to join a non-independent trade union (i.e. one under the domination of, or subject to interference by, an employer). A dismissal is fair if it is the practice in accordance with a union membership agreement (i.e. a closed shop agreement) for employees of the same class as the dismissed employee to belong to a specified trade union or to one of a number of specified unions, and the reason for the dismissal was that the employee was not a member of, or refused to become or remain a member of such a union. However, in such a case the dismissal *will* be unfair if the employee genuinely objects on grounds of religious belief to being a member of any trade union whatsoever. Dismissals which are unfair by virtue of these provisions are referred to as being for an inadmissible reason.

---

1 Trade Union and Labour Relations Act 1974, Sched. 1, para. 6(4)—(6).

Selection for redundancy

28.46 As we saw in para. 28.43, one of the reasons on which an employer can rely on an allegation of unfair dismissal is redundancy. If he does so, the employee may show that the circumstances constituting the redundancy applied equally to one or more other employees in the same undertaking who held positions similar to that held by him and who have not been dismissed by the employer, and either:

a. that the reason for which he was selected for dismissal was an inadmissible one; or

b. that he was selected for dismissal in contravention of a customary arrangement or agreed procedure relating to redundancy and there were no special reasons justifying a departure from that arrangement or procedure in his case[1].

If the employee shows such matters, his dismissal is automatically unfair. but if he fails to do so, the employer must nevertheless show that the action was reasonable in the circumstances in treating redundancy as sufficient to dismiss the employee[2], in which case relevant considerations may be failure of procedure, failure to offer alternative work, and 'last in, first out'.

---

1   Trade Union and Labour Relations Act 1974, Sched. 1, para. 6(7).
2   *Ibid.*, Sched. 1, para. 6(8).

The special case of pregnancy

28.47   An employee is unfairly dismissed if she is dismissed because she is pregnant, or for any other reason connected with pregnancy, except the reason that because of her pregnancy she is incapable of adequately doing her job or cannot continue to do her job without their being a contravention of a statute. Even in this excepted case, the dismissal will be unfair if the employer has failed to offer alternative work where there is a suitable available vacancy[1]. The dismissed employee retains her statutory right to return to work if she notifies her employer of her intention to return[2].

---

1   Employment Protection Act 1975, s.34.
2   *Ibid.*, s.35.

The special case of lock-outs or strikes

28.48   Where, at the datesof the dismissal, the employer was conducting a lock-out, or the employee was taking part in a strike or other industrial action, an industrial tribunal is debarred from considering whether the dismissal was unfair unless the dismissal was selective, in that one or more of the employees who were locked out or who took part in the industrial action have been offered re-engagement, when the employee concerned has not, or have not been dismissed[1].

---

1   Trade Union and Labour Relations Act 1974, Sched. 1, para. 7.

Remedies

28.49   If an industrial tribunal upholds a complaint of unfair dismissal, it must explain to the employee that it has power in certain circumstances to order a. his reinstatement, or b. his re-engagement, and must ask him if he wishes such an order to be made[1]. If the employee wishes an order to be made; the tribunal should first consider whether to order reinstatement. An order for reinstatement is an order that the employer treat the employee in all respects as if he had not been dismissed. In considering whether to order reinstatement, the tribunal must take into account the employee's wishes, whether it is practicable for the employer to comply with the order, and, where the employee was in any way to blame for the dismissal, whether it would be just to order his reinstatement. If the tribunal decides not to order reinstatement, it must then consider whether to order re-engagement and on what terms. An order for re-engagement is an order that the employer take the employee back in employment comparable to that from which he was dismissed, or other suitable employment. The tribunal must specify the terms on which the re-engagement is to take place. In deciding whether to make such an order, the tribunal must consider the same factors as when deciding whether to order reinstatement. Save where the employee was partly to blame for the dismissal, re-engagement should be on terms which are, so far as is reasonably practicable, as favourable as an order for reinstatement[2].

---

1 Employment Protection Act 1975, s.71(1).
2 *Ibid.*, s.71(2)–(7).

28.50 If an employer fails fully to comply with an order for reinstatement or re-engagement, an industrial tribunal may award the employee compensation in respect of loss sustained by reason of the failure, up to a maximum of £5,200. If an order is not complied with at all, although it was practicable to do so, the tribunal will award unfair dismissal compensation plus an additional award of not less than 13 nor more than 26 weeks' pay (up to £100 per week) or, where the dismissal is for an inadmissible reason or is an act of discrimination[1], not less than 26 nor more than 52 weeks' pay[2].

---

1 Para. 28.27.
2 Employment Protection Act 1975, s.72.

28.51 If neither order is made, compensation is to be awarded. Compensation comprises two elements: the basic award and the compensatory award[1]. The basic award is calculated by reckoning backwards from the date of dismissal and allowing:

1½ weeks' pay for each year of continuous employment in which the employee was not below the age of 41;

1 weeks' pay for each such year in which the employee was below the age of 41 and not below the age of 22; and,

half a weeks' pay for each such year in which the employee was below the age of 22 and not below the age of 18.

Twenty years is the maximum number of years of employment which may be counted; £100 is the maximum weeks' pay.

The basic award may be reduced to the extent that the employee contributed to his dismissal; but not below two weeks' pay. If an employee receives a redundancy payment in respect of the same dismissal he will in the normal case receive no basic award[2].

The compensatory award is such amount, up to £5,200, that the tribunal considers just and equitable in all the circumstances having regard to the loss sustained by the employee in consequence of his employer's action[3]. Loss does not include injury to pride or feelings, but includes such matters as immediate and future loss of wages, loss arising from the manner of the dismissal, loss of protection in respect of unfair dismissal and loss of pension rights[4]. The award may be reduced to the extent that the employee contributed to his dismissal[5].

---

1 Employment Protection Act 1975, ss. 72(5) and 73.
2 *Ibid.*, ss. 74 and 75.
3 *Ibid.*, s.76.
4 *Norton Tool Company Ltd v Tewson* [1973] 1 All ER 183, [1972] ICR 501; *Tidman v Aveling Marshall Ltd* [1977] IRLR 218, EAT.
5 Employment Protection Act 1975, s.76.

REDUNDANCY

28.52 An employee may be entitled to a redundancy payment if he has been continuously employed for two years or more since the age of 18, and has been dismissed by reason of redundancy or laid off or kept on short time.

28.53 Dismissal in the context of redundancy is defined in the same way as in respect of unfair dismissal[1] (see para. 28.42). Events which operate to determine a contract of employment, such as the death of the employer, are regarded as being a dismissal by the employer[2]. An employee who gives notice to terminate his employment within the period of notice given to him by his employer is nonetheless treated as dismissed by his employer; but if the employer requires the employee to withdraw his 'anticipatory notice' and the employee refuses to do so, he may not, at the discretion of the tribunal, be entitled to a redundancy payment[3]. Where an employer dismisses for redundancy in a case where he might have dismissed for misconduct, then, provided the dismissal is without notice, or is with short notice, or is accompanied by a statement referring to the entitlement to dismiss for misconduct, the employee will lose his entitlement to redundancy payment[4].

---

1 Redundancy Payments Act 1965, s.3.
2 *Ibid.*, s.22.
3 *Ibid.*, s.4.
4 *Ibid.*, s.2(2).

28.54 An employee's dismissal is by reason of redundancy if it is attributable wholly or mainly to:

a. the fact that his employer has ceased, or intends to cease, to carry on the business for the purposes of which the employee was employed by him, or has ceased, or intends to cease, to carry on that business in the place where the employee was so employed; or

b. the fact that the requirements of that business for employees to carry out work of a particular kind, or for employees to carry out work of a particular kind in the place where he was so employed, have ceased or diminished or are expected to cease or diminish[1].

In proceedings relating to a redundancy payment before an industrial tribunal it is presumed, unless the contrary is proved, that the dismissal was by reason of redundancy[2].

As to the definition of redundancy, no difficulty is likely to arise on a claim that the employer has ceased to carry on business altogether, but difficult questions may arise as to 'the place where the employee was so employed'. What is meant here is the place where, under his contract of employment, the employee could be required to work[3]. Thus, an employee, whose contract included a term that he was prepared and willing to work at any place within the United Kingdom, was not dismissed for redundancy when he left his employment on being required by his employer to move from Norfolk to Scotland, there being insufficient work for him in Norfolk[4]. In the absence of an express term as to the 'mobility' of the employee, what terms may be implied is a question of law to be determined on all the evidence.

Paragraph b. of the definition of redundancy has been the source of many difficulties. When considering the requirements of the business, an industrial tribunal must consider the overall requirements of the business and not any changes in the allocation of duties between individuals[5]. Where an employee, whose job as a workshop manager had involved him largely in mechanical work, was required to undertake a greater amount of administrative work instead, and was dismissed because he could not adapt himself to the new methods introduced by his employers, he was held not to have been dismissed for redundancy. It was irrelevant that the duties in the new job specification were not identical with the duties formerly undertaken by the employee if the overall requirements of the business remained unchanged[6].

A change in the time at which work is done, e.g. a change to a shift system is not relevant in determining whether there has been a reduction in the requirements of the business for employees to carry out work of a particular kind[7]. It has been held that 'work of a particular kind' is distinguished from other work of the same general kind by requiring special aptitudes, skills or knowledge[8]. In *Vaux and*

Associated Breweries Ltd v Ward[9], a middle-aged barmaid was dismissed because her employers required younger and more glamorous women to work in their recently renovated public house. Her contention that she was redundant because the requirements of the business for barmaids of the old type had ceased was rejected. The work of the new barmaids was not of a different kind to that which she had been doing.

---

1 Redundancy Payments Act 1965, s.1.
2 *Ibid.*, s.9.
3 *Sutcliffe v Hawker Siddeley Aviation Ltd* [1973] ICR 560.
4 *Ibid.*
5 *North Riding Garages Ltd v Butterwick* [1967] 2 QB 56, [1967] 1 All ER 644, DC.
6 *Ibid.*
7 *Johnson v Nottinghamshire Combined Police Authority* [1974] 1 All ER 1082, [1974] ICR 170, CA.
8 *Amos v Max-Arc Ltd* [1973] ICR 46.
9 (1969) 7 KIR 308, DC.

Renewal or re-engagement

28.55 If the employer offers, before the employee's contract comes to an end, to renew the contract or to re-engage the employee under a new contract, on the terms that the renewal or re-engagement is to take effect either immediately on the ending of the old contract or within four weeks thereafter, and either the employment offered does not differ from the old employment as regards the capacity and place in which the employee would be employed and as to the other terms and conditions of employment, or the employment offered does differ but is suitable in relation to the employee, then, if the employee unreasonably refuses the offer he is not entitled to a redundancy payment[1]. If, pursuant to the employer's offer, the employee's contract is renewed or he is re-engaged, he is not regarded as having been dismissed on the ending of his previous contract. If the new or renewed contract differs in any way from the previous contract, the first four weeks of work under the contract are regarded as a trial period. A longer trial period may be agreed for the purposes of retraining the employee. If, for whatever reason, the employee terminates the employment during the trial period, or the employer does so for a reason connected with the new employment, the employee is treated as having been dismissed on the ending of his previous contract[2]. If the employee unreasonably terminates the employment during the trial period and the employment was suitable in relation to him, he is not entitled to a redundancy payment in respect of his dismissal from the previous employment[3].

---

1 Redundancy Payments Act 1965, s.2(3) and (5).
2 *Ibid.*, s.3(3) and (8).
3 *Ibid.*, s.2(6).

28.56 The provisions as to renewal and re-engagement apply where there has been a change of ownership of the business and the previous owner terminates the employee's contract of employment and the new owner offers renewal or re-engagement. Whether there has been a change in the ownership of the business depends on whether the new owner took over the business as a going concern, so that the business remained the same but in different hands, or whether he only took over the physical assets, using them in a different business[1]. In *Crompton v Truly Fair (International) Ltd*[2], a factory and its machinery which had been used for making children's clothes were sold and used to manufacture trousers. There was thus no change of ownership of the children's clothes business and employees who took up employment with the new owner of the factory were able to claim redundancy payments from the outgoing owner of the factory.

---

1 *Woodhouse v Peter Brotherhood* [1972] 2 QB 520, [1972] 3 All ER 91, CA.
2 [1975] ICR 359.

Lay-off and short-time

28.57 An employee, whose remuneration depends on his being provided with work, is laid-off in any week in which, because no work is provided, he is not entitled to remuneration. If in any week an employee earns less than half a weeks' pay because of a reduction in the amount of work provided for him, he is regarded as being on short-time for that week[1]. If an employee is laid off or kept on short-time for a period of four consecutive weeks or six weeks within a period of 13 weeks, he will be entitled to a redundancy payment if:

a. within four weeks from the end of the lay-off or short-time, he serves a notice on his employer indicating his intention to claim a redundancy payment; and

b. he terminates his employment with notice[2].

The employer may give the employee a counter-notice stating that he will contest liability, in which case the employee will not be entitled to a redundancy payment if it was reasonably to be expected that, in not more than four weeks from the employee's notice, the employee would enter on a period of employment (under the same contract) of not less than 13 weeks during which time he would not be laid-off or kept on short-time[3].

1 Redundancy Payments Act 1965, s.5.
2 *Ibid.*, s.6.
3 *Ibid.*

Payment

28.58 The amount of redundancy payment to which an employee is entitled is reckoned in the same way as the basic award for unfair dismissal[1] and is likewise subject to the limits of 20 years and £100 per week.

1 Para. 28.51.

Redundancy Fund

28.59 Where an employer is liable to pay, and has paid, a redundancy payment, he is entitled to a rebate out of the Redundancy Fund[1]. The amount of rebate is currently 41 per cent of the payment; but the Secretary of State has power to fix the amount by statutory instrument at one of 10 rates varying from 35 per cent to 80 per cent of the payment. Where the employer has defaulted or is insolvent, redundancy payments may be made to employees out of the Fund[2]. The Fund is financed from employer's national insurance contributions and from the National Loans Fund.

1 Redundancy Payments Act 1965, s.30.
2 *Ibid.*, s.32.

Procedure for handling redundancies

Consultation with Trade Unions
28.60 If an employer plans to make redundant an employee of a description in respect of which he recognises a trade union for collective bargaining purposes, he must at the earliest opportunity (in some cases,

there is a minimum period which must elapse between commencement of consultation and dismissal) consult representatives of the trade union about the dismissal. To this end he must inform them in writing of:

a. his reasons;

b. the numbers and descriptions of employees affected;

c. the total number of employees of any such description employed at the establishment in question;

d. the method of selection for redundancy; and

e. the period over which the dismissals are to take effect.

The employer must then consider representations made by the trade union representatives and reply to them, stating his reasons should he reject any representation. There is thus no obligation to reach agreement with the union. It is particularly provided that where the employer is proposing to make redundant 100 or more employees at one establishment within a period of 90 days or less, the consultation required must begin at least 90 days before the first of the dismissals takes effect; where the employer proposes to make redundant 10 or more employees at one establishment within a period of 30 days or less, the consultation must begin at least 60 days before the first dismissal takes effect. If there are special circumstances which make it not reasonably practicable for an employer to comply with any requirement relating to consultation, he must take such steps as are reasonably practicable in the circumstances towards compliance[1].

---

1 Employment Protection Act 1975, s.99.

28.61 If the employer fails to comply with any requirement relating to consultation, the trade union may present a complaint to an industrial tribunal. The employer may wish to show that there were special circumstances, such that it was not reasonably practicable for him to comply, but that he took all such steps as were reasonably practicable. If the tribunal upholds the union's complaint it will make a declaration to that effect and may also make a 'protective award', that is, an award that, for a specified period, the employer shall pay remuneration to employees who have been made redundant, or whom it is proposed to make redundant, and in respect of whom there was a failure to comply with the consultation requirements. The period specified, 'the protected period', may be of such length as the tribunal considers just and equitable in the circumstances, having regard to the employer's default, subject to statutory maxima. Remuneration paid to an employee under the contract of employment, or by way of damages for breach, in respect of any time within the protected period goes towards discharging the employer's liability under the protective award, and vice versa. If the employee continues to be employed during the protected period but is fairly dismissed by the employer for a reason other than redundancy or unreasonably leaves his employment, his rights under the protective award cease. If the employer offers the employee renewal or re-engagement which would take effect during the protected period, then, if the offer is of the same, or different but suitable, employment, and the employee unreasonably refuses the offer, the employee's rights under the award cease. If the offer is of different terms there is a trial period; if during the trial period, the employee resigns, for whatever reason, or the employer terminates the contract for a reason related to the new employment, the employee remains entitled under the protective award, unless he acted unreasonably in resigning[1]. If the employer fails, wholly or in part to pay an employee under the award, the employee may complain to an industrial tribunal. If the complaint is upheld, the tribunal will order the employer to pay the amount owed[2].

---

1 Employment Protection Act 1975, s.102; cf. para. 28.55.
2 *Ibid.*, s.103.

Notification to Department of Employment[1]

28.62 An employer who proposes to make redundant 100 or more employees at one establishment within 90 days or less, or 10 or more employees at one establishment within 30 days or less must notify the Secretary of State, in writing, of his intentions – in the former case at least 90 days before the first dismissal takes place, in the latter case at least 60 days before the first dismissal takes place. If he recognises a trade union in respect of the relevant descriptions of employees he must send a copy of the notice to the union. The Department can require further information from the employer; if special circumstances make it impracticable for the employer to comply, he must take such steps as are practicable towards compliance. Failure to comply may lead to a reduction of the redundancy rebate to the employer by an amount (up to one-tenth) which the Secretary of State considers appropriate. The employer may appeal against a reduction to an industrial tribunal, but he runs the risk that the tribunal may reduce the rebate further. Instead of the redundancy rebate being reduced, the employer may be prosecuted for failure to notify the Secretary of State.

---

1 Employment Protection Act 1975, ss. 100, 104 and 105.

Time off to look for work
28.63 An employee who is given notice of dismissal for redundancy is entitled, before the notice expires, to reasonable time off during

working hours to look for a new job or to make arrangements for training for future employment. An employee qualifies for this right, if, on the expiry of the requisite notice period, he will have been continuously employed for two years. He is entitled to be paid up to two-fifths of a weeks' pay in respect of time off during the notice period. This right does not affect his contractual right to remuneration, but this will be set off against the statutory payment and vice versa. If the employer unreasonably refuses time off, the employee is entitled to up to two-fifths of a weeks' pay on top of any contractual entitlement, and the employee may complain to an industrial tribunal that his employer has unreasonably refused time off or failed to pay any sum to which the employee is entitled in that respect. If the tribunal upholds the complaint, it will make a declaration to that effect and order the employer to pay the amount due[1].

---

1 Employment Protection Act 1975, s.61.

LIABILITY FOR SAFETY AT WORK

28.64 An employee injured at work may have two causes of action against his employer:

a. for breach of the common law duty of care,

b. where applicable, for breach of statutory duty.

In addition to this civil liability, an employer may incur criminal penalties for breaches of legislation dealing with safety.

Common law duty

28.65 The employer's duty under common law is to take reasonable care[1] in all the circumstances of the case[2] to avoid reasonably foreseeable dangers to his employees. For convenience we treat this general duty as comprising three separate aspects: the duty to provide a safe system of work, the duty to employ reasonably competent fellow employees, and the duty to provide safe plant, machinery and premises. However, it is important to remember that there is in fact one general duty to take reasonable care[3]. An action for breach of the common law duty of care may be founded in contract, on the basis of breach of an implied term in the contract, or in tort for negligence. It is usual to sue in tort.

The common law duty of care lies on the employer personally and he cannot escape liability by showing that he has delegated the duty to provide for safety to, for example, a safety officer[4].

1 *Latimer v AEC Ltd* [1953] AC 643, [1953] 2 All ER 449, HL.
2 *Paris v London Borough of Stepney* [1951] AC 376, [1951] 1 All ER 42, HL: para. 20.20.
3 *Wilson v Tyneside Window Cleaning Co* [1958] 2 QB 110, [1958] 2 All ER 265, CA.
4 *Wilsons and Clyde Coal Co v English* [1938] AC 57, [1937] 3 All ER 628, HL.

Safe system of work
28.66 The employer must plan the work with due regard to safety. Thus, an employer was held to be in breach of his duty by permitting a crane to swing stones over the heads of employees working in a quarry, with the result that an employee was injured by falling stones. The fact that the employees continued to work in the knowledge of the risk did not mean that they continued to work consenting to the risk of injury[1]. In planning the work, the employer must recognise that employees become careless about risks involved in their jobs, and that the fact that a practice has grown up of doing a particular job in a particular way does not, necessarily, mean that to adopt that practice is to employ reasonable care[2].

An experienced workman dealing with a familiar and obvious risk may not reasonably need the same attention or the same precautions as an inexperienced man[3]. In the case of the skilled and experienced worker, it may be necessary only to *provide* safety equipment such as goggles, belts or spats; in the case of the inexperienced man it may be necessary actually to exhort him to use the equipment. A failure to provide safety equipment for an experienced worker may not result in an employer losing an action for breach of common law duty where it is shown that the accident would have occurred in any event because the employee refused to use the equipment[4].

1 *Smith v Charles Baker & Sons* [1891] AC 325, HL.
2 *Cavanagh v Ulster Weaving Co Ltd* [1960] AC 145, [1959] 2 All ER 745, HL.
3 *Qualcast (Wolverhampton) Ltd v Haynes* [1959] AC 743, [1959] 2 All ER 38, HL.
4 *McWilliams v Sir William Arrol & Co Ltd* [1962] 1 All ER 623, [1962] 1 WLR 295, HL; para. 20.24.

Competent fellow employees
28.67 In *Hudson v Ridge Manufacturing Co Ltd*[1] an employee was injured by being tripped up by a fellow employee who had, to the employer's knowledge, engaged in such 'horse-play' for a number of years. The employer was held to be liable for not removing a foreseeable source of danger, the fellow employee. Clearly, the employer would

not be in breach of this duty where he had no reason to expect the employee would do anything dangerous. It should be noted that the employer is here liable for his own negligence in not taking reasonable care for his employees' safety; the action is not based on vicarious liability for the acts of the employee.

---

1 [1957] 2 QB 348, [1957] 2 All ER 229.

Safe plant, machinery and premises
28.68 The employer must take reasonable care to provide safe plant, machinery and premises. Thus, an employer was held liable for sending an employee on a long journey in an unheated van in cold weather whereby the employee suffered frostbite[1]. In another case, an employee slipped on a 'duck-board' which was in a slippery condition, and was injured. Although at the time she was seeking to wash a tea cup for her own purposes her employer was held liable. The obligation to provide safe plant etc. extends to cover all acts which are normally and reasonably incidental to a day's work[2].

---

1 *Bradford v Robinson Rentals Ltd* [1967] 1 All ER 267, [1967] 1 WLR 337.
2 *Davidson v Handley Page Ltd* [1945] 1 All ER 235, CA.

28.69 Where an employee suffers an injury *in the course of his employment* because of a defect in equipment provided by his employer for the purposes of the business, and the defect is attributable wholly or in part to the fault of a third party (e.g. the manufacturer or supplier of the equipment), the injury is deemed to be *also* attributable to the employer's negligence[1]. Thus, the employee may sue his employer rather than pursuing the manufacturer or supplier; the employer may then seek a contribution from the third party[2].

---

1 Employer's Liability (Defective Equipment) Act 1969.
2 Para. 21.34.

28.70 If the employee's own negligence contributes to his injury, any damages he receives from his employer will be reduced accordingly[1]. Under the Employer's Liability (Compulsory Insurance) Act 1969 all employers must insure against liability to employees for personal injury arising in the course of employment.

---

1 We discuss contributory negligence in paras. 21.39—21.43.

Health and Safety at Work etc. Act 1974

28.71 The aim of this Act is to provide the framework on which a comprehensive body of provisions regulating health and safety at work will be built. It is intended that existing legislative provisions e.g. the Factories Act 1961 and the Offices, Shops and Railway Premises Act 1963, which were designed to deal piecemeal with health and safety matters in particular employment situations, will be progressively replaced by a system of regulations and codes of practice founded on the general duties laid down in the Act. For the moment the 1974 Act and earlier legislation exist side by side, but enforcement of all safety legislation is regulated by the Health and Safety at Work Act.

28.72 The Act itself contains a number of general duties, imposed particularly on employers, but also on the self-employed, on employees and on those who manufacture or supply articles for use at work, to take such steps as are reasonably practicable to ensure safety. Breach of these duties gives rise to *criminal* liability[1]; the relevant sections do not per se confer a right of action for breach of statutory duty[2].

It is the duty of every employer to ensure, so far as reasonably practicable, the health, safety and welfare at work of all his employees. In particular, this involves providing and maintaining, so far as is reasonably practicable, safe plant, safe premises and a safe system of work; ensuring that 'articles and substances' are, so far as is reasonably practicable, safe and free from health risks in use, storage etc.; providing such information, training, instruction and supervision as is necessary to ensure the health and safety of his employees, and ensuring that the working environment is, so far as is reasonably practicable, free from risks to health and adequate as regards facilities and arrangements for welfare.

The employer must provide his employees with a written statement of his health and safety policy and the organisation and arrangements for carrying it out. He must consult with safety representatives, appointed by relevant trade unions to represent the employees, with a view to promoting and developing health and safety at the place of work and to checking the effectiveness of measures taken to that end[3].

---

1 Health and Safety at Work etc. Act 1974, s.33.
2 *Ibid.*, s.47.
3 *Ibid.*, s.2.

28.73 Employers and the self-employed must conduct their undertakings so that, so far as is reasonably practicable, people other than employees are not thereby exposed to risks to health and safety[1].

Those having control of certain prescribed premises must use the best practicable means to prevent harmful emissions into the atmosphere[2].

---

1   Health and Safety at Work etc. Act 1974, s.3.
2   *Ibid.*, s.5.

28.74   It is the duty of those who design, manufacture, import or supply any article or substance for use at work to ensure, so far as is reasonably practicable, that it will be safe and without health risks when properly used; to carry out necessary testing and examination to that end; and to ensure that adequate information is provided as to its use. Those who erect or install an article for use at work must ensure, so far as is reasonably practicable, that nothing about the way in which it is erected or installed makes it unsafe or a risk to health when properly used[1].

---

1   Health and Safety at Work etc. Act 1974, s.6.

28.75   Finally, and importantly, it is the duty of every employee at work to take reasonable care for the health and safety of himself and others and to co-operate with his employer in complying with his statutory obligations[1].

---

1   Health and Safety at Work etc. Act 1974, s.7.

28.76   The Act establishes two government bodies concerned with health and safety at work, the Health and Safety Commission and the Health and Safety Executive. The Commission is responsible for developing health and safety policy, for disseminating information on health and safety, for making proposals for health and safety regulations and for drafting and approving codes of practice on health and safety. The Executive, which is subordinate to the Commission, is responsible via its inspectorate for the enforcement of health and safety legislation. We consider enforcement in paras. 28.81 and 28.82.

Factories Act 1961

28.77   This Act will ultimately be replaced by regulations and codes of practice made under the Health and Safety at Work etc. Act 1974. For the moment, it remains in force. Its provisions apply only to 'a factory'. A factory is any premises in which or within the precincts of which, persons are employed in manual labour in any process for or incidental to:

a. the making of any article or part of any article; or

b. the altering, repairing, ornamenting, finishing, cleaning, or washing, or the breaking up or demolition of any article; or

c. the adapting for sale of any article; or

d. the slaughtering of cattle; or

e. the confinement of such animals while awaiting slaughter;

being premises in which, or within the precincts of which, the work is carried on by way of trade or for purposes of gain and to or over which the employer of the persons employed therein has the right to access or control.

'Factory' also includes 'inter alia' packing and bottling plants, printing works and film sets[1].

---

1 Factories Act 1961, s.175.

28.78 The Factories Act contains general provisions dealing with health, safety and welfare in factories and specific provisions dealing with working conditions, accidents and diseases, and the employment of women and young persons in factories. We shall here deal only with the provisions relating to fencing of machinery[1].

---

1 Factories Act 1961, ss. 12—16.

28.79 Every part of electric generators, motors and rotary converters, and every flywheel connected thereto, must be securely fenced, unless in such a position or of such construction as to be as safe to every person employed or working on the premises as it would be if securely fenced. Every moving part of any other prime mover must be securely fenced[1]. Every part of transmission machinery[2] and every *dangerous* part of any machinery[3], other than prime movers and transmission machinery, must be securely fenced subject to the proviso as to position and construction. The interpretation of these provisions, in particular of s.14 which refers to the fencing of dangerous parts of machinery, has given rise to much case law.

---

1 Factories Act 1961, s.12.
2 *Ibid.*, s.13.
3 *Ibid.*, s.14.

28.80   Under s.14, it is only *dangerous* parts of machinery which must be fenced. A part is dangerous if it is a foreseeable cause of injury to anybody acting in a way in which a human being may reasonably be expected to act in circumstances which may reasonably be expected to occur[1]. Once it is established that a part of machinery is dangerous and that there is thus a duty to fence it, it matters not that a particular accident happened in a quite unexpected way. Thus, where a drill operator was injured when swarf from the metal he was drilling wound round his hand pulling it into contact with the drill, his employer was held liable for insecurely fencing the drill[2].

The section requires that *parts* of machinery should be fenced; thus there is no obligation to fence a machine if it is dangerous as a whole, but without having dangerous parts. Where an employee was injured by being trapped between two parts of a mobile crane, the House of Lords, in imposing liability on the employer, held that the question was not whether the crane was a 'vehicle' or a 'machine' but whether, being part of the equipment of the factory, it contained 'machinery'[3]. It is only parts of machinery that need be fenced and not materials; for example, a workpiece held in the machinery by a chuck and moving under power, or the lashing end of wire being drawn through a hole onto a drum[4]. Further, there is no duty to fence merely because of the proximity of a moving part of machinery to some stationary object extraneous to the machine. Thus, there was no duty to fence where an employee injured his arm between the rising platform of a pneumatic hoist and a separate conveyor belt support[5]. However, there is an obligation to fence where a part of machinery in juxtaposition with the material used in the machine is dangerous. Thus, the employer was liable for breach of statutory duty where an employee's fingers were caught between an iron bar and the upper rollers of the machine into which he was feeding it[6]. The fence which these sections require is intended to keep the worker out, not to keep the machine or its product in[7]. Thus, there was no breach of statutory duty where an employee was injured by wood thrown off a block of wood by a circular saw into which it was being fed[8], nor where the bit of an electric drill shattered and injured an employee[9].

A part of machinery is not securely fenced if, in the ordinary course of human affairs, danger may reasonably be anticipated in its use not only to workmen who are prudent, alert and skilled and intent on their task, but also to the careless or inattentive worker whose inadvertent or indolent conduct may expose him to the risk of injury or death from the unguarded part[10]. However, a fence does not necessarily cease to be secure if, by some act of perverted and deliberate ingenuity, the guard can be forced or circumvented[11]. Thus, the employer was not liable for breach of statutory duty to an employee whose fingers were injured when she forced her hand through a hole three inches in diameter to remove dough from the rotating arm of a macaroni extruding machine[12].

The obligation to fence dangerous parts of machinery is unqualified. Thus, it is no defence that to securely fence a part of machinery would be to render it unusable. Where an employee injured his thumb on a grinding wheel, his employer was held liable despite the fact that to totally fence the wheel would make it useless[13]. However, the Secretary of State is given power to modify or extend the duty to fence by regulations, and regulations are now in force covering the fencing of, for example, abrasive wheels and woodworking machines such as circular saws.

An employee has the benefit of the fencing provisions even though he is not acting in the course of his employment[14]. The provisions are limited to machinery used in the factory and do not extend to machinery emerging as a product of the factory[15]. All fencing required by the Act must be of substantial construction, and constantly maintained and kept in position while the parts required to be fenced are in motion or in use, except when the parts of the machine are necessarily exposed for examination or lubrication[16].

1 *Walker v Bletchley Flettons Ltd* [1937] 1 All ER 170, CA.
2 *Millard v Serck Tubes Ltd* [1969] 1 All ER 598, [1969] 1 WLR 211, CA.
3 *British Railways Board v Liptrot* [1969] AC 136, [1967] 2 All ER 1072, HL.
4 *Bullock v G. John Power (Agencies) Ltd* [1956] 1 All ER 498, [1956] 1 WLR 171, CA.
5 *Pearce v Stanley-Bridges Ltd* [1965] 2 All ER 594, [1965] 1 WLR 931, CA.
6 *Midland and Low Moor Iron and Steel Co Ltd v Cross* [1965] AC 343, [1964] 3 All ER 752, HL.
7 *Nicholls v F. Austin (Leyton) Ltd* [1946] AC 493, [1946] 2 All ER 92, HL.
8 *Ibid.*
9 *Close v Steel Co of Wales* [1962] AC 367, [1962] 2 All ER 953, HL.
10 *John Summers & Sons Ltd v Frost* [1955] AC 740, [1955] 1 All ER 870, HL.
11 *Carr v Mercantile Produce Co Ltd* [1949] 2 KB 601, [1949] 2 All ER 531.
12 *Ibid.*
13 *John Summers and Sons Ltd v Frost* [1955] AC 740, [1955] 1 All ER 870, HL.
14 *Uddin v Associated Portland Cement Manufacturers Ltd* [1965] 2 QB 582, [1965] 2 All ER 213, CA.
15 *Parvin v Morton Machine Co Ltd* [1952] AC 515, [1952] 1 All ER 670, HL.
16 Factories Act 1961, s.16.

Enforcement of safety legislation

28.81   Certain safety provisions, e.g. the 'fencing code' of the Factories Act 1961, may be enforced by an employee bringing an action for damages for breach of statutory duty (which we discussed in paras. 21.1 to 21.5). Inspectors of the Health and Safety Executive may prosecute for breach of the safety legislation, and for failure to comply with a notice such as is referred to in the next paragraph.

28.82   If an inspector is of the opinion that a person is contravening a statutory provision, he may serve on him an 'improvement notice' detailing the nature of the contravention and requiring that it be remedied within a specified period[1]. If particular activities appear to an inspector to involve a risk of serious personal injury, he may serve a 'prohibition notice' detailing the matters which give rise to the risk and any relevant statutory provision and directing that the activities shall not be carried on until the risks and any associated contravention of the legislation have been remedied. The notice may take effect either immediately or after a specified period[2]. A person on whom an improvement or prohibition notice has been served may appeal to an industrial tribunal which may affirm, cancel or modify the notice[3]. An inspector may seize any article or substance which he believes to be a cause of imminent danger of serious personal injury and cause it to be rendered harmless, by destruction if necessary[4].

---

1 Health and Safety at Work etc. Act 1974, s.21.
2 *Ibid.*, s.22.
3 *Ibid.*, s.24.
4 *Ibid.*, s.25.

SOCIAL SECURITY
Unemployment benefit

28.83   A person who is unemployed will be entitled to unemployment benefit if a specified minimum amount of contributions has been made to the national insurance scheme. In respect of unemployment benefit, the relevant contributions are paid both by the employee and the employer, the amount of the contributions being a fixed percentage of the employee's earnings per week between an upper and a lower limit. The unemployed person must be capable of work on the day in question to qualify[1]. There is no entitlement to benefit for the first three days of unemployment[2], and thereafter entitlement lasts for 312 days[3]. After that time a person, while still entitled to non-contributory supplementary benefit, must re-qualify for unemployment benefit. Subject to the contribution conditions, a person re-qualifies after 13 weeks' full-time employment[4]. Increases to the flat rate benefit are paid in respect of dependants[5], and, after the thirteenth day of unemployment, a person becomes entitled, for 156 days, to earnings-related supplement of the benefit[6]. The amount of benefit cannot exceed 85 per cent of earnings[7].

---

1 Social Security Act 1975, s.17.
2 *Ibid.*, s.14.

3 *Ibid.*, s.18.
4 *Ibid.*
5 *Ibid.*, ss. 41, 44.
6 *Ibid.*, s.14.
7 *Ibid.*, Sched. 6.

28.84 If a person becomes unemployed because of a stoppage of work due to a trade dispute at his place of work, then, unless he proves he is not participating in or directly interested in the trade dispute, he is disqualified from receiving unemployment benefit so long as the stoppage continues[1]. A stoppage of work may come to an end even though the dispute continues, since it ends when the employer has all the workers he requires. A person may have a direct interest in a dispute, even though he is not participating in it, if the outcome of the dispute is likely to affect him, not at a number of removes, but virtually automatically without further contingencies. In *Punton v Ministry of Pensions and National Insurance (No 2)*[2], a 'plater's helper' was held to be directly interested in a demarcation dispute between shipwrights and platers as he had a direct interest in the volume of work done by platers. On the other hand, a paint shop worker at a car factory was held by a National Insurance Commissioner not to be directly interested in a pay dispute involving assembly line workers. A favourable outcome to the dispute might at some time affect his pay, but not automatically.

1 Social Security Act 1975, s.19.
2 [1963] 2 All ER 693.

28.85 A person is also disqualified from receiving unemployment benefit for up to six weeks if:

a. he lost his employment as a result of misconduct; or

b. he voluntarily left his job without good cause, or

c. he has without good cause refused or failed to apply for a situation notified to him as vacant in suitable employment, or

d. he has neglected to avail himself of reasonable opportunities of suitable employment[1].

1 Social Security Act 1975, s.20.

Industrial injuries

28.86 If a person suffers personal injury caused by accident arising out of and in the course of his employment, he is entitled to industrial injuries benefit[1]. Benefit takes three forms: injury benefit, disablement benefit and industrial death benefit.

Injury benefit This is payable, for 156 days after the accident, excluding the first three days, to a person who by reason of such injury is incapable of work[2].

Disablement benefit If as a result of the accident a person suffers loss of physical or mental faculty or disfigurement he is entitled to disablement benefit, but not while he is entitled to injury benefit[3]. If the extent of disablement is assessed by a medical board at less than 20 per cent, benefit takes the form of a gratuity, which may be paid in instalments. If the disablement is assessed at 20 per cent or more, benefit takes the form of a pension, which is subject to increases where the person is incapable of work, or of following his regular occupation, and likely to remain so, or is severely disabled or is in need of constant attendance or in-patient hospital treatment[4].

Industrial death benefit If a person dies as a result of the accident, his widow, if she was residing with him or was entitled to receive maintenance from him, is entitled to death benefit which takes the form of a pension for life or until remarriage. On remarriage a gratuity is payable. Benefit is not payable where the widow is cohabiting with a man[5].

---

1 Social Security Act 1975, s.50.
2 *Ibid.*, s.56.
3 *Ibid.*, s.57.
4 *Ibid.*, ss. 58–63.
5 *Ibid.*, s.67.

28.87 For entitlement to benefit to arise, injury must have arisen from 'accident', which denotes an unlooked for mishap or an untoward event which is not expected or designed[1], and the accident must arise out of and in the course of the employment. If it arises in the course of employment it is deemed, unless the contrary is proved, also to have arisen out of the employment[2]. It is not necessary, for an accident to have arisen out of and in the course of employment, that the employee was doing something in pursuance of a duty owed to his employer. Thus, a person doing something reasonably incidental to his employment, such as taking a tea break or lunch in the canteen, is still acting in the course of his employment[3]. However, a police constable who suffered a leg injury while playing football for his constabulary, which he was expected, but not contractually obliged to do, was not injured in the course of employment. It was no part of his work to play football[4].

---

1 *Fenton v J. Thorley & Co Ltd* [1903] AC 443, HL.
2 Social Security Act 1975, s.50.

3 *Re v Industrial Injuries Commr, ex parte Amalgamated Engineering Union (No 2)* [1966] 2 QB 31, [1966] 1 All ER 97, CA.
4 *R v National Insurance Commr, ex parte Michael* [1977] 2 All ER 420, [1977] 1 WLR 109, CA.

28.88 It is specifically provided that an accident arises out of and in the course of employment notwithstanding that, at the time, the employee is acting in contravention of any regulations, or orders given by his employer, or without instructions from his employer, provided that the accident would otherwise have been considered to have arisen in the course of employment and the act was done for the purpose of, and in connection with, the employer's business[1].

If an employee is injured in an accident when travelling to or from work as a passenger in a vehicle which is operated by, on behalf of, or by arrangement with, his employer, but which is not being operated in the ordinary course of a public transport service, the accident is deemed to arise out of and in the course of employment, notwithstanding that the employee is not obliged to travel in the vehicle[2].

If an accident happens to an employee in or about premises at which he is for the time being employed on his employer's business, it is deemed to arise out of and in the course of employment if it happens while the employee is taking steps, on an actual or supposed emergency at the premises, to rescue, succour or protect people who are, or who are thought to be, injured or in danger, or to avert or minimise serious damage to property[3].

If an accident arises in the course of employment and either is caused by another person's misconduct, negligence or skylarking, or by the behaviour or presence of an animal, or is caused by or consists in the employee being struck by an object or by lightning, it is deemed to arise out of the employment, unless the employee directly or indirectly induced or contributed to it by his conduct outside the employment or by an act not incidental to the employment[4].

1 Social Security Act 1975, s.52.
2 *Ibid.*, s.53.
3 *Ibid.*, s.54.
4 *Ibid.*, s.55.

28.89 Provision is made for industrial injuries benefit to be paid to persons suffering certain diseases prescribed as being a risk of their particular occupations and not a risk common to all[1].

1 Social Security Act 1975, s.76.

Claims for benefit

28.90   A claim for any social security benefit is made to an insurance officer, against whose decision appeal lies to a local tribunal and thence to a National Insurance Commissioner. Questions relating to disablement under the industrial injuries scheme are determined by medical boards from whom appeal lies to a medical appeal tribunal[1].

---

1   Social Security Act 1975, ss. 93–109.

Index

Acceptance
  of bill of exchange, 24.54
  of goods, 22.69, 22.70
  of tender, 5.7—5.11, 5.15
Advertisements, 5.5, 23.20—23.22
Advocates, 2.50, 2.51
Affirmation of contract
  after breach, 10.13, 10.55, 10.56
  by representee, 14.11
  lapse of time as evidence, 14.11
  loss mitigation, 12.10
  meaning and effect, 10.8, 10.9,
    14.37
Affreightment, Contract of, 27.9, 27.33,
  27.36
Agency contract, 10.37, 18.21—18.43
Agents
  appointment, 18.7
  authority of, 5.11, 18.32—18.38
  betting and gaming, 15.7, 15.8
  characteristics of, 18.1
  contracting on own behalf, 18.48
  disclosed and undisclosed principal,
    18.39, 19.41
  liabilities of, 18.47, 21.30
  mercantile agents, 18.36, 22.30
  obligations of, 18.15—18.20
  of necessity, 18.13
  purporting to act as, 18.50
  ratification of transactions,
    18.8—18.12
  relationship with principal, 18.4,
    18.6—18.12, 24.7
  remuneration entitlement,
    18.21—18.22
  third party's rights against, 18.49,
    18.50

Agents (*cont.*)
  transfer of title, 22.29
  types of, 18.52
Agreements *See also* names of types
  of agreement: e.g. Hire purchase
  agreement, Maintenance
  agreement
  as basis for contract, 5.2
  condition precedent, subject to,
    5.27
  discharging contract, 6.32, 6.35
  enforceability, 7.9
  inaccurate record of, 13.18
  inconclusive, 5.23
  legal relations, without, 6.2
  subject to contract, 7.14
  to agree, 5.24, 5.26
  to sell, 22.3
  void and illegal, 15.14, 15.58,
    15.60
Air, Carriage by, 27.41
All England Reports, 3.50
Anticipatory breach of contract, 10.13,
  12.10
Appeal proceedings
  criminal, 2.20
  from lower courts, 2.4, 2.6—2.8,
    2.22
  Judicial Committee of Privy Council,
    2.35
  jurisdictions of higher courts,
    2.16—2.21, 2.25—2.30
Appropriation of payments, 9.7—9.10,
  23.35
Arbitration
  arbitrators, referees and umpires,
    2.42, 2.48

All references are to paragraph numbers

Arbitration (*cont.*)
  awards, validity of, 2.45, 2.46
  clause, 11.13n, 15.15
  employment terms, 28.25
  jurisdiction of courts, 2.48
  procedures, 2.12, 2.40–2.43
  statutory reference to, 2.47
Articles of Association, 4.9
Assignment
  absolute, criteria for, 19.6
  binding on communication, 19.14
  by way of charge, 19.6, 19.15
  choses in action, 19.2–19.16
  conditional, 19.6
  enforcement of, 19.15
  equitable, 19.8, 19.9
  form of, 19.5, 19.12
  insurance policy, of, 25.7–25.9,
    25.24–25.25
  involuntary, 19.21
  negotiation compared with, 24.2
  notice of, 19.7
  novation compared with, 19.18
  rights of assignee, 19.16
  statutory assignment, 19.4

Bailment
  carrier as bailee, 27.2
  consumer hire agreement, 23.12
  duties of bailee, 26.7
  insurance, right to, 25.11
  lien of bailee, 26.27
  meaning, 6.9, 26.1
  pledges, 26.15–26.19
  transactions, types and status,
    26.1–26.6
Bankruptcy
  agent and principal, effects on, 18.29
  involuntary assignment in, 19.24
  jurisdictions, 2.10, 2.13, 2.16
  rights and liabilities in, 19.24–19.27
Banks
  collecting banker, 24.80–24.85
  definition, 24.65
  duties of banker, 24.79
  letter of credit, 6.20
  regulations concerning cheques,
    24.5–24.16
  relation with customers, 24.78,
    24.79
Barristers, 2.50, 3.50
Betting and Gaming *See* Gaming
    Contract; Wagering Contract

Bill of Exchange
  acceptance of, 24.54
  cheque, compared with, 24.87
  delivery, 24.17
  status of, 7.5, 24.3
Bill of lading
  as evidence of contract, 27.9, 27.10
  assignment of, 19.3, 27.10
  exemption clause in, 10.36
  functions and procedures,
    27.27–27.31
  terms in, 27.32
Bill of sale, 7.5, 26.22
Blackstone's Commentaries, 3.51
Breach of care, 20.3 *et seq.*
Breach of contract
  action by misrepresentee, 8.8, 14.18
  anticipatory, 10.12, 10.13
  damages for *See* Damages, action for
  fundamental, 10.53, 10.54, 10.57,
    10.58
  liability, 10.23, 10.41
  losses caused by *See* Losses, recovery
    of
  meaning, 10.1
  performance failure, 9.14–9.16,
    10.18
  remedies for *See* Remedies for
    breach
  repudiatory, 10.4
  third party, enforcement for, 6.26
Bribery, 18.19, 28.12
British nationality, 2.19, 4.18, 4.19
Burden of contract, 6.28
Byelaws, 3.12

Capacity to contract
  clubs and societies, 4.16
  companies, 4.8
  mental patients, 16.19
  minors, 16.1–16.18
  partnerships, 4.15
Carriage, contract of
  by air, 27.41
  by rail, 27.8
  by road, 27.6, 27.7
  by sea, 27.9 *et seq.*
  dangerous goods, 27.21
  generally, 27.1–27.46
  rights and duties of carriers,
    27.3–27.8
  types of carrier, 27.2
Cartels, 15.33, 15.39, 15.41, 15.48

All references are to paragraph numbers

Case stated, 2.18
Certiorari, 2.18
Chancery, Court of, 1.11, 1.12
Chancery Division, 2.13, 2.15, 2.16
Charge, assignment by way of, 19.6,
    19.15
Charterparty
    affirmation of, 10.8
    bill of lading compared with, 27.10
    breach of, 10.21, 10.54
    cesser clause, 27.16
    exemption clause, 10.44, 27.15
    frustration of, 11.8, 11.11, 11.18
    meaning, 27.9, 27.11
    terms in, 8.17, 10.20, 27.12—27.22
Cheques
    alteration of, 24.25
    crossing of, 24.58—24.63
    dating of, 24.11
    definition of, 24.3, 24.4
    discharge of, 24.22
    dishonouring of, 24.44, 24.68
    holder in due course, 24.17, 24.82,
        24.85
    holder's rights and duties,
        24.26—24.46, 24.55, 24.59
    payment of gaming debts, 9.4, 15.9
    provisions applicable to,
        24.57—24.64
    validity requirements, 24.5—24.12
    wages payments by, 28.20
Children, proceedings concerning, 2.5,
    2.7, 2.19, 4.23
Choses in action
    assignment, 19.2—19.16
    enforcement of, 19.10
    future, 19.15
    insurance policy as, 25.8
    legal and equitable differentiated,
        19.10—19.12
    meaning, 19.2
    mortgage of, 19.6, 26.21
Chronological table of the Statutes, 3.9
Civil Law, 1.2, 1.7
Coke's Institutes, 3.51
Collateral contract
    parol evidence rule, 8.7
    representation in, 8.10
    to illegal contracts, 15.64
    validity, 6.21, 15.32
Commercial court, 2.18, 2.42
Commercial Law, 1.7
Commission merchant, 18.2

Committal proceedings, 2.3
Common Law, 1.8—1.11, 1.13, 3.25
Common Market Law Reports, 3.50
Companies
    as legal persons, 4.1, 4.7
    contractual capacity, 4.8
    disclosure of facts, 14.27
    domicile and residence, 4.24, 4.27
    formation of, 4.3, 4.9, 10.44
    law relating to, 1.7
    'lifting the veil', 4.6
    objects, alteration of, 4.12
    officers, liability of, 24.15
    powers of, 4.5
Compensation
    consumer credit termination, in,
        23.48
    courts' jurisdiction, 12.2, 12.7
    fine as, 21.1
    performance before frustration, for,
        11.17
    sale of goods rescission, 13.9
    single lump sum, 12.14
    statutory exclusion, 21.45
    unfair dismissal, for, 28.51
Condition
    breach of, 10.31
    implied, meaning, 22.47
    meaning, 10.19, 22.39, 22.40
    operation of, 5.27
Condition precedent, 5.27, 10.14n
Conditional sale agreement, 23.41,
    23.47, 23.65, 23.78
Consideration
    actions held to constitute, 6.7,
        6.11—6.17
    adequacy and sufficiency, 6.6, 6.10
    agreement to discharge, supporting,
        6.32, 6.36
    bill or cheque, supporting, 24.12
    binding contract, as factor in,
        6.1—6.6
    contracts without, 7.3
    equitable assignment, in, 19.11,
        19.15
    'executed' and 'executory', meaning,
        6.4
    failure of, payment recovery, 11.14,
        16.11, 17.7
    money as, 22.7
    not provided, remedies where, 12.18
    novation of contractual obligation,
        19.19

All references are to paragraph numbers

Consideration (*cont.*)
  past consideration, 6.4
  privity, relation with, 6.18, 6.19
  promisee's need to prove, 6.18
  third party provision for exemption,
    10.37
Constitutional Law, 1.7
Consumer
  as party to contract, 10.42, 10.43
  avoidance of liability towards, 10.47
Consumer Credit Agreements
  breach of, 23.32, 23.39
  cancellation of, 23.27—23.31
  conditional sale agreements, 23.41,
    23.47, 23.65, 23.78
  'cooling off' period, 23.29
  entry into agreements, 23.24—23.29
  exempt agreements, 23.11
  extortionate credit bargains, 14.38
  hire agreement, 23.64
  installation charge, 23.41, 23.48
  judicial control, 2.10, 23.59—23.70
  legislation, 23.1 *et seq.*
  licensing, 23.17—23.23
  linked transactions, 23.15
  payments, 23.30, 23.35, 23.45
  securities, 23.52—23.57
  termination, 23.44—23.51
  transfer of possession, 23.30
  types of, 23.4 *et seq.*
  variation of agreement, 23.36
Consumer hire agreement, 23.12 *et seq.*
Consumer Protection Advisory
  Committee, 10.60
Contract *See also names of types of*
  contract; e.g. Agency contract;
  Employment contract
  affirmation *See* Affirmation of
    contract
  bailment as, 26.3 *See also* Bailment
  basic requirements, 5.2
  bi-lateral and unilateral, 6.3
  breach of *See* Breach of contract
  by specialty, 7.4
  capacity to contract *See* Capacity
    to contract
  charterparty as, 10.21 *See also*
    Charterparty
  conditions *See* Condition
  definition, 1.4
  discharge *See* Discharge of contract
  enforcement *See* Enforcement of
    contract

Contract (*cont.*)
  See also names of types of
  contract; e.g. Agency contract;
  Employment contract
  forms of, 5.2, 6.35, 7.2, 7.5
  gratuitous services, 6.8
  honour clause, 6.2
  illegal *See* Illegal contract
  jurisdiction over actions in, 2.9, 2.18
  land, sale of, 5.27
  legal relations intention, 6.2
  memorandum or note, 7.12
  mistake as to terms, 13.15 *See also*
    Mistake
  oral, 1.4, 7.12
  penalty clause, 12.12 *See also*
    Penalty
  representations, intentions
    regarding, 8.9—8.14
  repudiation of *See* Repudiation of
    contract
  rescission, effect of, 6.35 *See also*
    Rescission of contract
  termination, generally, 6.31
  terms, contractual *See* Contractual
    terms
  time of the essence, 9.16, 9.17
  to assign, 19.15 *See also* Assignment
  ultra vires, 4.9—4.12
  uncertainty, need to dispel, 5.24,
    5.25
  under seal, 7.2—7.4, 12.26, 18.45
  validity *See* Validity of contract
  void, 15.1, 15.3
  waiver, alteration by, 6.33
Contract for differences, 15.3
Contractual rights
  assignment of, 19.2
  devolution on death, 19.22
  in bankruptcy, 19.25
  novation, transfer by, 19.17
Contractual terms
  ascertainment of accuracy, 8.12,
    8.14
  business efficacy implication, 8.22
  classification of, 10.20
  construction by courts, 10.20
  express terms, 8.2, 22.41
  implied terms, 8.17—8.23,
    22.42—22.45
  intermediate terms, 10.21
  misrepresentation in, 14.17
  opinion as, 8.13

All references are to paragraph numbers

Contractual terms (*cont.*)
performance of *See* Performance of
obligations
proof of oral terms, 8.8
reasonableness requirement, 10.49
representation as, 8.9, 8.11, 8.12
rescission entitlement, 10.22
statement of fact, 8.13
warranty, meaning, 10.20
written document, exclusions from,
8.6
Contributory negligence, 21.39—21.43,
28.70
Conventions, International, 3.27
Conversion, 26.8—26.10
County courts, 2.8—2.13, 2.18, 2.53
Court of Appeal, 2.13, 2.20, 2.24, 2.26,
3.41
Court of Chancery, 1.11, 1.12
Court of Common Pleas, 1.11
Court of Justice (EEC), 2.32, 2.33
Court of Kings Bench, 1.11
Court of Protection, 2.37, 16.19
Court of the Exchequer, 1.11
Courts
civil actions procedure, 1.3
common law courts, 1.11
hierarchy, 3.38—3.47
judicial precedent, 3.35, 3.38, 3.45
jurisdiction and powers —
criminal, 1.3, 2.3
construction of terms, 10.20
damages, quantification of, 12.7
determination of powers, 4.2
exemption clauses, 10.27, 10.31
interpretation of law, 3.51
legal aid discretion, 2.59
rescission refusal, 14.11
specific performance orders,
12.19
unliquidated damages, 12.11
record, contents of, 3.50
relation with European Court, 2.34,
3.39
systems before 1873 . . . 1.10
Covenant. 7.3
Credit
canvassing, control of, 23.23
consumer credit *See* Consumer
credit
letter of, 6.20
Credit sale agreement, 23.79
Creditor, 9.7—9.13, 9.18—9.21

Criminal injuries compensation, 1.3
Crown court
appeal to, 2.4
circuits of, 2.8, 2.21
jurisdiction, 2.3, 2.22, 2.23
relation with other courts, 2.14,
2.17, 2.19
tiers, distinctions between, 2.21
Crown immunity, 4.17
Custom
agent's liability, 18.46
as source of law, 3.52
terms implied by, 8.17

Damage
mitigation of, 12.9
remoteness of, 12.3—12.6,
20.26—20.29
Damages, action for
breach of contract, for, 1.4, 10.2,
10.5, 10.13
collateral contract, breach of, 15.56
illegal contract, party to, 15.51
indemnity compared with, 14.15
limitation periods, 12.26
misrepresentation, for, 8.8, 14.13,
14.18
on rescission for breach, 12.1
quantum meruit claim as alternative,
12.16
relief in equity, 13.8
tort, remedy in, 21.47
unawareness of plaintiff, 12.28
where no consideration provided,
12.18
Damages, award of
as remedy, 12.2, 12.6, 14.14, 24.53,
24.78
assessment, 1.3
delay in, interest rates, 12.15
in lieu of rescission, 14.14
intention of parties, relevance, 12.14
liquidated and unliquidated, 12.11
'loss of bargain' rule, 14.14
'out of pocket' rule, 14.14
quantification, 12.7, 14.14
taxation liability, 12.8
third party, payment to, 6.27
Death
effect on contract, 11.5, 23.38
tort as cause, 21.31—21.33
Debts
accounts stated, meaning, 16.13

All references are to paragraph numbers

Debts (*cont.*)
  acknowledgements, 12.30
  assignment of part, 19.6
  discharge, form of, 6.36
  forgoing as consideration, 6.13
  in equity, 6.14
  limitation of actions, 12.35
  notice of assignment, 19.13
  novation, 19.17
  payment of
    appropriation, 9.7, 12.25
    by third party, 9.19
    cash and cheques, 6.13, 9.13
    gaming debts, 15.9
    obligation to seek and pay, 9.2
    percentage arrangements, 6.16
    postal payments, 9.5
    quasi contract, 17.2, 17.3
    receipts, 9.6
    refusal of tender, 9.12
    tender under protest, 9.13
  revival of remedy, 12.29—12.31
  time limitation, 9.13
  variation of contract, 6.32
  writ of execution, 22.38
Deeds, 7.4
Defamation, 2.53, 21.6—21.8
Del credere agent, 18.52
Delivery of bill or cheque, 24.17, 24.19, 24.39
Delivery of goods *See also* Carriage, contract of
  carrier's duty, 27.3
  contractual terms, 22.63—22.68, 22.71
  refusal to take, 22.82, 22.85
  remedies for non-delivery, 22.73—22.75
Demurrage, 10.53, 27.10
Discharge of bill or cheque, 24.22—24.24
Discharge of contract
  accord and satisfaction, 6.36
  by frustration, 11.1—11.18
  by payment, 9.3—9.10
  by performance, 9.2—9.21
  by variation, 6.35
  consideration, position regarding, 6.31—6.36
  form, relevance of, 6.35
  guarantee, contract of, 26.37
  meaning and methods, 8.24
  unilateral, 6.36

Disclosure, duty of, 14.26, 14.27
Divisional courts, 3.43
Domestic proceedings, 2.5, 2.10, 2.19
Domicile, 4.21—4.24
Drunkenness, 16.19, 16.20
Duress, 14.28—14.30
Duty of care, 20.3 *et seq.*

EEC legislation, 3.4 *See also* European Communities Legislation
Employee
  continuous employment, 28.17, 28.18
  dismissal, 28.36—28.51
  duties of, 28.11—28.14, 28.75
  employment protection, 28.26
  independent contractor compared, 28.2
  lay-off and short-time, 28.57
  negligence liability, 10.41
  pregnancy of, 28.26, 28.47
  redundancy *See* Redundancy
  unemployment benefit, 28.83—28.85
Employer
  agreements between employers, 15.20
  as landlord, 28.20
  breach of statutory duty, 21.1
  duties of, 28.15—28.16, 28.65—28.85
  duty of care, 20.20, 20.24, 20.30, 21.24
  liability —
    employees and private contractors, 28.2
    insurance, 25.17
    vicarious, 21.15—21.20
  redundancy procedures, 28.60—28.62
  relationship with employees, 28.2—28.5
  sex discrimination, 28.27—28.31
Employment, contract of
  appeal tribunal, 2.25, 2.38
  collective agreements, legal status, 6.2
  demotion as breach, 12.2
  discharge by frustration, 11.5, 11.6
  dismissal, 28.36—28.51
  implied terms, 8.21
  injunction for breach, 12.23, 12.24
  minors, 16.6

All references are to paragraph numbers

Employment, contract of (*cont.*)
redundancy payment, 28.18
renewal, 28.55—28.56
severable parts of, 11.18
specific performance order, 12.18
terms, statement of, 28.16
trade restraint clause, 15.19
wrongful dismissal, 10.9. 11.6
Enforcement of contract
breach of statute, performance in,
15.54
consideration, need for, 6.3
for beneficiary, 6.23, 6.24, 6.26
gaming and wagering contracts, 15.5
illegal contracts, 15.50, 15.61
methods other than by action, 7.16
oral contract of indemnity, 7.8
performance of obligations, 7.17,
7.18
severance of void parts, 15.28—15.30
specific performance order, 6.26,
7.18
supply of necessaries to minor, 16.5
variation enforcement, 6.33
writing, need to be evidence in, 7.6
Entire Obligation, 10.14, 10.16, 10.17
Equal Opportunities Commission, 28.31
Equal pay, 28.32, 28.33
Equitable assignment, 19.8—19.15
Equitable interest, 4.28
Equitable relief, 12.32
Equity
as source of law, 1.8, 1.11, 1.12
contract alteration remedy, 6.34
debts in, 6.14
duress in, 14.30
jurisdiction of County Court, 2.9
mistake, contract based on, 13.8
specific performance remedy, 7.17
trusts, rule regarding, 6.25
Estoppel, doctrine of, 6.14n, 6.15
European Communities Legislation
Council and Commission, 3.29, 3.30
EEC nationals, status of, 4.18
interpretation of legislation, 3.34
national application of legislation,
3.28
Official Journal, 3.33
restrictive trade practices law, 15.39
review by European Court, 3.32
sources of, 3.28—3.30
treaties, 3.28
ultra vires contracts, 4.11

European Court, 2.32—2.34, 3.28, 3.50
Evidence of contract, 7.18, 8.4—8.8
Exclusive dealing agreements, 15.23,
15.41
Exemption clauses
ambiguity in, 10.32
application limitations, 10.34—10.36
fundamental breach liability, 10.53,
10.57, 10.58
inconsistent undertakings, 10.35
meaning, 10.23, 12.12
notice requirements, 10.26—10.29
reasonableness requirement, 10.45
secondary contract, evasion by,
10.51
third party, position of, 10.36,
10.37, 10.38
tortious liability, exclusion of, 10.33
validity, 10.24, 10.25, 10.40—10.49
Extortionate credit bargains,
23.67—23.69

Factor, 18.52
Factories Acts, 28.77—28.82
Fair Trading, Director General of
actions, powers of, 10.60
consumer protection function, 23.2
licensing authority, 23.17
registration of agreements, 15.36
Fair Trading Act, 14.38
Family arrangements contracts, 14.25
Family Division, 2.6, 2.19
Fiduciary relationships, 14.26, 14.32,
14.33, 18.19
Fire insurance, 25.10—25.13
Forebearance to sue, 6.7
Forgery, 24.16
Form of contract
discharge agreement, 6.35
evidence in writing, 7.6—7.11
procedural requirements, 5.2
under seal, 7.2
written, 7.5
Fraudulent misrepresentation
action for damages, 14.14
minor, contract induced by, 16.17
recovery of payment, 15.63
Freight, 27.35—27.37
Frustration, doctrine of
circumstances giving rise to,
11.2—11.11

All references are to paragraph numbers

Frustration, doctrine of (*cont.*)
  compensation for performance,
    11.17
  discharge as effect, 10.1, 11.13
  employment contracts, 11.5, 11.6
  leases, applicability, 11.12
  meaning, 11.1, 11.2
  perishing of goods, 22.26
  severable contracts, 11.18
Fundamental breach, 10.53–10.54,
    10.57–10.58

Gaming contract, 15.4 *et seq.*
Goods
  bailment of, *See* Bailment
  carriage of *See* Carriage, contract of
  insurance of, 25.2
  meaning, 22.4, 22.9–22.10
  minor's necessaries, 16.3, 16.5
  mortgage of, 26.22
  possession on agreement
    cancellation, 23.30
  protected goods, 23.41
  rejection by buyer, 22.77–22.79
  re-possession by creditor,
    23.41–23.42, 23.48
  resale prices, 6.30, 15.42–15.45
  restrictive agreements, 15.34
  transfer of property in, 22.14–22.21
Goodwill, purchase of, 15.22
Guarantees, 7.6–7.9, 26.31–26.37

Habeas Corpus, 2.18
Halsbury's Statutes of England, 3.33
Health and safety at work, 28.71–28.76
High Court
  appeals to House of Lords, 2.29
  arbitration, powers in, 2.42, 2.48
  constitution of, 2.14, 2.53
  jurisdiction, 2.11, 2.42, 3.44
Hire purchase agreement *See also*
    Consumer Credit; Sale of goods
  definition, 23.71
  forms of, 23.72–23.74
  implied contractual terms, 8.18
  liability avoidance, 10.46, 10.47
  linked transactions, 23.15
  obligations under, 23.75–23.77
Honour clause, 6.2
House of Lords, 2.29, 2.30, 3.40

Illegal contract
  crime, agreement to commit, 15.58
  examples, 15.46 *et seq.*, 15.57
  immorality as factor, 15.59
  penalty not affecting prohibition,
    15.49
  performance, manner of, 15.52
Incapacitation, 10.11, 11.2
Incorporated Council of Law Reporting,
    3.50
Indemnity
  agent's entitlement, 18.23
  clause, unreasonable, 10.43
  contract of, 7.8
  insurance contract, 25.5
  misrepresentee, claim by, 14.15
  surety, entitlement of, 17.2
Independent contractors, 21.21–21.29,
    28.2
Index to the Statutes in force, 3.9
Indorsement of cheques
  definition, 24.13
  forgery, 24.56, 24.73
  irregularity, 24.74
  types of, 24.21
  validity, 24.20
Industrial tribunal
  redundancy payments, 28.54, 28.61
  sex discrimination, 28.30
  unfair dismissal, 28.42, 28.49
Information agreements, 15.34
Injunction, 12.20, 12.24, 21.48
Injuries
  causes, 20.25, 21.4, 22.62
  damages for *See* Damages, award of
  industrial, 28.86–28.90
  likelihood of, 20.19
  rescuers, sustained by, 21.37
Innocent misrepresentation, 14.14
Inns of Court, 2.50
Insanity *See* Mental Disorder
Insurance contract *See also specific
    types of insurance,* e.g. Fire
    Insurance
  beneficiaries' rights, 6.20
  definition, 25.1
  disclosure, intending assured's duty,
    14.24, 25.4
  employer's liability, 25.17
  evidence, policy as, 25.4
  exemption clause, in, 10.44
  frustration, position on, 11.18
  indemnity policies, 25.5, 25.6

All references are to paragraph numbers

Insurance contract (*cont.*)
  See also specific types of
  insurance, e.g. Fire insurance
  legal right, need for, 15.3, 25.2
  subrogation, 25.6
  transfer of, 25.9
International law *See also* European
  Communities Legislation
  carriage of goods by sea,
    27.33–27.34
  conventions, 3.27, 27.33, 27.41
  diplomatic immunity, 4.2
  infringement presumption, 3.25
  national application, 3.28, 3.31
  persuasive precedents, 3.47
International supply contracts, 10.50
Interpretation of legislation
  rules, 3.18–3.21
  whole enactment consideration, 3.23
Invitation to treat, 5.4

Judge
  functions of, 1.11, 2.55, 3.18
  qualifications and retirement, 2.8,
    2.14
Judicial precedent, 3.26, 3.35,
  3.40–3.50
Jury, 2.3, 2.53–2.55
Justice of the Peace, 2.2

Knowhow agreements, 15.35

Labour law, 1.7, 1.9
Land, contract for sale of
  beneficiary, enforcement by, 6.24
  exemption clauses, 10.44
  form of, 7.6, 7.10, 7.12
  part performance, acts of, 7.18
  specific enforcement, 12.18
Land, interests in, 2.16, 4.29
Land Charges Register, 4.29
Land mortgage, 23.58
Landlord and tenant
  alteration of contract, 6.34
  County court jurisdiction, 2.10
  occupiers liability, 20.35–20.45
Lands Tribunal, 2.25
Law Commission, 3.2
Law Journal Reports, 3.50
'Law Lords', 2.28

Law reports, 3.50
Law Society, 2.51
Law Times Reports, 3.50
'Leap-frog' appeals, 2.29
Lease
  contract requirements, 7.2
  frustration doctrine applicability,
    11.12
  mistake in, effect of, 13.6, 13.9
  specific performance order, 12.18
Legal aid, 2.56–2.59
Legal executives, 2.52
Legal interest, 4.28
Legal relations, 6.2
Legal tender, 9.13
Legislation
  as source of law, 1.8, 3.2
  autonomic, 3.16
  delegated, 3.11, 3.13–3.15
  European Communities *See*
    European Communities
    Legislation
  forms of, 1.9, 3.4, 3.10, 3.26
  interpretation, 3.17
  'special parliamentary procedure',
    3.12
Legitimacy, 2.19, 4.23
Letter of credit, 6.20
Liability insurance, 25.14–25.19
Lien
  meaning, 22.89
  types of, 26.25–26.30
Life assurance, 25.20–25.25
Limitation of actions
  equitable relief, 12.32
  in tort, 21.46
  minors and mental patients, 12.27
  time periods, 12.25, 12.26
  unawareness of plaintiff, 12.28
Liquidated damages, 12.11
Lloyds Law Reports, 3.50
Loans *See also* Debts
  for gaming debts, 15.11
  to minor, 16.13, 16.14, 16.17
Lord Chancellor, 1.12, 2.15, 2.37,
  2.38
Lords of Appeal in Ordinary, 2.28
Losses, recovery of
  avoidable losses, 12.9
  goods carried by sea, 27.38–27.40
  lost profits, 12.8
  penalty clause, 12.12, 12.13
  rules and limitations, 12.3–12.6

All references are to paragraph numbers

Magistrates, 2.2, 2.3, 2.21
Magistrates' Courts
    appeals from, 2.4, 2.6
    constitution of, 2.2
    judicial precedent affecting, 3.38
    jurisdiction, 2.2, 2.3, 2.5
    reporting restrictions, 2.5
Maintenance agreements, 15.16
Maintenance orders, 2.5
Mandamus, 2.18
Manufacturer's duty of care,
    20.31—20.34
Marine insurance, 7.5
Market overt, 22.35
Marriage brokage agreements, 15.14,
    15.31
Master of the Rolls, 2.24
Masters of Chancery Division, 2.15
Masters of Queens Bench Division, 2.17
Memorandum of Association, 4.8
Memorandum or note of contract,
    7.12—7.15
Mental disorder
    contractual capacity in, 16.19
    domicile question, 4.23
    limitation of actions, 12.27
    suicide, 25.22
Mercantile agents, 18.36, 18.52, 22.30
Merchantable quality, 22.49—22.54
Minors
    as agents, 18.5
    contracts of, 16.1, 16.8—16.10,
        16.15
    credit canvassing control, 23.23
    debts of, 16.9
    domicile, 4.23
    liability for torts, 16.16
    limitation of actions, 12.27
    meaning, 16.1
    special legal provisions, 4.2
Misrepresentation
    active, 14.2, 14.8 *et seq.*
    address to person misled, 14.5
    contractual term, as, 8.8
    exemption clause, contents of, 10.34
    inducement to contract, 14.6
    liability for, limitation, 14.21
    mistake induced by, 14.1
    non-disclosure, through, 14.4, 14.23,
    of fact, 14.4
    of law, 14.4
    remedies for, 14.8—14.18

Mistake
    contract void for, 13.1 *et seq.*
    documents, in, 13.18, 13.19
    identity of party, as to,
        13.10—13.13
    in law and in equity, 13.9
    not shared by parties, 13.10—13.17
    shared mistake, 13.2—13.9
    subject matter, as to, 13.14
    terms of contract, as to, 13.15
Mitigation of loss, 12.9, 12.10
Mortgage, 23.58, 25.11, 26.20

Nationality, 4.18, 4.19, 4.20
Negligence
    as tort, 1.5, 20.2
    avoidance of liability for, 10.41
    carrier, liability of, 27.2, 27.5,
        27.15
    cheque, in drawing, 24.72
    contributory, 20.29
    employee, of, 28.13
    employer, of, 28.65—28.85
    exemption clause, 10.33
    foreseeability of risk, 12.5
    insurance against liability, 25.14
    mis-statements as, 20.12—20.14
    nervous shock caused by, 20.9
Negligent misrepresentation, 14.14
Negotiable instruments, 19.3, 24.2,
    24.18
Notice *See under relevant topic* e.g.
    Assignment
Novation, 19.17—19.19, 25.9
Nuisance, 21.11—21.13

Obiter Dicta, 3.55, 3.37, 3.47
Obligation, contractual, 9.2, 10.14,
    10.17 *See also* Performance of
    obligations
Offer, 5.3, 5.4, 5.8, 5.17—5.21
Opinion as representation, 14.4

Parliament, 3.4, 3.25
Parol evidence, 8.2n, 8.10
Part performance of obligations, 7.17,
    7.18
Partnership
    actions, jurisdiction, 2.16

All references are to paragraph numbers

Partnership (*cont.*)
  change in membership, 19.19
  debts, 16.9
  features of, 4.13, 4.15
  limited, meaning, 4.15
  residence of, 4.27
Patrials, 4.18, 4.19
Payment
  acknowledgement of claim, 12.29,
    12.30
  after frustrating event, 11.16
  appropriation of, 9.7—9.10, 12.25,
    23.35
  before frustration, 11.14—11.17
  carrier's rights, 27.4
  consumer credit, 23.45
  defective performance, refusal to
    pay for, 10.4
  employer's duty, 28.15, 28.18 *See
    also* Wages
  gaming debts, 15.9
  in due course, 24.23
  lost after posting, 9.5
  partial, 12.31
  proof of, 9.6
  quasi-contract, in, 17.1
  recovery *See* Recovery of Payment
  refusal by buyer, 22.86—22.94
  to agent, 18.40
Penalty
  clause, meaning, 12.12
  lump sum, compensation as, 12.14
Performance of obligations
  after frustrating event, 11.16
  change in law affecting, 11.7
  changed circumstances, in, 11.4
  contractual requirements, 9.2
  death, rights and duties on, 19.23
  defective, refusal to accept, 10.4
  failure —
    breach of contract, as, 10.18
    entire obligation, 10.14
    lawful excuse, 10.1
    remedies for, 10.2, 12.1
    time limitation, 9.16
  fault rendering impossible, 11.11
  frustration, discharge by, 10.15
  illegality from manner of, 15.52
  partial, 10.15, 11.17
  prevention, 10.11, 10.15, 11.3,
    11.5
  refusal to accept, 9.11, 9.14
  refusal to carry out, 14.3

Performance of obligations (*cont.*)
  rescission, effect of, 10.7
  severable obligations, 10.17
  third party, by, 9.18, 9.20
  time for, 9.15—9.17
  time of the essence, 9.17
Pledge, 26.15—26.19
Postal acceptance rule, 5.15
Postal payments, 9.5
Power of attorney, 18.25, 18.45
Premises, 20.35—20.45
Privity of contract
  collateral contract, 6.21
  consideration, relation with, 6.18,
    6.19
  exceptions to doctrine, 6.20
  meaning and effect, 6.1, 6.19
  trusts, evasion by use of, 6.25
  third party, exemption clause
    position, 10.36—10.38
Privy Council, Judicial Committee of,
    2.35, 3.47
Probate, 2.9, 2.16, 3.50
Prohibition Order, 2.18
Promise, 8.13, 10.19, 10.35
Promissory estoppel, 6.14, 6.15, 6.34,
    28.17
Promissory notes, 7.5, 24.88
Proof
  in fundamental breach, 10.54
  of negligence, 20.22
  of payment, 9.6
Property *See also* Title, transfer of
  destruction, effect on contract, 11.3
  insurance of, 25.5
  interests in, types of, 4.28
  meaning, 22.6
  rules relating to, 1.6
  title to, jurisdiction, 2.19
  transfer of, 22.11—22.13
Proprietary right, 1.6
Purchaser without notice, 4.29, 14.37

Quantum Meruit, 11.2, 12.16, 17.1
Quasi-Contract, 11.14, 11.15, 12.16,
    17.1, 17.8
Quasi-Estoppel, 6.14
Queen's Bench Division, 2.17, 2.18
Queen's Counsel, 2.50

Racial discrimination, 28.35
Rail, Carriage by, 27.8

All references are to paragraph numbers

Ratio Decidendi, 3.35, 3.36
Receipt, 9.6
Recorders (Crown Court), 2.21
Recovery of loss, 12.3–12.9,
    27.38–27.40
Recovery of payment
    advance payment, breach after,
        17.7
    consumer credit, 23.30
    failing enforcement, 15.63
    from stakeholder, 17.9
    goods rejection, on, 22.78
    hire agreement, 23.64
    illegal or void contract, 15.62, 17.7,
        25.2
    mistake, paid under, 17.4, 17.5
Rectification of documents, 13.18
Redundancy
    defence to unfair dismissal, 28.43
    determination of, 28.54
    payment entitlement, 28.52, 28.53,
        28.58
    procedures, 28.60–28.63
    selection for, 28.46
Refinancing agreements, 26.23
Registrars (County Court), 2.8
Registration of companies, 4.9, 4.20
Remedies for breach
    damages action as, 1.4 *See also*
        Damages, action for
    generally, 12.1
    injunction, 6.26, 12.20
    limitation of actions, 12.25, 12.26
    rescission, 10.4–10.6 *See also*
        Rescission of contract
    revival of, 12.29
    specific performance decree,
        12.17–12.19
Remoteness of damage, 12.3–12.6,
    20.26–20.29
Renunciation of obligations,
    10.10–10.12
Representations, 8.10–8.15
Repudiation of contract, 9.14–9.16,
    16.10, 16.11
Repudiatory breach, 10.4–10.6,
    10.9–10.14
Res Ipsa Loquitur, 20.22
Resale prices, 15.42–15.45
Rescission of contract
    bars to right to, 14.11
    duty of injured party, 12.10

Rescission of contract *(cont.)*
    effect on contractual obligations,
        10.7
    entitlement of injured party, 10.2,
        10.10, 10.22
    for breach, 10.2–10.6, 10.57, 12.1
    for duress, 14.30, 14.37
    for misrepresentation, 14.9, 14.19,
        15.63
    grounds for, 10.18
    indemnity ancillary to, 14.16
    injured party without option, 10.9
    insurer's right, 25.4
    methods and procedure, 10.4, 14.10
    refusal of, court's powers, 14.12
    rejection of whole consignment as,
        10.21
    restitution requirement, 14.11
    void contract, compared with, 13.9
Residence, 4.25–4.27
Restrictive practices court
    appeals from, 2.25
    functions of, 2.36, 10.60, 14.38
    reference to, 15.37
Restrictive trade practices
    goods and services agreements,
        15.34
    goodwill, purchase of, 15.22
    registration of agreements, 15.36
    tests of validity, 15.18
    types of, 15.17–15.27
Right to sue
    affirmation of contract, on, 10.8,
        10.56
    agents and principals, 18.36,
        18.41–18.45
    cheques, enforcement of, 24.13,
        24.40
    collateral contract, 15.56
    contract, parties to, 6.1, 6.19
    forebearance as consideration, 6.7
    gratuitous services, 6.8
    illegal contracts, 15.48, 15.55
    in tort, 21.46
    non-gaming wagers, 15.10
    third party, of, 6.27, 10.38, 10.39
Rights *in rem,* 4.28
Road haulage, 27.6–27.7
Road traffic insurance, 25.18
Royal Courts of Justice, 2.15

Safety at work, 28.64–28.65

All references are to paragraph numbers

Sale of goods contract
  defective goods, 22.62
  delivery and acceptance, 22.63
  disposal, right of, 22.22
  fitness for purpose, 22.55—22.58
  form of contract, 22.8
  frustration, 11.18
  implied terms, 8.18
  international sales, 22.99
  international supply contract, 10.50
  liability avoidance, 10.46—10.48
  meaning, 22.2—22.5
  mentally disturbed persons, 16.20
  minor, supply to, 16.5
  motor vehicles, 22.34
  perishing of the goods, 22.23—22.27
  quality, relevance of, 13.4—13.7
  remedies for breach, 22.72—22.94
  repudiation on breach, 22.77
  sale by description, 22.47
  sale by sample, 22.60
  second sale, 22.31, 22.32
  seller unpaid, remedies, 22.86—22.94
  shipment of goods, 22.95—22.98
  specific performance, 12.18n
  statutory control, 22.1
  terms of, 22.39 *et seq.*
  third party, resale by, 6.30
  title, transfer of, 22.28
Salvage, 25.6
Satisfaction, 6.36
Sea, carriage by *See also* Affreightment,
    contract of; Bill of Lading;
    Charterparty
  average loss, 27.38 -27.40
  generally, 27.9—27.40
  international rules, 27.33—27.34
Securities
  consumer credit agreements,
      23.52—23.57
  gaming legislation, 15.10
  in bailment, 26.14—26.24
Sentencing jurisdiction, 2.3, 2.22, 2.26
Service, contract for, 16.4, 16.5, 28.3
Sex discrimination, 28.27—28.31, 28.33
Shareholders, 4.4, 4.5
Signatures
  document validity, 13.19, 24.7
  forgery by agent, 18.11
  liability on cheques, 24.15
  non est factum, 13.19, 13.20
Small claims actions, 2.12
Social security, 28.83—28.90

Solicitors, 2.51
Solus agreements, 15.35, 15.41
Sources of law, 3.48, 3.51, 3.52
Sovereign immunity, 4.17
Special procedure orders, 3.12
Specific performance
  claim by injured party, 10.2
  decree as remedy, 12.1,
      12.17—12.19, 22.74
  injunction compared with, 12.24
  refusal of remedy, 13.17
  sale of goods contracts, 12.18n
Statutes
  application to UK, 3.25
  citation of, 3.5, 3.7, 3.23
  consolidatory statutes, 3.3
  copies, availability, 3.6
  interpretation, 3.17, 3.23—3.26
  parts of, 3.23
  presumptions regarding, 3.25
  repeal of, 3.9, 3.25
Statutory Instruments, 3.11, 3.32
Stock Exchange dealings, 15.3
Strikes and lockouts, 28.18, 28.48,
      28.84
Suicide, 25.22
Supreme Court of Judicature, 2.14,
      2.17
Sweepstake, 15.3

Tender of acts, 9.14
Tender of payment, 9.12, 9.13
Tender of performance, 9.11, 9.14,
      10.1
Tenders, 5.6, 5.10
Third party
  agents, rights against, 18.49, 18.50
  contractual obligations transfer,
      6.17, 19.19
  contractual rights transfer, 19.2,
      19.17
  damages payments to, 6.27
  debts paid by, 9.19
  duty of care to, 20.5
  exemption clause, position under,
      10.36—10.38
  insurer, rights against, 25.16, 25.18,
      25.19
  misrepresentation, effect of, 14.9
  performance of duty owed to, 6.17
  principal and agent, dealings with,
      18.39—18.42
  right to sue on cheque, 6.20

All references are to paragraph numbers

Title, transfer of
  implied undertakings, 22.43
  in assignment, 19.13
  in conditional sale agreement, 23.78
  in sale of goods, 22.28
  negotiable instruments, 24.2
  on rescission, 14.9, 14.10
  seller with voidable title, 22.36,
    22.37
Tort
  defences to, 21.35—21.46
  joint tortfeasors, 21.34
  jurisdiction, 2.9
  meaning, 1.5, 20.1
  minor's liability, 16.16
  remedies, 21.47—21.50
Tracing of goods, 4.12
Trade secrets, 15.19
Trade unions
  employment protection rights, 28.26
  legal status, 4.14, 6.2
  redundancy consultations, 28.60,
    28.61
Trading stamps, 22.61
Trespassers, 20.45
Tribunals, 2.39 *See also* Arbitration
Truck Acts, 28.20
Trustee in bankruptcy, 19.25, 19.26
Trusts
  execution of, 2.16
  insurance, right to, 25.11
  meaning, 4.28
  privity rule evasion by, 6.25

Ultra vires contracts, 4.9—4.12
Unconscionable bargains, 14.36
Undue influence, 14.31—14.38
Unfair dismissal
  complaint procedures, 28.42
  reasons for dismissal, 28.45
  remedies, 28.49—28.51
  test for unfairness, 11.6
Unincorporated Associations, 4.13

Validity of contract
  arbitration clause validity, 15.15
  attribute of party, mistake, 13.12

Validity of contract (*cont.*)
  breach of statute in performance,
    15.53
  collateral contract, 15.32
  duress, procured under, 14.28 *et seq.*
  equity following law, 13.17
  goodwill, purchase of, 15.22
  grounds for invalidity, 15.1
  identity of party, mistake, 13.10,
    13.11
  intoxication, 16.19
  mental disorder, 16.19
  misrepresentation inducing mistake,
    14.1
  mistake, effect of, 13.1 *et seq.*
  negatively voidable, types of, 16.15
  quality of goods, mistake as to, 13.5
  rescission, valid until election, 14.9
Variation of contract, 6.31, 6.32, 6.33,
  6.35
Verdict, 2.55
Vicarious liability, 21.14 *et seq.*
Voidable contracts, 15.12, 16.9, 16.12

Wagering contracts, 15.2 *et seq.*, 25.2
Wages
  coin and banknotes requirement,
    28.20
  deductions permitted, 28.20—28.22
  Fair Wages Resolution, 28.24
  statement, 28.19
  wages councils, 28.23
Waiver of contract, 6.33
Warranty
  as contractual term, 10.19—10.20,
    22.39
  condition, compared with, 22.40
  implied, 22.45
  remedies for breach, 22.80
Weekly Law Reports, 3.50
Winding-up of companies
  jurisdiction, 2.10, 2.16
  'lifting the veil' during, 4.7
  shareholders' liabilities, 4.5, 4.6
Writ of execution, 22.38
Wrongful dismissal
  damages for, 12.8
  meaning, 28.40
  test for, 11.6

All references are to paragraph numbers